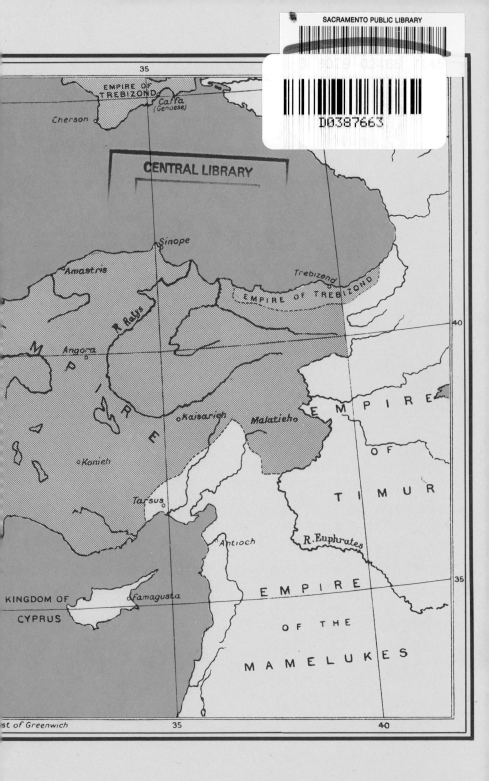

35

EMPIRE OF
TREBIZOND

Caffa
(Genoese)

Cherson

Sinope

Amastris

Trebizond

EMPIRE OF TREBIZOND

R. Rays

40

Angora

E
M
P
I
R
E

Kaisarieh

Malatieho

E M P I R E

O F

T I M U R

Konieh

Tarsus

Antioch

R. Euphrates

35

KINGDOM OF

Famagusta

CYPRUS

E M P I R E

O F   T H E

M A M E L U K E S

THE DECLINE AND FALL OF THE ROMAN EMPIRE

VOLUME VII

AMS PRESS · NEW YORK

MEDAL OF MAHOMET II, BY COSTANZO

THE HISTORY

OF THE

DECLINE AND FALL OF THE
ROMAN EMPIRE

BY

EDWARD GIBBON

EDITED

WITH INTRODUCTION, NOTES, AND APPENDICES

BY

J. B. BURY, D.Litt., LL.D.

CORRESPONDING MEMBER OF THE IMPERIAL ACADEMY OF SCIENCES, ST. PETERSBURG
FELLOW OF KING'S COLLEGE AND REGIUS PROFESSOR OF MODERN HISTORY
IN THE UNIVERSITY OF CAMBRIDGE

IN SEVEN VOLUMES

VOLUME VII

WITH NINETEEN ILLUSTRATIONS AND MAP AND PLAN

METHUEN & CO. LTD.
36 ESSEX STREET W.C.
LONDON
1914

Library of Congress Cataloging in Publication Data
Gibbon, Edward, 1737-1794.
The history of the decline and fall of the Roman Empire.
Reprint of the 1909-14 ed.
1. Rome—History—Empire, 30 B.C.-476 A.D.
2. Byzantine Empire—History.
I. Bury, John Bagnell, 1861-1927, ed.
II. Title.
DG311.G5   1974   937′.06   78-168113
ISBN 0-404-02820-9 (set)

Reprinted by arrangement with Methuen & Company Ltd., London, England
From the edition of 1914, London
First AMS edition published in 1974
Manufactured in the United States of America
International Standard Book Number : Complete set : 0-404-02820-9
Volume VII : 0-404-02827-6
AMS PRESS INC.
NEW YORK, N.Y. 10003

CONTENTS OF THE SEVENTH VOLUME

CHAPTER LXIV

Conquests of Zingis Khan and the Moguls from China to Poland—Escape of Constantinople and the Greeks—Origin of the Ottoman Turks in Bithynia—Reigns and Victories of Othman, Orchan, Amurath the First, and Bajazet the First—Foundation and Progress of the Turkish Monarchy in Asia and Europe—Danger of Constantinople and the Greek Empire

CHAPTER LXV

Elevation of Timour or Tamerlane to the Throne of Samarcand—His Conquests in Persia, Georgia, Tartary, Russia, India, Syria, and Anatolia—His Turkish War—Defeat and Captivity of Bajazet—Death of Timour—Civil War of the Sons of Bajazet—Restoration of the Turkish Monarchy by Mahomet the First—Siege of Constantinople by Amurath the Second

CHAPTER LXVI

Application of the Eastern Emperors to the Popes—Visits to the West, of John the First, Manuel, and John the Second, Palæologus—Union of the Greek and Latin Churches, Promoted by the Council of Basil, and Concluded at Ferrara and Florence—State of Literature at Constantinople—Its Revival in Italy by the Greek Fugitives—Curiosity and Emulation of the Latins

CONTENTS OF THE SEVENTH VOLUME vii

CHAPTER LXVII

Schism of the Greeks and Latins—Reign and Character of Amurath the Second—Crusade of Ladislaus, King of Hungary—His Defeat and Death —John Huniades— Scanderbeg— Constantine Palæologus last Emperor of the East

CHAPTER LXVIII

Reign and Character of Mahomet the Second—Siege, Assault, and Final Conquest of Constantinople by the Turks—Death of Constantine Palæologus—Servitude of the Greeks—Extinction of the Roman Empire in the East—Consternation of Europe—Conquests and Death of Mahomet the Second

CHAPTER LXIX

*State of Rome from the Twelfth Century—Temporal Dominion of the Popes—Sedi-
tions of the City—Political Heresy of Arnold of Brescia—Restoration of the
Republic—The Senators—Pride of the Romans—Their Wars—They are deprived of the Election and Presence of the Popes who retire to Avignon—The
Jubilee—Noble Families of Rome—Feud of the Colonna and Ursini*

CHAPTER LXX

Character and Coronation of Petrarch—Restoration of the Freedom and Government of Rome by the Tribune Rienzi—His Virtues and Vices, his Expulsion and Death—Return of the Popes from Avignon—Great Schism of the West—Re-union of the Latin Church—Last Struggles of Roman Liberty—Statutes of Rome—Final Settlement of the Ecclesiastical State

CHAPTER LXXI

Prospect of the Ruins of Rome in the Fifteenth Century—Four Cases of Decay and Destruction—Example of the Coliseum—Renovation of the City— Conclusion of the whole Work

APPENDIX

(*By the Editor*)

MAP AND PLAN

ILLUSTRATIONS

(SELECTED BY O. M. DALTON, M.A., F.S.A.)

THE DECLINE AND FALL OF THE ROMAN EMPIRE

VOLUME VII

THE HISTORY

OF THE

DECLINE AND FALL OF THE ROMAN EMPIRE

CHAPTER LXIV

Conquests of Zingis Khan and the Moguls from China to Poland —Escape of Constantinople and the Greeks—Origin of the Ottoman Turks in Bithynia—Reigns and Victories of Othman, Orchan, Amurath the First, and Bajazet the First—Foundation and Progress of the Turkish Monarchy in Asia and Europe—Danger of Constantinople and the Greek Empire

FROM the petty quarrels of a city and her suburbs, from the cowardice and discord of the falling Greeks, I shall now ascend to the victorious Turks, whose domestic slavery was ennobled by martial discipline, religious enthusiasm, and the energy of the national character. The rise and progress of the Ottomans, the present sovereigns of Constantinople, are connected with the most important scenes of modern history; but they are founded on a previous knowledge of the great eruption of the Moguls and Tartars, whose rapid conquests may be compared with the primitive convulsions of nature, which have agitated and altered the surface of the globe. I have long since asserted my claim to introduce the nations, the immediate or remote authors of the fall of the Roman empire; nor can I refuse myself to those events which, from their uncommon magnitude, will interest a philosophic mind in the history of blood.[1]

---

[1] The reader is invited to review the chapters of the third and fourth volumes; the manners of pastoral nations, the conquests of Attila and the Huns, which were composed at a time when I entertained the wish, rather than the hope, of concluding my history.

Zingis
[Chingiz]
Khan, first
emperor of
the Moguls
and Tar-
tars, A.D.
1206-1227 From the spacious highlands between China, Siberia, and the Caspian Sea, the tide of emigration and war has repeatedly been poured. These ancient seats of the Huns and Turks were occupied in the twelfth century by many pastoral tribes of the same descent and similar manners, which were united and led to conquest by the formidable Zingis. In his ascent to great-
[Temujin] ness, that barbarian (whose private appellation was Temugin) had trampled on the necks of his equals. His birth was noble ; but it was in the pride of victory that the prince or people deduced his seventh ancestor from the immaculate conception
[Yissugay] of a virgin.[2] His father had reigned over thirteen hordes, which composed about thirty or forty thousand families ; above two-thirds refused to pay tithes or obedience to his infant son ;
[A.D. 1175] and, at the age of thirteen, Temugin fought a battle against his rebellious subjects. The future conqueror of Asia was re-duced to fly and to obey ; but he rose superior to his fortune ; and, in his fortieth year, he had established his fame and dominion over the circumjacent tribes. In a state of society in which policy is rude and valour is universal, the ascendant of one man must be founded on his power and resolution to punish his enemies and recompense his friends. His first military league was ratified by the simple rites of sacrificing an horse and tasting of a running stream : Temugin pledged himself to divide with his followers the sweets and the bitters of life ; and, when he had shared among them his horses and apparel, he was rich in their gratitude and his own hopes. After his first victory, he placed seventy caldrons on the fire, and seventy of the most guilty rebels were cast headlong into the boiling water. The sphere of his attraction was continually enlarged by the ruin of the proud and the submission of the prudent ; and the boldest chieftains might tremble, when
[Wang
Khan] they beheld, enchased in silver, the skull of the khan of the

---

[2] [The miraculous origin of the race of Chingiz Khan appears in Turkish and Chinese as well as in Mongol legend. The family to which he belonged was called the Borjigen ; it seems to have been of Turkish origin on the female side, but Mongol on the male (Cahun, Intr. à l'histoire de l'Asie, p. 203). It possessed lands and high prestige among the Mongol tribes to the north of China between the rivers Selinga and Orchon. It is important to realise that the Mongols were not very numerous. In the Mongol empire, as it is called, which Chingiz Khan created, the Mongolian element was small. What he did was to create a great Turkish empire under Mongol domination.]

Keraites,[3] who under the name of Prester John had corresponded with the Roman pontiff and the princes of Europe. The ambition of Temugin condescended to employ the arts of superstition; and it was from a naked prophet, who could ascend to heaven on a white horse, that he accepted the title of Zingis,[4] the *Most Great;* and a divine right to the conquest and dominion of the earth. In a general *couroultai*, or diet, he was seated on a felt, which was long afterwards revered as a relic, and solemnly proclaimed Great Khan or emperor of the Moguls [5] and Tartars.[6] Of these kindred though rival names, the former had given birth to the Imperial race; and the latter has been extended, by accident or error, over the spacious wilderness of the north.

The code of laws which Zingis dictated to his subjects was His laws adapted to the preservation of domestic peace and the exercise of foreign hostility. The punishment of death was inflicted on

[3] The Khans of the Keraites [Karaits] were most probably incapable of reading the pompous epistles composed in their name by the Nestorian missionaries, who endowed them with the fabulous wonders of an Indian kingdom. Perhaps these Tartars (the Presbyter or Priest John) had submitted to the rites of baptism and ordination (Assemann. Bibliot. Orient. tom. iii. p. ii. p. 487-503). [Sir H. Howorth has shown very clearly (Hist. of the Mongols, i. p. 696 *sqq.*) that the Karaits were Turks, not Mongols. Their territory was near the Upper Orchon, between the rivers Selinga and Kernlen. They were Christians. Their chief Tughril received the title of Wang (" king ") from the (Manchu) Emperor of Northern China for his services in 1193 against the Naiman Turks of the regions of the Altai and Upper Irtish. Chingiz also took part in this war, and his services were recognised by the title of Dai Ming, " high Brightness ". For an account of Prester John—the name by which the Karait khans were known in the west—and the legends attached to him, see Howorth, i. cap. x. p. 534 *sqq.*]

[4] Since the history and tragedy of Voltaire, *Gengis*, at least in French, seems to be the more fashionable spelling; but Abulghazi Khan must have known the true name of his ancestor. His etymology appears just; *Zin*, in the Mogul tongue, signifies *great*, and *gis* is the superlative termination (Hist. Généalogique des Tartars, part iii. p. 194, 195). From the same idea of magnitude the appellation of *Zingis* is bestowed on the ocean. [Chingiz (= very great, or autocrat) represents the true spelling. He also bore the title Sutu Bodgo, " son of Heaven ".]

[5] The name of Moguls has prevailed among the Orientals, and still adheres to the titular sovereign, the Great Mogul of Hindostan. [Mongol, Mogul and (Arabic) Mughal are all attempts to represent a name which among the true Mongols is pronounced something between Moghol (or Mool) and Mongol, but never with the *u* sound. See Tarīkh-i-Rashīdī, tr. Elias and Ross, p. 73 note.]

[6] The Tartars (more properly Tatars) were descended from Tatar Khan, the brother of Mogul Khan (see Abulghazi, part i. and ii.), and once formed a horde of 70,000 families on the borders of Kitay (p. 103-112). In the great invasion of Europe (A.D. 1238), they seem to have led the vanguard; and the similitude of the name of *Tartarei* recommended that of Tartars to the Latins (Matth. Paris, p. 398, &c.). [The Tatars seem to have been a mixture of Manchus and Turks. In one of the old Turkish inscriptions of A.D. 733 (cp. above, vol. iv. p. 575) Tatars are mentioned.]

the crimes of adultery, murder, perjury, and the capital thefts
of an horse or ox; and the fiercest of men were mild and just
in their intercourse with each other. The future election of
the great khan was vested in the princes of his family and the
heads of the tribes; and the regulations of the chase were
essential to the pleasures and plenty of a Tartar camp. The
victorious nation was held sacred from all servile labours, which
were abandoned to slaves and strangers; and every labour was
servile except the profession of arms. The service and discipline of the troops, who were armed with bows, scymetars
and iron maces, and divided by hundreds, thousands, and ten
thousands, were the institutions of a veteran commander. Each
officer and soldier was made responsible, under pain of death,
for the safety and honour of his companions; and the spirit of
conquest breathed in the law that peace should never be granted
unless to a vanquished and suppliant enemy.[7]   But it is the
religion of Zingis that best deserves our wonder and applause.
The Catholic inquisitors of Europe, who defended nonsense by
cruelty, might have been confounded by the example of a
barbarian, who anticipated the lessons of philosophy [8] and
established by his laws a system of pure theism and perfect
toleration. His first and only article of faith was the existence
of one God, the author of all good, who fills, by his presence,
the heavens and earth, which he has created by his power.
The Tartars and Moguls were addicted to the idols of their
peculiar tribes; and many of them had been converted by the
foreign missionaries to the religions of Moses, of Mahomet, and
of Christ. These various systems in freedom and concord were
taught and practised within the precincts of the same camp;
and the Bonze, the Imam, the Rabbi, the Nestorian, and the
Latin priest enjoyed the same honourable exemption from
service and tribute. In the mosque of Bochara, the insolent
victor might trample the Koran under his horse's feet, but the
calm legislator respected the prophets and pontiffs of the most
hostile sects. The reason of Zingis was not informed by book;

[7] [The code drawn up by Chingiz was called Yāsāk or Law. (On it, see Sir
H. Howorth's paper in the *Indian Antiquary*, July, 1882.) The cruelties of
Chingiz were always the simple execution of the laws: he was never capricious.]
[8] A singular conformity may be found between the religious laws of Zingis Khan
and of Mr. Locke (Constitutions of Carolina, in his works, vol. iv. p. 535, 4to
edition, 1777).

the khan could neither read nor write; and, except the tribe of the Igours, the greatest part of the Moguls and Tartars were as illiterate as their sovereign.[9] The memory of their exploits was preserved by tradition; sixty-eight years after the death of Zingis, these traditions were collected and transcribed;[10] the brevity of their domestic annals may be supplied by the Chinese,[11] Persians,[12] Armenians,[13] Syrians,[14] Arabians,[15] Greeks,[16]

[9] [When Chingiz conquered the Naiman Turks of the Altai regions, c. 1203-4, the vizir of the Naiman king passed into his service and became his chancellor. This minister was an Ūigur and had Ūigur successors. Through these Uigurs, the Uigur alphabet (derived from the Syriac) was adopted by the Mongols, and the old Turkish script (of the Orchon incriptions, see above, vol. iv. p. 575) became obsolete. On the Uigurs see Vámbéry's Uigurische Sprachmonumente und das Kudatku Bilik, 1870.]

[10] In the year 1294, by the command of [Mahmūd Ghāzān] Cazan, khan of Persia, the fourth [fifth] in descent from Zingis. From these traditions, his vizir, Fadlallah [Rashīd ad-Dīn], composed a Mogul history in the Persian language, which has been used by Petit de la Croix (Hist. de Genghizcan, p. 537-539) [see D'Ohsson, Hist. des Mongols, i. 627 sqq. For Rashīd's Jāmi al-Tawārīkh see Appendix 1]. The Histoire Généalogique des Tatars (à Leyde, 1726, in 12mo, 2 tomes) was translated by the Swedish prisoners in Siberia, from the Mogul Ms. of Abulgasi Bahadur Khan, a descendant of Zingis, who reigned over the Usbeks of Charasm, or Carizme (A.D. 1644-1663). He is of most value and credit for the names, pedigrees, and manners of his nation. Of his nine parts, the 1st descends from Adam to Mogul Khan; the iid, from Mogul to Zingis; the iiid, is the life of Zingis; the ivth, vth, vith and viith, the general history of his four sons and their posterity; the viiith and ixth, the particular history of the descendants of Sheibani Khan, who reigned in Maurenahar and Charasm. [The work of Abulghazi has been edited and translated by Des Maisons (St. Petersburg, 1870). For Jūzjānī and Juvainī see Appendix 1.]

[11] Histoire de Gentchiscan, et de toute la Dinastie des Mongous ses Successeurs, Conquérans de la Chine; tirée de l'Histoire de la Chine, par le R. P. Gaubil, de la Société de Jésus, Missionaire à Pekin; à Paris, 1739, in 4to. This translation is stamped with the Chinese character of domestic accuracy and foreign ignorance. [It has been superseded by the Russian work of the Père Hyacinth, on the first four Khans of the house of Chingiz, 1829. A contemporary Chinese work by Men-Hun has been translated by Vasil'ev in the ivth vol. of the Transactions of the Russian Arch. Soc., Oriental Sect.]

[12] See the Histoire du Grand Genghizcan, premier Empereur des Mogols et Tartares, par M. Petit de la Croix, à Paris, 1710, in 12mo [it has been translated into English]: a work of ten years' labour, chiefly drawn from the Persian writers, among whom Nisavi, the secretary of sultan Gelaleddin, has the merit and prejudices of a contemporary. A slight air of romance is the fault of the originals, or the compiler. See likewise the articles of *Genghizcan, Mohammed, Gelaleddin,* &c., in the Bibliothèque Orientale of d'Herbelot. [Several histories of the Mongols have appeared in the 19th century: D'Ohsson, Histoire des Mongols, 1852; Wolff, Geschichte der Mongolen oder Tataren, 1872; Quatremère, Histoire des Mongoles de la Perse, 1836; Howorth, History of the Mongols, Part 1, 1876, Part 2 (in 2 vols.), 1880 (on the "Tartars" of Russia and Central Asia); Part 3, 1888 (on Mongols of Persia); Cahun, Introduction à l'Histoire de l'Asie, 1896. For later Mongols of Central Asia, see the Tarīkh-i-Rashīdī of Mirzā Muhammad Haidar Dughlāt, transl. by E. D. Ross, ed. by N. Elias, 1895; for which, and for Schmidt, Geschichte der Ost-Mongolen, cp. App. 1. For Chingiz Khan: Erdmann, Temudschin der Unerschütterliche, 1862; R. K. Douglas, Life of Jinghiz Khān, 1877; Howorth, *op. cit.* Pt. 1. Gibbon does not mention: Pallas, Sammlungen historischer

Russians,[17] Poles,[18] Hungarians [19] and Latins ; [20] and each nation

Nachrichten über die Mongolischen Völkerschaften, which appeared at St. Petersburg in 1776, 2 vols.]

[13] Haithonus, or Aithonus, an Armenian prince, and afterwards a monk of Premontré (Fabric. Bibliot. Lat. medii Ævi, tom. i. p. 34), dictated, in the French language, his book De Tartaris, his old fellow-soldiers. It was immediately translated into Latin, and is inserted in the Novus Orbis of Simon Grynæus (Basil, 1555, in folio). [See above, vol. vi. p. 553. For Haithon I. see Appendix 1.]

[14] Zingis Khan, and his first successors, occupy the conclusion of the ixth Dynasty of Abulpharagius (vers. Pocock, Oxon. 1663, in 4to) ; and his xth Dynasty is that of the Moguls of Persia. Assemannus (Bibliot. Orient. tom. ii.) has extracted some facts from his Syriac writings, and the lives of the Jacobite maphrians or primates of the East.

[15] Among the Arabians, in language and religion, we may distinguish Abulfeda, sultan of Hamah in Syria, who fought in person, under the Mamaluke standard, against the Moguls.

[16] Nicephorus Gregoras (l. ii. c. 5, 6) has felt the necessity of connecting the Scythian and Byzantine histories. He describes, with truth and elegance, the settlement and manners of the Moguls of Persia, but he is ignorant of their origin, and corrupts the names of Zingis and his sons.

[17] M. Levesque (Histoire de Russie, tom. ii.) has described the conquest of Russia by the Tartars, from the patriarch Nicon and the old chronicles. [See Soloviev, Istoriia Rossii, vol. iii. cap. ii. p. 820 sqq.]

[18] For Poland, I am content with the Sarmatia Asiatica et Europaea of Matthew à Michou, or de Michoviâ, a canon and physician of Cracow (A.D. 1506), inserted in the Novus Orbis of Grynæus. Fabric. Bibliot. Latin. mediæ et infimæ Ætatis, tom. v. p. 56. [The most important Polish source is the Historia Polonica of Johannes Dlugossius (who lived in the 15th century and died 1480). His works have been edited in 14 vols. by Alexander Przezdziecki (1867-87) and the Hist. Pol. occupies vols. x.-xiv. Roepell's Geschichte Polens, vol. i. (1840). Only one contemporary Polish chronicle has survived: the Annals of the Cracow Chapter, Mon. Germ. Hist. Scr., xix. 582 sqq.]

[19] I should quote Thuroczius, the oldest general historian (pars ii. c. 74, p. 150), in the first volume of the Scriptores Rerum Hungaricarum, did not the same volume contain the original narrative of a contemporary, an eye-witness, and a sufferer (M. Rogerii, Hungari, Varadiensis Capituli Canonici, Carmen miserabile, seu Historia super Destructione Regni Hungariæ, Temporibus Belæ IV. Regis per Tartaros factâ, p. 292-321) [it will be found in Endlicher, Rer. Hung. Monum. Arpadiana, p. 255 sqq.] ; the best picture that I have ever seen of all the circumstances of a barbaric invasion. [Gibbon omits to mention another contemporary account (of great importance) of the invasion of Hungary, by Thomas Archdeacon of Spalato, in his Historia Salonitana, published in Schwandtner's Scriptores Hung., vol. iii.]

[20] Matthew Paris has represented, from authentic documents, the danger and distress of Europe (consult the word Tartari in his copious Index). [It has been conjectured that among the documents used by Matthew were anti-Semitic fly-leaves, accusing the Jews of inviting and helping the Mongols, Strakosch-Grassmann, Der Einfall der Mongolen, p. 116.] From motives of zeal and curiosity, the court of the great Khan, in the xiiith century, was visited by two friars, John de Plano Carpini and William Rubruquis, and by Marco Polo, a Venetian gentleman. The Latin relations of the two former are inserted in the first volume of Hackluyt : the Italian original, or version, of the third (Fabric. Bibliot. Latin. medii Ævi, tom. ii. p. 198 ; tom. v. p. 25) may be found in the second tome of Ramusio. [Colonel H. Yule's English translation, The Book of Ser Marco Polo the Venetian, in 2 vols., 1875, with plans and illustrations, and most valuable elucidations and bibliography, has been re-edited (3rd ed.) by H. Cordier, 1903, and is indispensable to the study of the traveller. A new edition of Rubruquis along with John de Plano Carpini, by R. Beazley, appeared in 1903. The account of a journey among the Mongols by

will deserve credit in the relation of their own disasters and defeats.[21]

The arms of Zingis and his lieutenants successively reduced the hordes of the desert, who pitched their tents between the wall of China and the Volga; and the Mogul emperor became the monarch of the pastoral world, the lord of many millions of shepherds and soldiers, who felt their united strength, and were impatient to rush on the mild and wealthy climates of the south. His ancestors had been the tributaries of the Chinese emperors; and Temugin himself had been disgraced by a title of honour and servitude.[22] The court of Pekin was astonished by an embassy from its former vassal, who in the tone of the king of nations exacted the tribute and obedience which he had paid, and who affected to treat the *Son of Heaven* as the most contemptible of mankind. An haughty answer disguised their secret apprehensions; and their fears were soon justified by the march of innumerable squadrons, who pierced on all sides the feeble rampart of the great wall. Ninety cities were stormed, or starved, by the Moguls; ten only escaped; and Zingis, from a knowledge of the filial piety of the Chinese, covered his vanguard with their captive parents: an unworthy and, by degrees, a fruitless abuse of the virtues of his enemies. His

His invasion of China, A.D. 1210-1214

another traveller, Ascellinus, is printed in Fejér, Codex diplomaticus Hungariæ, iv. 1, 428 *sqq.*]

[21] In his great History of the Huns, M. de Guignes has most amply treated of Zingis Khan and his successors. See tom. iii. 1. xv.-xix., and in the collateral articles of the Seljukians of Roum, tom. ii. 1. xi., the Carizmians, 1. xiv., and the Mamalukes, tom. iv. 1. xxi.; consult likewise the tables of the 1st volume. He is ever learned and accurate; yet I am only indebted to him for a general view, and some passages of Abulfeda, which are still latent in the Arabic text.

[22] [The people who ruled over Northern China at this time were the Niu-Chi or Man-Chu. (They called themselves Aisin, " golden," which the Chinese translated by Kin, and hence they are generally called the Kin dynasty.) They had conquered Northern China in 1120 from the Kara-Khitay Turks who had held it since 1004. Chingiz, who was always punctilious in matters of form, chose his moment when the Emperor Chang-Tsong, to whom he had taken a feudal oath, was dead (1208); then he openly refused allegiance to the successor. He had prepared the way for the overthrow of the Niu-Chi by the conquest of the land of the Hia (north of Tibet, and west of the great bend of the Hoang Ho : the country of the Tanguts), which was then a republic of brigands, who (with their capital at Ning-Hia on the Hoang Ho), commanding the routes to the west, were a pest both to the southern and the northern Chinese empires. Cahun, Intr. à l'histoire de l'Asie, p. 248. Chingiz in conquering the Hia thus appeared as a public benefactor, but really seized a key position both in regard to China and in regard to the routes to the west through Dzungaria and through Cashgaria. On the Kin empire see the Histoire de l'empire de Kin ou empire d'or, Aisin Gurun-i Suduri Bithe, transl. by C. de Harlez, 1887.]

invasion was supported by the revolt of an hundred thousand
Khitans, who guarded the frontier; yet he listened to a treaty;
and a princess of China, three thousand horses, five hundred
youths, and as many virgins, and a tribute of gold and silk,
were the price of his retreat. In his second expedition, he compelled the Chinese emperor to retire beyond the yellow river
to a more southern residence. The siege of Pekin [23] was long
and laborious: the inhabitants were reduced by famine to deci-
mate and devour their fellow-citizens; when their ammunition was spent, they discharged ingots of gold and silver from
their engines; but the Moguls introduced a mine to the centre
of the capital; and the conflagration of the palace burnt above
thirty days. China was desolated by Tartar war and domestic
faction; and the five northern provinces were added to the
empire of Zingis.

In the West, he touched the dominions of Mohammed, sultan
of Carizme, who reigned from the Persian Gulf to the borders
of India and Turkestan; and who, in the proud imitation of
Alexander the Great, forgot the servitude and ingratitude of his
fathers to the house of Seljuk.[24] It was the wish of Zingis to
establish a friendly and commercial intercourse with the most
powerful of the Moslem princes; nor could he be tempted by
the secret solicitations of the caliph of Bagdad, who sacrificed
to his personal wrongs the safety of the church and state. A
rash and inhuman deed provoked and justified the Tartar arms
in the invasion of the southern Asia. A caravan of three ambassadors and one hundred and fifty merchants was arrested

[Treaty A.D. 1215]

[Kai-fong = Pian-King]

[A.D. 1216]

of Carizme, Trans-oxiana, and Persia, A.D. 1218-1224

[23] More properly *Yen-king*, an ancient city, whose ruins still appear some furlongs to the south-east of the modern *Pekin*, which was built by Cublai Khan
(Gaubil, p. 146). Pe-king and Nan-king are vague titles, the courts of the north
and of the south. The identity and change of names perplex the most skilful
readers of the Chinese geography (p. 177). [When the Karā-Khitay Turks (under
their chiefs the Ye-Lu family) conquered Northern China in 1004, they took Yen as
their capital; it is now called Pe-king, "capital of the north". "Khitan" is the
Chinese form of Khitay.]

[24] [In the last quarter of the 11th cent., Anushtigīn a Turkish slave was appointed governor of Carizme (Khwārizm) by the Sultan Malik Shāh. His son
took the title of Carizme Shāh, and his grandson Atsiz made himself independent
of the Seljuk sultans in the second quarter of the 12th cent. Alā ad-Dīn Mohammad (A.D. 1199-1220) made this principality of Carizme (which Atsiz and Tukush
(1172-1199) had already extended as far as Jand in the north and Ispahan in the
west) into a great realm, subduing Persia and Transoxiana, overthrowing the
Ghōrid dynasty of Afghanistan, and invading Eastern Turkestan (the kingdom of
the Karā-Khitay).]

and murdered at Otrar,[25] by the command of Mohammed; nor was it till after a demand and denial of justice, till he had prayed and fasted three nights on a mountain, that the Mogul emperor appealed to the judgment of God and his sword. Our European battles, says a philosophic writer,[26] are petty skirmishes, if compared to the numbers that have fought and fallen in the fields of Asia. Seven hundred thousand Moguls and Tartars are said to have marched under the standard of Zingis and his four sons. In the vast plains that extend to the north of the Sihon or Jaxartes, they were encountered by four hundred thousand soldiers of the Sultan; and in the first battle, which was suspended by the night, one hundred and sixty thousand Carizmians were slain. Mohammed was astonished by the multitude and valour of his enemies:[27] he withdrew from the scene of danger, and distributed his troops in the frontier towns, trusting that the barbarians, invincible in the field, would be repulsed by the length and difficulty of so many regular sieges. But the prudence of Zingis had formed a body of Chinese engineers, skilled in the mechanic arts, informed, perhaps, of the secret of gunpowder, and capable, under his discipline, of attacking a foreign country with more vigour and success than they had defended their own. The Persian historians will relate the sieges and reduction of Otrar, Cogende, Bochara, Samarcand, Carizme, Herat, Merou, Nisabour, Balch, and Candahar; and the conquest of the rich and populous

[25] [On the middle Jaxartes. It was the capital of the Gūr-Khans of the Turkish kingdom of Karā-Khitay. Gibbon omits to mention the conquest of this kingdom (the south-western provinces of the modern empire of China) by Chingiz, before he came face to face with the Carizmian empire.]

[26] M. de Voltaire, Essai sur l'Histoire Générale, tom. iii. c. 60, p. 8. His account of Zingis and the Moguls contains, as usual, much general sense and truth, with some particular errors.

[27] [The strategical ability displayed in the campaigns of Chingiz and his successors has been well brought out by Cahun. It is wholly an error to regard the Mongol conquests as achieved merely by numbers and intrepid physical bravery. The campaigns were carefully planned out—not by Chingiz himself, he only considered, and approved or rejected, the plans submitted to him by his military advisers. He knew how to choose able generals (Samuka and Subutai were two of the most illustrious), but he did not interfere with them in their work. The invasion of the Carizmian empire was carried out thus: a Mongol army which had just conquered the land of Cashgar advanced over the great southern pass into Fergana and descended upon Khojend. The main army advanced by the great northern gate, through Dzungaria and the Ili regions, to Otrār on the Jaxartes. Half the army spread up the river to take or mask the Carizmian fortresses and join hands at Khojend with the corps from Cashgar. The other half, under Chingiz himself, marched straight across the Red Sand Desert upon Bochara. Cahun, *op. cit.*, p. 285. Success was rendered easy by the strategical mistakes of Mohammad.]

countries of Transoxiana, Carizme, and Chorasan. The destructive hostilities of Attila and the Huns have long since been elucidated by the example of Zingis and the Moguls; and in this more proper place I shall be content to observe that, from the Caspian to the Indus, they ruined a tract of many hundred miles, which was adorned with the habitations and labours of mankind, and that five centuries have not been sufficient to repair the ravages of four years. The Mogul emperor encouraged or indulged the fury of his troops; the hope of future possession was lost in the ardour of rapine and slaughter; and the cause of the war exasperated their native fierceness by the pretence of justice and [A.D. 1220] revenge. The downfall and death of the sultan Mohammed, who expired unpitied and alone in a desert island of the Caspian Sea, is a poor atonement for the calamities of which he was the author. Could the Carizmian empire have been saved by a [Jalal ad-Din] single hero, it would have been saved by his son Gelaleddin, whose active valour repeatedly checked the Moguls in the career of victory. Retreating, as he fought, to the banks of the Indus, he was oppressed by their innumerable host, till, in the last moment of despair, Gelaleddin spurred his horse into the waves, swam one of the broadest and most rapid rivers of Asia, and extorted the admiration and applause of Zingis himself. It was in this camp that the Mogul emperor yielded with reluctance to the murmurs of his weary and wealthy troops, who sighed for the enjoyment of their native land. Incumbered with the spoils of Asia, he slowly measured back his footsteps, betrayed some pity for the misery of the vanquished, and declared his intention of rebuilding the cities which had been swept away by the tempest of his arms. After he had repassed the Oxus and Jaxartes, he was joined by two generals, whom he had detached with thirty thousand horse, to subdue the western provinces of Persia. They had trampled on the nations which opposed their passage, penetrated through the gates of Derbend, traversed the Volga and the desert, and accomplished the circuit of the Caspian Sea, by an expedition which had never been attempted and has never been repeated. The return of Zingis was signalised by the overthrow of the rebellious or independent kingdoms of His death, Tartary; and he died in the fulness of years and glory, with A.D. 1227 his last breath exhorting and instructing his sons to achieve the conquest of the Chinese empire.

The harem of Zingis was composed of five hundred wives and concubines; and of his numerous progeny, four sons, illustrious by their birth and merit, exercised under their father the principal offices of peace and war. Toushi [28] was his great huntsman, Zagatai [29] his judge, Octai his minister, and Tuli his general; and their names and actions are often conspicuous in the history of his conquests. Firmly united for their own and the public interest, the three brothers and their families were content with dependent sceptres; and Octai, by general consent, was proclaimed Great Khan, or emperor of the Moguls and Tartars. He was succeeded by his son Gayuk, after whose death the empire devolved to his cousins, Mangou and Cublai, the sons of Tuli, and the grandsons of Zingis.[30] In the sixty-eight years of his four first successors, the Moguls subdued almost all Asia and a large portion of Europe. Without confining myself to the order of time, without expatiating on the detail of events, I shall present a general picture of the progress of their arms: I. In the East; II. in the South; III. in the West; and, IV. in the North.

I. Before the invasion of Zingis, China was divided into two empires or dynasties of the North and South [31]; and the difference of origin and interest was smoothed by a general conformity of laws, language, and national manners. The Northern empire, which had been dismembered by Zingis, was

Conquests of the Moguls under the successors of Zingis, A.D. 1227-1295

[Ogotay]

[Kuyuk, A.D. 1241-1248]

Of the Northern empire of China, A.D. 1234

[The Kin empire— Manchu dynasty]

[28] [Jūjī received the realm of Kará-Khitay, and his son Bātū obtained possession of the Khanate of Kipchak, see below, p. 16.]

[29] Zagatai [Chagatāy] gave his name to his dominions of Maurenahar [Ma-warā-l-nahr], or Transoxiana [along with part of Kashgar, Balkh, and Ghazna]; and the Moguls of Hindostan, who emigrated from that country, are styled Zagatais by the Persians. This certain etymology, and the similar example of Uzbek, Nogai, &c. may warn us not absolutely to reject the derivations of a national, from a personal, name. [The succession of the Chagatāy Khans of Transoxiana is very uncertain. On this branch see Oliver's monograph, "The Chaghatai Mughals," in Journal of Royal Asiatic Society, vol. xx. Cp. the list in Lane-Poole's Mohammadan Dynasties, p. 242.]

[30] [Mangū (1251-1257) appointed his brother Khubilāy governor of the southern provinces. On Mangū's death Khubilāy defeated the attempts of the line of Jūjī to recover the chief Khanate, and reigned till 1294. He transferred the royal residence from Karakorum to Peking.]

[31] In Marco Polo and the Oriental geographers, the names of Cathay and Mangi distinguish the Northern and Southern empires, which, from A.D. 1234 to 1279, were those of the Great Khan and of the Chinese. The search of Cathay, after China had been found, excited and misled our navigators of the sixteenth century, in their attempts to discover the north-east passage. [Cp. Cathay and the Way Thither: a collection of all minor notices of China previous to the sixteenth century, translated and edited by Col. H. Yule, 2 vols. 1866.]

finally subdued seven years after his death.   After the loss of
Pekin, the emperor had fixed his residence at Kaifong, a city
many leagues in circumference, and which contained, according to the Chinese annals, fourteen hundred thousand families
of inhabitants and fugitives.   He escaped from thence with
only seven horsemen, and made his last stand in a third
capital, till at length the hopeless monarch, protesting his
innocence and accusing his fortune, ascended a funeral pile,
and gave orders that, as soon as he had stabbed himself, the
fire should be kindled by his attendants.   The dynasty of the
[The south-*Song*, the native and ancient sovereigns of the whole empire,
ern empire, survived above forty-five years the fall of the Northern usurpers ;
native
Chinese and the perfect conquest was reserved for the arms of Cublai.
dynasty] During this interval, the Moguls were often diverted by foreign
wars ; and, if the Chinese seldom dared to meet their victors in
the field, their passive courage presented an endless succession
of cities to storm and of millions to slaughter.   In the attack
and defence of places, the engines of antiquity and the Greek
fire were alternately employed; the use of gunpowder, in
cannon and bombs, appears as a familiar practice;[32] and the
sieges were conducted by the Mahometans and Franks, who
[Khubilay] had been liberally invited into the service of Cublai.   After
passing the great river, the troops and artillery were conveyed
along a series of canals, till they invested the royal residence
of Hamcheu, or Quinsay, in the country of silk, the most delicious climate of China.   The emperor, a defenceless youth,
surrendered his person and sceptre ; and, before he was sent in
exile into Tartary, he struck nine times the ground with his
forehead, to adore in prayer or thanksgiving the mercy of the
Of the Great Khan.   Yet the war (it was now styled a rebellion) was
Southern,
A.D. 1279 still maintained in the southern provinces from Hamcheu to
Canton ; and the obstinate remnant of independence and hos-

[32] I depend on the knowledge and fidelity of the Père Gaubil, who translates
the Chinese text of the annals of the Moguls or Yuen (p. 71, 93, 153); but I am
ignorant at what time these annals were composed and published.   The two uncles
of Marco Polo, who served as engineers at the siege of Siengyangfou (l. ii. c. 61,
in Ramusio, tom. ii.; see Gaubil, p. 155, 157) must have felt and related the effects
of this destructive powder, and their silence is a weighty and almost decisive objection.   I entertain a suspicion that the recent discovery was carried from Europe
to China by the caravans of the xvth century, and falsely adopted as an old national
discovery before the arrival of the Portuguese and Jesuits in the xvith.   Yet the
Père Gaubil affirms that the use of gunpowder has been known to the Chinese
above 1600 years.   [For Chinese Annals see Appendix 1.]

tility was transported from the land to the sea. But, when the fleet of the *Song* was surrounded and oppressed by a superior armament, their last champion leaped into the waves with his infant emperor in his arms. "It is more glorious," he cried, "to die a prince than to live a slave." An hundred thousand Chinese imitated his example; and the whole empire, from Tonkin to the great wall, submitted to the dominion of Cublai. His boundless ambition aspired to the conquest of Japan; his fleet was twice shipwrecked; and the lives of an hundred thousand Moguls and Chinese were sacrificed in the fruitless expedition. But the circumjacent kingdoms, Corea, [Corea won, A.D. 1241] Tonkin, Cochinchina, Pegu, Bengal and Thibet, were reduced in different degrees of tribute and obedience by the effort or terror of his arms. He explored the Indian Ocean with a fleet of a thousand ships; they sailed in sixty-eight days, most probably to the isle of Borneo, under the equinoctial line; and, though they returned not without spoil or glory, the emperor was dissatisfied that the savage king had escaped from their hands.

II. The conquest of Hindostan by the Moguls was reserved [Of Persia. and the empire of the Caliphs, A.D. 1258] in a later period for the house of Timour; but that of Iran, or Persia, was achieved by Holagou [33] Khan, the grandson of Zingis, the brother and lieutenant of the two successive emperors, Mangou and Cublai. I shall not enumerate the crowd of sultans, emirs, and atabeks, whom he trampled into dust; but the extirpation of the *Assassins*, or Ismaelians [34] of Persia, may be considered as a service to mankind. Among the hills to the south of the Caspian, these odious sectaries had reigned with impunity above an hundred and sixty years; and their prince, or imam, established his lieutenant to lead and govern the colony of

---

[33] [Hūlāgū. His reign in Persia began in A.D. 1256. His dynasty was called the Il Khāns, that is "Khāns of the Ils" or tribes (*i.e.* provincial). Hammer has made them the subject of a book: Geschichte der Ilchane, 1842. The Syriac Life (translated from the Persian) of the Nestorian Patriarch Jabalaha III., throws interesting light on the relation of the Il Khans to the surrounding powers. It has been edited in the Latin version by R. Hilgenfeld (Leipzig, 1896). See also J. B. Chabot, Histoire de Mar Jabalaha III. et du moine Rabban Çauma, 1895.]

[34] All that can be known of the Assassins of Persia and Syria, is poured from the copious, and even profuse, erudition of M. Falconet, in two *Mémoires* read before the Academy of Inscriptions (tom. xvii. p. 127-170). [One of the princes Jelal ad-Dīn Hasan had sent his submission to Chingiz: it was his son Rukn ad-Dīn who fought with Hūlāgū. On the Assassins see Hammer's History of the Assassins, transl. by O. C. Wood, 1835.]

Mount Libanus, so famous and formidable in the history of the crusades [35]. With the fanaticism of the Koran, the Ismaelians had blended the Indian transmigration and the visions of their own prophets; and it was their first duty to devote their souls and bodies in blind obedience to the vicar of God. The daggers of his missionaries were felt both in the East and West; the Christians and the Moslems enumerate, and perhaps multiply, the illustrious victims that were sacrificed to the zeal, avarice, or resentment of *the old man* (as he was corruptly styled) *of the mountain.* But these daggers, his only arms, were broken by the sword of Holagou, and not a vestige is left of the enemies of mankind, except the word *assassin*, which, in the most odious sense, has been adopted in the languages of Europe. The extinction of the Abbassides cannot be indifferent to the spectators of their greatness and decline. Since the fall of their Seljukian tyrants, the caliphs had recovered their lawful dominion of Bagdad and the Arabian Irak; but the city was distracted by theological factions, and the commander of the faithful was lost in a harem of seven hundred concubines. The invasion of the Moguls he encountered with feeble arms and haughty embassies. "On the divine decree," said the caliph Mostasem, "is founded the throne of the sons of Abbas: and their foes shall surely be destroyed in this world and in the next. Who is this Holagou that dares to arise against them? If he be desirous of peace, let him instantly depart from the sacred territory, and perhaps he may obtain from our clemency the pardon of his fault." This presumption was cherished by a perfidious vizir, who assured his master that, even if the barbarians had entered the city, the women and children, from the terraces, would be sufficient to overwhelm them with stones. But, when Holagou touched the phantom, it instantly vanished into smoke. After a siege of two months, Bagdad was stormed and sacked by the Moguls; and their savage commander pronounced the death of the caliph Mostasem, the last of the temporal successors of Mahomet; whose noble kinsmen, of the race of Abbas, had reigned in Asia above five hundred years. What-

---

[35] The Ismaelians of Syria, 40,000 assassins, had acquired or founded ten castles in the hills above Tortosa. About the year 1280, they were extirpated by the Mamalukes. [See Guyard, Un grand-Maître des Assassins, in the Journal asiatique, 1877.]

ever might be the designs of the conqueror, the holy cities of Mecca and Medina [36] were protected by the Arabian desert; but the Moguls spread beyond the Tigris and Euphrates, pillaged Aleppo and Damascus, and threatened to join the Franks in the deliverance of Jerusalem. Egypt was lost, had she been defended only by her feeble offspring; but the Mamalukes had breathed in their infancy the keenness of a Scythian air: equal in valour, superior in discipline, they met the Moguls in many a well-fought field; and drove back the stream of hostility to the eastward of the Euphrates. But it overflowed with resistless violence the kingdoms of Armenia and Anatolia, of which the former was possessed by the Christians, and the latter by the Turks. The sultans of Iconium opposed some resistance to the Mogul arms, till Azzadin sought a refuge among the Greeks of Constantinople, and his feeble successors, the last of the Seljukian dynasty, were finally extirpated by the khans of Persia. [Of Anatolia, A.D. 1242-1272] [Izz-al-Din, A.D. 1245-1257] [A.D. 1300]

III. No sooner had Octai subverted the northern empire of China, than he resolved to visit with his arms the most remote countries of the West.[37] Fifteen hundred thousand Moguls and Tartars were inscribed on the military roll; of these the Great Khan selected a third [38] which he entrusted to the command of his nephew Batou, the son of Tuli; [39] who reigned over his father's conquests to the north of the Caspian Sea. After a festival of forty days, Batou set forwards on this great expedition; and such was the speed and ardour of his innumerable squadrons that in less than six years they had measured a line of ninety degrees of longitude, a fourth part of the circumference of the globe. The great rivers of Asia and Europe, the Volga and Kama, the Don and Borysthenes, the Vistula and Danube, they either swam with their horses, or passed on the ice, or [Of Kipzak, Russia, Poland, Hungary, &c. A.D. 1235-1245]

---

[36] As a proof of the ignorance of the Chinese in foreign transactions, I must observe that some of their historians extend the conquests of Zingis himself to Medina, the country of Mahomet (Gaubil, p. 42).

[37] [On the history of the Mongols in the West and the Golden Horde, see Hammer's Geschichte der goldenen Horde, 1840, and Howorth's History of the Mongols, part ii. In May, 1334, the Moorish traveller Ibn Batūta visited the camp of Uzbeg Khan of the Golden Horde (Voyages, ed. and transl. Defrémery and Sanguinetti, vol. ii. 1877).]

[38] [The numbers given in the western sources are mere metaphors for immensity. Cp. Cahun, op. cit., p. 343-344; Strakosch-Grassmann, Der Einfall der Mongolen in Mitteleuropa, p. 182-184. The total number of the Mongols may have been about 100,000.]

[39] [Bātū was son of Jūjī (not of Tulūy).]

traversed in leathern boats, which followed the camp and transported their waggons and artillery. By the first victories of Batou,[40] the remains of national freedom were eradicated in the immense plains of Turkestan and Kipzak.[41] In his rapid progress, he overran the kingdoms, as they are now styled, of Astracan and Cazan; and the troops which he detached towards Mount Caucasus explored the most secret recesses of Georgia and Circassia. The civil discord of the great dukes or princes of Russia betrayed their country to the Tartars. They spread from Livonia to the Black Sea, and both Moscow and Kiow, the modern and the ancient capitals, were reduced to ashes: a temporary ruin, less fatal than the deep and perhaps indelible mark which a servitude of two hundred years has imprinted on the character of the Russians.[42] The Tartars ravaged with equal fury the countries which they hoped to possess and those which they were hastening to leave. From the permanent conquest of Russia, they made a deadly, though transient, inroad into the heart of Poland and as far as the borders of Germany. The cities of Lublin and Cracow were obliterated; they approached the shores of the Baltic; and in the battle of Lignitz,

[Battle of Wahlstatt near Liegnitz, 9th April, A.D. 1241] they defeated the dukes of Silesia, the Polish palatines, and the great master of the Teutonic order,[43] and filled nine sacks with the right ears of the slain. From Lignitz, the extreme point of their western march, they turned aside to the invasion of Hungary;[44] and the presence or spirit of Batou inspired the

[40] [Bātū was only nominally the leader. The true commander was Subutai, who deserves to be remembered among the great generals of the world for the brilliant campaign of 1241. See Appendix 2.]

[41] The *Dashte Kipzak* [Dasht-i-Kipchāk] or plain of Kipzak, extends on either side of the Volga, in a boundless space towards the Jaik and Borysthenes, and is supposed to contain the primitive name and nation of the Cossacks.

[42] [Riazan was taken 21st December, 1237; then Moscow; then Vladimir, the Grand Duke's capital, 7th January, 1238; then the Grand Duke's army was routed, 4th March. Subutai did not go farther north-westward than Torjok; he turned to subdue the Caucasian regions, the valley of the Don and the land of the Kipchaks. This occupied him till the end of 1239. Then he advanced on Kiev, and ruined it, with an exceptional and deliberate malice, which requires some explanation. Kiev was at this time a most prosperous and important centre of commerce with the East. From this time forward Venice had a monopoly of trade with the extreme East. Now the Venetian merchants of the Crimea were on very good terms with the Mongols. It has been plausibly suggested by M. Cahun that in the destruction of Kiev the Mongols acted under Venetian influence (*op. cit.*, p. 350).]

[43] [And a band of Knights Templar of France.]

[44] [This is not correct. The battle of Liegnitz was gained by the right wing of the Mongol army. The advance into Hungary, under Bātū and Subutai, was simultaneous. See Appendix 2.]

host of five hundred thousand men : the Carpathian hills could
not be long impervious to their divided columns ; and their ap- [Defeat of
proach had been fondly disbelieved till it was irresistibly felt. battle of
The king, Bela the Fourth, assembled the military force of his April, A.D.
counts and bishops ; but he had alienated the nation by adopt- 1241]
ing a vagrant horde of forty thousand families of Comans ; and
these savage guests were provoked to revolt by the suspicion of
treachery and the murder of their prince.   The whole country
north of the Danube was lost in a day, and depopulated in a
summer ; and the ruins of cities and churches were overspread
with the bones of the natives, who expiated the sins of their
Turkish ancestors.   An ecclesiastic, who fled from the sack of [Roger of
Waradin, describes the calamities which he had seen or suffered ; Wardein]
and the sanguinary rage of sieges and battles is far less atrocious
than the treatment of the fugitives, who had been allured from
the woods under a promise of peace and pardon, and who were
coolly slaughtered as soon as they had performed the labours of
the harvest and vintage.   In the winter, the Tartars passed the
Danube on the ice, and advanced to Gran or Strigonium, a
German colony, and the metropolis of the kingdom.   Thirty
engines were planted against the walls ; the ditches were filled
with sacks of earth and dead bodies ; and, after a promiscuous
massacre, three hundred noble matrons were slain in the presence of the khan.   Of all the cities and fortresses of Hungary,
three alone survived the Tartar invasion, and the unfortunate
Bela hid his head among the islands of the Adriatic.

The Latin world was darkened by this cloud of savage
hostility ; a Russian fugitive carried the alarm to Sweden ; and
the remote nations of the Baltic and the ocean trembled at the
approach of the Tartars,[45] whom their fear and ignorance were
inclined to separate from the human species.   Since the invasion of the Arabs in the eighth century, Europe had never
been exposed to a similar calamity ; and, if the disciples of
Mahomet would have oppressed her religion and liberty, it
might be apprehended that the shepherds of Scythia would

---

[45] In the year 1238, the inhabitants of Gothia (*Sweden*) and Frise were prevented,
by their fear of the Tartars, from sending, as usual, their ships to the herring
fishery on the coast of England ; and, as there was no exportation, forty or fifty of
these fish were sold for a shilling (Matthew Paris, p. 396).   It is whimsical enough
that the orders of a Mogul Khan, who reigned on the borders of China, should
have lowered the price of herrings in the English market.

extinguish her cities, her arts, and all the institutions of civil society. The Roman pontiff attempted to appease and convert these invincible pagans by a mission of Franciscan and Dominican friars; but he was astonished by the reply of the khan, that the sons of God and of Zingis were invested with a divine power to subdue or extirpate the nations; and that the Pope would be involved in the universal destruction, unless he visited in person, and as a suppliant, the royal horde. The emperor Frederic the Second embraced a more generous mode of defence; and his letters to the kings of France and England and the princes of Germany represented the common danger, and urged them to arm their vassals in this just and rational crusade.[46]   The Tartars themselves were awed by the fame and valour of the Franks; the town of Neustadt in Austria was bravely defended against them by fifty knights and twenty crossbows; and they raised the siege on the appearance of a German army. After wasting the adjacent kingdoms of Servia, Bosnia, and Bulgaria, Batou slowly retreated from the Danube to the Volga to enjoy the rewards of victory in the city and palace of Serai, which started at his command from the midst of the desert.[47]

Of Siberia,
A.D. 1242,
&c.
IV. Even the poor and frozen regions of the north attracted the arms of the Moguls: Sheibani Khan, the brother of the great Batou, led an horde of fifteen thousand families into the wilds of Siberia; and his descendants reigned at Tobolskoy above three centuries, till the Russian conquest. The spirit of enterprise which pursued the course of the Oby and Yenisei must

---

[46] I shall copy his characteristic or flattering epithets of the different countries of Europe : Furens ac fervens ad arma Germania, strenuæ militiæ genetrix et alumna Francia, bellicosa et audax Hispania, virtuosa viris et classe munita fertilis Anglia, impetuosis bellatoribus referta Alemannia, navalis Dacia, indomita Italia, pacis ignara Burgundia, inquieta Apulia, cum maris Græci, Adriatici, et Tyrrheni insulis pyraticis et invictis, Cretâ, Cypro, Sicilia, cum Oceano conterminis insulis et regionibus, cruenta Hybernia, cum agili Walliâ, palustris Scotia, glacialis Norwegia, suam electam militiam sub vexillo Crucis destinabunt, &c. (Matthew Paris, p. 498).

[47] [The news of the death of the Grand Khan Ogotai recalled Bātū and Subutai to the East. The Mongols left Siebenbürgen in summer, 1242, Bulgaria in the following winter. Europe did not deceive itself. It was fully conscious that the Mongols could have extended their conquests if they had chosen. As Roger puts it, they disdained to conquer Germany—Tartari aspernabantur Theutomain expugnare (Miserabile Carmen, in M. G. H. 29, p. 564). On the position of the capital of the Golden Horde, Serai, the chief works are Grigor'ev, O miestopolozhenii stolitsy zolotoi Ordy Saraia, 1845 ; and Brun, O rezidentsii chanov zolotoi Ordy do vremen Dzhanibeka (in the publications of the 3rd Archeological Congress at Kiev), 1878. Brun attempts to show that there were two (old) Serais,—the elder, nearer the Caspian Sea, not far from the village of Selitrian, the later at Tsarev.]

have led to the discovery of the Icy Sea. After brushing away
the monstrous fables, of men with dogs' heads and cloven feet,
we shall find that, fifteen years after the death of Zingis, the
Moguls were informed of the name and manners of the Samo-
yedes in the neighbourhood of the polar circle, who dwelt in
subterraneous huts, and derived their furs and their food from
the sole occupation of hunting.[48]

While China, Syria, and Poland were invaded at the same The suc-
time by the Moguls and Tartars, the authors of the mighty cessors of Zingis, A.D.
mischief were content with the knowledge and declaration 1227-1259
that their word was the sword of death. Like the first
caliphs, the first successors of Zingis seldom appeared in person
at the head of their victorious armies. On the banks of the
Onon and Selinga, the royal or *golden horde* exhibited the
contrast of simplicity and greatness ; of the roasted sheep and
mare's milk which composed their banquets ; and of a distribution in one day of five hundred waggons of gold and silver.
The ambassadors and princes of Europe and Asia were compelled to undertake this distant and laborious pilgrimage ;
and the life and reign of the great dukes of Russia, the kings
of Gregoria and Armenia, the sultans of Iconium, and the
emirs of Persia, were decided by the frown or smile of the
Great Khan. The sons and grandsons of Zingis had been accustomed to the pastoral life ; but the village of Caracorum[49]
was gradually ennobled by their election and residence. A
change of manners is implied in the removal of Octai and
Mangou from a tent to an house ; and their example was
imitated by the princes of their family and the great officers
of the empire. Instead of the boundless forest, the inclosure
of a park afforded the more indolent pleasures of the chase ;
their new habitations were decorated with painting and sculpture ; their superfluous treasures were cast in fountains, and

---

[48] See Carpin's relation in Hakluyt, vol. i. p. 30. The pedigree of the khans
of Siberia is given by Abulghazi (part viii. p. 485-495). Have the Russians found
no Tartar chronicles at Tobolskoi ?

[49] The Map of d'Anville and the Chinese Itineraries (de Guignes, tom. i. p. 57)
seem to mark the position of Holin, or Caracorum, about six hundred miles to the
north-west of Pekin. The distance between Selinginsky and Pekin is near 2000
Russian versts, between 1300 and 1400 English miles (Bell's Travels, vol. ii. p. 67).
[For the situation of Caracorum, at a place still called Kara-Kharam, on the north
bank of the Orchon, see Geographical Magazine for July, 1874, p. 137 ; Yule's
Marco Polo, vol. i. p. 228-229.]

basons, and statues of massy silver; and the artists of China
and Paris vied with each other in the service of the Great
Khan.[50] Caracorum contained two streets, the one of Chinese
mechanics, the other of Mahometan traders; and the places of
religious worship, one Nestorian church, two mosques, and
twelve temples of various idols, may represent, in some degree,
the number and division of inhabitants. Yet a French missionary declares that the town of St. Denys, near Paris, was
more considerable than the Tartar capital; and that the whole
palace of Mangou was scarcely equal to a tenth part of that
Benedictine abbey. The conquests of Russia and Syria might
amuse the vanity of the Great Khans; but they were seated
on the borders of China; the acquisition of that empire was
the nearest and most interesting object; and they might learn
from their pastoral economy that it is for the advantage of the
shepherd to protect and propagate his flock. I have already
celebrated the wisdom and virtue of a mandarin who prevented
the desolation of five populous and cultivated provinces. In
a spotless administration of thirty years, this friend of his
country and of mankind continually laboured to mitigate or
suspend the havoc of war; to save the monuments, and to
rekindle the flame, of science; to restrain the military commander by the restoration of civil magistrates; and to instil
the love of peace and justice into the minds of the Moguls.
He struggled with the barbarism of the first conquerors; but
his salutary lessons produced a rich harvest in the second generation. The northern and by degrees the southern empire
acquiesced in the government of Cublai, the lieutenant and
afterwards the successor of Mangou; and the nation was
loyal to a prince who had been educated in the manners of
China. He restored the forms of her venerable constitution;
and the victors submitted to the laws, the fashions, and even
the prejudices of the vanquished people. This peaceful triumph,
which has been more than once repeated, may be ascribed, in
a great measure, to the numbers and servitude of the Chinese.
The Mogul army was dissolved in a vast and populous country;
and their emperors adopted with pleasure a political system

adopt the manners of China, A.D. 1259-1368

---

[50] Rubruquis found at Caracorum his countryman *Guillaume Boucher, orfèvre
de Paris*, who had executed, for the khan, a silver tree, supported by four lions,
and ejecting four different liquors. Abulghazi (part iv. p. 336) mentions the painters
of Kitay or China.

which gives to the prince the solid substance of despotism and leaves to the subject the empty names of philosophy, freedom, and filial obedience. Under the reign of Cublai, letters and commerce, peace and justice, were restored ; the great canal of five hundred miles was opened from Nankin to the capital ; [Period of the Yuen dynasty] he fixed his residence at Pekin,[51] and displayed in his court the magnificence of the greatest monarch of Asia. Yet this learned prince declined from the pure and simple religion of his great ancestor ; he sacrificed to the idol Fo ; and his blind attachment to the lamas of Thibet and the bonzes of China [52] provoked the censure of the disciples of Confucius. His successors polluted the palace with a crowd of eunuchs, physicians, and astrologers, while thirteen millions of their subjects were consumed in the provinces by famine. One hundred and forty years after the death of Zingis, his degenerate race, the dynasty of the Yuen, was expelled by a revolt of the native Chinese ; [53] [A.D. 1268] and the Mogul emperors were lost in the oblivion of the desert. Before this revolution, they had forfeited their supremacy over the dependent branches of their house, the khans of Kipzak and Russia, the khans of Zagatai or Transoxiana, and the khans of Iran or Persia. By their distance and power, these royal lieu- [Division of the Mogul empire, A.D. 1259-1300] tenants had soon been released from the duties of obedience ; and, after the death of Cublai, they scorned to accept a sceptre or a title from his unworthy successors. According to their respective situation, they maintained the simplicity of the pastoral life or assumed the luxury of the cities of Asia; but the princes and their hordes were alike disposed for the reception of a foreign worship. After some hesitation between the Gospel and the Koran, they conformed to the religion of Mahomet ; and, while they adopted for their brethren the Arabs and Persians, they renounced all intercourse with the ancient Moguls, the idolaters of China.

In this shipwreck of nations, some surprise may be excited

---

[51] [Which was called Khān Baligh, City of the Khān.]

[52] The attachment of the khans and the hatred of the mandarins, to the bonzes and lamas (Duhalde, Hist. de la Chine, tom. i. p. 502, 503) seems to represent them as the priests of the same god, of the Indian *Fo*, whose worship prevails among the sects of Hindostan, Siam, Thibet, China, and Japan. But this mysterious subject is still lost in a cloud, which the researches of our Asiatic Society may gradually dispel.

[53] [Under Chu Yuen Chang who became emperor and founded the Ming dynasty.]

Escape of Constantinople and the Greek empire from the Moguls, A.D. 1240-1304

by the escape of the Roman empire, whose relics, at the time of the Mogul invasion, were dismembered by the Greeks and Latins. Less potent than Alexander, they were pressed, like the Macedonian, both in Europe and Asia, by the shepherds of Scythia; and, had the Tartars undertaken the siege, Constantinople must have yielded to the fate of Pekin, Samarcand, and Bagdad. The glorious and voluntary retreat of Batou from the Danube was insulted by the vain triumph of the Franks and Greeks; [54] and in a second expedition death surprised him in full march to attack the capital of the Cæsars. His brother

[Bγraka, 1256-66 A.D.]

Borga carried the Tartar arms into Bulgaria and Thrace; but he was diverted from the Byzantine war by a visit to Novogorod, in the fifty-seventh degree of latitude, where he numbered the inhabitants and regulated the tributes of Russia. The Mogul khan formed an alliance with the Mamalukes against his brethren of Persia; three hundred thousand horse penetrated through the gates of Derbend; and the Greeks might rejoice in the first example of domestic war. After the recovery of Constantinople, Michael Palæologus,[55] at a distance from his court and army, was surprised and surrounded in a Thracian castle by twenty thousand Tartars. But the object of their march was a private interest; they came to the deliverance of Azzadin,[56] the Turkish sultan; and were content with his person and the treasure of the emperor. Their general Noga, whose name is perpetuated in the hordes of Astracan, raised a formid-

[Mangu-Timur, A.D. 1266-1280]

able rebellion against Mengo Timour, the third of the khans of Kipzak; obtained in marriage Maria, the natural daughter of Palæologus; and guarded the dominions of his friend and father. The subsequent invasions of a Scythian cast were those of outlaws and fugitives; and some thousands of Alani and Comans, who had been driven from their native seats, were reclaimed from a vagrant life and enlisted in the service of the empire. Such was the influence in Europe of the invasion of the Moguls. The first terror of their arms secured

[54] Some repulse of the Moguls in Hungary (Matthew Paris, p. 545, 546) might propagate and colour the report of the union and victory of the kings of the Franks on the confines of Bulgaria. Abulpharagius (Dynast. p. 310), after forty years, beyond the Tigris, might be easily deceived.

[55] See Pachymer, l. iii. c. 25, and l. ix. c. 26, 27 ; and the false alarm at Nice, l. iii. c. 27 [28]. Nicephorus Gregoras, l. iv. c. 6.

[56] [Izz ad-Dīn II. reigned A.D. 1245-1257.]

rather than disturbed the peace of the Roman Asia. The sultan of Iconium solicited a personal interview with John Vataces; and his artful policy encouraged the Turks to defend their barrier against the common enemy.[57] That barrier indeed was soon overthrown; and the servitude and ruin of the Seljukians exposed the nakedness of the Greeks. The formidable Holagou threatened to march to Constantinople at the head of four hundred thousand men; and the groundless panic of the citizens of Nice will present an image of the terror which he had inspired. The accident of a procession, and the sound of a doleful litany, "From the fury of the Tartars, good Lord, deliver us," had scattered the hasty report of an assault and massacre. In the blind credulity of fear, the streets of Nice were crowded with thousands of both sexes, who knew not from what or to whom they fled; and some hours elapsed before the firmness of the military officers could relieve the city from this imaginary foe. But the ambition of Holagou and his successors was fortunately diverted by the conquest of Bagdad and a long vicissitude of Syrian wars; their hostility to the Moslems inclined them to unite with the Greeks and Franks;[58] and their generosity or contempt had offered the kingdom of Anatolia as the reward of an Armenian vassal. The fragments of the Seljukian monarchy were disputed by the emirs who had occupied the cities or the mountains; but they all confessed the supremacy of the khans of Persia; and he often interposed his authority, and sometimes his arms, to check their depredations, and to preserve the peace and balance of his Turkish frontier. The death of Cazan,[59] one of the greatest and most accomplished princes of the house of Zingis, removed this salutary control; and the decline of the Moguls gave a free scope to the rise and progress of the OTTOMAN EMPIRE.[60]

Decline of the Mogul Khans of Persia, A.D. 1304, 31st May

---

[57] G. Acropolita, p. 36, 37 [c. 41].   Nic. Gregoras, l. ii. c. 6, l. iv. c. 5.

[58] Abulpharagius, who wrote in the year 1284, declares that the Moguls, since the fabulous defeat of Batou, had not attacked either the Franks or Greeks; and of this he is a competent witness. Hayton, likewise, the Armeniac prince, celebrates their friendship for himself and his nation.

[59] Pachymer gives a splendid character of Cazan Khan, the rival of Cyrus and Alexander (l. xii. c. 1). In the conclusion of his history (l. xiii. c. 36), he *hopes* much from the arrival of 30,000 Tochars, or Tartars, who were ordered by the successor of Cazan [Ghāzān Mahmūd, A.D. 1295-1304; his successor was Uljāitu, A.D. 1304-1316] to restrain the Turks of Bithynia, A.D. 1308.

[60] The origin of the Ottoman dynasty is illustrated by the critical learning of MM. de Guignes (Hist. des Huns, tom. iv. p. 329-337), and d'Anville (Empire Turc,

Origin of
the Otto-
mans, A.D.
1240, &c.
After the retreat of Zingis, the sultan Gelaleddin of Carizme had returned from India to the possession and defence of his Persian kingdoms. In the space of eleven years, that hero fought in person fourteen battles; and such was his activity that
[A.D. 1220-
1231]
he led his cavalry, in seventeen days, from Teflis to Kerman, a march of a thousand miles.[61] Yet he was oppressed by the jealousy of the Moslem princes and the innumerable armies of the Moguls; and after his last defeat Gelaleddin perished ignobly in the mountains of Curdistan. His death dissolved a veteran and adventurous army, which included under the name of Cariz-mians, or Corasmins, many Turkman hordes that had attached themselves to the sultan's fortune. The bolder and more powerful chiefs invaded Syria and violated the holy sepulchre of
[Ala-ad-Din
I. A.D. 1219-
1236]
Jerusalem; the more humble engaged in the service of Aladin, sultan of Iconium; and among these were the obscure fathers of the Ottoman line.[62] They had formerly pitched their tents near the southern banks of the Oxus, in the plains of Mahan and Nesa; and it is somewhat remarkable that the same spot should have produced the first authors of the Parthian and Turkish
[Death of
Sulayman,
A.D. 1231]
empires. At the head or in the rear of a Carizmian army, Soliman Shah was drowned in the passage of the Euphrates;
[Ertughrul]
his son, Orthogrul, became the soldier and subject of Aladin,
[In Phry-
gia]
and established at Surgut,[63] on the banks of the Sangar, a camp
Reign of
Othman,
A.D. 1299-
1326
of four hundred families, or tents, whom he governed fifty-two years both in peace and war. He was the father of Thaman, or Athman, whose Turkish name has been melted into the appella-tion of the caliph Othman;[64] and, if we describe that pastoral chief as a shepherd and a robber, we must separate from those characters all idea of ignominy and baseness. Othman possessed, and perhaps surpassed, the ordinary virtues of a soldier; and the circumstances of time and place were propitious to his independ-ence and success. The Seljukian dynasty was no more; and the

p. 14-22), two inhabitants of Paris, from whom the Orientals may learn the history and geography of their own country.

[61] [Jalāl ad-Dīn Mangbarti, A.D. 1220-1231.]

[62] [They were a clan of the tribe of Oghuz.]

[Sugut (Turkish name = " willow "), south of Malagina on the way to Dory-læum, is mentioned by Anna Comnena (Σαγουδάους, xv. 2). Othmän was born in A.D. 1258. Gibbon has shown his critical faculty in neglecting the confused and false accounts of the Greek historians, Phrantzes and Chalcondyles, of the deeds of Ertughrul.]

[64] [This is the correct form of the name –Othmän. The name of the people is Othmänli; Ottoman is a corruption.]

distance and decline of the Mogul khans soon enfranchised him from the control of a superior. He was situate on the verge of the Greek empire; the Koran sanctified his *gazi*, or holy war, against the infidels; and their political errors unlocked the passes of Mount Olympus, and invited him to descend into the plains of Bithynia. Till the reign of Palæologus, these passes had been vigilantly guarded by the militia of the country, who were repaid by their own safety and an exemption from taxes. The emperor abolished their privilege and assumed their office; but the tribute was rigorously collected, the custody of the passes was neglected, and the hardy mountaineers degenerated into a trembling crowd of peasants without spirit or discipline. It was on the twenty-seventh of July, in the year twelve hundred and ninety-nine of the Christian æra, that Othman first invaded the territory of Nicomedia[65]; and the singular accuracy of the date seems to disclose some foresight of the rapid and destructive growth of the monster. The annals of the twenty-seven years of his reign would exhibit a repetition of the same inroads; and his hereditary troops were multiplied in each campaign by the accession of captives and volunteers. Instead of retreating to the hills, he maintained the most useful and defensible posts; fortified the towns and castles which he had first pillaged; and renounced the pastoral life for the baths and palaces of his infant capitals. But it was not till Othman was oppressed by age and infirmities that he received the welcome news of the conquest of Prusa, which had been surrendered by [A.D. 1326] famine or treachery to the arms of his son Orchan. The glory of Othman is chiefly founded on that of his descendants; but the Turks have transcribed or composed a royal testament of his last counsels of justice and moderation.[66]

[65] See Pachymer, l. x. c. 25, 26; l. xiii. c. 33, 34, 36; and concerning the guard of the mountains, l. i. c. 3-6; Nicephorus Gregoras, l. vii. c. 1; and the first book of Laonicus Chalcondyles, the Athenian.

[66] I am ignorant whether the Turks have any writers older than Mahomet II., nor can I reach beyond a meagre chronicle (Annales Turcici ad annum 1550), translated by John Gaudier, and published by Leunclavius (ad calcem Laonic. Chalcond. p. 311-350) with copious pandects, or commentaries. The History of the Growth and Decay (A.D. 1300-1683) of the Othman empire was translated into English from the Latin Ms. of Demetrius Cantemir, Prince of Moldavia (London, 1734, in folio). The author is guilty of strange blunders in Oriental History; but he was conversant with the language, the annals, and institutions of the Turks. Cantemir partly draws his materials from the Synopsis of Saadi Effendi of Larissa, dedicated in the year 1696 to sultan Mustapha, and a valuable abridgment of the original historians. In one of the Ramblers, Dr. Johnson praises Knolles (a

From the conquest of Prusa we may date the true æra of the Ottoman empire. The lives and possessions of the Christian subjects were redeemed by a tribute or ransom of thirty thousand crowns of gold; and the city, by the labours of Orchan, assumed the aspect of a Mahometan capital; Prusa was decorated with a mosque, a college, and a hospital of royal foundation; the Seljukian coin was changed for the name and impression of the new dynasty; and the most skilful professors of human and divine knowledge attracted the Persian and Arabian students from the ancient schools of Oriental learning. The office of vizir was instituted for Aladin, the brother of Orchan; and a different habit distinguished the citizens from the peasants, the Moslems from the infidels. All the troops of Othman had consisted of loose squadrons of Turkman cavalry, who served without pay and fought without discipline; but a regular body of infantry was first established and trained by the prudence of his son.[67] A great number of volunteers was enrolled with a small stipend, but with the permission of living at home, unless they were summoned to the field; their rude manners and seditious temper disposed Orchan to educate his young captives as his soldiers and those of the prophet; but the Turkish peasants were still allowed to mount on horseback and follow his standard, with the appellation and the hopes of *freebooters*. By these arts he formed an army of twenty-five thousand Moslems; a train of battering engines was framed for

General History of the Turks to the present year, London, 1603) as the first of historians, unhappy only in the choice of his subject. Yet I much doubt whether a partial and verbose compilation from Latin writers, thirteen hundred folio pages of speeches and battles, can either instruct or amuse an enlightened age, which requires from the historian some tincture of philosophy and criticism. [See Appendix 1.]

[67] [Alā ad-Dīn was a political thinker. Having resigned all claim to a share in Othman's inheritance he spent some years in retirement and thought, and then gave to his brother the result of his meditations. Orchan made him vizir and followed his suggestions. The chief reforms introduced by Alā ad-Dīn were three. (1) The regulation of Turkish dress is mentioned in the text. (2) The introduction of an independent Ottoman coinage. Hitherto the Seljuk money circulated. The historian Sad ad-Dīn (transl. Bratutti, i. p. 40) states that the first Ottoman coins, gold and silver, with Orchan's name, were issued in 1328. There are no dates on Orchan's coins. (3) The institution of the Janissaries (Yani Chari, " new soldiery "), probably in A.D. 1330 (cp. Sad ad-Dīn, *ib.* p. 42). This used to be wrongly ascribed to Murad I. (so Marsigli, Stato militare, i. 67, and Gibbon). Compare Hammer, Geschichte des osmanischen Reiches, i. 97 *sqq.* Alā ad-Dīn clearly grasped the fact that an establishment of well-trained infantry was indispensable. A regular body of cavalry was also established at the same time. The regular troops received pay; whereas the great general levy of cavalry performed military service for their fiefs.]

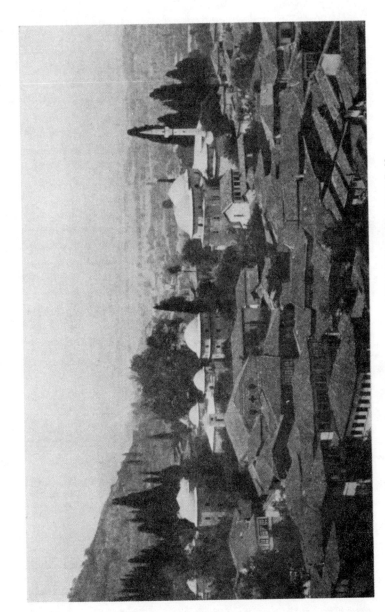

BROUSSA (PRUSA), SHOWING THE MOSQUE OF MURAD II

the use of sieges; and the first successful experiment was made on the cities of Nice and Nicomedia. Orchan granted a safe-conduct to all who were desirous of departing with their families and effects; but the widows of the slain were given in marriage to the conquerors; and the sacrilegious plunder, the books, the vases, and the images were sold or ransomed at Constantinople. The emperor, Andronicus the Younger, was vanquished and wounded by the son of Othman; [68] he subdued the whole province or kingdom of Bithynia, as far as the shores of the Bosphorus and Hellespont; and the Christians confessed the justice and clemency of a reign which claimed the voluntary attachment of the Turks of Asia. Yet Orchan was content with the modest title of emir; and in the list of his compeers, the princes of Roum or Anatolia,[69] his military forces were surpassed by the emirs of Ghermian and Caramania, each of whom could bring into the field an army of forty thousand men. Their dominions were situate in the heart of the Seljukian kingdom; but the holy warriors, though of inferior note, who formed new principalities on the Greek empire, are more conspicuous in the light of history. The maritime country from the Propontis to the Mæander and the isle of Rhodes, so long threatened and so often pillaged, was finally lost about the thirtieth year of Andronicus the Elder.[70] Two Turkish chieftains, Sarukhan and

His conquest of Bithynia, A.D. 1326-1339

[Battle of Pelekanon, A.D. 1329]

[Reduction of Bithynia completed, A.D. 1340]

Division of Anatolia among the Turkish emirs, A.D. 1300, &c.

[68] Cantacuzene, though he relates the battle and heroic flight of the younger Andronicus (l. ii. c. 6-8), dissembles, by his silence, the loss of Prusa, Nice and Nicomedia, which are fairly confessed by Nicephorus Gregoras (l. viii. 15; ix. 9, 13; xi. 6). It appears that Nice was taken by Orchan in 1330, and Nicomedia in 1339, which are somewhat different from the Turkish dates. [Capture of Nicomedia, A.D. 1326; battle of Pelekanon, A.D. 1329; capture of Nicæa, A.D. 1330; reduction of Karāsī (the ancient Mysia, including Pergamus) after A.D. 1340. See Zinkeisen, Geschichte des osmanischen Reiches in Europa, i. 102-117. For the position of Pelekanon, on the northern coast of the Gulf of Ismid, see J. Milioponlos, Byzantinische Zeitschrift, ix. 473 sq.]

[69] The partition of the Turkish emirs is extracted from two contemporaries, the Greek Nicephorus Gregoras (l. vii. 1), and the Arabian Marakeschi (de Guignes, tom. ii. P. ii. p. 76-77). See likewise the first book of Laonicus Chalcondyles.

[70] Pachymer, l. xiii. c. 13. [The western coast of Asia Minor south of Karāsī (Mysia) was not incorporated in the Ottoman realm till the reign of Bayezid I. The most powerful rival of the Ottomans in Asia, at this time, was the state of Caramania (which reached from the Sangarius to the Pamphylian sea, and included Galatia, Eastern Phrygia, Lycaonia, Pisidia and Pamphylia). Murad took Angora (Ancyra) in A.D. 1360, and in 1386 he inflicted a demoralising defeat on the Caramanian Sultan in the battle of Iconium. In 1391 the prince of Sarūkhān (the regions of the Hermus, including Sardis and Magnesia) and the prince of Aidin (south of Sarūkhān, reaching to south of the Mæander) submitted, and likewise the lord of Mentesia (Caria, including Miletus). At the same time Bayezid subdued Kermiyān (Western Phrygia) and Tekka (Lycia), and the western part of Caramania. In 1393

Aidin, left their names to their conquests and their conquests to their posterity. The captivity or ruin of the *seven* churches of Asia was consummated; and the barbarous lords of Ionia and Lydia still trample on the monuments of classic and Christian antiquity. In the loss of Ephesus, the Christians deplored the fall of the first angel, the extinction of the first candlestick of the Revelations;[71] the desolation is complete; and the temple of Diana or the church of Mary will equally elude the search of the curious traveller. The circus and three stately theatres of Laodicea are now peopled with wolves and foxes; Sardes is reduced to a miserable village; the God of Mahomet, without a rival or a son, is invoked in the mosques of Thyatira and Pergamus; and the populousness of Smyrna is supported by the foreign trade of the Franks and Armenians. Philadelphia alone has been saved by prophecy or courage. At a distance from the sea, forgotten by the emperors, encompassed on all sides by the Turks, her valiant citizens defended their religion and freedom above four-score years, and at length capitulated with the proudest of the Ottomans. Among the Greek colonies and churches of Asia, Philadelphia is still erect, a column in a scene of ruins: a pleasing example that the paths of honour and safety may sometimes be the same.[72] The servitude of Rhodes was delayed above two centuries by the establishment of the knights of St. John of Jerusalem.[73] Under the discipline of the order that island emerged into fame and opulence; the noble and warlike monks were renowned by land and sea; and the bulwark of Christendom provoked and repelled the arms of the Turks and Saracens.

Loss of the Asiatic provinces, A.D. 1312, &c.

The knights of Rhodes, A.D. 1310, 15th Aug.-A.D. 1523, 1st Jan.

the principality of Kastamunīyā (in Paphlagonia, including Sinope) was conquered; and with the exception of the eastern parts of Caramania all the little Seljuk states of Anatolia were in the hands of the Ottomans. Cp. the table in S. Lane-Poole's Mohammadan Dynasties, p. 134. See below, p. 35.]

[71] See the Travels of Wheeler and Spon, of Pococke and Chandler, and more particularly Smith's Survey of the Seven Churches of Asia, p. 205-276. The more pious antiquaries labour to reconcile the promises and threats of the author of the Revelations with the *present* state of the seven cities. Perhaps it would be more prudent to confine his predictions to the characters and events of his own times. [For Ephesus and the temple of Diana see Wood's Discoveries at Ephesus, 1877. For recent excavations at Ephesus, since 1895, by Austrian archæologists see the Jahreshefte of the Austrian archæological Institute.]

[72] [The date of the Ottoman capture of Philadelphia is uncertain (cp. Finlay, History of Greece, iii., p. 469, note). Probably A.D. 1391.]

[73] Consult the fourth book of the Histoire de l'Ordre de Malthe, par l'Abbé de Vertot. That pleasing writer betrays his ignorance in supposing that Othman, a freebooter of the Bithynian hills, could besiege Rhodes by sea and land.

The Greeks, by their intestine divisions, were the authors of their final ruin.[74] During the civil wars of the elder and younger Andronicus, the son of Othman achieved, almost without resistance, the conquest of Bithynia ; and the same disorders encouraged the Turkish emirs of Lydia and Ionia to build a fleet, and to pillage the adjacent islands and the seacoast of Europe. In the defence of his life and honour, Cantacuzene was tempted to prevent or imitate his adversaries by calling to his aid the public enemies of his religion and country. Amir, the son of Aidin, concealed under a Turkish garb the humanity and politeness of a Greek ; he was united with the great domestic by mutual esteem and reciprocal services ; and their friendship is compared, in the vain rhetoric of the times, to the perfect union of Orestes and Pylades.[75] On the report of the danger of his friend, who was persecuted by an ungrateful court, the prince of Ionia assembled at Smyrna a fleet of three hundred vessels, with an army of twenty-nine thousand men ; sailed in the depth of winter, and cast anchor at the mouth of the Hebrus. From thence, with a chosen band of two thousand Turks, he marched along the banks of the river, and rescued the empress, who was besieged in Demotica by the wild Bulgarians. At that disastrous moment the life or death of his beloved Cantacuzene was concealed by his flight into Servia ; but the grateful Irene, impatient to behold her deliverer, invited him to enter the city, and accompanied her message with a present of rich apparel and an hundred horses. By a peculiar strain of delicacy the gentle barbarian refused, in the absence of an unfortunate friend, to visit his wife or to taste the luxuries of the palace ;

First passage of the Turks into Europe, A.D. 1341-1347

[Omar?]

[Didymoteichos]

---

[74] [For the success of the Ottomans, " the last example of the conquest of a numerous Christian population by a small number of Musulman invaders, and of the colonisation of civilised countries by a race ruder than the native population," Finlay assigns three particular causes (History of Greece, iii. p. 475). " 1. The superiority of the Ottoman tribe over all contemporary nations in religious convictions and in moral and military conduct. 2. The number of different races that composed the population of the country between the Adriatic and the Black Sea, the Danube and the Aegean. 3. The depopulation of the Greek empire, the degraded state of its judicial and civil administration, and the demoralisation of the Hellenic race."]

[75] Nicephorus Gregoras has expatiated with pleasure on this amiable character (l. xii. 7 ; xiii. 4, 10 ; xiv. 1, 9 ; xvi. 6). Cantacuzene speaks with honour and esteem of his ally (l. iii. c. 56, 57, 63, 64, 66-68, 86, 89, 95, 96) ; but he seems ignorant of his own sentimental passion for the Turk, and indirectly denies the possibility of such unnatural friendship (l. iv. c. 40).

sustained in his tent the rigour of the winter ; and rejected the hospitable gift, that he might share the hardships of two thousand companions, all as deserving as himself of that honour and distinction. Necessity and revenge might justify his predatory excursions by sea and land ; he left nine thousand five hundred men for the guard of his fleet ; and persevered in the fruitless search of Cantacuzene, till his embarkation was hastened by a fictitious letter, the severity of the season, the clamours of his independent troops, and the weight of his spoil and captives. In the prosecution of the civil war, the prince of Ionia twice returned to Europe ; joined his arms with those of the emperor ; besieged Thessalonica, and threatened Constantinople. Calumny might affix some reproach on his imperfect aid, his hasty departure, and a bribe of ten thousand crowns, which he accepted from the Byzantine court; but his friend was satisfied ; and the conduct of Amir is excused by the more sacred duty of defending against the Latins his hereditary dominions. The maritime power of the Turks had united the pope, the king of Cyprus, the republic of Venice, and the order of St. John, in a laudable crusade ; their galleys invaded the coast of Ionia ; and Amir was slain with an arrow, in the attempt to wrest from the Rhodian knights the citadel of Smyrna.[76] Before his death, he generously recommended another ally of his own nation, not more sincere or zealous than himself, but more able to afford a prompt and powerful succour, by his situation along the Propontis and in the front of Constantinople. By the prospect of a more advantageous treaty, the Turkish prince of Bithynia was detached from his engagements with Anne of Savoy ; and the pride of Orchan dictated the most solemn protestations that, if he could obtain the daughter of Cantacuzene, he would invariably fulfil the duties of a subject and a son. Parental tenderness was silenced by the voice of ambition ; the Greek clergy connived at the marriage of a Christian princess with a sectary of Mahomet; and the father of Theodora describes, with shameful satisfaction, the dishonour of the purple.[77] A body of Turkish

Marriage of Orchan with a Greek princess [A.D. 1346]

---

[76] After the conquest of Smyrna by the Latins, the defence of this fortress was imposed by Pope Gregory XI. on the Knights of Rhodes (see Vertot, l. v.).

[77] See Cantacuzenus, l. iii. c. 95. Nicephoras Gregoras, who, for the light of Mount Thabor, brands the emperor with the names of tyrant and Herod, excuses, rather than blames, this Turkish marriage, and alleges the passion and power of

cavalry attended the ambassadors, who disembarked from thirty vessels before his camp of Selybria. A stately pavilion was erected, in which the empress Irene passed the night with her daughters. In the morning, Theodora ascended a throne, which was surrounded with curtains of silk and gold ; the troops were under arms ; but the emperor alone was on horseback. At a signal the curtains were suddenly withdrawn, to disclose the bride, or the victim, encircled by kneeling eunuchs and hymenæal torches : the sound of flutes and trumpets proclaimed the joyful event ; and her pretended happiness was the theme of the nuptial song, which was chaunted by such poets as the age could produce. Without the rites of the church, Theodora was delivered to her barbarous lord ; but it had been stipulated that she should preserve her religion in the harem of Boursa ; and her father celebrates her charity and devotion in this ambiguous situation. After his peaceful establishment on the throne of Constantinople, the Greek emperor visited his Turkish ally, who, with four sons, by various wives, expected him at Scutari, on the Asiatic shore. The two princes partook, with seeming cordiality, of the pleasures of the banquet and the chase ; and Theodora was permitted to repass the Bosphorus, and to enjoy some days in the society of her mother. But the friendship of Orchan was subservient to his religion and interest ; and in the Genoese war he joined without a blush the enemies of Cantacuzene.

In the treaty with the empress Anne, the Ottoman prince had inserted a singular condition, that it should be lawful for him to sell his prisoners at Constantinople or transport them into Asia. A naked crowd of Christians of both sexes and every age, of priests and monks, of matrons and virgins, was exposed in the public market ; the whip was frequently used to quicken the charity of redemption ; and the indigent Greeks deplored the fate of their brethren, who were led away to the worst evils of temporal and spiritual bondage.[78] Cantacuzene was reduced to subscribe the same terms ; and their execution must

Establishment of the Ottomans in Europe, A.D. 1353 [1358]

Orchan, ἐγγύτατος, καὶ τῇ δυνάμει τοὺς κατ' αὐτὸν ἤδη Περσικοὺς (*Turkish*) ὑπεραίρων Σατράπας (l. xv. 5). He afterwards celebrates his kingdom and armies. See his reign in Cantemir, p. 24-30.

[78] The most lively and concise picture of this captivity may be found in the history of Ducas (c. 8), who fairly transcribes what Cantacuzene confesses with a guilty blush !

have been still more pernicious to the empire ; a body of ten
thousand Turks had been detached to the assistance of the
empress Anne; but the entire forces of Orchan were exerted
in the service of his father. Yet these calamities were of a
transient nature ; as soon as the storm had passed away, the
fugitives might return to their habitations ; and at the conclusion of the civil and foreign wars Europe was completely
evacuated by the Moslems of Asia. It was in his last quarrel
with his pupil that Cantacuzene inflicted the deep and deadly
wound, which could never be healed by his successors, and
which is poorly expiated by his theological dialogues against
the prophet Mahomet. Ignorant of their own history, the
modern Turks confound their first and their final passage of the
Hellespont,[79] and describe the son of Orchan as a nocturnal
robber, who, with eighty companions, explores by stratagem
an hostile and unknown shore. Soliman, at the head of ten
thousand horse, was transported in the vessels, and entertained
as a friend, of the Greek emperor. In the civil wars of
Romania, he performed some service and perpetrated more
mischief ; but the Chersonesus was insensibly filled with a
Turkish colony; and the Byzantine court solicited in vain the
restitution of the fortresses of Thrace. After some artful delays between the Ottoman prince and his son, their ransom was
valued at sixty thousand crowns, and the first payment had
been made, when an earthquake shook the walls and cities of
the provinces; the dismantled places were occupied by the
Turks; and Gallipoli, the key of the Hellespont, was rebuilt
and repeopled by the policy of Soliman. The abdication of
Cantacuzene dissolved the feeble bands of domestic alliance ;
and his last advice admonished his countrymen to decline a
rash contest, and to compare their own weakness with the
numbers and valour, the discipline and enthusiasm, of the
Moslems. His prudent counsels were despised by the headstrong vanity of youth, and soon justified by the victories of

---

[79] In this passage, and the first conquests in Europe, Cantemir (p. 27, &c.)
gives a miserable idea of his Turkish guides ; nor am I much better satisfied with
Chalcondyles (l. i. p. 12, &c. [p. 25, ed. Bonn]). They forget to consult the most
authentic record, the ivth book of Cantacuzene. I likewise regret the last books,
which are still manuscript, of Nicephorus Gregoras. [They have been since published. See above, vol. vi. p. 542. The Ottomans captured the little fortress of
Tzympe, near Gallipoli, in 1356, and Gallipoli itself in 1358. For Tzympe, cp.
Cantacuzenus, iv. 33 ; vol. iii. p. 242, ed. Bonn.]

the Ottomans. But, as he practised in the field the exercise Death of Orchan of the *jerid*, Soliman was killed by a fall from his horse; and his son and the aged Orchan wept and expired on the tomb of his [A.D. 1360] valiant son.

But the Greeks had not time to rejoice in the death of their The reign and Euro-enemies ; and the Turkish scymetar was wielded with the same pean con-quests of spirit by Amurath the First, the son of Orchan and the brother Amurath I. of Soliman. By the pale and fainting light of the Byzantine 1389, Sept. annals,[80] we can discern that he subdued without resistance the whole province of Romania or Thrace, from the Hellespont to Mount Hæmus and the verge of the capital ; and that Hadrian-ople was chosen for the royal seat of his government and religion in Europe.[81] Constantinople, whose decline is almost coeval with her foundation, had often, in the lapse of a thousand years, been assaulted by the barbarians of the East and West ; but never till this fatal hour had the Greeks been surrounded, both in Asia and Europe, by the arms of the same hostile monarchy. Yet the prudence or generosity of Amurath postponed for a while this easy conquest ; and his pride was satisfied with the frequent and humble attendance of the emperor John Palæologus and his four sons, who followed at his summons the court and camp of the Ottoman prince. He marched against the Sclavonian nations between the Danube and the Adriatic, the Bulgarians, Servians, Bosnians, and Albanians ; and these warlike tribes who had so often insulted the majesty of the empire, were repeatedly broken by his destructive inroads. Their countries did not abound either in gold or silver ; nor were their rustic hamlets and townships enriched by commerce or decorated by the arts of luxury. But the natives of the soil have been distinguished in every age by their hardiness of mind and body ; and they were converted by a prudent institution into the firmest and most faithful supporters

[80] After the conclusion of Cantacuzene and Gregoras, there follows a dark interval of an hundred years. George Phranza, Michael Ducas, and Laonicus Chalcondyles, all three wrote after the taking of Constantinople.

[81] [Hadrianople was taken in 1361, Philippopolis in 1362. In the next year (1363) a federate army of the Servians (under Urosh V.), Bosnians and Walachians marched to deliver Hadrianople, but were defeated by a far inferior force on the banks of the Maritza. (Cp. Sad ad-Dīn, tr. Bratutti, i. p. 91 *sqq.*) In 1365 Murad established his residence at Hadrianople. In 1373-4 he pressed into Macedonia. In 1375 the Bulgarian prince Shishman became his vassal. In 1385 Sophia was captured. It should be noted that in 1365 Murad made a treaty with the important commercial city of Ragusa.]

of the Ottoman greatness.[82] The vizir of Amurath reminded his sovereign that, according to the Mahometan law, he was entitled to a fifth part of the spoil and captives ; and that the duty might easily be levied, if vigilant officers were stationed at Gallipoli, to watch the passage, and to select for his use the stoutest and most beautiful of the Christian youth. The advice was followed ; the edict was proclaimed ; many thousands of the European captives were educated in religion and arms ; and the new militia was consecrated and named by a celebrated dervish. Standing in the front of their ranks, he stretched the sleeve of his gown over the head of the foremost soldier, and his blessing was delivered in these words : "Let them be called Janizaries (*Yengi cheri*, or new soldiers) ; may their countenance be ever bright ! their hand victorious ! their sword keen ! may their spear always hang over the heads of their enemies ; and, wheresoever they go, may they return with a *white face !*"[83] Such was the origin of these haughty troops, the terror of the nations, and sometimes of the sultans themselves. Their valour has declined, their discipline is relaxed, and their tumultuary array is incapable of contending with the order and weapons of modern tactics ; [84] but at the time of their institution, they possessed a decisive superiority in war ; since a regular body of infantry, in constant exercise and pay, was not maintained by any of the princes of Christendom. The Janizaries fought with the zeal of proselytes against their *idola-trous* countrymen ; and in the battle of Cossova the league and independence of the Sclavonian tribes was finally crushed.[85] As

The Jani-
zaries
[Yani
Chari]

[A.D. 1389]

---

[82] See Cantemir, p. 37-41, with his own large and curious annotations. [The institution of the Janissaries is here wrongly ascribed to Murad ; it belongs to the reign of Orchan. See above, p. 26, note 67.]

[83] *White* and *black* face are common and proverbial expressions of praise and reproach in the Turkish language. Hic *niger* est, hunc tu Romane caveto, was likewise a Latin sentence.

[84] [They were abolished (massacred) by the sultan Mahmūd II. in 1826.]

[85] [Lazarus, the Kral of Servia, won important successes over Ottoman invaders of Bosnia in 1387. This emboldened the other Slavs of the Balkan peninsula. Shishman of Bulgaria revolted, and this led to the direct incorporation of Bulgaria in the Ottoman empire. The Servian Kral, who was the leader of the Slavs in their struggle to maintain their independence, took the field at the head of a federate army in spring, 1389. He was supported by the King of Bosnia, the princes of Croatia, Albania and Chlum (afterwards Herzegovina) and Walachia ; and there were some Bulgarians (who had escaped the wreck of their country) and Hungarian auxiliaries in his army. The battle was fought, 15th June, on the Kosovo-polje or Amselfeld (blackbird field) on the banks of the Lab, west of Pristina. The name of the Servian who stabbed Murad was Milosh Obilić (or Kobilović). See the Turkish historian Nesri's account of the campaign (Hungarian translation by Thúry in Török történetírók, i. p. 32 *sqq.*). For the general history of the Slavonic struggles

the conqueror walked over the field, he observed that the greatest part of the slain consisted of beardless youths; and listened to the flattering reply of his vizir, that age and wisdom would have taught them not to oppose his irresistible arms. But the sword of his Janizaries could not defend him from the dagger of despair; a Servian soldier started from the crowd of dead bodies, and Amurath was pierced in the belly with a mortal wound. The grandson of Othman was mild in his temper, modest in his apparel, and a lover of learning and virtue; but the Moslems were scandalized at his absence from public worship; and he was corrected by the firmness of the mufti, who dared to reject his testimony in a civil cause: a mixture of servitude and freedom not unfrequent in Oriental history.[86]

The character of Bajazet, the son and successor of Amurath, is strongly expressed in his surname of *Ilderim* or the lightning; and he might glory in an epithet which was drawn from the fiery energy of his soul and the rapidity of his destructive march. In the fourteenth year of his reign,[87] he incessantly moved at the head of his armies, from Boursa to Hadrianople, from the Danube to the Euphrates; and, though he strenuously laboured for the propagation of the law, he invaded, with impartial ambition, the Christian and Mahometan princes of Europe and Asia. From Angora to Amasia and Erzeroum, the northern regions of Anatolia were reduced to his obedience; he stripped of their hereditary possessions his brother emirs, of Ghermian and Caramania, of Aidin and Sarukhan; and after the conquest of Iconium the ancient kingdom of the Seljukians again revived in the Ottoman dynasty. Nor were the conquests of Bajazet less rapid or important in Europe. No sooner had he imposed a regular form of servitude on the Servians and Bulgarians, than he passed the Danube to seek new enemies

The reign of Bajazet I. Ilderim, A.D. 1389-1403, 9th March

[Brusa= Prusa]

His conquests, from the Euphrates to the Danube

---

against the Turks see Rački's articles in the Rad (South Slavonic Journal), vols. ii. iii. and iv.; on the battle of Kosovo, iii. p. 91.]

[86] See the life and death of Morad, or Amurath I., in Cantemir (p. 33-45), the 1st book of Chalcondyles, and the Annales Turcici of Leunclavius. According to another story, the sultan was stabbed by a Croat in his tent: and this accident was alleged to Busbequius (Epist. i. p. 98), as an excuse for the unworthy precaution of pinioning, as it were, between two attendants, an ambassador's arms when he is introduced to the royal presence.

[87] The reign of Bajazet I. or Ilderim Bayazid, is contained in Cantemir (p. 46), the iid book of Chalcondyles, and the Annales Turcici. The surname of Ilderim, or lightning, is an example that the conquerors and poets of every age have *felt* the truth of a system which derives the sublime from the principle of terror.

and new subjects in the heart of Moldavia.[88]   Whatever yet
adhered to the Greek empire in Thrace, Macedonia, and
Thessaly, acknowledged a Turkish master.   An obsequious
bishop led him through the gates of Thermopylæ into Greece;
and we may observe, as a singular fact, that the widow of a
Spanish chief, who possessed the ancient seat of the oracle of
Delphi, deserved his favour by the sacrifice of a beauteous
daughter.   The Turkish communication between Europe and
Asia had been dangerous and doubtful, till he stationed at
Gallipoli a fleet of galleys, to command the Hellespont and
intercept the Latin succours of Constantinople.   While the
monarch indulged his passions in a boundless range of injustice
and cruelty, he imposed on his soldiers the most rigid laws of
modesty and abstinence; and the harvest was peaceably reaped
and sold within the precincts of his camp.[89]   Provoked by the
loose and corrupt administration of justice, he collected, in a
house, the judges and lawyers of his dominions, who expected
that in a few moments the fire would be kindled to reduce
them to ashes.   His ministers trembled in silence; but an
Æthiopian buffoon presumed to insinuate the true cause of
the evil; and future venality was left without excuse by annex-
ing an adequate salary to the office of Cadhi.[90]   The humble
title of Emir was no longer suitable to the Ottoman greatness;
and Bajazet condescended to accept a patent of Sultan from
the caliphs who served in Egypt under the yoke of the Mamalukes:[91] a last and frivolous homage that was yielded by force
to opinion, by the Turkish conquerors to the house of Abbas
and the successors of the Arabian prophet.   The ambition of
the sultan was inflamed by the obligation of deserving this

---

[88] Cantemir, who celebrates the victories of the great Stephen over the Turks
(p. 47), had composed the ancient and modern state of his principality of Moldavia,
which has been long promised, and is still unpublished.

[89] [The reign of Bayezid [Bāyezīd] was marked by a general corruption of
morals and manners, propagated by the example of the court—especially of
Bayezid himself and his grand vizir, Ali Pasha.   See Zinkeisen, Geschichte des
osmanischen Reiches, i. p. 384-6.]

[90] Leunclav. Annal. Turcici, p. 318, 319.   The venality of the cadhis has long
been an object of scandal and satire; and, if we distrust the observations of our
travellers, we may consult the feeling of the Turks themselves (d'Herbelot, Bibliot.
Orientale, p. 216, 217, 229, 230).

[91] The fact, which is attested by the Arabic history of Ben Schounah [Ibn-
Shihna], a contemporary Syrian (de Guignes, Hist. des Huns, tom. iv. p. 336),
destroys the testimony of Saad Effendi and Cantemir (p. 14, 15), of the election of
Othman to the dignity of Sultan.

august title; and he turned his arms against the kingdom of
Hungary, the perpetual theatre of the Turkish victories and
defeats. Sigismond, the Hungarian king, was the son and
brother of the emperors of the West; his cause was that of
Europe and the church; and, on the report of his danger, the
bravest knights of France and Germany were eager to march
under his standard and that of the cross. In the battle of Battle of
Nicopolis, Bajazet defeated a confederate army of an hundred A.D. 1396,
thousand Christians, who had proudly boasted that, if the sky 28th Sept.
should fall, they could uphold it on their lances. The far
greater part were slain or driven into the Danube; and Sigismond, escaping to Constantinople by the river and the Black
Sea, returned after a long circuit to his exhausted kingdom.[92]
In the pride of victory, Bajazet threatened that he would
besiege Buda; that he would subdue the adjacent countries of Germany and Italy; and that he would feed his horse
with a bushel of oats on the altar of St. Peter at Rome. His
progress was checked, not by the miraculous interposition of
the apostle, not by a crusade of the Christian powers, but by
a long and painful fit of the gout. The disorders of the moral,
are sometimes corrected by those of the physical, world; and
an acrimonious humour falling on a single fibre of one man
may prevent or suspend the misery of nations.

Such is the general idea of the Hungarian war; but the Crusade
disastrous adventure of the French has procured us some tivity of
memorials which illustrate the victory and character of Baja- the French
zet.[93] The duke of Burgundy, sovereign of Flanders, and uncle A.D. 1396-
1398

---

[92] See the Decades Rerum Hungaricarum (Dec. iii. l. ii. p. 379) of Bonfinius, an
Italian, who, in the xvth century, was invited into Hungary to compose an eloquent
history of that kingdom. Yet, if it be extant and accessible I should give the preference to some homely chronicle of the time and country. [There is an account
of the battle by John Schiltberger of Munich (who was made prisoner), in his story
of his Bondage and Travels, 1394-1427, which has been translated into English
by J. B. Telfer, 1879 (Hakluyt Society). Mirtschea the Great, prince of Walachia,
who had been made prisoner at Kosovo, was also engaged at Nicopolis, as the ally
of Sigismund; but seeing that the battle was hopeless, he drew off his forces in
good time. He was followed by a Turkish force to Walachia, and defeated it near
Craiova. For his rôle cp. the pamphlet of Charles I. (King of Roumania), Nikopolis,
1396-1877-1902, published in Breslau, 1905. On the confusion in the Turkish
historians on the Nicopolis campaign, see Thúry, Török történetírók, i. p. 50, note.]

[93] I should not complain of the labour of this work, if my materials were always
derived from such books as the Chronicle of honest Froissard (vol. iv. c. 67, 69, 72,
74, 79-83, 85, 87, 89), who read little, inquired much, and believed all. The original Mémoires of the Maréchal de Boucicault (Partie i. c. 22-28) add some facts,
but they are dry and deficient, if compared with the pleasant garrulity of Froissard.

of Charles the Sixth, yielded to the ardour of his son, John count of Nevers; and the fearless youth was accompanied by four princes, *his* cousins, and those of the French monarch. Their inexperience was guided by the Sire de Coucy, one of the best and oldest captains of Christendom; [94] but the constable, admiral, and marshal of France [95] commanded an army which did not exceed the number of a thousand knights and squires. These splendid names were the source of presumption and the bane of discipline. So many might aspire to command that none were willing to obey; their national spirit despised both their enemies and their allies; and in the persuasion that Bajazet *would* fly or *must* fall, they began to compute how soon they should visit Constantinople, and deliver the holy sepulchre. When their scouts announced the approach of the Turks,[96] the gay and thoughtless youths were at table, already heated with wine; they instantly clasped their armour, mounted their horses, rode full speed to the vanguard, and resented as an affront the advice of Sigismond, which would have deprived them of the right and honour of the foremost attack. The battle of Nicopolis would not have been lost, if the French would have obeyed the prudence of the Hungarians; but it might have been gloriously won, had the Hungarians imitated the valour of the French. They dispersed the first line, consisting of the troops of Asia; forced a rampart of stakes, which had been planted against the cavalry; broke, after a bloody conflict, the Janizaries themselves; and were at

[Very important is the Chronique du religieux de Saint Denys, published in a French translation under the title Histoire de Charles VI., roy de France, in 1663. The original Latin was first published by Bellaguet (in 6 vols.) in 1839-52. There is a study on the work by H. Delaborde, La vraie Chronique du Religieux de Saint Denis, 1890.]

[94] An accurate Memoir on the life of Enguerrand VII. Sire de Coucy, has been given by the Baron de Zurlauben (Hist. de l'Académie des Inscriptions, tom. xxv.). His rank and possessions were equally considerable in France and England; and, in 1375, he led an army of adventurers into Switzerland, to recover a large patrimony which he claimed in right of his grandmother, the daughter of the emperor Albert I. of Austria (Sinner, Voyage dans la Suisse Occidentale, tom. i. p. 118-124).

[95] That military office, so respectable at present, was still more conspicuous when it was divided between two persons (Daniel, Hist. de la Milice Françoise, tom. ii. p. 5). One of these, the marshal of the crusade, was the famous Boucicault, who afterwards defended Constantinople, governed Genoa, invaded the coast of Asia, and died in the field of Azincour.

[96] [Bayezid was engaged in besieging Constantinople when he received news that the Franks were besieging Nicopolis.]

length overwhelmed by the numerous squadrons [97] that issued
from the woods, and charged on all sides this handful of
intrepid warriors. In the speed and secrecy of his march, in
the order and evolutions of the battle, his enemies felt and
admired the military talents of Bajazet. They accuse his
cruelty in the use of victory. After reserving the count of
Nevers, and four-and-twenty lords, whose birth and riches
were attested by his Latin interpreters, the remainder of the
French captives, who had survived the slaughter of the day,
were led before his throne; and, as they refused to abjure
their faith, were successively beheaded in his presence. The
sultan was exasperated by the loss of his bravest Janizaries;
and if it be true that, on the eve of the engagement, the
French had massacred their Turkish prisoners,[98] they might
impute to themselves the consequences of a just retaliation.
A knight, whose life had been spared, was permitted to return
to Paris, that he might relate the deplorable tale and solicit
the ransom of the noble captives. In the meanwhile the
count of Nevers, with the princes and barons of France, were
dragged along in the marches of the Turkish camp, exposed as
a grateful trophy to the Moslems of Europe and Asia, and
strictly confined at Boursa, as often as Bajazet resided in his
capital. The sultan was pressed each day to expiate with
their blood the blood of his martyrs; but he had pronounced
that they should live, and either for mercy or destruction his
word was irrevocable. He was assured of their value and
importance by the return of the messenger, and the gifts and
intercessions of the kings of France and of Cyprus. Lusignan
presented him with a gold salt-cellar of curious workmanship
and of the price of ten thousand ducats; and Charles the
Sixth dispatched by the way of Hungary a cast of Norwegian
hawks, and six horse-loads of scarlet cloth, of fine linen of
Rheims, and of Arras tapestry, representing the battles of the
great Alexander. After much delay, the effect of distance
rather than of art, Bajazet agreed to accept a ransom of two
hundred thousand ducats for the count of Nevers and the
surviving princes and barons; the marshal Boucicault, a famous
warrior, was of the number of the fortunate; but the admiral

---

[97] [About half the Turkish army, which amounted altogether to about 100,000.]
[98] For this odious fact, the Abbé de Vertot quotes the Hist. Anonyme de St.
Denys [see above, note 93], l. xvi. c. 10, 11 (Ordre de Malthe, tom. ii. p. 310).

of France had been slain in the battle; and the constable, with the Sire de Coucy, died in the prison of Boursa. This heavy demand, which was doubled by incidental costs, fell chiefly on the duke of Burgundy, or rather on his Flemish subjects, who were bound by the feudal laws to contribute for the knighthood and captivity of the eldest son of their lord. For the faithful discharge of the debt, some merchants of Genoa gave security to the amount of five times the sum: a lesson to those warlike times that commerce and credit are the links of the society of nations. It had been stipulated in the treaty that the French captives should swear never to bear arms against the person of their conqueror; but the onerous restraint was abolished by Bajazet himself. "I despise," said he to the heir of Burgundy, "thy oaths and thy arms. Thou art young, and mayest be ambitious of effacing the disgrace or misfortune of thy first chivalry. Assemble thy powers, proclaim thy design, and be assured that Bajazet will rejoice to meet thee a second time in a field of battle." Before their departure, they were indulged in the freedom and hospitality of the court of Boursa. The French princes admired the magnificence of the Ottoman, whose hunting and hawking equipage was composed of seven thousand huntsmen, and seven thousand falconers.[99] In their presence, and at his command, the belly of one of his chamberlains was cut open, on a complaint against him for drinking the goat's milk of a poor woman. The strangers were astonished by this act of justice; but it was the justice of a sultan who disdains to balance the weight of evidence or to measure the degrees of guilt.

The emperor John Palæologus, A.D. 1355, 8th Jan.-A.D. 1391

After his enfranchisement from an oppressive guardian, John Palæologus remained thirty-six years the helpless and, as it should seem, the careless spectator of the public ruin.[100] Love, or rather lust, was his only vigorous passion; and in the embraces of the wives and virgins of the city the Turkish slave forgot the dishonour of the emperor of the *Romans*. Andronicus, his eld-

[99] Sherefeddin Ali (Hist. de Timour Bec, l. v. c. 13) allows Bajazet a round number of 12,000 officers and servants of the chase. A part of his spoils was afterwards displayed in a hunting-match of Timour: 1. Hounds with satin housings; 2. leopards with collars set with jewels; 3. Grecian greyhounds; and, 4. dogs from Europe, as strong as African lions (*idem*, l. vi. c. 15). Bajazet was particularly fond of flying his hawks at cranes (Chalcondyles, l. ii. p. 35 [p. 67, ed. Bonn]).

[100] For the reigns of John Palæologus and his son Manuel, from 1354 to 1402, see Ducas, c. 9-15, Phranza, l. i. c. 16-21, and the ist and iid books of Chalcondyles, whose proper subject is drowned in a sea of episode.

est son, had formed, at Hadrianople, an intimate and guilty friendship with Sauzes, the son of Amurath; and the two youths conspired against the authority and lives of their parents. The presence of Amurath in Europe soon discovered and dissipated their rash counsels; and, after depriving Sauzes of his sight,[101] the Ottoman threatened his vassal with the treatment of an accomplice and an enemy, unless he inflicted a similar punishment on his own son. Palæologus trembled and obeyed; and a cruel precaution involved in the same sentence the childhood and innocence of John, the son of the criminal. But the operation was so mildly, or so unskilfully, performed that the one retained the sight of an eye and the other was afflicted only with the infirmity of squinting. Thus excluded from the succession, the two princes were confined in the tower of Anema; and the piety of Manuel, the second son of the reigning monarch, was rewarded with the gift of the Imperial crown. But at the end of two years the turbulence of the Latins and the levity of the Greeks produced a revolution; and the two emperors were buried in the tower from whence the two prisoners were exalted to the throne. Another period of two years afforded Palæologus and Manuel the means of escape. It was contrived by the magic or subtlety of a monk, who was alternately named the angel or the devil. They fled to Scutari; their adherents armed in their cause; and the two Byzantine factions displayed the ambition and animosity with which Cæsar and Pompey had disputed the empire of the world. The Roman world was now contracted to a corner of Thrace, between the Propontis and the Black Sea, about fifty miles in length and thirty in breadth: a space of ground not more extensive than the lesser principalities of Germany or Italy, if the remains of Constantinople had not still represented the wealth and populousness of a kingdom. To restore the public peace, it was found necessary to divide this fragment of the empire; and, while Palæologus and Manuel were left in possession of the capital, almost all that lay without the walls was ceded to the blind princes, who fixed their residence at Rhodosto and Selybria.[102] In the tranquil slumber of royalty, the passions of John Palæologus survived his rea-

Discord of the Greeks

[A.D. 1381]

[Rhaedestus, Selymbria]

---

[101] [And beheading him. The prince's name, Saudshi, is given rightly by Chalcondyles: Saûzes, but Ducas and Phrantzes give wrong names.]

[102] [A confirmation of this treaty by the Patriarch Nilus (1380-8) is published in the Sitzungsberichte of the Vienna Academy, 1851, p. 345.]

son and his strength; he deprived his favourite and heir of a blooming princess of Trebizond; and, while the feeble emperor laboured to consummate his nuptials, Manuel, with an hundred of the noblest Greeks, was sent on a peremptory summons to the Ottoman *porte*. They served with honour in the wars of Bajazet; but a plan of fortifying Constantinople excited his jealousy; he threatened their lives; the new works were instantly demolished; and we shall bestow a praise, perhaps above the merit of Palæologus, if we impute this last humiliation as the cause of his death.

The earliest intelligence of that event was communicated to Manuel, who escaped with speed and secrecy from the palace of Boursa to the Byzantine throne. Bajazet affected a proud indifference at the loss of this valuable pledge; and, while he pursued his conquests in Europe and Asia, he left the emperor to struggle with his blind cousin, John of Selybria, who, in eight years of civil war, asserted his right of primogeniture. At length the ambition of the victorious sultan pointed to the conquest of Constantinople; but he listened to the advice of his vizir, who represented that such an enterprise might unite the powers of Christendom in a second and more formidable crusade. His

epistle to the emperor was conceived in these words: "By the divine clemency, our invincible scymetar has reduced to our obedience almost all Asia, with many and large countries in Europe, excepting only the city of Constantinople; for beyond the walls thou hast nothing left. Resign that city; stipulate thy reward; or tremble for thyself and thy unhappy people at the consequences of a rash refusal." But his ambassadors were instructed to soften their tone, and to propose a treaty, which was subscribed with submission and gratitude. A truce of ten years was purchased by an annual tribute of thirty thousand crowns of gold; the Greeks deplored the public toleration of the law of Mahomet; and Bajazet enjoyed the glory of establishing a Turkish cadhi and founding a royal mosque in the metropolis of the Eastern church.[103] Yet this truce was soon violated by the restless sultan. In the cause of the prince of Selybria, the lawful emperor,[104] an army of Ottomans again threatened Con-

---

[103] Cantemir, p. 50-53. Of the Greeks, Ducas alone (c. 13, 15) acknowledges the Turkish cadhi at Constantinople. Yet even Ducas dissembles the mosque.

[104] [The Sultan had forced John to come forward as pretender to the throne, extorting a secret promise that he would hand over Constantinople to himself.]

stantinople; and the distress of Manuel implored the protection of the king of France. His plaintive embassy obtained much pity, and some relief; and the conduct of the succour was entrusted to the marshal Boucicault,[105] whose religious chivalry was inflamed by the desire of revenging his captivity on the infidels. He sailed with four ships of war from Aiguesmortes to the [A.D. 1399] Hellespont; forced the passage, which was guarded by seventeen Turkish galleys; landed at Constantinople a supply of six hundred men at arms and sixteen hundred archers; and reviewed them in the adjacent plain, without condescending to number or array the multitude of Greeks. By his presence, the blockade was raised both by sea and land; the flying squadrons of Bajazet were driven to a more respectful distance; and several castles in Europe and Asia were stormed by the emperor and the marshal, who fought with equal valour by each other's side. But the Ottomans soon returned with an increase of numbers; and the intrepid Boucicault, after a year's struggle, resolved to evacuate a country which could no longer afford either pay or provisions for his soldiers. The marshal offered to conduct Manuel to the French court, where he might solicit in person a supply of men and money; and advised in the meanwhile that, to extinguish all domestic discord, he should leave his blind competitor on the throne. The proposal was embraced; the prince of Selybria was introduced to the capital; and such was the public misery that the lot of the exile seemed more fortunate than that of the sovereign. Instead of applauding the success of his vassal, the Turkish sultan claimed the city as his own; and, on the refusal of the emperor John, Constantinople was more closely pressed by the calamities of war and famine. Against such an enemy prayers and resistance were alike unavailing; and the savage would have devoured his prey, if, in the fatal moment, he had not been overthrown by another savage stronger than himself. By the victory of Timour, or Tamerlane, the fall of Constantinople was delayed about fifty years; and this important though accidental service may justly introduce the life and character of the Mogul conqueror.

[105] Mémoires du bon Messire Jean le Maingre, dit *Boucicault*, Maréchal de France, partie i. c. 30-35.

CHAPTER LXV

Elevation of Timour, or Tamerlane, to the throne of Samarcand—His Conquests in Persia, Georgia, Tartary, Russia, India, Syria, and Anatolia—His Turkish War —Defeat and Captivity of Bajazet—Death of Timour— Civil War of the Sons of Bajazet—Restoration of the Turkish Monarchy by Mahomet the First—Siege of Constantinople by Amurath the Second

Histories of Timour, or Tamerlane

THE conquest and monarchy of the world was the first object of the ambition of TIMOUR. To live in the memory and esteem of future ages was the second wish of his magnanimous spirit. All the civil and military transactions of his reign were diligently recorded in the journals of his secretaries [1]; the authentic narrative was revised by the persons best informed of each particular transaction; and it is believed in the empire and family of Timour that the monarch himself composed the *commentaries* [2] of his life and the *institutions* [3]

[1] These journals were communicated to Sherefeddin, or Cherefeddin Ali, a native of Yezd, who composed in the Persian language a history of Timour Beg [entitled Zafar Nāma = Book of Victory] which has been translated into French by M. Petis de la Croix (Paris, 1722, in 4 vols. 12mo), and has always been my faithful guide. [Translated into English under the title, The History of Timur Beg (in 2 vols.) 1723.] His geography and chronology are wonderfully accurate; and he may be trusted for public facts, though he servilely praises the virtue and fortune of the hero. Timour's attention to procure intelligence from his own and foreign countries may be seen in the Institutions, p. 215, 217, 349, 351. [There is an older Life of Timur, bearing the same title as that of Sheref ad-Din (Book of Victory). It was written by Nizām Shāmī, at the command of Timur himself. The work has never been published, but an edition is promised by Professor E. Denison Ross from a Ms. in the British Museum dated 1434. See note in Skrine and Ross, The Heart of Asia, p. 168.]

[2] These commentaries are yet unknown in Europe; but Mr. White gives some hope that they may be imported and translated by his friend Major Davy, who had read in the East this "minute and faithful narrative of an interesting and eventful period". [See Appendix 1.]

[3] I am ignorant whether the original institution, in the Turkish or Mogul language, be still extant. The Persic version, with an English translation and most valuable index, was published (Oxford, 1783, in 4to) by the joint labours of Major Davy and Mr. White, the Arabic professor. This work has been since translated from the Persic into French (Paris, 1787) by M. Langlès, a learned Orientalist, who has added the Life of Timour and many curious notes.

PORTRAIT OF A MONGOL, BY SOME CONSIDERED TO REPRESENT
TIMUR, FROM A PERSIAN MS. OF THE 16TH CENTURY
COLLECTION OF J. P. MORGAN, ESQ.

of his government.[4] But these cares were ineffectual for the preservation of his fame, and these precious memorials in the Mogul or Persian language were concealed from the world, or at least from the knowledge of Europe. The nations which he vanquished exercised a base and impotent revenge; and ignorance has long repeated the tale of calumny,[5] which had disfigured the birth and character, the person, and even the name of *Tamerlane*.[6] Yet his real merit would be enhanced, rather than debased, by the elevation of a peasant to the throne of Asia; nor can his lameness be a theme of reproach, unless he had the weakness to blush at a natural, or perhaps an honourable, infirmity.

In the eyes of the Moguls, who held the indefeasible succession of the house of Zingis, he was doubtless a rebel-subject; yet he sprang from the noble tribe of Berlass : his fifth ancestor, Carashar Nevian, had been the vizir of Zagatai, in his new realm of Transoxiana; and, in the ascent of some generations, the branch of Timour is confounded, at least by the females,[7] with the Imperial stem.[8] He was born forty miles to the

---

[4] Shaw Allum, the present Mogul, reads, values, but cannot imitate, the institutions of his great ancestor. The English translator relies on their internal evidence; but, if any suspicions should arise of fraud and fiction, they will not be dispelled by Major Davy's letter. The Orientals have never cultivated the art of criticism; the patronage of a prince, less honourable perhaps, is not less lucrative than that of a bookseller; nor can it be deemed incredible that a Persian, the *real* author, should renounce the credit, to raise the value and price, of the work.

[5] The original of the tale is found in the following work, which is much esteemed for its florid elegance of style : *Ahmedis Arabsiadae* (Ahmed Ebn Arabshaw) *Vitae et Rerum gestarum Timuri. Arabice et Latine. Edidit Samuel Henricus Manger. Franequerae,* 1767, 2 *tom. in* 4to. This Syrian author is ever a malicious and often an ignorant enemy; the very titles of his chapters are injurious; as how the wicked, as how the impious, as how the viper, &c. The copious article of Timur, in Bibliothèque Orientale, is of a mixed nature, as d'Herbelot indifferently draws his materials (p. 877-888) from Khondemir Ebn Schounah, and the Lebtarikh.

[6] *Demir* or *Timour* [Tīmūr] signifies, in the Turkish language, iron; and *Beg* is the appellation of a lord or prince. By the change of a letter or accent it is changed into *Lenc* [Lang] or lame; and a European corruption confounds the two words in the name of Tamerlane. [Timur's lameness was due to an arrow wound in the foot, received in a battle in Sīstān, when he was conquering the countries south of the Oxus, before he won Transoxiana.]

[7] After relating some false and foolish tales of Timour *Lenc*, Arabshah is compelled to speak truth, and to own him for a kinsman of Zingis, per mulieres (as he peevishly adds) laqueos Satanæ (pars i. c. i. p. 25). The testimony of Abulghazi Khan (p. ii. c. 5, p. v. c. 4) is clear, unquestionable and decisive. [M. Cahun also agrees that the claim to connexion with the family of Chingiz was justified.]

[8] According to one of the pedigrees, the fourth ancestor of Zingis, and the ninth of Timour, were brothers; and they agreed that the posterity of the elder should succeed to the dignity of Khan, and that the descendants of the younger should fill

south of Samarcand, in the village of Sebzar,[9] in the fruitful territory of Cash, of which his fathers were the hereditary chiefs, as well as of a toman of ten thousand horse.[10] His

[A.D. 1335] birth[11] was cast on one of those periods of anarchy which announce the fall of the Asiatic dynasties and open a new field to adventurous ambition. The khans of Zagatai were extinct; the emirs aspired to independence; and their domestic feuds could only be suspended by the conquest and tyranny of the

[Jata] khans of Kashgar, who with an army of Getes or Calmucks,[12]

His first adventures, A.D. 1361-1370 invaded the Transoxian kingdom. From the twelfth year of his age Timour had entered the field of action; in the twenty-fifth, he stood forth as the deliverer of his country[13]; and the eyes and wishes of the people were turned towards an hero

the office of their minister and general. This tradition was at least convenient to justify the *first* steps of Timour's ambition (Institutions, p. 24, 25, from the Ms. fragments of Timour's History).

[9] [Not Sebzewār but Shehr-i-sebz. The province of Kesh had been given as a fief to Taragai, Timur's father, by Kazghan, the emir or governor of Transoxiana.]

[10] See the preface of Sherefeddin, and Abulfeda's Geography (Chorasmiæ, &c. Descriptio, p. 60, 61), in the 3d volume of Hudson's Minor Greek Geographers. [Timur's family, the Barlas, belonged to the clan of the Kurikan (or Kureken), a Turkish clan mentioned in one of the old Turkish inscriptions of A.D. 733 (see above, vol. iv. p. 575). Thus Timur was a Turk not a Mongol. Cp. Cahun, Intr. à l'histoire de l'Asie, p. 444-445.]

[11] See his nativity in Dr. Hyde (Syntagma Dissertat. tom. ii. p. 466), as it was cast by the astrologers of his grandson Ulugh Beg. He was born A.D. 1336, 9th April, 11° 57' P. M. lat. 36. I know not whether they can prove the great conjunction of the planets from whence, like other conquerors and prophets, Timour derived the surname of Saheb Keran, or master of the conjunctions (Bibliot. Orient. p. 878). [Ulugh Beg founded his observatory at Samarcand in 1428. The "Gurganian" astronomical tables were calculated there.]

[12] In the institutions of Timour, these subjects of the Khan of Kashgar are most improperly styled Ouzbegs, or Uzbeks, a name which belongs to another branch and country of Tartars (Abulghazi, p. v. c. 5; p. vii. c. 5). Could I be sure that this word is in the Turkish original, I would boldly pronounce that the Institutions were framed a century after the death of Timour, since the establishment of the Uzbeks in Transoxiana. [The people of the Kirghiz steppes now came to be known as Uzbegs, and the reading in Timur's Institutes is quite genuine. Gibbon, with others, probably thought the Jātā were Getae. It is like the inveterate mistake (into which he also falls) of confounding the Goths with the Getae (who were Dacians). Jātā is regularly used for Mogolistān in the Zafar Nāma. It is a nickname, meaning "ne'er-do-well," applied to Central Asian Mongols by their neighbours. Petis da la Croix translated it Geta.]

[13] [Timur had not entered the field of action so early. He says in his Memoirs that from the age of twelve he could receive his visitors with dignity. At eighteen he was a good knight, skilled in the science of venery, and amused himself with reading pious books, playing chess, and exercising himself in arms. At twenty-two, we find him taking part (A.D. 1458) in an expedition of Kazghan the emir against the Iranians of Khorasan. On Kazghan's death, Timur (by the advice of the religious orders of Islam) supported the Chagatāy sultan Taghlak-Timur, who first made him emir of Transoxiana, and then deposed him in favour of his own son. Then Timur took to the desert.]

who suffered in their cause. The chiefs of the law and of the
army had pledged their salvation to support him with their
lives and fortunes; but in the hour of danger they were silent
and afraid; and, after waiting seven days on the hills of Samarcand, he retreated to the desert with only sixty horsemen.
The fugitives were overtaken by a thousand Getes, whom he
repulsed with incredible slaughter, and his enemies were forced
to exclaim, "Timour is a wonderful man; fortune and the
divine favour are with him ". But in this bloody action his own
followers were reduced to ten, a number which was soon diminished by the desertion of three Carizmians.[14] He wandered in
the desert with his wife, seven companions, and four horses;
and sixty-two days was he plunged in a loathsome dungeon, from
whence he escaped by his own courage and the remorse of the
oppressor. After swimming the broad and rapid stream of the
Jihoon, or Oxus, he led during some months the life of a vagrant
and outlaw, on the borders of the adjacent states. But his fame
shone brighter in adversity; he learned to distinguish the friends
of his person, the associates of his fortune, and to apply the
various characters of men for their advantage, and above all for
his own. On his return to his native country, Timour was successively joined by the parties of his confederates, who anxiously
sought him in the desert; nor can I refuse to describe, in his
pathetic simplicity, one of their fortunate encounters. He presented himself as a guide to three chiefs, who were at the head
of seventy horse. " When their eyes fell upon me," says Timour,
" they were overwhelmed with joy; and they alighted from their
horses; and they came and kneeled; and they kissed my stirrup.
I also came down from my horse, and took each of them in my
arms. And I put my turban on the head of the first chief; and
my girdle, rich in jewels and wrought with gold, I bound on
the loins of the second; and the third I clothed in my own coat.
And they wept and I wept also; and the hour of prayer was
arrived and we prayed. And we mounted our horses and came
to my dwelling; and I collected my people and made a feast."
His trusty bands were soon increased by the bravest of the
tribes; he led them against a superior foe; and after some
vicissitudes of war the Getes were finally driven from the king- [Uzbegs]

[14] [Timur himself says he had ten left; Sheref ad-Dīn says seven. The name of
Timur's brave wife, who was with him throughout his adventures, was Oljai.]

dom of Transoxiana. He had done much for his own glory;
but much remained to be done, much art to be exerted, and
some blood to be spilt, before he could teach his equals to obey
him as their master. The birth and power of emir Houssein
compelled him to accept a vicious and unworthy colleague,
whose sister was the best beloved of his wives. Their union
was short and jealous; but the policy of Timour, in their frequent quarrels, exposed his rival to the reproach of injustice
and perfidy; and, after a small defeat, Houssein was slain by
some sagacious friends, who presumed, for the last time, to dis-
obey the commands of their lord. At the age of thirty-four,[15] and
in a general diet, or *couroultai*, he was invested with *Imperial*
command; but he affected to revere the house of Zingis; and,
while the emir Timour reigned over Zagatai and the East, a
nominal khan served as a private officer in the armies of his
servant. A fertile kingdom, five hundred miles in length and
in breadth, might have satisfied the ambition of a subject; but
Timour aspired to the dominion of the world; and before his
death the crown of Zagatai was one of the twenty-seven crowns
which he had placed on his head. Without expatiating on the
victories of thirty-five campaigns; without describing the lines
of march, which he repeatedly traced over the continent of Asia;
I shall briefly represent his conquests in I. Persia, II. Tartary,
and III. India [16]; and from thence proceed to the more interesting narrative of his Ottoman war.

He ascends
the throne
of Zagatai
[and is
crowned at
Balkh], A.D.
1370 [1369]
[8th] April

I. For every war, a motive of safety or revenge, of honour
or zeal, of right or convenience, may be readily found in the
jurisprudence of conquerors. No sooner had Timour re-united
to the patrimony of Zagatai the dependent countries of Carizme
and Candahar, than he turned his eyes towards the kingdoms
of Iran or Persia. From the Oxus to the Tigris that extensive
country was left without a lawful sovereign since the death of
Abousaid, the last of the descendants of the great Holacou.[17]

His con-
quests, A.D.
1370-1400
I. of Persia,
A.D. 1380-
1393
[Conquest
of Khor-
asan, A.D.
1381]

---

[15] The 1st book of Sherefeddin is employed on the private life of the hero; and
he himself, or his secretary (Institutions, p. 3-77), enlarges with pleasure on the
thirteen designs and enterprises which most truly constitute his *personal* merit.
It even shines through the dark colouring of Arabshah, p. i. c. 1-12.

[16] The conquests of Persia, Tartary and India, are represented in the iid and
iiid books of Sherefeddin, and by Arabshah, c. 13-55. Consult the excellent Indexes
to the Institutions.

[17] [Rather Mūsā A.D. 1336; Abū Sa'īd reigned 1316-1335. See Lane-Poole,
Mohammadan Dynasties, p. 220.]

Peace and justice had been banished from the land above forty years ; and the Mogul invader might seem to listen to the cries of an oppressed people.   Their petty tyrants might have opposed him with confederate arms; they separately stood and successively fell; and the difference of their fate was only marked by the promptitude of submission or the obstinacy of resistance. Ibrahim, prince of Shirwan or Albania, kissed the footstool of the Imperial throne.   His peace-offerings of silks, horses, and jewels were composed, according to the Tartar fashion, each article of nine pieces; but a critical spectator observed that there were only eight slaves.   "I myself am the ninth," replied Ibrahim, who was prepared for the remark; and his flattery was rewarded by the smile of Timour.[18]   Shah Mansour, prince of Fars or the proper Persia, was one of the least powerful, but most dangerous, of his enemies.   In a battle under the walls of Shiraz, he broke, with three or four thousand soldiers, the *coul* or main body of thirty thousand horse, where the emperor fought in person.   No more than fourteen or fifteen guards remained near the standard of Timour; he stood firm as a rock, and received on his helmet two weighty strokes of a scymetar ; [19] the Moguls rallied ; the head of Mansour was thrown at his feet, and he declared his esteem of the valour of a foe by extirpating all the males of so intrepid a race.   From Shiraz, his troops advanced to the Persian Gulf; and the richness and weakness of Ormuz [20] were displayed in an annual tribute of six hundred thousand dinars of gold.   Bagdad was no longer the city of peace, the seat of the caliphs; but the noblest conquest of Holacou could not be overlooked by his ambitious successor.   The whole

[18] The reverence of the Tartars for the mysterious number of *nine* is declared by Abulghazi Khan, who, for that reason, divides his Genealogical History into nine parts.

[19] According to Arabshah (p. i. c. 28, p. 183), the coward Timour ran away to his tent, and hid himself from the pursuit of Shah Mansour under the women's garments.   Perhaps Sherefeddin (l. ii. c. 25) has magnified his courage.

[20] The history of Ormuz is not unlike that of Tyre.   The old city, on the continent, was destroyed by the Tartars, and renewed [in the 14th cent.] in a neighbouring island without fresh water or vegetation.   The kings of Ormuz, rich in the Indian trade and the pearl fishery, possessed large territories both in Persia and Arabia ; but they were at first the tributaries of the sultans of Kerman, and at last were delivered (A.D. 1505) by the Portuguese tyrants from the tyranny of their own vizirs (Marco Polo, l. i. c. 15, 16, fol. 7, 8 ; Abulfeda Geograph. tabul. xi. p. 261, 262 ; an original Chronicle of Ormuz, in Texeira, or Stevens' History of Persia, p. 376-416, and the Itineraries inserted in the 1st volume of Ramusio ; of Ludovico Barthema (1503), fol. 167 ; of Andrea Corsali (1517), fol. 202, 203 ; and of Odoardo Barbessa (in 1516), fol. 315-318).

course of the Tigris and Euphrates, from the mouth to the sources of those rivers, was reduced to his obedience. He entered Edessa; and the Turkmans of the black sheep were chastised for the sacrilegious pillage of a caravan of Mecca. In the mountains of Georgia, the native Christians still braved the law and the sword of Mahomet; by three expeditions he obtained the merit of the *gazie*, or holy war; and the Prince of Teflis became his proselyte and friend.

II. Of Turkestan, A.D. 1370-1383

II. A just retaliation might be urged for the invasion of Turkestan, or the Eastern Tartary. The dignity of Timour could not endure the impunity of the Getes; he passed the Sihoon, subdued the kingdom of Cashgar, and marched seven times into the heart of their country. His most distant camp was two months' journey, or four hundred and eighty leagues to the north-east of Samarcand; and his emirs, who traversed the river Irtish, engraved in the forests of Siberia a rude memorial of their exploits. The conquest of Kipzak, or the Western Tartary,[21] was founded on the double motive of aiding

[A.D. 1375]

the distressed and chastising the ungrateful. Toctamish, a fugitive prince, was entertained and protected in his court; the ambassadors of Auruss Khan were dismissed with an haughty denial, and followed on the same day by the armies of Zagatai; and their success established Toctamish in the Mogul empire

[A.D. 1376]

of the North. But, after a reign of ten years, the new khan forgot the merits and the strength of his benefactor, the base usurper, as he deemed him, of the sacred rights of the house of

[A.D. 1387]

Zingis. Through the gates of Derbend, he entered Persia at

---

[21] Arabshah had travelled into Kipzak, and acquired a singular knowledge of the geography, cities, and revolutions of that northern region (p. i. c. 45-49). [The position of Tōktámish cannot be understood without a knowledge of the relations of the rulers of the Golden Horde. Orda, the eldest son of Jūjī (eldest son of Chingiz Khan) had succeeded his father in the rule over the tribes north of the Jaxartes. The tribes of the Western Kipchak (the regions of the Volga and Ural, north of the Caspian) had been conquered by Bātū, a younger son of Jūjī (see above, pp. 15, 16). Tūka-Tīmūr, another son, ruled over Great Bulgaria on the Middle Volga; and a fourth, named Shaybān, was lord of the Kirghiz Kazaks, in Siberia, to the north of Orda's land. The tribes ruled over by all these brothers and their descendants were included under the "Golden Horde," which derived its name from the Sir Orda, the *golden camp* of the Khan. The tribes under the line of Orda were called the White Horde; and the Khans of this line were nominally the head of the family. The tribes subject to Bātū's line were the Blue Horde, and they were far the most important. The line of Bātū came to an end in 1358, and after twenty years of anarchy Tōktámish won the Khanate with Timur's help in 1378. Tōktámish was a descendant of Orda, and had won the lordship of the White Horde in 1376. Under him the Khanate of the Golden Horde reasserted itself in Russia, and Moscow was burned in 1382.]

the head of ninety thousand horse; with the innumerable forces of Kipzak, Bulgaria, Circassia, and Russia, he passed the Sihoon, burnt the palaces of Timour, and compelled him, amidst the winter snows, to contend for Samarcand and his life. After a mild expostulation, and a glorious victory, the emperor resolved on revenge; and by the east and the west of the Caspian and the Volga, he twice invaded Kipzak with such mighty[22] powers that thirteen miles were measured from his right to his left wing. In a march of five months, they rarely beheld the footsteps of man; and their daily subsistence was often trusted to the fortune of the chase. At length the armies encountered each other; but the treachery of the standard-bearer, who, in the heat of action, reversed the Imperial standard of Kipzak, determined the victory of the Zagatais; [A.D. 1391] and Toctamish (I speak the language of the Institutions) gave the tribe of Toushi to the wind of desolation.[23] He fled to the Christian duke of Lithuania; again returned to the banks of the Volga; and, after fifteen battles with a domestic rival, at last perished in the wilds of Siberia. The pursuit of a flying enemy carried Timour into the tributary provinces of Russia; a duke of the reigning family was made prisoner amidst the ruins of his capital; and Yeletz, by the pride and ignorance of the Orientals, might easily be confounded with the genuine metropolis of the nation. Moscow trembled at the approach of the Tartar, and the resistance would have been feeble, since the hopes of the Russians were placed in a miraculous image of the Virgin, to whose protection they ascribed the casual and voluntary retreat of the conqueror. Ambition and prudence recalled him to the south, the desolate country was exhausted, and the Mogul soldiers were enriched with an immense spoil of precious furs, of linen of Antioch,[24] and of ingots of gold and

Of Kipzak, Russia, &c. A.D. 1390-1396

[Flight of Toctamish to Siberia, A.D. 1399]

---

[22] [Timur routed Tōktāmish in 1391 at Urtupa, and in 1395 on the Terek. By thus destroying the power of the Khanate of the Golden Horde, Timur involuntarily delivered Russia.]

[23] Institutions of Timour, p. 123, 125. Mr. White, the editor, bestows some animadversion on the superficial account of Sherefeddin (l. iii. c. 12-14), who was ignorant of the designs of Timour, and the true springs of action. [M. Charmoy contributed to the 3rd vol. of the Transactions of the Academy of St. Petersburg an important account of these campaigns of Timur.]

[24] The furs of Russia are more credible than the ingots. But the linen of Antioch has never been famous; and Antioch was in ruins. I suspect that it was some manufacture of Europe, which the Hanse merchants had imported by the way of Novogorod.

silver.[25] On the banks of the Don, or Tanais, he received an humble deputation from the consuls and merchants of Egypt,[26] Venice, Genoa, Catalonia, and Biscay, who occupied the commerce and city of Tana, or Azoph, at the mouth of the river. They offered their gifts, admired his magnificence, and trusted his royal word. But the peaceful visit of an emir, who explored the state of the magazines and harbour, was speedily followed by the destructive presence of the Tartars. The city was reduced to ashes ; the Moslems were pillaged and dismissed ; but all the Christians who had not fled to their ships were condemned either to death or slavery.[27] Revenge prompted him to burn the cities of Serai and Astrachan, the monuments of rising civilisation ; and his vanity proclaimed that he had penetrated to the region of perpetual daylight, a strange phenomenon, which authorised his Mahometan doctors to dispense with the obligation of evening prayer.[28]

III. Of Hindostan, A.D. 1398, 1399 III. When Timour first proposed to his princes and emirs the invasion of India or Hindostan,[29] he was answered by a murmur of discontent : " The rivers ! and the mountains and deserts ! and the soldiers clad in armour ! and the elephants, destroyers of men ! " But the displeasure of the emperor was more dreadful than all these terrors ; and his superior reason

---

[25] M. Levesque (Hist. de Russie, tom. ii. p. 247. Vie de Timour, p. 64-67, before the French version of the Institutes) has corrected the error of Sherefeddin, and marked the true limit of Timour's conquests. His arguments are superfluous, and a simple appeal to the Russian annals is sufficient to prove that Moscow, which six years before had been taken by Toctamish [A.D. 1382], escaped the arms of a more formidable invader.

[26] An Egyptian consul from Grand Cairo is mentioned in Barbaro's voyage to Tana in 1436, after the city had been rebuilt (Ramusio, tom. ii. fol. 92).

[27] The sack of Azoph is described by Sherefeddin (l. iii. c. 55), and much more particularly by the author of an Italian chronicle (Andreas de Redusiis de Quero, in Chron. Tarvisiano, in Muratori, Script. Rerum Italicarum, tom. xix. p. 802-805). He had conversed with the Mianis, two Venetian brothers, one of whom had been sent a deputy to the camp of Timour, and the other had lost at Azoph three sons and 12,000 ducats. [After the disintegration of the Golden Horde by Tīmūr, the house of Tūka-Tīmūr (see above, note 21) begins to come into prominence. Members of this house established the three Khanates of Kazan, the Crimea, and Kazimov.]

[28] Sherefeddin only says (l. iii. c. 13) that the rays of the setting, and those of the rising, sun were scarcely separated by any interval : a problem which may be solved in the latitude of Moscow (the 56th degree) with the aid of the Aurora Borealis and a long summer twilight. But a day of forty days (Khondemir apud d'Herbelot, p. 880) would rigorously confine us within the polar circle.

[29] For the Indian war, see the Institutions (p. 129-139), the fourth book of Sherefeddin, and the history of Ferishta (in Dow, vol. ii. p. 1-20), which throws a general light on the affairs of Hindostan.

was convinced that an enterprise of such tremendous aspect was safe and easy in the execution. He was informed by his spies of the weakness and anarchy of Hindostan ; the soubahs of the provinces had erected the standard of rebellion ; and the perpetual infancy of sultan Mahmoud was despised even in the harem of Delhi. The Mogul army moved in three great divisions ; and Timour observes with pleasure that the ninety-two squadrons of a thousand horse most fortunately corresponded with the ninety-two names or epithets of the prophet Mahomet. Between the Jihoon and the Indus, they crossed one of the ridges of mountains, which are styled by the Arabian geographers the Stony Girdles of the Earth. The highland robbers were subdued or extirpated ; but great numbers of men and horses perished in the snow; the emperor himself was let down a precipice on a portable scaffold ; the ropes were one hundred and fifty cubits in length ; and, before he could reach the bottom, this dangerous operation was five times repeated. Timour crossed the Indus at the ordinary passage of Attok ; and successively traversed, in the footsteps of Alexander, the *Punjab*, or five rivers,[30] that fall into the master-stream. From Attok to Delhi the high road measures no more than six hundred miles ; but the two conquerors deviated to the south-east ; and the motive of Timour was to join his grandson who had achieved by his command the conquest of Moultan. On the eastern bank of the Hyphasis, on the edge of the desert, the Macedonian hero halted and wept; the Mogul entered the desert, reduced the fortress of Batnir, and stood in arms before the gates of Delhi, a great and flourishing city, which had subsisted three centuries under the dominion of the Mahometan kings. The siege, more especially of the [A.D. 1398] castle, might have been a work of time; but he tempted, by the appearance of weakness, the sultan Mahmoud and his vizir to descend into the plain, with ten thousand cuirassiers, forty thousand of his foot-guards, and one hundred and twenty elephants, whose tusks are said to have been armed with sharp and poisoned daggers. Against these monsters, or rather against the imagination of his troops, he condescended to use

---

[30] The rivers of the Punjab, the five eastern branches of the Indus, have been laid down for the first time with truth and accuracy in Major Rennell's incomparable map of Hindostan. In his Critical Memoir he illustrates with judgment and learning the marches of Alexander and Timour.

some extraordinary precautions of fire and a ditch, of iron spikes and a rampart of bucklers ; but the event taught the Moguls to smile at their own fears ; and, as soon as these unwieldy animals were routed, the inferior species (the men of India) disappeared from the field. Timour made his triumphal entry into the capital of Hindostan ; and admired, with a view to imitate, the architecture of the stately mosque ; but the order or licence of a general pillage and massacre polluted the festival of his victory. He resolved to purify his soldiers in the blood of the idolaters, or Gentoos, who still surpass, in the proportion of ten to one, the numbers of the Moslems. In this pious design, he advanced one hundred miles to the northeast of Delhi, passed the Ganges, fought several battles by land and water, and penetrated to the famous rock of Coupele, the statue of the cow, that *seems* to discharge the mighty river, whose source is far distant among the mountains of Thibet.[31] His return was along the skirts of the northern hills ; nor could this rapid campaign of one year justify the strange foresight of his emirs that their children in a warm climate would degenerate into a race of Hindoos.

His war against Sultan Bajazet, A.D. 1400, 1st Sept.

[His return to Samarcand, A.D. 1399, May]

It was on the banks of the Ganges that Timour was informed, by his speedy messengers, of the disturbances which had arisen on the confines of Georgia and Anatolia, of the revolt of the Christians, and the ambitious designs of the sultan Bajazet. His vigour of mind and body was not impaired by sixty-three years and innumerable fatigues ; and, after enjoying some tranquil months in the palace of Samarcand, he proclaimed a new expedition of seven years into the western countries of Asia.[32] To the soldiers who had served in the Indian war, he granted the choice of remaining at home or following their prince ; but the troops of all the provinces and kingdoms of Persia were commanded to assemble at Ispahan and wait the

---

[31] The two great rivers, the Ganges and Burrampooter [Brahmapootra], rise in Thibet, from the opposite ridges of the same hills, separate from each other to the distance of 1200 miles, and, after a winding course of 2000 miles, again meet in one point near the gulf of Bengal. Yet, so capricious is fame that the Burrampooter is a late discovery, while his brother Ganges has been the theme of ancient and modern story. Coupele, the scene of Timour's last victory, must be situate near Loldong, 1100 miles from Calcutta ; and, in 1774, a British camp ! (Rennell's Memoir, p. 7, 59, 90, 91, 99).

[32] See the institutions, p. 141, to the end of the 1st book, and Sherefeddin (l. v. c. 1-16), to the entrance of Timour into Syria.

arrival of the Imperial standard.   It was first directed against
the Christians of Georgia, who were strong only in their rocks,
their castles, and the winter-season ; but these obstacles were
overcome by the zeal and perseverance of Timour ; the rebels
submitted to the tribute or the Koran ; and, if both religions
boasted of their martyrs, that name is more justly due to the
Christian prisoners, who were offered the choice of abjuration
or death.   On his descent from the hills, the emperor gave
audience to the first ambassadors of Bajazet, and opened the
hostile correspondence of complaints and menaces, which fermented two years before the final explosion.   Between two
jealous and haughty neighbours, the motives of quarrel will
seldom be wanting.   The Mogul and Ottoman conquests now
touched each other in the neighbourhood of Erzerum and the
Euphrates ; nor had the doubtful limit been ascertained by time
and treaty.   Each of these ambitious monarchs might accuse
his rival of violating his territory, of threatening his vassals,
and protecting his rebels ; and, by the name of rebels, each
understood the fugitive princes, whose kingdoms he had usurped
and whose life or liberty he implacably pursued.   The resemblance of character was still more dangerous than the opposition of interest ; and, in their victorious career, Timour was
impatient of an equal, and Bajazet was ignorant of a superior.
The first epistle [33] of the Mogul emperor must have provoked
instead of reconciling the Turkish sultan, whose family and
nation he affected to despise.[34]   " Dost thou not know that the
greatest part of Asia is subject to our arms and our laws ? that
our invincible forces extend from one sea to the other ? that
the potentates of the earth form a line before our gate ? and
that we have compelled Fortune herself to watch over the
prosperity of our empire ?   What is the foundation of thy insolence and folly ?   Thou has fought some battles in the woods

---

[33] We have three copies of these hostile epistles in the Institutions (p. 147), in
Sherefeddin (l. v. c. 14), and in Arabshah (tom. ii. c. 19, p. 183-201), which agree
with each other in the spirit and substance, rather than in the style.   It is probable
that they have been translated, with various latitude, from the Turkish original into
the Arabic and Persian tongues.   [The genuineness of these letters is doubtful.]

[34] The Mogul emir distinguishes himself and his countrymen by the name of
Turks, and stigmatizes the race and nation of Bajazet with the less honourable
epithet of Turkmans.   Yet I do not understand how the Ottomans could be descended
from a Turkman sailor ; those inland shepherds were so remote from the sea and
all maritime affairs.

of Anatolia ; contemptible trophies ! Thou hast obtained some victories over the Christians of Europe ; thy sword was blessed by the apostle of God ; and thy obedience to the precept of the Koran, in waging war against the infidels, is the sole considera-tion that prevents us from destroying thy country, the frontier and bulwark of the Moslem world. Be wise in time ; re-flect ; repent ; and avert the thunder of our vengeance, which is yet suspended over thy head. Thou art no more than a pismire ; why wilt thou seek to provoke the elephants ? Alas ! they will trample thee under their feet." In his replies, Bajazet poured forth the indignation of a soul which was deeply stung by such unusual contempt. After retorting the basest reproaches on the thief and rebel of the desert, the Ottoman recapitulates his boasted victories in Iran, Touran, and the Indies ; and labours to prove that Timour had never triumphed, unless by his own perfidy and the vices of his foes. " Thy armies are innumerable : be they so ; but what are the arrows of the flying Tartar against the scymetars and battle-axes of my firm and invincible Janizaries ? I will guard the princes who have implored my protection ; seek them in my tents. The cities of Arzingan and Erzeroum are mine ; and, unless the tribute be duly paid, I will demand the arrears under the walls of Tauris and Sultania." The ungovernable rage of the Sultan at length betrayed him to an insult of a more domestic kind : " If I fly from my arms," said he, " may *my* wives be thrice divorced from my bed ; but, if thou hast not courage to meet me in the field, mayest thou again receive *thy* wives after they have thrice endured the embraces of a stranger ".[35] Any violation, by word or deed, of the secrecy of the harem is an unpardonable offence among the Turkish nations [36] ; and the political quarrel of the two monarchs was embittered by private and personal resentment. Yet in his first expedition Timour

[35] According to the Koran (c. ii. p. 27, and Sale's Discourses, p. 134), a Musul-man who had thrice divorced his wife (who had thrice repeated the words of a divorce) could not take her again, till after she had been married *to*, and repudiated *by*, another husband ; an ignominious transaction, which it is needless to aggravate by supposing that the first husband must see her enjoyed by a second before his face (Rycaut's State of the Ottoman Empire, l. ii. c. 21).

[36] The common delicacy of the Orientals, in never speaking of their women, is ascribed in a much higher degree by Arabshah to the Turkish nations ; and it is remarkable enough that Chalcondyles (l. ii. p. 55 [p. 105, ed. Bonn]) had some knowledge of the prejudice and the insult.

was satisfied with the siege and destruction of Suvas, or Sebaste, [A.D. 1401] a strong city on the borders of Anatolia ; and he revenged the indiscretion of the Ottoman on a garrison of four thousand Armenians, who were buried alive for the brave and faithful discharge of their duty.[37] As a Musulman, he seemed to respect the pious occupation of Bajazet, who was still engaged in the blockade of Constantinople ; and, after this salutary lesson, the Mogul conqueror checked his pursuit, and turned aside to the invasion of Syria and Egypt. In these transactions, the Ottoman prince, by the Orientals, and even by Timour, is styled the *Kaissar of Roum*, the Cæsar of the Romans : a title which, by a small anticipation, might be given to a monarch who possessed the provinces, and threatened the city, of the successors of Constantine.[38]

Timour invades Syria, A.D. 1400

The military republic of the Mamalukes still reigned in Egypt and Syria ; but the dynasty of the Turks was overthrown by that of the Circassians ;[39] and their favourite Barkok, from a slave and a prisoner, was raised and restored to the throne. In the midst of rebellion and discord, he braved the menaces, corresponded with the enemies, and detained the ambassadors, of the Mogul, who patiently expected his decease, to revenge the crimes of the father on the feeble reign of his son Farage. The Syrian emirs[40] were assembled at Aleppo to repel the invasion ; they confided in the fame and discipline of the Mamalukes, in the temper of their swords and lances, of the purest steel of Damascus, in the strength of their walled cities, and in the populousness of sixty thousand villages ; and, instead of sustaining a siege, they threw open their gates and arrayed

---

[37] [And he put to death Bayezid's eldest son Ertogrul.]
[38] For the style of the Moguls, see the Institutions (p. 131, 147), and for the Persians, the Bibliothèque Orientale (p. 882) ; but I do not find that the title of Cæsar has been applied by the Arabians, or assumed by the Ottomans themselves. [From Timur to Bayezid the name is an insult ; he will not give him a Musulman title.]
[39] See the reigns of Barkok and Pharadge, in M. de Guignes (tom. iv. l. xxii.), who from the Arabic texts of Aboulmahasen, Ebn Schounah, and Aintabi has added some acts to our common stock of materials. [In 1390 the Bahrī dynasty made way for the Burjī dynasty, founded by Al-Zāhir Sayf al-Dīn Barkūk, who in 1398 was succeeded by Al-Nāsir Nāsir al-Dīn Faraj.]
[40] For these recent and domestic transactions, Arabshah, though a partial, is a credible, witness (tom. i. c. 64-68 ; tom. ii. c. 1-14). Timour must have been odious to a Syrian ; but the notoriety of facts would have obliged him, in some measure, to respect his enemy and himself. His bitters may correct the luscious sweets of Sherefeddin (l. v. c. 17-29).

their forces in the plain.   But these forces were not cemented
by virtue and union ; and some powerful emirs had been seduced
to desert or betray their more loyal companions.   Timour's
front was covered with a line of Indian elephants, whose turrets
were filled with archers and Greek fire ; the rapid evolutions
of his cavalry completed the dismay and disorder; the Syrian
crowds fell back on each other; many thousands were stifled
or slaughtered in the entrance of the great street; the Moguls
entered with the fugitives; and, after a short defence, the
citadel, the impregnable citadel of Aleppo, was surrendered by
cowardice or treachery.   Among the suppliants and captives,
Sacks
Aleppo,
A.D. 1400,
11th Nov. Timour distinguished the doctors of the law, whom he invited
to the dangerous honour of a personal conference.[41]   The Mo-
gul prince was a zealous Musulman ; but his Persian schools
had taught him to revere the memory of Ali and Hosein ; and
he had imbibed a deep prejudice against the Syrians, as the
enemies of the son of the daughter of the apostle of God.   To
these doctors he proposed a captious question, which the casuists
of Bochara, Samarcand, and Herat were incapable of resolving.
" Who are the true martyrs, of those who are slain on my side,
or on that of my enemies ? "   But he was silenced, or satisfied,
by the dexterity of one of the cadhis of Aleppo, who replied,
in the words of Mahomet himself, that the motive, not the en-
sign, constitutes the martyr; and that the Moslems of either
party, who fight only for the glory of God, may deserve that
sacred appellation.   The true succession of the caliphs was a
controversy of a still more delicate nature, and the frankness of
a doctor, too honest for his situation, provoked the emperor to
exclaim, " Ye are as false as those of Damascus : Moawiyah was
an usurper, Yezid a tyrant, and Ali alone is the lawful successor
of the prophet ".   A prudent explanation restored his tranquillity ; and he passed to a more familiar topic of conversation.
" What is your age ? " said he to the cadhi.   " Fifty years."
" It would be the age of my eldest son.   You see me here
(continued Timour) a poor, lame, decrepit mortal.   Yet by my
arm has the Almighty been pleased to subdue the kingdoms of
Iran, Touran, and the Indies.   I am not a man of blood ; and

---

[41] These interesting conversations appear to have been copied by Arabshah
(tom. i. c. 68, p. 625-645) from the Cadhi and historian Ebn Schounah, a principal
actor.   Yet how could he be alive seventy-five years afterwards (d' Herbelot, p. 792) ?

God is my witness that in all my wars I have never been the
aggressor, and that my enemies have always been the authors
of their own calamity." During this peaceful conversation, the
streets of Aleppo streamed with blood, and re-echoed with the
cries of mothers and children, with the shrieks of violated virgins.
The rich plunder that was abandoned to his soldiers might
stimulate their avarice; but their cruelty was enforced by the
peremptory command of producing an adequate number of heads,
which, according to his custom, were curiously piled in columns
and pyramids; the Moguls celebrated the feast of victory, while
the surviving Moslems passed the night in tears and in chains.
I shall not dwell on the march of the destroyer from Aleppo to
Damascus, where he was rudely encountered, and almost overthrown, by the armies of Egypt. A retrograde motion was
imputed to his distress and despair: one of his nephews deserted
to the enemy; and Syria rejoiced in the tale of his defeat, when
the sultan was driven, by the revolt of the Mamalukes, to escape with precipitation and shame to his palace of Cairo.
Abandoned by their prince, the inhabitants of Damascus still
defended their walls; and Timour consented to raise the siege,
if they would adorn his retreat with a gift or ransom; each
article of nine pieces. But no sooner had he introduced himself into the city, under colour of a truce, than he perfidiously
violated the treaty; imposed a contribution of ten millions of Damascus,
gold; and animated his troops to chastise the posterity of those 23rd Jan.
Syrians who had executed or approved the murder of the grandson of Mahomet. A family which had given honourable burial
to the head of Hosein, and a colony of artificers whom he sent
to labour at Samarcand, were alone reserved in the general
massacre; and, after a period of seven centuries, Damascus
was reduced to ashes, because a Tartar was moved by religious
zeal to avenge the blood of an Arab.[42] The losses and fatigues
of the campaign obliged Timour to renounce the conquest of
Palestine and Egypt; but in his return to the Euphrates he
delivered Aleppo to the flames; and justified his pious motive
by the pardon and reward of two thousand sectaries of Ali, who

---

[42] [The destruction attributed to Timur has been greatly exaggerated. That
he did not burn the mosque of Damascus is proved by its remains. (It had been
partly burnt in a tumult in 1068.) Compare the remarks of Cahun, *op. cit.*, p. 495-
497.]

were desirous to visit the tomb of his son. I have expatiated
on the personal anecdotes which mark the character of the
Mogul hero; but I shall briefly mention [43] that he erected on
the ruins of Bagdad a pyramid of ninety thousand heads; again
visited Georgia; encamped on the banks of Araxes; and proclaimed his resolution of marching against the Ottoman emperor. Conscious of the importance of the war, he collected
his forces from every province; eight hundred thousand men
were enrolled on his military list; [44] but the splendid commands
of five and ten thousand horse may be rather expressive of the
rank and pension of the chiefs than of the genuine number of
effective soldiers.[45] In the pillage of Syria, the Moguls had acquired immense riches; but the delivery of their pay and arrears for
seven years more firmly attached them to the Imperial standard.

During this diversion of the Mogul arms, Bajazet had two
years to collect his forces for a more serious encounter. They
consisted of four hundred thousand horse and foot,[46] whose
merit and fidelity were of an unequal complexion. We may
discriminate the Janizaries, who have been gradually raised to
an establishment of forty thousand men; a national cavalry,
the Spahis of modern times; twenty thousand cuirassiers of
Europe, clad in black and impenetrable armour; the troops of
Anatolia, whose princes had taken refuge in the camp of Timour,
and a colony of Tartars, whom he had driven from Kipzak, and
to whom Bajazet had assigned a settlement in the plains of
Hadrianople. The fearless confidence of the sultan urged him

Margin notes:
and Bag-
dad, A.D.
1401, 23rd
July

Invades
Anatolia,
A.D. 1402

[Sipahis]

---

[43] The marches and occupations of Timour between the Syrian and Ottoman
wars, are represented by Sherefeddin (l. v. c. 29-43) and Arabshah (tom. ii. c.
15-18).

[44] This number of 800,000 was extracted by Arabshah, or rather by Ebn
Schounah, ex rationario Timuri, on the faith of a Carizmian officer (tom. i. c. 68,
p. 617); and it is remarkable enough that a Greek historian (Phranza, l. i. c. 29)
adds no more than 20,000 men. Poggius reckons 1,000,000; another Latin contemporary (Chron. Tarvisianum, apud Muratori, tom. xix. p. 800) 1,100,000; and
the enormous sum of 1,600,000 is attested by a German soldier who was present at
the battle of Angora (Leunclav. ad Chalcondyl. l. iii. p. 82). Timour, in his Institutions, has not deigned to calculate his troops, his subjects, or his revenues.

[45] A wide latitude of non-effectives was allowed by the Great Mogul for his own
pride and the benefit of his officers. Bernier's patron was Penge-Hazari, commander of 5000 horse, of which he maintained no more than 500 (Voyages, tom. i.
p. 288, 289).

[46] Timour himself fixes at 400,000 men the Ottoman army (Institutions, p. 153),
which is reduced to 150,000 by Phranza (l. i. c. 29), and swelled by the German
soldier to 1,400,000. It is evident that the Moguls were the more numerous.
[The forces of Bayezid are put at 90,000 by Sad ad-Din (tr. Bratutti, 214). Of
course the number given by Timur cannot be accepted.]

to meet his antagonist; and, as if he had chosen that spot for revenge, he displayed his banners near the ruins of the unfortunate Suvas. In the meanwhile, Timour moved from the Araxes through the countries of Armenia and Anatolia : his boldness was secured by the wisest precautions; his speed was guided by order and discipline; and the woods, the mountains, and the rivers were diligently explored by the flying squadrons, who marked his road and preceded his standard. Firm in his plan of fighting in the heart of the Ottoman kingdom, he avoided their camp; dexterously inclined to the left; occupied Cæsarea; traversed the salt desert and the river Halys ; and invested Angora : while the sultan, immoveable and ignorant in his post, compared the Tartar swiftness to the crawling of a snail.[47] He returned on the wings of indignation to the relief of Angora ; and, as both generals were alike impatient for action, the plains round that city were the scene of a memorable battle, which has immortalised the glory of Timour and the shame of Bajazet. For this signal victory, the Mogul emperor was indebted to himself, to the genius of the moment, and the discipline of thirty years. He had improved the tactics, without violating the manners, of his nation,[48] whose force still consisted in the missile weapons, and rapid evolutions, of a numerous cavalry. From a single troop to a great army, the mode of attack was the same : a foremost line first advanced to the charge, and was supported in a just order by the squadrons of the great vanguard. The general's eye watched over the field, and at his command the front and rear of the right and left wings successively moved forwards in their several divisions, and in a direct or oblique line ; the enemy was pressed by eighteen or twenty attacks ; and each attack afforded a chance of victory. If they all proved fruitless or unsuccessful, the occasion was worthy of the emperor himself, who gave the signal of advancing to the standard and main body, which he led in person.[49] But in the

Battle of Angora, A.D. 1402, 28th [20th] July

---

[47] It may not be useless to mark the distances between Angora and the neighbouring cities, by the journeys of the caravans, each of twenty or twenty-five miles ; to Smyrna 20, to Kiotahia [i.e. Kutaya = Cotiæum] 10, to Boursa 10, to Cæsarea 8, to Sinope 10, to Nicomedia 9, to Constantinople 12 or 13 (see Tournefort, Voyage au Levant, tom. ii. lettre 21).

[48] See the Systems of Tactics in the Institutions, which the English editors have illustrated with elaborate plans (p. 373-407).

[49] The Sultan himself (says Timour) must then put the foot of courage into the stirrup of patience. A Tartar metaphor, which is lost in the English, but preserved in the French, version of the Institutes (p. 156, 157).

battle of Angora, the main body itself was supported, on the
flanks and in the rear, by the bravest squadrons of the reserve,
commanded by the sons and grandsons of Timour. The conqueror of Hindostan ostentatiously shewed a line of elephants,
the trophies, rather than the instruments, of victory: the use
of the Greek fire was familiar to the Moguls and Ottomans;
but, had they borrowed from Europe the recent invention of
gunpowder and cannon, the artificial thunder, in the hands of
either nation, must have turned the fortune of the day.[50]   In
that day, Bajazet displayed the qualities of a soldier and a chief;
but his genius sunk under a stronger ascendant; and, from
various motives, the greatest part of his troops failed him in
the decisive moment. His rigour and avarice had provoked a
mutiny among the Turks; and even his son Soliman too hastily
withdrew from the field. The forces of Anatolia, loyal in their
revolt, were drawn away to the banners of their lawful princes.
His Tartar allies had been tempted by the letters and emissaries
of Timour;[51] who reproached their ignoble servitude under the
slaves of their fathers, and offered to their hopes the dominion
of their new, or the liberty of their ancient, country. In the
right wing of Bajazet, the cuirassiers of Europe charged with
faithful hearts and irresistible arms; but these men of iron were
soon broken by an artful flight and headlong pursuit; and the
Janizaries, alone, without cavalry or missile weapons, were encompassed by the circle of the Mogul hunters. Their valour
was at length oppressed by heat, thirst, and the weight of
numbers; and the unfortunate sultan, afflicted with the gout
in his hands and feet, was transported from the field on the
fleetest of his horses. He was pursued and taken by the titular
khan of Zagatai; and after his capture, and the defeat of the
Ottoman powers, the kingdom of Anatolia submitted to the
conqueror, who planted his standard at Kiotahia, and dispersed
on all sides the ministers of rapine and destruction. Mirza
Mehemmed Sultan, the eldest and best beloved of his grand-

Defeat and captivity of Bajazet

[50] The Greek fire, on Timour's side, is attested by Sherefeddin (l. v. c. 47); but
Voltaire's strange suspicion that some cannon, inscribed with strange characters,
must have been sent by that monarch to Delhi is refuted by the universal silence of
contemporaries.
[51] Timour has dissembled this secret and important negotiation with the Tartars,
which is indisputably proved by the joint evidence of the Arabian (tom. i. c. 47, p.
391), Turkish (Annal. Leunclav. p. 321), and Persian historians (Khondemir, apud
d'Herbelot, p. 882). [And cp. Ducas, p. 35, ed. Bonn.]

sons, was dispatched to Boursa with thirty thousand horse; and such was his youthful ardour that he arrived with only four thousand at the gates of the capital, after performing in five days a march of two hundred and thirty miles. Yet fear is still more rapid in its course; and Soliman, the son of Bajazet, had already passed over to Europe with the royal treasure. The spoil, however, of the palace and city was immense; the inhabitants had escaped; but the buildings, for the most part of wood, were reduced to ashes. From Boursa, the grandson of Timour advanced to Nice, even yet a fair and flourishing city; and the Mogul squadrons were only stopped by the waves of the Propontis. The same success attended the other mirzas and emirs in their excursions; and Smyrna, defended by the zeal and courage of the Rhodian knights, alone deserved the presence of the emperor himself. After an obstinate defence, the place was taken by storm; all that breathed was put to the sword; and the heads of the Christian heroes were launched from the engines, on board of two carracks, or great ships of Europe, that rode at anchor in the harbour. The Moslems of Asia rejoiced in their deliverance from a dangerous and domestic foe, and a parallel was drawn between the two rivals, by observing that Timour, in fourteen days, had reduced a fortress which had sustained seven years the siege, or at least the blockade, of Bajazet.[52]

The *iron cage* in which Bajazet was imprisoned by Tamer- The story lane, so long and so often repeated as a moral lesson, is now cage rejected as a fable by the modern writers, who smile at the vulgar credulity.[53]   They appeal with confidence to the Persian

---

[52] For the war of Anatolia, or Roum, I add some hints in the Institutions, to the copious narratives of Sherefeddin (l. v. c. 44-65) and Arabshah (tom. ii. c. 20-35). On this part only of Timour's history, it is lawful to quote the Turks (Cantemir, p. 53-55, Annal. Leunclav. p. 320-322), and the Greeks (Phranza, l. i. c. 29, Ducas, c. 15-17, Chalcondyles, l. iii.). [Add Sad ad-Dīn's account of the battle, tr. Bratutti, i. p. 213 *sqq.*]

[53] The scepticism of Voltaire (Essai sur l'Histoire Générale, c. 88) is ready on this, as on every, occasion to reject a popular tale, and to diminish the magnitude of vice and virtue; and on most occasions his incredulity is reasonable.   [The fable of the iron cage is fully discussed by Hammer (Gesch. des osmanischen Reiches, i. 252-6); who refers to three points unknown to Gibbon: (1) the silence of the eye-witness, John Schiltberger, whom we have already seen captured in the battle of Nicopolis, and who was again captured by the Mongols at Angora; (2) the evidence of the two oldest Ottoman historians, Neshri and Ashikpashazādé; (3) the discussion and denial of the story by the later Ottoman historian Sad ad-Dīn. Hammer points out that the story arose out of a misconception of the words of Ashikpashazādé and Neshri, who state that a litter, furnished with bars like a

history of Sherefeddin Ali, which has been given to our curiosity in a French version, and from which I shall collect and abridge a more specious narrative of this memorable transaction.

disapproved by the Persian historian of Timour: No sooner was Timour informed [54] that the captive Ottoman was at the door of his tent, than he graciously stepped forwards to receive him, seated him by his side, and mingled with just reproaches a soothing pity for his rank and misfortune. " Alas ! " said the emperor, " the decree of fate is now accomplished by your own fault : it is the web which you have woven, the thorns of the tree which yourself have planted. I wished to spare, and even to assist, the champion of the Moslems ; you braved our threats ; you despised our friendship ; you forced us to enter your kingdom with our invincible armies. Behold the event. Had you vanquished, I am not ignorant of the fate which you reserved for myself and my troops. But I disdain to retaliate ; your life and honour are secure ; and I shall express my gratitude to God by my clemency to man." The royal captive shewed some signs of repentance, accepted the humiliation of a robe of honour, and embraced with tears his son Mousa, who, at his request, was sought and found among the captives of the field. The Ottoman princes were lodged in a splendid pavilion ; and the respect of the guards could be surpassed only by their vigilance. On the arrival of the harem from Boursa, Timour restored the queen Despina and her daughter to their father and husband ; but he piously required that the Servian princess, who had hitherto been indulged in the profession of Christianity, should embrace without delay the religion of the prophet. In the feast of victory, to which Bajazet was invited, the Mogul emperor placed a crown on his head and a sceptre in his hand, with a solemn assurance of restoring him with an increase of glory to the throne of his ancestors. But the effect of this promise was disappointed by the sultan's untimely death : amidst the care of the most skilful physicians, he expired of an apoplexy at Akshehr, the Antioch of Pisidia, about nine months after his defeat. The victor dropped a tear over his grave ; his body, with royal

[δέσποινα = queen]

cage, was provided for Bayezid. Such litters were the kind of vehicle regularly used for conveying a prince's harem.]

[54] [According to Ducas, Timur was playing chess at the moment of Bayezid's arrival (p. 37).]

pomp, was conveyed to the mausoleum which he had erected at Boursa; and his son Mousa, after receiving a rich present of gold and jewels, of horses and arms, was invested by a patent in red ink with the kingdom of Anatolia.

Such is the portrait of a generous conqueror, which has been extracted from his own memorials, and dedicated to his son and grandson, nineteen years after his decease; [55] and, at a time when the truth was remembered by thousands, a manifest falsehood would have implied a satire on his real conduct. Weighty, indeed, is this evidence, adopted by all the Persian histories; [56] yet flattery, more especially in the East, is base and audacious; and the harsh and ignominious treatment of Bajazet is attested by a chain of witnesses, some of whom shall be produced in the order of their time and country. 1. The reader has not forgot the garrison of French, whom the marshal Boucicault left behind him for the defence of Constantinople. They were on the spot to receive the earliest and most faithful intelligence of the overthrow of their great adversary; and it is more than probable that some of them accompanied the Greek embassy to the camp of Tamerlane. From their account, the *hardships* of the prison and death of Bajazet are affirmed by the marshal's servant and historian, within the distance of seven years.[57]   2. The name of Poggius the Italian [58] is deservedly famous among the revivers of learning in the fifteenth century. His elegant dialogue on the vicissitudes of fortune [59] was composed in his fiftieth year,

attested, 1. by the French

2. by the Italians

---

[55] See the history of Sherefeddin (l. v. c. 49, 52, 53, 59, 60). This work was finished at Shiraz, in the year 1424, and dedicated to Sultan Ibrahim, the son of Sharokh, the son of Timour, who reigned in Farsistan in his father's lifetime.

[56] After the perusal of Khondemir, Ebn Schounah, &c., the learned d'Herbelot (Bibliot. Orientale, p. 882) may affirm that this fable is not mentioned in the most authentic histories; but his denial of the visible testimony of Arabshah leaves some room to suspect his accuracy.

[57] Et fut lui-même (*Bajazet*) pris, et mené en prison, en laquelle mourut de *dure mort!* Mémoires de Boucicault, p. i. c. 37. These Memoirs were composed while the Marshal was still governor of Genoa, from whence he was expelled in the year 1409 by a popular insurrection (Muratori, Annali d'Italia, tom. xii. p. 473, 474). [On Boucicaut's Memoirs and Life see Delaville Le Roulx, La France en Orient au 14ᵐᵉ siècle. Expéditions du Maréchal Boucicaut, 2 vols., 1886.]

[58] The reader will find a satisfactory account of the life and writings of Poggius in the Poggiana, an entertaining work of M. Lenfant [A.D. 1720], and in the Bibliotheca Latina mediæ et infimæ Ætatis of Fabricius (tom. v. p. 305-308). Poggius was born in the year 1380, and died in 1459.

[59] The dialogue de Varietate Fortunæ (of which a complete and elegant edition has been published at Paris in 1723, in 4to) was composed a short time before the death of Pope Martin V. (p. 5), and consequently about the end of the year 1430.

twenty-eight years after the Turkish victory of Tamerlane,[60] whom he celebrates as not inferior to the illustrious barbarians of antiquity. Of his exploits and discipline, Poggius was informed by several ocular witnesses; nor does he forget an example so apposite to his theme as the Ottoman monarch, whom the Scythian confined like a wild beast in an iron cage and exhibited a spectacle to Asia. I might add the authority of two Italian chronicles, perhaps of an earlier date, which would prove at least that the same story, whether false or true, was imported into Europe with the first tidings of the revolution.[61] 3. At the time when Poggius flourished at Rome, Ahmed Ebn Arabshah composed at Damascus the florid and malevolent history of Timour, for which he had collected materials in his journeys over Turkey and Tartary.[62] Without any possible correspondence between the Latin and the Arabian writer, they agree in the fact of the iron cage; and their agreement is a striking proof of their common veracity. Ahmed Arabshah likewise relates another outrage, which Bajazet endured, of a more domestic and tender nature. His indiscreet mention of women and divorces was deeply resented by the jealous Tartar. In the feast of victory, the wine was served by female cup-bearers; and the sultan beheld his own concubines and wives confounded among the slaves, and exposed, without a veil, to the eyes of intemperance. To escape a similar indignity, it is said that his successors, except in a single instance, have abstained from legitimate nuptials; and the Ottoman practice and belief, at least in the sixteenth century, is attested by the observing Busbequius,[63] ambassador from the court of Vienna to the great Soliman. 4. Such is the separation of language that the testimony of a Greek is not less inde-

3. by the Arabs

4. by the Greeks

[60] See a splendid and elegant encomium of Tamerlane, p. 36-39, ipse enim novi (says Poggius) qui fuere in ejus castris. . . . Regem vivum cepit, caveâque in modum feræ inclusum per omnem Asiam circumtulit egregium admirandumque spectaculum fortunæ.

[61] The Chronicon Tarvisianum (in Muratori, Script. Rerum Italicarum, tom. xix. p. 800), and the Annales Estenses (tom. xviii. p. 974). The two authors, Andrea de Redusiis de Quero and James de Delayto, were both contemporaries, and both chancellors, the one of Trevigi, the other of Ferrara. The evidence of the former is the most positive.

[62] See Arabshah, tom. ii. c. 28, 34. He travelled in regiones Rumæas, A.H. 839 (A.D. 1435, 27th July), tom. ii. c. 2, p. 13.

[63] Busbequius in Legatione Turcicâ, epist. i. p. 52. Yet his respectable authority is somewhat shaken by the subsequent marriages of Amurath II. with a Servian, and of Mahomet II. with an Asiatic, princess (Cantemir, p. 83, 93).

pendent than that of a Latin or an Arab. I suppress the names of Chalcondyles and Ducas, who flourished in a later period, and who speak in a less positive tone; but more attention is due to George Phranza,[64] protovestiare of the last emperors, and who was born a year before the battle of Angora. Twenty-two years after that event, he was sent ambassador to Amurath the Second; and the historian might converse with some veteran Janizaries, who had been made prisoners with the sultan and had themselves seen him in his iron cage. 5. The last evidence, in every sense, is that of the Turkish annals, which have been consulted or transcribed by Leunclavius, Pocock, and Cantemir.[65] They unanimously deplore the captivity of the iron cage; and some credit may be allowed to national historians, who cannot stigmatize the Tartar without uncovering the shame of their king and country. 5. by the Turks

From these opposite premises, a fair and moderate conclusion may be deduced. I am satisfied that Sherefeddin Ali has faithfully described the first ostentatious interview, in which the conqueror, whose spirits were harmonized by success, affected the character of generosity. But his mind was insensibly alienated by the unseasonable arrogance of Bajazet; the complaints of his enemies, the Anatolian princes, were just and vehement; and Timour betrayed a design of leading his royal captive in triumph to Samarcand. An attempt to facilitate his escape, by digging a mine under the tent, provoked the Mogul emperor to impose a harsher restraint; and, in his perpetual marches, an iron cage on a waggon might be invented, not as a wanton insult, but as a rigorous precaution. Timour had read in some fabulous history a similar treatment of one of his predecessors, a king of Persia; and Bajazet was condemned to represent the person, and expiate the guilt, of the Roman Cæsar.[66] But the strength of his mind and body fainted under the trial, and his premature death might, with- Probable conclusion

Death of Bajazet, A.D. 1403, 9th March

---

[64] See the testimony of George Phranza (l. i. c. 29), and his life in Hanckius (de Script. Byzant. p. i. c. 40). Chalcondyles and Ducas speak in general terms of Bajazet's *chains*.

[65] Annales Leunclav. p. 321; Pocock, Prolegomen. ad Abulpharag. Dynast.; Cantemir, p. 55. [See above, note 53.]

[66] A Sapor, king of Persia, had been made prisoner, and inclosed in the figure of a cow's hide, by Maximian, or Galerius Cæsar. Such is the fable related by Eutychius (Annal. tom. i. p. 421, vers. Pocock). The recollection of the true history (Decline and Fall, &c., vol. i. p. 400 *sq.*) will teach us to appreciate the knowledge of the Orientals of the ages which precede the Hegira.

out injustice, be ascribed to the severity of Timour. He warred not with the dead; a tear and a sepulchre were all that he could bestow on a captive who was delivered from his power; and, if Mousa, the son of Bajazet, was permitted to reign over the ruins of Boursa, the greatest part of the province of Anatolia had been restored by the conqueror to their lawful sovereigns.

Term of the conquests of Timour, A.D. 1403

From the Irtish and Volga to the Persian Gulf, and from the Ganges to Damascus and the Archipelago, Asia was in the hand of Timour; his armies were invincible, his ambition was boundless, and his zeal might aspire to conquer and convert the Christian kingdoms of the West, which already trembled at his name. He touched the utmost verge of the land; but an insuperable, though narrow sea, rolled between the two continents of Europe and Asia; [67] and the lord of so many *tomans*, or myriads of horse, was not master of a single galley. The two passages of the Bosphorus and Hellespont, of Constantinople and Gallipoli, were possessed, the one by the Christians, the other by the Turks. On this great occasion, they forgot the difference of religion, to act with union and firmness in the common cause. The double straits were guarded with ships and fortifications; and they separately withheld the transports which Timour demanded of either nation, under the pretence of attacking their enemy. At the same time, they soothed his pride with tributary gifts and suppliant embassies, and prudently tempted him to retreat with the honours of victory. Soliman, the son of Bajazet, implored his clemency for his father and himself; accepted, by a red patent, the investiture of the kingdom of Romania, which he already held by the sword; and reiterated his ardent wish of casting himself in person at the feet of the king of the world. The Greek emperor [68] (either John or Manuel) submitted to pay the same tribute which he had stipulated with the Turkish sultan, and

---

[67] Arabshah (tom. ii. c. 25) describes, like a curious traveller, the straits of Gallipoli and Constantinople. To acquire a just idea of these events, I have compared the narratives and prejudices of the Moguls, Turks, Greeks, and Arabians. The Spanish ambassador mentions this hostile union of the Christians and Ottomans (Vie de Timour, p. 96).

[68] Since the name of Cæsar had been transferred to the sultans of Roum, the Greek princes of Constantinople (Sherefeddin, l. v. c. 54) were confounded with the Christian *lords* of Gallipoli, Thessalonica, &c. under the title of *Tekkur*, which is derived by corruption from the genitive τοῦ κυρίου (Cantemir, p. 51).

SAMARCAND: THE GUR AMIR, OR TOMB OF TIMUR

ratified the treaty by an oath of allegiance, from which he could absolve his conscience as soon as the Mogul arms had retired from Anatolia. But the fears and fancy of nations ascribed to the ambitious Tamerlane a new design of vast and romantic compass: a design of subduing Egypt and Africa, marching from the Nile to the Atlantic Ocean, entering Europe by the Straits of Gibraltar, and, after imposing his yoke on the kingdoms of Christendom, of returning home by the deserts of Russia and Tartary. This remote and perhaps imaginary danger was averted by the submission of the sultan of Egypt; the honours of the prayer and the coin attested at Cairo the supremacy of Timour; and a rare gift of a *giraffe*, or camelopard, and nine ostriches, represented at Samarcand the tribute of the African world. Our imagination is not less astonished by the portrait of a Mogul, who, in his camp before Smyrna, meditates and almost accomplishes the invasion of the Chinese empire.[69] Timour was urged to this enterprise by national honour and religious zeal. The torrents which he had shed of Musulman blood could be expiated only by an equal destruction of the infidels; and, as he now stood at the gates of paradise, he might best secure his glorious entrance by demolishing the idols of China, founding mosques in every city, and establishing the profession of faith in one God and his prophet Mahomet. The recent expulsion of the house of Zingis was an insult on the Mogul name; and the disorders of the empire afforded the fairest opportunity for revenge. The illustrious Hongvou, founder of the dynasty of *Ming*, died four years before the battle of Angora; and his grandson, a weak and unfortunate youth, was burnt in a palace, after a million of Chinese had perished in the civil war.[70] Before he evacuated Anatolia, Timour dispatched beyond the Sihoon a numerous army, or rather colony, of his old and new subjects, to open the road, to subdue the Pagan Calmucks and Mungals, and to found cities and magazines in the desert; and, by the diligence of his lieutenant, he soon received a perfect map and

[69] See Sherefeddin, l. v. c. 4, who marks, in a just itinerary, the road to China, which Arabshah (tom. ii. c. 33) paints in vague and rhetorical colours.
[70] Synopsis Hist. Sinicæ, p. 74-76 (in the ivth part of the relations de Thévenot), Duhalde, Hist. de la Chine (tom. i. p. 507, 508, folio edition); and for the chronology of the Chinese Emperors, de Guignes, Hist. des Huns, tom. i. p. 71, 72.

description of the unknown regions from the source of the Irtish to the wall of China. During these preparations, the emperor achieved the final conquest of Georgia; passed the winter on the banks of the Araxes; appeased the troubles of Persia; and slowly returned to his capital, after a campaign of four years and nine months.

His triumph at Samarcand, A.D. 1404, July-A.D. 1405, 8th January

On the throne of Samarcand,[71] he displayed, in a short repose, his magnificence and power; listened to the complaints of the people; distributed a just measure of rewards and punishments; employed his riches in the architecture of palaces and temples; and gave audience to the ambassadors of Egypt, Arabia, India, Tartary, Russia, and Spain, the last of whom presented a suit of tapestry which eclipsed the pencil of the Oriental artists. The marriage of six of the emperor's grandsons was esteemed an act of religion as well as of paternal tenderness; and the pomp of the ancient caliphs was revived in their nuptials. They were celebrated in the gardens of Canighul, decorated with innumerable tents and pavilions, which displayed the luxury of a great city, and the spoils of a victorious camp. Whole forests were cut down to supply fuel for the kitchens; the plain was spread with pyramids of meat and vases of every liquor, to which thousands of guests were courteously invited. The orders of the state and the nations of the earth were marshalled at the royal banquet; nor were the ambassadors of Europe (says the haughty Persian) excluded from the feast; since even the *casses*, the smallest of fish, find their place in the ocean.[72] The public joy was testified by illuminations and masquerades; the trades of Samarcand passed in review; and every trade was emulous to execute some quaint device, some marvellous pageant, with the materials of their peculiar art. After the marriage-contracts had been ratified by the cadhis, the bridegrooms and their brides retired to their

---

[71] For the return, triumph, and death of Timour, see Sherefeddin (l. vi. c. 1-30) and Arabshah (tom. ii. c. 35-47).

[72] Sherefeddin (l. xi. c. 24) mentions the ambassadors of one of the most potent sovereigns of Europe. We know that it was Henry III. King of Castile; and the curious relation of his two embassies is still extant, Mariana, Hist. Hispan. l. xix. c. 11, tom. ii. p. 329, 330. Advertissement à l'Hist. de Timur Bec, p. 28-33. There appears likewise to have been some correspondence between the Mogul emperor and the court of Charles VII. King of France (Histoire de France, par Velly et Villaret, tom. xii. p. 336). [The account of Ruy Gonzalez de Clavijo of his embassy to the court of Timour in 1403-6, has been translated, with elucidations, by Clements R. Markham, for the Hakluyt Society, 1859.]

nuptial chambers; nine times, according to the Asiatic fashion, they were dressed and undressed; and at each change of apparel pearls and rubies were showered on their heads, and contemptuously abandoned to their attendants. A general indulgence was proclaimed; every law was relaxed, every pleasure was allowed; the people was free, the sovereign was idle; and the historian of Timour may remark that, after devoting fifty years to the attainment of empire, the only happy period of his life were the two months in which he ceased to exercise his power. But he was soon awakened to the cares of government and war. The standard was unfurled for the invasion of China: the emirs made their report of two hundred thousand, the select and veteran soldiers of Iran and Turan; their baggage and provisions were transported by five hundred great waggons, and an immense train of horses and camels; and the troops might prepare for a long absence, since more than six months were employed in the tranquil journey of a caravan from Samarcand to Pekin. Neither age nor the severity of the winter could retard the impatience of Timour; he mounted on horseback, passed the Sihoon on the ice, marched seventy-six parasangs, three hundred miles, from his capital, and pitched his last camp in the neighbourhood of Otrar, where he was expected by the angel of death. Fatigue, and the indiscreet use of iced water, accelerated the progress of his fever; and the conqueror of Asia expired in the seventieth year of his age, thirty-five years after he had ascended the throne of Zagatai. His designs were lost; his armies were disbanded; China was saved; and, fourteen years after his decease, the most powerful of his children sent an embassy of friendship and commerce to the court of Pekin.[73] *His death on the road to China, A.D. 1405, 1st April*

The fame of Timour has pervaded the East and West; his posterity is still invested with the Imperial *title*; and the admiration of his subjects, who revered him almost as a deity, may be justified in some degree by the praise or confession of his bitterest enemies.[74] Although he was lame of an hand and *Character and merits of Timour*

[73] See the translation of the Persian account of their embassy, a curious and original piece (in the ivth part of the Relations de Thévenot). They presented the emperor of China with an old horse which Timour had formerly rode. It was in the year 1419 that they departed from the court of Herat, to which place they returned in 1422 from Pekin. [Timur died in February, 1405, see Elias and Ross, Tarikh-i-Rashīdī, p. 54 note.]

[74] From Arabshah, tom. ii. c. 96. The bright or softer colours are borrowed rom Sherefeddin, d'Herbelot, and the Institutions. [In one important respect

foot, his form and stature were not unworthy of his rank;
and his vigorous health, so essential to himself and to the
world, was corroborated by temperance and exercise. In his
familiar discourse he was grave and modest, and, if he was
ignorant of the Arabic language, he spoke with fluency and
elegance the Persian and Turkish idioms. It was his delight
to converse with the learned on topics of history and science;
and the amusement of his leisure hours was the game of chess,
which he improved or corrupted with new refinements.[75] In
his religion, he was a zealous, though not perhaps an orthodox,
Musulman; [76] but his sound understanding may tempt us to
believe that a superstitious reverence for omens and prophecies,
for saints and astrologers, was only affected as an instrument
of policy. In the government of a vast empire, he stood alone
and absolute, without a rebel to oppose his power, a favourite
to seduce his affections, or a minister to mislead his judgment.
It was his firmest maxim that, whatever might be the consequence, the word of the prince should never be disputed or
recalled; but his foes have maliciously observed that the commands of anger and destruction were more strictly executed
than those of beneficence and favour. His sons and grandsons,
of whom Timour left six-and-thirty at his decease, were his
first and most submissive subjects; and, whenever they deviated
from their duty, they were corrected, according to the laws of

Gibbon's account of Timur and his work is deficient. He has not realised, or
brought out, the fact that the greatest result of Timur's empire was the victory of
Islam in Central Asia. Timur acted from the beginning in close co-operation with
the Musulman ecclesiastics of Transoxiana, and when he won supreme power, he
did away with the Mongol and Turkish legislative system of Chingiz and substituted the law of Islam. In regard to the very foundations of the political constitution there is a vast difference between the two systems. Chingiz and his successors
were subject to the law (the Yāsāk) and bound by its provisions; whereas according
to the principles of Islam the head of the state is not bound by the law, but is responsible only to God. Thus the will of the sovereign is set above the law. Timur
then broke completely with the Mongol tradition, such as it had been developed
under Chinese influence, and drew the Turks of Central Asia out of touch with the
far East. As the Mongol power in China was overthrown about the same time by
the revolution which set the Ming dynasty on the throne (A.D. 1370), this period
marks a general decline of Mongol influence in Asia.]

[75] His new system was multiplied from 32 pieces and 64 squares, to 56 pieces
and 110 or 130 squares. But, except in his court, the old game has been thought
sufficiently elaborate. The Mogul emperor was rather pleased than hurt with the
victory of a subject; a chess-player will feel the value of this encomium!

[76] See Sherefeddin, l. v. c. 15, 25. Arabshah (tom. ii. c. 96, p. 801, 803) re-
proves the impiety of Timour and the Moguls, who almost preferred to the Koran
the Yacsa, or Law of Zingis (cui Deus maledicat): nor will he believe that Sharokh
had abolished the use and authority of that Pagan code.

Zingis, with the bastonade, and afterwards restored to honour and command. Perhaps his heart was not devoid of the social virtues ; perhaps he was not incapable of loving his friends and pardoning his enemies ; but the rules of morality are founded on the public interest; and it may be sufficient to applaud the *wisdom* of a monarch, for the liberality by which he is not impoverished, and for the justice by which he is strengthened and enriched. To maintain the harmony of authority and obedience, to chastise the proud, to protect the weak, to reward the deserving, to banish vice and idleness from his dominions, to secure the traveller and merchant, to restrain the depredations of the soldier, to cherish the labours of the husbandman, to encourage industry and learning, and, by an equal and modern assessment, to increase the revenue without increasing the taxes, are indeed the duties of a prince ; but, in the discharge of these duties, he finds an ample and immediate recompense. Timour might boast that, at his accession to the throne, Asia was the prey of anarchy and rapine, whilst under his prosperous monarchy, a child, fearless and unhurt, might carry a purse of gold from the East to the West. Such was his confidence of merit that from this reformation he derived excuse for his victories and a title to universal dominion. The four following observations will serve to appreciate his claim to the public gratitude ; and perhaps we shall conclude that the Mogul emperor was rather the scourge than the benefactor of mankind. 1. If some partial disorders, some local oppressions, were healed by the sword of Timour, the remedy was far more pernicious than the disease. By their rapine, cruelty, and discord, the petty tyrants of Persia might afflict their subjects ; but whole nations were crushed under the footsteps of the reformer. The ground which had been occupied by flourishing cities was often marked by his abominable trophies, by columns or pyramids of human heads. Astracan, Carizme, Delhi, Ispahan, Bagdad, Aleppo, Damascus, Boursa, Smyrna, and a thousand others, were sacked, or burnt, or utterly destroyed, in his presence, and by his troops ; and perhaps his conscience would have been startled if a priest or philosopher had dared to number the millions of victims whom he had sacrificed to the establishment of peace and order.[77]

[77] Besides the bloody passages of this narrative, I must refer to an anticipation in the third volume of the Decline and Fall, which, in a single note (p. 452, note 26),

2. His most destructive wars were rather inroads than conquests. He invaded Turkestan, Kipzak, Russia, Hindostan, Syria, Anatolia, Armenia, and Georgia, without a hope or a desire of preserving those distant provinces. From thence he departed, laden with spoil; but he left behind him neither troops to awe the contumacious, nor magistrates to protect the obedient, natives. When he had broken the fabric of their ancient government, he abandoned them to the evils which his invasion had aggravated or caused; nor were these evils compensated by any present or possible benefits. 3. The kingdoms of Transoxiana and Persia were the proper field which he laboured to cultivate and adorn as the perpetual inheritance of his family. But his peaceful labours were often interrupted, and sometimes blasted, by the absence of the conqueror. While he triumphed on the Volga or the Ganges, his servants, and even his sons, forgot their master and their duty. The public and private injuries were poorly redressed by the tardy rigour of inquiry and punishment; and we must be content to praise the Institutions of Timour, as the specious idea of a perfect monarchy. 4. Whatsoever might be the blessings of his administration, they evaporated with his life. To reign, rather than to govern, was the ambition of his children and grandchildren,[78] the enemies of each other and of the people. A fragment of the empire was upheld with some glory by Sharokh, his youngest son; but after *his* decease, the scene was again involved in darkness and blood; and before the end of a century Transoxiana and Persia were trampled by the Uzbeks from the North, and the Turkmans of the black and white sheep. The race of Timour would have been extinct, if an hero, his descendant in the fifth degree, had not fled before the Uzbek arms to the conquest of Hindostan. His successors (the Great Moguls [79]) extended their sway from the moun-

[Babar, his flight, A.D. 1504]

accumulates near 300,000 heads of the monuments of his cruelty. Except in Rowe's play on the fifth of November, I did not expect to hear of Timour's amiable moderation (White's preface, p. 7). Yet I can excuse a generous enthusiasm in the reader, and still more in the editor, of the Institutions.

[78] Consult the last chapters of Sherefeddin and Arabshah, and M. de Guignes (Hist. des Huns, tom. iv. l. xx.), Fraser's History of Nadir Shah (p. 1-62). The story of Timour's descendants is imperfectly told; and the second and third parts of Sherefeddin are unknown.

[79] Shah Allum [Shāh-Ālam, A.D. 1759-1806], the present Mogul, is in the fourteenth [rather fifteenth from Bābar, who was fifth from Timour] degree from Timour by Miran Shah, his third son. See the iid volume of Dow's History of Hindustan. [The shadowy survival of the Mogul empire ceased to exist in 1857.]

tains of Cashmir to Cape Comorin, and from Candahar to the Gulf of Bengal. Since the reign of Aurungzebe, their empire [Aurangzib, A.D. 1659-1707] has been dissolved ; their treasures of Delhi have been rifled by a Persian robber ; and the richest of their kingdoms is now possessed by a company of Christian merchants, of a remote island in the Northern Ocean.

Far different was the fate of the Ottoman monarchy. The [Civil wars of the sons of Bajazet, A.D. 1403-1421] massy trunk was bent to the ground, but no sooner did the hurricane pass away than it again rose with fresh vigour and more lively vegetation. When Timour, in every sense, had evacuated Anatolia, he left the cities without a palace, a treasure, or a king. The open country was overspread with hordes of shepherds and robbers of Tartar or Turkman origin ; the recent conquests of Bajazet were restored to the emirs, one of whom, in base revenge, demolished his sepulchre; and his five sons were eager, by civil discord, to consume the remnant of their patrimony. I shall enumerate their names in the order of their age and actions.[80] 1. It is doubtful, whether I [1. Mustapha] relate the story of the true *Mustapha*, or of an impostor who personated that lost prince.[81] He fought by his father's side in the battle of Angora ; but, when the captive sultan was permitted to inquire for his children, Mousa alone could be found ; and the Turkish historians, the slaves of the triumphant faction, are persuaded that his brother was confounded among the slain. If Mustapha escaped from that disastrous field, he was concealed twelve years from his friends and enemies, till he emerged in Thessaly and was hailed by a numerous party as the son and successor of Bajazet. His first defeat would have been his last, had not the true, or false, Mustapha been saved by the Greeks and restored, after the decease of his brother Mahomet, to liberty and empire. A degenerate mind seemed to argue his spurious birth; and, if, on the throne of Hadrianople, he was adored as the Ottoman sultan, his flight, his fetters, and an ignominious gibbet delivered the impostor

---

[80] The civil wars, from the death of Bajazet to that of Mustapha, are related, according to the Turks, by Demetrius Cantemir (p. 58-82). Of the Greeks, Chalcondyles (l. iv. and v.), Phranza (l. i. c. 30-32) and Ducas (c. 18-27), the last is the most copious and best informed.

[81] [It is difficult to decide whether he was an impostor, as the Ottoman, or genuine, as the Greek, historians allege. Zinkeisen leaves the question open (i. 383-384), but with an inclination to the former opinion ; Hammer argues for the view that the claimant was the true Mustapha, i. 297.]

to popular contempt.   A similar character and claim was asserted by several rival pretenders; thirty persons are said to have suffered under the name of Mustapha; and these frequent executions may perhaps insinuate that the Turkish court was not perfectly secure of the death of the lawful prince.   2.

2. Isa After his father's captivity, Isa [82] reigned for some time in the neighbourhood of Angora, Sinope, and the Black Sea ; and his ambassadors were dismissed from the presence of Timour with fair promises and honourable gifts.   But their master was soon deprived of his province and life by a jealous brother, the sovereign of Amasia ; and the final event [83] suggested a pious allusion that the law of Moses and Jesus, of *Isa* and *Mousa*, had been abrogated by the greater *Mahomet*.   3.

3. Soliman, A.D. 1403-1410 *Soliman* is not numbered in the list of the Turkish emperors; yet he checked the victorious progress of the Moguls, and after their departure united for a while the thrones of Hadrianople and Boursa.   In war, he was brave, active, and fortunate ; his courage was softened by clemency ; but it was likewise inflamed by presumption, and corrupted by intemperance and idleness.   He relaxed the nerves of discipline in a government where either the subject or the sovereign must continually tremble ; his vices alienated the chiefs of the army and the law ; and his daily drunkenness, so contemptible in a prince and a man, was doubly odious in a disciple of the prophet. In the slumber of intoxication, he was surprised by his brother Mousa ; and, as he fled from Hadrianople towards the Byzantine capital, Soliman was overtaken and slain in a bath, after

4. Mousa, A.D. 1410 a reign of seven years and ten months.   4. The investiture of Mousa degraded him as the slave of the Moguls ; his tributary kingdom of Anatolia was confined within a narrow limit, nor could his broken militia and empty treasury contend with the hardy and veteran bands of the sovereign of Romania.   Mousa fled in disguise from the palace of Boursa; traversed the Propontis in an open boat ; wandered over the Walachian and Servian hills ; and, after some vain attempts, ascended the throne of Hadrianople, so recently stained with the blood of

---

[82] Arabshah, tom. ii. c. 26, whose testimony on this occasion is weighty and valuable.   The existence of Isa (unknown to the Turks) is likewise confirmed by Sherefeddin (l. v. c. 57).

[83] [Mohammad defeated Isa in battle at Ulubad, A.D. 1403, and again in 1404 (Sad ad-Dīn, transl. Bratutti, p. 284).]

Soliman. In a reign of three years and a half, his troops were victorious against the Christians of Hungary and the Morea ; but Mousa was ruined by his timorous disposition and unseasonable clemency. After resigning the sovereignty of Anatolia, he fell a victim to the perfidy of his ministers and the superior ascendant of his brother Mahomet. 5. The final victory of Mahomet was the just recompense of his prudence and moderation. *5. Mahomet I. A.D. 1413-1421* Before his father's captivity, the royal youth had been entrusted with the government of Amasia, thirty days' journey from Constantinople and the Turkish frontier against the Christians of Trebizond and Georgia. The castle, in Asiatic warfare, was esteemed impregnable ; and the city of Amasia,[84] which is equally divided by the river Iris, rises on either side in the form of an amphitheatre, and represents, on a smaller scale, the image of Bagdad. In his rapid career, Timour appears to have overlooked this obscure and contumacious angle of Anatolia ; and Mahomet, without provoking the conqueror, maintained his silent independence, and chased from the province the last stragglers of the Tartar host. He relieved himself from the dangerous neighbourhood of Isa ; but in the contests of their more powerful brethren his firm neutrality was respected ; till, after the triumph of Mousa, he stood forth the heir and avenger of the unfortunate Soliman. Mahomet obtained Anatolia by treaty and Romania by arms ; and the soldier who presented him with the head of Mousa was rewarded as the benefactor of his king and country. *[Victory of Mohammad over Musa at Tsha-morlu, near Sophia]* The eight years of his sole and peaceful reign were usefully employed in banishing the vices of civil discord, and restoring, on a firmer basis, the fabric of the Ottoman monarchy.[85] His last care was. the choice of two vizirs, Bajazet and Ibrahim,[86] who might guide the youth of his son Amurath ; and such was their union and prudence that they concealed, above forty days, the emperor's death, till the arrival of his successor in the palace of Boursa. *Reign of Amurath II. A.D. 1421-1451, 9th Feb.* A new war was kindled in Europe by the prince, or impostor,

---

[84] Arabshah, *loc. citat.* Abulfeda, Geograph. tab. xvii. p. 302. Busbequius, epist. i. p. 96, 97, in Itinere C. P. et Amasiano.

[85] [Mohammad's character was marked by justice, mildness, and freedom from fanaticism.]

[86] The virtues of Ibrahim are praised by a contemporary Greek (Ducas, c. 25). His descendants are the sole nobles in Turkey ; they content themselves with the administration of his pious foundations, are excused from public offices, and receive two annual visits from the Sultan (Cantemir, p. 76).

Mustapha ; the first vizir lost his army and his head ; but the more fortunate Ibrahim, whose name and family are still revered, extinguished the last pretender to the throne of Bajazet, and closed the scene of domestic hostility.

Re-union of the Ottoman empire, A.D. 1421   In these conflicts, the wisest Turks, and indeed the body of the nation, were strongly attached to the unity of the empire ; and Romania and Anatolia, so often torn asunder by private ambition, were animated by a strong and invincible tendency of cohesion. Their efforts might have instructed the Christian powers ; and, had they occupied, with a confederate fleet, the straits of Gallipoli, the Ottomans, at least in Europe, must have been speedily annihilated. But the schism of the West, and the factions and wars of France and England, diverted the Latins from this generous enterprise ; they enjoyed the present respite without a thought of futurity ; and were often tempted by a momentary interest to serve the common enemy of their religion. A colony of Genoese,[87] which had been planted at Phocæa [88] on the Ionian coast, was enriched by the lucrative monopoly of alum [89]; and their tranquillity, under the Turkish empire, was secured by the annual payment of tribute. In the last civil war of the Ottomans, the Genoese governor, Adorno, a bold and ambitious youth, embraced the party of Amurath ; and undertook, with seven stout galleys, to transport him from Asia to Europe. The sultan and five hundred guards embarked on board the admiral's ship, which was manned by eight hundred of the bravest Franks. His life and liberty were in their hands ; nor can we, without reluctance, applaud the fidelity of Adorno, who, in the midst of the passage, knelt before him, and gratefully accepted a discharge of his arrears of tribute. They landed in sight of Mustapha and Gallipoli ; two thousand Italians, armed with lances and battle-axes, attended Amurath to the conquest

[87] See Pachymer (l. v. c. 29), Nicephorus Gregoras (l. ii. c. i.), Sherefeddin (l. v. c. 57), and Ducas (c. 25). The last of these, a curious and careful observer, is entitled, from his birth and station, to particular credit in all that concerns Ionia and the islands. Among the nations that resorted to New Phocæa he mentions the English ('Ιγγλῆνοι) : an early evidence of Mediterranean trade.

[88] For the spirit of navigation and freedom of ancient Phocæa, or rather of the Phocæans, consult the first book of Herodotus, and the Geographical Index of his last and learned French translator, M. Larcher (tom. vii. p. 299).

[89] Phocæa is not enumerated by Pliny (Hist. Nat. xxxv. 52) among the places productive of alum ; he reckons Egypt as the first, and for the second the isle of Melos, whose alum mines are described by Tournefort (tom. i. lettre iv.), a traveller and a naturalist. After the loss of Phocæa, the Genoese, in 1459, found that useful mineral in the isle of Ischia (Ismael. Bouillaud, ad Ducam, c. 25).

of Hadrianople; and this venal service was soon repaid by the ruin of the commerce and colony of Phocæa.

If Timour had generously marched at the request, and to the relief of, the Greek emperor, he might be entitled to the praise and gratitude of the Christians.[90] But a Musulman, who carried into Georgia the sword of persecution, and respected the holy warfare of Bajazet, was not disposed to pity or succour the *idolaters* of Europe. The Tartar followed the impulse of ambition; and the deliverance of Constantinople was the accidental consequence. When Manuel abdicated the government, it was his prayer, rather than his hope, that the ruin of the church and state might be delayed beyond his unhappy days; and, after his return from a western pilgrimage, he expected every hour the news of the sad catastrophe. On a sudden, he was astonished and rejoiced by the intelligence of the retreat, the overthrow, and the captivity of the Ottoman. Manuel [91] immediately sailed from Modon in the Morea; ascended the throne of Constantinople; and dismissed his blind competitor to an easy exile in the isle of Lesbos. The ambassadors of the son of Bajazet were soon introduced to his presence; but their pride was fallen, their tone was modest; they were awed by the just apprehension lest the Greeks should open to the Moguls the gates of Europe. Soliman saluted the emperor by the name of father; solicited at his hands the government or gift of Romania; and promised to deserve his favour by inviolable friendship, and the restitution of Thessalonica, with the most important places along the Strymon, the Propontis, and the Black Sea. The alliance of Soliman exposed the emperor to the enmity and revenge of Mousa. The Turks appeared in arms before the gates of Constantinople; but they were repulsed by sea and land; and, unless the city was guarded by some foreign mercenaries, the Greeks must have wondered at their own triumph. But, instead of prolonging the division of the Ottoman powers, the policy or passion of Manuel

Marginal note: State of the Greek empire. A.D. 1402-1425

---

[90] The writer who has the most abused this fabulous generosity is our ingenious Sir William Temple (his Works, vol. iii. p. 349, 350, 8vo edition), that lover of exotic virtue. After the conquest of Russia, &c. and the passage of the Danube, his Tartar hero relieves, visits, admires, and refuses the city of Constantine. His flattering pencil deviates in every line from the truth of history; yet his pleasing fictions are more excusable than the gross errors of Cantemir.

[91] For the reigns of Manuel and John, of Mahomet I. and Amurath II. see the Othman history of Cantemir (p. 70-95), and the three Greeks, Chalcondyles, Phranza, and Ducas, who is still superior to his rivals.

was tempted to assist the most formidable of the sons of Bajazet. He concluded a treaty with Mahomet, whose progress
was checked by the insuperable barrier of Gallipoli : the sultan
and his troops were transported over the Bosphorus; he was
hospitably entertained in the capital; and his successful sally
was the first step to the conquest of Romania. The ruin was
suspended by the prudence and moderation of the conqueror;
he faithfully discharged his own obligations, and those of Soliman; respected the laws of gratitude and peace; and left the
emperor guardian of his two younger sons, in the vain hope of
saving them from the jealous cruelty of their brother Amurath.
But the execution of his last testament would have offended the
national honour and religion; and the divan unanimously pronounced that the royal youths should never be abandoned to
the custody and education of a Christian dog. On this refusal,
the Byzantine councils were divided; but the age and caution
of Manuel yielded to the presumption of his son John; and
they unsheathed a dangerous weapon of revenge, by dismissing
the true or false Mustapha, who had long been detained as a
captive and hostage, and for whose maintenance they received
an annual pension of three hundred thousand aspers.[92] At the
door of his prison, Mustapha subscribed to every proposal; and
the keys of Gallipoli, or rather of Europe, were stipulated as
the price of his deliverance. But no sooner was he seated on
the throne of Romania than he dismissed the Greek ambassadors
with a smile of contempt, declaring, in a pious tone, that, at the
day of judgment, he would rather answer for the violation of an
oath than for the surrender of a Musulman city into the hands
of the infidels. The emperor was at once the enemy of the
two rivals; from whom he had sustained, and to whom he had
offered, an injury; and the victory of Amurath was followed, in
the ensuing spring, by the siege of Constantinople.[93]

[92] The Turkish asper (from the Greek ἄσπρος [= white]) is, or was, a piece of
white or silver money, at present much debased, but which was formerly equivalent
to the 54th part, at least, of a Venetian ducat, or sequin ; and the 300,000 aspers, a
princely allowance or royal tribute, may be computed at 2500l. sterling (Leunclav.
Pandect. Turc. p. 406-408). [Cantacuscino (in Sansovino, Historia Universale de
Turchi, fol. 11, v.) counts 54 aspers to a sultanin or ducat, and this was still the
value about the beginning of the 16th century, but in the reign of Selim I., before
1520, 60 aspers went to a ducat, and this value was maintained during the reigns of
Sulayman and Selim II.]

[93] For the siege of Constantinople in 1422, see the particular and contemporary
narrative of John Cananus, published by Leo Allatius, at the end of his edition of
Acropolita (p. 188-199).

The religious merit of subduing the city of the Cæsars attracted from Asia a crowd of volunteers, who aspired to the crown of martyrdom. Their military ardour was inflamed by the promise of rich spoils and beautiful females; and the sultan's ambition was consecrated by the presence and prediction of Seid Bechar, a descendant of the prophet,[94] who arrived in the camp, on a mule, with a venerable train of five hundred disciples. But he might blush, if a fanatic could blush, at the failure of his assurances. The strength of the walls resisted an army of two hundred thousand Turks[95]; their assaults were repelled by the sallies of the Greeks and their foreign mercenaries; the old resources of defence were opposed to the new engines of attack; and the enthusiasm of the dervish, who was snatched to heaven in visionary converse with Mahomet, was answered by the credulity of the Christians, who *beheld* the Virgin Mary, in a violet garment, walking on the rampart and animating their courage.[96] After a siege of two months, Amurath was recalled to Boursa by a domestic revolt, which had been kindled by Greek treachery, and was soon extinguished by the death of a guiltless brother. While he led his Janizaries to new conquests in Europe and Asia, the Byzantine empire was indulged in a servile and precarious respite of thirty years. Manuel sank into the grave; and John Palæologus was permitted to reign, for an annual tribute of three hundred thousand aspers, and the dereliction of almost all that he held beyond the suburbs of Constantinople.

In the establishment and restoration of the Turkish empire, the first merit must doubtless be assigned to the personal qualities of the sultans; since, in human life, the most important scenes will depend on the character of a single actor. By some shades of wisdom and virtue they may be discriminated from each other; but, except in a single instance, a period

Marginal notes:
Siege of Constantinople by Amurath II. A.D. 1422, 10th June-24th August

The emperor John Palæologus II. A.D. 1425, 21st July-A.D. 1448, 31st October

Hereditary succession and merit of the Ottomans

---

[94] Cantemir, p. 80. Cananus, who describes Seid Bechar, without naming him, supposes that the friend of Mahomet assumed, in his amours, the privilege of a prophet, and that the fairest of the Greek nuns were promised to the saint and his disciples.

[95] [This number, given by Ducas and Phrantzes, is obviously a gross exaggeration, perhaps a slip of the pen. Cp. Zinkeisen, i. 524 (and 527), who think the besiegers did not exceed 40,000 or 50,000. According to Cananus the first corps brought against the city was 10,000; then followed "another army" like a hail storm, p. 459, ed. Bonn.]

[96] For this miraculous apparition, Cananus appeals to the Musulman saint; but who will bear testimony for Seid Bechar?

of nine reigns and two hundred and sixty-five years, is occupied
from the elevation of Othman to the death of Soliman, by a
rare series of warlike and active princes, who impressed their
subjects with obedience and their enemies with terror. Instead of the slothful luxury of the seraglio, the heirs of royalty
were educated in the council and the field; from early youth
they were entrusted by their fathers with the command of
provinces and armies; and this manly institution, which was
often productive of civil war, must have essentially contributed
to the discipline and vigour of the monarchy. The Ottomans
cannot style themselves, like the Arabian caliphs, the descendants or successors of the apostle of God; and the kindred which
they claim with the Tartar khans of the house of Zingis appears
to be founded in flattery rather than in truth.[97] Their origin
is obscure; but their sacred and indefeasible right, which no
time can erase and no violence can infringe, was soon and un-
alterably implanted in the minds of their subjects. A weak
or vicious sultan may be deposed and strangled; but his inheritance devolves to an infant or an idiot; nor has the most
daring rebel presumed to ascend the throne of his lawful
sovereign.[98] While the transient dynasties of Asia have been
continually subverted by a crafty vizir in the palace or a victorious general in the camp, the Ottoman succession has been
confirmed by the practice of five centuries, and is now incorporated with the vital principle of the Turkish nation.

Education
and dis-
cipline of
the Turks   To the spirit and constitution of that nation a strong and
singular influence may, however, be ascribed. The primitive
subjects of Othman were the four hundred families of wandering Turkmans, who had followed his ancestors from the Oxus
to the Sangar; and the plains of Anatolia are still covered with
the white and black tents of their rustic brethren. But this
original drop was dissolved in the mass of voluntary and vanquished subjects who, under the name of Turks, are united by

---

[97] See Rycaut (l. i. c. 13). The Turkish sultans assume the title of Khan.
Yet Abulghazi is ignorant of his Ottoman cousins.

[98] The third grand vizir of the name of Kiuperli, who was slain at the battle of
Salankamen in 1691 (Cantemir, p. 382), presumed to say that all the successors of
Soliman had been fools or tyrants, and that it was time to abolish the race
(Marsigli Stato Militare, &c. p. 28). This political heretic was a good Whig, and
justified, against the French ambassador, the revolution of England (Mignot, Hist.
des Ottomans, tom. iii. p. 434). His presumption condemns the singular exception
of continuing offices in the same family.

MEDAL OF JOHN PALAEOLOGUS, BY PISANELLO

the common ties of religion, language, and manners. In the cities, from Erzeroum to Belgrade, that national appellation is common to all the Moslems, the first and most honourable inhabitants; but they have abandoned, at least in Romania, the villages and the cultivation of the land to the Christian peasants. In the vigorous age of the Ottoman government, the Turks were themselves excluded from all civil and military honours; and a servile class, an artificial people, was raised by the discipline of education to obey, to conquer, and to command.[99] From the time of Orchan and the first Amurath, the sultans were persuaded that a government of the sword must be renewed in each generation with new soldiers; and that such soldiers must be sought, not in effeminate Asia, but among the hardy and warlike natives of Europe. The provinces of Thrace, Macedonia, Albania, Bulgaria, and Servia became the perpetual seminary of the Turkish army; and, when the royal fifth of the captives was diminished by conquest, an inhuman tax, of the fifth child, or of every fifth year, was rigorously levied on the Christian families.[100] At the age of twelve or fourteen years,[101] the most robust youths were torn from their parents; their names were enrolled in a book; and from that moment they were clothed, taught, and maintained for the public service. According to the promise of their appearance, they were selected for the royal schools of Boursa, Pera, and Hadrianople, entrusted to the care of the bashaws, or dispersed in the houses of the Anatolian peasantry. It was the first care of their masters to instruct them in the Turkish language; their bodies were exercised by every labour that could fortify their strength; they learned to wrestle, to leap, to run, to shoot with the bow, and afterwards with the musket; till they were drafted into the chambers and companies of the Janizaries, and severely trained in the military or monastic discipline of the order. The youths most conspicuous for birth, talents, and beauty, were admitted into the inferior class of *Agiamo-*

---

[99] Chalcondyles (l. v.) and Ducas (c. 23) exhibit the rude lineaments of the Ottoman policy, and the transmutation of Christian children into Turkish soldiers.

[100] [It is uncertain at what time the rule of levying this tribute every 5th year was introduced; it had become established by the time of Selim I.; but the tribute was sometimes exacted oftener, and many witnesses say " every three years ". Cp. Zinkeisen, iii. p. 216.]

[101] [In earlier times, the age seems to have been younger—six or seven.]

[Ajami-
Oghlans] *glans*, or the more liberal rank of *Ichoglans*, of whom the former were attached to the palace, and the latter to the person of the prince. In four successive schools, under the rod of the white eunuchs, the arts of horsemanship and of darting the javelin were their daily exercise, while those of a more studious cast applied themselves to the study of the Koran and the knowledge of the Arabic and Persian tongues. As they advanced in seniority and merit, they were gradually dismissed to military, civil, and even ecclesiastical employments ; the longer their stay, the higher was their expectation ; till, at a mature period, they were admitted into the number of the forty agas, who stood before the sultan, and were promoted by his choice to the government of provinces and the first honours of the empire.[102] Such a mode of institution was admirably adapted to the form and spirit of a despotic monarchy. The ministers and generals were, in the strictest sense, the slaves of the emperor, to whose bounty they were indebted for their instruction and support. When they left the seraglio, and suffered their beards to grow as the symbol of enfranchisement, they found themselves in an important office, without faction or friendship, without parents and without heirs, dependent on the hand which had raised them from the dust, and which, on the slightest displeasure, could break in pieces these statues of glass, as they are aptly termed by the Turkish proverb.[103] In the slow and painful steps of education, their character and talents were unfolded to a discerning eye : the *man*, naked and alone, was reduced to the standard of his personal merit ; and, if the sovereign had wisdom to choose, he possessed a pure and boundless liberty of choice. The Ottoman candidates were trained by the virtues of abstinence to those of

[102] This sketch of the Turkish education and discipline is chiefly borrowed from Rycaut's State of the Ottoman Empire, the Stato Militare del' Imperio Ottomano of Count Marsigli (in Haya, 1732, in folio), and a Description of the Seraglio, approved by Mr. Greaves himself, a curious traveller, and inserted in the second volume of his works. [One important feature of the Ottoman education was that pains were taken to discover the natural faculties of each individual and to train him for the work to which he was best adapted. On the history of the Janissaries, their organisation and duties, the variations in their effective strength, see A. Djevad Bey, Etat militaire Ottoman, vol. i., 1882. There is a good brief account of the military establishment in Ranke's little work on the Ottoman Empire (Engl. transl. by Kelly, 1843).]

[103] From the series of 115 vizirs till the siege of Vienna (Marsigli, p. 13), their place may be valued at three years and a half purchase.

action ; by the habits of submission, to those of command. A similar spirit was diffused among the troops ; and their silence and sobriety, their patience and modesty, have extorted the reluctant praise of their Christian enemies.[104] Nor can the victory appear doubtful, if we compare the discipline and exercise of the Janizaries with the pride of birth, the independence of chivalry, the ignorance of the new levies, the mutinous temper of the veterans, and the vices of intemperance and disorder which so long contaminated the armies of Europe.

The only hope of salvation for the Greek empire and the adjacent kingdoms would have been some more powerful weapon, some discovery in the art of war, that should give them a decisive superiority over their Turkish foes. Such a weapon was in their hands ; such a discovery had been made in the critical moment of their fate. The chymists of China or Europe had found, by casual or elaborate experiments, that a mixture of saltpetre, sulphur, and charcoal produces, with a spark of fire, a tremendous explosion. It was soon observed that, if the expansive force were compressed in a strong tube, a ball of stone or iron might be expelled with irresistible and destructive velocity. The precise æra of the invention and application of gunpowder [105] is involved in doubtful traditions and equivocal language ; yet we may clearly discern that it was known before the middle of the fourteenth century ; and that, before the end of the same, the use of artillery in battles and sieges, by sea and land, was familiar to the states of Germany, Italy, Spain, France, and England.[106] The priority of nations is of small account ; none could derive any exclusive benefit from their previous or superior knowledge ; and in the common improvement they stood on the same level of relative power and military science. Nor was it

Invention and use of gunpowder

---

[104] See the entertaining and judicious letters of Busbequius.

[105] The 1st and 2d volumes of Dr. Watson's Chemical Essays contain two valuable discourses on the discovery and composition of gunpowder.

[106] On this subject, modern testimonies cannot be trusted. The original passages are collected by Ducange (Gloss. Latin. tom. i. p. 675, *Bombarda*). But in the early doubtful twilight, the name, sound, fire, and effect, that seem to express *our* artillery, may be fairly interpreted of the old engines and the Greek fire. For the English cannon at Crecy, the authority of John Villani (Chron. l. xii. c. 65) must be weighed against the silence of Froissard [and the English authorities]. Yet Muratori (Antiquit. Italiæ medii Ævi, tom. ii. Dissert. xxvi. p. 514, 515) has produced a decisive passage from Petrarch (de Remediis utriusque Fortunæ Dialog.), who, before the year 1344, execrates this terrestrial thunder, *nuper rara nunc communis*. [La Cabane, De la poudre à canon et de son introduction en France, 1845 ; Reinaud et Favé, Du feu grégois et des origines de la poudre à canon, 1860.]

possible to circumscribe the secret within the pale of the church ; it was disclosed to the Turks by the treachery of apostates and the selfish policy of rivals ; and the sultans had sense to adopt, and wealth to reward, the talents of a Christian engineer. The Genoese who transported Amurath into Europe must be accused as his preceptors ; and it was probably by their hands that his cannon was cast and directed at the siege of Constantinople.[107] The first attempt was indeed unsuccessful ; but in the general warfare of the age the advantage was on *their* side who were most commonly the assailants ; for a while the proportion of the attack and defence was suspended ; and this thundering artillery was pointed against the walls and turrets which had been erected only to resist the less potent engines of antiquity. By the Venetians, the use of gunpowder was communicated without reproach to the sultans of Egypt and Persia, their allies against the Ottoman power. The secret was soon propagated to the extremities of Asia ; and the advantage of the European was confined to his easy victories over the savages of the new world. If we contrast the rapid progress of this mischievous discovery with the slow and laborious advances of reason, science, and the arts of peace, a philosopher, according to his temper, will laugh or weep at the folly of mankind.

[107] The Turkish cannon, which Ducas (c. 30) first introduces before Belgrade (A.D. 1436), is mentioned by Chalcondyles (l. v. p. 123 [p. 231, ed. Bonn]) in 1422, at the siege of Constantinople.

CHAPTER LXVI

Applications of the Eastern Emperors to the Popes—Visits to the West, of John the First, Manuel, and John the Second, Palæologus—Union of the Greek and Latin Churches promoted by the Council of Basil, and concluded at Ferrara and Florence—State of Literature at Constantinople—Its Revival in Italy by the Greek Fugitives— Curiosity and Emulation of the Latins

IN the four last centuries of the Greek emperors, their friendly or hostile aspect towards the pope and the Latins may be observed as the thermometer of their prosperity or distress, as the scale of the rise and fall of the barbarian dynasties.[1] When the Turks of the house of Seljuk pervaded Asia and threatened Constantinople, we have seen at the Council of Placentia the suppliant ambassadors of Alexius imploring the protection of the common father of the Christians. No sooner had the arms of the French pilgrims removed the sultan from Nice to Iconium than the Greek princes resumed, or avowed, their genuine hatred and contempt for the schismatics of the West, which precipitated the first downfall of their empire. The date of the Mogul invasion is marked in the soft and charitable language of John Vataces. After the recovery of Constantinople, the throne of the first Palæologus was encompassed by foreign and domestic enemies; as long as the sword of Charles

Embassy of the younger Andronicus to Pope Benedict XII. A.D. 1339

---

[1] [The following works deal with the general history of the schism of the Greek and Latin Churches and the attempts at reunion : Maimbourg, Histoire du Schisme des Grecs, 2 vols., 1677 ; Pitzipios, L'église orientale, 1855 ; Pichler, Geschichte der kirchlichen Trennung zwischen Orient und Occident, 2 vols., 1864-5; Demitrakopulos, Ἱστορία τοῦ σχίσματος τῆς Λατινικῆς ἐκκλησίας ἀπὸ τῆς ὀρθοδόξου Ἑλληνικῆς, 1867 ; Lebedev, History of the Byzantine-Oriental Church from the end of the 11th to the middle of the 15th century (in Russian), 1892. See also for relations of East and West, W. Norden, Das Papsttum und Byzanz., 1903 ; Delaville de Roulx, La France en Orient, 1886 ; N. Jorga, Philippe de Mézières (1327-1405) et la croisade au xive siècle, 1896, and Latins et Grecs d'Orient et l'établissement des Turcs en Europe (1342-1362), in the Byzantinische Zeitschrift, xv. 179 *sqq.*, 1906 ; J. Gay, Le pape Clément VI. et les affaires d'Orient, 1904.]

was suspended over his head, he basely courted the favour of the
Roman pontiff, and sacrificed to the present danger his faith,
his virtue, and the affection of his subjects.   On the decease
of Michael, the prince and people asserted the independence of
their church and the purity of their creed ; the elder Andronicus
neither feared nor loved the Latins ; in his last distress, pride
was the safeguard of superstition ; nor could he decently retract
in his age the firm and orthodox declarations of his youth.   His
grandson, the younger Andronicus, was less a slave in his temper
and situation ; and the conquest of Bithynia by the Turks admonished him to seek a temporal and spiritual alliance with the
Western princes.   After a separation and silence of fifty years,
a secret agent, the monk Barlaam, was dispatched to Pope
Benedict the Twelfth ; and his artful instructions appear to
have been drawn by the master-hand of the great domestic.[2]
" Most holy father," was he commissioned to say, " the emperor
is not less desirous than yourself of an union between the two
churches ; but in this delicate transaction he is obliged to respect
his own dignity and the prejudices of his subjects.   The ways
of union are twofold, force and persuasion.   Of force, the
inefficacy has been already tried ; since the Latins have subdued
the empire, without subduing the minds, of the Greeks.   The
method of persuasion, though slow, is sure and permanent.
A deputation of thirty or forty of our doctors would probably
agree with those of the Vatican, in the love of truth and the unity
of belief ; but on their return, what would be the use, the recompense, of such agreement ? the scorn of their brethren, and the
reproaches of a blind and obstinate nation.   Yet that nation
is accustomed to reverence the general councils which have
fixed the articles of our faith ; and, if they reprobate the
decrees of Lyons, it is because the Eastern churches were
neither heard nor represented in that arbitrary meeting.   For
this salutary end it will be expedient, and even necessary, that
a well-chosen legate should be sent into Greece, to convene
the patriarchs of Constantinople, Alexandria, Antioch, and Jerusalem, and, with their aid, to prepare a free and universal synod.

*The argu-
ments for a
crusade
and union*

[2] This curious instruction was transcribed (I believe) from the Vatican archives
by Odoricus Raynaldus, in his Continuation of the Annals of Baronius (Romæ,
1646-1677, in 10 volumes in folio).   I have contented myself with the Abbé Fleury
(Hist. Ecclésiastique, tom. xx. p. 1-8), whose extracts I have always found to be
clear, accurate, and impartial.   [For Barlaam the Calabrian see below, p. 123.]

But at this moment," continued the subtle agent, "the empire is assaulted and endangered by the Turks, who have occupied four of the greatest cities of Anatolia. The Christian inhabitants have expressed a wish of returning to their allegiance and religion; but the forces and revenues of the emperor are insufficient for their deliverance; and the Roman legate must be accompanied, or preceded, by an army of Franks, to expel the infidels and open a way to the holy sepulchre." If the suspicious Latins should require some pledge, some previous effect of the sincerity of the Greeks, the answers of Barlaam were perspicuous and rational. " 1. A general synod can alone consummate the union of the churches: nor can such a synod be held till the three Oriental patriarchs, and a great number of bishops, are enfranchised from the Mahometan yoke. 2. The Greeks are alienated by a long series of oppression and injury: they must be reconciled by some act of brotherly love, some effectual succour, which may fortify the authority and arguments of the emperor and the friends of the union. 3. If some difference of faith or ceremonies should be found incurable, the Greeks, however, are the disciples of Christ, and the Turks are the common enemies of the Christian name. The Armenians, Cyprians, and Rhodians are equally attacked; and it will become the piety of the French princes to draw their swords in the general defence of religion. 4. Should the subjects of Andronicus be treated as the worst of schismatics, of heretics, of pagans, a judicious policy may yet instruct the powers of the West to embrace an useful ally, to uphold a sinking empire, to guard the confines of Europe; and rather to join the Greeks against the Turks than to expect the union of the Turkish arms with the troops and treasures of captive Greece." The reasons, the offers, and the demands of Andronicus were eluded with cold and stately indifference. The kings of France and Naples declined the dangers and glory of a crusade; the pope refused to call a new synod to determine old articles of faith; and his regard for the obsolete claims of the Latin emperor and clergy engaged him to use an offensive superscription: "To the *moderator*[3] of the Greeks, and the persons who style themselves the patriarchs of the Eastern

---

[3] The ambiguity of this title is happy or ingenious; and *moderator*, as synonymous to *rector*, *gubernator*, is a word of classical, and even Ciceronian, Latinity which may be found, not in the Glossary of Ducange, but in the Thesaurus of Robert Stephens.

churches ". For such an embassy, a time and character less propitious could not easily have been found.

Benedict the Twelfth[4] was a dull peasant, perplexed with scruples, and immersed in sloth and wine ; his pride might enrich with a third crown the papal tiara, but he was alike unfit for the regal and the pastoral office.

Negotiation of Cantacuzene with Clement VI. A.D. 1348 After the decease of Andronicus, while the Greeks were distracted by intestine war, they could not presume to agitate a general union of the Christians. But, as soon as Cantacuzene had subdued and pardoned his enemies, he was anxious to justify, or at least to extenuate, the introduction of the Turks into Europe and the nuptials of his daughter with a Musulman prince. Two officers of state, with a Latin interpreter, were sent in his name to the Roman court, which was transplanted to Avignon, on the banks of the Rhone, during a period of seventy years; they represented the hard necessity which had urged him to embrace the alliance of the miscreants, and pronounced by his command the specious and edifying sounds of union and crusade. Pope Clement the Sixth,[5] the successor of Benedict, received them with hospitality and honour, acknowledged the innocence of their sovereign, excused his distress, applauded his magnanimity, and displayed a clear knowledge of the state and revolutions of the Greek empire, which he had imbibed from the honest accounts of a Savoyard lady, an attendant of the empress Anne.[6] If Clement was ill endowed with the virtues of a priest, he possessed, however, the spirit and magnificence of a prince, whose liberal hand distributed benefices and kingdoms with equal facility. Under his reign,

---

[4] The first epistle (sine titulo) of Petrarch exposes the danger of the *bark* and the incapacity of the *pilot*. Hæc inter, vino madidus, ævo gravis ac soporifero rore perfusus, jamjam nutitat, dormitat, jam somno præceps, atque (utinam solus) ruit. . . . Heu quanto felicius patrio terram sulcasset aratro, quam scalmum piscatorium ascendisset. This satire engages his biographer to weigh the virtues and vices of Benedict XII., which have been exaggerated by Guelphs and Ghibelines, by Papists and Protestants (see Mémoires sur la Vie de Pétrarque, tom. i. p. 259 ; ii. not. 15, p. 13-16). He gave occasion to the saying, Bibamus Papaliter.

[5] See the original Lives of Clement VI. in Muratori (Script. Rerum Italicarum, tom. iii. p. ii. p. 550-589) ; Matteo Villani (Chron. l. iii. c. 43, in Muratori, tom. xiv. p. 186), who styles him, molto cavalleresco, poco religioso ; Fleury (Hist. Ecclés. tom. xx. p. 126) ; and the Vie de Pétrarque (tom. ii. p. 42-45). The Abbé de Sade treats him with the most indulgence ; but *he* is a gentleman as well as a priest.

[6] Her name (most probably corrupted) was Zampea. She had accompanied and alone remained with her mistress at Constantinople, where her prudence, erudition, and politeness deserved the praises of the Greeks themselves (Cantacuzen. l. i. c. 42).

Avignon was the seat of pomp and pleasure; in his youth he had surpassed the licentiousness of a baron; and the palace, nay, the bed-chamber of the pope was adorned, or polluted, by the visits of his female favourites. The wars of France and England were adverse to the holy enterprise; but his vanity was amused by the splendid idea; and the Greek ambassadors returned with two Latin bishops, the ministers of the pontiff. On their arrival at Constantinople, the emperor and the nuncios admired each other's piety and eloquence; and their frequent conferences were filled with mutual praises and promises, by which both parties were amused and neither could be deceived. "I am delighted," said the devout Cantacuzene, "with the project of our holy war, which must redound to my personal glory as well as to the public benefit of Christendom. My dominions will give a free passage to the armies of France: my troops, my galleys, my treasures, shall be consecrated to the common cause; and happy would be my fate, could I deserve and obtain the crown of martyrdom. Words are insufficient to express the ardour with which I sigh for the re-union of the scattered members of Christ. If my death could avail, I would gladly present my sword and my neck; if the spiritual phœnix could arise from my ashes, I would erect the pile and kindle the flame with my own hands." Yet the Greek emperor presumed to observe that the articles of faith which divided the two churches had been introduced by the pride and precipitation of the Latins: he disclaimed the servile and arbitrary steps of the first Palæologus; and firmly declared that he would never submit his conscience, unless to the decrees of a free and universal synod. "The situation of the times," continued he, "will not allow the pope and myself to meet either at Rome or Constantinople; but some maritime city may be chosen on the verge of the two empires, to unite the bishops, and to instruct the faithful, of the East and West." The nuncios seemed content with the proposition; and Cantacuzene affects to deplore the failure of his hopes, which were soon overthrown by the death of Clement and the different temper of his successor. His own life was prolonged, but it was prolonged in a cloister; and, except by his prayers, the humble monk was incapable of directing the counsels of his pupil or the state.[7]

---

[7] See this whole negotiation in Cantacuzene (l. iv. c. 9), who, amidst the praises and virtues which he bestows on himself, reveals the uneasiness of a guilty conscience.

Treaty of
John
Palæologus
I. with In-
nocent VI.
A.D. 1355
Yet, of all the Byzantine princes, that pupil, John Palæologus, was the best disposed to embrace, to believe, and to obey
the shepherd of the West.   His mother, Anne of Savoy, was
baptized in the bosom of the Latin church : her marriage with
Andronicus imposed a change of name, of apparel, and of worship ; but her heart was still faithful to her country and religion ; she had formed the infancy of her son, and she governed
the emperor, after his mind, or at least his stature, was enlarged
to the size of man.   In the first year of his deliverance and restoration, the Turks were still masters of the Hellespont ; the
son of Cantacuzene was in arms at Hadrianople ; and Palæologus could depend neither on himself nor on his people.   By his
mother's advice, and in the hope of foreign aid, he abjured the
rights both of the church and state ; and the act of slavery,[8]
subscribed in purple ink and sealed with the *golden* bull, was
privately entrusted to an Italian agent.   The first article of
the treaty is an oath of fidelity and obedience to Innocence the
Sixth and his successors, the supreme pontiffs of the Roman
and Catholic church.   The emperor promises to entertain, with
due reverence, their legates and nuncios ; to assign a palace for
their residence, and a temple for their worship ; and to deliver
his second son Manuel as the hostage of his faith.   For these
condescensions, he requires a prompt succour of fifteen galleys,
with five hundred men at arms and a thousand archers, to serve
against his Christian and Musulman enemies.   Palæologus engages to impose on his clergy and people the same spiritual
yoke ; but, as the resistance of the Greeks might be justly fore-
seen, he adopts the two effectual methods of corruption and
education.   The legate was impowered to distribute the vacant
benefices among the ecclesiastics who should subscribe the creed
of the Vatican ; three schools were instituted to instruct the
youth of Constantinople in the language and doctrine of the
Latins ; and the name of Andronicus, the heir of the empire,
was enrolled as the first student.   Should he fail in the measures
of persuasion or force, Palæologus declares himself unworthy to
reign ; transfers to the pope all regal and paternal authority ;
and invests Innocent with full power to regulate the family,

---

[8] See this ignominious treaty in Fleury (Hist. Ecclés. p. 151-154), from Raynaldus, who drew it from the Vatican archives. It was not worth the trouble of a
pious forgery.

the government, and the marriage of his son and successor.
But this treaty was neither executed nor published. The
Roman galleys were as vain and imaginary as the submission
of the Greeks; and it was only by the secrecy, that their sovereign escaped the dishonour, of this fruitless humiliation.

The tempest of the Turkish arms soon burst on his head; Visit of
and, after the loss of Hadrianople and Romania, he was inclosed John
Palæologus
in his capital, the vassal of the haughty Amurath, with the to Urban
V. at Rome.
miserable hope of being the last devoured by the savage. In A.D. 1369,
13th Octo-
this abject state, Palæologus embraced the resolution of em- ber, &c.
barking for Venice and casting himself at the feet of the pope.
He was the first of the Byzantine princes who had ever visited
the unknown regions of the West, yet in them alone he could
seek consolation or relief; and with less violation of his dignity
he might appear in the sacred college than at the Ottoman
Porte. After a long absence, the Roman pontiffs were returning from Avignon to the banks of the Tiber; Urban the Fifth,[9]
of a mild and virtuous character, encouraged or allowed the
pilgrimage of the Greek prince; and, within the same year,
enjoyed the glory of receiving in the Vatican the two imperial
shadows who represented the majesty of Constantine and Charlemagne. In this suppliant visit, the emperor of Constantinople,
whose vanity was lost in his distress, gave more than could be
expected of empty sounds and formal submissions. A previous
trial was imposed; and, in the presence of four cardinals, he
acknowledged, as a true Catholic, the supremacy of the pope
and the double procession of the Holy Ghost. After this purification, he was introduced to a public audience in the church
of St. Peter: Urban, in the midst of the cardinals, was seated
on his throne; the Greek monarch, after three genuflexions,
devoutly kissed the feet, the hands, and at length the mouth,
of the holy father, who celebrated high mass in his presence,
allowed him to lead the bridle of his mule, and treated him
with a sumptuous banquet in the Vatican. The entertainment
of Palæologus was friendly and honourable; yet some difference

[9] See the two first original Lives of Urban V. (in Muratori, Script. Rerum
Italicarum, tom. iii. p. ii. p. 623, 635), and the Ecclesiastical Annals of Spondanus
(tom. i. p. 573, A.D. 1369, No. 7) and Raynaldus (Fleury, Hist. Ecclés. tom. xx. p.
223, 224). Yet, from some variations, I suspect the papal writers of slightly mag-
nifying the genuflexions of Palæologus.

was observed between the emperors of the East and West;[10] nor could the former be entitled to the rare privilege of chanting the gospel in the rank of a deacon.[11] In favour of his proselyte Urban strove to rekindle the zeal of the French king and the other powers of the West; but he found them cold in the general cause and active only in their domestic quarrels. The last hope of the emperor was in an English mercenary, John Hawkwood,[12] or Acuto, who, with a band of adventurers, the White Brotherhood, had ravaged Italy from the Alps to Calabria; sold his services to the hostile states; and incurred a just excommunication by shooting his arrows against the papal residence. A special licence was granted to negotiate with the outlaw; but the forces, or the spirit, of Hawkwood were unequal to the enterprise; and it was for the advantage perhaps of Palæologus to be disappointed of a succour that must have been costly, that could not be effectual, and which might have been dangerous.[13] The disconsolate Greek[14] prepared for his return, but even his return was impeded by a most ignominious obstacle. On his arrival at Venice, he had borrowed large sums at exorbitant usury; but his coffers were empty, his creditors were impatient, and his person was detained as the best security for the payment. His eldest son Andronicus, the regent of Constantinople, was repeatedly urged to exhaust every resource,

[10] Paullo minus quam si fuisset Imperator Romanorum. Yet his title of Imperator Græcorum was no longer disputed (Vit. Urban V. p. 623).

[11] It was confined to the successors of Charlemagne, and to them only on Christmas Day. On all other festivals, these Imperial deacons were content to serve the pope, as he said mass, with the book and the *corporal*. Yet the Abbé de Sade generously thinks that the merits of Charles IV. might have entitled him, though not on the proper day (A.D. 1368, 1st November), to the whole privilege. He seems to affix a just value on the privilege and the man (Vie de Pétrarque, tom. iii. p. 735).

[12] Through some Italian corruptions, the etymology of *Falcone in bosco* (Matteo [rather, Filippo, the Continuer of Matteo] Villani, l. xi. c. 79, in Muratori, tom. xiv. p. 746) suggests the English word *Hawkwood*, the true name of our adventurous countryman (Thomas Walsingham, Hist. Anglican. inter Scriptores Camdeni, p. 184). After two and twenty victories and one defeat, he died, in 1394, General of the Florentines, and was buried with such honours as the republic has not paid to Dante or Petrarch (Muratori, Annali d'Italia, tom. xii. p. 212-371).

[13] This torrent of English (by birth or service) overflowed from France into Italy after the peace of Bretigny in 1360. Yet the exclamation of Muratori (Annali, tom. xii. p. 197) is rather true than civil. " Ci mancava ancor questo, che dopo essere calpestrata l'Italia da tanti masnadieri Tedeschi ed Ungheri, venissero fin dall' Inghilterra nuovi *cani* a finire di divorarla."

[14] Chalcondyles, l. i. p. 25, 26 [p. 50, ed. Bonn]. The Greek supposes his journey to the king of France, which is sufficiently refuted by the silence of the national historians. Nor am I much more inclined to believe that Palæologus departed from Italy, valde bene consolatus et contentus (Vit. Urban. V. p. 623).

CHALICE OF MANUEL PALAEOLOGUS IN THE MONASTERY OF VATOPEDI, MOUNT ATHOS and, even by stripping the churches, to extricate his father from captivity and disgrace. But the unnatural youth was insensible of the disgrace, and secretly pleased with the captivity of the emperor; the state was poor, the clergy was obstinate; nor could some religious scruple be wanting to excuse the guilt of his indifference and delay. Such undutiful neglect was severely reproved by the piety of his brother Manuel, who instantly sold or mortgaged all that he possessed, embarked for Venice, relieved his father, and pledged his own freedom to be responsible for the debt. On his return to Constantinople, the parent and king distinguished his two sons with suitable rewards; but the faith and manners of the slothful Palæologus had not been improved by his Roman pilgrimage; and his apostacy or conversion, devoid of any spiritual or temporal effects, was speedily forgotten by the Greeks and Latins.[15] *His return to Constantinople, A.D. 1370*

Thirty years after the return of Palæologus, his son and successor, Manuel, from a similar motive, but on a larger scale, again visited the countries of the West. In a preceding chapter, I have related his treaty with Bajazet, the violation of that treaty, the siege or blockade of Constantinople, and the French succour under the command of the gallant Boucicault.[16] By his ambassadors, Manuel had solicited the Latin powers; but it was thought that the presence of a distressed monarch would draw tears and supplies from the hardest barbarians;[17] and the marshal who advised the journey, prepared the reception, of the Byzantine prince. The land was occupied by the Turks; but the navigation of Venice was safe and open; Italy received him as the first, or at least as the second, of the Christian princes; Manuel was pitied as the champion and confessor of the faith; and the dignity of his behaviour prevented that pity from sinking into contempt. From Venice he proceeded to Padua and Pavia; and even the duke of Milan, a secret ally of Bajazet, gave him safe and honourable conduct to the verge of his dominions.[18] On the confines of *Visit of the emperor Manuel* *to the court of France, A.D. 1400, 3rd June;*

[15] His return in 1370, and the coronation of Manuel, 25th September, 1373 (Ducange, Fam. Byzant. p. 241), leaves some intermediate æra for the conspiracy and punishment of Andronicus.

[16] Mémoires de Boucicault, p. i. c. 35, 36.

[17] His journey into the west of Europe is slightly, and I believe reluctantly, noticed by Chalcondyles (l. ii. p. 44-50 [p. 84 *sqq.*, ed. Bonn]) and Ducas (c. 14).

[18] Muratori, Annali d'Italia, tom. xii. p. 406. John Galeazzo was the first and most powerful duke of Milan. His connexion with Bajazet is attested by Froissard; and he contributed to save and deliver the French captives of Nicopolis.

France,[19] the royal officers undertook the care of his person, journey, and expenses; and two thousand of the richest citizens, in arms and on horseback, came forth to meet him as far as Charenton, in the neighbourhood of the capital. At the gates of Paris, he was saluted by the chancellor and the parliament; and Charles the Sixth, attended by his princes and nobles, welcomed his brother with a cordial embrace. The successor of Constantine was clothed in a robe of white silk and mounted on a milk-white steed—a circumstance, in the French ceremonial, of singular importance. The white colour is considered as the symbol of sovereignty; and, in a late visit, the German emperor, after an haughty demand and a peevish refusal, had been reduced to content himself with a black courser. Manuel was lodged in the Louvre; a succession of feasts and balls, the pleasures of the banquet and the chase, were ingeniously varied by the politeness of the French, to display their magnificence and amuse his grief. He was indulged in the liberty of his chapel; and the doctors of the Sorbonne were astonished, and possibly scandalized, by the language, the rites, and the vestments of his Greek clergy. But the slightest glance on the state of the kingdom must teach him to despair of any effectual assistance. The unfortunate Charles, though he enjoyed some lucid intervals, continually relapsed into furious or stupid insanity; the reins of government were alternately seized by his brother and uncle, the dukes of Orleans and Burgundy, whose factious competition prepared the miseries of civil war. The former was a gay youth, dissolved in luxury and love; the latter was the father of John, count of Nevers, who had so lately been ransomed from Turkish captivity; and, if the fearless son was ardent to revenge his defeat, the more prudent Burgundy was content with the cost and peril of the first experiment. When Manuel had satiated the curiosity, and perhaps fatigued the
of England, patience, of the French, he resolved on a visit to the adjacent
A.D. 1400,
December island. In his progress from Dover, he was entertained at Canterbury with due reverence by the prior and monks of St.

---

[19] For the reception of Manuel at Paris, see Spondanus (Annal. Eccles. tom. i. p. 676, 677, A.D. 1400, No. 5), who quotes Juvenal des Ursins [Histoire de Charles VI., 1380-1422 (ed. in Buchon's Choix de Chroniques, vol. iv.)] and the monk of St. Denys; and Villaret (Hist. de France, tom. xii. p. 331-334), who quotes nobody, according to the last fashion of the French writers.

Austin; and, on Blackheath, King Henry the Fourth, with the English court, saluted the Greek hero (I copy our old historian), who, during many days, was lodged and treated in London as Emperor of the East.[20]   But the state of England was still more adverse to the design of the holy war.   In the same year, the hereditary sovereign had been deposed and murdered; the reigning prince was a successful usurper, whose ambition was punished by jealousy and remorse; nor could Henry of Lancaster withdraw his person or forces from the defence of a throne incessantly shaken by conspiracy and rebellion.   He pitied, he praised, he feasted, the emperor of Constantinople; but, if the English monarch assumed the cross, it was only to appease his people, and perhaps his conscience, by the merit or semblance of this pious intention.[21]   Satisfied, however, with gifts and honours, Manuel returned to Paris; and, after a residence of two years in the West, shaped his course through Germany and Italy, embarked at Venice, and patiently expected, in the Morea, the moment of his ruin or deliverance. Yet he had escaped the ignominious necessity of offering his religion to public or private sale.   The Latin church was distracted by the great schism; the kings, the nations, the universities, of Europe were divided in their obedience between the popes of Rome and Avignon; and the emperor, anxious to conciliate the friendship of both parties, abstained from any correspondence with the indigent and unpopular rivals.   His journey coincided with the year of the jubilee; but he passed through Italy without desiring or deserving the plenary indulgence which abolished the guilt or penance of the sins of the faithful.   The Roman pope was offended by this neglect; accused him of irreverence to an image of Christ; and exhorted the princes of Italy to reject and abandon the obstinate schismatic.[22]

His return to Greece, A.D. 1402

[20] A short note of Manuel in England is extracted by Dr. Hody from a Ms. at Lambeth (de Græcis illustribus, p. 14), C. P. Imperator, diu variisque et horrendis Paganorum insultibus coartatus, ut pro eisdem resistentiam triumphalem perquireret Anglorum Regem visitare decrevit, &c.   Rex (says Walsingham, p. 364) nobili apparatu . . . suscepit (ut debuit) tantum Heroa, duxitque Londonias, et per multos dies exhibuit gloriose, pro expensis hospitii sui solvens, et eum respiciens [dignis] tanto fastigio donativis.   He repeats the same in his Upodigma Neustriæ, p. 556).

[21] Shakespeare begins and ends the play of Henry IV. with that prince's vow of a crusade, and his belief that he should die in Jerusalem.

[22] This fact is preserved in the Historia Politica, A.D. 1391-1478, published by Martin Crusius (Turco-Græci, p. 1-43).   The image of Christ which the Greek emperor refused to worship was probably a work of sculpture.

Greek
knowledge
and de-
scriptions

During the period of the crusades, the Greeks beheld, with astonishment and terror, the perpetual stream of emigration that flowed, and continued to flow, from the unknown climates of the West. The visits of their last emperors removed the veil of separation, and they disclosed to their eyes the powerful nations of Europe, whom they no longer presumed to brand with the name of barbarians. The observations of Manuel and his more inquisitive followers have been preserved by a Byzantine historian of the times ; [23] his scattered ideas I shall collect and abridge ; and it may be amusing enough, perhaps instructive, to contemplate the rude pictures of Germany, France, and England, whose ancient and modern state are so familiar to *our* minds. I. GERMANY (says the Greek Chalcondyles) is of ample latitude from Vienna to the Ocean ; and it stretches (a strange geography !) from Prague in Bohemia to the river Tartessus and the Pyrenæan Mountains.[24]   The soil, except in figs and olives, is sufficiently fruitful ; the air is salubrious ; the bodies of the natives are robust and healthy ; and these cold regions are seldom visited with the calamities of pestilence or earthquakes. After the Scythians or Tartars, the Germans are the most numerous of nations ; they are brave and patient, and, were they united under a single head, their force would be irresistible. By the gift of the pope, they have acquired the privilege of choosing the Roman emperor ; [25] nor is any people more devoutly attached to the faith and obedience of the Latin patriarch. The greatest part of the country is divided among the princes and prelates ; but Strasburg, Cologne,

of Ger-
many

---

[23] The ¡Greek and Turkish history of Laonicus Chalcondyles ends with the winter of 1463, and the abrupt conclusion seems to mark that he laid down his pen in the same year. We know that he was an Athenian, and that some contemporaries of the same name contributed to the revival of the Greek language in Italy.   But in his numerous digressions the modest historian has never introduced himself ; and his editor Leunclavius, as well as Fabricius (Bibliot. Græc. tom. vi. p. 474), seems ignorant of his life and character.   For his descriptions of Germany, France and England, see l. ii. p. 36, 37 [p. 70 *sqq.*], 44-50 [p. 85 *sqq.*].

[24] I shall not animadvert on the geographical errors of Chalcondyles.   In this instance, he perhaps followed and mistook Herodotus (l. ii. c. 33), whose text may be explained (Herodote de Larcher, tom. ii. p. 219, 220), or whose ignorance may be excused.   Had these modern Greeks never read Strabo, or any of their lesser geographers ?

[25] A citizen of new Rome, while new Rome survived, would have scorned to dignify the German Ῥήξ with the titles of Βασιλεύς, or Αὐτοκράτωρ Ῥωμαίων ; but all pride was extinct in the bosom of Chalcondyles ; and he describes the Byzantine prince and his subjects by the proper, though humble names of Ἕλληνες and Βασιλεὺς Ἑλλήνων.   [Cp. above, vol. vi. p. 342.]

Hamburg, and more than two hundred free cities are governed by sage and equal laws, according to the will, and for the advantage, of the whole community. The use of duels, or single combats on foot, prevails among them in peace and war; their industry excels in all the mechanic arts; and the Germans may boast of the invention of gunpowder and cannon, which is now diffused over the greatest part of the world. II. The kingdom of France of FRANCE is spread above fifteen or twenty days' journey from Germany to Spain, and from the Alps to the British Ocean, containing many flourishing cities, and among these Paris, the seat of the king, which surpasses the rest in riches and luxury. Many princes and lords alternately wait in his palace and acknowledge him as their sovereign; the most powerful are the dukes of Bretagne and Burgundy, of whom the latter possesses the wealthy province of Flanders, whose harbours are frequented by the ships and merchants of our own and the more remote seas. The French are an ancient and opulent people; and their language and manners, though somewhat different, are not dissimilar from those of the Italians. Vain of the Imperial dignity of Charlemagne, of their victories over the Saracens, and of the exploits of their heroes, Oliver and Rowland,[26] they esteem themselves the first of the western nations; but this foolish arrogance has been recently humbled by the unfortunate events of their wars against the English, the inhabitants of the British Island. III. Britain, in the of England ocean and opposite to the shores of Flanders, may be considered either as one or as three islands; but the whole is united by a common interest, by the same manners, and by a similar government. The measure of its circumference is five thousand stadia: the land is overspread with towns and villages; though destitute of wine, and not abounding in fruit-trees, it is fertile in wheat and barley, in honey and wool; and much cloth is manufactured by the inhabitants. In populousness and power, in riches and luxury, London,[27] the metropolis of the isle, may

[26] Most of the old romances were translated in the xivth century into French prose, and soon became the favourite amusement of the knights and ladies in the court of Charles VI. If a Greek believed in the exploits of Rowland and Oliver, he may surely be excused, since the monks of St. Denys, the national historians, have inserted the fables of Archbishop Turpin in their Chronicles of France.

[27] Λονδίνη . . . δέ τε πόλις δυνάμει τε προέχουσα τῶν ἐν τῇ νήσῳ ταύτῃ πασῶν πόλεων, ὄλβῳ τε καὶ τῇ ἄλλῃ εὐδαιμονίᾳ οὐδεμιᾶς τῶν πρὸς ἐσπέραν λειπομένη [ii. p. 93, ed. Bonn]. Even since the time of Fitzstephen (the xiith century), London appears to have

claim a pre-eminence over all the cities of the West. It is
situate on the Thames, a broad and rapid river, which, at the
distance of thirty miles, falls into the Gallic Sea; and the daily
flow and ebb of the tide affords a safe entrance and departure
to the vessels of commerce. The king is the head of a powerful and turbulent aristocracy: his principal vassals hold their
estates by a free and unalterable tenure; and the laws define
the limits of his authority and their obedience. The kingdom
has been often afflicted by foreign conquest and domestic
sedition; but the natives are bold and hardy, renowned in
arms and victorious in war. The form of their shields or
targets is derived from the Italians, that of their swords from
the Greeks; the use of the long bow is the peculiar and
decisive advantage of the English. Their language bears no
affinity to the idioms of the continent; in the habits of domestic
life, they are not easily distinguished from their neighbours of
France; but the most singular circumstance of their manners
is their disregard of conjugal honour and of female chastity.
In their mutual visits, as the first act of hospitality, the guest
is welcomed in the embraces of their wives and daughters;
among friends, they are lent and borrowed without shame;
nor are the islanders offended at this strange commerce and its
inevitable consequences.[28] Informed as we are of the customs
of old England, and assured of the virtue of our mothers, we
may smile at the credulity, or resent the injustice, of the
Greek, who must have confounded a modest salute [29] with a
criminal embrace. But his credulity and injustice may teach
an important lesson: to distrust the accounts of foreign and
remote nations, and to suspend our belief of every tale that
deviates from the laws of nature and the character of man.[30]

maintained this pre-eminence of wealth and magnitude; and her gradual increase
has at least kept pace with the general improvement of Europe.

[28] If the double sense of the verb κυω (osculor, and in utero gero) be equivocal,
the context and pious horror of Chalcondyles can leave no doubt of his meaning
and mistake (p. 49). [There is no ambiguity. Chalcondyles uses the middle form
κύεσθαι instead of the active κύειν which is used in classical Greek; but there
is no second sense. Neither κύω nor κυῶ is ever used in the sense of κυνῶ (kiss).
It is only in the aorist (ἔκῦσα: ἔκῦσα) that there would be a danger of confusion.—
Cp. Phrantzes, iii. 2.]

[29] Erasmus (Epist. Fausto Andrelino) has a pretty passage on the English
fashion of kissing strangers on their arrival and departure, from whence, however,
he draws no scandalous inferences.

[30] Perhaps we may apply this remark to the community of wives among the
old Britons, as it is supposed by Cæsar and Dion (Dion Cassius, l. lxii. tom. ii. p. 1007

After his return, and the victory of Timour, Manuel reigned Indifference of Manuel towards the Latins, A.D. 1402-1417 many years in prosperity and peace. As long as the sons of Bajazet solicited his friendship and spared his dominions, he was satisfied with the national religion; and his leisure was employed in composing twenty theological dialogues for its defence.[31] The appearance of the Byzantine ambassadors at the council of Constance[32] announces the restoration of the Turkish power, as well as of the Latin church; the conquest of the sultans, Mahomet and Amurath, reconciled the emperor to the Vatican; and the siege of Constantinople almost tempted him to acquiesce in the double procession of the Holy Ghost. When Martin the Fifth ascended, without a rival, the chair of St. Peter, a friendly intercourse of letters and embassies was revived between the East and West. Ambition on one side and distress on the other His negotiations, A.D. 1417-1425 dictated the same decent language of charity and peace. The artful Greek expressed a desire of marrying his six sons to Italian princesses; and the Roman, not less artful, dispatched the daughter of the marquis of Montferrat, with a company of noble virgins, to soften, by their charms, the obstinacy of the schismatics. Yet, under this mask of zeal, a discerning eye will perceive that all was hollow and insincere in the court and church of Constantinople. According to the vicissitudes of danger and repose, the emperor advanced or retreated; alternately instructed and disavowed his ministers; and escaped from an importunate pressure by urging the duty of inquiry, the obligation of collecting the sense of his patriarchs and bishops, and the impossibility of convening them at a time when the Turkish arms were at the gates of his capital. From a review of the

---

[c. 6]), with Reimar's judicious annotation. The *Arreoy* of Otaheite, so certain at first, is become less visible and scandalous, in proportion as we have studied the manners of that gentle and amorous people.

[31] [Manuel composed in 26 dialogues a defence of orthodox Christianity against Islam. The whole work was entitled Διάλογος περὶ τῆς τῶν Χριστιανῶν θρησκείας πρός τινα Πέρσην, and grew out of conversations which Manuel had had at Ancyra in 1390 with a Turkish muterizis. Only the two first dialogues have been published (Migne, P.G. 156, p. 126 *sqq.*). Manuel wrote much, and most of his published works will be found in Migne, *tom. cit.* His letters have been edited by Legrand, 1893, and this volume contains the interesting essay of Manuel, "What Timur may have said to the conquered Bajazet". There is an excellent monograph on Manuel and his writings by Berger de Xivrey in the Mémoires de l'Institut de France, Ac. des Inscr. xix. 1 *sqq.* (1853).]

[32] See Lenfant, Hist. du Concile de Constance, tom. ii. p. 576; and for the ecclesiastical history of the times, the Annals of Spondanus; the Bibliothèque of Dupin, tom. xii.; and xxist and xxiid volumes of the History, or rather the Continuation of Fleury.

public transactions, it will appear that the Greeks insisted on three successive measures, a succour, a council, and a final reunion, while the Latins eluded the second, and only promised the first as a consequential and voluntary reward of the third. But we have an opportunity of unfolding the most secret His private
motives intentions of Manuel, as he explained them in a private conversation without artifice or disguise.   In his declining age the emperor had associated John Palæologus, the second of the name and the eldest of his sons, on whom he devolved the greatest part of the authority and weight of government.   One day, in the presence only of the historian Phranza,[33] his favourite chamberlain, he opened to his colleague and successor the true principle of his negotiations with the pope.[34]   "Our last resource," said Manuel, "against the Turks is their fear of our union with the Latins, of the warlike nations of the West, who may arm for our relief, and for their destruction.   As often as you are threatened by the miscreants, present this danger before their eyes.   Propose a council; consult on the means; but ever delay and avoid the convocation of an assembly, which cannot tend either to our spiritual or temporal emolument.   The Latins are proud; the Greeks are obstinate: neither party will recede or retract; and the attempt of a perfect union will confirm the schism, alienate the churches, and leave us, without hope or defence, at the mercy of the barbarians."   Impatient of this salutary lesson, the royal youth arose from his seat and departed in silence; and the wise monarch (continues Phranza) casting his eyes on me, thus resumed his discourse: "My son deems himself a great and heroic prince; but alas! our miserable age does not afford scope for heroism or greatness.   His daring spirit might have suited the happier times of our ancestors; but

---

[33] From his early youth, George Phranza, or Phranzes, was employed in the service of the state and palace; and Hanckius (de Script. Byzant. p. i. c. 40) has collected his life from his own writings. He was no more than four and twenty years of age at the death of Manuel, who recommended him, in the strongest terms, to his successor: Imprimis vero hunc Phranzen tibi commendo, qui ministravit mihi fideliter et diligenter (Phranzes, l. ii. c. 1). Yet the emperor John was cold, and he preferred the service of the despots of Peloponnesus.

[34] See Phranzes, l. ii. c. 13. While so many manuscripts of the Greek original are extant in the libraries of Rome, Milan, the Escurial, &c. it is a matter of shame and reproach that we should be reduced to the Latin version, or abstract, of James Pontanus, ad calcem Theophylact. Simocattæ (Ingolstadt, 1604), so deficient in accuracy and elegance (Fabric. Bibliot. Græc. tom. vi. p. 615-620). [See Appendix 1.]

the present state requires not an emperor, but a cautious steward
of the last relics of our fortunes.   Well do I remember the lofty
expectations which he built on our alliance with Mustapha; and
much do I fear that his rash courage will urge the ruin of our
house, and that even religion may precipitate our downfall."
Yet the experience and authority of Manuel preserved the
peace and eluded the council; till, in the seventy-eighth year His death
of his age, and in the habit of a monk, he terminated his career, [21st July, A.D. 1425]
dividing his precious moveables among his children and the poor,
his physicians, and his favourite servants.   Of his six sons,[35]
Andronicus the Second was invested with the principality of
Thessalonica, and died of a leprosy soon after the sale of that
city to the Venetians and its final conquest by the Turks.   Some [A.D. 1430]
fortunate incidents had restored Peloponnesus, or the Morea, to
the empire; and in his more prosperous days Manuel had fortified the narrow isthmus of six miles [36] with a stone wall and one
hundred and fifty-three towers.   The wall was overthrown by
the first blast of the Ottomans; the fertile peninsula might have
been sufficient for the four younger brothers, Theodore and Constantine, Demetrius and Thomas; but they wasted, in domestic
contests, the remains of their strength; and the least successful
of the rivals were reduced to a life of dependence in the
Byzantine palace.

The eldest of the sons of Manuel, John Palæologus the Second, Zeal of
was acknowledged, after his father's death, as the sole emperor John
Palæologus
of the Greeks.   He immediately proceeded to repudiate his wife II. A.D.
1425-1437
and to contract a new marriage with the princess of Trebizond;
beauty was in his eye the first qualification of an empress; and
the clergy had yielded to his firm assurance that, unless he
might be indulged in a divorce, he would retire to a cloister
and leave the throne to his brother Constantine.   The first, and
in truth the only, victory of Palæologus was over a Jew,[37] whom,

---

[35] See Ducange, Fam. Byzant. p. 243-248.

[36] The exact measure of the Hexamilion from sea to sea, was 3800 orgygiæ
[orgyiæ, ὀργυἱαι], or *toises*, of six Greek feet (Phranzes, l. i. c. 38), which would produce a Greek mile, still smaller than that of 660 French *toises*, which is assigned by
d'Anville as still in use in Turkey.   Five miles are commonly reckoned for the
breadth of the Isthmus.   See the Travels of Spon, Wheeler, and Chandler.

[37] The first objection of the Jews is on the death of Christ: if it were voluntary,
Christ was a suicide; which the emperor parries with a mystery.   They then dispute on the conception of the Virgin, the sense of the prophecies, &c. (Phranzes, l. ii.
c. 12, a whole chapter).

after a long and learned dispute, he converted to the Christian faith; and this momentous conquest is carefully recorded in the history of the times.   But he soon resumed the design of uniting the East and West; and, regardless of his father's advice, listened, as it should seem, with sincerity to the proposal of meeting the pope in a general council beyond the Adriatic. This dangerous project was encouraged by Martin the Fifth, and coldly entertained by his successor Eugenius, till, after a tedious negotiation, the emperor received a summons from a Latin assembly of a new character, the independent prelates of Basil, who styled themselves the representatives and judges of the Catholic church.

Corruption of the Latin church

The Roman pontiff had fought and conquered in the cause of ecclesiastical freedom; but the victorious clergy were soon exposed to the tyranny of their deliverer; and his sacred character was invulnerable to those arms which they found so keen and effectual against the civil magistrate.   Their great charter, the right of election, was annihilated by appeals, evaded by trusts or commendams, disappointed by reversionary grants, and superseded by previous and arbitrary reservations.[38] A public auction was instituted in the court of Rome: the cardinals and favourites were enriched with the spoils of nations; and every country might complain that the most important and valuable benefices were accumulated on the heads of aliens and absentees.   During their residence at Avignon, the ambition of the popes subsided in the meaner passions of avarice[39] and luxury: they rigorously imposed on the clergy the tributes of first-fruits and tenths; but they freely tolerated the impunity of vice, disorder, and corruption.   These manifold scandals were

Schism, A.D. 1377-1429

aggravated by the great schism of the West, which continued above fifty years.   In the furious conflicts of Rome and Avignon, the vices of the rivals were mutually exposed; and their precarious situation degraded their authority, relaxed their discipline,

---

[38] In the treatise delle Materie Beneficiarie of Fra Paolo (in the ivth volume of the last and best edition of his works), the papal system is deeply studied and freely described.   Should Rome and her religion be annihilated, this golden volume may still survive, a philosophical history and a salutary warning.

[39] Pope John XXII. (in 1334) left behind him, at Avignon, eighteen millions of gold florins, and the value of seven millions more in plate and jewels.   See the Chronicle of John Villani (l. xi. c. 20, in Muratori's Collection, tom. xiii. p. 765), whose brother received the account from the Papal treasurers.   A treasure of six or eight millions sterling in the xivth century is enormous, and almost incredible.

and multiplied their wants and exactions. To heal the wounds, Council of Pisa, A.D.
and restore the monarchy, of the church, the synods of Pisa 1409; of Constance,
and Constance [40] were successively convened; but these great as- A.D. 1414-1418
semblies, conscious of their strength, resolved to vindicate the
privileges of the Christian aristocracy. From a personal sentence against two pontiffs, whom' they rejected, and a third,
their acknowledged sovereign, whom they deposed, the fathers
of Constance proceeded to examine the nature and limits of the
Roman supremacy; nor did they separate till they had established
the authority, above the pope, of a general council. It was
enacted that, for the government and reformation of the church,
such assemblies should be held at regular intervals; and that
each synod, before its dissolution, should appoint the time and
place of the subsequent meeting. By the influence of the court of Basil, A.D. 1431-
of Rome, the next convocation at Sienna was easily eluded; 1443
but the bold and vigorous proceedings of the council of Basil [41]
had almost been fatal to the reigning pontiff, Eugenius the
Fourth. A just suspicion of his design prompted the fathers
to hasten the promulgation of their first decree, that the representatives of the church-militant on earth were invested
with a divine and spiritual jurisdiction over all Christians,
without excepting the pope; and that a general council could
not be dissolved, prorogued, or transferred, unless by their free
deliberation and consent. On the notice that Eugenius had
fulminated a bull for that purpose, they ventured to summon,

[40] A learned and liberal Protestant, M. Lenfant, has given a fair history of the
councils of Pisa, Constance, and Basil, in six volumes in quarto; but the last part
is the most hasty and imperfect, except in the account of the troubles of Bohemia.
[For the Council of Pisa see Erler, Zur Geschichte des Pisaner Conzils, 1884. The
history of the Council of Constance has been rewritten by L. Tosti, Storia del concilio di Costanza, 1853 (in 2 vols.), a work which has been translated into German
by W. Arnold (1860). See also F. Stuhr, Die Organisation und Geschäftsordnung
des Pisaner und Costanzer Konzils, 1891; and the document (Ein Tagebuch-fragment
über das Kostanzer Konzil) edited by Knöpfler in the Historisches Jahrbuch der
Görresgesellschaft, vol. xi. p. 267 sqq., 1890. Gibbon does not mention the big work
of Hardt: Magnum œcumenicum Constantiense concilium (6 vols.), 1697-1700 (Index,
1742).]

[41] The original acts or minutes of the council of Basil are preserved in the
public library, in twelve volumes in folio. Basil was a free city, conveniently situate
on the Rhine, and guarded by the arms of the neighbouring and confederate Swiss.
In 1459, the university was founded by Pope Pius II. (Æneas Sylvius), who had been
secretary to the council. But what is a council, or an university, to the presses of
Froben and the studies of Erasmus? [The first 3 vols. (1853-94) of the Vienna
Monumenta conciliorum generalium are devoted to the council of Basil. For the
union question see Mugnier, L'Expédition du concile de Bâle à Constantinople pour
l'union de l'église grecque à l'église latine (1437-8), 1892.]

Their op-
position to
Eugenius
IV. to admonish, to threaten, to censure, the contumacious successor of St. Peter. After many delays, to allow time for repentance, they finally declared that, unless he submitted within the term of sixty days, he was suspended from the exercise of all temporal and ecclesiastical authority. And to mark their jurisdiction over the prince as well as the priest, they assumed the government of Avignon, annulled the alienation of the sacred patrimony, and protected Rome from the imposition of new taxes. Their boldness was justified, not only by the general opinion of the clergy, but by the support and power of the first monarchs of Christendom: the emperor Sigismond declared himself the servant and protector of the synod; Germany and France adhered to their cause; the duke of Milan was the enemy of Eugenius; and he was driven from the Vatican by an insurrection of the Roman people. Rejected at the same time by his temporal and spiritual subjects, submission was his only choice; by a most humiliating bull, the pope repealed his own acts and ratified those of the council; incorporated his legates and cardinals with that venerable body; and *seemed* to resign himself to the decrees of the supreme legislature. Their fame pervaded the countries of the East; and it was in their presence that Sigismond received the ambassadors of the Turkish sultan,[42]

Negotia-
tions with
the Greeks,
A.D. 1434-
1437 who laid at his feet twelve large vases, filled with robes of silk and pieces of gold. The fathers of Basil aspired to the glory of reducing the Greeks, as well as the Bohemians, within the pale of the church; and their deputies invited the emperor and patriarch of Constantinople to unite with an assembly which possessed the confidence of the Western nations. Palæologus was not averse to the proposal; and his ambassadors were introduced with due honours into the Catholic senate. But the choice of the place appeared to be an insuperable obstacle, since he refused to pass the Alps or the sea of Sicily, and positively required that the synod should be adjourned to some convenient city in Italy, or at least on the Danube. The other articles of this treaty were more readily stipulated: it was agreed to defray the travelling expenses of the emperor, with a train of seven hundred persons,[43] to remit an immediate sum of eight

---

[42] This Turkish embassy, attested only by Crantzius, is related with some doubt by the annalist Spondanus, A.D. 1433, No. 25, tom. i. p. 824.

[43] Syropulus, p. 19. In this list, the Greeks appear to have exceeded the real numbers of the clergy and laity which afterwards attended the emperor and patriarch,

LATE BYZANTINE ART: PANEL PAINTING OF THE VIRGIN AND CHILD
UFFIZI GALLERY, FLORENCE

thousand ducats [44] for the accommodation of the Greek clergy; and in his absence to grant a supply of ten thousand ducats, with three hundred archers, and some galleys for the protection of Constantinople. The city of Avignon advanced the funds for the preliminary expenses; and the embarkation was prepared at Marseilles with some difficulty and delay.

In his distress, the friendship of Palæologus was disputed by the ecclesiastical powers of the West; but the dexterous activity of a monarch prevailed over the slow debates and inflexible temper of a republic. The decrees of Basil continually tended to circumscribe the despotism of the pope and to erect a supreme and perpetual tribunal in the church. Eugenius was impatient of the yoke; and the union of the Greeks might afford a decent pretence for translating a rebellious synod from the Rhine to the Po. The independence of the fathers was lost if they passed the Alps; Savoy or Avignon, to which they acceded with reluctance, were described at Constantinople as situate far beyond the Pillars of Hercules; [45] the emperor and his clergy were apprehensive of the dangers of a long navigation; they were offended by an haughty declaration that, after suppressing the *new* heresy of the Bohemians, the council would soon eradicate the *old* heresy of the Greeks. [46] On the side of Eugenius, all was smooth and yielding and respectful; and he invited the Byzantine monarch to heal, by his presence, the schism of the Latin, as well as of the Eastern, church. Ferrara, near the coast of the Adriatic, was proposed for their amicable interview; and with some indulgence of forgery and theft a

(margin note: John Palæologus embarks in the pope's galleys, A.D. 1437, 4th Nov.)

but which are not clearly specified by the great ecclesiarch. The 75,000 florins which they asked in this negotiation of the pope (p. 9) were more than they could hope or want.

[44] I use indifferently the words *ducat* and *florin*, which derive their names, the former from the *dukes* of Milan, the latter from the republic of *Florence*. These gold pieces, the first that were coined in Italy, perhaps in the Latin world, may be compared, in weight and value, to one-third of the English guinea.

[45] At the end of the Latin version of Phranzes, we read a long Greek epistle or declamation of George of Trebizond, who advises the emperor to prefer Eugenius and Italy. He treats with contempt the schismatic assembly of Basil, the barbarians of Gaul and Germany, who had conspired to transport the chair of St. Peter beyond the Alps: οἱ ἄθλιοί (says he) σε καὶ τὴν μετὰ σοῦ σύνοδον ἔξω τῶν Ἡρακλείων στηλῶν καὶ πέρα Γαδήρων ἐξάξουσι. Was Constantinople unprovided with a map? [The writings of the humanist George of Trebizond, on the union question, will be found in Migne, P. G., vol. 161, 829 *sqq*.]

[46] Syropulus (p. 26-31) attests his own indignation, and that of his countrymen; and the Basil deputies, who excused the rash declaration, could neither deny nor alter an act of the council.

surreptitious decree was procured, which transferred the synod, with its own consent, to that Italian city.   Nine galleys were equipped for this service at Venice and in the isle of Candia; their diligence anticipated the slower vessels of Basil.   The Roman admiral was commissioned to burn, sink, and destroy; [47] and these priestly squadrons might have encountered each other in the same seas where Athens and Sparta had formerly contended for the pre-eminence of glory.   Assaulted by the importunity of the factions, who were ready to fight for the possession of his person, Palæologus hesitated before he left his palace and country on a perilous experiment.   His father's advice still dwelt on his memory; and reason must suggest that, since the Latins were divided among themselves, they could never unite in a foreign cause.   Sigismond dissuaded the unseasonable adventure; his advice was impartial, since he adhered to the council; and it was enforced by the strange belief that the German Cæsar would nominate a Greek his heir and successor in the empire of the West.[48]   Even the Turkish sultan was a counsellor whom it might be unsafe to trust, but whom it was dangerous to offend.   Amurath was unskilled in the disputes, but he was apprehensive of the union, of the Christians.   From his own treasures, he offered to relieve the wants of the Byzantine court; yet he declared, with seeming magnanimity, that Constantinople should be secure and inviolate in the absence of her sovereign.[49]   The resolution of Palæologus was decided by the most splendid gifts and the most specious promises.   He wished to escape, for a while, from a scene of danger and distress; and, after dismissing, with an ambiguous answer, the messengers of the council, he declared his intention of embarking in the Roman galleys.   The age of the patriarch

---

[47] Condolmieri, the Pope's nephew and admiral, expressly declared, ὅτι ὁρισμὸν ἔχει παρὰ τοῦ Πάπα ἵνα πολεμήσῃ ὅπου ἂν εὕρῃ τὰ κάτεργα τῆς Συνόδου, καὶ εἰ δυνήθῃ καταδύσῃ καὶ ἀφανίσῃ.   The naval orders of the synod were less peremptory, and, till the hostile squadrons appeared, both parties tried to conceal their quarrel from the Greeks.

[48] Syropulus mentions the hopes of Palæologus (p. 36), and the last advice of Sigismond (p. 57).   At Corfu, the Greek emperor was informed of his friend's death; had he known it sooner, he would have returned home (p. 79).

[49] Phranzes himself, though from different motives, was of the advice of Amurath (l. ii. c. 13).   Utinam ne synodus ista unquam fuisset, si tantas offensiones et detrimenta paritura erat.   This Turkish embassy is likewise mentioned by Syropulus (p. 58); and Amurath kept his word.   He might threaten (p. 125, 219), but he never attacked, the city.

Joseph was more susceptible of fear than of hope; he trembled at the perils of the sea, and expressed his apprehension that his feeble voice, with thirty, perhaps, of his orthodox brethren, would be oppressed in a foreign land by the power and numbers of a Latin synod. He yielded to the royal mandate, to the flattering assurance that he would be heard as the oracle of nations, and to the secret wish of learning from his brother of the West to deliver the church from the yoke of kings.[50] The five cross-bearers, or dignitaries of St. Sophia, were bound to attend his person; and one of these, the great ecclesiarch or preacher, Sylvester Syropulus,[51] has composed [52] a free and curious history of the false union.[53] Of the clergy that reluctantly obeyed the summons of the emperor and the patriarch, submission was the first duty, and patience the most useful virtue. In a chosen list of twenty bishops, we discover the metropolitan titles of Heraclea and Cyzicus, Nice and Nicomedia, Ephesus and Trebizond, and the personal merit of Mark and Bessarion, who, in the confidence of their learning and eloquence, were promoted to the episcopal rank. Some monks and philosophers were named to display the science and sanctity of the Greek church; and the service of the choir was performed by a select band of singers and musicians. The patriarchs of Alexandria, Antioch, and Jerusalem appeared by their genuine or fictitious deputies, the primate of Russia represented a

---

[50] The reader will smile at the symplicity with which he imparted these hopes to his favourites: τοιαύτην πληροφορίαν σχήσειν ἤλπιζε καὶ διὰ τοῦ Πάπα ἐθάρρει ἐλευθερῶσαι τὴν ἐκκλησίαν ἀπὸ τῆς ἀποτεθείσης αὐτοῦ δουλείας παρὰ τοῦ βασιλέως (p. 92). Yet it would have been difficult for him to have practised the lessons of Gregory VII.

[51] The Christian name of Sylvester is borrowed from the Latin Calendar. In modern Greek, πουλος, as a diminutive, is added to the end of words; nor can any reasoning of Creyghton, the editor, excuse his changing into Sguropulus (Sguros, fuscus) the Syropulus of his own manuscript, whose name is subscribed with his own hand in the acts of the council of Florence. Why might not the author be of Syrian extraction? [The name Syropulos occurs repeatedly in the Collection of Letters (dating from the 14th century) in the Florentine Codex S. Marco, 356. See Krumbacher, Gesch. der byzantinischen Litteratur, p. 485.]

[52] From the conclusion of the history, I should fix the date to the year 1444, four years after the synod, when the great ecclesiarch had abdicated his office (sectio xii. p. 330-350). His passions were cooled by time and retirement; and, although Syropulus is often partial, he is never intemperate.

[53] Vera historia unionis non verae inter Graecos et Latinos (Hagae Comitis, 1660, in folio) was first published with a loose and florid version, by Robert Creyghton, chaplain to Charles II. in his exile. The zeal of the editor has prefixed a polemic title, for the beginning of the original is wanting. Syropulus may be ranked with the best of the Byzantine writers for the merit of his narration, and even of his style; but he is excluded from the orthodox collections of the Councils.

national church, and the Greeks might contend with the Latins in the extent of their spiritual empire. The precious vases of St. Sophia were exposed to the winds and waves, that the patriarch might officiate with becoming splendour; whatever gold the emperor could procure was expended in the massy ornaments of his bed and chariot;[54] and, while they affected to maintain the prosperity of their ancient fortune, they quarrelled for the division of fifteen thousand ducats, the first alms of the Roman pontiff. After the necessary preparations, John Palæologus, with a numerous train, accompanied by his brother Demetrius, and the most respectable persons of the church and state, embarked in eight vessels with sails and oars, which steered through the Turkish straits of Gallipoli to the Archipelago, the Morea, and the Adriatic Gulf.[55]

His triumphal entry at Venice, A.D. 1438, 9th Feb.

After a tedious and troublesome navigation of seventy-seven days, this religious squadron cast anchor before Venice; and their reception proclaimed the joy and magnificence of that powerful republic. In the command of the world, the modest Augustus had never claimed such honours from his subjects as were paid to his feeble successor by an independent state. Seated on the poop, on a lofty throne, he received the visit, or, in the Greek style, the *adoration*, of the Doge and senators.[56] They sailed in the Bucentaur, which was accompanied by twelve stately galleys; the sea was overspread with innumerable gondolas of pomp and pleasure; the air resounded with music and acclamations; the mariners, and even the vessels, were dressed in silk and gold; and in all the emblems and pageants the Roman eagles were blended with the lions of St. Mark. The triumphal procession, ascending the great canal, passed under the bridge of the Rialto; and the eastern strangers

[54] Syropulus (p. 63) simply expresses his intention: ἵν᾽ οὕτω πομπάων ἐν ᾽Ιτάλοις μέγας βασιλεὺς παρ᾽ ἐκείνων νομίζοιτο; and the Latin of Creyghton may afford a specimen of his florid paraphrase. Ut pompâ circumductus noster Imperator Italiæ populis aliquis deauratus Jupiter crederetur, aut Crœsus ex opulentâ Lydiâ. [In the Greek citation πομπάων is unintelligible, but so it stands in Creyghton's text. Evidently Syropulus wrote πομπεύων.]

[55] Although I cannot stop to quote Syropulus for every fact, I will observe that the navigation of the Greeks from Constantinople to Venice and Ferrara is contained in the ivth section (p. 67-100), and that the historian has the uncommon talent of placing each scene before the reader's eye.

[56] At the time of the synod, Phranzes was in Peloponnesus; but he received from the despot Demetrius a faithful account of the honourable reception of the emperor and patriarch, both at Venice and Ferrara (Dux . . . sedentem Imperatorem *adorat*), which are more slightly mentioned by the Latins (l. ii. c. 14-16).

gazed with admiration on the palaces, the churches, and the populousness of a city that seems to float on the bosom of the waves.[57] They sighed to behold the spoils and trophies with which it had been decorated after the sack of Constantinople. After an hospitable entertainment of fifteen days, Palæologus pursued his journey by land and water, from Venice to Ferrara; and on this occasion the pride of the Vatican was tempered by policy to indulge the ancient dignity of the emperor of the East. He made his entry on a *black* horse; but a milk-white into Ferrara, 28th steed, whose trappings were embroidered with golden eagles, Feb. was led before him; and the canopy was borne over his head by the princes of Este, the sons or kinsmen of Nicholas, marquis of the city, and a sovereign more powerful than himself.[58] Palæologus did not alight till he reached the bottom of the staircase; the pope advanced to the door of the apartment; refused his proffered genuflexion; and, after a paternal embrace, conducted the emperor to a seat on his left hand. Nor would the patriarch descend from his galley, till a ceremony, almost equal, had been stipulated between the bishops of Rome and Constantinople. The latter was saluted by his brother with a kiss of union and charity; nor would any of the Greek ecclesiastics submit to kiss the feet of the Western primate. On the opening of the synod, the place of honour in the centre was claimed by the temporal and ecclesiastical chiefs; and it was only by alleging that his predecessors had not assisted in person at Nice or Chalcedon that Eugenius could evade the ancient precedents of Constantine and Marcian. After much debate, it was agreed that the right and left sides of the church should be occupied by the two nations; that the solitary chair of St. Peter should be raised the first of the Latin line; and that the throne of the Greek emperor, at the head of his clergy, should be equal and opposite to the second place, the vacant seat of the emperor of the West.[59]

[57] The astonishment of a Greek prince and a French ambassador (Mémoires de Philippe de Comines, l. vii. c. 18) at the sight of Venice abundantly proves that in the xvth century it was the first and most splendid of the Christian cities. For the spoils of Constantinople at Venice, see Syropulus (p. 87).

[58] Nicholas III. of Este reigned forty-eight years (A.D. 1393-1441), and was lord of Ferrara, Modena, Reggio, Parma, Rovigo, and Commachio. See his life in Muratori (Antichità Estense, tom. ii. p. 159-201).

[59] The Latin vulgar was provoked to laughter at the strange dresses of the Greeks, and especially the length of their garments, their sleeves, and their beards;

Council of
the Greeks
and Latins
at Ferrara
and Flor-
ence, A.D.
1438, 8th
Oct.-A.D.
1439, 6th
July

But, as soon as festivity and form had given place to a more serious treaty, the Greeks were dissatisfied with their journey, with themselves, and with the pope. The artful pencil of his emissaries had painted him in a prosperous state; at the head of the princes and prelates of Europe, obedient, at his voice, to believe and to arm. The thin appearance of the universal synod of Ferrara betrayed his weakness; and the Latins opened the first session with only five archbishops, eighteen bishops, and ten abbots, the greatest part of whom were the subjects or countrymen of the Italian pontiff. Except the duke of Burgundy, none of the potentates of the West condescended to appear in person or by their ambassadors; nor was it possible to suppress the judicial acts of Basil against the dignity and person of Eugenius, which were finally concluded by a new election. Under these circumstances, a truce or delay was asked and granted, till Palæologus could expect from the consent of the Latins some temporal reward for an unpopular union; and, after the first session, the public proceedings were adjourned above six months. The emperor, with a chosen band of his favourites and *Janizaries*, fixed his summer residence at a pleasant spacious monastery, six miles from Ferrara; forgot, in the pleasures of the chase, the distress of the church and state; and persisted in destroying the game, without listening to the just complaints of the marquis or the husbandman.[60] In the meanwhile, his unfortunate Greeks were exposed to all the miseries of exile and poverty; for the support of each stranger, a monthly allowance was assigned of three or four gold florins; and, although the entire sum did not amount to seven hundred florins, a long arrear was repeatedly incurred by the indigence or policy of the Roman court.[61] They sighed for a speedy

nor was the emperor distinguished, except by the purple colour, and his diadem or tiara with a jewel on the top (Hody de Græcis Illustribus, p. 31). Yet another spectator confesses that the Greek fashion was piu grave e piu degna than the Italian (Vespasiano, in Vit. Eugen. IV. in Muratori, tom. xxv. p. 261).

[60] For the emperor's hunting, see Syropulus (p. 143, 144, 191). The pope had sent him eleven miserable hawks; but he bought a strong and swift horse that came from Russia. The name of *Janizaries* may surprise; but the name, rather than the institution, had passed from the Ottoman to the Byzantine court, and is often used in the last age of the empire.

[61] The Greeks obtained, with much difficulty, that, instead of provisions, money should be distributed, four florins *per* month to the persons of honourable rank, and three florins to their servants, with an addition of thirty more to the emperor, twenty-five to the patriarch, and twenty to the prince or despot Demetrius. The payment of the first month amounted to 691 florins, a sum which will not allow us

deliverance, but their escape was prevented by a triple chain: a passport from their superiors was required at the gates of Ferrara; the government of Venice had engaged to arrest and send back the fugitives; and inevitable punishment awaited them at Constantinople: excommunication, fines, and a sentence which did not respect the sacerdotal dignity, that they should be stripped naked and publicly whipped.[62] It was only by the alternative of hunger or dispute that the Greeks could be persuaded to open the first conference; and they yielded with extreme reluctance to attend, from Ferrara to Florence, the rear of a flying synod. This new translation was urged by inevitable necessity: the city was visited by the plague; the fidelity of the marquis might be suspected; the mercenary troops of the duke of Milan were at the gates; and, as they occupied Romagna, it was not without difficulty and danger that the pope, the emperor, and the bishops explored their way through the unfrequented paths of the Apennine.[63]

Yet all these obstacles were surmounted by time and policy. The violence of the fathers of Basil rather promoted than injured the cause of Eugenius: the nations of Europe abhorred the schism, and disowned the election, of Felix the Fifth, who was successively a duke of Savoy, an hermit, and a pope; and the great princes were gradually reclaimed by his competitor to a favourable neutrality and a firm attachment. The legates, with some respectable members, deserted to the Roman army, which insensibly rose in numbers and reputation: the council of Basil was reduced to thirty-nine bishops and three hundred of the inferior clergy;[64] while the Latins of Florence could produce the subscriptions of the pope himself, eight cardinals, two

to reckon above 200 Greeks of every condition (Syropulus, p. 104, 105). On the 20th October, 1438, there was an arrear of four months; in April, 1439, of three; and of five and a half in July, at the time of the union (p. 172, 225, 271).

[62] Syropulus (p. 141, 142, 204, 221) deplores the imprisonment of the Greeks, and the tyranny of the emperor and patriarch.

[63] The wars of Italy are most clearly represented in the xiiith volume of the Annals of Muratori. The schismatic Greek, Syropulus (p. 145), appears to have exaggerated the fear and disorder of the pope in his retreat from Ferrara to Florence, which is proved by the acts to have been somewhat more decent and deliberate.

[64] Syropulus is pleased to reckon seven hundred prelates in the council of Basil. The error is manifest, and perhaps voluntary. That extravagant number could not be supplied by all the ecclesiastics, of every degree, who were present at the council, nor by all the absent bishops of the West, who, expressly or tacitly, might adhere to its decrees.

patriarchs, eight archbishops, fifty-two bishops, and forty-five abbots, or chiefs of religious orders. After the labour of nine months, and the debates of twenty-five sessions, they attained the advantage and glory of the reunion of the Greeks. Four principal questions had been agitated between the two churches: 1. The use of unleavened bread in the communion of Christ's body; 2. The nature of purgatory; 3. The supremacy of the pope; and 4. The single or double procession of the Holy Ghost. The cause of either nation was managed by ten theological champions: the Latins were supported by the inexhaustible eloquence of Cardinal Julian; and Mark of Ephesus and Bessarion of Nice were the bold and able leaders of the Greek forces. We may bestow some praise on the progress of human reason by observing that the first of these questions was *now* treated as an immaterial rite, which might innocently vary with the fashion of the age and country. With regard to the second, both parties were agreed in the belief of an intermediate state of purgation for the venial sins of the faithful; and, whether their souls were purified by elemental fire was a doubtful point, which in a few years might be conveniently settled on the spot by the disputants. The claims of supremacy appeared of a more weighty and substantial kind; yet, by the Orientals the Roman bishop had ever been respected as the first of the five patriarchs; nor did they scruple to admit that his jurisdiction should be exercised agreeable to the holy canons: a vague allowance which might be defined or eluded by occasional convenience. The procession of the Holy Ghost from the Father alone, or from the Father and the Son, was an article of faith which had sunk much deeper into the minds of men; and in the sessions of Ferrara and Florence the Latin addition of *filioque* was subdivided into two questions, whether it were legal, and whether it were orthodox. Perhaps it may not be necessary to boast on this subject of my own impartial indifference; but I must think that the Greeks were strongly supported by the prohibition of the council of Chalcedon against adding any article whatsoever to the creed of Nice or rather of Constantinople.[65] In earthly affairs, it is not easy to conceive

---

[65] The Greeks, who disliked the union, were unwilling to sally from this strong fortress (p. 178, 193, 195, 202, of Syropulus). The shame of the Latins was aggravated by their producing an old Ms. of the second council of Nice, with *filioque* in the Nicene creed. A palpable forgery! (p. 173).

how an assembly of legislators can bind their successors invested
with powers equal to their own. But the dictates of inspiration
must be true and unchangeable ; nor should a private bishop,
or a provincial synod, have presumed to innovate against the
judgment of the Catholic church. On the substance of the
doctrine, the controversy was equal and endless : reason is confounded by the procession of a deity ; the gospel, which lay on
the altar, was silent ; the various texts of the fathers might be
corrupted by fraud or entangled by sophistry ; and the Greeks
were ignorant of the characters and writings of the Latin saints.[66]
Of this, at least, we may be sure, that neither side could be convinced by the arguments of their opponents. Prejudice may be
enlightened by reason, and a superficial glance may be rectified
by a clear and more perfect view of an object adapted to our
faculties. But the bishops and monks had been taught from
their infancy to repeat a form of mysterious words ; their
national and personal honour depended on the repetition of
the same sounds ; and their narrow minds were hardened and
inflamed by the acrimony of a public dispute.

While they were lost in a cloud of dust and darkness, the
pope and emperor were desirous of a seeming union, which
could alone accomplish the purposes of their interview ; and
the obstinacy of public dispute was softened by the arts of
private and personal negotiation. The patriarch Joseph had
sunk under the weight of age and infirmities ; his dying voice
breathed the counsels of charity and concord, and his vacant
benefice might tempt the hopes of the ambitious clergy. The
ready and active obedience of the archbishops of Russia and
Nice, of Isidore and Bessarion, was prompted and recompensed
by their speedy promotion to the dignity of cardinals. Bessarion,
in the first debates, had stood forth the most strenuous and eloquent champion of the Greek church ; and, if the apostate, the
bastard, was reprobated by his country,[67] he appears in ecclesi-

Negotiations with the Greeks

---

[66] Ὡς ἐγὼ (said an eminent Greek) ὅταν εἰς ναὸν εἰσέλθω Λατίνων οὐ προσκυνῶ τινα
τῶν ἐκεῖσε ἁγίων, ἐπεὶ οὐδὲ γνωρίζω τινά (Syropulus, p. 109). See the perplexity of the
Greeks (p. 217, 218, 252, 253, 273).

[67] See the polite altercation of Mark and Bessarion in Syropulus (p. 257), who
never dissembles the vices of his own party, and fairly praises the virtues of the
Latins. [The works of Bessarion are collected in Migne's Greek Patrology, vol.
clxi., where Bandini's monograph on his life and writings (1777) is reprinted.
There are two recent monographs : Le Cardinal Bessarion, by H. Vast (1878), and
a Russian monograph by A. Sadov (1883). The writings of his opponent Markos

astical story a rare example of a patriot who was recommended
to court favour by loud opposition and well-timed compliance.
With the aid of his two spiritual coadjutors, the emperor applied
his arguments to the general situation and personal characters
of the bishops, and each was successively moved by authority
and example. Their revenues were in the hands of the Turks,
their persons in those of the Latins ; an episcopal treasure,
three robes and forty ducats, were soon exhausted ; [68] the hopes
of their return still depended on the ships of Venice and the
alms of Rome; and such was their indigence that their arrears,
the payment of a debt, would be accepted as a favour and
might operate as a bribe.[69] The danger and relief of Constantinople might excuse some prudent and pious dissimulation ;
and it was insinuated that the obstinate heretics who should
resist the consent of the East and West would be abandoned
in a hostile land to the revenge or justice of the Roman pontiff.[70] In the first private assembly of the Greeks, the formulary
of union was approved by twenty-four, and rejected by twelve,
members; but the five *cross-bearers* of St. Sophia, who aspired
to represent the patriarch, were disqualified by ancient discipline; and their right of voting was transferred to an obsequious
train of monks, grammarians, and profane laymen. The will
of the monarch produced a false and servile unanimity, and no
more than two patriots had courage to speak their own sentiments, and those of their country. Demetrius, the emperor's
brother, retired to Venice, that he might not be witness of
the union; and Mark of Ephesus, mistaking perhaps his pride
for his conscience, disclaimed all communion with the Latin
heretics, and avowed himself the champion and confessor of

Eugenikos, metropolitan of Ephesus, will be found in Migne, P. G., vols. clx. and
clxi. There is a Greek work on these two men by N. Kalogeras (Μάρκος ὁ Εὐγενικὸς
καὶ Βησσαρίων ὁ Καρδινάλις, 1893). Cp. J. Dräseke, Byzantinische Zeitschrift, iv.
145 *sqq.*, and Zeitschrift für Kirchengeschichte, xii. 91 *sqq.*]

[68] For the poverty of the Greek bishops, see a remarkable passage of Ducas
(c. 31). One had possessed, for his whole property, three old gowns, &c. By
teaching one-and-twenty years in his monastery, Bessarion himself had collected
forty gold florins ; but of these, the archbishop had expended twenty-eight in his
voyage from Peloponnesus, and the remainder at Constantinople (Syropulus, p. 127).

[69] Syropulus denies that the Greeks received any money before they had subscribed the act of union (p. 283); yet he relates some suspicious circumstances ;
and their bribery and corruption are positively affirmed by the historian Ducas.

[70] The Greeks most piteously express their own fears of exile and perpetual
slavery (Syropul. p. 196); and they were strongly moved by the emperor's threats
(p. 260).

the orthodox creed.[71] In the treaty between the two nations several forms of consent were proposed, such as might satisfy the Latins without dishonouring the Greeks ; and they weighed the scruples of words and syllables, till the theological balance trembled with a slight preponderance in favour of the Vatican. It was agreed (I must intreat the attention of the reader), that the Holy Ghost proceeds from the Father *and* the Son, as from one principle and one substance; that he proceeds *by* the Son, being of the same nature and substance; and that he proceeds from the Father *and* the Son, by one *spiration* and production. It is less difficult to understand the articles of the preliminary treaty: that the pope should defray all the expenses of the Greeks in their return home; that he should annually maintain two galleys and three hundred soldiers for the defence of Constantinople; that all the ships which transported pilgrims to Jerusalem should be obliged to touch at that port ; that, as often as they were required, the pope should furnish ten galleys for a year, or twenty-six months; and that he should powerfully solicit the princes of Europe, if the emperor had occasion for land-forces.

The same year, and almost the same day, were marked by the deposition of Eugenius at Basil, and, at Florence, by his reunion of the Greeks and Latins. In the former synod (which he styled indeed an assembly of dæmons), the pope was branded with the guilt of simony, perjury, tyranny, heresy, and schism ; [72] and declared to be incorrigible in his vices, unworthy of any title, and incapable of holding any ecclesiastical office. In the latter, he was revered as the true and holy vicar of Christ, who, after a separation of six hundred years, had reconciled the Catholics of the East and West, in one fold and under one shepherd. The act of union was subscribed by the pope, the emperor, and the principal members of both churches ; even by those who, like Syropulus,[73] had been deprived of the right of

Eugenius deposed at Basil, A.D. 1438. 25th June

Reunion of the Greeks of Florence, A.D. 1438. 6th July

---

[71] I had forgot another popular and orthodox protester : a favourite hound, who usually lay quiet on the foot-cloth of the emperor's throne; but who barked most furiously while the act of union was reading, without being silenced by the soothing or the lashes of the royal attendants (Syropul. p. 265, 266).

[72] From the original Lives of the Popes, in Muratori's Collection (tom. iii. p. 2, tom. xxv.), the manners of Eugenius IV. appear to have been decent, and even exemplary. His situation, exposed to the world and to his enemies, was a restraint, and is a pledge.

[73] Syropulus, rather than subscribe, would have assisted, as the least evil, at the

voting. Two copies might have sufficed for the East and West; but Eugenius was not satisfied, unless four authentic and similar transcripts were signed and attested as the monuments of his victory.[74] On a memorable day, the sixth of July, the successors of St. Peter and Constantine ascended their thrones; the two nations assembled in the cathedral of Florence; their representatives, Cardinal Julian, and Bessarion, Archbishop of Nice, appeared in the pulpit, and, after reading, in their respective tongues, the act of union, they mutually embraced, in the name and the presence of their applauding brethren. The pope and his ministers then officiated according to the Roman liturgy; the creed was chanted with the addition of *filioque;* the acquiescence of the Greeks was poorly excused by their ignorance of the harmonious, but inarticulate, sounds;[75] and the more scrupulous Latins refused any public celebration of the Byzantine rite. Yet the emperor and his clergy were not totally unmindful of national honour. The treaty was ratified by their consent: it was tacitly agreed that no innovation should be attempted in their creed or ceremonies; they spared, and secretly respected, the generous firmness of Mark of Ephesus; and, on the decease of the patriarch, they refused to elect his successor, except in the cathedral of St. Sophia. In the distribution of public and private rewards, the liberal pontiff exceeded their hopes and his promises; the Greeks, with less pomp and pride, returned by the same road of Ferrara and Venice; and their reception at Constantinople was such as will be described in the following chapter.[76] The success of the first trial encouraged Eugenius to repeat the same edifying scenes; and the deputies

Their return to Constantinople, A.D. 1440, 1st Feb.

ceremony of the union. He was compelled to do both; and the great ecclesiarch poorly excuses his submission to the emperor (p. 290-292).

[74] None of these original acts of union can at present be produced. Of the ten Mss. that are preserved (five at Rome, and the remainder at Florence, Bologna, Venice, Paris, and London), nine have been examined by an accurate critic (M. de Brequigny), who condemns them for the variety and imperfections of the Greek signatures. Yet several of these may be esteemed as authentic copies, which were subscribed at Florence before (26th August, 1439) the final separation of the Pope and emperor (Mémoires de l'Académie des Inscriptions, tom. xliii. p. 287-311). [On these copies see Hefele, Conciliengeschichte, vol. vii. part 2, p. 757 *sqq.* The true original is the copy which is kept under glass in the Laurentian Library at Florence. The text of the Union decree—in Greek, in Latin, and a German translation—is given in Hefele, *ib.*, pp. 742-753.]

[75] Ἡμῖν δὲ ὡς ἄσημοι ἐδόκουν φῶναι (Syropul. p. 297).

[76] In their return, the Greeks conversed at Bologna with the ambassadors of England; and, after some questions and answers, these impartial strangers laughed at the pretended union of Florence (Syropul. p. 307).

A CENTRE OF LATE BYZANTINE CIVILIZATION: RUINS OF MISTRA IN THE MOREA

COLLECTION DES HAUTES ÉTUDES

of the Armenians, the Maronites, the Jacobites of Syria and Egypt, the Nestorians, and the Ethiopians, were successively introduced, to kiss the feet of the Roman pontiff, and to announce the obedience and the orthodoxy of the East. These Oriental embassies, unknown in the countries which they presumed to represent,[77] diffused over the West the fame of Eugenius; and a clamour was artfully propagated against the remnant of a schism in Switzerland and Savoy, which alone impeded the harmony of the Christian world. The vigour of opposition was succeeded by the lassitude of despair : the council of Basil was silently dissolved ; and Felix, renouncing the tiara, again withdrew to the devout or delicious hermitage of Ripaille.[78] A general peace was secured by mutual acts of oblivion and indemnity ; all ideas of reformation subsided ; the popes continued to exercise and abuse their ecclesiastical despotism ; nor has Rome been since disturbed by the mischiefs of a contested election.[79] *Final peace of the church, A.D. 1449*

The journeys of three emperors were unavailing for their temporal, or perhaps their spiritual, salvation ; but they were productive of a beneficial consequence, the revival of the Greek learning in Italy, from whence it was propagated to the last nations of the West and North. In their lowest servitude and depression, the subjects of the Byzantine throne were still possessed of a golden key that could unlock the treasures of antiquity ; *State of the Greek language at Constantinople, A.D. 1300-1453*

[77] So nugatory, or rather so fabulous, are these reunions of the Nestorians, Jacobites, &c. that I have turned over, without success, the Bibliotheca Orientalis of Assemannus, a faithful slave of the Vatican.

[78] Ripaille is situated near Thonon in Savoy, on the southern side of the lake of Geneva. It is now a Carthusian abbey; and Mr. Addison (Travels into Italy, vol. ii. p. 147, 148, of Baskerville's edition of his works) has celebrated the place and the founder. Æneas Sylvius, and the fathers of Basil, applaud the austere life of the ducal hermit; but the French and Italian proverbs most unluckily attest the popular opinion of his luxury.

[79] In this account of the councils of Basil, Ferrara, and Florence, I have consulted the original acts, which fill the xviith and xviiith tomes of the edition of Venice, and are closed by the perspicuous, though partial, history of Augustin Patricius, an Italian of the xvth century. They are digested and abridged by Dupin (Bibliothèque Ecclés. tom. xii.) and the continuator of Fleury (tom. xxii.); and the respect of the Gallican church for the adverse parties confines their members to an awkward moderation. [An English translation of Gorski's (Russian) History of the Council of Florence, appeared in 1861 (ed. by Neale). Kalligas wrote an important essay on it, which is published in his Μελέται καὶ λόγοι (1882) pp. 1-181. See also Dräseke Zum Kircheneinigungsversuch des Jahres 1439, in Byz. Zeitsch. v. p. 572 *sqq.;* Frommann, Kritische Beiträge zur Geschichte der florentinischen Kircheneinigung, 1862. The full story of the Councils of Constance, Basil, Ferrara, and Florence is contained in vol. vii., parts i. and ii., of Hefele's Conciliengeschichte.]

of a musical and prolific language, that gives a soul to the objects of sense and a body to the abstractions of philosophy. Since the barriers of the monarchy, and even of the capital, had been trampled under foot, the various barbarians had doubtless corrupted the form and substance of the national dialect; and ample glossaries have been composed, to interpret a multitude of words of Arabic, Turkish, Sclavonian, Latin, or French origin.[80] But a purer idiom was spoken in the court and taught in the college; and the flourishing state of the language is described, and perhaps embellished, by a learned Italian,[81] who, by a long residence and noble marriage,[82] was naturalised at Constantinople about thirty years before the Turkish conquest. "The vulgar speech," says Philelphus,[83] "has been depraved by the people, and infected by the multitude of strangers and merchants, who every day

[80] In the first attempt, Meursius collected 3600 Græco-barbarous words, to which in a second edition, he subjoined 1800 more; yet what plenteous gleanings did he leave to Portius, Ducange, Fabrotti, the Bollandists, &c! (Fabric. Bibliot. Græc. tom. x. p. 101, &c.). *Some* Persic words may be found in Xenophon, and some Latin ones in Plutarch; and such is the inevitable effect of war and commerce; but the form and substance of the language were not affected by this slight alloy. [On foreign words in Greek see: G. Meyer, Neugriechische Studien, ii. (Slavonic, Albanian, and Roumanian loanwords in modern Greek), iii. and iv. (Latin and Romance loanwords), in the Sitzungsberichte of the Vienna Academy, vol. cxxx., 1894, and vol. cxxxii., 1895; K. Dieterich, Zu den lateinisch-romanischen Lehnwörtern im Neugriechischen, in Byzantinische Zeitschift, x. 587 *sqq.* and xi. 506 *sqq.* Also F. Miklosich, Die slavischen Elemente im Neugriechischen, *ib.*, vol. lxiii., 1870; and Die türkischen Elemente in den südosteuropäischen Sprachen, in the Denkschriften of the Vienna Acad., vols. xxxiv., xxxv., xxxviii. (1884, 1886, 1890). D. C. Hesseling, Zu den germanischen Elementen des Neugriechischen, in Byzantinische Zeitschrift, xii. 595 *sqq.*]

[81] The life of Francis Philelphus, a sophist, proud, restless, and rapacious, has been diligently composed by Lancelot (Mémoires de l'Académie des Inscriptions, tom. x. p. 691-751), and Tiraboschi (Istoria della Letteratura Italiana, tom. vii. p. 282-294), for the most part from his own letters. His elaborate writings, and those of his contemporaries, are forgotten; but their familiar epistles still describe the men and the times. [G. Voigt, Die Wiederbelebung des klassischen Alterthums, 3rd ed., 1893; T. Klette, Beiträge zur Geschichte und Litteratur der italienischen Gelehrtenrenaissance, 1890 (part iii. contains Greek Letters of Philelphus). Legrand, Centdix lettres grecques de François Filelfe, 1892.]

[82] He married, and had perhaps debauched, the daughter of John, and the grand-daughter of Manuel, Chrysoloras. She was young, beautiful, and wealthy; and her noble family was allied to the Dorias of Genoa and the emperors of Constantinople.

[83] Græci quibus lingua depravata non sit . . . ita loquuntur vulgo hâc etiam tempestate ut Aristophanes comicus, aut Euripides tragicus, ut oratores omnes, ut historiographi, ut philosophi . . . literati autem homines et doctius et emendatius . . . Nam viri aulici veterem sermonis dignitatem atque elegantiam retinebant in primisque ipsæ nobiles mulieres; quibus cum nullum esset omnino cum viris peregrinis commercium, merus ille ac purus Græcorum sermo servabatur intactus (Philelph. Epist. ad ann. 1451, apud Hodium, p. 188, 189). He observes in another passage, uxor illa mea Theodora locutione erat admodum moderatâ et suavi et maxime Atticâ.

flock to the city and mingle with the inhabitants. It is from the
disciples of such a school that the Latin language received the
versions of Aristotle and Plato, so obscure in sense, and in
spirit so poor. But the Greeks who have escaped the contagion
are those whom *we* follow; and they alone are worthy of our
imitation. In familiar discourse, they still speak the tongue of
Aristophanes and Euripides, of the historians and philosophers
of Athens; and the style of their writings is still more elaborate
and correct. The persons who, by their birth and offices, are
attached to the Byzantine court are those who maintain, with
the least alloy, the ancient standard of elegance and purity;
and the native graces of language most conspicuously shine
among the noble matrons, who are excluded from all intercourse with foreigners. With foreigners do I say? They live
retired and sequestered from the eyes of their fellow-citizens.
Seldom are they seen in the streets; and, when they leave their
houses, it is in the dusk of evening, on visits to the churches and
their nearest kindred. On these occasions, they are on horseback, covered with a veil, and encompassed by their parents,
their husbands, or their servants." [84]

Among the Greeks, a numerous and opulent clergy was
dedicated to the service of religion; their monks and bishops
have ever been distinguished by the gravity and austerity of
their manners; nor were they diverted, like the Latin priests,
by the pursuits and pleasures of a secular or even military life.
After a large deduction for the time and talents that were lost
in the devotion, the laziness, and the discord of the church and
cloister, the more inquisitive and ambitious minds would explore
the sacred and profane erudition of their native language. The
ecclesiastics presided over the education of youth; the schools
of philosophy and eloquence were perpetuated till the fall of
the empire; and it may be affirmed that more books and more
knowledge were included within the walls of Constantinople
than could be dispersed over the extensive countries of the
West. [85] But an important distinction has been already noticed: Compari-
the Greeks were stationary or retrograde, while the Latins were son of the
Greeks and
Latins

[84] Philelphus, absurdly enough, derives this Greek or Oriental jealousy from
the manners of ancient Rome.
[85] See the state of learning in the xiiith and xivth centuries, in the learned and
judicious Mosheim (Institut. Hist. Eccles. p. 434-440, 490-494).

advancing with a rapid and progressive motion. The nations were excited by the spirit of independence and emulation ; and even the little world of the Italian states contained more people and industry than the decreasing circle of the Byzantine empire. In Europe, the lower ranks of society were relieved from the yoke of feudal servitude ; and freedom is the first step to curiosity and knowledge. The use, however rude and corrupt, of the Latin tongue had been preserved by superstition ; the universities, from Bologna to Oxford,[86] were peopled with thousands of scholars ; and their misguided ardour might be directed to more liberal and manly studies. In the resurrection of science, Italy was the first that cast away her shroud ; and the eloquent Petrarch, by his lessons and his example, may justly be applauded as the first harbinger of day. A purer style of composition, a more generous and rational strain of sentiment, flowed from the study and imitation of the writers of ancient Rome ; and the disciples of Cicero and Virgil approached, with reverence and love, the sanctuary of their Grecian masters. In the sack of Constantinople, the French, and even the Venetians, had despised and destroyed the works of Lysippus and Homer ; the monuments of art may be annihilated by a single blow ; but the immortal mind is renewed and multiplied by the copies of the pen ; and such copies it was the ambition of Petrarch and his friends to possess and understand. The arms of the Turks undoubtedly pressed the flight of the Muses ; yet we may tremble at the thought that Greece might have been overwhelmed, with her schools and libraries, before Europe had emerged from the deluge of barbarism ; that the seeds of science might have been scattered by the winds, before the Italian soil was prepared for their cultivation.

The most learned Italians of the fifteenth century have con-

[86] At the end of the xvth century, there existed in Europe about fifty universities, and of these the foundation of ten or twelve is prior to the year 1300. They were crowded in proportion to their scarcity. Bologna contained 10,000 students, chiefly of the civil law. In the year 1357, the number at Oxford had decreased from 30,000 to 6000 scholars (Henry's History of Great Britain, vol. iv. p. 478). Yet even this decrease is much superior to the present list of the members of the university. [These numbers are grossly exaggerated. See H. Rashdall, Universities of Europe in the Middle Ages, vol. ii., pt. ii., where a short chapter (xiii.) is devoted to the subject. He concludes (p. 589) that " the maximum number at Oxford was something between 1500 and 3000. By about 1438 the numbers had fallen to under 1000." He thinks it improbable that the number at Bologna or at Paris ever went beyond about 6000 or 7000.]

fessed and applauded the restoration of Greek literature, after Revival of the Greek learning in Italy a long oblivion of many hundreds years.[87] Yet in that country, and beyond the Alps, some names are quoted : some profound scholars, who, in the darker ages, were honourably distinguished by their knowledge of the Greek tongue ; and national vanity has been loud in the praise of such rare examples of erudition. Without scrutinising the merit of individuals, truth must observe that their science is without a cause and without an effect ; that it was easy for them to satisfy themselves and their more ignorant contemporaries ; and that the idiom, which they had so marvellously acquired, was transcribed in few manuscripts, and was not taught in any university of the West. In a corner of Italy it faintly existed as the popular, or at least as the ecclesiastical, dialect.[88] The first impression of the Doric and Ionic colonies has never been completely erased ; the Calabrian churches were long attached to the throne of Constantinople ; and the monks of St. Basil pursued their studies in Mount Athos and the schools of the East. Calabria was the native country of Barlaam, who has already appeared as a sectary and an ambassador ; and Barlaam was the first who revived, beyond the Alps, the memory, or at least the writings, of Homer.[89] Lessons of Barlaam, A.D. 1339

[87] Of those writers, who professedly treat of the restoration of the Greek learning in Italy, the two principal are Hodius, Dr. Humphrey Hody (de Græcis Illustribus, Linguæ Græcæ Literarumque humaniorum Instauratoribus ; Londini, 1742, in large octavo), and Tiraboschi (Istoria della Letteratura Italiana, tom. v. p. 364-377, tom. vii. p. 112-143). The Oxford professor is a laborious scholar, but the librarian of Modena enjoys the superiority of a modern and national historian. [Cp. above, note 81. Legrand, Biographie hellénique, vol. i., 1885. J. A. Symonds, The Renaissance in Italy, ii., The Revival of Learning, 1877. Therianos, in the first volume of his biography of Koraês (Ἀδαμάντιος Κοραῆς, 1889), gives a good summary of the movement. G. Fioretto, Gli umanisti, o lo studio del Latino e del Greco nel secolo xv. in Italia, 1881. R. C. Jebb, The Classical Renaissance, cap. xvi., in the Cambridge Modern History, vol. i., 1902. See also the excellent monograph on Vittorino da Feltre, dealing with the education of the Humanist teachers in Italy, by W. H. Woodward, 1897.]

[88] In Calabriâ quæ olim magna Græcia dicebatur, coloniis Græcis repletâ, remansit quædam linguæ veteris cognitio (Hodius, p. 2). If it were eradicated by the Romans, it was revived and perpetuated by the monks of St. Basil, who possessed seven convents at Rossano alone (Giannone, Istoria di Napoli, tom. i. p. 520). [Greek is still spoken by a population of about 20,000 in both the heel and the toe of Italy—in the land of Otranto and in the territory of Bova ; these two dialects differ considerably. Comparetti, Saggi dei dialetti greci dell' Italia meridionale, 1866 ; Morosi, Studi sui dialetti greci della Terra d'Otranto, 1870, and Dialetti romaici del mandamento di Bova in Calabria, 1874 ; Pellegrini, Il dialetto greco-calabro di Bova, 1880 ; H. F. Tozer, The Greek-speaking Population of Southern Italy, in Journal of Hellenic Studies, x. p. 11 sqq.]

[89] Ii Barbari (says Petrarch, the French and Germans) vix non dicam libros sed nomen Homeri audiverunt. Perhaps, in that respect, the xiiith century was less

He is described, by Petrarch and Boccace,[90] as a man of a
diminutive stature, though truly great in the measure of learning and genius ; of a piercing discernment, though of a slow
and painful elocution. For many ages (as they affirm) Greece
had not produced his equal in the knowledge of history, grammar,
and philosophy ; and his merit was celebrated in the attestations of the princes and doctors of Constantinople. One of
these attestations is still extant ; and the emperor Cantacuzene,
the protector of his adversaries, is forced to allow that Euclid,
Aristotle, and Plato were familiar to that profound and subtle
logician.[91] In the court of Avignon, he formed an intimate
connexion with Petrarch,[92] the first of the Latin scholars ; and
the desire of mutual instruction was the principle of their

Studies of
Petrarch,
A.D. 1339-
1374

literary commerce. The Tuscan applied himself with eager
curiosity and assiduous diligence to the study of the Greek
language ; and, in a laborious struggle with the dryness and
difficulty of the first rudiments, he began to reach the sense,
and to feel the spirit, of poets and philosophers whose minds
were congenial to his own. But he was soon deprived of the
society and lessons of this useful assistant. Barlaam relinquished his fruitless embassy ; and, on his return to Greece,
he rashly provoked the swarms of fanatic monks by attempting
to substitute the light of reason to that of their navel. After
a separation of three years, the two friends again met in the
court of Naples ; but the generous pupil renounced the fairest
occasion of improvement ; and by his recommendation Barlaam
was finally settled in a small bishopric of his native Calabria.[93]
The manifold avocations of Petrarch, love and friendship, his

happy than the age of Charlemagne. [Barlaam was a native of Seminaria in
Calabria. His work (against the Roman church) περὶ τῆς ἀρχῆς τοῦ πάπα is published in Migne, P. G., 151, p. 1256 sqq. There is an account of Barlaam's work in
T. Uspenski's essay, Philosophskoe i bogoslovkoe dvizhenie v xiv viekie, printed in
his Ocherki, p. 246-364 (1892).]

[90] See the character of Barlaam in Boccace, de Genealog. Deorum, l. xv. c. 6.
[91] Cantacuzen. l. ii. c. 36.
[92] For the connexion of Petrarch and Barlaam, and the two interviews at
Avignon in 1339 and at Naples in 1342, see the excellent Mémoires sur la Vie de
Pétrarque, tom. i. p. 406-410, tom. ii. p. 75-77. [G. Mandolori, Fra Barlaamo
Calabrese, maestro del Petrarca, 1888 ; P. de Nolhac, Pétrarque et l'humanisme,
1892 (new ed. 1907). On Petrarch see further below, chap. lxx. ad init.]

[93] The bishopric to which Barlaam retired was the old Locri, in the middle ages
Scta Cyriaca, and by corruption Hieracium, Gerace (Dissert. Chorographica Italiæ
medii Ævi, p. 312). The dives opum of the Norman times soon lapsed into poverty,
since even the church was poor : yet the town still contains 3000 inhabitants (Swinburne, p. 340).

various correspondence and frequent journeys, the Roman
laurel, and his elaborate compositions in prose and verse, in
Latin and Italian, diverted him from a foreign idiom ; and, as
he advanced in life, the attainment of the Greek language was
the object of his wishes rather than of his hopes.   When he
was about fifty years of age, a Byzantine ambassador, his friend,
and a master of both tongues, presented him with a copy of
Homer ; and the answer of Petrarch is at once expressive of
his eloquence, gratitude, and regret.   After celebrating the
generosity of the donor, and the value of a gift more precious
in his estimation than gold or rubies, he thus proceeds : " Your
present of the genuine and original text of the divine poet, the
fountain of all invention, is worthy of yourself and of me ; you
have fulfilled your promise and satisfied my desires.   Yet your
liberality is still imperfect : with Homer you should have given
me yourself : a guide, who could lead me into the fields of light,
and disclose to my wondering eyes the specious miracles of the
Iliad and Odyssey.   But, alas ! Homer is dumb, or I am deaf ;
nor is it in my power to enjoy the beauty which I possess.   I
have seated him by the side of Plato, the prince of poets near
the prince of philosophers ; and I glory in the sight of my
illustrious guests.   Of their immortal writings, whatever had
been translated into the Latin idiom, I had already acquired ;
but, if there be no profit, there is some pleasure in beholding
these venerable Greeks in their proper and national habit.   I
am delighted with the aspect of Homer ; and, as often as I
embrace the silent volume, I exclaim, with a sigh, Illustrious
bard ! with what pleasure should I listen to thy song, if my
sense of hearing were not obstructed and lost by the death of
one friend, and in the much lamented absence of another !
Nor do I yet despair ; and the example of Cato suggests some
comfort and hope, since it was in the last period of age that he
attained the knowledge of the Greek letters." [94]

The prize which eluded the efforts of Petrarch was obtained Of Boccace,
by the fortune and industry of his friend Boccace,[95] the father A.D. 1360, &c.

[94] I will transcribe a passage from this epistle of Petrarch (Famil. ix. 2) : Donasti
Homerum non in alienum sermonem violento alveo derivatum, sed ex ipsis Græci
eloquii scatebris, et qualis divino illi profluxit ingenio. . . . Sine tuâ voce Homerus
tuus apud me mutus, immo, vero ego apud illum surdus sum. Gaudeo tamen vel
adspectu solo, ac sæpe illum amplexus atque suspirans dico, O magne vir ! &c.

[95] For the life and writings of Boccace, who was born in 1313, and died in 1375,
Fabricius (Bibliot. Latin. medii Ævi, tom. i. p. 248, &c.) and Tiraboschi (tom. v.

of the Tuscan prose.   That popular writer, who derives his reputation from the Decameron, an hundred novels of pleasantry
and love, may aspire to the more serious praise of restoring in
Italy the study of the Greek language.   In the year one thousand three hundred and sixty, a disciple of Barlaam, whose
name was Leo or Leontius Pilatus, was detained in his way to
Avignon by the advice and hospitality of Boccace, who lodged
the stranger in his house, prevailed on the republic of Florence
to allow him an annual stipend, and devoted his leisure to the
first Greek professor who taught the language in the Western

Leo Pilatus countries of Europe.   The appearance of Leo might disgust the
first Greek
professor most eager disciple : he was clothed in the mantle of a philo-
at Flor-
ence, and sopher, or a mendicant; his countenance was hideous ; his face
in the
West, A.D. was overshadowed with black hair ; his beard long and uncombed ;
1360-1363
his deportment rustic ; his temper gloomy and inconstant ; nor
could he grace his discourse with the ornaments or even the
perspicuity of Latin elocution.   But his mind was stored with
a treasure of Greek learning ; history and fable, philosophy and
grammar, were alike at his command ; and he read the poems
of Homer in the schools of Florence.   It was from his explanation that Boccace composed and transcribed a literal prose
version of the Iliad and Odyssey, which satisfied the thirst
of his friend Petrarch, and which perhaps, in the succeeding
century, was clandestinely used by Laurentius Valla, the Latin
interpreter.   It was from his narratives that the same Boccace
collected the materials for his treatise on the genealogy of the
heathen gods : a work, in that age, of stupendous erudition,
and which he ostentatiously sprinkled with Greek characters and
passages, to excite the wonder and applause of his more ignorant
readers.[96]   The first steps of learning are slow and laborious :
no more than ten votaries of Homer could be enumerated in
all Italy ; and neither Rome nor Venice nor Naples could add
a single name to this studious catalogue.   But their numbers

p. 83, 439-451) may be consulted.   The editions, versions, imitations of his novels
are innumerable.   Yet he was ashamed to communicate that trifling and perhaps
scandalous work to Petrarch his respectable friend, in whose letters and memoirs he
conspicuously appears.
    [96] Boccace indulges an honest vanity : Ostentationis causâ Græca carmina adscripsi
. . . jure utor meo ; meum est hoc decus, mea gloria scilicet inter Etruscos Græcis
uti carminibus.   Nonne ego fui qui Leontium Pilatum, &c. (de Genealogiâ Deorum,
l. xv. c. 7, a work, which, though now forgotten, has run through thirteen or fourteen
editions).   [It was Leontius Pilatus himself who translated Homer.]

would have multiplied, their progress would have been accelerated, if the inconstant Leo, at the end of three years, had
not relinquished an honourable and beneficial station. In his
passage, Petrarch entertained him at Padua a short time: he
enjoyed the scholar, but was justly offended with the gloomy
and unsocial temper of the man. Discontented with the world
and with himself, Leo depreciated his present enjoyments, while
absent persons and objects were dear to his imagination. In
Italy, he was a Thessalian; in Greece, a native of Calabria; in
the company of the Latins, he disdained their language, religion, and manner: no sooner was he landed at Constantinople,
than he again sighed for the wealth of Venice and the elegance
of Florence. His Italian friends were deaf to his importunity;
he depended on their curiosity and indulgence, and embarked
on a second voyage; but, on his entrance into the Adriatic, the
ship was assailed by a tempest, and the unfortunate teacher,
who, like Ulysses, had fastened himself to the mast, was struck
dead by a flash of lightning. The humane Petrarch dropped a
tear on his disaster; but he was most anxious to learn whether
some copy of Euripides or Sophocles might not be saved from
the hands of the mariners.[97]

But the faint rudiments of Greek learning, which Petrarch _{Founda-}
had encouraged and Boccace had planted, soon withered and Greek lan-
expired. The succeeding generation was content for a while Italy by
with the improvement of Latin eloquence; nor was it before Chrysolo-
the end of the fourteenth century that a new and perpetual 1390-1415
flame was rekindled in Italy.[98] Previous to his own journey,
the emperor Manuel dispatched his envoys and orators to im-
plore the compassion of the Western princes. Of these envoys,
the most conspicuous or the most learned was Manuel Chrysoloras,[99] of noble birth, and whose Roman ancestors are supposed

[97] Leontius, or Leo Pilatus, is sufficiently made known by Hody (p. 2-11), and the
Abbé de Sade (Vie de Pétrarque, tom. iii. p. 625-634, 670-673), who has very happily
caught the lively and dramatic manner of his original.
[98] Dr. Hody (p. 54) is angry with Leonard Aretin, Guarinus, Paulus Jovius, &c.,
for affirming that the Greek letters were restored in Italy *post septingentos annos;*
as if, says he, they had flourished till the end of the viith century. These writers
most probably reckoned from the last period of the exarchate; and the presence of the
Greek magistrates and troops at Ravenna and Rome must have preserved, in some
degree, the use of their native tongue.
[99] See the article of Emmanuel, or Manuel Chrysoloras, in Hody (p. 12-54), and
Tiraboschi (tom. vii. p. 113-118). The precise date of his arrival floats between the
years 1390 and 1400, and is only confined by the reign of Boniface IX. [The Greek

to have migrated with the great Constantine. After visiting the courts of France and England, where he obtained some contributions and more promises, the envoy was invited to assume the office of a professor ; and Florence had again the honour of this second invitation. By his knowledge, not only of the Greek but of the Latin tongue, Chrysoloras deserved the stipend and surpassed the expectation of the republic; his school was frequented by a crowd of disciples of every rank and age ; and one of these, in a general history, has described his motives and his success. " At that time," says Leonard Aretin,[100] " I was a student of the civil law ; but my soul was inflamed with the love of letters ; and I bestowed some application on the sciences of logic and rhetoric. On the arrival of Manuel, I hesitated whether I should desert my legal studies or relinquish this golden opportunity; and thus, in the ardour of youth, I communed with my own mind—Wilt thou be wanting to thyself and thy fortune ? Wilt thou refuse to be introduced to a familiar converse with Homer, Plato, and Demosthenes ? with those poets, philosophers, and orators, of whom such wonders are related, and who are celebrated by every age as the great masters of human science ? Of professors and scholars in civil law, a sufficient supply will always be found in our universities ; but a teacher, and such a teacher, of the Greek language, if he once be suffered to escape, may never afterwards be retrieved. Convinced by these reasons, I gave myself to Chrysoloras ; and so strong was my passion that the lessons which I had imbibed in the day were the constant subject of my nightly dreams." [101] At the same time and place the Latin classics were explained by John of Ravenna, the domestic pupil of Petrarch ; [102] the Italians, who illustrated their age and country, were formed in

[c. A.D. 1397-1400]

Grammar of Chrysoloras was printed in Venice in 1484. For the chronology of his life cp. Klette, *op. cit.* part i.]

[100] The name of *Aretinus* has been assumed by five or six natives of *Arezzo* in Tuscany, of whom the most famous and the most worthless lived in the xvith century. Leonardus Brunus Aretinus, the disciple of Chrysoloras, was a linguist, an orator, and an historian, the secretary of four successive popes, and the chancellor of the republic of Florence, where he died, A.D. 1444, at the age of seventy-five (Fabric. Bibliot. medii Ævi, tom. i. p. 190, &c. ; Tiraboschi, tom. vii. p. 33-38).

[101] See the passage in Aretin. Commentario Rerum suo Tempore in Italiâ gestarum, apud Hodium, p. 28-30.

[102] In this domestic discipline, Petrarch, who loved the youth, often complains of the eager curiosity, restless temper, and proud feelings, which announce the genius and glory of a riper age (Mémoires sur Pétrarque, tom. iii. p. 700-709).

this double school ; and Florence became the fruitful seminary
of Greek and Roman erudition.[103]   The presence of the emperor
recalled Chrysoloras from the college to the court, but he afterwards taught at Pavia and Rome with equal industry and ap- [At Pavia, c. A.D. 1402]
plause.   The remainder of his life, about fifteen years, was
divided between Italy and Constantinople, between embassies [In Con-
and lessons.   In the noble office of enlightening a foreign na- stanti-
tion, the grammarian was not unmindful of a more sacred duty nople, A.D. 1403]
to his prince and country ; and Emanuel Chrysoloras died at [A.D. 1415]
Constance, on a public mission from the emperor to the council.

After his example, the restoration of the Greek letters in The Greeks
Italy was prosecuted by a series of emigrants, who were desti- in Italy, A.D. 1400-
tute of fortune, and endowed with learning, or at least with 1500
language.   From the terror or oppression of the Turkish arms
the natives of Thessalonica and Constantinople escaped to a
land of freedom, curiosity, and wealth.   The synod introduced
into Florence the lights of the Greek church and the oracles
of the Platonic philosophy; and the fugitives who adhered to
the union had the double merit of renouncing their country
not only for the Christian but for the Catholic cause.   A patriot
who sacrifices his party and conscience to the allurements of
favour may be possessed, however, of the private and social
virtues; he no longer hears the reproachful epithets of slave
and apostate ; and the consideration which he acquires among
his new associates will restore in his own eyes the dignity of
his character.   The prudent conformity of Bessarion was re- Cardinal
warded with the Roman purple ; he fixed his residence in Italy ; &c.
and the Greek cardinal, the titular patriarch of Constantinople,
was respected as the chief and protector of his nation.[104]   His
abilities were exercised in the legations of Bologna, Venice,

[103] Hinc Græcae Latinæque scholæ exortæ sunt, Guarino Philelpho, Leonardo
Aretino, Caroloque, ac plerisque aliis tanquam ex equo Trojano prodeuntibus,
quorum emulatione multa ingenia deinceps ad laudem excitata sunt (Platina in
Bonifacio IX.).   Another Italian writer adds the names of Paulus Petrus Vergerius,
Omnibonus [Ognibene da Lonigo], Vincentius, Poggius, Franciscus Barbarus, &c.
But I question whether a rigid chronology would allow Chrysoloras *all* these
eminent scholars (Hodius, p. 25-27, &c.).   [Vergerius (who *was* one of his pupils)
wrote the epitaph on Chrysoloras which is to be seen in the kitchen of the Hôtel
Insel at Constance.]

[104] See in Hody the article of Bessarion (p. 136-177).   Theodora Gaza [of
Thessalonica], George of Trebizond, and the rest of the Greeks whom I have
named or omitted, are inserted in their proper chapters of his learned work.   See
likewise Tiraboschi, in the 1st and 2d parts of the vith tome.   [See Legrand's
work quoted above, note 87.]

Germany, and France; and his election to the chair of St. Peter floated for a moment on the uncertain breath of a conclave.[105] His ecclesiastical honours diffused a splendour and pre-eminence over his literary merit and service: his palace was a school; as often as the cardinal visited the Vatican, he was attended by a learned train of both nations;[106] of men applauded by themselves and the public; and whose writings, now overspread with dust, were popular and useful in their own times. I shall not attempt to enumerate the restorers of Grecian literature in the fifteenth century; and it may be sufficient to mention with gratitude the names of Theodore Gaza, of George of Trebizond, of John Argyropulus, and Demetrius Chalcondyles, who taught their native language in the schools of Florence and Rome. Their labours were not inferior to those of Bessarion, whose purple they revered, and whose fortune was the secret object of their envy. But the lives of these grammarians were humble and obscure; they had declined the lucrative paths of the church; their dress and manners secluded them from the commerce of the world; and, since they were confined to the merit, they might be content with the rewards, of learning. From this character Janus Lascaris[107] will deserve an exception. His eloquence, politeness, and Imperial descent recommended him to the French monarchs; and in the same cities he was alternately employed to teach and to negotiate. Duty and interest prompted them to cultivate the study of the Latin language; and the most successful attained the faculty of writing and speaking with fluency and elegance in a foreign idiom. But they ever retained the inveterate vanity of their country: their praise, or at least their esteem, was reserved for the national writers, to whom they owed their fame and subsist-

Their faults and merits

---

[105] The cardinals knocked at his door, but his conclavist refused to interrupt the studies of Bessarion: "Nicholas," said he, "thy respect hath cost thee an hat, and me the tiara ".

[106] Such as George of Trebizond, Theodore Gaza, Argyropulus, Andronicus of Thessalonica, Philelphus, Poggius, Blondus, Nicholas Perrot, Valla, Campanus, Platina, &c. Viri (says Hody, with the pious zeal of a scholar) nullo ævo perituri (p. 156).

[107] He was born before the taking of Constantinople, but his honourable life was stretched far into the xvith century (A.D. 1535). Leo X. and Francis I. were his noblest patrons, under whose auspices he founded the Greek colleges of Rome and Paris (Hody, p. 247-275). He left posterity in France; but the counts de Vintimille, and their numerous branches, derive the name of Lascaris from a doubtful marriage, in the xiiith century, with the daughter of a Greek emperor (Ducange, Fam. Byzant. p. 224-230).

ence; and they sometimes betrayed their contempt in licentious criticism or satire on Virgil's poetry and the oratory of Tully.[108] The superiority of these masters arose from the familiar use of a living language; and their first disciples were incapable of discerning how far they had degenerated from the knowledge, and even the practice, of their ancestors. A vicious pronunciation,[109] which they introduced, was banished from the schools by the reason of the succeeding age. Of the power of the Greek accents they were ignorant; and those musical notes, which, from an Attic tongue and to an Attic ear, must have been the secret soul of harmony, were to their eyes, as to our own, no more than mute or unmeaning marks, in prose superfluous and troublesome in verse.[109a] The art of grammar they truly possessed; the valuable fragments of Apollonius and Herodian were transfused into their lessons; and their treatises of syntax and etymology, though devoid of philosophic spirit, are still useful to the Greek student. In the shipwreck of the Byzantine libraries, each fugitive seized a fragment of treasure, a copy of some author, who without his industry, might have perished; the transcripts were multiplied by an assiduous, and sometimes an elegant, pen; and the text was corrected and explained by their own comments or those of the elder scholiasts. The sense, though not the spirit, of the Greek classics was interpreted to

---

[108] Two of his epigrams against Virgil, and three against Tully, are preserved and refuted by Franciscus Floridus, who can find no better names than Græculus ineptus et impudens (Hody, p. 274). In our own times, an English critic has accused the Æneid of containing multa languida, nugatoria, spiritu et majestate carminis heroici defecta: many such verses as he, the said Jeremiah Markland, would have been ashamed of owning (præfat. ad Statii Sylvas, p. 21, 22).

[109] Emanuel Chrysoloras, and his colleagues, are accused of ignorance, envy, or avarice (Sylloge, &c. tom. ii. p. 235). The modern Greek [Greeks ?] pronounce the β as a V consonant, and confound three vowels (η ι υ) and several diphthongs [$\epsilon\iota$, $o\iota$, $\upsilon\iota$]. Such was the vulgar pronunciation which the stern Gardiner maintained by penal statutes in the University of Cambridge; but the monosyllable $\beta\eta$ represented to an Attic ear the bleating of sheep; and a bell-wether is better evidence than a bishop or a chancellor. The treatises of those scholars, particularly Erasmus, who asserted a more classical pronunciation, are collected in the Sylloge of Havercamp (2 vols. in octavo, Lugd. Bat. 1736, 1740); but it is difficult to paint sounds by words; and in their reference to modern use they can be understood only by their respective countrymen. We may observe that our peculiar pronunciation of the θ, *th*, is approved by Erasmus (tom. ii. p. 130) [θ is so pronounced in modern Greek].

[109a] [It is to be observed however that the system of accent-notation was first introduced by the Alexandrines. Gibbon assumes that the meaning of the accents was in ancient times entirely different from their meaning in modern Greek. This is improbable. But it is still a problem how the Greeks conciliated their accentuation with the rhythms of their verses.]

the Latin world; the beauties of style evaporate in a version; but the judgment of Theodore Gaza selected the more solid works of Aristotle and Theophrastus, and their natural histories of animals and plants opened a rich fund of genuine and experimental science.[110]

The Platonic philosophy Yet the fleeting shadows of metaphysics were pursued with more curiosity and ardour.   After a long oblivion, Plato was revived in Italy by a venerable Greek,[111] who taught in the [Cosimo de' Medici] house of Cosmo of Medicis.   While the synod of Florence was involved in theological debate, some beneficial consequences might flow from the study of his elegant philosophy; his style is the purest standard of the Attic dialect; and his sublime thoughts are sometimes adapted to familiar conversation, and sometimes adorned with the richest colours of poetry and eloquence.   The dialogues of Plato are a dramatic picture of the life and death of a sage; and, as often as he descends from the clouds, his moral system inculcates the love of truth, of our country, and of mankind.   The precept and example of Socrates recommended a modest doubt and liberal inquiry; and, if the Platonists, with blind devotion, adored the visions and errors of their divine master, their enthusiasm might correct the dry dogmatic method of the Peripatetic school.   So equal, yet so opposite, are the merits of Plato and Aristotle that they may be balanced in endless controversy; but some spark of freedom may be produced by the collision of adverse servitude.   The modern Greeks were divided between the two sects; with more fury than skill they fought under the banner of their leaders; and the field of battle was removed in their flight from Constantinople to Rome.   But this philosophic debate

[110] [On Theodore Gaza see the biographical essay of L. Stein in the Archiv für Geschichte der Philosophie, ii. p. 426 *sqq.*, 1889.]

[111] George Gemistus Pletho, a various and voluminous writer, the master of Bessarion and all the Platonists of the times.   He visited Italy in his old age, and soon returned to end his days in Peloponnesus.   See the curious Diatribe of Leo Allatius de Georgiis, in Fabricius (Bibliot. Græc. tom. x. p. 739-756).   [The study of Plato was revived in the 11th century by Michael Psellus.   For Plethon see H. F. Tozer, A Byzantine Reformer, in the Journal of Hellenic Studies, vii. p. 353 *sqq.*, 1886; and F. Schultze, Geschichte der Philosophie der Renaissance, vol. i., 1874. The Memoir on the state of the Peloponnesus, which he addressed to the emperor Manuel, is edited by Ellissen in his Analekten der mittel- und neugriechischen Litteratur, vol. iv., part ii., with a German translation.   Plethon's works are collected in Migne's P. G. vol. clx.   On the theological side of his works see W. Gass, Gennadius und Pletho, Aristotelismus und Platonismus in der griechischen Kirche, 1844.]

soon degenerated into an angry and personal quarrel of grammarians; and Bessarion, though an advocate for Plato, protected the national honour, by interposing the advice and
authority of a mediator. In the gardens of the Medici, the
academical doctrine was enjoyed by the polite and learned;
but their philosophic society was quickly dissolved; and, if the
writings of the Attic sage were perused in the closet, the more
powerful Stagirite continued to reign the oracle of the church
and school.[112]

I have fairly represented the literary merits of the Greeks;
yet it must be confessed that they were seconded and surpassed
by the ardour of the Latins. Italy was divided into many independent states; and at that time it was the ambition of princes
and republics to vie with each other in the encouragement and
reward of literature. The fame of Nicholas the Fifth[113] has
not been adequate to his merits. From a plebeian origin he
raised himself by his virtue and learning: the character of the
man prevailed over the interest of the pope; and he sharpened
those weapons which were soon pointed against the Roman
church.[114] He had been the friend of the most eminent
scholars of the age; he became their patron; and such was the
humility of his manners that the change was scarcely discernible
either to them or to himself. If he pressed the acceptance of a
liberal gift, it was not as the measure of desert, but as the proof
of benevolence; and, when modest merit declined his bounty,
"Accept it," would he say with a consciousness of his own
worth; "you will not always have a Nicholas among ye". The
influence of the holy see pervaded Christendom; and he exerted
that influence in the search, not of benefices, but of books.
From the ruins of the Byzantine libraries, from the darkest
monasteries of Germany and Britain, he collected the dusty
manuscripts of the writers of antiquity; and, wherever the

Emulation and progress of the Latins

Nicholas V. A.D. 1447-1455

---

[112] The state of the Platonic philosophy in Italy is illustrated by Boivin (Mém.
de l'Acad. des Inscriptions, tom. ii. p. 715-729) and Tiraboschi (tom. vi. p. i. p.
259-288).

[113] See the life of Nicholas V. by two contemporary authors, Janottus Manettus
(tom. iii. p. ii. p. 905-962), and Vespasian of Florence (tom. xxv. p. 267-290), in
the collection of Muratori; and consult Tiraboschi (tom. vi. p. i. p. 46-52, 109), and
Hody in the articles of Theodore Gaza, George of Trebizond, &c.

[114] Lord Bolingbroke observes, with truth and spirit, that the popes, in this instance,
were worse politicians than the muftis, and that the charm which had bound mankind
for so many ages was broken by the magicians themselves (Letters on the Study of
History, l. vi. p. 165, 166, octavo edition, 1779).

original could not be removed, a faithful copy was transcribed and transmitted for his use.　The Vatican, the old repository for bulls and legends, for superstition and forgery, was daily replenished with more precious furniture ; and such was the industry of Nicholas that in a reign of eight years he formed a library of five thousand volumes.　To his munificence the Latin world was indebted for the versions of Xenophon, Diodorus, Polybius, Thucydides, Herodotus, and Appian ; of Strabo's Geography, of the Iliad, of the most valuable works of Plato and Aristotle, of Ptolemy and Theophrastus, and of the fathers of the Greek church.　The example of the Roman pontiff was preceded or imitated by a Florentine merchant, who governed the republic without arms and without a title.　Cosmo of Medicis [115] was the father of a line of princes, whose name and age are almost synonymous with the restoration of learning ; his credit was ennobled into fame ; his riches were dedicated to the service of mankind ; he corresponded at once with Cairo and London ; and a cargo of Indian spices and Greek books was often imported in the same vessel.　The genius and education of his grandson Lorenzo rendered him, not only a patron, but a judge and candidate, in the literary race.　In his palace, distress was entitled to relief, and merit to reward ; his leisure hours were delightfully spent in the Platonic academy ; he encouraged the emulation of Demetrius Chalcondyles and Angelo Politian ; and his active missionary, Janus Lascaris, returned from the East with a treasure of two hundred manuscripts, fourscore of which were as yet unknown in the libraries of Europe.[116]　The rest of Italy was animated by a similar spirit, and the progress of the nation repaid the liberality of her princes.　The Latins held the exclusive property of their own literature ; and these disciples of Greece were soon capable of transmitting and improving the lessons which they had imbibed.　After a short succession

Margin note: Cosmo and Lorenzo of Medicis, A.D. 1428-1492

[115] See the literary history of Cosmo and Lorenzo of Medicis, in Tiraboschi (tom. vi. p. i. l. i. c. 2), who bestows a due measure of praise on Alphonso of Arragon, king of Naples, the dukes of Milan, Ferrara, Urbino, &c.　The republic of Venice has deserved the least from the gratitude of scholars.

[116] Tiraboschi (tom. vi. p. i. p. 104), from the preface of Janus Lascaris to the Greek Anthology, printed at Florence, 1494.　Latebant (says Aldus in his preface to the Greek Orators, apud Hodium, p. 249) in Atho Thraciæ monte.　Eas Lascaris . . . in Italiam reportavit.　Miserat enim ipsum Laurentius ille Medices in Græciam ad inquirendos simul et quantovis emendos pretio bonos libros.　It is remarkable enough that the research was facilitated by sultan Bajazet II.

of foreign teachers, the tide of emigration subsided ; but the language of Constantinople was spread beyond the Alps ; and the natives of France, Germany, and England [117] imparted to their country the sacred fire which they had kindled in the schools of Florence and Rome.[118] In the productions of the mind, as in those of the soil, the gifts of nature are excelled by industry and skill ; the Greek authors, forgotten on the banks of the Ilissus, have been illustrated on those of the Elbe and the Thames ; and Bessarion or Gaza might have envied the superior science of the barbarians : the accuracy of Budæus, the taste of Erasmus, the copiousness of Stephens, the erudition of Scaliger, the discernment of Reiske or of Bentley. On the side of the Latins, the discovery of printing was a casual advantage ; but this useful art has been applied by Aldus, and his innumerable successors, to perpetuate and multiply the works of antiquity.[119] A single manuscript imported from Greece is revived in ten thousand copies ; and each copy is fairer than the original. In this form, Homer and Plato would peruse with more satisfaction their own writings ; and their scholiasts must resign the prize to the labours of our western editors.

Before the revival of classic literature, the barbarians in Europe were immersed in ignorance ; and their vulgar tongues were marked with the rudeness and poverty of their manners. The students of the more perfect idioms of Rome and Greece were introduced to a new world of light and science ; to the society of the free and polished nations of antiquity ; and to

Use and abuse of ancient learning

---

[117] The Greek language was introduced into the University of Oxford in the last years of the xvth century, by Grocyn, Linacer, and Latimer, who had all studied at Florence under Demetrius Chalcondyles. See Dr. Knight's curious Life of Erasmus. Although a stout academical patriot, he is forced to acknowledge that Erasmus learned Greek at Oxford and taught it at Cambridge.

[118] The jealous Italians were desirous of keeping a monopoly of Greek learning. When Aldus was about to publish the Greek scholiasts on Sophocles and Euripides, Cave (say they), cave hoc facias, ne *Barbari* istis adjuti domi maneant, et pauciores in Italian ventitent (Dr. Knight, in his Life of Erasmus, p. 365, from Beatus Rhenanus).

[119] The press of Aldus Manutius, a Roman, was established at Venice about the year 1494. He printed above sixty considerable works of Greek literature, almost all for the first time ; several containing different treatises and authors, and of several authors two, three, or four editions (Fabric. Bibliot. Græc. tom. xiii. p. 605, &c.). Yet his glory must not tempt us to forget that the first Greek book, the Grammar of Constantine Lascaris, was printed at Milan in 1476 ; and that the Florence Homer of 1488 displays all the luxury of the typographical art. See the Annales Typographici of Mattaire and the Bibliographie Instructive of De Bure, a knowing bookseller of Paris. [A. F. Didot, Alde Manuce et l'hellénisme à Venise, 1875.]

a familiar converse with those immortal men who spoke the sublime language of eloquence and reason. Such an intercourse must tend to refine the taste, and to elevate the genius, of the moderns; and yet, from the first experiments, it might appear that the study of the ancients had given fetters, rather than wings, to the human mind. However laudable, the spirit of imitation is of a servile cast; and the first disciples of the Greeks and Romans were a colony of strangers in the midst of their age and country. The minute and laborious diligence which explored the antiquities of remote times might have improved or adorned the present state of society: the critic and metaphysician were the slaves of Aristotle ; the poets, historians, and orators were proud to repeat the thoughts and words of the Augustan age; the works of nature were observed with the eyes of Pliny and Theophrastus ; and some pagan votaries professed a secret devotion to the gods of Homer and Plato.[120]   The Italians were oppressed by the strength and number of their ancient auxiliaries: the century after the deaths of Petrarch and Boccace was filled with a crowd of Latin imitators, who decently repose on our shelves; but in that æra of learning it will not be easy to discern a real discovery of science, a work of invention or eloquence, in the popular language of the country.[121]   But, as soon as it had been deeply saturated with the celestial dew, the soil was quickened into vegetation and life; the modern idioms were refined ; the classics of Athens and Rome inspired a pure taste and a generous emulation ; and in Italy, as afterwards in France and England, the pleasing reign of poetry and fiction was succeeded by the light of speculative and experimental philosophy. Genius may anti-

[120] I will select three singular examples of this classic enthusiasm. 1. At the synod of Florence, Gemistus Pletho said in familiar conversation to George of Trebizond, that in a short time mankind would unanimously renounce the Gospel and the Koran for a religion similar to that of the Gentiles (Leo Allatius, apud Fabricium, tom. x. p. 751). 2. Paul II. persecuted the Roman academy which had been founded by Pomponius Lætus ; and the principal members were accused of heresy, impiety, and *paganism* (Tiraboschi, tom. vi. p. i. p. 81, 82). [Cp. Burckhardt, Die Cultur der Renaissance in Italien, ii. 252.] 3. In the next century, some scholars and poets in France celebrated the success of Jodelle's tragedy of Cleopatra by a sacrifice of Bacchus ; and, it is said, by the sacrifice of a goat (Bayle, Dictionnaire, JODELLE ; Fontenelle, tom. iii. p. 56-61). Yet the spirit of bigotry might often discern a serious impiety in the sportive play of fancy and learning.

[121] The survivor of Boccace died in the year 1375 ; and we cannot place before 1480 the composition of the Morgante Maggiore of Pulci, and the Orlando Inamorato of Boyardo (Tiraboschi, tom. vi. p. ii. p. 174-177).

cipate the season of maturity; but in the education of a people, as in that of an individual, memory must be exercised, before the powers of reason and fancy can be expanded; nor may the artist hope to equal or surpass, till he has learned to imitate, the works of his predecessors.

CHAPTER LXVII

Schism of the Greeks and Latins—Reign and Character of Amurath the Second—Crusade of Ladislaus, King of Hungary—His Defeat and Death—John Huniades—Scanderbeg—Constantine Palæologus, last Emperor of the East

Comparison of Rome and Constantinople

THE respective merits of Rome and Constantinople are compared and celebrated by an eloquent Greek, the father of the Italian schools.[1]   The view of the ancient capital, the seat of his ancestors, surpassed the most sanguine expectations of Emanuel Chrysoloras; and he no longer blamed the exclamation of an old sophist, that Rome was the habitation, not of men, but of gods.   Those gods and those men had long since vanished; but, to the eye of liberal enthusiasm, the majesty of ruin restored the image of her ancient prosperity.   The monuments of the consuls and Cæsars, of the martyrs and apostles, engaged on all sides the curiosity of the philosopher and the Christian; and he confessed that in every age the arms and religion of Rome were destined to reign over the earth.   While Chrysoloras admired the venerable beauties of the mother, he was not forgetful of his native country, her fairest daughter, her Imperial colony; and the Byzantine patriot expatiates with zeal and truth on the eternal advantages of nature and the more transitory glories of art and dominion, which adorned, or had adorned, the city of Constantine.   Yet the perfection of the copy still redounds (as he modestly observes) to the honour of the original; and parents are delighted to be renewed, and

[1] The epistle of Emanuel Chrysoloras to the emperor John Palæologus will not offend the eye or ear of a classical student (ad calcem Codini de Antiquitatibus C. P. p. 107-126). The superscription suggests a chronological remark that John Palæologus II. was associated in the empire before the year 1414, the date of Chrysoloras's death. A still earlier date, at least 1408, is deduced from the age of his youngest sons Demetrius and Thomas, who were both *Porphyrogeniti* (Ducange, Fam. Byzant. p. 244, 247).

LATE BYZANTINE ARCHITECTURE: CHURCH OF THE EVANGELISTRIA AT MISTRA

even excelled, by the superior merit of their children. "Constantinople," says the orator, "is situate on a commanding point, between Europe and Asia, between the Archipelago and the Euxine. By her interposition, the two seas and the two continents are united for the common benefit of nations; and the gates of commerce may be shut or opened at her command. The harbour, encompassed on all sides by the sea and the continent, is the most secure and capacious in the world. The walls and gates of Constantinople may be compared with those of Babylon; the towers are many; each tower is a solid and lofty structure; and the second wall, the outer fortification, would be sufficient for the defence and dignity of an ordinary capital. A broad and rapid stream may be introduced into the ditches; and the artificial island may be encompassed, like Athens,[2] by land or water." Two strong and natural causes are alleged for the perfection of the model of new Rome. The royal founder reigned over the most illustrious nations of the globe; and, in the accomplishment of his designs, the power of the Romans was combined with the art and science of the Greeks. Other cities have been reared to maturity by accident and time; their beauties are mingled with disorder and deformity; and the inhabitants, unwilling to remove from their natal spot, are incapable of correcting the errors of their ancestors and the original vices of situation or climate. But the free idea of Constantinople was formed and executed by a single mind; and the primitive model was improved by the obedient zeal of the subjects and successors of the first monarch. The adjacent isles were stored with an inexhaustible supply of marble; but the various materials were transported from the most remote shores of Europe and Asia; and the public and private buildings, the palaces, churches, aqueducts, cisterns, porticoes, columns, baths, and hippodromes, were adapted to the greatness of the capital of the East. The superfluity of wealth was spread along the shores of Europe and Asia; and the Byzantine territory, as far as the Euxine, the Hellespont, and the long wall, might be considered as a populous suburb and a perpetual garden. In this

---

[2] Somebody observed, that the city of Athens might be circumnavigated (τις εἶπεν τὴν πόλιν τῶν Ἀθηναίων δύνασθαι καὶ παραπλεῖν καὶ περιπλεῖν). But what may be true in a rhetorical sense of Constantinople cannot be applied to the situation of Athens, five miles from the sea, and not intersected or surrounded by any navigable streams.

flattering picture, the past and the present, the times of prosperity and decay, are artfully confounded; but a sigh and a
confession escape from the orator, that his wretched country
was the shadow and sepulchre of its former self.   The works
of ancient sculpture had been defaced by Christian zeal or
barbaric violence; the fairest structures were demolished; and
the marbles of Paros or Numidia were burnt for lime or applied to the meanest uses.   Of many a statue, the place was
marked by an empty pedestal; of many a column, the size was
determined by a broken capital; the tombs of the emperors
were scattered on the ground; the stroke of time was accelerated
by storms and earthquakes; and the vacant space was adorned,
by vulgar tradition, with fabulous monuments of gold and silver.
From these wonders, which lived only in memory or belief, he
distinguishes, however, the porphyry pillar, the column and colossus of Justinian,[3] and the church, more especially the dome, of
St. Sophia: the best conclusion, since it could not be described
according to its merits, and after it no other object could deserve to be mentioned.   But he forgets that a century before
the trembling fabrics of the colossus and the church had been
saved and supported by the timely care of Andronicus the
Elder.   Thirty years after the emperor had fortified St. Sophia
with two new buttresses, or pyramids, the eastern hemisphere
suddenly gave way; and the images, the altars, and the sanctuary were crushed by the falling ruin.   The mischief indeed
was speedily repaired; the rubbish was cleared by the incessant
labour of every rank and age; and the poor remains of riches
and industry were consecrated by the Greeks to the most
stately and venerable temple of the East.[4]

    [3] Nicephorus Gregoras has described the colossus of Justinian (l. vii. 12); but
his measures are false and inconsistent.   The editor, Boivin, consulted his friend
Girardon; and the sculptor gave him the true proportions of an equestrian statue.
That of Justinian was still visible to Peter Gyllius, not on the column, but in the
outward court of the seraglio; and he was at Constantinople when it was melted
down and cast into a brass cannon (de Topograph. C. P. l. ii. c. 17).   [The equestrian
statue of Justinian was in the Augusteum.   What seems to be the base of the statue has
been found near the Church of SS. Sergius and Bacchus (the Kutchuk Aya Sophia)
with an inscription beginning: Ἐπιβίσι (sic) ἐπὶ τοὺς ἵππους σου καὶ ἡ ἱππασία σου
σωτηρία (from Habakkuk iii. 8).   See Mordtmann, Esquisse topographique, § 97
(p. 55).]
    [4] See the decay and repairs of St. Sophia, in Nicephorus Gregoras (l. vii. 12; l.
xv. 2).   The building was propped by Andronicus in 1317, the eastern hemisphere
fell in 1345.   The Greeks, in their pompous rhetoric, exalt the beauty and holiness
of the church, an earthly heaven, the abode of angels, and of God himself, &c.   [Cp.
Cantacuzenus, i. p. 30, ed. Bonn.   See Lethaby and Swainson, Sancta Sophia, p. 124
and p. 152.]

The last hope of the falling city and empire was placed in the harmony of the mother and daughter, in the maternal tenderness of Rome and the filial obedience of Constantinople. In the synod of Florence, the Greeks and Latins had embraced, and subscribed, and promised; but these signs of friendship were perfidious or fruitless;[5] and the baseless fabric of the union vanished like a dream.[6] The emperor and his prelates returned in the Venetian galleys; but, as they touched at the Morea and the isles of Corfu and Lesbos, the subjects of the Latins complained that the pretended union would be an instrument of oppression. No sooner did they land on the Byzantine shore than they were saluted, or rather assailed, with a general murmur of zeal and discontent. During their absence, above two years, the capital had been deprived of its civil and ecclesiastical rulers; fanaticism fermented in anarchy; the most furious monks reigned over the conscience of women and bigots; and the hatred of the Latin name was the first principle of nature and religion. Before his departure for Italy, the emperor had flattered the city with the assurance of a prompt relief and a powerful succour; and the clergy, confident in their orthodoxy and science, had promised themselves and their flocks an easy victory over the blind shepherds of the West. The double disappointment exasperated the Greeks; the conscience of the subscribing prelates was awakened; the hour of temptation was past; and they had more to dread from the public resentment than they could hope from the favour of the emperor or the pope. Instead of justifying their conduct, they deplored their weakness, professed their contrition, and cast themselves on the mercy of God and of their brethren. To the reproachful question, What had been the event or use of their Italian synod? they answered, with sighs and tears, "Alas! we have made a new faith; we have exchanged piety for impiety; we have betrayed the immaculate sacrifice; and we are become

The Greek schism after the council of Florence, A.D. 1440-1448

---

[5] The genuine and original narrative of Syropulus (p. 312-351) opens the schism from the first *office* of the Greeks at Venice to the general opposition at Constantinople of the clergy and people.

[6] On the schism of Constantinople, see Phranza (l. ii. c. 17), Laonicus Chalcondyles (l. vi. p. 155, 156 [pp. 292 *sqq.* ed. B.]), and Ducas (c. 31); the last of whom writes with truth and freedom. Among the moderns we may distinguish the continuator of Fleury (tom. xxii. p. 338, &c., 401, 420, &c.) and Spondanus (A.D. 1440-30). The sense of the latter is drowned in prejudice and passion, as soon as Rome and religion are concerned.

Azymites". (The Azymites were those who celebrated the communion with unleavened bread; and I must retract or qualify
the praise which I have bestowed on the growing philosophy
of the times.) "Alas! we have been seduced by distress, by
fraud, and by the hopes and fears of a transitory life. The
hand that has signed the union should be cut off; and the
tongue that has pronounced the Latin creed deserves to be
torn from the root." The best proof of their repentance was
an increase of zeal for the most trivial rites and the most in-
comprehensible doctrines; and an absolute separation from all,
without excepting their prince, who preserved some regard for
honour and consistency. After the decease of the patriarch
Joseph, the archbishops of Heraclea and Trebizond had courage
to refuse the vacant office; and Cardinal Bessarion preferred the
warm and comfortable shelter of the Vatican. The choice of
the emperor and his clergy was confined to Metrophanes of
Cyzicus: he was consecrated in St. Sophia, but the temple
was vacant; the cross-bearers abdicated their service; the infection spread from the city to the villages; and Metrophanes
discharged, without effect, some ecclesiastical thunders against
a nation of schismatics. The eyes of the Greeks were directed
to Mark of Ephesus, the champion of his country; and the
sufferings of the holy confessor were repaid with a tribute of
admiration and applause. His example and writings propagated
the flame of religious discord; age and infirmity soon removed
him from the world; but the gospel of Mark was not a law of
forgiveness; and he requested with his dying breath that none
of the adherents of Rome might attend his obsequies or pray
for his soul.[7]

---

[7] [Since the publication of the De Ecclesiæ occidentalis atque Orientalis perpe-
tuâ consensione of Leo Allatius, it has been generally supposed that a Synod, held
at St. Sophia in A.D. 1450, under the auspices of the Emperor Constantine, repudiated the Acts of the Council of Florence. Allatius (c. 1380) gave an account of
the "Acts" of this Synod, and condemned them as spurious, on account of some
obvious blunders which appeared in their Title. An edition of these Acts was
shortly afterwards published by Dositheus, Patriarch of Jerusalem, in his Τόμος
καταλλαγῆς, p. 454 *sqq.*; but in the Title, in his edition, the blunders were corrected,
and he defended the genuineness of the document. But, quite apart from the title,
the document is marked by anachronisms and blunders which have been recently
exposed by Ch. Papaioannu. This Russian scholar has submitted the Acts to
a thorough-going criticism (Akty tak nazyvaemago posliedniago Sophiiskago So-
bora (1450 g.) i ich istoricheskoe dostoinstvo, in Vizantiiskii Vremennik, ii. p. 394
sqq., 1895), and has shown convincingly not only that the Acts are spurious but that
no such Synod was ever held. The first Synod that rejected the decrees of Florence

The schism was not confined to the narrow limits of the Byzantine empire. Secure under the Mamaluke sceptre, the three
patriarchs of Alexandria, Antioch, and Jerusalem assembled a
numerous synod ; disowned their representatives at Ferrara and
Florence ; condemned the creed and council of the Latins ; and
threatened the emperor of Constantinople with the censures of
the Eastern church. Of the sectaries of the Greek communion,
the Russians were the most powerful, ignorant, and superstitious.
Their primate, the cardinal Isidore, hastened from Florence to
Moscow,[8] to reduce the independent nation under the Roman
yoke. But the Russian bishops had been educated at Mount
Athos ; and the prince and people embraced the theology of
their priests. They were scandalized by the title, the pomp,
the Latin cross, of the legate, the friend of those impious men
who shaved their beards and performed the divine office with
gloves on their hands and rings on their fingers. Isidore was condemned by a synod ; his person was imprisoned in a monastery ;
and it was with extreme difficulty that the cardinal could escape
from the hands of a fierce and fanatic people.[9] The Russians
refused a passage to the missionaries of Rome, who aspired to
convert the pagans beyond the Tanais ;[10] and their refusal was
justified by the maxim that the guilt of idolatry is less dam-
nable than that of schism. The errors of the Bohemians were

was that of A.D. 1484. The Synod of 1450 was invented and the Acts forged
probably not later than the beginning of the 17th century. One of the anachronisms which the unknown forger committed was making Marcus of Ephesus take
part in the Synod. But Marcus had died before 1448; probably (as Papaioannu
shows, pp. 398-399) in 1447.]

[8] Isidore was metropolitan of Kiow, but the Greeks subject to Poland have removed that see from the ruins of Kiow to Lemberg or Leopold [Lvov] (Herbestein,
in Ramusio, tom. ii. p. 127). On the other hand, the Russians transferred their
spiritual obedience to the archbishop, who became, in 1588, the patriarch of Moscow
(Levesque, Hist. de Russie, tom. iii. p. 188, 190, from a Greek Ms. at Turin, Iter et
labores Archiepiscopi Arsenii).

[9] The curious narrative of Levesque (Hist. de Russie, tom. ii. p. 242-247) is extracted from the patriarchal archives. The scenes of Ferrara and Florence are described by ignorance and passion ; but the Russians are credible in the account of
their own prejudices.

[10] The Shamanism, the ancient religion of the Samanæans and Gymnosophists,
has been driven by the more popular Bramins from India into the northern deserts ;
the naked philosophers were compelled to wrap themselves in fur ; but they insensibly sunk into wizards and physicians. The Mordvans and Tcheremisses, in the
European Russia, adhere to this religion, which is formed on the earthly model of
one King or God, his ministers or angels, and the rebellious spirits who oppose his
government. As these tribes of the Volga have no images, they might more justly
retort on the Latin missionaries the name of Idolaters (Levesque, Hist. des Peuples
soumis à la domination des Russes, tom. i. p. 194-237, 423-460).

excused by their abhorrence for the pope; and a deputation of
the Greek clergy solicited the friendship of those sanguinary
enthusiasts.[11]   While Eugenius triumphed in the union and
orthodoxy of the Greeks, his party was contracted to the walls,
or rather to the palace, of Constantinople.   The zeal of Palæologus had been excited by interest ; it was soon cooled by opposition : an attempt to violate the national belief might endanger
his life and crown ; nor could the pious rebels be destitute of
foreign and domestic aid.   The sword of his brother Demetrius,
who, in Italy, had maintained a prudent and popular silence,
was half unsheathed in the cause of religion ; and Amurath, the
Turkish sultan, was displeased and alarmed by the seeming
friendship of the Greeks and Latins.

Reign and
character
of Amu-
rath II. A.D.
1421-1451,
February

"Sultan Murad, or Amurath, lived forty-nine, and reigned
thirty years, six months, and eight days.   He was a just and
valiant prince, of a great soul, patient of labours, learned,
merciful, religious, charitable ; a lover and encourager of the
studious, and of all who excelled in any art or science ; a good
emperor, and a great general.   No man obtained more or
greater victories than Amurath ; Belgrade alone withstood his
attacks.   Under his reign, the soldier was ever victorious, the
citizen rich and secure.   If he subdued any country, his first
care was to build mosques and caravanseras, hospitals, and
colleges.   Every year he gave a thousand pieces of gold to
the sons of the Prophet ; and sent two thousand five hundred
to the religious persons of Mecca, Medina, and Jerusalem." [12]
This portrait is transcribed from the historian of the Othman
empire ; but the applause of a servile and superstitious people
has been lavished on the worst of tyrants ; and the virtues
of a sultan are often the vices most useful to himself, or

[11] Spondanus, Annal. Eccles. tom. ii. A.D. 1451, No. 13.   The epistle of the
Greeks, with a Latin version, is extant in the college library at Prague.
[12] See Cantemir, History of the Othman Empire, p. 94.   Murad, or Morad, may
be correct; but I have preferred the popular name to that obscure diligence which
is rarely successful in translating an Oriental into the Roman alphabet.   [A Burgundian knight, Bertrandon de la Brocquière (see below, p. 165, note 62), gives the
following description of Murad :—
"He is a little short thick man, with the physiognomy of a Tartar.   He has a
broad and brown face, high cheek bones, a round beard, a great and crooked nose, with
little eyes ; but they say he is kind, good, generous, and willingly gives away lands
and money. . . . He is thought not to love war, and this seems to be well founded.
. . . He loves liquor and those who drink hard." He threw a Moor into prison who
ventured to admonish him against indulgence in wine (T. Wright's Early Travels in
Palestine, p. 346-347).]

most agreeable to his subjects. A nation ignorant of the equal benefits of liberty and law must be awed by the flashes of arbitrary power : the cruelty of a despot will assume the character of justice ; his profusion, of liberality ; his obstinacy, of firmness. If the most reasonable excuse be rejected, few acts of obedience will be found impossible ; and guilt must tremble where innocence cannot always be secure. The tranquillity of the people and the discipline of the troops were best maintained by perpetual action in the field ; war was the trade of the Janizaries ; and those who survived the peril and divided the spoil applauded the generous ambition of their sovereign. To propagate the true religion was the duty of a faithful Musulman : the unbelievers were *his* enemies, and those of the Prophet ; and, in the hands of the Turks, the scymetar was the only instrument of conversion. Under these circumstances, however, the justice and moderation of Amurath are attested by his conduct and acknowledged by the Christians themselves ; who consider a prosperous reign and a peaceful death as the reward of his singular merits. In the vigour of his age and military power, he seldom engaged in a war till he was justified by a previous and adequate provocation ; the victorious sultan was disarmed by submission ; and in the observance of treaties his word was inviolate and sacred.[13] The Hungarians were commonly the aggressors ; he was provoked by the revolt of Scanderbeg ; and the perfidious Caramanian was twice vanquished and twice pardoned by the Ottoman monarch. Before he invaded the Morea, Thebes had been surprised by the despot ; in the conquest of Thessalonica,[14] the grandson of Bajazet might dispute the recent purchase of the Venetians ; and, after the first siege of Constantinople, the sultan was never tempted, by the distress, the absence, or the injuries, of Palæologus, to extinguish the dying light of the Byzantine empire.

[13] See Chalcondyles (l. vii. p. 186, 198), Ducas (c. 33) and Marinus Barletius (in Vit. Scanderbeg, p. 145, 146). In his good faith towards the garrison of Sfetigrade he was a lesson and example to his son Mahomet.

[14] [There is an account of Murad's conquest of Thessalonica, A.D. 1430, by John Anagnostes (publ. at the end of the Bonn edition of Phrantzes, p. 484 *sqq.*), written in imitation of the account of the Saracen siege in A.D. 904 by Cameniates. Two popular Greek ballads on the capture are given in Passow's Popularia Carmina Græciæ recentioris, cxciv. cxcv. (cp. Miss F. M'Pherson, Journal of Hellenic Studies, x. p. 86, 87). The lines occur :—

πῆραν τὴν πόλι, πῆραν τὴν, πῆραν τὴν Σαλονίκη,
πῆραν καὶ τὴν ἁγιὰ Σοφιὰ, τὸ μέγα μοναστῆρι.]

His double
abdication,
A.D. 1442-1   But the most striking feature in the life and character of Amurath is the double abdication of the Turkish throne; and, were not his motives debased by an alloy of superstition, we must praise the royal philosopher,[15] who, at the age of forty, could discern the vanity of human greatness. Resigning the sceptre to his son, he retired to the pleasant residence of Magnesia; but he retired to the society of saints and hermits. It was not till the fourth century of the Hegira that the religion of Mahomet had been corrupted by an institution so adverse to his genius; but in the age of the crusades the various orders of Dervishes were multiplied by the example of the Christian, and even the Latin, monks.[16]   The lord of nations submitted to fast, and pray, and turn round in endless rotation with the fanatics who mistook the giddiness of the head for the illumination of the spirit.[17]   But he was soon awakened from this dream of enthusiasm by the Hungarian invasion; and his obedient son was the foremost to urge the public danger and the wishes of the people. Under the banner of their veteran leader, the Janizaries fought and conquered; but he withdrew from the field of Varna, again to pray, to fast, and to turn round with his Magnesian brethren. These pious occupations were again interrupted by the danger of the state. A victorious army disdained the inexperience of their youthful ruler; the city of Hadrianople was abandoned to rapine and slaughter; and the unanimous divan implored his presence to appease the tumult, and prevent the rebellion, of the Janizaries. At the well-known voice of their master, they trembled and obeyed; and the reluctant sultan was compelled to support his splendid servitude, till, at the end of four years, he was relieved by the angel of death. Age or disease, misfortune or caprice, have tempted several princes to descend from the throne; and they have had

[15] Voltaire (Essai sur l'Histoire Générale, c. 89, p. 283, 284) admires *le Philosophe Turc;* would he have bestowed the same praise on a Christian prince for retiring to a monastery? In his way, Voltaire was a bigot, an intolerant bigot.

[16] See the articles *Dervische, Fakir, Nasser, Rohbaniat,* in d'Herbelot's Bibliothèque Orientale. Yet the subject is superficially treated from the Persian and Arabian writers. It is among the Turks that these orders have principally flourished.

[17] Rycaut (in the Present State of the Ottoman Empire, p. 242-268) affords much information, which he drew from his personal conversation with the heads of the dervishes, most of whom ascribed their origin to the time of Orchan. He does not mention the *Zichidae* of Chalcondyles (l. vii. p. 286), among whom Amurath retired; the *Seids* of that author are the descendants of Mahomet.

leisure to repent of their irretrievable step. But Amurath alone, in the full liberty of choice, after the trial of empire and solitude, has *repeated* his preference of a private life.

After the departure of his Greek brethren, Eugenius had not been unmindful of their temporal interest; and his tender regard for the Byzantine empire was animated by a just appre-hension of the Turks, who approached, and might soon invade, the borders of Italy. But the spirit of the crusades had expired; and the coldness of the Franks was not less unreasonable than their headlong passion. In the eleventh century, a fanatic monk could precipitate Europe on Asia for the recovery of the holy sepulchre; but, in the fifteenth, the most pressing motives of religion and policy were insufficient to unite the Latins in the defence of Christendom. Germany was an inexhaustible store-house of men and arms; [18] but that complex and languid body required the impulse of a vigorous hand; and Frederic the Third was alike impotent in his personal character and his Im-perial dignity. A long war had impaired the strength, without satiating the animosity, of France and England; [19] but Philip, duke of Burgundy, was a vain and magnificent prince; and he enjoyed, without danger or expense, the adventurous piety of his subjects, who sailed, in a gallant fleet, from the coast of Flanders to the Hellespont. The maritime republics of Venice and Genoa were less remote from the scene of action; and their hostile fleets were associated under the standard of St. Peter. The kingdoms of Hungary and Poland, which covered, as it were, the interior pale of the Latin church, were the most nearly concerned to oppose the progress of the Turks. Arms were the patrimony of the Scythians and Sarmatians; and these nations might appear equal to the contest, could they point, against the common foe, those swords that were so wantonly drawn in bloody and domestic quarrels. But the same spirit

Marginal note: Eugenius forms a league against the Turks. A.D. 1443

[18] In the year 1431, Germany raised 40,000 horse, men at arms, against the Hussites of Bohemia (Lenfant, Hist. du Concile de Basle, tom. i. p. 318). At the siege of Nuys [Neuss] on the Rhine, in 1474, the princes, prelates, and cities sent their respective quotas; and the bishop of Munster (qui n'est pas des plus grands) furnished 1400 horse, 6000 foot, all in green, with 1200 waggons. The united armies of the king of England and the duke of Burgundy scarcely equalled one-third of this German host (Mémoires de Philippe de Comines, l. iv. c. 2). At present, six or seven hundred thousand men are maintained in constant pay and admirable discipline by the powers of Germany.

[19] It was not till the year 1444, that France and England could agree on a truce of some months (see Rymer's Fœdera, and the chronicles of both nations).

was adverse to concord and obedience ; a poor country and a
limited monarch are incapable of maintaining a standing force;
and the loose bodies of Polish and Hungarian horse were not
armed with the sentiments and weapons which, on some occasions, have given irresistible weight to the French chivalry.
Yet, on this side, the designs of the Roman pontiff and the
[Juliano   eloquence of Cardinal Julian, his legate, were promoted by the
Cesarini] circumstances of the times ; [20] by the union of the two crowns
on the head of Ladislaus,[21] a young and ambitious soldier ; by
the valour of an hero, whose name, the name of John Huniades,
was already popular among the Christians and formidable to the
Turks.   An endless treasure of pardons and indulgences were
scattered by the legate ; many private warriors of France and
Germany enlisted under the holy banner ; and the crusade
derived some strength, or at least some reputation, from the
[George   new allies, both of Europe and Asia.   A fugitive despot of
Brankovic] Servia exaggerated the distress and ardour of the Christians
beyond the Danube, who would unanimously rise to vindicate
their religion and liberty.   The Greek emperor,[22] with a spirit
unknown to his fathers, engaged to guard the Bosphorus, and
to sally from Constantinople at the head of his national and
mercenary troops.   The sultan of Caramania [23] announced the
retreat of Amurath and a powerful diversion in the heart of
Anatolia ; and, if the fleets of the West could occupy at the
same moment the straits of the Hellespont, the Ottoman monarchy would be dissevered and destroyed.   Heaven and earth
must rejoice in the perdition of the miscreants ; and the legate,
with prudent ambiguity, instilled the opinion of the invisible,

[20] In the Hungarian crusade, Spondanus (Annal. Eccles. A.D. 1443, 1444) has
been my leading guide. He has diligently read, and critically compared, the Greek
and Turkish materials, the historians of Hungary, Poland, and the West. His
narrative is perspicuous ; and, where he can be free from a religious bias, the judgment
of Spondanus is not contemptible.

[21] I have curtailed the harsh letter (Wladislaus) which most writers affix to his
name, either in compliance with the Polish pronunciation, or to distinguish him from
his rival the infant Ladislaus of Austria. Their competition for the crown of Hungary
is described by Callimachus (l. i. ii. p. 447-486), Bonfinius (Decad. iii. l. iv.), Spondanus, and Lenfant.

[22] The Greek historians, Phranza, Chalcondyles, and Ducas, do not ascribe to
their prince a very active part in this crusade, which he seems to have promoted by
his wishes and injured by his fears.

[23] Cantemir (p. 88) ascribes to his policy the original plan, and transcribes his
animating epistle to the king of Hungary. But the Mahometan powers are seldom
informed of the state of Christendom ; and the situation and correspondence of the
knights of Rhodes must connect them with the sultan of Caramania.

perhaps the visible, aid of the Son of God and his divine mother.

Of the Polish and Hungarian diets, a religious war was the unanimous cry; and Ladislaus, after passing the Danube, led an army of his confederate subjects as far as Sophia, the capital of the Bulgarian kingdom.[24] In this expedition they obtained two signal victories, which were justly ascribed to the valour and conduct of Huniades. In the first, with a vanguard of ten thousand men, he surprised the Turkish camp; in the second, he vanquished and made prisoner the most renowned of their generals, who possessed the double advantage of ground and numbers. The approach of winter and the natural and artificial obstacles of Mount Hæmus arrested the progress of the hero, who measured a narrow interval of six days' march from the foot of the mountains to the hostile towers of Hadrianople and the friendly capital of the Greek empire. The retreat was undisturbed; and the entrance into Buda was at once a military and religious triumph. An ecclesiastical procession was followed by the king and his warriors on foot; he nicely balanced the merits and rewards of the two nations; and the pride of conquest was blended with the humble temper of Christianity. Thirteen bashaws, nine standards, and four thousand captives were unquestionable trophies; and, as all were willing to believe and none were present to contradict, the crusaders multiplied, with unblushing confidence, the myriads of Turks whom they had left on the field of battle.[25] The most solid proof and the most salutary consequence of victory was a deputation from the divan to solicit peace, to restore Servia, to ransom the prisoners, and to evacuate the Hungarian frontier. By this treaty, the rational objects of the war were obtained: the king, the despot, and Huniades himself, in the diet of Segedin, were satisfied with public and private emolument; a truce of ten years was concluded; and the followers of Jesus and Mahomet, who swore on the Gospel and the Koran, attested the word of God as the guardian of truth and the avenger of perfidy. In the place of

Ladislaus, king of Poland and Hungary, marches against them [A.D. 1443]

[Battle of Nitzch, 3rd Nov.]

[Battle of Kunoviza, 25th Dec.]

The Turkish peace [The Peace of Szegedin]

---

[24] [For this expedition see Katona, Histor. crit. reg. Hung. Stirpis mixtae, vi. p. 245 sqq.; Nesri (in Thúry's Török történetirók, vol. i.) p. 58; the Anonymous of 1486, ib. p. 18, 19; Sad ad-Dīn, ib. p. 136 sqq.; Zinkeisen, Gesch. des osmanischen Reiches, i. 611 sqq.]

[25] In their letters to the emperor Frederic III. the Hungarians slay 30,000 Turks in one battle, but the modest Julian reduces the slaughter to 6000 or even 2000 infidels (Æneas Sylvius in Europ. c. 5, and epist. 44, 81, apud Spondanum).

the Gospel, the Turkish ministers had proposed to substitute the Eucharist, the real presence of the Catholic deity; but the Christians refused to profane their holy mysteries; and a superstitious conscience is less forcibly bound by the spiritual energy, than by the outward and visible symbols, of an oath.[26]

Violation of the peace, A.D. 1444 During the whole transaction the cardinal-legate had observed a sullen silence, unwilling to approve, and unable to oppose, the consent of the king and people. But the diet was not dissolved before Julian was fortified by the welcome intelligence that Anatolia was invaded by the Caramanian, and Thrace by the Greek emperor; that the fleets of Genoa, Venice, and Burgundy were masters of the Hellespont; and that the allies, informed of the victory, and ignorant of the treaty, of Ladislaus, impatiently waited for the return of his victorious army. "And is it thus," exclaimed the cardinal,[27] "that you will desert their expectations and your own fortune? It is to them, to your God, and your fellow-Christians, that you have pledged your faith; and that prior obligation annihilates a rash and sacrilegious oath to the enemies of Christ. His vicar on earth is the Roman pontiff; without whose sanction you can neither promise nor perform. In his name I absolve your perjury and sanctify your arms; follow my footsteps in the paths of glory and salvation; and, if still ye have scruples, devolve on my head the punishment and the sin." This mischievous casuistry was seconded by his respectable character and the levity of popular assemblies. War was resolved on the same spot where peace had so lately been sworn; and, in the execution of the treaty, the Turks were assaulted by the Christians to whom, with some reason, they might apply the epithet of Infidels. The falsehood of Ladislaus to his word and oath was palliated by the religion of the times; the most perfect, or at least the most popular, excuse would have been the success of his arms and

---

[26] See the origin of the Turkish war, and the first expedition of Ladislaus, in the vth and vith books of the iiid Decad of Bonfinius, who, in his division and style, copies Livy with tolerable success. Callimachus (l. ii. p. 487-496) is still more pure and authentic.

[27] I do not pretend to warrant the literal accuracy of Julian's speech, which is variously worded by Callimachus (l. iii. p. 505-507), Bonfinius (Dec. iii. l. vi. p. 457, 458), and other historians, who might indulge their own eloquence, while they represent one of the orators of the age. But they all agree in the advice and arguments for perjury, which in the field of controversy are fiercely attacked by the Protestants and feebly defended by the Catholics. The latter are discouraged by the misfortune of Varna.

the deliverance of the Eastern church. But the same treaty
which should have bound his conscience had diminished his
strength. On the proclamation of the peace, the French and
German volunteers departed with indignant murmurs; the Poles
were exhausted by distant warfare, and perhaps disgusted with
foreign command; and their palatines accepted the first licence
and hastily retired to their provinces and castles. Even Hungary was divided by faction or restrained by a laudable scruple;
and the relics of the crusade that marched in the second expedition were reduced to an inadequate force of twenty thousand
men. A Walachian chief, who joined the royal standard with his
vassals, presumed to remark that their numbers did not exceed
the hunting retinue that sometimes attended the sultan; and
the gift of two horses of matchless speed might admonish
Ladislaus of his secret foresight of the event. But the despot
of Servia, after the restoration of his country and children, was
tempted by the promise of new realms; and the inexperience
of the king, the enthusiasm of the legate, and the martial
presumption of Huniades himself were persuaded that every
obstacle must yield to the invincible virtue of the sword and
the cross. After the passage of the Danube, two roads might
lead to Constantinople and the Hellespont: the one direct,
abrupt, and difficult, through the mountains of Hæmus; the
other more tedious and secure, over a level country, and along
the shores of the Euxine; in which their flanks, according to
the Scythian discipline, might always be covered by a moveable
fortification of waggons. The latter was judiciously preferred:
the Catholics marched through the plains of Bulgaria, burning,
with wanton cruelty, the churches and villages of the Christian
natives; and their last station was at Warna, near the sea-shore,
on which the defeat and death of Ladislaus have bestowed a
memorable name.[28]

It was on this fatal spot that, instead of finding a con- Battle of
federate fleet to second their operations, they were alarmed by Warna,
the approach of Amurath himself, who had issued from his A.D. 1444,
10th Nov.

[28] Warna, under the Grecian name of Odessus, was a colony of the Milesians
which they denominated from the hero Ulysses (Cellarius, tom. i. p. 374; d'Anville, tom. i. p. 312). According to Arrian's Periplus of the Euxine (p. 24, 25, in
the first volume of Hudson's Geographers), it was situate 1740 stadia, or furlongs,
from the mouth of the Danube, 2140 from Byzantium, and 360 to the north of a
ridge or promontory of Mount Hæmus which advances into the sea.

Magnesian solitude and transported the forces of Asia to the defence of Europe. According to some writers, the Greek emperor had been awed, or seduced, to grant the passage of the Bosphorus; and an indelible stain of corruption is fixed on the Genoese, or the pope's nephew, the Catholic admiral, whose mercenary connivance betrayed the guard of the Hellespont.[29] From Hadrianople, the sultan advanced, by hasty marches, at the head of sixty thousand men; and, when the cardinal and Huniades had taken a nearer survey of the numbers and order of the Turks, these ardent warriors proposed the tardy and impracticable measure of a retreat. The king alone was resolved to conquer or die; and his resolution had almost been crowned with a glorious and salutary victory. The princes were opposite to each other in the centre; and the Beglerbegs, or generals of Anatolia and Romania, commanded on the right and left against the adverse divisions of the despot and Huniades. The Turkish wings were broken on the first onset; but the advantage was fatal; and the rash victors, in the heat of the pursuit, were carried away far from the annoyance of the enemy or the support of their friends. When Amurath beheld the flight of his squadrons, he despaired of his fortune and that of the empire: a veteran Janizary seized his horse's bridle; and he had magnanimity to pardon and reward the soldier who dared to perceive the terror, and arrest the flight, of his sovereign. A copy of the treaty, the monument of Christian perfidy, had been displayed in the front of battle; and it is said that the sultan in his distress, lifting his eyes and his hands to heaven, implored the protection of the God of truth; and called on the prophet Jesus himself to avenge the impious mockery of his name and religion.[30] With inferior numbers and disordered ranks, the king of Hungary rushed forwards in the confidence of victory, till his career was stopped by the impenetrable phalanx of the Janizaries. If we may credit the Ottoman annals, his horse was pierced by the javelin of

[29] [It is difficult to understand what the Papal fleet was doing. The place where Murad crossed is uncertain. The Turkish sources differ; they agree only that he did not cross at Gallipoli. Cp. Thúry's note, *op. cit.* p. 21.]

[30] Some Christian writers affirm that he drew from his bosom the host or wafer on which the treaty had *not* been sworn. The Moslems suppose, with more simplicity, an appeal to God and his prophet Jesus, which is likewise insinuated by Callimachus (l. iii. p. 516, Spondan. A.D. 1444, No. 8).

Amurath[31]; he fell among the spears of the infantry; and a Turkish soldier proclaimed with a loud voice, " Hungarians, behold the head of your king ! " The death of Ladislaus was the signal of their defeat. On his return from an intemperate pursuit, Huniades deplored his error and the public loss; he strove to rescue the royal body, till he was overwhelmed by the tumultuous crowd of the victors and vanquished; and the last efforts of his courage and conduct were exerted to save the remnant of his Walachian cavalry. Ten thousand Christians were slain in the disastrous battle of Warna. The loss of the Turks, more considerable in numbers, bore a smaller proportion, to their total strength; yet the philosophic sultan was not ashamed to confess that his ruin must be the consequence of a second and similar victory. At his command, a column was erected on the spot where Ladislaus had fallen; but the modest inscription, instead of accusing the rashness, recorded the valour, and bewailed the misfortune, of the Hungarian youth.[32]

Before I lose sight of the field of Warna, I am tempted to pause on the character and story of two principal actors, the cardinal Julian, and John Huniades. Julian[33] Cæsarini was born of a noble family of Rome; his studies had embraced both the Latin and Greek learning, both the sciences of divinity and law; and his versatile genius was equally adapted to the schools,

Death of Ladislaus

The Cardinal Julian

---

[31] A critic will always distrust these *spolia opima* of a victorious general, so difficult for valour to obtain, so easy for flattery to invent (Cantemir, p. 90, 91). Callimachus (l. iii. p. 517) more simply and probably affirms, supervenientibus Janizaris, telorum multitudine non tam confossus est quam obrutus.

[32] Besides some valuable hints from Æneas Sylvius, which are diligently collected by Spondanus, our best authorities are three historians of the xvth century, Philippus Callimachus (de rebus a Vladislao Polonorum atque Hungarorum Rege gestis, libri iii. in Bel. [= Schwandtner] Script. Rerum Hungaricarum, tom. i. p. 433-518), Bonfinius (decad iii. l. v. p. 460-467), and Chalcondyles (l. vii. p. 165-179). The two first were Italians, but they passed their lives in Poland and Hungary (Fabric. Bibliot. Latin. med. et infimæ Ætatis, tom. i. p. 324; Vossius de Hist. Latin. l. iii. c. 8, 11; Bayle, Dictionnaire, BONFINIUS). A small tract of Fælix Petancius, chancellor of Segnia (ad calcem Cuspinian. de Cæsaribus, p. 716-722), represents the theatre of the war in the xvth century. [The story of the Varna campaign by Callimachus or Philip Buonaccorsi has recently been edited by Kwiatkovski in vol. vi. of the Monum. Polon. Hist. (1893). See also the authorities cited in Katóna, *op. cit.*, vol. vi., and the Turkish writers cited above, note 24. A full account of the battle will be found in Hammer, i. p. 355-357, and in Zinkeisen, i. p. 689 *sqq.* There is a description of the battle in Greek verse by Paraspondylus Zoticus who professes to have been an eye-witness. It has been edited (with Hungarian notes) by W. Pecz, 1894; and it was included in Legrand's Collections de Monuments, Nouvelle série, v. p. 51 *sqq.*]

[33] M. Lenfant has described the origin (Hist. du Concile de Basle, tom. i. p. 247, &c.), and Bohemian campaign (p. 315, &c.), of Cardinal Julian. His services at Basil and Ferrara, and his unfortunate end, are occasionally related by Spondanus and the continuator of Fleury.

the camp, and the court. No sooner had he been invested with
the Roman purple than he was sent into Germany to arm the
empire against the rebels and heretics of Bohemia. The spirit
of persecution is unworthy of a Christian ; the military profession ill becomes a priest ; but the former is excused by the
times ; and the latter was ennobled by the courage of Julian,
who stood dauntless and alone in the disgraceful flight of the
German host. As the pope's legate, he opened the council of
Basil; but the president soon appeared the most strenuous champion of ecclesiastical freedom ; and an opposition of seven years
was conducted by his ability and zeal. After promoting the
strongest measures against the authority and person of Eugenius,
some secret motive of interest or conscience engaged him to
desert, on a sudden, the popular party. The cardinal withdrew
himself from Basil to Ferrara ; and, in the debates of the Greeks
and Latins, the two nations admired the dexterity of his arguments and the depth of his theological erudition.[34] In his Hungarian embassy we have already seen the mischievous effects of
his sophistry and eloquence, of which Julian himself was the
first victim. The cardinal, who performed the duties of a priest
and a soldier, was lost in the defeat of Warna. The circumstances of his death are variously related ; but it is believed
that a weighty incumbrance of gold impeded his flight, and
tempted the cruel avarice of some Christian fugitives.

John Cor-
vinus
Huniades

From an humble or at least a doubtful origin, the merit of
John Huniades promoted him to the command of the Hungarian
armies. His father was a Walachian, his mother a Greek : her
unknown race might possibly ascend to the emperors of Constantinople ; and the claims of the Walachians, with the surname
of Corvinus, from the place of his nativity, might suggest a thin
pretence for mingling his blood with the patricians of ancient
Rome.[35] In his youth, he served in the wars of Italy, and was
retained, with twelve horsemen, by the bishop of Zagrab ; the

[34] Syropulus honourably praises the talents of an enemy (p. 117) : τοιαῦτά τινα
εἶπεν ὁ Ἰουλιανός, πεπλατυσμένως ἄγαν καὶ λογικῶς, καὶ μετ' ἐπιστήμης καὶ δεινότητος
ῥητορικῆς.
[35] See Bonfinius, decad iii. l. iv. p. 423. Could the Italian historian pronounce,
or the king of Hungary hear, without a blush, the absurd flattery which confounded
the name of a Walachian village with the casual though glorious epithet of a single
branch of the Valerian family at Rome ? [For the Walachian origin of Hunyady, cp.
Xénopol, Histoire des Roumains, i. p. 264.]

valour of the *white knight* [36] was soon conspicuous ; he increased
his fortunes by a noble and wealthy marriage ; and in the defence
of the Hungarian borders he won, in the same year, three battles
against the Turks. By his influence, Ladislaus of Poland obtained the crown of Hungary ; and the important service was
rewarded by the title and office of Waivod of Transylvania. The
first of Julian's crusades added two Turkish laurels on his brow ;
and in the public distress the fatal errors of Warna were forgotten. During the absence and minority of Ladislaus of Austria,
the titular king, Huniades was elected supreme captain and governor of Hungary ; and, if envy at first was silenced by terror, a
reign of twelve years supposes the arts of policy as well as of
war. Yet the idea of a consummate general is not delineated
in his campaigns; the white knight fought with the hand rather
than the head, as the chief of desultory barbarians, who attack
without fear and fly without shame ; and his military life is composed of a romantic alternative of victories and escapes. By the
Turks, who employed his name to frighten their perverse children, he was corruptly denominated *Jancus Lain*, or the Wicked ;
their hatred is the proof of their esteem ; the kingdom which he
guarded was inaccessible to their arms; and they felt him most
daring and formidable, when they fondly believed the captain of
his country irrecoverably lost. Instead of confining himself to
a defensive war, four years after the defeat of Warna he again
penetrated into the heart of Bulgaria ; and in the plain of Cossova sustained, till the third day, the shock of the Ottoman
army, four times more numerous than his own. As he fled alone
through the woods of Walachia, the hero was surprised by two
robbers; but, while they disputed a gold chain that hung at his
neck, he recovered his sword, slew the one, terrified the other ;
and, after new perils of captivity or death, consoled by his
presence an afflicted kingdom. But the last and most glorious
action of his life was the defence of Belgrade against the powers
of Mahomet the Second in person. After a siege of forty days, His defence
of Bel-
the Turks, who had already entered the town, were compelled grade, and
death, A.D.
to retreat ; and the joyful nations celebrated Huniades and 1456, 22nd
July-4th
Sept.

[36] Philip de Comines (Mémoires, l. vi. c. 13), from the tradition of the times,
mentions him with high encomiums, but under the whimsical name of the Chevalier
Blanc de Valaigne (Valachia). The Greek Chalcondyles, and the Turkish Annals
of Leunclavius, presume to accuse his fidelity or valour. [Teleki, A Hunyadiak
kora Magyarországon (The Age of the Hunyadys in Hungary), vols. 1-5, 1852-7.]

Belgrade as the bulwarks of Christendom.[37]   About a month
after this great deliverance, the champion expired ; and his most
splendid epitaph is the regret of the Ottoman prince, who sighed
that he could no longer hope for revenge against the single antagonist who had triumphed over his arms.   On the first vacancy
of the throne, Matthias Corvinus, a youth of eighteen years of
age, was elected and crowned by the grateful Hungarians.   His
reign was prosperous and long.   Matthias aspired to the glory of
a conqueror and a saint ; but his purest merit is the encouragement of learning ; and the Latin orators and historians, who
were invited from Italy by the son, have shed the lustre of their
eloquence on the father's character.[38]

Birth and education of Scander- derbeg, prince of Albania, A.D. 1404-1413, &c.

In the list of heroes, John Huniades and Scanderbeg are commonly associated ; [39] and they are both entitled to our notice,
since their occupation of the Ottoman arms delayed the ruin of
the Greek empire.   John Castriot, the father of Scanderbeg,[40]

---

[37] See Bonfinius (decad iii. l. viii. p. 492) and Spondanus (A.D. 1456, No. 1-7).
Huniades shared the glory of the defence of Belgrade with Capistran, a Franciscan
friar ; and in their respective narratives neither the saint nor the hero condescends
to take notice of his rival's merit.   [On John Capistrano see Hermann, Capistranus
triumphans seu historia fundamentalis de S. Joanne Cap., 1700 ; Cataneo, Vita di
S. Giovanni da Capistrano, 1691 ; Guérard, S. Jean de Capistran et son temps,
1865.   The last campaign of Hunyady is the subject of a monograph by Kiss
(Hunyadi János utolsó hadjárata, 1857).   The siege of Belgrade has been treated
fully by R. N. Bain in the Eng. Historical Review for July, 1892.]

[38] See Bonfinius, decad iii. l. viii.-decad iv. l. viii.   The observations of Spondanus on the life and character of Matthias Corvinus are curious and critical (A.D.
1464, No. 1 ; 1475, No. 6 ; 1476, No. 14-16 ; 1490, No. 4, 5).   Italian fame was the
object of his vanity.   His actions are celebrated in the Epitome Rerum Hungaricarum (p. 322-412) of Peter Ranzanus, a Sicilian.   His wise and facetious sayings
are registered by Galeotus Martius of Narni (528-568) ; and we have a particular
narrative of his wedding and coronation.   These three tracts are all contained in
the first vol. of Bel's Scriptores Rerum Hungaricarum.   [The best monograph on
Matthias Corvinus is that of W. Fraknói which has appeared in a German translation (from the Hungarian) in 1891.   It is furnished with interesting illustrations.]

[39] They are ranked by Sir William Temple, in his pleasing Essay on Heroic
Virtue (Works, vol. iii. p. 385), among the seven chiefs who have deserved, without
wearing, a royal crown ; Belisarius, Narses, Gonsalvo of Cordova, William first prince
of Orange, Alexander duke of Parma, John Huniades, and George Castriot, or Scanderbeg.

[40] I could wish for some simple authentic memoirs of a friend of Scanderbeg,
which would introduce me to the man, the time, and the place.   In the old and
national history of Marinus Barletius, a priest of Scodra (de Vitâ, Moribus, et
Rebus gestis Georgii Castrioti, &c. libri xiii. p. 367, Argentorat. 1537, in fol.),
his gaudy and cumbersome robes are stuck with many false jewels.   See likewise
Chalcondyles, l. vii. p. 185 [p. 350, ed. B.] ; l. viii. p. 229 [p. 432].   [Besides the
contemporary authority, Barletius, we know indirectly of another contemporary
source written by an anonymous man of Antivari.   This work (Historia Scanderbegi
edita per quendam Albanensem) was printed at Venice in 1480, but is now lost.
But it is known to us through Giammaria Biemmi, who used it for his Istoria di
Giorgio Castriota, detto Scander Begh, 1742.   The best modern work on the life

SIGNOR·SCANDERBEGO

PORTRAIT OF SCANDERBEG, FROM THE "LIFE" BY M. BARLETIUS,
A.D. 1537

was the hereditary prince of a small district of Epirus or Albania,
between the mountains and the Adriatic Sea.   Unable to contend with the sultan's power, Castriot submitted to the hard
conditions of peace and tribute ; he delivered his four sons as the
pledges of his fidelity ; and the Christian youths, after receiving
the mark of circumcision, were instructed in the Mahometan
religion, and trained in the arms and arts of Turkish policy.[41]
The three elder brothers were confounded in the crowd of slaves ;
and the poison to which their deaths are ascribed cannot be verified or disproved by any positive evidence.   Yet the suspicion is
in a great measure removed by the kind and paternal treatment
of George Castriot, the fourth brother, who, from his tender
youth, displayed the strength and spirit of a soldier.   The successive overthrow of a Tartar and two Persians, who carried a [A.D. 1429]
proud defiance to the Turkish court, recommended him to the
favour of Amurath, and his Turkish appellation of Scanderbeg
(*Iskender beg*), or the lord Alexander, is an indelible memorial
of his glory and servitude.   His father's principality was reduced
into a province ; but the loss was compensated by the rank and
title of Sanjiak, a command of five thousand horse, and the
prospect of the first dignities of the empire.   He served with
honour in the wars of Europe and Asia ; and we may smile at
the art or credulity of the historian, who supposes that in every
encounter he spared the Christians, while he fell with a thundering arm on his Musulman foes.   The glory of Huniades is
without reproach : he fought in the defence of his religion and
country ; but the enemies who applaud the patriot have branded
his rival with the name of traitor and apostate.   In the eyes of [Death of
the Christians the rebellion of Scanderbeg is justified by his Scanderbeg's
father's wrongs, the ambiguous death of his three brothers, his father, A·D
1433]
own degradation, and the slavery of his country ; and they adore
the generous though tardy zeal with which he asserted the faith
and independence of his ancestors.   But he had imbibed from
his ninth year the doctrines of the Koran ; he was ignorant of
the Gospel ; the religion of a soldier is determined by authority
and habit ; nor is it easy to conceive what new illumination at

and exploits of Scanderbeg is that of Julius Pisko : Skanderbeg, 1894 ; a number
of new documents are printed in an appendix.]
    [41] His circumcision, education, &c. are marked by Marinus with brevity and
reluctance (l. i. p. 6, 7).

the age of forty [42] could be poured into his soul. His motives
would be less exposed to the suspicion of interest or revenge,
had he broken his chain from the moment that he was sensible
of its weight; but a long oblivion had surely impaired his
original right; and every year of obedience and reward had
cemented the mutual bond of the sultan and his subject. If
Scanderbeg had long harboured the belief of Christianity and
the intention of revolt, a worthy mind must condemn the base
dissimulation, that could serve only to betray, that could promise
only to be forsworn, that could actively join in the temporal and
spiritual perdition of so many thousands of his unhappy brethren.
Shall we praise a secret correspondence with Huniades, while he

His revolt from the Turks, A.D. 1443, 28th Nov. commanded the vanguard of the Turkish army? shall we excuse
the desertion of his standard, a treacherous desertion, which
abandoned the victory to the enemies of his benefactor? In
the confusion of a defeat, the eye of Scanderbeg was fixed on
the Reis Effendi, or principal secretary; with a dagger at his
breast, he extorted a firman or patent for the government of
Albania; and the murder of the guiltless scribe and his train
prevented the consequences of an immediate discovery. With
some bold companions, to whom he had revealed his design, he
escaped in the night, by rapid marches, from the field of battle
to his paternal mountains. The gates of Croya were opened to
the royal mandate; and no sooner did he command the fortress
than George Castriot dropped the mask of dissimulation, abjured
the Prophet and the sultan, and proclaimed himself the avenger
of his family and country. The names of religion and liberty
provoked a general revolt: the Albanians, a martial race, were
unanimous to live and die with their hereditary prince; and the
Ottoman garrisons were indulged in the choice of martyrdom or

[Assembly at Alessio, 2nd March, A.D. 1444] baptism. In the assembly of the states of Epirus, Scanderbeg
was elected general of the Turkish war; and each of the allies
engaged to furnish his respective proportion of men and money.
From these contributions, from his patrimonial estate, and from
the valuable salt-pits of Selina, he drew an annual revenue of

---

[42] Since Scanderbeg died, A.D. 1466, in the 63d year of his age (Marinus, l. xiii.
p. 370), he was born in 1403 [1404]; since he was torn from his parents by the
Turks when he was *novennis* (Marinus, l. i. p. 1, 6), that event must have happened in 1412 [or 1413], nine years before the accession of Amurath II., who must
have inherited, not acquired, the Albanian slave. Spondanus has remarked this
inconsistency, A.D. 1431, No. 31; 1443, No. 14.

two hundred thousand ducats;[43] and the entire sum, exempt from the demands of luxury, was strictly appropriated to the public use. His manners were popular; but his discipline was severe; and every superfluous vice was banished from his camp; his example strengthened his command; and under his conduct the Albanians were invincible in their own opinion and that of their enemies. The bravest adventurers of France and Germany His valour were allured by his fame and retained in his service; his standing militia consisted of eight thousand horse and seven thousand foot; the horses were small, the men were active; but he viewed with a discerning eye the difficulties and resources of the mountains; and, at the blaze of the beacons, the whole nation was distributed in the strongest posts. With such unequal arms, Scanderbeg resisted twenty-three years the powers of the Ottoman empire; and two conquerors, Amurath the Second and his greater son, were repeatedly baffled by a rebel whom they pursued with seeming contempt and implacable resentment. At the head of sixty thousand horse and forty thousand Janizaries,[44] [A.D. 1449] Amurath entered Albania: he might ravage the open country, occupy the defenceless towns, convert the churches into mosques, circumcise the Christian youths, and punish with death his adult and obstinate captives, but the conquests of the sultan were confined to the petty fortress of Sfetigrade; and the garrison, invincible to his arms, was oppressed by a paltry artifice and a superstitious scruple.[45] Amurath retired with shame and loss from the walls of Croya, the castle and residence of the Castriots; the march, the siege, the retreat, were harassed by a vexatious and almost invisible adversary;[46] and the disappointment might tend to embitter, perhaps to shorten, the last days of the sultan.[47]

[43] His revenue and forces are luckily given by Marinus (l. ii. p. 44).

[44] [Biemmi says that the total number of fighting men did not exceed 70,000; see Pisko, p. 47.]

[45] There were two Dibras, the upper and lower, the Bulgarian and Albanian: the former, 70 miles from Croya (l. i. p. 17), was contiguous to the fortress of Sfetigrade, whose inhabitants refused to drink from a well into which a dead dog had traitorously been cast (l. v. p. 139, 140). We want a good map of Epirus. [The site of Sfetigrad is uncertain. It was in the Upper Dibre, and perhaps near Trebiste. See Pisko, p. 18 note; and for the mode of its capture, p. 50, 51.]

[46] Compare the Turkish narrative of Cantemir (p. 92) with the pompous and prolix declamation in the ivth, vth, and vith books of the Albanian priest, who has been copied by the tribe of strangers and moderns.

[47] In honour of his hero, Barletius (l. vi. p. 188-192) kills the sultan, by disease indeed, under the walls of Croya. But this audacious fiction is disproved by the Greeks and Turks, who agree in the time and manner of Amurath's death at Hadrianople.

In the fulness of conquest, Mahomet the Second still felt at his bosom this domestic thorn ; his lieutenants were permitted to negotiate a truce ; and the Albanian prince may justly be praised as a firm and able champion of his national independence.   The enthusiasm of chivalry and religion has ranked him with the names of Alexander and Pyrrhus, nor would they blush to ac-knowledge their intrepid countryman ; but his narrow dominion and slender powers must leave him at an humble distance below the heroes of antiquity, who triumphed over the East and the Roman legions.   His splendid achievements, the bashaws whom he encountered, the armies that he discomfited, and the three thousand Turks who were slain by his single hand, must be weighed in the scales of suspicious criticism.   Against an illit-erate enemy, and in the dark solitude of Epirus, his partial biographers may safely indulge the latitude of romance ; but their fictions are exposed by the light of Italian history ; and

[Scander-beg in the kingdom of Naples, A.D. 1461, middle of August-c. December]

they afford a strong presumption against their own truth by a fabulous tale of his exploits, when he passed the Adriatic with eight hundred horse to the succour of the king of Naples.[48] Without disparagement to his fame, they might have owned that he was finally oppressed by the Ottoman powers ; in his extreme danger, he applied to Pope Pius the Second for a refuge

and death [at Alessio], A.D. 1467, 17th Jan.

in the ecclesiastical state ; and his resources were almost ex-hausted, since Scanderbeg died a fugitive at Lissus, on the Venetian territory.[49]   His sepulchre was soon violated by the Turkish conquerors ; but the Janizaries, who wore his bones

[A.D. 1479]

enchased in a bracelet, declared by this superstitious amulet their involuntary reverence for his valour.   The instant ruin of his country may redound to the hero's glory ; yet, had he balanced the consequences of submission and resistance, a patriot, perhaps,

---

[48] See the marvels of his Calabrian expedition in the ixth and xth books of Marinus Barletius, which may be rectified by the testimony or silence of Muratori (Annali d'Italia, tom. xiii. p. 291), and his original authors (Joh. Simonetta de Rebus Francisci Sfortiæ, in Muratori, Script. Rerum Ital. tom. xxi. p. 728, et alios).   The Albanian cavalry, under the name of *Stradiots*, soon became famous in the wars of Italy (Mémoires de Comines, l. viii. c. 5).   [The date of Scander-beg's expedition to Italy is fixed by Pisko (p. 86-88) by means of new documents. According to Antonius Guidobonus, the ambassador of Milan at Venice, the troops which Scanderbeg took with him numbered 2000 foot and 1000 horse.]

[49] Spondanus, from the best evidence and the most rational criticism, has re-duced the giant Scanderbeg to the human size (A.D. 1461, No. 20 ; 1463, No. 9 ; 1465, No. 12, 13 ; 1467, No. 1).   His own letter to the pope, and the testimony of Phranza (l. iii. c. 28), a refugee in the neighbouring isle of Corfu, demonstrate his last distress, which is awkwardly concealed by Marinus Barletius (l. x.).

would have declined the unequal contest which must depend on the life and genius of one man. Scanderbeg might indeed be supported by the rational though fallacious hope that the pope, the king of Naples, and the Venetian republic would join in the defence of a free and Christian people, who guarded the sea-coast of the Adriatic and the narrow passage from Greece to Italy. His infant son was saved from the national shipwreck; the Castriots [50] were invested with a Neapolitan dukedom, and their blood continues to flow in the noblest families of the realm. A colony of Albanian fugitives obtained a settlement in Calabria, and they preserve at this day the language and manners of their ancestors.[51]

In the long career of the decline and fall of the Roman empire, I have reached at length the last reign of the princes of Constantinople, who so feebly sustained the name and majesty of the Cæsars.[52] On the decease of John Palæologus, who survived about four years the Hungarian crusade,[53] the royal family, by the death of Andronicus and the monastic profession of Isidore, was reduced to three princes, Constantine, Demetrius, and Thomas, the surviving sons of the emperor Manuel. Of these the first and the last were far distant in the Morea; but Demetrius, who possessed the domain of Selybria, was in the suburbs, at the head of a party; his ambition was not chilled by the public distress; and his conspiracy with the Turks and the schismatics had already disturbed the peace of his country. The funeral of the late emperor was accelerated with singular and even suspicious haste; the claim of Demetrius to the vacant throne was justified by a trite and flimsy sophism, that he was born in the purple, the eldest son of his father's reign. But the empress-mother, the senate and soldiers, the clergy and

[margin: Constantine, the last of the Roman or Greek emperors, A.D. 1448, 1st Nov.-A.D. 1453, 29th May]

[margin: [Selymbria]]

---

[50] See the family of the Castriots in Ducange (Fam. Dalmaticæ, &c. xviii. p. 348-350).

[51] This colony of Albanese is mentioned by Mr. Swinburne (Travels into the Two Sicilies, vol. i. p. 350-354).

[52] [Constantine is generally numbered as Constantine XI., but Gibbon (who counts Constantine, son of Romanus I., as Constantine VIII.; see above, vol v. p. 222) makes him Constantine XII. He was distinguished by the surname Dragases, derived through his mother Irene, who was daughter of Constantine Dragases, a Servian prince.]

[53] The chronology of Phranza is clear and authentic; but, instead of four years and seven months, Spondanus (A.D. 1445, No. 7) assigns seven or eight years to the reign of the last Constantine, which he deduces from a spurious epistle of Eugenius IV. to the king of Ethiopia.

people, were unanimous in the cause of the lawful successor;
and the despot Thomas, who, ignorant of the change, accident-
ally returned to the capital, asserted with becoming zeal the
interest of his absent brother.   An ambassador, the historian
Phranza, was immediately dispatched to the court of Hadrianople.   Amurath received him with honour, and dismissed him
with gifts; but the gracious approbation of the Turkish sultan
announced his supremacy, and the approaching downfall of the
Eastern empire.   By the hands of two illustrious deputies, the
[Jan. A.D. 1449] Imperial crown was placed at Sparta on the head of Constantine.[54]   In the spring, he sailed from the Morea, escaped the
encounter of a Turkish squadron, enjoyed the acclamations of his
subjects, celebrated the festival of a new reign, and exhausted
by his donatives the treasure, or rather the indigence, of the
state.   The emperor immediately resigned to his brothers the
possession of the Morea, and the brittle friendship of the two
princes, Demetrius and Thomas, was confirmed in their mother's
presence by the frail security of oaths and embraces.   His next
occupation was the choice of a consort.   A daughter of the doge
of Venice had been proposed; but the Byzantine nobles objected
the distance between an hereditary monarch and an elective
magistrate; and in their subsequent distress the chief of that
powerful republic was not unmindful of the affront.   Constantine afterwards hesitated between the royal families of Trebizond and Georgia; and the embassy of Phranza represents in his
public and private life the last days of the Byzantine empire.[55]

Embassies of Phranza, A.D. 1450- 1452   The *protovestiare*, or great chamberlain, Phranza, sailed
from Constantinople as minister of a bridegroom; and the relics
of wealth and luxury were applied to his pompous appearance.
His numerous retinue consisted of nobles and guards, of physicians and monks; he was attended by a band of music; and the
term of his costly embassy was protracted above two years.   On
his arrival in Georgia or Iberia, the natives from the towns and
villages flocked around the strangers; and such was their simplicity that they were delighted with the effects, without understanding the cause, of musical harmony.   Among the crowd was
an old man, above an hundred years of age, who had formerly

---

[54] [The ceremony was not renewed at Constantinople.   The emperor desired to
avoid any occasion for quarrels between the Unionists and anti-Unionists.]
[55] Phranza (l. iii. c. 1-6) deserves credit and esteem.

been carried away a captive by the barbarians,[56] and who amused his hearers with a tale of the wonders of India,[57] from whence he had returned to Portugal by an unknown sea.[58] From this hospitable land Phranza proceeded to the court of Trebizond, where he was informed by the Greek prince of the recent decease of Amurath. Instead of rejoicing in the deliverance, the experienced statesman expressed his apprehension that an ambitious youth would not long adhere to the sage and pacific system of his father. After the sultan's decease, his Christian wife Maria,[59] the daughter of the Servian despot, had been honourably restored to her parents: on the fame of her beauty and merit, she was recommended by the ambassador as the most worthy object of the royal choice; and Phranza recapitulates and refutes the specious objections that might be raised against the proposal. The majesty of the purple would ennoble an unequal alliance; the bar of affinity might be removed by liberal alms and the dispensation of the church; the disgrace of Turkish nuptials had been repeatedly overlooked; and, though the fair Maria was near fifty years of age, she might yet hope to give an heir to the empire. Constantine listened to the advice, which was transmitted in the first ship that sailed from Trebizond; but the factions of the court opposed his marriage; and it was finally prevented by the pious vow of the sultana, who ended her days in the monastic profession. Reduced to the first alternative, the choice of Phranza was decided in favour of a Georgian princess; and the vanity of her father was dazzled by the glorious alliance. Instead of demanding, according to the

[56] Suppose him to have been captured in 1394, in Timour's first war in Georgia (Sherefeddin, l. iii. c. 50), he might follow his Tartar master into Hindostan in 1398, and from thence sail to the spice-islands.

[57] The happy and pious Indians lived 150 years, and enjoyed the most perfect productions of the vegetable and mineral kingdoms. The animals were on a large scale: dragons seventy cubits, ants (the *formica Indica*) nine inches long, sheep like elephants, elephants like sheep. Quidlibet audendi, &c.

[58] He sailed in a country vessel from the spice-islands to one of the ports of the exterior India; invenitque navem grandem *Ibericam*, quâ in *Portugalliam* est delatus. This passage, composed in 1477 (Phranza, l. iii. c. 30), twenty years before the discovery of the Cape of Good Hope, is spurious or wonderful. But this new geography is sullied by the old and incompatible error which places the source of the Nile in India.

[59] Cantemir (p. 83), who styles her the daughter of Lazarus Ogli, and the Helen of the Servians, places her marriage with Amurath in the year 1424. It will not easily be believed that in six and twenty years' cohabitation the Sultan corpus ejus non tetigit. After the taking of Constantinople, she fled to Mahomet II. (Phranza, l. iii. c. 22).

primitive and national custom, a price for his daughter,[60] he
offered a portion of fifty-six thousand, with an annual pension
of five thousand, ducats; and the services of the ambassador
were repaid by an assurance that, as his son had been adopted in
baptism by the emperor, the establishment of his daughter should
be the peculiar care of the empress of Constantinople.   On the
return of Phranza, the treaty was ratified by the Greek monarch,
who with his own hand impressed three vermilion crosses on the
Golden Bull, and assured the Georgian envoy that in the spring
his galleys should conduct the bride to her Imperial palace.   But
Constantine embraced his faithful servant, not with the cold approbation of a sovereign, but with the warm confidence of a
friend, who, after a long absence, is impatient to pour his secrets
into the bosom of his friend.   " Since the death of my mother
and of Cantacuzene, who alone advised me without interest or
passion,[61] I am surrounded," said the emperor, "by men whom
I can neither love nor trust nor esteem.   You are not a stranger
to Lucas Notaras, the great admiral : obstinately attached to his
own sentiments, he declares, both in private and public, that his
sentiments are the absolute measure of my thoughts and actions.
The rest of the courtiers are swayed by their personal or factious
views; and how can I consult the monks on questions of policy
and marriage?   I have yet much employment for your diligence
and fidelity.   In the spring you shall engage one of my brothers
to solicit the succour of the Western powers; from the Morea
you shall sail to Cyprus on a particular commission; and from
thence proceed to Georgia to receive and conduct the future empress."   "Your commands," replied Phranza, "are irresistible;
but deign, great Sir," he added, with a serious smile, "to consider that, if I am thus perpetually absent from my family, my
wife may be tempted either to seek another husband or to throw
herself into a monastery."   After laughing at his apprehensions,
the emperor more gravely consoled him by the pleasing assurance that *this* should be his last service abroad, and that he
destined for his son a wealthy and noble heiress; for himself,
the important office of great logothete, or principal minister of

State of the
Byzantine
court

---

[60] The classical reader will recollect the offers of Agamemnon (Iliad, I., v. 144)
and the general practice of antiquity.
[61] Cantacuzene (I am ignorant of his relation to the emperor of that name) was
great domestic, a firm assertor of the Greek creed, and a brother of the queen of
Servia, whom he visited with the character of ambassador (Syropulus, p. 37, 38, 45).

state. The marriage was immediately stipulated; but the office, however incompatible with his own, had been usurped by the ambition of the admiral. Some delay was requisite to negotiate a consent and an equivalent; and the nomination of Phranza was half declared and half suppressed, lest it might be displeasing to an insolent and powerful favourite. The winter was spent in the preparations of his embassy; and Phranza had resolved that the youth his son should embrace this opportunity of foreign travel, and be left, on the appearance of danger, with his maternal kindred of the Morea. Such were the private and public designs, which were interrupted by a Turkish war, and finally buried in the ruins of the empire.[62]

[62] [A Burgundian knight, Bertrandon de la Brocquière, returning from a pilgrimage to Jerusalem, visited Constantinople in 1432, and has left us a very interesting description of life in that city, and also of Murad's court at Hadrianople. Legrand D'Aussy published this work (Voyage d'Outremer et Retour de Jérusalem en France) in 1804, and it has been re-edited by C. Schefer, 1892. An English edition appeared in T. Wright's Early Travels in Palestine (ed. Bohn, 1848, p. 283-382).

Finlay writes (Hist. of Greece, iii. p. 492): "Court processions, religious ceremonies, and national vanity amused and consoled the Greeks as they hastened along the path of degradation and ruin. Dramatic representations of sacred subjects were performed in the Church of St. Sophia, as musical exhibitions had been celebrated in earlier days. Exercises of archery and imitations of Turkish horsemanship replaced the military pageants and the games of the hippodrome which had been the delight of the Byzantine populace in better days."]

CHAPTER LXVIII

*Reign and Character of Mahomet the Second—Siege, Assault,
and final Conquest, of Constantinople, by the Turks—
Death of Constantine Palæologus—Servitude of the
Greeks—Extinction of the Roman Empire in the East—
Consternation of Europe—Conquests and Death of
Mahomet the Second*

Character
of
Mahomet
II.

THE siege of Constantinople by the Turks attracts our
first attention to the person and character of the great
destroyer.   Mahomet the Second [1] was the son of the
second Amurath ; and, though his mother has been decorated
with the titles of Christian and princess, she is more probably confounded with the numerous concubines who peopled from every
climate the harem of the sultan.   His first education and sentiments were those of a devout Musulman ; and, as often as he
conversed with an infidel, he purified his hands and face by the
legal rights of ablution.   Age and empire appear to have relaxed
this narrow bigotry ; his aspiring genius disdained to acknowledge a power above his own ; and in his looser hours he presumed (it is said) to brand the prophet of Mecca as a robber
and impostor.   Yet the Sultan persevered in a decent reverence
for the doctrine and discipline of the Koran ; [2] his private indiscretion must have been sacred from the vulgar ear ; and we
should suspect the credulity of strangers and sectaries, so prone

---

[1] For the character of Mahomet II. it is dangerous to trust either the Turks or
the Christians.   The most moderate picture appears to be drawn by Phranza (l. i.
c. 33), whose resentment had cooled in age and solitude ; see likewise Spondanus
(A.D. 1451, No. 11), and the continuator of Fleury (tom. xxii. p. 552), the *Elogia* of
Paulus Jovius (l. iii. p. 164-166), and the Dictionnaire de Bayle (tom. iii. p. 272-
279).   [Cp. Critobulus, i. 5, in Müller, Frag. Hist. Gr., v. part 2 ; Zinkeisen, Gesch.
des osmanischen Reiches, ii. 468 *sqq. ;* Pears, Destruction of the Greek Empire, p. 206
sqq.]

[2] Cantemir (p. 115), and the mosques which he founded, attest his public regard
for religion.   Mahomet freely disputed with the patriarch Gennadius on the two
religions (Spond. A.D. 1453, No. 22).

to believe that a mind which is hardened against truth must be armed with superior contempt for absurdity and error. Under the tuition of the most skilful masters, Mahomet advanced with an early and rapid progress in the paths of knowledge ; and, besides his native tongue, it is affirmed that he spoke or understood five languages,[3] the Arabic, the Persian, the Chaldæan or Hebrew, the Latin, and the Greek. The Persian might, indeed, contribute to his amusement, and the Arabic to his edification ; and such studies are familiar to the Oriental youth. In the intercourse of the Greeks and Turks, a conqueror might wish to converse with the people over whom he was ambitious to reign ; his own praises in Latin poetry [4] or prose [5] might find a passage to the royal ear ; but what use or merit could recommend to the statesman or the scholar the uncouth dialect of his Hebrew slaves ? The history and geography of the world were familiar to his memory ; the lives of the heroes of the East, perhaps of the West,[6] excited his emulation ; his skill in astrology is excused by the folly of the times, and supposes some rudiments

[3] Quinque linguas præter suam noverat ; Græcam, Latinam, Chaldaicam, Persicam. The Latin translator of Phranza has dropt the Arabic, which the Koran must recommend to every Musulman. [The Greek text of Phranza, i. 32 (p. 95, ed. Bonn) has Ἀραβικήν. The historian Critobulus (for whom see Appendix 1) gives us the means of criticizing this statement of Phrantzes. He says (i. 5, 2) that Mohammad was thoroughly conversant with Arabic and Persian and had studied Greek philosophical works (Aristotelian and Stoic) that were translated into those languages. He repeats this statement, v. 10, 4, and describes the Sultan studying the cosmographical diagrams of Ptolemy. Villoison (Notices et extraits des Manuscrits, vol. viii. part 2, p. 22) quotes from a description of Mohammad given by Nicolaus Sagundinus to King Alfonso of Aragon, in Jan. 1453, the statement that the Sultan kept by him two physicians, one versed in Latin, the other in Greek ; and they instructed him in ancient history.]

[4] Philelphus, by a Latin Ode, requested and obtained the liberty of his wife's mother and sisters from the conqueror of Constantinople. It was delivered into the sultan's hands by the envoys of the duke of Milan. Philelphus himself was suspected of a design of retiring to Constantinople ; yet the orator often sounded the trumpet of holy war (see his Life by M. Lancelot, in the Mémoires de l'Académie des Inscriptions, tom. x. p. 718, 724, &c.). [The Letter of Philelphus to Mohammad, 11th March, 1454, is published in his biography by Rosmini (1805), vol. ii. p. 305.]

[5] Robert Valturio published at Verona, in 1483, his twelve books, de Re Militari, in which he first mentions the use of bombs. By his patron Sigismond Malatesta, prince of Rimini, it had been addressed with a Latin epistle to Mahomet II.

[6] According to Phranza, he assiduously studied the lives and actions of Alexander, Augustus, Constantine and Theodosius. I have read somewhere that Plutarch's Lives were translated by his orders into the Turkish language. If the sultan himself understood Greek, it must have been for the benefit of his subjects. Yet these Lives are a school of freedom as well as of valour. [Critobulus (i. 5, 1) says that Mohammad's examples were Alexander, Pompey and Cæsar—πρὸς Ἀλέξανδρον ἑώρα καὶ Πομπηΐους καὶ Καίσαρας καὶ τοὺς κατ' ἐκείνους βασιλεῖς τε καὶ στρατηγούς.]

of mathematical science ; and a profane taste for the arts is
betrayed in his liberal invitation and reward of the painters of
Italy.[7]   But the influence of religion and learning were employed without effect on his savage and licentious nature.   I
will not transcribe, nor do I firmly believe, the stories of his
fourteen pages, whose bellies were ripped open in search of a
stolen melon ; or of the beauteous slave, whose head he severed
from her body, to convince the Janizaries that their master was
not the votary of love.[8]   His sobriety is attested by the silence
of the Turkish annals, which accuse three, and three only, of
the Ottoman line of the vice of drunkenness.[9]   But it cannot
be denied that his passions were at once furious and inexorable ;
that in the palace, as in the field, a torrent of blood was spilt
on the slightest provocation ; and that the noblest of the captive
youth were often dishonoured by his unnatural lust.   In the
Albanian war, he studied the lessons, and soon surpassed the
example, of his father ; and the conquest of two empires, twelve
kingdoms, and two hundred cities, a vain and flattering account,
is ascribed to his invincible sword.   He was doubtless a soldier,
and possibly a general ; Constantinople has sealed his glory ;
but, if we compare the means, the obstacles, and the achievements, Mahomet the Second must blush to sustain a parallel
with Alexander or Timour.   Under his command, the Ottoman
forces were always more numerous than their enemies ; yet
their progress was bounded by the Euphrates and the Adriatic ;
and his arms were checked by Huniades and Scanderbeg, by
the Rhodian knights, and by the Persian king.

His reign,
A.D. 1451,
Feb. 9-A.D.
1481, July 2

In the reign of Amurath, he twice tasted of royalty, and
twice descended from the throne ; his tender age was incapable
of opposing his father's restoration, but never could he forgive

---

[7] The famous Gentile Bellino, whom he had invited from Venice, was dismissed
with a chain and collar of gold, and a purse of 3000 ducats.   With Voltaire I laugh
at the foolish story of a slave purposely beheaded, to instruct the painter in the
action of the muscles. [Bellini painted a portrait of Mohammad, which is extant.
It passed into the possession of Sir Henry Layard.   For Bellini at the Sultan's
court (1479-80) see L. Thuasne, Gentile Bellini et Sultan Mohammed II.]

[8] [The story is an invention, and is likewise rejected by Thuasne (*op. cit.* p. 53
sqq.), who points out that a similar story was told about Parrhasius (see the elder
Seneca's Controversiæ, x. 5).]

[9] These Imperial drunkards were Soliman I., Selim II., and Amurath IV.
(Cantemir, p. 61).   The sophis of Persia can produce a more regular succession ;
and in the last age our European travellers were the witnesses and the companions
of their revels.

the vizirs who had recommended that salutary measure. His nuptials were celebrated with the daughter of a Turkman emir; and, after a festival of two months, he departed from Hadrian-ople with his bride to reside in the government of Magnesia. Before the end of six weeks, he was recalled by a sudden message from the divan, which announced the decease of Amurath and the mutinous spirit of the Janizaries. His speed and vigour commanded their obedience; he passed the Helle-spont with a chosen guard; and, at a distance of a mile from Hadrianople, the vizirs and emirs, the imams and cadhis, the soldiers and the people, fell prostrate before the new sultan. They affected to weep, they affected to rejoice; he ascended the throne at the age of twenty-one years, and removed the cause of sedition by the death, the inevitable death, of his infant brothers.[10] The ambassadors of Europe and Asia soon appeared to congratulate his accession, and solicit his friend-ship; and to all he spoke the language of moderation and peace. The confidence of the Greek emperor was revived by the solemn oaths and fair assurances with which he sealed the ratification of the treaty; and a rich domain on the banks of the Strymon was assigned for the annual payment of three hundred thousand aspers, the pension of an Ottoman prince who was detained at his request in the Byzantine court. Yet the neighbours of Mahomet might tremble at the severity with which a youthful monarch reformed the pomp of his father's household; the expenses of luxury were applied to those of ambition, and an useless train of seven thousand falconers was either dismissed from his service or enlisted in his troops. In the first summer of his reign, he visited with an army the Asiatic provinces; but, after humbling the pride, Mahomet accepted the submission, of the Caramanian, that he might not be diverted by the smallest obstacle from the execution of his great design.[11]

The Mahometan, and more especially the Turkish, casuists

---

[10] Calapin, one of these royal infants, was saved from his cruel brother, and baptized at Rome under the name of Callistus Othomannus. The emperor Frederic III. presented him with an estate in Austria, where he ended his life; and Cuspinian, who in his youth conversed with the aged prince at Vienna, applauds his piety and wisdom (de Cæsaribus, p. 672, 673).

[11] See the accession of Mahomet II. in Ducas (c. 33), Phranza (l. i. c. 33, l. ii. c. 2), Chalcondyles (l. vii. p. 199 [p. 376, ed. Bonn]), and Cantemir (p. 96).

have pronounced that no promise can bind the faithful against the interest and duty of their religion; and that the sultan may abrogate his own treaties and those of his predecessors. The justice and magnanimity of Amurath had scorned this immoral privilege; but his son, though the proudest of men, could stoop from ambition to the basest arts of dissimulation and deceit.   Peace was on his lips, while war was in his heart: he incessantly sighed for the possession of Constantinople; and the Greeks, by their own indiscretion, afforded the first pretence of the fatal rupture.[12]   Instead of labouring to be forgotten, their ambassadors pursued his camp, to demand the payment and even the increase of their annual stipend: the divan was importuned by their complaints, and the vizir, a secret friend of the Christians, was constrained to deliver the sense of his brethren. "Ye foolish and miserable Romans," said Calil, "we know your devices, and ye are ignorant of your own danger! the scrupulous Amurath is no more; his throne is occupied by a young conqueror, whom no laws can bind and no obstacles can resist; and, if you escape from his hands, give praise to the divine clemency, which yet delays the chastisement of your sins.   Why do ye seek to affright us by vain and indirect menaces?   Release the fugitive Orchan, crown him sultan of Romania; call the Hungarians from beyond the Danube; arm against us the nations of the West; and be assured that you will only provoke and precipitate your ruin."   But, if the fears of the ambassadors

[12] Before I enter on the siege of Constantinople, I shall observe that, except the short hints of Cantemir and Leunclavius, I have not been able to obtain any Turkish account of this conquest; such an account as we possess of the siege of Rhodes by Soliman II. (Mémoires de l'Académie des Inscriptions, tom. xxvi. p. 723-769).   I must therefore depend on the Greeks, whose prejudices, in some degree, are subdued by their distress.   Our standard texts are those of Ducas (c. 34-42), Phranza (l. iii. c. 7-20), Chalcondyles (l. viii. p. 201-214 [p. 380 *sqq.*, ed. Bonn]), and Leonardus Chiensis (Historia C. P. a Turco expugnatæ, Norimberghæ, 1544, in 4to, 20 leaves [more accessible in Reusner's Epistolæ Turcicæ, i. p. 113 *sqq.*, or in the Chronica Turcica of Lonicerus, i. p. 315 *sqq.*]).   The last of these narratives is the earliest in date, since it was composed in the isle of Chios, the 16th of August, 1453, only seventy-nine days after the loss of the city, and in the first confusion of ideas and passions.   Some hints may be added from an epistle of Cardinal Isidore (in Farragine Rerum Turcicarum, ad calcem Chalcondyl. Clauseri, Basil, 1556 [and in Reusner's Epistolæ Turcicæ, i. 104]) to Pope Nicholas V., and a tract of Theodosius Zygomala, which he addressed, in the year 1581, to Martin Crusius (Turco-Græcia, l. i. p. 74-98, Basil, 1584).   The various facts and materials are briefly though critically reviewed by Spondanus (A.D. 1453, No. 1-27).   The hearsay-relations of Monstrelet and the distant Latins, I shall take leave to disregard. [See for other authorities Appendix 3.]

were alarmed by the stern language of the vizir, they were
soothed by the courteous audience and friendly speeches of the
Ottoman prince; and Mahomet assured them that on his return
to Hadrianople he would redress the grievances, and consult the
true interests, of the Greeks. No sooner had he repassed the
Hellespont than he issued a mandate to suppress their pension
and to expel their officers from the banks of the Strymon: in
this measure he betrayed an hostile mind; and the second order
announced, and in some degree commenced, the siege of Constantinople. In the narrow pass of the Bosphorus, an Asiatic
fortress had formerly been raised by his grandfather: in the
opposite situation, on the European side, he resolved to erect
a more formidable castle; and a thousand masons were commanded to assemble in the spring, on a spot named Asomaton,
about five miles from the Greek metropolis.[13] Persuasion is the [March 26]
resource of the feeble; and the feeble can seldom persuade:
the ambassadors of the emperor attempted, without success, to
divert Mahomet from the execution of his design. They represented, that his grandfather had solicited the permission of
Manuel to build a castle on his own territories; but that this
double fortification, which would command the strait, could
only tend to violate the alliance of the nations, to intercept the
Latins who traded in the Black Sea, and perhaps to annihilate
the subsistence of the city. "I form no enterprise," replied the
perfidious sultan, "against the city; but the empire of Constantinople is measured by her walls. Have you forgot the
distress to which my father was reduced, when you formed a
league with the Hungarians; when they invaded our country by
land, and the Hellespont was occupied by the French galleys?
Amurath was compelled to force the passage of the Bosphorus;
and your strength was not equal to your malevolence. I was
then a child at Hadrianople; the Moslems trembled; and for a

---

[13] The situation of the fortress, and the topography of the Bosphorus, are best
learned from Peter Gyllius (de Bosphoro Thracio, l. ii. c. 13 [cp. p. 169]), Leunclavius (Pandect. p. 445), and Tournefort (Voyage dans le Levant, tom. ii. lettre
xv. p. 443, 444); but I must regret the map or plan which Tournefort sent to the
French minister of the marine. The reader may turn back to Chap. xvii. [vol. ii.]
of this history. [The building of the fortress is well described by Critobulus, i. 10
and 11 (p. 59-62). The place is now called Rumili Hissari, Castle of Rumelia.
The village of Asomaton is the modern Arnaut kioï, a little to the north of Bebek.
Compare Mordtmann, Belagerung und Eroberung Constantinopels, p. 17, 18; Paspates, Πολιορκία καὶ ἄλωσις τῆς Κωνστ., p. 78 sqq.; Pears, Destruction of the Greek
Empire, p. 164.]

while the *Gabours* [14] insulted our disgrace.   But, when my father
had triumphed in the field of Warna, he vowed to erect a fort
on the western shore, and that vow it is my duty to accomplish.
Have ye the right, have ye the power, to control my actions on my
own ground?   For that ground *is* my own : as far as the shores
of the Bosphorus, Asia is inhabited by the Turks, and Europe is
deserted by the Romans.   Return, and inform your king that
the present Ottoman is far different from his predecessors ; that
his resolutions surpass *their* wishes ; and that *he* performs more
than *they* could resolve.   Return in safety ; but the next who
delivers a similar message may expect to be flayed alive."   After
this declaration, Constantine, the first of the Greeks in spirit as
in rank,[15] had determined to unsheath the sword, and to resist
the approach and establishment of the Turks on the Bosphorus.
He was disarmed by the advice of his civil and ecclesiastical
ministers, who recommended a system less generous, and even
less prudent, than his own, to approve their patience and long-
suffering, to brand the Ottoman with the name and guilt of an
aggressor, and to depend on chance and time for their own safety
and the destruction of a fort which could not be long maintained
in the neighbourhood of a great and populous city.   Amidst hope
and fear, the fears of the wise and the hopes of the credulous,
the winter rolled away ; the proper business of each man, and
each hour, was postponed ; and the Greeks shut their eyes
against the impending danger, till the arrival of the spring and
the sultan decided the assurance of their ruin.

He builds a
fortress on
the Bos-
phorus,
A.D. 1452,
March

Of a master who never forgives, the orders are seldom dis-
obeyed.   On the twenty-sixth of March, the appointed spot of
Asomaton was covered with an active swarm of Turkish artificers ; and the materials by sea and land were diligently transported from Europe and Asia.[16]   The lime had been burnt in

---

[14] The opprobrious name which the Turks bestow on the Infidels is expressed
Καβουρ by Ducas, and *Giaour* by Leunclavius and the moderns.   The former term
is derived by Ducange (Gloss. Græc. tom. i. p. 530) from καβουρον, in vulgar Greek a
tortoise, as denouncing a retrograde motion from the faith.   But, alas ! *Gabour* is
no more than *Gheber*, which was transferred from the Persian to the Turkish language, from the worshippers of fire to those of the crucifix (d'Herbelot, Bibliot.
Orient. p. 375).

[15] Phranza does justice to his master's sense and courage : Calliditatem hominis
non ignorans Imperator prior arma movere constituit, and stigmatizes the folly of
the cum sacri tum profani proceres, which he had heard, amentes spe vanâ pasci.
Ducas was not a privy counsellor.

[16] Instead of this clear and consistent account, the Turkish Annals (Cantemir,
p. 97) revived the foolish tale of the ox's hide, and Dido's stratagem in the founda-

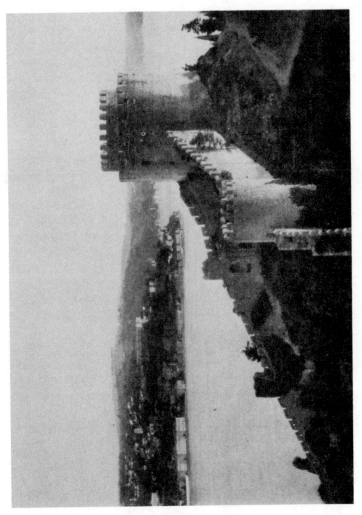

RUMILI HISSAR ON THE BOSPHORUS

Cataphrygia; the timber was cut down in the woods of Heraclea
and Nicomedia; and the stones were dug from the Anatolian
quarries. Each of the thousand masons was assisted by two
workmen; and a measure of two cubits was marked for their
daily task. The fortress [17] was built in a triangular form; each
angle was flanked by a strong and massy tower; one on the
declivity of the hill, two along the sea-shore; a thickness of
twenty-two feet was assigned for the walls, thirty for the
towers; and the whole building was covered with a solid platform of lead. Mahomet himself pressed and directed the work
with indefatigable ardour; his three viziers claimed the honour
of finishing their respective towers; the zeal of the cadhis emulated that of the Janizaries; the meanest labour was ennobled
by the service of God and the sultan; and the diligence of the
multitude was quickened by the eye of a despot, whose smile
was the hope of fortune, and whose frown was the messenger of
death. The Greek emperor beheld with terror the irresistible
progress of the work; and vainly strove, by flattery and gifts,
to assuage an implacable foe, who sought, and secretly fomented,
the slightest occasion of a quarrel. Such occasions must soon
and inevitably be found. The ruins of stately churches, and even
the marble columns which had been consecrated to St. Michael
the archangel, were employed without scruple by the profane
and rapacious Moslems; and some Christians, who presumed to
oppose the removal, received from their hands the crown of martyrdom. Constantine had solicited a Turkish guard to protect
the fields and harvests of his subjects: the guard was fixed; but
their first order was to allow free pasture to the mules and
horses of the camp, and to defend their brethren if they should
be molested by the natives. The retinue of an Ottoman chief
had left their horses to pass the night among the ripe corn: the
damage was felt; the insult was resented; and several of both

tion of Carthage. These annals (unless we are swayed by an antichristian prejudice)
are far less valuable than the Greek historians.

[17] In the dimensions of this fortress, the old castle of Europe, Phranza does not
exactly agree with Chalcondyles, whose description has been verified on the spot
by his editor Leunclavius. [Phrantzes (p. 234) gives the breadth of the towers as
25 feet, and this nearly agrees with Critobulus (i. 11, 4) who says "12 cubits,"
i.e., 24 feet. Chalcondyles says 22 feet, and Ducas "30 spans," i.e., 22½ feet. Critobulus alone gives the height of the wall, 100 feet, and adds that in size the fortress
resembled not a fortress but a little town (πολίχνη). The fort was completed in
August.]

nations were slain in a tumultuous conflict.   Mahomet listened
with joy to the complaint; and a detachment was commanded
to exterminate the guilty village: the guilty had fled; but forty
innocent and unsuspecting reapers were massacred by the soldiers.   Till this provocation, Constantinople had been open to
the visits of commerce and curiosity: on the first alarm, the
gates were shut; but the emperor, still anxious for peace, released on the third day his Turkish captives,[18] and expressed, in
a last message, the firm resignation of a Christian and a soldier.
"Since neither oaths, nor treaty, nor submission, can secure
peace, pursue," said he to Mahomet, "your impious warfare.
My trust is in God alone: if it should please him to mollify
your heart, I shall rejoice in the happy change; if he delivers
the city into your hands, I submit without a murmur to his
holy will.   But, until the Judge of the earth shall pronounce
between us, it is my duty to live and die in the defence of my
people."   The sultan's answer was hostile and decisive; his
fortifications were completed; and before his departure for
Hadrianople he stationed a vigilant Aga and four hundred Janizaries to levy a tribute of the ships of every nation that should
pass within the reach of their cannon.   A Venetian vessel, refusing obedience to the new lords of the Bosphorus, was sunk
with a single bullet.   The master and thirty sailors escaped in
the boat; but they were dragged in chains to the *Porte;* the
chief was impaled; his companions were beheaded; and the
historian Ducas [19] beheld, at Demotica, their bodies exposed to
the wild beasts.   The siege of Constantinople was deferred till
the ensuing spring; but an Ottoman army marched into the
Morea to divert the force of the brothers of Constantine.   At
this æra of calamity, one of these princes, the despot Thomas,
was blessed or afflicted with the birth of a son, "the last
heir," says the plaintive Phranza, "of the last spark of the
Roman empire".[20]

The Turk-
ish war,
June;

Sept. 1

[The ship
of Antonio
Rizzo,
Nov. 26]

A.D. 1453,
Jan. 17

[18] Among these were some pages of Mahomet, so conscious of his inexorable
rigour that they begged to lose their heads in the city unless they could return
before sunset.

[19] Ducas, c. 35.   Phranza (l. iii. c. 3), who had sailed in his vessel, commemorates
the Venetian pilot as a martyr. [Cp. Niccolò Barbaro, p. 2 (ed. Cornet). Other
Venetian vessels were more successful.]

[20] Auctum est Palæologorum genus, et Imperii successor, parvæque Romanorum
scintillæ heres natus, Andreas, &c. (Phranza, l. iii. c. 7).   The strong expression
was inspired by his feelings.

The Greeks and the Turks passed an anxious and sleepless Preparations for the siege of Constantinople, A.D. 1452, September—A.D. 1453, April winter: the former were kept awake by their fears, the latter by their hopes; both by the preparations of defence and attack; and the two emperors, who had the most to lose or to gain, were the most deeply affected by the national sentiment. In Mahomet, that sentiment was inflamed by the ardour of his youth and temper: he amused his leisure with building at Hadrianople [21] the lofty palace of Jehan Numa (the watch-tower of the world); but his serious thoughts were irrevocably bent on the conquest of the city of Cæsar. At the dead of night, about the second watch, he started from his bed, and commanded the instant attendance of his prime vizir. The message, the hour, the prince, and his own situation alarmed the guilty conscience of Calil Basha, who had possessed the confi- [Halil Pasha] dence, and advised the restoration, of Amurath. On the accession of the son, the vizir was confirmed in his office and the appearances of favour; but the veteran statesman was not insensible that he trod on a thin and slippery ice, which might break under his footsteps and plunge him in the abyss. His friendship for the Christians, which might be innocent under the late reign, had stigmatized him with the name of Gabour Ortachi, or foster brother of the infidels; [22] and his avarice entertained a venal and treasonable correspondence, which was detected and punished after the conclusion of the war. On receiving the royal mandate, he embraced, perhaps for the last time, his wife and children; filled up a cup with pieces of gold, hastened to the palace, adored the sultan, and offered, according to the Oriental custom, the slight tribute of his duty and gratitude.[23] "It is not my wish," said Mahomet, "to resume my gifts, but rather to heap and multiply them on thy head. In my turn, I ask a present far more valuable and important,— Constantinople." As soon as the vizir had recovered from his

[21] Cantemir, p. 97, 98. The sultan was either doubtful of his conquest or ignorant of the superior merits of Constantinople. A city or a kingdom may sometimes be ruined by the Imperial fortune of their sovereign.

[22] Σύντροφος, by the president Cousin, is translated père nourricier, most correctly indeed from the Latin version; but in his haste he has overlooked the note by which Ismael Boillaud (ad Ducam, c. 35) acknowledges and rectifies his own error.

[23] The Oriental custom of never appearing without gifts before a sovereign or a superior is of high antiquity, and seems analogous with the idea of sacrifice, still more ancient and universal. See the examples of such Persian gifts, Ælian, Hist. Var. l. i. c. 31-33.

surprise, "The same God," said he, "who has already given thee so large a portion of the Roman empire, will not deny the remnant, and the capital. His providence and thy power assure thy success; and myself, with the rest of thy faithful slaves, will sacrifice our lives and fortunes." "Lala" [24] (or preceptor), continued the sultan, "do you see this pillow? all the night, in my agitation, I have pulled it on one side and the other; I have risen from my bed, again have I lain down; yet sleep has not visited these weary eyes. Beware of the gold and silver of the Romans; in arms we are superior; and with the aid of God, and the prayers of the prophet, we shall speedily become masters of Constantinople." To sound the disposition of his soldiers, he often wandered through the streets alone and in disguise; and it was fatal to discover the sultan, when he wished to escape from the vulgar eye. His hours were spent in delineating the plan of the hostile city; in debating with his generals and engineers, on what spot he should erect his batteries; on which side he should assault the walls; where he should spring his mines; to what place he should apply his scaling-ladders; and the exercises of the day repeated and proved the lucubrations of the night.

The great cannon of Mahomet

[Urban]

Among the implements of destruction, he studied with peculiar care the recent and tremendous discovery of the Latins; and his artillery surpassed whatever had yet appeared in the world. A founder of cannon, a Dane or Hungarian,[25] who had been almost starved in the Greek service, deserted to the Moslems, and was liberally entertained by the Turkish sultan. Mahomet was satisfied with the answer to his first question, which he eagerly pressed on the artist. "Am I able to cast a cannon capable of throwing a stone or ball of sufficient size to batter the walls of Constantinople? I am not ignorant of their strength, but, were they more solid than those of Babylon, I could oppose an engine of superior power; the position and management of that

---

[24] The *Lala* of the Turks (Cantemir, p. 34) and the *Tata* of the Greeks (Ducas, c. 35) are derived from the natural language of children; and it may be observed that all such primitive words which denote their parents are the simple repetition of one syllable, composed of a labial or dental consonant and an open vowel (des Brosses, Mécanisme des Langues, tom. i. p. 231-247).

[25] [Orban ('Ορβανός) was a Hungarian; no authority says that he was a Dane. Gibbon has mistaken the phrase of Chalcondyles who pedantically describes him as a "Dacian" (Δάξ), p. 385, ed. Bonn. τηλεβολιστής is the word Chalcondyles uses for a "gunner". Strictly Orban was a τηλεβολοποιός.]

engine must be left to your engineers." On this assurance, a
foundry was established in Hadrianople: the metal was prepared; and, at the end of three months, Urban produced a piece
of brass ordnance of stupendous and almost incredible magnitude; a measure of twelve palms is assigned to the bore; and
the stone bullet weighed above six hundred pounds.[26] A vacant
place before the new palace was chosen for the first experiment;
but, to prevent the sudden and mischievous effects of astonishment and fear, a proclamation was issued that the cannon would
be discharged the ensuing day. The explosion was felt or heard
in the circuit of an hundred furlongs: the ball, by the force of
gunpowder, was driven above a mile; and on the spot where it
fell, it buried itself a fathom deep in the ground. For the con-
veyance of this destructive engine,[27] a frame or carriage of thirty
waggons was linked together and drawn along by a team of sixty
oxen; two hundred men on both sides were stationed to poise
and support the rolling weight; two hundred and fifty workmen
marched before to smooth the way and repair the bridges; and
near two months were employed in a laborious journey of one
hundred and fifty miles. A lively [28] philosopher derides, on this
occasion, the credulity of the Greeks, and observes, with much
reason, that we should always distrust the exaggerations of a
vanquished people. He calculates that a ball, even of two
hundred pounds, would require a charge of one hundred and
fifty pounds of powder; and that the stroke would be feeble and
impotent, since not a fifteenth part of the mass could be inflamed
at the same moment. A stranger as I am to the act of destruction, I can discern that the modern improvements of artillery
prefer the number of pieces to the weight of metal; the quick-

[The great cannon starts, beginning of February, A.D. 1453]

[Arrival, end of March]

[26] The Attic talent weighed about sixty minæ, or avoirdupois pounds (see Hooper
on Ancient Weights, Measures, &c.); but among the modern Greeks that classic
appellation was extended to a weight of one hundred or one hundred and twenty-
five pounds (Ducange, τάλαντον). Leonardus Chiensis measured the ball or stone
of the *second* cannon : Lapidem, qui palmis undecim ex meis ambibat in gyro. [The
palma, or span, being reckoned at 8 inches, it is calculated that the ball would have
weighed 1456 lb. avoirdupois. Mordtmann, *op. cit.*, p. 36. Critobulus, i. 29, describes another enormous cannon.]

[27] [According to Zorzo Dolfin, Assedio e presa di Cpli, § 16 (Paspates, *op. cit.*
p. 120 n.) the cannon was conveyed *in pieces.*]

[28] See Voltaire (Hist. Générale, c. xci. p. 294, 295). He was ambitious of universal monarchy; and the poet frequently aspires to the name and style of an
astronomer, a chemist, &c. [Mordtmann (*loc. cit.*) says that stone balls, measuring from 72 to 88 inches round, have been found in the Arsenal, in the walls of
Galata, and elsewhere.]

ness of the fire to the sound, or even the consequence, of a single explosion.   Yet I dare not reject the positive and unanimous evidence of contemporary writers; nor can it seem improbable that the first artists, in their rude and ambitious efforts, should have transgressed the standard of moderation.   A Turkish cannon, more enormous than that of Mahomet, still guards the entrance of the Dardanelles; and, if the use be inconvenient, it has been found on a late trial that the effect was far from contemptible.   A stone bullet of *eleven* hundred pounds weight was once discharged with three hundred and thirty pounds of powder; at the distance of six hundred yards, it shivered into three rocky fragments, traversed the strait, and, leaving the waters in a foam, again rose and bounded against the opposite hill.[29]

While Mahomet threatened the capital of the East, the Greek emperor implored with fervent prayers the assistance of earth and heaven.   But the invisible powers were deaf to his supplications; and Christendom beheld with indifference the fall of Constantinople, while she derived at least some promise of supply from the jealous and temporal policy of the sultan of Egypt. Some states were too weak, and others too remote; by some the danger was considered as imaginary, by others as inevitable : the Western princes were involved in their endless and domestic quarrels ; and the Roman pontiff was exasperated by the falsehood or obstinacy of the Greeks.   Instead of employing in their favour the arms and treasures of Italy, Nicholas the Fifth had foretold their approaching ruin ; and his honour was engaged in the accomplishment of his prophecy.   Perhaps he was softened by the last extremity of their distress ; but his compassion was tardy; his efforts were faint and unavailing; and Constantinople had fallen, before the squadrons of Genoa and Venice could sail from their harbours.[30]   Even the princes of the Morea and of the Greek islands affected a cold neutrality : the Genoese colony of Galata negotiated a private treaty ; and the sultan indulged them in the delusive hope that by his clemency they

Marginal note: Mahomet II. forms the siege of Constantinople, A.D. 1453, April 6

---

[29] The Baron de Tott (tom. iii. p. 85-89), who fortified the Dardanelles against the Russians, describes in a lively, and even comic, strain his own prowess and the consternation of the Turks.   But that adventurous traveller does not possess the art of gaining our confidence.

[30] Non audivit, indignum ducens, says the honest Antoninus ; but, as the Roman court was afterwards grieved and ashamed, we find the more courtly expression of Platina, in animo fuisse pontifici juvare Græcos, and the positive assertion of Æneas Sylvius, structam classem, &c. (Spond. A.D. 1453, No. 3).

might survive the ruin of the empire. A plebeian crowd, and
some Byzantine nobles, basely withdrew from the danger of
their country ; and the avarice of the rich denied the emperor,
and reserved for the Turks, the secret treasures which might
have raised in their defence whole armies of mercenaries.[31] The
indigent and solitary prince prepared, however, to sustain his
formidable adversary ; but, if his courage were equal to the peril,
his strength was inadequate to the contest. In the beginning
of the spring, the Turkish vanguard swept the towns and villages
as far as the gates of Constantinople : submission was spared and
protected ; whatever presumed to resist was exterminated with
fire and sword. The Greek places on the Black Sea, Mesembria, [Missivri,
Acheloum, and Bizon, surrendered on the first summons ; Sely- Achiallu, Viza]
bria alone[32] deserved the honours of a siege or blockade ; and the [Silivri]
bold inhabitants, while they were invested by land, launched
their boats, pillaged the opposite coast of Cyzicus, and sold their
captives in the public market. But on the approach of Mahomet
himself all was silent and prostrate ; he first halted at the
distance of five miles ; and from thence advancing in battle-
array planted before the gate of St. Romanus the Imperial
standard ; and, on the sixth day of April, formed the memorable
siege of Constantinople.

The troops of Asia and Europe extended on the right and left Forces of
from the Propontis to the harbour ; the Janizaries in the front the Turks ;
were stationed before the sultan's tent ; the Ottoman line was
covered by a deep entrenchment ; and a subordinate army inclosed the suburb of Galata, and watched the doubtful faith of
the Genoese. The inquisitive Philelphus, who resided in Greece
about thirty years before the siege, is confident that all the
Turkish forces, of any name or value, could not exceed the
number of sixty thousand horse and twenty thousand foot ; and

---

[31] Antonin. in Prooem.—Epist. Cardinal. Isidor. apud Spondanum ; and Dr.
Johnson, in the tragedy of Irene, has happily seized this characteristic circumstance :—

> The groaning Greeks dig up the golden caverns,
> The accumulated wealth of hoarding ages ;
> That wealth which, granted to their weeping prince,
> Had rang'd embattled nations at their gates.

[32] [The Tower of St. Stephen, on the sea of Marmora, two hours from the city, was
also stormed and the garrison beheaded. Critobulus (i. 32) mentions that Mohammad himself, after his arrival, stormed the forts of Studion and Therapeion ; the
latter is Therapia on the Bosphorus. He also sent his admiral Paltogles to capture
the fort of the Prince's island (ib. 33), for which see Pears, op. cit. p. 253. These facts
are recorded by Critobulus alone.]

he upbraids the pusillanimity of the nations who had tamely yielded to a handful of barbarians. Such, indeed, might be the regular establishment of the *Capiculi*,[33] the troops of the Porte who marched with the prince and were paid from his royal treasury. But the bashaws, in their respective governments, maintained or levied a provincial militia; many lands were held by a military tenure; many volunteers were attracted by the hope of spoil; and the sound of the holy trumpet invited a swarm of hungry and fearless fanatics, who might contribute at least to multiply the terrors, and in a first attack to blunt the swords, of the Christians. The whole mass of the Turkish powers is magnified by Ducas, Chalcondyles, and Leonard of Chios, to the amount of three or four hundred thousand men; but Phranza was a less remote and more accurate judge; and his precise definition of two hundred and fifty-eight thousand does not exceed the measure of experience and probability.[34] The navy of the besiegers was less formidable: the Propontis was overspread with three hundred and twenty sail; but of these no more than eighteen could be rated as galleys of war; and the far greater part must be degraded to the condition of

---

[33] The palatine troops are styled *Capiculi*, the provincials, *Seratculi*: and most of the names and institutions of the Turkish militia existed before the *Canon Nameh* of Soliman II., from which, and his own experience, Count Marsigli has composed his Military State of the Ottoman empire. [Mohammad pitched his headquarters on the hill of Maltepe, a short distance from the middle part of the land wall, opposite to the gate of St. Romanus (Top Kapussi) and the part of the wall known as Myriandrion (cp. Mordtmann, Esquisse topographique de Constantinople, p. 24). The Anatolic army (under Isaac) was on his right, stretching to the sea of Marmora, the Rumeliot (under Karatzas) on his left, towards the Golden Horn. A special force was committed to Zagan Pasha, and posted behind Galata, on the ground which is now Pera, to watch the Genoese; and Zagan was also to survey the building of a bridge across the Golden Horn to the north point of Constantinople (Porta Cynegii, Aiwan Kapussi). See Critobulus, i. 27 (p. 75); N. Barbaro, p. 30.— The numbers of the besieging army are given as follows: Phrantzes, 258,000; Critobulus, over 300,000 (not counting camp followers, &c.); Chalcondyles, 400,000; Ducas, over 400,000 (p. 267), but his particular items (p. 283) amount to 260,000; Leonardus, over 300,000; N. Barbaro, 160,000; the Thrênos of Constantinople, 217,000. Tedardi, a Florentine witness (for whose work see Appendix 3), nearly agrees with Barbaro; counting 140,000 fighting men and 60,000 traders, tailors, &c., who followed the army in hope of gain (Informacion, p. 21). Mordtmann is inclined to accept the number of Barbaro; and cp. Pears, *op. cit.* p. 223. It is to be observed that there were a large number of Christians in the Turkish army according to Tedardi (the Thrênos gives the number at 30,000; l. 752).]

[34] The observation of Philelphus is approved by Cuspinian in the year 1508 (de Cæsaribus, in Epilog. de Militiâ Turcicâ, p. 697). Marsigli proves that the effective armies of the Turks are much less numerous than they appear. In the army that besieged Constantinople, Leonardus Chiensis reckons no more than 15,000 Janizaries. [The usual strength of the Ottoman army on an important expedition was about 100,000. For Mohammad's fleet cp. Pears, *op. cit.* p. 232-5.]

storeships and transports, which poured into the camp fresh supplies of men, ammunition, and provisions. In her last decay, of the Greeks Constantinople was still peopled with more than an hundred thousand inhabitants ; but these numbers are found in the accounts, not of war, but of captivity ; and they mostly consisted of mechanics, of priests, of women, and of men devoid of that spirit which even women have sometimes exerted for the common safety. I can suppose, I could almost excuse, the reluctance of subjects to serve on a distant frontier, at the will of a tyrant ; but the man who dares not expose his life in the defence of his children and his property has lost in society the first and most active energies of nature. By the emperor's command, a particular inquiry had been made through the streets and houses, how many of the citizens, or even of the monks, were able and willing to bear arms for their country. The lists were intrusted to Phranza ; [35] and, after a diligent addition, he informed his master, with grief and surprise, that the national defence was reduced to four thousand nine hundred and seventy *Romans*. [4973] Between Constantine and his faithful minister, this comfortless secret was preserved ; and a sufficient proportion of shields, cross-bows, and muskets was distributed from the arsenal to the city-bands. They derived some accession from a body of two [Arrival of Giustini-thousand strangers, under the command of John Justiniani, a ani, Jan. noble Genoese ; [36] a liberal donative was advanced to these auxili-1453] aries ; and a princely recompense, the isle of Lemnos, was promised to the valour and victory of their chief. A strong chain [Harbour blocked by was drawn across the mouth of the harbour ; [37] it was supported chain, April 2] by some Greek and Italian vessels of war and merchandise ; and the ships of every Christian nation, that successively arrived from Candia and the Black Sea, were detained for the public service. Against the powers of the Ottoman empire, a city of the extent of thirteen, perhaps of sixteen, miles was defended by a scanty

[35] Ego eidem (Imp.) tabellas extribui non absque dolore et mœstitiâ, mansitque apud nos duos aliis occultus numerus (Phranza, l. iii. c. 3). With some indulgence for national prejudices, we cannot desire a more authentic witness, not only of public facts, but of private counsels. [In addition to the *Romans* Phrantzes counts about 2000 foreigners. His statement as to the total number is confirmed by Tedardi.]

[36] [All these strangers had not come with Giustiniani ; he brought 700 (Barbaro, p. 13) or perhaps only 400 (Critobulus, i. 25 ; Leonardus, p. 319).]

[37] [For the chain see above, vol. ii. p. 153. A part of the chain is preserved in the court of the church of St. Irene, and may be seen figured in Mordtmann's Esquisse Topographique, p. 49. Cp. above, vol. vi. p. 410.]

garrison of seven or eight thousand soldiers.   Europe and Asia
were open to the besiegers ; but the strength and provisions of
the Greeks must sustain a daily decrease ; nor could they indulge
the expectation of any foreign succour or supply.[38]

False
union of
the two
churches,
A.D. 1452,
Dec. 12

The primitive Romans would have drawn their swords in the
resolution of death or conquest.   The primitive Christians might
have embraced each other, and awaited in patience and charity
the stroke of martyrdom.   But the Greeks of Constantinople
were animated only by the spirit of religion, and that spirit was
productive only of animosity and discord.   Before his death, the
emperor John Palæologus had renounced the unpopular measure
of an union with the Latins ; nor was the idea revived, till the
distress of his brother Constantine imposed a last trial of flattery
and dissimulation.[39]   With the demand of temporal aid, his
ambassadors were instructed to mingle the assurance of spiritual
obedience ; his neglect of the church was excused by the urgent
cares of the state ; and his orthodox wishes solicited the presence
of a Roman legate.   The Vatican had been too often deluded ;
yet the signs of repentance could not decently be overlooked ;
a legate was more easily granted than an army ; and, about

[Nov. A.D.
1452]

six months before the final destruction, the cardinal Isidore of
Russia appeared in that character with a retinue of priests and
soldiers.   The emperor saluted him as a friend and father ; respectfully listened to his public and private sermons ; and with
the most obsequious of the clergy and laymen subscribed the act
of union, as it had been ratified in the council of Florence.   On
the twelfth of December, the two nations, in the church of St.

---

[38] [Since the fourth century, various emperors had improved the fortifications of
the city.   Heraclius had strengthened the Palace of Blachern on the west (at the
time of the Avar siege) by a new wall, between the Tower of Anemas and the
Xyloporta ; and Leo V. had built another wall outside the wall of Heraclius.   In
the twelfth century Manuel Comnenus built a wall enclosing the quarter called
Caligaria, from the Tower of Anemas to the gate of Xylokerkos (or Kerkoporta).
The Gate of Caligaria (Egri Kapu) was in this new wall of Manuel.   The ineffective
siege of Constantinople by Murad in 1432 moved John Palæologus to repair and
strengthen the whole outer line of wall, and inscriptions recording this are found
on the towers.   The fortifications on the seaside, the walls along the Golden Horn
and the Propontis, were restored in the 9th century.   It is interesting to find an
inscription on a tower (near the Porta Contoscali) stating that it was repaired by
George Brankovič, Despot of Servia, in 1448.   In 1453 George contributed troops to
the army of Mohammad.]

[39] In Spondanus, the narrative of the union is not only partial but imperfect.
The bishop of Pamiers died in 1642, and the history of Ducas, which represents
these scenes (c. 36, 37) with such truth and spirit, was not printed till the year
1649.

Sophia, joined in the communion of sacrifice and prayer; and the names of the two pontiffs were solemnly commemorated: the names of Nicholas the Fifth, the vicar of Christ, and of the patriarch Gregory, who had been driven into exile by a rebellious people.

But the dress and language of the Latin priest who officiated at the altar were an object of scandal; and it was observed with horror that he consecrated a cake or wafer of *unleavened* bread and poured cold water into the cup of the sacrament. A national historian acknowledges with a blush that none of his countrymen, not the emperor himself, were sincere in this occasional conformity.[40] Their hasty and unconditional submission was palliated by a promise of future revisal; but the best or the worst of their excuses was the confession of their own perjury. When they were pressed by the reproaches of their honest brethren, "Have patience," they whispered, "have patience till God shall have delivered the city from the great dragon who seeks to devour us. You shall then perceive whether we are truly reconciled with the Azymites." But patience is not the attribute of zeal; nor can the arts of a court be adapted to the freedom and violence of popular enthusiasm. From the dome of St. Sophia, the inhabitants of either sex and of every degree rushed in crowds to the cell of the monk Gennadius,[41] to consult the oracle of the church. The holy man was invisible; entranced, as it should seem, in deep meditation or divine rapture; but he had exposed on the door of his cell a speaking tablet; and they successively withdrew, after reading these tremendous words: " O miserable Romans! why will ye abandon the truth? and why, instead of confiding in God, will ye put your trust in the Italians? In losing your faith, you will lose your city. Have mercy on me, O Lord! I protest, in thy presence,

(marginal note: Obstinacy and fanaticism of the Greeks)

[40] Phranza, one of the conforming Greeks, acknowledges that the measure was adopted only propter spem auxilii; he affirms with pleasure that those who refused to perform their devotion in St. Sophia, extra culpam et in pace essent (l. iii. c. 20).

[41] His primitive and secular name was George Scholarius, which he changed for that of Gennadius, either when he became a monk [in the monastery of the Pantokrator] or a patriarch. His defence, at Florence, of the same union which he so furiously attacked at Constantinople, has tempted Leo Allatius (Diatrib. de Georgiis, in Fabric. Bibliot. Græc. tom. x. p. 760-786) to divide him into two men; but Renaudot (p. 343-383) has restored the identity of his person, and the duplicity of his character. [Monographs by C. Sathas, Γεώργιος Σχολάριος, 1865; T. E. Evangelides, Γεννάδιος β' ὁ Σχολάριος, 1896; I. Dräseke, Zu Georgios Scholarios, in Byzantinische Zeitschrift, iv. 561 sqq. The writings of Gennadius are collected in Migne, P.G. 160.]

that I am innocent of the crime.   O miserable Romans! consider, pause, and repent.   At the same moment that you renounce the religion of your fathers, by embracing impiety, you
submit to a foreign servitude." According to the advice of
Gennadius, the religious virgins, as pure as angels and as proud
as dæmons, rejected the act of union and abjured all communion
with the present and future associates of the Latins; and their
example was applauded and imitated by the greatest part of
the clergy and people. From the monastery, the devout Greeks
dispersed themselves in the tavern; drank confusion to the
slaves of the pope;[42] emptied their glasses in honour of the
image of the holy Virgin; and besought her to defend against
Mahomet the city which she had formerly saved from Chosroes
and the Chagan. In the double intoxication of zeal and wine,
they valiantly exclaimed, " What occasion have we for succour, or
union, or Latins? far from us be the worship of the Azymites! "
During the winter that preceded the Turkish conquest, the
nation was distracted by this epidemical frenzy; and the season
of Lent, the approach of Easter, instead of breathing charity and
love, served only to fortify the obstinacy and influence of the
zealots. The confessors scrutinised and alarmed the conscience
of their votaries, and a rigorous penance was imposed on those
who had received the communion from a priest who had given
an express or tacit consent to the union. His service at the
altar propagated the infection to the mute and simple spectators
of the ceremony; they forfeited, by the impure spectacle, the
virtue of their sacerdotal character; nor was it lawful, even in
danger of sudden death, to invoke the assistance of their prayers
or absolution. No sooner had the church of St. Sophia been
polluted by the Latin sacrifice than it was deserted as a Jewish
synagogue, or an heathen temple, by the clergy and people;
and a vast and gloomy silence prevailed in that venerable dome,
which had so often smoked with a cloud of incense, blazed with
innumerable lights, and resounded with the voice of prayer and
[Lucas
Notaras]   thanksgiving. The Latins were the most odious of heretics and
infidels; and the first minister of the empire, the great duke,
was heard to declare that he had rather behold, in Constanti-

---

[42] [Ubertinus Pusculus (ii. 1. 498 *sqq.*, ed. Ellissen, p. 36-7) narrates that Gennadius suborned a Bohemian heretic, who happened to be in the city, to stir up the
people against the Union and inveigh against the Pope.]

nople, the turban of Mahomet than the pope's tiara or a cardinal's hat.[43] A sentiment so unworthy of Christians and patriots was familiar and fatal to the Greeks: the emperor was deprived of the affection and support of his subjects; and their native cowardice was sanctified by resignation to the divine decree or the visionary hope of a miraculous deliverance.

Of the triangle which composes the figure of Constantinople, the two sides along the sea were made inaccessible to an enemy: the Propontis by nature, and the harbour by art. Between the two waters, the basis of the triangle, the land-side was protected by a double wall and a deep ditch of the depth of one hundred feet.[44] Against this line of fortification, which Phranza, an eye-witness, prolongs to the measure of six miles,[45] the Ottomans directed their principal attack; and the emperor, after distributing the service and command of the most perilous stations, undertook the defence of the external wall. In the first days of the siege, the Greek soldiers descended into the ditch, or sallied into the field; but they soon discovered that, in the proportion of their numbers, one Christian was of more value than twenty Turks; and, after these bold preludes, they were prudently content to maintain the rampart with their missile weapons. Nor should this prudence be accused of pusillanimity. The nation was indeed pusillanimous and base; but the last Constantine deserves the name of an hero; his noble band of volunteers was inspired with Roman virtue; and the foreign auxiliaries supported the honour of the Western chivalry. The incessant volleys of lances and arrows were accompanied with the smoke, the sound, and the fire of their musketry and cannon. Their small arms discharged at the same time either five or even ten balls of lead of the size of a walnut; and, according to the closeness of the ranks and the force of the powder, several breast-

[Marginal note:] Siege of Constantinople by Mahomet II., A.D. 1453, April 6-May 29

---

[43] Φακιόλιον, καλύπτρα, may be fairly translated a cardinal's hat. The difference of the Greek and Latin habits embittered the schism.

[44] [Niccolò Barbaro, p. 14, 15, mentions that during the last two weeks of March, a Venetian sea-captain named Diedo, with the crews of his vessels, was employed by the emperor to dig a ditch in front of a portion of the wall near the Porta Caligaria (Egri Kapu). This was a weak spot.]

[45] We are obliged to reduce the Greek miles to the smallest measure which is preserved in the wersts of Russia, of 547 French *toises*, and of 104¾ to a degree. The six miles of Phranza do not exceed four English miles (D'Anville, Mesures Itinéraires, p. 61, 123, &c.). [Cp. Critobulus, i, 28; he gives 126 stadia (15¾ miles) as the circuit of the city, allowing 48 for the land wall, 35 for the side of the Golden Horn. For the walls cp. above, vol. ii. p. 159, n. 33.]

plates and bodies were transpierced by the same shot. But the
Turkish approaches were soon sunk in trenches or covered with
ruins. Each day added to the science of the Christians; but
their inadequate stock of gunpowder was wasted in the operations of each day. Their ordnance was not powerful either in
size or number; and, if they possessed some heavy cannon, they
feared to plant them on the walls, lest the aged structure should
be shaken and overthrown by the explosion.[46] The same destructive secret had been revealed to the Moslems; by whom
it was employed with the superior energy of zeal, riches, and
[Bombardment begins, April 12] despotism. The great cannon of Mahomet has been separately
noticed: an important and visible object in the history of the
times; but that enormous engine was flanked by two fellows
almost of equal magnitude;[47] the long order of the Turkish
artillery was pointed against the walls; fourteen batteries thundered at once on the most accessible places; and of one of these it
is ambiguously expressed that it was mounted with one hundred
and thirty guns, or that it discharged one hundred and thirty
bullets. Yet, in the power and activity of the sultan, we may
discern the infancy of the new science. Under a master who
counted the moments, the great cannon could be loaded and

[46] At indies doctiores nostri facti paravere contra hostes machinamenta, quæ
tamen avare dabantur. Pulvis erat nitri modica, exigua; tela modica; bombardæ,
si aderant incommoditate loci, primum hostes offendere maceriebus alveisque tectos
non poterant. Nam siquæ magnæ erant, ne murus concuteretur noster, quiesce-
bant. This passage of Leonardus Chiensis is curious and important. [The Turks
had directed twelve large cannons (apart from the fourteen batteries) against the land
wall; three against the Tekfour Serai Palace, four against the Gate of Romanus,
three against the Gate of Selymbria, and two against the Golden Gate. For the
gates see the Plan of the City above, vol. ii. p. 159. The chief place of assault
was in the Lycus Valley, which lay between the Gates of Hadrianople (Porta Charisii) on the north, and Romanus on the south. Here was the Pempton or Fifth
Military Gate. Dethier suggested, and Pears (op. cit. p. 429 sqq.) has made it vir-
tually certain, that by the "Gate of Romanus" in the accounts of the siege is
meant, not the old gate of that name, but the Pempton. This assumption alone
is consistent with the circumstances of the final attack. The present name of the old
gate of S. Romanus, Top Kapu = Cannon Gate, seems to have been due to reverse
transference. It must have been originally given to the Pempton, where the big gun
was placed (Pears, op. cit. p. 435). (It may be noted here that the Porta Polyandri is not
to be identified, as it has usually been, with the Porta Charisii, but with the Porta
Rhesii (or Rhegii); see Th. Preger in Byzantinische Zeitschrift, xiv. 272 sqq.) The
dangerous and important post at the "S. Romanus Gate" was defended by 3000
men (including 500 Genoese), under the command of the Emperor and Giustiniani,
who were supported by Don Francisco of Toledo, a relative of the Emperor.]

[47] According to Chalcondyles and Phranza, the great cannon burst: an accident
which, according to Ducas, was prevented by the artist's skill. It is evident that
they do not speak of the same gun.

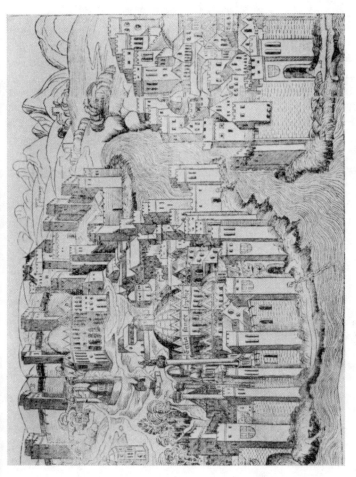

CONSTANTINOPLE: FROM THE NUREMBERG CHRONICLE OF A.D. 1493

fired no more than seven times in one day.[48]   The heated metal
unfortunately burst ; several workmen were destroyed ; and the
skill of an artist was admired, who bethought himself of pre-
venting the danger and the accident, by pouring oil, after each
explosion, into the mouth of the cannon.

The first random shots were productive of more sound than
effect ; and it was by the advice of a Christian that the engineers
were taught to level their aim against the two opposite sides of
the salient angles of a bastion.[49] However imperfect, the weight
and repetition of the fire made some impression on the walls ;
and the Turks, pushing their approaches to the edge of the ditch,
attempted to fill the enormous chasm and to build a road to the
assault.[50]   Innumerable fascines and hogsheads and trunks of
trees were heaped on each other ; and such was the impetuosity
of the throng that the foremost and the weakest were pushed
headlong down the precipice and instantly buried under the accumulated mass.   To fill the ditch was the toil of the besiegers ;
to clear away the rubbish was the safety of the besieged ; and,
after a long and bloody conflict, the web that had been woven
in the day was still unravelled in the night.   The next resource
of Mahomet was the practice of mines ; but the soil was rocky ;
in every attempt he was stopped and undermined by the Christian engineers ; nor had the art been yet invented of replenishing
those subterraneous passages with gunpowder and blowing whole
towers and cities into the air.[51] A circumstance that distinguishes
the siege of Constantinople is the reunion of the ancient and
modern artillery.   The cannon were intermingled with the mechanical engines for casting stones and darts ;[52] the bullet and

Attack and defence

[48] Near an hundred years after the siege of Constantinople, the French and
English fleets in the Channel were proud of firing 300 shot in an engagement of
two hours (Mémoires de Martin du Bellay, l. x. in the Collection Générale, tom.
xxi. p. 239).

[49] [The Christian who gave the advice was an envoy of John Hunyady. He
could not resist criticizing the shooting of the inexperienced Turkish gunners.]

[50] I have selected some curious facts, without striving to emulate the bloody
and obstinate eloquence of the Abbé de Vertot, in his prolix descriptions of the
sieges of Rhodes, Malta, &c.   But that agreeable historian had a turn for romance,
and, as he wrote to please the Order, he has adopted the same spirit of enthusiasm
and chivalry.

[51] The first theory of mines with gunpowder appears in 1480, in a Ms. of George
of Sienna (Tiraboschi, tom. vi. p. i. p. 324).   They were first practised at Sarza-
nella, in 1487 ; but the honour and improvement in 1503 is ascribed to Peter of
Navarre, who used them with success in the wars of Italy (Hist. de la Ligue de
Cambray, tom. ii. p. 93-97).

[52] [Cp. Blanchin and Tedardi, Informacion, p. 22 (for this work see Appendix 3).]

the battering-ram were directed against the same walls; nor had the discovery of gunpowder superseded the use of the liquid and unextinguishable fire. A wooden turret of the largest size was advanced on rollers; this portable magazine of ammunition and fascines was protected by a threefold covering of bulls' hides; incessant volleys were securely discharged from the loop-holes; in the front, three doors were contrived for the alternate sally and retreat of the soldiers and workmen. They ascended by a staircase to the upper platform, and, as high as the level of that platform, a scaling ladder could be raised by pulleys to form a bridge and grapple with the adverse rampart. By these various arts of annoyance, some as new as they were pernicious to the Greeks, the tower of St. Romanus was at length overturned; after a severe struggle, the Turks were repulsed from the breach and interrupted by darkness; but they trusted that with the return of light they should renew the attack with fresh vigour and decisive success. Of this pause of action, this interval of hope, each moment was improved by the activity of the emperor and Justiniani, who passed the night on the spot, and urged the labours which involved the safety of the church and city. At the dawn of day, the impatient sultan perceived, with astonishment and grief, that his wooden turret had been reduced to ashes: the ditch was cleared and restored; and the tower of St. Romanus was again strong and entire. He deplored the failure of his design; and uttered a profane exclamation that the word of the thirty-seven thousand prophets should not have compelled him to believe that such a work, in so short a time, should have been accomplished by the infidels.

The generosity of the Christian princes was cold and tardy; but, in the first apprehension of a siege, Constantine had negotiated, in the isles of the Archipelago, the Morea, and Sicily, the most indispensable supplies. As early as the beginning of April, five[53] great ships, equipped for merchandise and war, would

[The helepolis near the Romanus Gate, May 18]

[May 19]

Succour and victory of four ships

[four]

---

[53] It is singular that the Greeks should not agree in the number of these illustrious vessels; the *five* of Ducas, the *four* of Phranza and Leonardus [and Barbaro and Pusculus], and the *two* of Chalcondyles [and Sad ad-Dīn, ii. p. 137], must be extended to the smaller, or confined to the larger, size. Voltaire, in giving one of these ships to Frederic III., confounds the emperors of the East and West. [Critobulus does not mention the Imperial ship but only the three Italian ships, which, he says, were sent by the Pope with provisional help till he should prepare a large armament, i. 39. Ducas describes them as Genoese merchant vessels. The date of the engagement is known from Barbaro (p. 23, 24), who supplies the chronology of the siege.]

have sailed from the harbour of Chios, had not the wind blown obstinately from the north.[54] One of these ships bore the Imperial flag; the remaining four belonged to the Genoese; and [three] they were laden with wheat and barley, with wine, oil, and vegetables, and, above all, with soldiers and mariners, for the service of the capital. After a tedious delay, a gentle breeze, and, on the second day, a strong gale from the south, carried them through the Hellespont and the Propontis; but the city was already invested by sea and land; and the Turkish fleet, at the entrance of the Bosphorus, was stretched from shore to shore, in the form of a crescent, to intercept, or at least to repel, these bold auxiliaries.[55] The reader who has present to his mind the geographical picture of Constantinople, will conceive and admire the greatness of the spectacle. The five Christian ships con-[April 20] tinued to advance with joyful shouts, and a full press both of sails and oars, against an hostile fleet of three hundred vessels;[56] and the rampart, the camp, the coasts of Europe and Asia, were lined with innumerable spectators, who anxiously awaited the event of this momentous succour. At the first view, that event could not appear doubtful: the superiority of the Moslems was beyond all measure or account; and, in a calm, their numbers and valour must inevitably have prevailed. But their hasty and imperfect navy had been created, not by the genius of the people, but by the will of the sultan. In the height of their prosperity, the Turks have acknowledged that, if God had given them the earth, he had left the sea to the infidels;[57] and a series of defeats, a rapid progress of decay, has established the truth of their modest confession. Except eighteen galleys of some force, the rest of their

[54] In bold defiance, or rather in gross ignorance, of language and geography, the President Cousin detains them at Chios with a south, and wafts them to Constantinople with a north, wind.

[55] [The fleet had arrived on April 12 (a small part of it had arrived earlier, on the same day as Mohammad, April 2, according to Phrantzes, p. 237). It weighed anchor, and made its headquarters at Diplokionion, now Beshik Tash, on the Thracian side of the Bosphorus, at a short distance north of the mouth of the Golden Horn.]

[56] [Our authorities give very various statements as to the strength of the Turkish fleet. Critobulus (i. 22) says 350 (not counting ships of freight); Phrantzes, 480 (comparing p. 237 with p. 239 ed. Bonn); Marino Sanuto (Muratori, S. R. I. xxii. 1148), 375; Leonardus, 250; Chalcondyles, 230; Pusculus (4, 332), 170; Barbaro, 145. Cp. Pears, *op. cit.* p. 233, n. 3.]

[57] The perpetual decay and weakness of the Turkish navy may be observed in Rycaut (State of the Ottoman Empire, p. 372-378), Thévenot (Voyages, p. i. p. 229-242), and Tott (Mémoires, tom. iii.); the last of whom is always solicitous to amuse and amaze his reader.

fleet consisted of open boats, rudely constructed and awkwardly managed, crowded with troops and destitute of cannon; and, since courage arises in a great measure from the consciousness of strength, the bravest of the Janizaries might tremble on a new element. In the Christian squadron, five stout and lofty ships were guided by skilful pilots, and manned with the veterans of Italy and Greece, long practised in the arts and perils of the sea. Their weight was directed to sink or scatter the weak obstacles that impeded their passage; their artillery swept the waters; their liquid fire was poured on the heads of the adversaries who, with the design of boarding, presumed to approach them; and the winds and waves are always on the side of the ablest navigators. In this conflict, the Imperial vessel, which had been almost overpowered, was rescued by the Genoese; but the Turks, in a distant and closer attack, were twice repulsed with considerable loss. Mahomet himself sat on horseback on the beach, to encourage their valour by his voice and presence, by the promise of reward, and by fear more potent than the fear of the enemy. The passions of his soul, and even the gestures of his body,[58] seemed to imitate the actions of the combatants; and, as if he had been the lord of nature, he spurred his horse with a fearless and impotent effort into the sea. His loud reproaches, and the clamours of the camp, urged the Ottomans to a third attack, more fatal and bloody than the two former; and I must repeat, though I cannot credit, the evidence of Phranza, who affirms, from their own mouth, that they lost above twelve thousand men in the slaughter of the day.[59] They fled in disorder to the shores of Europe and Asia, while the Christian squadron, triumphant and unhurt, steered along the Bosphorus and securely anchored within the chain of the harbour. In the confidence of victory, they boasted that the whole Turkish power must have yielded to their arms; but the admiral, or captain-bashaw, found some consolation for a

[58] I must confess that I have before my eyes the living picture which Thucydides (l. vii. c. 71) has drawn of the passions and gestures of the Athenians in a naval engagement in the great harbour of Syracuse. [The account in the text seems to suppose that the conflict was in the Propontis, close to the entrance of the Golden Horn, but it was actually in the Golden Horn. See Pears, *op. cit.* p. 26 *sqq.*]

[59] [Leonardus says 10,000. Critobulus gives more reasonable numbers, but he, writing from the Turkish point of view, may have been inclined to understate the Turkish losses. He says that a little more that 100 were killed, and more than 300 wounded.]

painful wound in his eye, by representing that accident as the cause of his defeat. Baltha Ogli was a renegade of the race of the Bulgarian princes ; his military character was tainted with the unpopular vice of avarice ; and, under the despotism of the prince or people, misfortune is a sufficient evidence of guilt. His rank and services were annihilated by the displeasure of Mahomet. In the royal presence, the captain-bashaw was extended on the ground by four slaves, and received one hundred strokes with a golden rod ;[60] his death had been pronounced ; and he adored the clemency of the sultan, who was satisfied with the milder punishment of confiscation and exile. The introduction of this supply revived the hopes of the Greeks, and accused the supineness of their Western allies. Amidst the deserts of Anatolia and the rocks of Palestine, the millions of the crusades had buried themselves in a voluntary and inevitable grave ; but the situation of the Imperial city was strong against her enemies, and accessible to her friends ; and a rational and moderate armament of the maritime states might have saved the relics of the Roman name and maintained a Christian fortress in the heart of the Ottoman empire. Yet this was the sole and feeble attempt for the deliverance of Constantinople ; the more distant powers were insensible of its danger ; and the ambassador of Hungary, or at least of Huniades, resided in the Turkish camp, to remove the fears, and to direct the operations, of the sultan.[61]

It was difficult for the Greeks to penetrate the secret of the divan ; yet the Greeks are persuaded that a resistance, so obstinate and surprising, had fatigued the perseverance of Mahomet. He began to meditate a retreat, and the siege would have been speedily raised, if the ambition and jealousy of the second vizir had not opposed the perfidious advice of Calil Bashaw, who still

Mahomet transports his navy over land

---

[60] According to the exaggeration or corrupt text of Ducas (c. 38), this golden bar was of the enormous and incredible weight of 500 libræ, or pounds. Bouillaud's reading of 500 drachms, or five pounds, is sufficient to exercise the arm of Mahomet and bruise the back of his admiral.

[61] Ducas, who confesses himself ill informed of the affairs of Hungary, assigns a motive of superstition, a fatal belief that Constantinople would be the term of the Turkish conquests. See Phranza (l. iii. c. 20) and Spondanus. [The Hungarian envoy had come to announce that Hunyady had resigned the government to Ladislaus, the young king, and to return the document, in which a truce between Turkey and Hungary had been signed in 1451, and ask for the counterpart which had been signed by Hunyady. The embassy was thus a move intended to suggest to Mohammad that Hungary *might* come to the rescue of the Emperor.]

maintained a secret correspondence with the Byzantine court.
The reduction of the city appeared to be hopeless, unless a
double attack could be made from the harbour as well as from
the land; but the harbour was inaccessible : an impenetrable
chain was now defended by eight large ships, more than twenty
of a smaller size, with several galleys and sloops ; and, instead
of forcing this barrier, the Turks might apprehend a naval sally
and a second encounter in the open sea.   In this perplexity, the
genius of Mahomet conceived and executed a plan of a bold and
marvellous cast,[62] of transporting by land his lighter vessels and
military stores from the Bosphorus into the higher part of the
harbour.   The distance is about ten miles ; the ground is un-
even, and was overspread with thickets ; and, as the road must
be opened behind the suburb of Galata, their free passage or
total destruction must depend on the option of the Genoese.[63]
But these selfish merchants were ambitious of the favour of
being the last devoured ; and the deficiency of art was supplied
by the strength of obedient myriads.   A level way was covered
with a broad platform of strong and solid planks ; and to render
them more slippery and smooth, they were anointed with the
fat of sheep and oxen.   Fourscore [64] light galleys and brigantines
of fifty and thirty oars were disembarked on the Bosphorus
shore ; arranged successively on rollers ; and drawn forwards
by the power of men and pulleys.   Two guides or pilots were
stationed at the helm and the prow of each vessel ; the sails
[April 22-
23] were unfurled to the winds ; and the labour was cheered by song
and acclamation.   In the course of a single night, this Turkish
fleet painfully climbed the hill, steered over the plain, and was

[62] [N. Barbaro says that the idea was suggested to the Sultan by a Christian
(p. 27).]
[63] [Paspatès suggested (*op. cit.* p. 136) that, starting from Diplokionion (Beshik-
tash) the ships sailed up the hill of Staurodromion, and descended to the little bay
of Kasimpasha in the Golden Horn.   The distance was between two and three miles.
But Pears (*op. cit.* p. 272 *sqq.*) has made it probable that they started from Tophana,
near the mouth of the Bosphorus, and were hauled up the steep ridge to the level which
is now the Grande Rue de Péra, and thence down to the Golden Horn.   Critobulus
(who gives the best description of the transport, i. 42) says that the distance was 8
stadia, and this suits, taking the stadium as about a furlong.   According to Michael
the Janissary (for his Memoirs see Appendix 3) " the batteries kept up an incessant
cannonade that night," to distract attention (Mijatovich, Constantine : Last Emperor of the Greeks, p. 163).]
[64] [The number of ships is given by Barbaro as 72, by Tedardi as between 70
and 80, by Critobulus as 67 (Chalcondyles 70, Ducas 80).]

launched from the declivity into the shallow waters of the
harbour, far above the molestation of the deeper vessels of the
Greeks.   The real importance of this operation was magnified
by the consternation and confidence which it inspired ; but the
notorious, unquestionable fact was displayed before the eyes,
and is recorded by the pens, of the two nations.[65]   A similar
stratagem has been repeatedly practised by the ancients;[66] the
Ottoman galleys (I must again repeat) should be considered as
large boats ; and, if we compare the magnitude and the distance,
the obstacles and the means, the boasted miracle [67] has perhaps
been equalled by the industry of our own times.[68]   As soon as
Mahomet had occupied the upper harbour with a fleet and army, [May 19,
he constructed, in the narrowest part, a bridge, or rather mole, bridge completed]
of fifty cubits in breadth and one hundred in length; it was
formed of casks and hogsheads, joined with rafters linked with
iron, and covered with a solid floor.   On this floating battery
he planted one of his largest cannon, while the fourscore galleys,
with troops and scaling-ladders, approached the most accessible
side, which had formerly been stormed by the Latin conquerors.
The indolence of the Christians has been accused for not destroying these unfinished works ; but their fire, by a superior
fire, was controlled and silenced ; nor were they wanting in a
nocturnal attempt to burn the vessels as well as the bridge [69] of

[65] The unanimous testimony of the four Greeks is confirmed by Cantemir (p. 96)
from the Turkish annals; but I could wish to contract the distance of *ten* miles
and to prolong the term of *one* night.

[66] Phranza relates two examples of a similar transportation over the six miles of
the isthmus of Corinth : the one fabulous, of Augustus after the battle of Actium ;
the other true, of Nicetas, a Greek general, in the xth century.   To these he might
have added a bold enterprise of Hannibal, to introduce his vessels into the harbour
of Tarentum (Polybius, l. viii. p. 749, edit. Gronov [c. 36]).   [Cp. also Thucydides,
iii. 15, 81 ; iv. 8; and the dragging of the Syracusan fleet of Dionysius I. over
the isthmus of Motya, a distance of 2½ miles, on a wooden road (Diodorus, xiv.
50 ; Polyænus, v. 2).   In 1097 an Imperial squadron was transported across land
into Lake Ascanias, to operate against Nicæa.]

[67] A Greek of Candia, who had served the Venetians in a similar undertaking
(Spond. A.D. 1438, No. 37), might possibly be the adviser and agent of Mahomet.
[The Venetians conveyed ships from the river Adige to L. Garda.]

[68] I particularly allude to our own embarkations on the lakes of Canada, in the
years 1776 and 1777, so great in the labour, so fruitless in the event.

[69] [Barbaro states that the bridge was not completed till May 19; and he
places this attempt to burn the vessels on April 28.   Gibbon follows Phrantzes.
Ducas also mentions (p. 277, ed. Bonn) an attempt to burn the Turkish ships, and
attributes its failure to the treachery of the Genoese of Galata who revealed it to
Mohammad.   Ducas mentions the construction of the bridge *after* this unlucky
enterprise.   Critobulus relates how Mohammad foiled a plan of the Greeks to confine his ships to the little harbour (Kasim Pasha) ; and he places this episode after

[April 28] the sultan.   His vigilance prevented their approach; their foremost galliots were sunk or taken; forty youths, the bravest of Italy and Greece, were inhumanly massacred at his command; nor could the emperor's grief be assuaged by the just though cruel retaliation of exposing from the walls the heads of two Distress of hundred and sixty Musulman captives.   After a siege of forty the city days, the fate of Constantinople could no longer be averted. The diminutive garrison was exhausted by a double attack; the fortifications, which had stood for ages against hostile violence, were dismantled on all sides by the Ottoman cannon; many breaches were opened; and near the gate of St. Romanus four towers had been levelled with the ground.[70]   For the payment of his feeble and mutinous troops, Constantine was compelled to despoil the churches, with the promise of a fourfold restitution; and his sacrilege offered a new reproach to the enemies of the union.   A spirit of discord impaired the remnant of the Christian strength; the Genoese and Venetian auxiliaries asserted the pre-eminence of their respective service; and Justiniani and the Great Duke, whose ambition was not extinguished by the common danger, accused each other of treachery and cowardice.

Preparations of the Turks for the general assault, May 26
During the siege of Constantinople, the words of peace and capitulation had been sometimes pronounced; and several embassies had passed between the camp and the city.[71]   The Greek emperor was humbled by adversity; and would have yielded to any terms compatible with religion and royalty.[72]

the building of the bridge (i. 44).   It seems from this that Ducas has mixed together the incident recorded by Phrantzes with that recorded by Critobulus.]

[70] [The Turks also essayed mining operations against the Caligaria region (south of Blachernæ), where the ground was most favourable.   But all their mines (the first was discovered on May 16, see Barbaro, p. 41) were foiled by the skill of a German engineer, Johannes Grant, who was entrusted with the defence of this part of the wall.   Cp. Phrantzes, p. 254, and Tedardi, Informacion, p. 25.]

[71] Chalcondyles and Ducas differ in the time and circumstances of the negotiation; and, as it was neither glorious nor salutary, the faithful Phranza spares his prince even the thought of a surrender.

[72] [The author of the Slavonic relation of the siege (see Appendix 3) states that a council was held on May 3, and that all the military officers, the senators, and the patriarch advised the emperor to leave the city, and attempt to create a diversion.   "The emperor" (the passage is thus translated by Ch. Mijatovich, op. cit. p. 173) "listened to all this quietly and patiently.   At last, after having been for some time in deep thought, he began to speak: ' I thank all for the advice which you have given me.   I know that my going out of the city might be of some benefit to me, inasmuch as all that you foresee might really happen.   But it is impossible for me to go away!   How could I leave the churches of our Lord and his servants the clergy, and the throne, and my people in such a plight?   What would

The Turkish sultan was desirous of sparing the blood of his
soldiers; still more desirous of securing for his own use the
Byzantine treasures; and he accomplished a sacred duty in presenting to the *Gabours* the choice of circumcision, of tribute, or [May 23]
of death.[73] The avarice of Mahomet might have been satisfied
with an annual sum of one hundred thousand ducats; but his
ambition grasped the capital of the East; to the prince he
offered a rich equivalent, to the people a free toleration or a
safe departure; but, after some fruitless treaty, he declared his
resolution of finding either a throne or a grave under the walls
of Constantinople. A sense of honour and the fear of universal
reproach forbade Palæologus to resign the city into the hands of
the Ottomans; and he determined to abide the last extremities
of war. Several days were employed by the sultan in the
preparations of the assault; and a respite was granted by his
favourite science of astrology, which had fixed on the twenty-
ninth of May as the fortunate and fatal hour. On the evening
of the twenty-seventh, he issued his final orders; assembled
in his presence the military chiefs; and dispersed his heralds
through the camp to proclaim the duty and the motives of the
perilous enterprise. Fear is the first principle of a despotic
government; and his menaces were expressed in the Oriental
style, that the fugitives and deserters, had they the wings of
a bird,[74] should not escape from his inexorable justice. The

the world say about me? I pray you, my friends, in future do not say to me anything else but: "Nay, sire, do not leave us!" Never, never will I leave you! I
am resolved to die here with you!' And saying this, the emperor turned his head
aside, because tears filled his eyes; and with him wept the patriarch and all who
were there."]

[73] [On this mission Mohammad sent his brother-in-law Ismail Hamza, lord of
Sinope and Castamboly, who was on friendly terms with Constantine. The incident
is entirely omitted by Barbaro, Phrantzes, and Critobulus.]

[74] These wings (Chalcondyles, l. viii. p. 208) are no more than an Oriental
figure; but, in the tragedy of Irene, Mahomet's passion soars above sense and
reason :—

> Should the fierce North, upon his frozen wings,
> Bear him aloft above the wondering clouds,
> And seat him in the Pleiads' golden chariot—
> Thence should my fury drag him down to tortures.

Besides the extravagance of the rant, I must observe, 1. That the operation of the
winds must be confined to the *lower* region of the air. 2. That the name, etymology, and fable of the Pleiads are purely Greek (Scholiast ad Homer, Σ. 686;
Eudocia in Ioniâ, p. 399; Apollodor. l. iii. c. 10; Heine, p. 229, Not. 682), and
had no affinity with the astronomy of the East (Hyde ad Ulugbeg, Tabul. in
Syntagma Dissert. tom. i. p. 40, 42; Goguet, Origine des Arts, &c. tom. vi. p.
73-78; Gebelin, Hist. du Calendrier, p. 73), which Mahomet had studied. 3. The
golden chariot does not exist either in science or fiction; but I much fear that Dr.

greatest part of his bashaws and Janizaries were the offspring of
Christian parents; but the glories of the Turkish name were
perpetuated by successive adoption; and, in the gradual change
of individuals, the spirit of a legion, a regiment, or an *oda* is
kept alive by imitation and discipline. In this holy warfare,
the Moslems were exhorted to purify their minds with prayer,
their bodies with seven ablutions; and to abstain from food
till the close of the ensuing day. A crowd of dervishes visited
the tents, to instil the desire of martyrdom, and the assurance
of spending an immortal youth amidst the rivers and gardens of
paradise and in the embraces of the black-eyed virgins. Yet
Mahomet principally trusted to the efficacy of temporal and
visible rewards. A double pay was promised to the victorious
troops: " The city and the buildings," said Mahomet, " are mine;
but I resign to your valour the captives and the spoil, the
treasures of gold and beauty; be rich and be happy. Many
are the provinces of my empire: the intrepid soldier who first
ascends the walls of Constantinople shall be rewarded with the
government of the fairest and most wealthy; and my gratitude
shall accumulate his honours and fortunes above the measure
of his own hopes." Such various and potent motives diffused
among the Turks a general ardour, regardless of life and impatient for action; the camp re-echoed with the Moslem shouts
of " God is God, there is but one God, and Mahomet is the
apostle of God "; [75] and the sea and land, from Galata to the seven
towers, were illuminated by the blaze of their nocturnal fires.

[Sunday]

Far different was the state of the Christians; who, with loud
and impotent complaints, deplored the guilt, or the punishment,
of their sins. The celestial image of the Virgin had been exposed in solemn procession; but their divine patroness was deaf
to their entreaties: they accused the obstinacy of the emperor
for refusing a timely surrender; anticipated the horrors of their
fate; and sighed for the repose and security of Turkish servitude.

Last fare-
well of the
emperor
and the
Greeks
[Monday,
May 28]

Johnson has confounded the Pleiads with the great bear or waggon, the zodiac with
a northern constellation :—

Ἄρκτον θ᾽ ἣν καὶ ἅμαξαν ἐπίκλησιν καλέουσι.

[75] Phranza quarrels with these Moslem acclamations, not for the name of God,
but for that of the Prophet: the pious zeal of Voltaire is excessive, and even ridiculous. [There was a great illumination in the Turkish camp on the night of the
24th May, when the Sultan first proclaimed his plan for a general assault (Barbaro,
p. 46; it is mentioned also by the Slavonic chronicle). Gibbon refers to the illumination on May 27.]

The noblest of the Greeks, and the bravest of the allies, were summoned to the palace, to prepare them, on the evening of the twenty-eighth, for the duties and dangers of the general assault. The last speech of Palæologus was the funeral oration of the Roman Empire:[76] he promised, he conjured, and he vainly attempted to infuse the hope which was extinguished in his own mind. In this world all was comfortless and gloomy; and neither the gospel nor the church have proposed any conspicuous recompense to the heroes who fall in the service of their country. But the example of their prince and the confinement of a siege had armed these warriors with the courage of despair; and the pathetic scene is described by the feelings of the historian Phranza, who was himself present at this mournful assembly. They wept, they embraced; regardless of their families and fortunes, they devoted their lives; and each commander, departing to his station, maintained all night a vigilant and anxious watch on the rampart. The emperor, and some faithful companions, entered the dome of St. Sophia, which in a few hours was to be converted into a mosque; and devoutly received, with tears and prayers, the sacrament of the holy communion. He reposed some moments in the palace, which resounded with cries and lamentations; solicited the pardon of all whom he might have injured;[77] and mounted on horseback to visit the guards and explore the motions of the enemy. The distress and fall of the last Constantine are more glorious than the long prosperity of the Byzantine Cæsars.

In the confusion of darkness an assailant may sometimes succeed; but, in this great and general attack, the military judgment and astrological knowledge of Mahomet advised him to expect the morning,[78] the memorable twenty-ninth of May,

The general assault.
May 29
[Tuesday]

---

[76] I am afraid that this discourse was composed by Phranza himself; and it smells so grossly of the sermon and the convent that I almost doubt whether it was pronounced by Constantine. Leonardus assigns him another speech, in which he addresses himself more respectfully to the Latin auxiliaries. [The speeches in Phrantzes and Leonardo "are substantially identical, and do not vary more than would do two independent reports written some months after the delivery of a speech in our own time" (Pears, *op. cit.* p. 328).]

[77] This abasement, which devotion has sometimes extorted from dying princes, is an improvement of the gospel doctrine of the forgiveness of injuries; it is more easy to forgive 490 times than once to ask pardon of an inferior.

[78] [So the eye-witnesses, Phrantzes and Barbaro. But Critobulus and Ducas set the beginning of the final assault on the 28th, and make the fighting go on all night. Cp. Pears, p. 334.]

in the fourteen hundred and fifty-third year of the Christian æra. The preceding night had been strenuously employed : the troops, the cannon, and the fascines were advanced to the edge of the ditch, which, in many parts, presented a smooth and level passage to the breach ; and his fourscore galleys almost touched, with the prows and their scaling-ladders, the less defensible walls of the harbour.   Under pain of death, silence was enjoined ; but the physical laws of motion and sound are not obedient to discipline or fear ; each individual might suppress his voice and measure his footsteps ; but the march and labour of thousands must inevitably produce a strange confusion of dissonant clamours, which reached the ears of the watchmen of the towers.   At daybreak, without the customary signal of the morning-gun, the Turks assaulted the city by sea and land ; and the similitude of a twined or twisted thread has been applied to the closeness and continuity of their line of attack.[79]   The foremost ranks consisted of the refuse of the host, a voluntary crowd, who fought without order or command ; of the feebleness of age or childhood, of peasants and vagrants, and of all who had joined the camp in the blind hope of plunder and martyrdom.   The common impulse drove them onwards to the wall ; the most audacious to climb were instantly precipitated ; and not a dart, not a bullet of the Christians was idly wasted on the accumulated throng. But their strength and ammunition were exhausted in this laborious defence ; the ditch was filled with the bodies of the slain ; they supported the footsteps of their companions ; and of this devoted vanguard the death was more serviceable than the life.   Under their respective bashaws and sanjaks, the troops of Anatolia and Romania were successively led to the charge : their progress was various and doubtful ; but, after a conflict of two hours, the Greeks still maintained and improved their advantage ; and the voice of the emperor was heard, encouraging his soldiers to achieve, by a last effort, the deliverance of their country.   In that fatal moment, the Janizaries arose, fresh, vigorous, and invincible.   The sultan himself on horseback, with an iron mace in his hand, was the spectator and judge of their valour ; he was surrounded by ten thousand of his domestic troops, whom he reserved for the decisive occasion ; and the

[79] Besides the 10,000 guards, and the sailors and the marines, Ducas numbers in this general assault 250,000 Turks, both horse and foot.

tide of battle was directed and impelled by his voice and eye. His numerous ministers of justice were posted behind the line, to urge, to restrain, and to punish ; and, if danger was in the front, shame and inevitable death were in the rear of the fugitives. The cries of fear and of pain were drowned in the martial music of drums, trumpets, and attaballs ; and experience has proved that the mechanical operation of sounds, by quickening the circulation of the blood and spirits, will act on the human machine more forcibly than the eloquence of reason and honour. From the lines, the galleys, and the bridge, the Ottoman artillery thundered on all sides ; and the camp and city, the Greeks and the Turks, were involved in a cloud of smoke, which could only be dispelled by the final deliverance or destruction of the Roman empire. The signal combats of the heroes of history or fable amuse our fancy and engage our affections ; the skilful evolutions of war may inform the mind, and improve a necessary though pernicious science. But, in the uniform and odious pictures of a general assault, all is blood, and horror, and confusion ; nor shall I strive, at the distance of three centuries and a thousand miles, to delineate a scene of which there could be no spectators, and of which the actors themselves were incapable of forming any just or adequate idea.

The immediate loss of Constantinople may be ascribed to the bullet, or arrow, which pierced the gauntlet of John Justiniani.[80] The sight of his blood, and the exquisite pain, appalled the courage of the chief, whose arms and counsel were the firmest rampart of the city. As he withdrew from his station in quest of a surgeon, his flight was perceived and stopped by the indefatigable emperor. "Your wound," exclaimed Palæologus, "is slight; the danger is pressing; your presence is necessary ; and whither will you retire ? " " I will retire," said the trembling Genoese, " by the same road which God has opened to the Turks ; " and at these words he hastily

[80] [At 3 o'clock in the morning a breach in the outer wall near the gate of " St. Romanus" had been made by a cannon, and the Turks pressed into the space between the outer and inner walls. They were repelled at last, mainly through the efforts of the Venetians (according to Barbaro) ; but it was soon necessary to bring up the reserves which (under Theodore Palæologus and Demetrius Cantacuzenus) were posted at the Church of the Holy Apostles. It was at this moment, when these reserve troops were driving back the Turks, that Giustiniani was wounded (in the leg, Phrantzes ; in the hand, Chalcondyles and Ducas ; under the armpit, Zorzo Dolfin and Leonardus ; in the arm, Pusculus : in the chest, Critobulus).]

passed through one of the breaches of the inner wall.   By this
pusillanimous act, he stained the honours of a military life ;
and the few days which he survived in Galata, or the isle of
Chios, was embittered by his own and the public reproach.[81]
His example was imitated by the greatest part of the Latin
auxiliaries, and the defence began to slacken when the attack
was pressed with redoubled vigour.   The number of the Ottomans was fifty, perhaps an hundred, times superior to that of
the Christians ; the double walls were reduced by the cannon
to an heap of ruins ; in a circuit of several miles, some places
must be found more easy of access or more feebly guarded ;
and, if the besiegers could penetrate in a single point, the
whole city was irrecoverably lost.   The first who deserved the
[Hasan of Ulubad] sultan's reward was Hassan, the Janizary, of gigantic stature
and strength.   With his scymetar in one hand and his buckler
in the other, he ascended the outward fortification ; of the
thirty Janizaries, who were emulous of his valour, eighteen
perished in the bold adventure.   Hassan and his twelve companions had reached the summit: the giant was precipitated
from the rampart ; he rose on one knee, and was again oppressed
by a shower of darts and stones.   But his success had proved
that the achievement was possible: the walls and towers were
instantly covered with a swarm of Turks ; and the Greeks, now
driven from the vantage-ground, were overwhelmed by increasing multitudes.[82]   Amidst these multitudes, the emperor,[83] who

[81] In the severe censure of the flight of Justiniani, Phranza expresses his own
feelings and those of the public.   For some private reasons, he is treated with more
lenity and respect by Ducas ; but the words of Leonardus Chiensis express his
strong and recent ·indignation, gloriæ salutis suique oblitus.   In the whole series
of their Eastern policy, his countrymen, the Genoese, were always suspected, and
often guilty.   [" The dialogue between Constantine and Giustiniani given in the
pages of Gibbon is evidently a rhetorical invention.   None of the historians were
present, and who of those present could report any conversation with accuracy at
such a moment ? "   Finlay, History of Greece, iii. p. 520 note.   Barbaro, who is
throughout severe on the Genoese, is markedly hostile to Giustiniani.   The facts
that the wound actually proved mortal, and that Giustiniani's valour and distinguished services are extolled by all the Greek writers, are a sufficient answer to
the accusations of cowardice and failure in duty.]

[82] [In this account of the last conflict Gibbon has omitted a highly important
fact which hastened the capture of the city.   This fact is not mentioned by
Phrantzes ; it rests on the authority of Ducas (p. 280-5) and is confirmed by a
short statement of Critobulus (i. 60 ad fin.).   North of the Porta Charisii, south
of the Porta Caligaria, in a transverse wall which connects the inner and outer
Theodosian walls, there is a small postern (found by M. Paspates) which is
called the Kerkoporta by Ducas (wrongly ?).   It was always kept shut, but had
been opened by Giustiniani's orders for the purpose of a possible sortie.   Some

TOP AND BOTTOM OF A GRANT IN GREEK CONCEDING COMMERCIAL
PRIVILEGES TO THE GENOESE THE WEEK AFTER THE CAPTURE OF
CONSTANTINOPLE IN 1453: ABOVE IS THE MONOGRAM OF MAHOMET II;
BELOW, THE SIGNATURE OF THE VIZIER

accomplished all the duties of a general and a soldier, was long seen, and finally lost. The nobles who fought round his person sustained, till their last breath, the honourable names of Palæologus and Cantacuzene: his mournful exclamation was heard, "Cannot there be found a Christian to cut off my head?"[84] and his last fear was that of falling alive into the hands of the infidels.[85] The prudent despair of Constantine cast away the purple; amidst the tumult, he fell by an unknown hand, and his body was buried under a mountain of the slain. After his death, resistance and order were no more; the Greeks fled towards the city; and many were pressed and stifled in the narrow pass of the gate of St. Romanus. The victorious Turks rushed through the breaches of the inner wall; and, as they advanced into the streets, they were soon joined by their brethren, who had forced the gate Phenar on the side of the

Death of the emperor Constantine Palæologus

of the Greeks who were fighting in the space between the inner and the outer wall, pressed by the enemy, retreated through the Kerkoporta, and fifty Turks followed them, as they neglected to shut the gate. More Turks soon pressed in, and others mounted the walls, captured the tower close to the gate, and set up the Ottoman standards on the walls. The retreat of the Greeks, who were outside the inner wall, by the Kerkoporta was now cut off, and seeing the flags of the foe on the battlements they thronged back through the Porta Charseæ, which was then left undefended, so that the Turks could enter by this gate too. The Turks who thus penetrated seem to have betaken themselves at first to the harbour side of the city, and some time elapsed before the combatants at the Gate of St. Romanus, where the fight was raging most hotly, learned what had happened. Phrantzes (without explaining) describes the arrival of the tidings (p. 285). A cry was heard on the harbour side: "The fort is taken, the standards of the foe are on the towers!" Then Constantine spurred his horse into the thick of the fray. On the Kerkoporta, see Van Millingen, Byzantine Constantinople, p. 89 sqq.; Pears, op. cit. p. 342.]

[83] Ducas kills him with two blows of Turkish soldiers; Chalcondyles wounds him in the shoulder, and then tramples him in the gate. The grief of Phranza carrying him among the enemy escapes from the precise image of his death; but we may, without flattery, apply these noble lines of Dryden:—

As to Sebastian, let them search the field;
And, where they find a mountain of the slain,
Send one to climb, and looking down beneath,
There they will find him at his manly length,
With his face up to heaven, in that red monument
Which his good sword had digg'd.

[84] Spondanus (A.D. 1453, No. 10), who has hopes of his salvation, wishes to absolve this demand from the guilt of suicide.

[85] Leonardus Chiensis very properly observes that the Turks, had they known the emperor, would have laboured to save and secure a captive so acceptable to the sultan. [It appears that Constantine fell in the space between the inner and outer walls (Ducas, p. 283), near the Gate of St. Romanus (Phrantzes, p. 287). Critobulus is mistaken in saying that it was near the Kerkoporta (i. 60). Theodore Spandugino Cantacusino in his work "Dell' origine et imperio de Turchi" (ed. 1564, p. 195) describes Constantine as rejecting the proposals which were made to him to flee to the harbour, and crying, "God forbid that I should live an Emperor without enjoying the Empire! I will die with my city!"]

harbour.[86]   In the first heat of the pursuit, about two thousand Christians were put to the sword; but avarice soon prevailed over cruelty; and the victors acknowledged that they should immediately have given quarter, if the valour of the emperor and his chosen bands had not prepared them for a similar opposi-

Loss of the city and empire

tion in every part of the capital.   It was thus, after a siege of fifty-three days, that Constantinople, which had defied the power of Chosroes, the Chagan, and the caliphs, was irretrievably subdued by the arms of Mahomet the Second.   Her empire only had been subverted by the Latins; her religion was trampled in the dust by the Moslem conquerors.[87]

The Turks enter and pillage Constantinople

The tidings of misfortune fly with a rapid wing; yet such was the extent of Constantinople that the more distant quarters might prolong, some moments, the happy ignorance of their ruin.[88]   But in the general consternation, in the feelings of selfish or social anxiety, in the tumult and thunder of the assault, a *sleepless* night and morning must have elapsed; nor can I believe that many Grecian ladies were awakened by the Janizaries from a sound and tranquil slumber.   On the assurance of the public calamity, the houses and convents were instantly deserted; and the trembling inhabitants flocked together in the streets, like an herd of timid animals, as if accumulated weakness could be productive of strength, or in the vain hope that amid the crowd each individual might be safe and invisible.   From every part of the capital, they flowed into the church of St. Sophia: in the space of an hour, the sanctuary, the choir, the nave, the upper and lower galleries, were filled with the multitudes of fathers and husbands, of women and children, of priests, monks, and religious virgins; the doors were barred on the inside, and they sought protection from the sacred dome which they had so lately abhorred as a profane and polluted edifice.   Their confidence was founded on

[86] Cantemir, p. 96.   The Christian ships in the mouth of the harbour had flanked and retarded this naval attack.   [Cp. Barbaro, p. 56; Critobulus, i. 65.]

[87] Chalcondyles most absurdly supposes that Constantinople was sacked by the Asiatics in revenge for the ancient calamities of Troy; and the grammarians of the xvth century are happy to melt down the uncouth appellation of Turks into the more classical name of *Teucri*.

[88] When Cyrus surprised Babylon during the celebration of a festival, so vast was the city, and so careless were the inhabitants, that much time elapsed before the distant quarters knew that they were captives.   Herodotus (l. i. c. 191), and Usher (Annal. p. 78), who has quoted from the prophet Jeremiah a passage of similar import.

the prophecy of an enthusiast or impostor, that one day the
Turks would enter Constantinople, and pursue the Romans as far
as the column of Constantine in the square before St. Sophia;
but that this would be the term of their calamities; that an
angel would descend from heaven, with a sword in his hand,
and would deliver the empire, with that celestial weapon, to
a poor man seated at the foot of the column. "Take this
sword," would he say, "and avenge the people of the Lord."
At these animating words, the Turks would instantly fly, and
the victorious Romans would drive them from the West, and
from all Anatolia, as far as the frontiers of Persia. It is on
this occasion that Ducas, with some fancy and much truth,
upbraids the discord and obstinacy of the Greeks. "Had that
angel appeared," exclaims the historian, "had he offered to
exterminate your foes if you would consent to the union of
the church, even then, in that fatal moment, you would have
rejected your safety or have deceived your God." [89]

While they expected the descent of the tardy angel, the doors were broken with axes; and, as the Turks encountered no resistance, their bloodless hands were employed in selecting
and securing the multitude of their prisoners. Youth, beauty,
and the appearance of wealth attracted their choice; and the
right of property was decided among themselves by a prior
seizure, by personal strength, and by the authority of command.
In the space of an hour, the male captives were bound with
cords, the females with their veils and girdles. The senators
were linked with their slaves; the prelates with the porters of
the church; and young men of a plebeian class with noble maids,
whose faces had been invisible to the sun and their nearest
kindred. In this common captivity, the ranks of society were
confounded; the ties of nature were cut asunder; and the inexorable soldier was careless of the father's groans, the tears of
the mother, and the lamentations of the children. The loudest

Captivity of the Greeks

[89] This lively description is extracted from Ducas (c. 39), who two years afterwards was sent ambassador from the prince of Lesbos to the sultan (c. 44). Till
Lesbos was subdued in 1463 (Phranza, l. iii. c. 27), that island must have been full
of the fugitives of Constantinople, who delighted to repeat, perhaps to adorn, the
tale of their misery. [The terrible description of the wasting of Constantinople
given by Critobulus (i. 61-63), who wrote as a friend of the Turks, proves that the
other historians have not exaggerated the frightful scenes. He has an interesting
notice of the destruction of books sacred and profane (c. 62, 3); some were destroyed, but "the greater number of them" were sold for small sums, cp. Ducas,
p. 312.]

in their wailings were the nuns, who were torn from the altar
with naked bosoms, outstretched hands, and dishevelled hair;
and we should piously believe that few could be tempted to
prefer the vigils of the harem to those of the monastery. Of
these unfortunate Greeks, of these domestic animals, whole
strings were rudely driven through the streets; and, as the
conquerors were eager to return for more prey, their trembling
pace was quickened with menaces and blows. At the same
hour, a similar rapine was exercised in all the churches and
monasteries, in all the palaces and habitations of the capital;
nor could any palace, however sacred or sequestered, protect
the persons or the property of the Greeks. Above sixty thousand [90] of this devoted people were transported from the city to
the camp and fleet; exchanged or sold according to the caprice
or interest of their masters, and dispersed in remote servitude
through the provinces of the Ottoman empire. Among these
we may notice some remarkable characters. The historian
Phranza, first chamberlain and principal secretary, was involved
with his family in the common lot. After suffering four months
the hardships of slavery, he recovered his freedom; in the ensuing winter he ventured to Hadrianople, and ransomed his wife
from the *mir bashi*, or master of horse; but his two children, in
the flower of youth and beauty, had been seized for the use of
Mahomet himself. The daughter of Phranza died in the seraglio,
perhaps a virgin; his son, in the fifteenth year of his age, preferred death to infamy, and was stabbed by the hand of the
royal lover.[91] A deed thus inhuman cannot surely be expiated
by the taste and liberality with which he released a Grecian
matron and her two daughters, on receiving a Latin ode from
Philelphus, who had chosen a wife in that noble family.[92] The
pride or cruelty of Mahomet would have been most sensibly
gratified by the capture of a Roman legate; but the dexterity

[90] [So Leonardus, p. 334; according to Critobulus, 50,000, and the same authority gives the number of slain among the defenders, throughout the siege and in the
final capture, as 4000.]

[91] See Phranza, l. iii. c. 20, 21. His expressions are positive: Ameras suâ manu
jugulavit . . . volebat enim eo turpiter et nefarie abuti. Me miserum et infelicem.
Yet he could only learn from report the bloody or impure scenes that were acted in
the dark recesses of the seraglio.

[92] See Tiraboschi (tom. vi. p. i. p. 290), and Lancelot (Mém. de l'Académie des
Inscriptions, tom. x. p. 718). I should be curious to learn how he could praise
the public enemy, whom he so often reviles as the most corrupt and inhuman of
tyrants.

of Cardinal Isidore eluded the search, and he escaped from Galata in a plebeian habit.[93]

The chain and entrance of the outward harbour was still occupied by the Italian ships of merchandise and war. They had signalised their valour in the siege; they embraced the moment of retreat, while the Turkish mariners were dissipated in the pillage of the city. When they hoisted sail, the beach was covered with a suppliant and lamentable crowd; but the means of transportation were scanty; the Venetians and Genoese selected their countrymen; and, notwithstanding the fairest promises of the sultan, the inhabitants of Galata evacuated their houses and embarked with their most precious effects.

In the fall and the sack of great cities, an historian is con- Amount of the spoil demned to repeat the tale of uniform calamity; the same effects must be produced by the same passions; and, when those passions may be indulged without control, small, alas! is the difference between civilised and savage man. Amidst the vague exclamations of bigotry and hatred, the Turks are not accused of a wanton or immoderate effusion of Christian blood; but, according to their maxims (the maxims of antiquity), the lives of the vanquished were forfeited; and the legitimate reward of the conqueror was derived from the service, the sale, or the ransom, of his captives of both sexes.[94] The wealth of Constantinople had been granted by the sultan to his victorious troops; and the rapine of an hour is more productive than the industry of years. But, as no regular division was attempted of the spoil, the respective shares were not determined by merit; and the rewards of valour were stolen away by the followers of the camp, who had declined the toil and danger of the battle. The narrative of their depredations could not afford either amusement or instruction; the total amount, in the last poverty of the empire, has been valued at four millions of ducats;[95] and of this sum a

[93] The Commentaries of Pius II. suppose that he craftily placed his cardinal's hat on the head of a corpse, which was cut off and exposed in triumph, while the legate himself was bought and delivered as a captive of no value. The great Belgic Chronicle adorns his escape with new adventures, which he suppressed (says Spondanus, A.D. 1453, No. 15) in his own letters, lest he should lose the merit and reward of suffering for Christ.

[94] Busbequius expatiates with pleasure and applause on the rights of war and the use of slavery among the ancients and the Turks (de Legat. Turcicâ, epist. iii. p. 161).

[95] This sum is specified in a marginal note of Leunclavius (Chalcondyles, l. viii. p. 211), but in the distribution to Venice, Genoa, Florence, and Ancona, of 50, 20,

small part was the property of the Venetians, the Genoese, the Florentines, and the merchants of Ancona. Of these foreigners, the stock was improved in quick and perpetual circulation; but the riches of the Greeks were displayed in the idle ostentation of palaces and wardrobes, or deeply buried in treasures of ingots and old coin, lest it should be demanded at their hands for the defence of their country. The profanation and plunder of the monasteries and churches excited the most tragic complaints. The dome of St. Sophia itself, the earthly heaven, the second firmament, the vehicle of the cherubim, the throne of the glory of God,[96] was despoiled of the oblations of ages; and the gold and silver, the pearls and jewels, the vases and sacerdotal ornaments, were most wickedly converted to the service of mankind. After the divine images had been stripped of all that could be valuable to a profane eye, the canvas, or the wood, was torn, or broken, or burnt, or trod under foot, or applied, in the stables or the kitchen, to the vilest uses. The example of sacrilege was imitated, however, from the Latin conquerors of Constantinople; and the treatment which Christ, the Virgin, and the saints had sustained from the guilty Catholic might be inflicted by the zealous Musulman on the monuments of idolatry. Perhaps, instead of joining the public clamour, a philosopher will observe that in the decline of the arts the workmanship could not be more valuable than the work, and that a fresh supply of visions and miracles would speedily be renewed by the craft of the priest and the credulity of the people. He will more seriously deplore the loss of the Byzantine libraries, which they destroyed or scattered in the general confusion: one hundred and twenty thousand manuscripts are said to have disappeared;[97] ten volumes might be purchased for a single ducat; and the same ignominious price, too high perhaps for a shelf of theology, included the whole works of Aristotle and Homer, the noblest productions of the science and literature of ancient Greece. We may reflect with pleasure that an inestimable portion of our classic treasures was safely deposited in Italy; and that the mechanics of a German

20, and 15,000 ducats, I suspect that a figure has been dropt. Even with the restitution, the foreign property would scarcely exceed one-fourth.

[96] See the enthusiastic praises and lamentations of Phranza (l. iii. c. 17).

[97] See Ducas (c. 43), and an epistle, 15th July, 1453, from Laurus Quirinus to Pope Nicholas V. (Hody de Græcis, p. 192, from a Ms. in the Cotton Library). [Cp. above, p, 203, note 89.]

town had invented an art which derides the havoc of time and barbarism.

From the first hour [98] of the memorable twenty-ninth of May, disorder and rapine prevailed in Constantinople till the eighth hour of the same day; when the sultan himself passed in triumph through the gate of St. Romanus. He was attended by his viziers, bashaws, and guards, each of whom (says a Byzantine historian) was robust as Hercules, dexterous as Apollo, and equal in battle to any ten of the race of ordinary mortals. The conqueror [99] gazed with satisfaction and wonder on the strange though splendid appearance of the domes and palaces, so dissimilar from the style of Oriental architecture. In the hippodrome, or *atmeidan*, his eye was attracted by the twisted columns of the three serpents; and, as a trial of his strength, he shattered with his iron mace or battle-axe the under-jaw of one of these monsters, [100] which in the eye of the Turks were the idols or talismans of the city. At the principal door of St. Sophia, he alighted from his horse and entered the dome; [101] and such was his jealous regard for that monument of his glory that, on observing a zealous Musulman in the act of breaking the marble pavement, he admonished him with his scymetar that, if the spoil and captives were granted to the soldiers, the public and private buildings had been reserved for the prince. By his command the metropolis of the Eastern church was transformed into a mosque: the rich and portable instruments of superstition had been removed; the crosses were thrown down; and the walls, which were covered with images and mosaics, were washed and purified and restored to a state of naked simplicity.[102] On the same day, or on the ensuing Friday, the *muezin* or crier ascended the most lofty turret, and proclaimed the *ezan*, or public invitation, in the name of God and his prophet; the imam preached; and Mahomet the Second performed the *namaz* of prayer and thanksgiving on

Mahomet II. visits the city, St. Sophia, the palace, &c.

[98] The Julian calendar, which reckons the days and hours from midnight, was used at Constantinople. But Ducas seems to understand the natural hours from sunrise.

[99] See the Turkish Annals, p. 329, and the Pandects of Leunclavius, p. 448.

[100] I have had occasion (vol. ii. p. 162) to mention this curious relic of Grecian antiquity.

[101] [According to the Slavonic Relation, he stooped down at the threshold of the church, took some earth, and scattered it on his head, in token of humiliation to God. In the same source it is stated that, at the prayers of the priests who met him in St. Sophia, he issued a proclamation to stay the pillage, c. 21-22.]

[102] [Covered with whitewash.]

the great altar, where the Christian mysteries had so lately been celebrated before the last of the Cæsars.[103] From St. Sophia he proceeded to the august but desolate mansion of an hundred successors of the great Constantine; but which, in a few hours, had been stripped of the pomp of royalty. A melancholy reflection on the vicissitudes of human greatness forced itself on his mind; and he repeated an elegant distich of Persian poetry, "The spider has wove his web in the imperial palace; and the owl hath sung her watch-song on the towers of Afrasiab ".[104]

Yet his mind was not satisfied, nor did the victory seem complete, till he was informed of the fate of Constantine; whether he had escaped, or been made prisoner, or had fallen in the battle. Two Janizaries claimed the honour and reward of his death: the body, under a heap of slain, was discovered by the golden eagles embroidered on his shoes; the Greeks acknowledged with tears the head of their late emperor; and, after exposing the bloody trophy,[105] Mahomet bestowed on his rival the honours of a decent funeral. After his decease, Lucas Notaras, great duke,[106] and first minister of the empire, was the most important prisoner. When he offered his person and his treasures at the foot of the throne, "And why," said the indignant sultan, "did you not employ these treasures in the defence of your prince and country?" "They were yours," answered the slave; "God had reserved them for your hands." "If he reserved them for me," replied the despot, "how have you presumed to withhold them so long by a fruitless and fatal resistance?" The great duke alleged the obstinacy of the strangers, and some secret encouragement from the Turkish vizir; and from this perilous interview he was at length dismissed with the

[103] We are obliged to Cantemir (p. 102) for the Turkish account of the conversion of St. Sophia, so bitterly deplored by Phranza and Ducas. It is amusing enough to observe in what opposite lights the same object appears to a Musulman and a Christian eye.

[104] This distich, which Cantemir gives in the original, derives new beauties from the application. It was thus that Scipio repeated, in the sack of Carthage, the famous prophecy of Homer. The same generous feeling carried the mind of the conqueror to the past or the future.

[105] I cannot believe, with Ducas (see Spondanus, A.D. 1453, No. 13), that Mahomet sent round Persia, Arabia, &c., the head of the Greek emperor; he would surely content himself with a trophy less inhuman.

[106] Phranza was the personal enemy of the great duke; nor could time, or death, or his own retreat to a monastery, extort a feeling of sympathy or forgiveness [iii. 9]. Ducas is inclined to praise and pity the martyr; Chalcondyles is neuter; but we are indebted to him for the hint of the Greek conspiracy.

assurance of pardon and protection. Mahomet condescended
to visit his wife, a venerable princess, oppressed with sickness
and grief; and his consolation for her misfortunes was in the
most tender strain of humanity and filial reverence. A similar
clemency was extended to the principal officers of state, of whom
several were ransomed at his expense; and during some days he
declared himself the friend and father of the vanquished people.
But the scene was soon changed; and before his departure the
hippodrome streamed with the blood of his noblest captives.
His perfidious cruelty is execrated by the Christians. They
adorn with the colours of heroic martyrdom the execution of
the great duke and his two sons; and his death is ascribed to
the generous refusal of delivering his children to the tyrant's
lust.[107] Yet a Byzantine historian has dropt an unguarded word
of conspiracy, deliverance, and Italian succour: such treason
may be glorious; but the rebel who bravely ventures has justly
forfeited his life; nor should we blame a conqueror for destroying the enemies whom he can no longer trust. On the eighteenth
of June, the victorious sultan returned to Hadrianople; and smiled
at the base and hollow embassies of the Christian princes, who
viewed their approaching ruin in the fall of the Eastern empire.

Constantinople had been left naked and desolate, without a
prince or a people. But she could not be despoiled of the
incomparable situation which marks her for the metropolis of
a great empire; and the genius of the place will ever triumph
over the accidents of time and fortune. Boursa and Hadrianople,
the ancient seats of the Ottomans, sunk into provincial towns;
and Mahomet the Second established his own residence, and
that of his successors, on the same commanding spot which had
been chosen by Constantine.[108] The fortifications of Galata,
which might afford a shelter to the Latins, were prudently
destroyed; but the damage of the Turkish cannon was soon
repaired; and before the month of August great quantities of

He re-peoples and adorns Constanti-nople

---

[107] [So Ducas, p. 303 *sqq.* Chalcondyles, p. 402. Pusculus, iv. 1071. Critobulus says generally that Notaras and his sons were put to death by the advice of
the Sultan's counsellors (i. 73, 9).]

[108] For the restitution of Constantinople and the Turkish foundations, see Cantemir (p. 102-109), Ducas (c. 42), with Thévenot, Tournefort, and the rest of our
modern travellers. [Cp. Zinkeisen, *op. cit.* ii. p. 5-8.] From a gigantic picture of
the greatness, population, &c., of Constantinople and the Ottoman empire (Abrégé
de l'Histoire Ottomane, tom. i. p. 16-21), we may learn that in the year 1586 the
Moslems were less numerous in the capital than the Christians or even the Jews.

lime had been burnt for the restoration of the walls of the capital. As the entire property of the soil and buildings, whether public or private, or profane or sacred, was now transferred to the conqueror, he first separated a space of eight furlongs from the point of the triangle for the establishment of his seraglio, or palace. It is here, in the bosom of luxury, that the *Grand Signor* (as he has been emphatically named by the Italians) appears to reign over Europe and Asia; but his person on the shores of the Bosphorus may not always be secure from the insults of an hostile navy. In the new character of a mosque, the cathedral of St. Sophia was endowed with an ample revenue, crowned with lofty minarets, and surrounded with groves and fountains, for the devotion and refreshment of the Moslems. The same model was imitated in the *jami*, or royal mosques; and the first of these was built by Mahomet himself, on the ruins of the church of the Holy Apostles and the tombs of the Greek emperors. On the third day after the conquest, the grave of Abu Ayub, or Job, who had fallen in the first siege of the Arabs, was revealed in a vision; and it is before the sepulchre of the martyr that the new sultans are girded with the sword of empire.[109] Constantinople no longer appertains to the Roman historian; nor shall I enumerate the civil and religious edifices that were profaned or erected by its Turkish masters: the population was speedily renewed; and before the end of September five thousand families of Anatolia and Romania had obeyed the royal mandate, which enjoined them, under pain of death, to occupy their new habitations in the capital.[110] The throne of Mahomet was guarded by the numbers and fidelity of his Moslem subjects; but his rational policy aspired to collect the remnant of the Greeks; and they returned in crowds, as soon as they were assured of their lives, their liberties, and the free exercise of their religion.[111] In the

---

[109] The *Turbé*, or sepulchral monument of Abu Ayub, is described and engraved in the Tableau Général de l'Empire Ottoman (Paris, 1787, in large folio), a work of less use, perhaps, than magnificence (tom. i. p. 305, 306).

[110] [Subsequently 4000 Servians were settled in Constantinople; 2000 Peloponnesian families after the reduction of the Peloponnesus; two-thirds of the population of Amastris, the Genoese colony on the Black Sea; also Trapezus, Sinope, Caffa, Eubœa, Samothrace, &c., were forced, when they were conquered, to augment the population of the capital. See Zinkeisen, *loc. cit.*]

[111] [The first volume of a history of the Greek Church under Turkish rule by Prof. Lebedev appeared in 1896. It is entitled, Istoriia greko-vostochnoi tserkvi pod vlastiiu Turok, ot padeniia Konstantinopolia do nastoiaschago vremeni.]

election and investiture of a patriarch, the ceremonial of the Byzantine court was revived and imitated. With a mixture of satisfaction and horror, they beheld the sultan on his throne, who delivered into the hands of Gennadius the crosier, or pastoral staff, the symbol of his ecclesiastical office; who conducted the patriarch to the gate of the seraglio, presented him with an horse richly caparisoned, and directed the vizirs and bashaws to lead him to the palace which had been allotted for his residence.[112] The churches of Constantinople were shared between the two religions : their limits were marked ; and, till it was infringed by Selim, the grandson of Mahomet, the Greeks[113] enjoyed above sixty years the benefit of this equal partition. Encouraged by the ministers of the divan, who wished to elude the fanaticism of the sultan, the Christian advocates presumed to allege that this division had been an act, not of generosity but of justice ; not a concession, but a compact ; and that, if one half of the city had been taken by storm, the other moiety had surrendered on the faith of a sacred capitulation. The original grant had indeed been consumed by fire ; but the loss was supplied by the testimony of three aged Janizaries who remembered the transaction ; and their venal oaths are of more weight in the opinion of Cantemir than the positive and unanimous consent of the history of the times.[114]

[112] Phranza (l. iii. c. 19) relates the ceremony, which has possibly been adorned in the Greek reports to each other, and to the Latins. The fact is confirmed by Emanuel Malaxus, who wrote, in vulgar Greek, the history of the Patriarchs after the taking of Constantinople, inserted in the Turco-Græcia of Crusius (l. v. p. 106-184). [C. Sathas has shewn that the Historia Patriarchica was not the work of Malaxus but of Damascenus Studites, to whom he also ascribes the Historia Politica, which is likewise printed in Turco-Græcia.] But the most patient reader will not believe that Mahomet adopted the Catholic form, " Sancta Trinitas quæ mihi donavit imperium te in patriarcham novæ Romæ deligit ".

[113] From the Turco-Græcia of Crusius, &c. Spondanus (A.D. 1453, No. 21 ; 1458, No. 16) describes the slavery and domestic quarrels of the Greek Church. The patriarch who succeeded Gennadius threw himself in despair into a well.

[114] Cantemir (p. 101-105) insists on the unanimous consent of the Turkish historians, ancient as well as modern, and argues that they would not have violated the truth to diminish their national glory, since it is esteemed more honourable to take a city by force than by composition. But 1. I doubt this consent, since he quotes no particular historian, and the Turkish Annals of Leunclavius affirm, without exception, that Mahomet took Constantinople *per vim* (p. 329). 2. The same argument may be turned in favour of the Greeks of the times, who would not have forgotten this honourable and salutary treaty. Voltaire, as usual, prefers the Turks to the Christians. [This fable, recorded in the Hist. Patriarch. p. 156, is connected with the reign of Sulayman, not with that of his father Selim. Finlay has pointed out that it involves a chronological mistake. The date given is 1537 and the vizir named, as interesting himself in the cause of the Greeks, is Tulphi. But the Lufti —who is meant—was vizir in 1539-1541. See History of Greece, v. p. 142.]

Extinction
of the Im-
perial
families of
Comnenus
and Palæo-
logus

The remaining fragments of the Greek kingdom in Europe and Asia I shall abandon to the Turkish arms; but the final extinction of the two last dynasties [115] which have reigned in Constantinople should terminate the decline and fall of the Roman empire in the East. The despots of the Morea, Demetrius and Thomas, [116] the two surviving brothers of the name of PALÆOLOGUS, were astonished by the death of the emperor Constantine and the ruin of the monarchy. Hopeless of defence, they prepared, with the noble Greeks who adhered to their fortune, to seek a refuge in Italy, beyond the reach of the Ottoman thunder. Their first apprehensions were dispelled by the victorious sultan, who contented himself with a tribute of twelve thousand ducats; and, while his ambition explored the continent and the islands in search of prey, he indulged the Morea in a respite of seven years. But this respite was a period of grief, discord, and misery. The *hexamilion*, the rampart of the Isthmus, so often raised and so often subverted, could not long be defended by three hundred Italian archers: the keys of Corinth were seized by the Turks; they returned from their summer excursions with a train of captives and spoil; and the complaints of the injured Greeks were heard with indifference and disdain. [117] The Albanians, a vagrant tribe of shepherds and robbers, filled the peninsula with rapine and murder; the two despots implored the dangerous and humiliating aid of a neighbouring bashaw; and, when he had quelled the revolt, his lessons inculcated the rule of their future conduct. Neither the ties of blood, nor the oaths which they repeatedly pledged in the communion and before the altar, nor the stronger pressure of necessity, could reconcile or suspend their domestic quarrels. They ravaged each other's patrimony with fire and sword; the alms and succours of the West were consumed in civil hostility;

[115] For the genealogy and fall of the Comneni of Trebizond, see Ducange (Fam. Byzant. p. 195); for the last Palæologi, the same accurate antiquarian (p. 244, 247, 248). The Palæologi of Montferrat were not extinct till the next century; but they had forgotten their Greek origin and kindred.

[116] In the worthless story of the disputes and misfortunes of the two brothers, Phranza (l. iii. c. 21-30) is too partial on the side of Thomas, Ducas (c. 44, 45) is too brief, and Chalcondyles (l. viii. ix. x.) too diffuse and digressive.

[117] [The misgovernment of the Poloponnesus in the 15th century is illustrated by the discourses of Gemistus Plethon addressed to the Emperor Manuel and his son the despot Theodore, proposing political reforms. They were published by Canter in his edition of the Eclogæ of Stobaeus (1575), and have been edited (with German translation) by Ellissen. See above, p. 132, note 111.]

and their power was only exerted in savage and arbitrary executions. The distress and revenge of the weaker rival invoked their supreme lord ; and, in the season of maturity and revenge, Mahomet declared himself the friend of Demetrius, and marched into the Morea with an irresistible force. When he had taken possession of Sparta, " You are too weak," said the sultan, " to control this turbulent province. I will take your daughter to my bed ; and you shall pass the remainder of your life in security and honour." Demetrius sighed, and obeyed ; surrendered his daughter and his castles ; followed to Hadrianople his sovereign and son ; and received, for his own maintenance, and that of his followers, a city in Thrace, and the adjacent isles of Imbros, Lemnos, and Samothrace. He was joined the next year by a companion of misfortune, the last of the COMNENIAN race, who, after the taking of Constantinople by the Latins, had founded a new empire on the coast of the Black Sea.[118] In the progress of his Anatolian conquests, Mahomet invested, with a fleet and army, the capital of David, who presumed to style himself Emperor of Trebizond ;[119] and the negotiation was comprised in a short and peremptory question, " Will you secure your life and treasures by resigning your kingdom ? or had you rather forfeit your kingdom, your treasures, and your life ? " The feeble Comnenus was subdued by his own fears, and the example of a Musulman neighbour, the prince of Sinope,[120] who, on a similar summons, had yielded a fortified city with four hundred cannon and ten or twelve thousand soldiers. The capitulation of Trebizond was faithfully performed ; and the emperor, with his family, was transported to a castle in Romania ; but on a slight suspicion of corresponding with the Persian king, David and the whole

Loss of the Morea, A.D. 1460 ;

of Trebizond, A.D. 1461

[118] See the loss or conquest of Trebizond in Chalcondyles (l. ix. p. 263-266 [p. 494 *sqq.* ed. Bonn]), Ducas (c. 45), Phranza (l. iii. c. 27), and Cantemir (p. 107). [The last days of the Empire of Trebizond are described by Finlay in History of Greece, iv. p. 400 *sqq.*]

[119] Though Tournefort (tom. iii. lettre xvii. p. 179) speaks of Trebizond as mal peuplée, Peyssonel, the latest and most accurate observer, can find 100,000 inhabitants (Commerce de la Mer Noire, tom. ii. p. 72, and for the province, p. 53-90). Its prosperity and trade are perpetually disturbed by the factious quarrels of two *odas* of Janizaries, in one of which 30,000 Lazi are commonly enrolled (Mémoires de Tott, tom. iii. p. 16, 17).

[120] Ismael Beg, prince of Sinope or Sinople, was possessed (chiefly from his copper mines) of a revenue of 200,000 ducats (Chalcond. l. ix. p. 258, 259). Peyssonel (Commerce de la Mer Noire, tom. ii. p. 100) ascribes to the modern city 60,000 inhabitants. This account seems enormous ; yet it is by trading with a people that we become acquainted with their wealth and numbers.

Comnenian race were sacrificed to the jealousy or avarice of the conqueror. Nor could the name of father long protect the unfortunate Demetrius from exile and confiscation : his abject submission moved the pity and contempt of the sultan; his followers were transplanted to Constantinople ; and his poverty was alleviated by a pension of fifty thousand aspers, till a monastic habit and a tardy death released Palæologus from an earthly master. It is not easy to pronounce whether the servitude of Demetrius or the exile of his brother Thomas [121] be the most inglorious. On the conquest of the Morea, the despot escaped to Corfu, and from thence to Italy, with some naked adherents ; his name, his sufferings, and the head of the apostle St. Andrew entitled him to the hospitality of the Vatican ; and his misery was prolonged by a pension of six thousand ducats from the pope and cardinals. His two sons, Andrew and Manuel, were educated in Italy ; but the eldest, contemptible to his enemies and burdensome to his friends, was degraded by the baseness of his life and marriage. A title was his sole inheritance ; and that inheritance he successively sold to the kings of France and Arragon.[122] During this transient prosperity, Charles the Eighth was ambitious of joining the empire of the East with the kingdom of Naples : in a public festival, he assumed the appellation and the purple of *Augustus :* the Greeks rejoiced, and the Ottoman already trembled, at the approach of the French chivalry.[123] Manuel Palæologus, the second son, was tempted to revisit his native country : his return might be grateful, and could not be dangerous, to the Porte ; he was maintained at Constantinople in safety and ease; and an honourable train of Christians and Moslems attended him to the grave. If there be some animals of so generous a nature that they refuse to propagate in a

---

[121] Spondanus (from Gobelin, Comment. Pii II. l. v.) relates the arrival and reception of the despot Thomas at Rome (A.D. 1461, No. 3).

[122] By an act dated A.D. 1494, 6th Sept., and lately transmitted from the archives of the Capitol to the royal library of Paris, the despot Andrew Palæologus, reserving the Morea, and stipulating some private advantages, conveys to Charles VIII. King of France, the empires of Constantinople and Trebizond (Spondanus, A.D. 1495, No. 2). M. de Foncemagne (Mém. de l'Académie des Inscriptions, tom. xvii. p. 539-578) has bestowed a dissertation on this national title, of which he had obtained a copy from Rome.

[123] See Philippe de Comines (l. vii. c. 14), who reckons with pleasure the number of Greeks who were prepared to rise, sixty miles of an easy navigation, eighteen days' journey from Valona to Constantinople, &c. On this occasion the Turkish empire was saved by the policy of Venice.

LATE BYZANTINE ART: FIGURES FROM A FRESCO IN THE CHURCH OF
THE PERIBLEPTOS AT MISTRA
COLLECTION DES HAUTES ÉTUDES

domestic state, the last of the Imperial race must be ascribed
to an inferior kind: he accepted from the sultan's liberality two
beautiful females; and his surviving son was lost in the habit
and religion of a Turkish slave.

The importance of Constantinople was felt and magnified in
its loss: the pontificate of Nicholas the Fifth, however peaceful
and prosperous, was dishonoured by the fall of the Eastern
empire; and the grief and terror of the Latins revived, or seemed
to revive, the old enthusiasm of the crusades. In one of the
most distant countries of the West, Philip, duke of Burgundy,
entertained, at Lisle in Flanders, an assembly of his nobles; and
the pompous pageants of the feast were skilfully adapted to their
fancy and feelings.[124] In the midst of the banquet, a gigantic
Saracen entered the hall, leading a fictitious elephant with a
castle on his back; a matron in a mourning robe, the symbol of
religion, was seen to issue from the castle; she deplored her
oppression and accused the slowness of her champions; the
principal herald of the golden fleece advanced, bearing on his
fist a live pheasant, which, according to the rites of chivalry, he
presented to the duke. At this extraordinary summons, Philip,
a wise and aged prince, engaged his person and powers in the
holy war against the Turks; his example was imitated by the
barons and knights of the assembly; they swore to God, the
Virgin, the ladies, and the *pheasant*; and their particular vows
were not less extravagant than the general sanction of their
oath. But the performance was made to depend on some future
and foreign contingency; and, during twelve years, till the last
hour of his life, the duke of Burgundy might be scrupulously,
and perhaps sincerely, on the eve of his departure. Had every
breast glowed with the same ardour; had the union of the
Christians corresponded with their bravery; had every country,
from Sweden [125] to Naples, supplied a just proportion of cavalry
and infantry, of men and money, it is indeed probable that
Constantinople would have been delivered, and that the Turks
might have been chased beyond the Hellespont or the Euphrates.

Grief and terror of Europe, A.D. 1453

[124] See the original feast in Olivier de la Marche (Mémoires, p. i. c. 29, 30), with
the abstract and observations of M. de St. Palaye (Mémoires sur la Chevalerie, tom.
i. p. iii. p. 182-185). The peacock and the pheasant were distinguished as royal
birds.

[125] It was found by an actual enumeration that Sweden, Gothland, and Finland
contained 1,800,000 fighting men, and consequently were far more populous than at
present.

But the secretary of the emperor, who composed every epistle and attended every meeting, Æneas Sylvius,[126] a statesman and orator, describes from his own experience the repugnant state and spirit of Christendom. "It is a body," says he, "without an head ; a republic without laws or magistrates. The pope and the emperor may shine as lofty titles, as splendid images ; but *they* are unable to command, and none are willing to obey ; every state has a separate prince, and every prince has a separate interest. What eloquence could unite so many discordant and hostile powers under the same standard ? Could they be assembled in arms, who would dare to assume the office of general ? What order could be maintained ?—what military discipline ? Who would undertake to feed such an enormous multitude ? Who would understand their various languages, or direct their stranger and incompatible manners ? What mortal could reconcile the English with the French, Genoa with Arragon, the Germans with the natives of Hungary and Bohemia ? If a small number enlisted in the holy war, they must be overthrown by the infidels ; if many, by their own weight and confusion." Yet the same Æneas, when he was raised to the papal throne, under the name of Pius the Second, devoted his life to the prosecution

[A.D. 1459] of the Turkish war. In the council of Mantua, he excited some sparks of a false or feeble enthusiasm ; but, when the pontiff

[A.D. 1464] appeared at Ancona, to embark in person with the troops, engagements vanished in excuses ; a precise day was adjourned to an indefinite term ; and his effective army consisted of some German pilgrims, whom he was obliged to disband with indulgences and alms. Regardless of futurity, his successors and the powers of Italy were involved in the schemes of present and domestic ambition ; and the distance or proximity of each object determined, in their eyes, its apparent magnitude. A more enlarged view of their interest would have taught them to maintain a defensive and naval war against the common enemy ; and the support of Scanderbeg and his brave Albanians might

---

[126] In the year 1454, Spondanus has given, from Æneas Sylvius, a view of the state of Europe, enriched with his own observations. That valuable annalist, and the Italian Muratori, will continue the series of events from the year 1453 to 1481, the end of Mahomet's life, and of this chapter. [The chief work on Æneas Sylvius is that of G. Voigt : Enea Silvio de' Piccolomini als Papst Pius II. und sein Zeitalter (in 3 vols.), 1857-63. There is a special monograph by O. von Heinemann on his agitation against the Turks : Æneas Sylvius als Prediger eines allgemeinen Kreuzzuges gegen die Türken, 1855.]

CONSTANTINOPLE : THE MOSQUE OF SELIM

have prevented the subsequent invasion of the kingdom of
Naples. The siege and sack of Otranto by the Turks diffused
a general consternation; and Pope Sixtus was preparing to fly
beyond the Alps, when the storm was instantly dispelled by the
death of Mahomet the Second, in the fifty-first year of his age.[127] Death of
Mahomet
His lofty genius aspired to the conquest of Italy: he was pos- II. A.D. 1481,
May 3, or
sessed of a strong city and a capacious harbour; and the same July 2
reign might have been decorated with the trophies of the NEW
and the ANCIENT ROME.[128]

[127] Besides the two annalists, the reader may consult Giannone (Istoria Civile,
tom. iii. p. 449-455) for the Turkish invasion of the kingdom of Naples. [See the
Diarium Parmense (p. 350 *sqq.*) in the xxiid volume of Muratori; the Relazione
della presa di Otranto (by a commissario of the Duke of Bari) in the Archivio
storico per le province Napolitane, vi. i. 74-162, 169-176 (1880); Joannis Albini
Lucani de gestis regum Neap. ab Aragonia qui extant libri iv., 1689; Antonio
de Ferrariis, Successi dell' armata turchesca nella città d'Otranto nell' anno
MCCCLXXX, 1612.] For the reign and conquests of Mahomet II. I have occasionally used the Memorie Istoriche de' Monarchi Ottomanni di Giovanni Sagredo
(Venezia, 1677, in 4to). In peace and war, the Turks have ever engaged the attention of the republic of Venice. All her dispatches and archives were open to a
procurator of St. Mark, and Sagredo is not contemptible either in sense or style.
Yet he too bitterly hates the infidels; he is ignorant of their language and manners;
and his narrative, which allows only seventy pages to Mahomet II. (p. 69-140), becomes more copious and authentic as he approaches the years 1640 and 1644, the
term of the historic labours of John Sagredo. [Mohammad died on 3rd May, cp.
Zinkeisen, ii. p. 468.]

[128] As I am now taking an everlasting farewell of the Greek empire, I shall briefly
mention the great collection of Byzantine writers, whose names and testimonies
have been successively repeated in this work. The Greek presses of Aldus and the
Italians were confined to the classics of a better age; and the first rude editions of
Procopius, Agathias, Cedrenus, Zonaras, &c., were published by the learned diligence of the Germans. The whole Byzantine series (36 volumes in folio) has
gradually issued (A.D. 1648, &c.), from the royal press of the Louvre, with some
collateral aid from Rome and Leipsic; but the Venetian edition (A.D. 1729), though
cheaper and more copious, is not less inferior in correctness than in magnificence
to that of Paris. The merits of the French editors are various; but the value of
Anna Comnena, Cinnamus, Villehardouin, &c., is enhanced by the historical notes
of Charles du Fresne du Cange. His supplemental works, the Greek Glossary, the
Constantinopolis Christiana, the Familiæ Byzantinæ, diffuse a steady light over the
darkness of the Lower Empire.

CHAPTER LXIX

*State of Rome from the Twelfth Century—Temporal Dominion
of the Popes—Seditions of the City—Political Heresy of
Arnold of Brescia—Restoration of the Republic—The
Senators—Pride of the Romans—Their Wars—They are
deprived of the Election and Presence of the Popes, who
retire to Avignon—The Jubilee—Noble Families of Rome
—Feud of the Colonna and Ursini*

State and
revolu-
tions of
Rome, A.D.
1100-1500

IN the first ages of the decline and fall of the Roman empire
our eye is invariably fixed on the royal city which had
given laws to the fairest portion of the globe.   We contemplate her fortunes, at first with admiration, at length with
pity, always with attention ; and, when that attention is diverted,
from the capital to the provinces, they are considered as so many
branches which have been successively severed from the Imperial
trunk.   The foundation of a second Rome on the shores of the
Bosphorus has compelled the historian to follow the successors of
Constantine ; and our curiosity has been tempted to visit the
most remote countries of Europe and Asia, to explore the causes
and the authors of the long decay of the Byzantine monarchy.
By the conquest of Justinian we have been recalled to the banks
of the Tiber, to the deliverance of the ancient metropolis ; but
that deliverance was a change, or perhaps an aggravation, of
servitude.   Rome had been already stripped of her trophies,
her gods, and her Cæsars ; nor was the Gothic dominion more
inglorious and oppressive than the tyranny of the Greeks.   In
the eighth century of the Christian æra, a religious quarrel, the
worship of images, provoked the Romans to assert their independence ; their bishop became the temporal as well as the
spiritual father of a free people; and of the Western empire,
which was restored by Charlemagne, the title and image still

decorate the singular constitution of modern Germany.[1] The name of Rome must yet command our involuntary respect ; the climate (whatsoever may be its influence) was no longer the same ;[2] the purity of blood had been contaminated through a thousand channels ; but the venerable aspect of her ruins, and the memory of past greatness, rekindled a spark of the national character. The darkness of the middle ages exhibits some scenes not unworthy of our notice. Nor shall I dismiss the present work till I have reviewed the state and revolutions of the ROMAN CITY, which acquiesced under the absolute dominion of the Popes about the same time that Constantinople was enslaved by the Turkish arms.

In the beginning of the twelfth century,[3] the æra of the first crusade, Rome was revered by the Latins, as the metropolis of the world, as the throne of the pope and the emperor, who, from the eternal city, derived their title, their honours, and the right or exercise of temporal dominion. After so long an interruption, it may not be useless to repeat that the successors of Charlemagne and the Othos were chosen beyond the Rhine in a national diet ; but that these princes were content with the humble names of kings of Germany and Italy, till they had passed the Alps and the Apennine, to seek their Imperial crown on the banks of the Tiber.[4] At some distance from the city, their

The French and German emperors of Rome, A.D. 1000-1100

---

[1] [But no longer, as the Roman empire ceased to exist in 1806 (August) when Francis II. resigned the Imperial Crown. He had taken the new title of Emperor of Austria in 1804.]

[2] The Abbé Dubos, who, with less genius than his successor Montesquieu, has asserted and magnified the influence of climate, objects to himself the degeneracy of the Romans and Batavians. To the first of these examples he replies, 1. That the change is less real than apparent, and that the modern Romans prudently conceal in themselves the virtues of their ancestors. 2. That the air, the soil, and the climate of Rome have suffered a great and visible alteration (Réflexions sur la Poésie et sur la Peinture, part ii. sect. 16). [The chief work now on the subject of this and the two following chapters is Gregorovius, Geschichte der Stadt Rom in Mittelalter, 8 vols., 1886-94, which has been excellently translated into English by Mrs. Hamilton, 7 vols., 1894-1900.]

[3] The reader has been so long absent from Rome, that I would advise him to recollect or review the 49th chapter, in the 5th volume of this history.

[4] The coronation of the German Emperors at Rome, more especially in the xith century, is best represented from the original monuments by Muratori (Antiquitat. Italiæ medii Ævi, tom. i. dissertat. ii. p. 99, &c.) and Cenni (Monument. Domin. Pontif., tom. ii. diss. .vi. p. 261), the latter of whom I only know from the copious extract of Schmidt (Hist. des Allemands, tom. iii. p. 255-266). [Cenni quotes the *Ordo coronationis* given by Cencius Camerarius, which critics variously refer to Henry III. and Henry VI. See Waitz, Die Formeln der deutschen Königs- und der römischen Kaiserkrönung vom 10ten bis 12ten Jahrhundert (in the Abhandlungen of the Göttingen Gesellschaft der Wiss., 1873, No. 18) ; and Schwarzer, Die Ordines

approach was saluted by a long procession of the clergy and
people with palms and crosses; and the terrific emblems of
wolves and lions, of dragons and eagles, that floated in the
military banners, represented the departed legions and cohorts
of the republic. The royal oath to maintain the liberties of
Rome was thrice reiterated, at the bridge,[5] the gate, and on the
stairs of the Vatican ; and the distribution of a customary donative feebly imitated the magnificence of the first Cæsars. In
the church of St. Peter,[6] the coronation was performed by his
successor ;[7] the voice of God was confounded with that of the
people; and the public consent was declared in the acclamations
of "Long life and victory to our lord the pope ! Long life and
victory to our lord the emperor! Long life and victory to the
Roman and Teutonic armies !"[8] The names of Cæsar and

der Kaiserkrönung (in Forschungen zur deutschen Geschichte, xxii. 161 *sqq*., 1882).
The coronations of the 9th century have been treated by W. Sickel in his article on
Die Kaiserkrönungen von Karl bis Berengar, in the Historische Zeitschrift, N.F.
xlvi. 1 *sqq.*]

[5] [The emperor "first took an oath to the Romans at the little bridge on the
Neronian field faithfully to observe the rights and usages of the city. On the day
of the coronation he made his entrance through the Porta Castella close to St.
Angelo and here repeated the oath. The clergy and the corporations of Rome
greeted him at the church of St. Maria Traspontina on a legendary site called the
Terebinthus of Nero" (Gregorovius, *op. cit.*, Eng. Tr. iv. 59).]

[6] [It may be noted that Henry V., crowned at St. Peter's A.D. 1111, 13th April,
was the first emperor crowned at Rome who was not crowned in the city.]

[7] [The interesting ceremony at St. Peter's—as it was performed in the 12th
century at all events—deserves more particular notice. Gregorovius thus describes
it (*ib.* p. 59, 60) : Having arrived at the steps, the king dismounted and "stooped
to kiss the pope's foot, tendered the oath to be an upright protector of the Church,
and was adopted by him as the son of the Church. With solemn song both king
and pope entered the Church of St. Maria in Turri beside the steps of St. Peter's,
and here the king was formally made Canon of the Cathedral. He then
advanced, conducted by the Lateran Count of the Palace and by the Primicerius
of the Judges, to the silver door of the cathedral, where he prayed and the Bishop
of Albano delivered the first oration. Innumerable mystic ceremonies awaited the
king in St. Peter's itself. Here a short way from the entrance was the Rota Por-
phyretica, a round porphyry stone inserted in the pavement, on which the king and
pope knelt. The imperial candidate here made his Confession of Faith, the Car-
dinal-bishop of Portus placed himself in the middle of the Rota and pronounced
the second oration. The king was then draped in new vestments, was made a
cleric in the sacristy by the pope, was clad with a tunic, dalmatica, pluviale, mitre
and sandals, and was then led to the altar of St. Maurice, whither his wife, after
similar but less fatiguing ceremonies, accompanied him. The Bishop of Ostia here
anointed the king on the right arm and the neck and delivered the third oration."
After this followed the chief ceremony. The pope placed a ring on the king's
finger, girt him with a sword, and placed the crown on his head. Then the
emperor, having taken off these symbols, "ministered to the pope as subdeacon at
mass. The Count Palatine afterwards removed the sandals and put the red
imperial boots with the spurs of St. Maurice upon him."]

[8] Exercitui Romano et Teutonico ! The latter was both seen and felt ; but the
former was no more than magni nominis umbra.

Augustus, the laws of Constantine and Justinian, the example of Charlemagne and Otho, established the supreme dominion of the emperors; their title and image was engraved on the papal coins; [9] and their jurisdiction was marked by the sword of justice, which they delivered to the præfect of the city. But every Roman prejudice was awakened by the name, the language, and the manners, of a barbarian lord. The Cæsars of Saxony or Franconia were the chiefs of a feudal aristocracy; nor could they exercise the discipline of civil and military power, which alone secures the obedience of a distant people, impatient of servitude, though perhaps incapable of freedom. Once, and once only, in his life, each emperor, with an army of Teutonic vassals, descended from the Alps. I have described the peaceful order of his entry and coronation; but that order was commonly disturbed by the clamour and sedition of the Romans, who encountered their sovereign as a foreign invader: his departure was always speedy, and often shameful; and, in the absence of a long reign, his authority was insulted, and his name was forgotten. The progress of independence in Germany and Italy undermined the foundations of the Imperial sovereignty, and the triumph of the popes was the deliverance of Rome.

Of her two sovereigns, the emperor had precariously reigned by the right of conquest; but the authority of the pope was founded on the soft, though more solid, basis of opinion and habit. The removal of a foreign influence restored and endeared the shepherd to his flock. Instead of the arbitrary or venal nomination of a German court, the vicar of Christ was freely chosen by the college of cardinals, most of whom were either natives or inhabitants of the city. The applause of the magistrates and people confirmed his election; and the ecclesiastical power that was obeyed in Sweden and Britain had been ultimately derived from the suffrage of the Romans. The same suffrage

Authority of the popes in Rome,

from affection:

---

[9] Muratori has given the series of the papal coins (Antiquitat. tom. ii. diss. xxvii. p. 548-554). He finds only two more early than the year 800; fifty are still extant from Leo III. to Leo IX. with the addition of the reigning emperor; none remain of Gregory VII. or Urban II.; but in those of Paschal II. he seems to have renounced this badge of dependence. [There are no Papal denarii between Benedict VII. (ob. A.D. 984) and Leo IX. But, as Gregorovius observes (*op. cit.* iv. p. 78 note), this is an accident, for coins must have been struck. In the 11th century we have one coin of Leo IX. and one of Paschal II. The interval between Paschal and Benedict XI. (ob. A.D. 1304) is filled by the coinage of the Senate; but, after the installation of the Senate, "solidi Papæ" (sous of the Pope) are still spoken of. See Gregorovius, *ib.* p. 498.]

gave a prince, as well as a pontiff, to the capital. It was universally believed that Constantine had invested the popes with the temporal dominion of Rome; and the boldest civilians, the most profane sceptics, were satisfied with disputing the right of the emperor and the validity of his gift. The truth of the fact, the authenticity of his donation, was deeply rooted in the ignorance and tradition of four centuries; and the fabulous origin was lost in the real and permanent effects. The name of *Dominus*, or Lord, was inscribed on the coin of the bishops; their

right; title was acknowledged by acclamations and oaths of allegiance; and, with the free or reluctant consent of the German Cæsars, they had long exercised a supreme or subordinate jurisdiction over the city and patrimony of St. Peter. The reign of the popes, which gratified the prejudices, was not incompatible with the liberties of Rome; and a more critical inquiry would have revealed a still nobler source of their power: the gratitude of a nation, whom they had rescued from the heresy and oppression of the Greek tyrant. In an age of superstition, it should seem that the union of the royal and sacerdotal characters would mutually fortify each other, and that the keys of paradise would be the surest pledge of earthly obedience. The sanctity of the

virtue; office might indeed be degraded by the personal vices of the man; but the scandals of the tenth century were obliterated by the austere and more dangerous virtues of Gregory the Seventh and his successors; and, in the ambitious contests which they maintained for the rights of the church, their sufferings or their success must equally tend to increase the popular veneration. They sometimes wandered in poverty and exile, the victims of persecution; and the apostolic zeal with which they offered themselves to martyrdom must engage the favour and sympathy of every Catholic breast. And sometimes, thundering from the Vatican, they created, judged, and deposed the kings of the world; nor could the proudest Roman be disgraced by submitting to a priest whose feet were kissed, and whose stirrup was held, by the successors of Charlemagne.[10] Even the temporal interest of the city should have protected in peace

---

[10] See Ducange, Gloss. mediæ et infimæ Latinitat. tom. vi. p. 364, 365, STAFFA. This homage was paid by kings to archbishops, and by vassals to their lords (Schmidt, tom. iii. p. 262); and it was the nicest policy of Rome to confound the marks of filial and of feudal subjection.

and honour the residence of the popes; from whence a vain and
lazy people derived the greatest part of their subsistence and
riches. The fixed revenue of the popes was probably impaired: benefits
many of the old patrimonial estates, both in Italy and the provinces, had been invaded by sacrilegious hands; nor could the
loss be compensated by the claim rather than the possession of
the more ample gifts of Pepin and his descendants. But the
Vatican and Capitol were nourished by the incessant and increasing swarms of pilgrims and suppliants; the pale of Christianity
was enlarged, and the pope and cardinals were overwhelmed by
the judgment of ecclesiastical and secular causes. A new jurisprudence had established in the Latin church the right and
practice of appeals; [11] and, from the North and West, the bishops
and abbots were invited or summoned to solicit, to complain, to
accuse, or to justify, before the threshold of the apostles. A
rare prodigy is once recorded, that two horses, belonging to the
Archbishops of Mentz and Cologne, repassed the Alps, yet laden
with gold and silver; [12] but it was soon understood that the
success, both of the pilgrims and clients, depended much less on
the justice of their cause than on the value of their offering.
The wealth and piety of these strangers were ostentatiously
displayed; and their expenses, sacred or profane, circulated in
various channels for the emolument of the Romans.

Such powerful motives should have firmly attached the Incon-
voluntary and pious obedience of the Roman people to their supersti-
spiritual and temporal father. But the operation of prejudice tion
and interest is often disturbed by the sallies of ungovernable
passion. The Indian who fells the tree that he may gather the
fruit,[13] and the Arab who plunders the caravans of commerce,
are actuated by the same impulse of savage nature, which over-

[11] The appeals from all the churches to the Roman Pontiff are deplored by the
zeal of St. Bernard (de Consideratione, l. iii. tom. ii. p. 431-442, edit. Mabillon,
Venet, 1750), and the judgment of Fleury (Discours sur l'Hist. Ecclésiastique, iv.
and vii.). But the saint, who believed in the false decretals, condemns only the abuse
of these appeals; the more enlightened historian investigates the origin, and rejects
the principles, of this new jurisprudence.

[12] Germanici . . . summarii non levatis sarcinis onusti nihilominus repatriant
inviti. Nova res! quando hâctenus aurum Roma refudit? Et nunc Romanorum
consilio id usurpatum non credimus (Bernard, de Consideratione, l. iii. c. 3, p.
437). The first words of the passage are obscure, and probably corrupt.

[13] Quand les sauvages de la Louisiane veulent avoir du fruit, ils coupent l'arbre
au pied et cueillent le fruit. Voilà le gouvernement despotique (Esprit des Loix, l.
v. c. 13); and passion and ignorance are always despotic.

looks the future in the present, and relinquishes for momentary
rapine the long and secure possession of the most important
blessings.   And it was thus that the shrine of St. Peter was
profaned by the thoughtless Romans, who pillaged the offerings,
and wounded the pilgrims, without computing the number and
value of similar visits, which they prevented by their inhospitable
sacrilege.   Even the influence of superstition is fluctuating and
precarious; and the slave, whose reason is subdued, will often
be delivered by his avarice or pride.   A credulous devotion for
the fables and oracles of the priesthood most powerfully acts on
the mind of a barbarian; yet such a mind is the least capable of
preferring imagination to sense, of sacrificing to a distant motive,
to an invisible, perhaps an ideal, object, the appetites and interests
of the present world.   In the vigour of health and youth, his
practice will perpetually contradict his belief; till the pressure
of age, or sickness, or calamity, awakens his terrors and com-
pels him to satisfy the double debt of piety and remorse.   I have
already observed that the modern times of religious indifference
are the most favourable to the peace and security of the clergy.
Under the reign of superstition they had much to hope from the
ignorance, and much to fear from the violence, of mankind.   The
wealth, whose constant increase must have rendered them the
sole proprietors of the earth, was alternately bestowed by the
repentant father and plundered by the rapacious son; their
persons were adored or violated; and the same idol, by the
hands of the same votaries, was placed on the altar or trampled
in the dust.   In the feudal system of Europe, arms were the title
of distinction and the measure of allegiance; and amidst their
tumult the still voice of law and reason was seldom heard or
obeyed.   The turbulent Romans disdained the yoke, and insulted the impotence, of their bishop; [14] nor would his education
or character allow him to exercise, with decency or effect, the
power of the sword.   The motives of his election and the frail-
ties of his life were exposed to their familiar observation; and

Seditions of Rome against the popes

---

[14] In a free conversation with his countryman Adrian IV. John of Salisbury
accuses the avarice of the pope and clergy: Provinciarum deripiunt spolia, ac si
thesauros Crœsi studeant reparare.   Sed recte cum eis agit Altissimus, quoniam et
ipsi aliis et sæpe vilissimis hominibus dati sunt in direptionem (de Nugis Curialium,
l. vi. c. 24, p. 387).   In the next page, he blames the rashness and infidelity of the
Romans, whom their bishops vainly strove to conciliate by gifts instead of virtues.
It is pity that this miscellaneous writer has not given us less morality and erudition,
and more pictures of himself and the times.

proximity must diminish the reverence which his name and his decrees impressed on a barbarous world. This difference has not escaped the notice of our philosophic historian : " though the name and authority of the court of Rome were so terrible in the remote countries of Europe, which were sunk in profound ignorance, and were entirely unacquainted with its character and conduct, the pope was so little revered at home that his inveterate enemies surrounded the gates of Rome itself and even controlled his government in that city ; and the ambassadors, who, from a distant extremity of Europe, carried to him the humble, or rather abject, submissions of the greatest potentate of the age, found the utmost difficulty to make their way to him and to throw themselves at his feet ".[15]

Since the primitive times, the wealth of the popes was exposed to envy, their power to opposition, and their persons to violence. But the long hostility of the mitre and the crown increased the numbers, and inflamed the passions, of their enemies. The deadly factions of the Guelphs and Ghibelines, so fatal to Italy, could never be embraced with truth or constancy by the Romans, the subjects and adversaries both of the bishop and emperor; but their support was solicited by both parties; and they alternately displayed in their banners the keys of St. Peter and the German eagle. Gregory the Seventh, who may be adored or detested as the founder of the papal monarchy, was driven from Rome, and died in exile at Salerno. Six-and-thirty of his successors,[16] till their retreat to Avignon, maintained an unequal

Successors of Gregory VII. A.D. 1086-1305

---

[15] Hume's History of England, vol. i. p. 419. The same writer has given us, from Fitz Stephen, a singular act of cruelty perpetrated on the clergy by Geoffrey, the father of Henry II. " When he was master of Normandy, the chapter of Seez presumed, without his consent, to proceed to the election of a bishop; upon which, he ordered all of them, with the bishop elect, to be castrated, and made all their testicles be brought him in a platter." Of the pain and danger they might justly complain ; yet, since they had vowed chastity, he deprived them of a superfluous treasure.

[16] From Leo IX. and Gregory VII. an authentic and contemporary series of the lives of the Popes, by the Cardinal of Arragon [Nicolò Roselli (ob. A.D. 1362)], Pandulphus Pisanus, Bernard Guido, &c. is inserted in the Italian historians of Muratori (tom. iii. p. i. p. 277-685), and has been always before my eyes. [This collection of Lives, printed by Muratori under the false title of the Cardinal of Aragon, is contained in the Liber Censuum sanctæ Romanæ Ecclesiæ (which is noticed above, vol. vi. p. 194 note). The Lives were also published, as Acta Vaticana, by Baronius in his Annales ecclesiastici (scattered about under the various years) ; and his text is said to be better than that of Muratori. There is a new edition of the Liber Censuum (put together A.D. 1192 by Cencius Camerarius) by P. Fabre. On the whole subject cp. Fabre's Etude sur le Liber censuum de l'église romaine, 1892.]

contest with the Romans; their age and dignity were often violated ; and the churches, in the solemn rites of religion, were polluted with sedition and murder. A repetition [17] of such capricious brutality, without connection or design, would be tedious and disgusting; and I shall content myself with some events of the twelfth century, which represent the state of the popes and the city. On Holy Thursday, while Paschal officiated before the altar, he was interrupted by the clamours of the multitude, who imperiously demanded the confirmation of a favourite magistrate.[18] His silence exasperated their fury ; his pious refusal to mingle the affairs of earth and heaven was encountered with menaces and oaths, that he should be the cause and the witness of the public ruin. During the festival of Easter, while the bishop and the clergy, barefoot and in procession, visited the tombs of the martyrs, they were twice assaulted, at the bridge of St. Angelo and before the Capitol, with volleys of stones and darts. The houses of his adherents were levelled with the ground; Paschal escaped with difficulty and danger ; he levied an army in the patrimony of St. Peter ; and his last days were embittered by suffering and inflicting the calamities of civil war. The scenes that followed the election of his successor Gelasius the Second were still more scandalous to the church and city. Cencio Frangipani,[19] a potent and factious baron, burst into the assembly furious, and in arms : the cardinals were stripped, beaten, and trampled under foot ; and he seized, without pity or respect, the vicar of Christ by the throat. Gelasius was dragged by his hair along the ground,

Paschal II. A.D. 1090-1118

[A.D. 1116]

Gelasius II. A.D. 1118, 1119

[Frangipane]

---

[17] The dates of years in the margin may, throughout this chapter, be understood as tacit references to the Annals of Muratori, my ordinary and excellent guide. He uses, and indeed quotes, with the freedom of a master, his great Collection of the Italian Historians, in xxviii. volumes ; and, as that treasure is in my library, I have thought it an amusement, if not a duty, to consult the originals.

[18] [The magistrate meant is the Prefect of the City (cp. below, p. 237), the criminal judge of Rome. His election often caused party conflicts. Paschal wished a son of Pierleone to be chosen, and the riot was marked by an attack on the fortress of the Pierleoni near the theatre of Marcellus.]

[19] I cannot refrain from transcribing the high-coloured words of Pandulphus Pisanus (p. 384) : Hoc audiens inimicus pacis atque turbator jam fatus Centius Frajapane, more draconis immanissimi sibilans, et ab imis pectoribus trahens longa suspiria, accinctus retro gladio sine more cucurrit, valvas ac fores confregit. Ecclesiam furibundus introiit, inde custode remoto papam per gulam accepit, distraxit, pugnis calcibusque percussit, et tanquam brutum animal intra limen ecclesiæ acriter calcaribus cruentavit ; et latro tantum dominum per capillos et brachia, Jesu bono interim dormiente, detraxit, ad domum usque deduxit, inibi catenavit et inclusit.

MEDIÆVAL ROME: THE CLOISTERS OF THE LATERAN

buffeted with blows, wounded with spurs, and bound with an
iron chain in the house of his brutal tyrant. An insurrection
of the people delivered their bishop; the rival families opposed
the violence of the Frangipani ; and Cencio, who sued for pardon,
repented of the failure rather than of the guilt of his enterprise.
Not many days had elapsed when the pope was again assaulted
at the altar. While his friends and enemies were engaged in a
bloody contest, he escaped in his sacerdotal garments. In this
unworthy flight, which excited the compassion of the Roman
matrons, his attendants were scattered or unhorsed ; and, in the
fields behind the church of St. Peter, his successor was found
alone and half dead with fear and fatigue. Shaking the dust
from his feet, the *apostle* withdrew from a city in which his
dignity was insulted and his person was endangered ; and the
vanity of sacerdotal ambition is revealed in the involuntary confession that one emperor was more tolerable than twenty.[20]
These examples might suffice ; but I cannot forget the sufferings of two pontiffs of the same age, the second and third of the
name of Lucius. The former, as he ascended in battle-array to Lucius II.
assault the Capitol, was struck on the temple by a stone, and A.D. 1144, 1145
expired in a few days ; [21] the latter was severely wounded in Lucius III.
the persons of his servants.[22] In a civil commotion several of A.D. 1181-1185
his priests had been made prisoners ; and the inhuman Romans,
reserving one as a guide for his brethren, put out their eyes,
crowned them with ludicrous mitres, mounted them on asses,
with their faces to the tail, and extorted an oath that in this
wretched condition they should offer themselves as a lesson to
the head of the church. Hope or fear, lassitude or remorse, the
characters of the men and the circumstances of the times, might
sometimes obtain an interval of peace and obedience ; and the
pope was restored with joyful acclamations to the Lateran or
Vatican, from whence he had been driven with threats and

[20] Ego coram Deo et Ecclesiâ dico si unquam possibile esset, mallem unum
imperatorem quam tot dominos (Vit. Gelas. II. p. 398). [Henry V., called in by
the Frangipani, appeared in Rome on 11th March, 1119. Gelasius escaped to Gaeta.
Gregorovius appropriately observes that " the flight to Gaeta was repeated 729 years
later in the history of Pius IX." (iv. 383).]

[21] [Godfrey of Viterbo, in Muratori, vii. p. 461.]

[22] [The sources for this outrage on Lucius III. (who finally sought the emperor's
protection at Verona, where he died) are : Sigebertus Gemblacensis, Auctarium
Aquicinense, ad ann. 1184 (Bethmann's ed. of Sigibert in the Monum. Germ. Hist.
vi. p. 300 *sqq.* has superseded all others) ; Albertus Stadensis (= Annales Stadenses,
in Mon. Germ. Hist. xvi.) ad 1183.]

violence.   But the root of mischief was deep and perennial; [23]
and a momentary calm was preceded and followed by such
tempests as had almost sunk the bark of St. Peter.   Rome continually presented the aspect of war and discord ; the churches
and palaces were fortified and assaulted by the factions and
Calixtus II. families; and, after giving peace to Europe, Calixtus the Second
A.D. 1119-
1124   alone had resolution and power to prohibit the use of private
Innocent arms in the metropolis.[24]   Among the nations who revered the
II. A.D.
1130-1143 apostolic throne, the tumults of Rome provoked a general indignation ; and, in a letter to his disciple Eugenius the Third,
St. Bernard, with the sharpness of his wit and zeal, has stigmatized the vices of the rebellious people.[25]   " Who is ignorant,"
Character says the monk of Clairvaux, " of the vanity and arrogance of the
of the
Romans by Romans ? a nation nursed in sedition, cruel, untractable, and
St. Ber-
nard   scorning to obey, unless they are too feeble to resist.   When
they promise to serve, they aspire to reign ; if they swear allegiance, they watch the opportunity of revolt ; yet they vent their
discontent in loud clamours, if your doors or your counsels are
shut against them.   Dexterous in mischief, they have never
learned the science of doing good.   Odious to earth and heaven,
impious to God, seditious among themselves, jealous of their
neighbours, inhuman to strangers, they love no one, by no one
are they beloved ; and, while they wish to inspire fear, they live
in base and continual apprehension.   They will not submit ;
they know not [25a] how to govern; faithless to their superiors, in-
tolerable to their equals, ungrateful to their benefactors, and
alike impudent in their demands and their refusals.   Lofty in
promise, poor in execution : adulation and calumny, perfidy
and treason, are the familiar arts of their policy."   Surely this
dark portrait is not coloured by the pencil of Christian charity ; [26]

[23] [As Gregorovius puts it (iv. 609) : " The spirit of Arnold still survived in Rome,
and each Pope was obliged to win toleration for himself or else to live in exile".]

[24] [Calixtus also forbade the fortification of churches. See Mansi, Concilia, xxi.
285. He restored the Lateran.]

[25] Quid tam notum seculis quam protervia et cervicositas Romanorum ? Gens
insueta paci, tumultui assueta, gens immitis et intractabilis usque adhuc, subdi
nescia, nisi cum non valet resistere (de Considerat. l. iv. c. 2, p. 441). The saint
takes breath, and then begins again : Hi, invisi terræ et cælo, utrique injecere
manus, &c. (p. 443).

[25a] [I have inserted *not*, which is omitted;in the quarto and subsequent editions.
St. Bernard's words are, præesse non norunt (De Consid. iv. 2, in Migne, Patr. Lat.
182, p. 774.)]

[26] As a Roman citizen, Petrarch takes leave to observe that Bernard, though a
saint, was a man ; that he might be provoked by resentment, and possibly repent of
his hasty passion, &c. (Mémoires sur la Vie de Pétrarque, tom. i. p. 330).

yet the features, however harsh and ugly, express a lively re-semblance of the Romans of the twelfth century.[27]

The Jews had rejected the Christ when he appeared among them in a plebeian character; and the Romans might plead their ignorance of his vicar when he assumed the pomp and pride of a temporal sovereign. In the busy age of the crusades, some sparks of curiosity and reason were rekindled in the Western world; the heresy of Bulgaria, the Paulician sect, was successfully transplanted into the soil of Italy and France ; the Gnostic visions were mingled with the simplicity of the Gospel; and the enemies of the clergy reconciled their passions with their conscience, the desire of freedom with the profession of piety.[28] The trumpet of Roman liberty was first sounded by Arnold of Brescia,[29] whose promotion in the church was confined to the lowest rank, and who wore the monastic habit rather as a garb of poverty than as an uniform of obedience. His adver-saries could not deny the wit and eloquence which they severely felt ; they confess with reluctance the specious purity of his morals; and his errors were recommended to the public by a mixture of important and beneficial truths. In his theological studies, he had been the disciple of the famous and unfortunate Abelard,[30] who was likewise involved in the suspicion of heresy;

Political heresy of Arnold of Brescia, A.D. 1140

[27] Baronius, in his index to the xiith volume of his Annals, has found a fair and easy excuse. He makes two heads, of Romani *Catholici* and *Schismatici ;* to the former, he applies all the good, to the latter all the evil, that is told of the city.

[28] The heresies of the xiith century may be found in Mosheim (Institut. Hist. Eccles. p. 419-427), who entertains a favourable opinion of Arnold of Brescia. In the 6th volume, I have described the sect of the Paulicians, and followed their migration from Armenia to Thrace and Bulgaria, Italy and France.

[29] The original pictures of Arnold of Brescia are drawn by Otho bishop of Frisingen (Chron. l. vii. c. 31, de Gestis Frederici I. l. i. c. 27, l. ii. c. 21), and in l. iii. of the Ligurinus [composed in A.D. 1186-7], a poem of Gunther, who flourished A.D. 1200, in the monastery of Paris [not Paris, but Päris, in Elsass], near Basil (Fabric. Bibliot. Latin. med. et infimæ Ætatis, tom. iii. p. 174, 175). The long passage that relates to Arnold, is produced by Guilliman (de Rebus Helveticis, l. iii. c. 5, p. 108). [Gibbon does not seem to know of the attack made on the genuineness of the poem " Ligurinus " by Senckenberg in his Parerga Gottingensia, i. (1737). Up to the year 1871, the orthodox view of critics was that the work was a forgery. But the authorship of Gunther was proved by Pannenborg in the Forschungen zur deutschen Geschichte, xi. p. 163 *sqq.* (1871).   Cp. his Programm " Der Verfasser des Ligurinus," 1883. There is a German translation of the poem by T. Vulpinus, 1889. On Arnold of Brescia, see Giesebrecht's monograph, Arnold von Brescia.]

[30] The wicked wit of Bayle was amused in composing, with much levity and learning, the articles of ABÉLARD, FOULQUES, HELOISE, in his Dictionnaire Critique. The dispute of Abelard and St. Bernard, of scholastic and positive divinity, is well understood by Mosheim (Institut. Hist. Eccles. p. 412-415).

but the lover of Eloisa was of a soft and flexible nature ; and his ecclesiastic judges were edified and disarmed by the humility of his repentance.   From this master Arnold most probably imbibed some metaphysical definitions of the Trinity, repugnant to the taste of the times; his ideas of baptism and the eucharist are loosely censured ; but a *political* heresy was the source of his fame and misfortunes.   He presumed to quote the declaration of Christ that his kingdom is not of this world : he boldly maintained that the sword and the sceptre were entrusted to the civil magistrate ; that temporal honours and possessions were lawfully vested in secular persons ; that the abbots, the bishops, and the pope himself must renounce either their state or their salvation ; and that, after the loss of their revenues, the voluntary tithes and oblations of the faithful would suffice, not indeed for luxury and avarice, but for a frugal life in the exercise of spiritual labours.   During a short time the preacher was revered as a patriot ; and the discontent, or revolt, of Brescia against her bishop was the first-fruits of his dangerous lessons.   But the favour of the people is less permanent than the resentment of the priest ; and, after the heresy of Arnold had been condemned [A.D. 1139] by Innocent the Second [31] in the general council of the Lateran, the magistrates themselves were urged by prejudice and fear to execute the sentence of the church.   Italy could no longer afford a refuge ; and the disciple of Abelard escaped beyond the Alps, till he found a safe and hospitable shelter in Zurich, now the first of the Swiss cantons.   From a Roman station,[32] a royal villa, a chapter of noble virgins, Zurich had gradually increased to a free and flourishing city, where the appeals of the Milanese were sometimes tried by the Imperial commissaries.[33]   In an age less

---

[31]   ——Damnatus ab illo
    Præsule, qui numeros vetitum contingere nostros
    Nomen ab *innocua* ducit laudabile vitâ.
We may applaud the dexterity and correctness of Ligurinus, who turns the unpoetical name of Innocent II. into a compliment. [For the acts of the Lateran Council see Mansi, Concil. xxi. p. 523 *sqq.*]

[32] A Roman inscription of Statio Turicensis has been found at Zurich (d'Anville, Notice de l'ancienne Gaule, p. 642-644) ; but it is without sufficient warrant that the city and canton have usurped and even monopolized the names of Tigurum and Pagus Tigurinus. [See Otto of Freisingen, Gesta Frederici, ii. 29.]

[33] Guilliman (de Rebus Helveticis, l. iii. c. 5, p. 106) recapitulates the donation (A.D. 833) of the emperor Lewis the Pious to his daughter the abbess Hildegardis. Curtim nostram Turegum in ducatu Alamanniæ in pago Durgaugensi, with villages, woods, meadows, waters, slaves, churches, &c., a noble gift.   Charles the Bald gave the jus monetæ, the city was walled under Otho I., and the line of the bishop

ripe for reformation, the præcursor of Zuinglius was heard with
applause; a brave and simple people imbibed, and long retained,
the colour of his opinions; and his art, or merit, seduced the
bishop of Constance, and even the pope's legate, who forgot,
for his sake, the interest of their master and their order. Their
tardy zeal was quickened by the fierce exhortations of St. Bernard;[34] and the enemy of the church was driven by persecution
to the desperate measure of erecting his standard in Rome itself,
in the face of the successor of St. Peter.

Yet the courage of Arnold was not devoid of discretion: he
was protected, and had perhaps been invited, by the nobles and
people; and in the service of freedom his eloquence thundered
over the seven hills. Blending in the same discourse the texts
of Livy and St. Paul, uniting the motives of gospel and of classic
enthusiasm, he admonished the Romans how strangely their
patience and the vices of the clergy had degenerated from the
primitive times of the church and the city. He exhorted them
to assert the inalienable rights of men and Christians; to restore
the laws and magistrates of the republic; to respect the *name* of
the emperor; but to confine their shepherd to the spiritual
government of his flock.[35] Nor could his spiritual government
escape the censure and control of the reformer; and the inferior
clergy were taught by his lessons to resist the cardinals, who
had usurped a despotic command over the twenty-eight regions
or parishes of Rome.[36] The revolution was not accomplished
without rapine and violence, the effusion of blood, and the

He exhorts the Romans to restore the republic, A.D. 1144-1154

of Frisingen,
> Nobile Turegum multarum copia rerum,

is repeated with pleasure by the antiquaries of Zurich.

[34] Bernard, epistol. cxcv. cxcvi. tom. i. p. 187-190. Amidst his invectives, he
drops a precious acknowledgment, qui utinam quam sanæ esset doctrinæ quam
districtæ est vitæ. He owns that Arnold would be a valuable acquisition for the
church. [Bernard himself—though he opposed Arnold as a heretic—strongly
condemned the temporal dominion of the Pope, in his De Consideratione. He
observes, for instance : nemo militans Deo implicet se negotiis secularibus. Cp.
Gregorovius, *op. cit.* iv. p. 483-4.]

[35] He advised the Romans,
> Consiliis armisque sua moderamina summa
> Arbitrio tractare suo : nil juris in hâc re
> Pontifici summo, modicum concedere regi
> Suadebat populo. Sic læsâ stultus utrâque
> Majestate, reum geminæ se fecerat aulæ.

Nor is the poetry of Gunther different from the prose of Otho.

[36] See Baronius (A.D. 1148, No. 38, 39) from the Vatican Mss. He loudly
condemns Arnold (A.D. 1141, No. 3) as the father of the political heretics whose
influence then hurt him in France.

demolition of houses; the victorious faction was enriched with the spoils of the clergy and the adverse nobles.   Arnold of Brescia enjoyed or deplored the effects of his mission; his reign continued above ten years, while two popes, Innocent the Second and Anastasius the Fourth, either trembled in the Vatican or wandered as exiles in the adjacent cities.   They were succeeded by a more vigorous and fortunate pontiff, Adrian the Fourth,[37] the only Englishman who has ascended the throne of St. Peter; and whose merit emerged from the mean condition of a monk, and almost a beggar, in the monastery of St. Albans.   On the first provocation, of a cardinal killed or wounded in the streets, he cast an interdict on the guilty people; and, from Christmas to Easter, Rome was deprived of the real or imaginary comforts of religious worship.   The Romans had despised their temporal prince: they submitted with grief and terror to the censures of their spiritual father; their guilt was expiated by penance, and the banishment of the seditious preacher was the price of their absolution.   But the revenge of Adrian was yet unsatisfied, and the approaching coronation of Frederic Barbarossa was fatal to the bold reformer, who had offended, though not in an equal degree, the heads of the church and state.   In their interview at Viterbo,[38] the pope represented to the emperor the furious ungovernable spirit of the Romans; the insults, the injuries, the fears, to which his person and his clergy were continually exposed; and the pernicious tendency of the heresy of Arnold, which must subvert the principles of civil as well as ecclesiastical subordination.   Frederic was convinced by these arguments, or tempted by the desire of the Imperial crown; in the balance of ambition, the innocence or life of an individual is of small account; and their common enemy was sacrificed to a moment of political concord.   After his retreat from Rome, Arnold had been protected by the viscounts of Campania, from whom he was extorted by the power of Cæsar: the præfect of the city pronounced his sentence; the martyr of freedom was burnt alive in the presence of a careless and ungrateful people; and his ashes were cast into the Tiber, lest the heretics should collect and worship the relics of their master.[39]   The clergy triumphed in

[Innocent II. A.D. 1130-43]

[Anastasius IV. A.D. 1153-4]

[Nicholas Breakspear, A.D. 1154-9]

[A.D. 1155]

[Frederick crowned, June 18, 1155]

His execution, A.D. 1155

---

[37] The English reader may consult the Biographia Britannica, ADRIAN IV., but our own writers have added nothing to the fame or merits of their countryman.

[38] [The meeting was close to Nepi.   See Muratori, Antiq. Ital. i. 117.]

[39] Besides the historian and poet already quoted, the last adventures of Arnold are related by the biographer of Adrian IV. (Muratori, Script. Rerum Ital. tom.

his death; with his ashes, his sect was dispersed; his memory still lived in the minds of the Romans. From his school they had probably derived a new article of faith, that the metropolis of the Catholic church is exempt from the penalties of excommunication and interdict. Their bishops might argue that the supreme jurisdiction, which they exercised over kings and nations, more specially embraced the city and diocese of the prince of the apostles. But they preached to the winds, and the same principle that weakened the effect, must temper the abuse, of the thunders of the Vatican.

The love of ancient freedom has encouraged a belief that as early as the tenth century, in their first struggles against the Saxon Othos, the commonwealth was vindicated and restored by the senate and people of Rome; that two consuls were annually elected among the nobles; and that ten or twelve plebeian magistrates revived the name and office of the tribunes of the commons.[40] But this venerable structure disappears before the light of criticism. In the darkness of the middle ages, the appellations of senators, of consuls, of the sons of consuls, may sometimes be discovered.[41] They were bestowed by the

Restoration of the Senate.
A.D. 1144
[1143]

iii. p. i. p. 441, 442). [The circumstances of the death of Arnold of Brescia are dark; it happened near Soracte, not in the city. Cp. Gregorovius, *op. cit.* iv. 544. A new and important source was discovered not many years ago—an anonymous Latin poem entitled Gesta Friderici imperatoris in Italia, describing the Lombard wars of Frederick Barbarossa up to the battle of Carcano in A.D. 1160. (It has been proposed to ascribe the authorship to Thadeus de Roma.) It was published in 1887 (Gesta di Federico I. in Italia) by E. Monaci, as vol. i. of the Fonti per la storia d'Italia. But the passage relating to Arnold of Brescia was printed in 1878 in vol. i. of the Archivio della Società Romana di storia patria.]

[40] Ducange (Gloss. Latinitatis mediæ et infimæ Ætatis, DECARCHONES, tom. ii. p. 726) gives me a quotation from Blondus (decad. ii. l. ii.): Duo consules ex nobilitate quotannis fiebant, qui ad vetustum consulum exemplar summæ rerum præessent. And in Sigonius (de Regno Italiæ, l. vi. Opp. tom. ii. p. 400) I read of the consuls and tribunes of the xth century. Both Blondus, and even Sigonius, too freely copied the classic method of supplying from reason or fancy the deficiency of records.

[41] In the panegyric of Berengarius (Muratori, Script. Rer. Ital. tom. ii. p. i. p. 408), a Roman is mentioned as consulis natus in the beginning of the xth century. Muratori (dissert. v.) discovers, in the years 952 and 956, Gratianus in Dei nomine consul et dux, Georgius consul et dux; and in 1015, Romanus, brother of Gregory VIII., proudly, but vaguely, styles himself consul et dux et omnium Romanorum senator. [No such body as a Senate existed in Rome from the 8th to the 12th century; and the word *Senatus* frequently occurring not only in chronicles but even in Acts of Councils signifies merely the Roman nobility. For example Benzo describes a meeting of the adherents of the Imperial party in A.D. 1062 as an "assembly of the Senate". Thus *senator* meant a noble. But it was sometimes assumed as a title in a more pregnant sense, implying municipal authority, as when Alberic styled himself *omnium Romanorum Senator;* and his father-in-law Theophylactus had already borne the title Consul or Senator of the Romans, and the

emperors, or assumed by the most powerful citizens, to denote their rank, their honours [42] and perhaps the claim of a pure and patrician descent; but they float on the surface, without a series or a substance, the titles of men, not the orders of government; [43] and it is only from the year of Christ one thousand one hundred and forty-four, that the establishment of the senate is dated, as a glorious æra, in the acts of the city.[44] A new constitution was hastily framed by private ambition or popular enthusiasm; nor could Rome, in the twelfth century, produce an antiquary to explain, or a legislator to restore, the harmony and proportions of the ancient model. The assembly of a free, of an armed people will ever speak in loud and weighty acclamations. But the regular distribution of the thirty-five tribes, the nice balance of the wealth and numbers of the centuries, the debates of the adverse orators, and the slow operation of votes and ballots could not easily be adapted by a blind multitude, ignor-

---

son of Theophylactus was called Son of the Consul, and his wife Theodora the Senatrix. Compare Gregorovius, *op. cit.* iii. p. 293-5. Though there is no reason to suppose that the Romans elected consuls annually in this age (10th century), it seems that "a Consul of the Romans was elected as Princeps of the nobility from its midst; confirmed by the Pope; and placed as a Patricius at the head of the jurisdiction and administration of the city". Gregorovius, *ib.* p. 253. The Counts of Tusculum used to style themselves Consuls and Senators of the Romans. Gregorovius, iv. p. 138.]

[42] As late as the xth century, the Greek emperors conferred on the dukes of Venice, Naples, Amalfi, &c. the title of ὕπατος, or consuls [consul?] (see Chron. Sagornini, *passim*); and the successors of Charlemagne would not abdicate any of their prerogatives. But, in general, the names of *consul* and *senator*, which may be found among the French and Germans, signify no more than count or lord (*Signeur*, Ducange, Glossar.). The monkish writers are often ambitious of fine classic words. [The title consul was borne in the 12th century, denoting the judiciary and ruling magistracy. Cp. Gregorovius, *op. cit.* iv. 459.]

[43] The most constitutional form is a diploma of Otho III. (A.D. 998), Consulibus senatus populique Romani; but the act is probably spurious. At the coronation of Henry I. A.D. 1014, the historian Dithmar (apud Muratori, Dissert. xxiii.) describes him, a senatoribus duodecim vallatum, quorum sex rasi barbâ alii prolixâ mystice incedebant cum baculis. The senate is mentioned in the panegyric of Berengarius (p. 406).

[44] [Just before this revolution the Romans had been involved in a war for the possession of Tivoli. The place had surrendered to the Pope, and they had demanded it from him. The revolution followed. "In 1143," says Gregorovius, "Rome made an attempt to form such an association of the different classes as had been formed in Milan, Pisa, Genoa, and other cities" (iv. p. 449). The lesser nobility joined the burghers, seized the Capitoline, declared themselves the Senate. Thus a free burgher class was established, and the despotism of the nobility who were the supporters of the Pope was overthrown: this is the significance of the revolution of 1143. The first civic constitution (1144) was framed under the influence of Jordan Pierleone.—Pope Lucius II. turned to Conrad III., but got no help. Then the Senate invited Conrad to come and rule in Rome (1149 or 1150). See Otto of Freisingen, i. 28.]

ant of the arts, and insensible of the benefits, of legal government. It was proposed by Arnold to revive and discriminate
the equestrian order; but what could be the motive or measure of such distinction?[45] The pecuniary qualification of the
knights must have been reduced to the poverty of the times:
those times no longer required their civil functions of judges
and farmers of the revenue; and their primitive duty, their
military service on horseback, was more nobly supplied by
feudal tenures and the spirit of chivalry. The jurisprudence
of the republic was useless and unknown; the nations and
families of Italy, who lived under the Roman and barbaric
laws, were insensibly mingled in a common mass; and some
faint tradition, some imperfect fragments, preserved the memory
of the Code and Pandects of Justinian. With their liberty,
the Romans might doubtless have restored the appellation and
office of consuls, had they not disdained a title so promiscuously
adopted in the Italian cities that it has finally settled on the
humble station of the agents of commerce in a foreign land.
But the rights of the tribunes, the formidable word that arrested
the public counsels, suppose, or must produce, a legitimate democracy. The old patricians were the subjects, the modern
barons the tyrants, of the state; nor would the enemies of
peace and order, who insulted the vicar of Christ, have long
respected the unarmed sanctity of a plebeian magistrate.[46]

In the revolution of the twelfth century, which gave a new
existence and æra to Rome, we may observe the real and important events that marked or confirmed her political independence. I. The Capitoline hill, one of her seven eminences,[47] is

The Capi-
tol

<hr>

[45] In ancient Rome, the equestrian order was not ranked with the senate and
people as a third branch of the republic till the consulship of Cicero, who assumes
the merit of the establishment (Plin. Hist. Natur. xxxiii. 3; Beaufort, République
Romaine, tom. i. p. 144-155).

[46] The republican plan of Arnold of Brescia is thus stated by Gunther:—

Quin etiam titulos urbis renovare vetustos;
Nomine plebeio secernere nomen equestre,
Jura tribunorum, sanctum reparare senatum,
Et senio fessas mutasque reponere leges.
Lapsa ruinosis, et adhuc pendentia muris
Reddere primævo Capitolia prisca nitori.

But of these reformations, some were no more than ideas, others no more than
words.

[47] After many disputes among the antiquaries of Rome, it seems determined
that the summit of the Capitoline hill next the river is strictly the Mons Tarpeius,
the Arx; and that, on the other summit, the church and convent of Araceli, the
barefoot friars of St. Francis occupy the temple of Jupiter (Nardini, Roma Antica,

about four hundred yards in length and two hundred in breadth. A flight of an hundred steps led to the summit of the Tarpeian rock; and far steeper was the ascent before the declivities had been smoothed and the precipices filled by the ruins of fallen edifices. From the earliest ages, the Capitol had been used as a temple in peace, a fortress in war: after the loss of the city, it maintained a siege against the victorious Gauls; and the sanctuary of empire was occupied, assaulted, and burnt, in the civil wars of Vitellius and Vespasian.[48] The temples of Jupiter and his kindred deities had crumbled into dust; their place was supplied by monasteries and houses; and the solid walls, the long and shelving porticoes, were decayed or ruined by the lapse of time. It was the first act of the Romans, an act of freedom, to restore the strength, though not the beauty, of the Capitol;[49] to fortify the seat of their arms and counsels; and, as often as they ascended the hill, the coldest minds must have glowed

The coin with the remembrance of their ancestors. II. The first Cæsars had been invested with the exclusive coinage of the gold and silver; to the senate they abandoned the baser metal of bronze or copper;[50] the emblems and legends were inscribed on a more ample field by the genius of flattery; and the prince was relieved from the care of celebrating his own virtues. The successors of Diocletian despised even the flattery of the senate: their royal officers at Rome, and in the provinces, assumed the sole direction of the mint; and the same prerogative was inherited by the Gothic kings of Italy, and the long series of the Greek, the French, and the German dynasties. After an abdication of eight hundred years, the Roman senate asserted

---

l. v. c. 11-16). [This conclusion is incorrect. Both the Tarpeian Rock and the Temple of Jupiter were on the western height; the Arx was on the eastern, which is now crowned by the Church of St. Maria in Aracœli. For the determination of the site of the temple, a passage in the *Graphia* (a collection of ceremonial formularies which was perhaps drawn up for Otto III., in imitation of the Byzantine ceremonials) was of great importance: "On the summit of the fortress over the Porticus Crinorum was the Temple of Jupiter and Moneta". This portico belonged to the Forum olitorium; as was shown by excavations in the Caffarelli gardens. Pope Anaclete II. ratified to the Abbot of St. Maria the possession of the Capitoline hill.]

[48] Tacit. Hist. iii. 69, 70.

[49] [The old Tabularium, in the saddle between the two summits, became the Senate-house. Cp. Gregorovius, *op. cit.* iv. 477.]

[50] This partition of the nobler and the baser metals between the emperor and senate must, however, be adopted, not as a positive fact, but as the probable opinion of the best antiquaries (see the Science des Médailles of the Père Joubert, tom. ii. p. 208-211, in the improved and scarce edition of the Baron de la Bastie).

this honourable and lucrative privilege; which was tacitly renounced by the popes, from Paschal the Second to the establishment of their residence beyond the Alps. Some of these republican coins of the twelfth and thirteenth centuries are shewn in the cabinets of the curious. On one of these, a gold medal, Christ is depictured, holding in his left hand a book with this inscription, "THE VOW OF THE ROMAN SENATE AND PEOPLE: ROME, THE CAPITAL OF THE WORLD"; on the reverse, St. Peter delivering a banner to a kneeling senator in his cap and gown, with the name and arms of his family impressed on a shield.[51] III. With the empire, the præfect of the city had declined to a municipal officer; yet he still exercised in the last appeal the civil and criminal jurisdiction; and a drawn sword, which he received from the successors of Otho, was the mode of his investiture and the emblem of his functions.[52] The dignity was confined to the noble families of Rome; the choice of the people was ratified by the pope; but a triple oath of fidelity must have often embarrassed the præfect in the conflict of adverse duties.[53] A servant, in whom they possessed but a third share, was dismissed by the independent Romans; in his place they elected a patrician; but this title, which Charlemagne had not disdained, was too lofty for a citizen or a subject; and, after the first fervour of rebellion, they consented without reluctance to the restoration of the præfect. About fifty years after this event, Innocent the Third, the most ambitious, or at least the most fortunate, of the pontiffs, delivered the Romans

The præfect of the city

A.D. 1198-1216

[51] In his xxviith dissertation on the Antiquities of Italy (tom. ii. p. 559-569), Muratori exhibits a series of the senatorian coins, which bore the obscure names of *Affortiati* [= of strong gold], *Infortiati*, *Provisini* [from Provins, in Champagne], *Paparini*. [Those which are perhaps earliest have ROMAN. PRICIPE round the image of St. Peter, and SENAT. POPVL. Q.R. round St. Paul.] During this period, all the popes, without excepting Boniface VIII., abstained from the right of coining, which was resumed by his successor Benedict XI. and regularly exercised in the court of Avignon.

[52] A German historian, Gerard of Reicherspeg (in Baluz. Miscell. tom. v. p. 64, apud Schmidt, Hist. des Allemands, tom. iii. p. 265), thus describes the constitution of Rome in the xith century: Grandiora urbis et orbis negotia spectant ad Romanum pontificem itemque ad Romanum Imperatorem; sive illius vicarium urbis præfectum, qui de suâ dignitate respicit utrumque, videlicet dominum papam cui facit hominum, et dominum imperatorum a quo accipit suæ potestatis insigne, scilicet gladium exertum. [Contelorius, De præfecto Urbis.]

[53] The words of a contemporary writer (Pandulph. Pisan. in Vit. Paschal. II. p. 357, 358) describe the election and oath of the præfect in 1118, inconsultis patribus . . . loca præfectoria . . . laudes præfectoriæ . . . comitiorum applausum . . . juraturam populo in ambonem sublevant . . . confirmari eum in urbe præfectum petunt.

and himself from this badge of foreign dominion; he invested the præfect with a banner instead of a sword, and absolved him from all dependence of oaths of service to the German emperors.[54] In his place an ecclesiastic, a present or future cardinal, was named by the pope to the civil government of Rome; but his jurisdiction has been reduced to a narrow

Number and choice of the senate

compass; and in the days of freedom the right or exercise was derived from the senate and people. IV. After the revival of the senate,[55] the conscript fathers (if I may use the expression) were invested with the legislative and executive power; but their views seldom reached beyond the present day; and that day was most frequently disturbed by violence and tumult. In its utmost plenitude, the order or assembly consisted of fifty-six senators,[56] the most eminent of whom were distinguished by the title of counsellors; they were nominated, perhaps annually, by the people; and a previous choice of their electors, ten persons in each region or parish, might afford a basis for a free and permanent constitution. The popes, who in this tempest submitted rather to bend than to break, confirmed by treaty the establishment and privileges of the senate, and expected from time, peace, and religion, the restoration of their government. The motives of public and private interest might sometimes draw from the Romans an occasional and temporary sacrifice of their claims; and they renewed their oath of allegiance to the successor of St. Peter and Constantine, the lawful head of the church and the republic.[57]

---

[54] Urbis præfectum ad ligiam fidelitatem recepit, et per mantum quod illi donavit de præfecturâ eum publice investivit, qui usque ad id tempus juramento fidelitatis imperatori fuit obligatus, et ab eo præfecturæ tenuit honorem (Gesta Innocent. III. in Muratori, tom. iii. p. i. p. 487).

[55] See Otho Frising. Chron. vii. 31, de Gest. Frederic. I. l. i. c. 27.

[56] Our countryman, Roger Hoveden, speaks of the single senators, of the *Capuzzi* family, &c. quorum temporibus melius regebatur Roma quam nunc (A.D. 1194) est temporibus lvi. senatorum (Ducange, Gloss. tom. vi. p. 191. SENATORES).

[57] Muratori (dissert. xlii. tom. iii. p. 785-788) has published an original treaty: Concordia inter D. nostrum papam Clementem III. et senatores populi Romani super regalibus et aliis dignitatibus urbis, &c. 44° senatus. The senate speaks, and speaks with authority: Reddimus ad præsens . . . habebimus . . . dabitis presbyteria . . . jurabimus pacem et fidelitatem, &c. A chartula De tenimentis Tusculani, dated in the 47th year of the same æra, and confirmed decreto amplissimi ordinis senatus, acclamatione P.R. publice Capitolio consistentis. It is there we find the difference of senatores consiliarii and simple senators (Muratori, dissert. xlii. tom. iii. ·p. 787-789). [The transactions here touched on belong to the revolution of A.D. 1188, which deserved a more particular notice. Pope Clement III. (1187-91) was forced to make a formal treaty, which implied a new constitution. The Pope was recognised as overlord; he had the right of investing the Senate;

The union and vigour of a public council was dissolved in a lawless city; and the Romans soon adopted a more strong and simple mode of administration. They condensed the name and authority of the senate in a single magistrate or two colleagues; and, as they were changed at the end of a year or of six months, the greatness of the trust was compensated by the shortness of the term. But in this transient reign, the senators of Rome indulged their avarice and ambition; their justice was perverted by the interest of their family and faction; and, as they punished only their enemies, they were obeyed only by their adherents. Anarchy, no longer tempered by the pastoral care of their bishop, admonished the Romans that they were incapable of governing themselves; and they sought abroad those blessings which they were hopeless of finding at home. In the same age, and from the same motives, most of the Italian republics were prompted to embrace a measure, which, however strange it may seem, was adapted to their situation, and productive of the most salutary effects.[58] They chose, in some foreign but friendly city, an impartial magistrate, of noble birth and unblemished character, a soldier and a statesman, recommended by the voice of fame and his country, to whom they delegated for a time the supreme administration of peace and war. The compact between the governor and the governed was sealed with oaths and subscriptions; and the duration of his power, the measure of his stipend, the nature of their mutual obligations, were defined with scrupulous precision. They swore to obey him as their lawful superior; he pledged his faith to unite the indifference of a stranger with the zeal of a patriot. At his choice four or six knights and civilians, his assessors in arms and justice, attended the *Podestà*,[59]

The office of senator

the Senators took an oath of loyalty to him; he had the right of coining, and enjoyed the old revenues of the see; he was bound to supply £100 a year for the walls of the city and to pay the militia; he abandoned Tusculum to the Romans to destroy, though it was under his protection. The Pope, by this agreement, gave up all legislative authority and rights of government; his power depended on his lands and estates. It is to be noted that this constitution completely ignored the Imperial authority. See Gregorovius, iv. p. 620.]

[58] Muratori (dissert. xlv. tom. iv. p. 64-92) has fully explained this mode of government; and the *Oculus Pastoralis*, which he has given at the end, is a treatise or sermon on the duties of these foreign magistrates.

[59] In the Latin writers, at least of the silver age, the title of *Potestas* was transferred from the office to the magistrate:—

Hujus qui trahitur prætextam sumere mavis;
An Fidenarum Gabiorumque esse *Potestas*.

(Juvenal. Satir. x. 99).

who maintained at his own expense a decent retinue of servants and horses; his wife, his son, his brother, who might bias the affections of the judge, were left behind; during the exercise of his office, he was not permitted to purchase land, to contract an alliance, or even to accept an invitation in the house of a citizen; nor could he honourably depart till he had satisfied the complaints that might be urged against his government.

Branca-
leone, A.D.
1252-1258

It was thus, about the middle of the thirteenth century, that the Romans called from Bologna the senator Brancaleone,[60] whose fame and merit have been rescued from oblivion by the pen of an English historian. A just anxiety for his reputation, a clear foresight of the difficulties of the task, had engaged him to refuse the honour of their choice; the statutes of Rome were suspended, and his office prolonged to the term of three years. By the guilty and licentious he was accused as cruel; by the clergy he was suspected as partial; but the friends of peace and order applauded the firm and upright magistrate by whom those blessings were restored. No criminals were so powerful as to brave, so obscure as to elude, the justice of the senator. By his sentence, two nobles of the Annibaldi family were executed on a gibbet; and he inexorably demolished, in the city and neighbourhood, one hundred and forty towers, the strong shelters of rapine and mischief. The bishop, as a simple bishop, was compelled to reside in his diocese; and the standard of Brancaleone was displayed in the field with terror and effect. His services were repaid by the ingratitude of a people unworthy of the happiness which they enjoyed. By the public robbers, whom he had provoked for their sake, the Romans were excited to depose and imprison their benefactor; nor would his life have been spared, if Bologna had not possessed a pledge for his safety. Before his departure, the prudent senator had required the exchange of thirty hostages of the noblest families of Rome: on

[60] See the life and death of Brancaleone, in the Historia Major of Matthew Paris, p. 741, 757, 792, 797, 799, 810, 823, 833, 836, 840. The multitude of pilgrims and suitors connected Rome and St. Albans; and the resentment of the English clergy prompted them to rejoice whenever the popes were humbled and oppressed. [There had been another revolution in A.D. 1191. Since 1143 the majority of the Senate had been plebeian; the nobles gained admission by degrees, and after the time of Clement III. and Celestine III. it numbered more patricians of ancient lineage than burghers or knights. Hence discontent and revolution. In 1191 the populace overthrew the Constitution and made Benedict Carushomo the *summus senator*. Under him the first municipal statute seems to have been issued. Epp. Innocentii III. lib. ii. n. 239. See Gregorovius, *op. cit.* iv. 632.]

the news of his danger, and at the prayer of his wife, they were more strictly guarded; and Bologna, in the cause of honour, sustained the thunders of a papal interdict. This generous resistance allowed the Romans to compare the present with the past; and Brancaleone was conducted from the prison to the Capitol amidst the acclamations of a repentant people. The remainder of his government was firm and fortunate; and, as soon as envy was appeased by death, his head, inclosed in a precious vase, was deposited on a lofty column of marble.[61]

The impotence of reason and virtue recommended in Italy a more effectual choice: instead of a private citizen, to whom they yielded a voluntary and precarious obedience, the Romans elected for their senator some prince of independent power, who could defend them from their enemies and themselves. Charles of Anjou and Provence, the most ambitious and warlike monarch of the age, accepted at the same time the kingdom of Naples from the pope and the office of senator from the Roman people.[62] As he passed through the city, in his road to victory, he received their oath of allegiance, lodged in the Lateran palace, and smoothed, in a short visit, the harsh features of his despotic character. Yet even Charles was exposed to the inconstancy of the people, who saluted with the same acclamations the passage of his rival, the unfortunate Conradin; and a powerful avenger, who reigned in the Capitol, alarmed the fears and jealousy of the popes. The absolute term of his life was superseded by a renewal every third year; and the enmity of Nicholas the Third obliged the Sicilian king to abdicate the government of Rome. In his bull, a perpetual law, the imperious pontiff asserts the truth, validity, and use of the donation of Constantine, not less essential to the peace of the city than to the independence of the church; establishes the annual election of the senator; and formally disqualifies all emperors, kings, princes, and persons

[61] Matthew Paris thus ends his account: Caput vero ipsius Brancaleonis in vase pretioso super marmoream columneam collocatum, in signum sui valoris et probitatis, quasi reliquias superstitiose nimis et pompose sustulerunt. Fuerat enim superborum potentum et malefactorum urbis malleus et exstirpator, et populi protector et defensor, veritatis et justitiæ imitator et amator (p. 840). A biographer of Innocent IV. (Muratori, Script. tom. iii. p. i. p. 591, 592) draws a less favourable portrait of this Ghibelline senator.

[62] The election of Charles of Anjou to the office of perpetual senator of Rome is mentioned by the historians in the viiith volume of the Collection of Muratori, by Nicholas de Jamsilla (p. 592), the monk of Padua (p. 724), Sabas Malaspina (l. ii. c. 9, p. 808), and Ricordano Malespini (c. 177, p. 999).

of an eminent and conspicuous rank.[63] This prohibitory clause was repealed in his own behalf by Martin the Fourth, who humbly solicited the suffrage of the Romans. In the presence, and by the authority, of the people, two electors conferred, not on the pope, but on the noble and faithful Martin, the dignity of senator and the supreme administration of the republic,[64] to hold during his natural life, and to exercise at pleasure by himself or his de-puties. About fifty years afterwards, the same title was granted to the emperor Lewis of Bavaria; and the liberty of Rome was acknowledged by her two sovereigns, who accepted a municipal office in the government of their own metropolis.

In the first moments of rebellion, when Arnold of Brescia had inflamed their minds against the church, the Romans artfully laboured to conciliate the favour of the empire, and to recommend their merit and services in the cause of Cæsar. The style of their ambassadors to Conrad the Third and Frederic the First is a mixture of flattery and pride, the tradition and the ignorance of their own history.[65] After some complaint of his silence and neglect, they exhort the former of these princes to pass the Alps and assume from their hands the Imperial crown. "We beseech your Majesty not to disdain the humility of your sons and vassals, not to listen to the accusations of our common enemies; who calumniate the senate as hostile to your throne, who sow the seeds of discord, that they may reap the harvest of

[63]The high-sounding bull of Nicholas III., which founds his temporal sovereignty on the donation of Constantine, is still extant; and, as it has been inserted by Boniface VIII. in the *Sexte* of the Decretals, it must be received by the Catholics, or at least by the Papists, as a sacred and perpetual law.

[64]I am indebted to Fleury (Hist. Ecclés. tom. xviii. p. 306) for an extract of this Roman act which he has taken from the Ecclesiastical Annals of Odericus Raynaldus, A.D. 1281, No. 14, 15.

[65]These letters and speeches are preserved by Otho [Otto], Bishop of Frisingen (Fabric. Bibliot. Lat. med. et infim. tom. v. p. 186, 187), perhaps the noblest of historians; he was son of Leopold, marquis of Austria; his mother, Agnes, was daughter of the emperor Henry IV.; and he was half-brother and uncle to Conrad III. and Frederic I. He has left, in seven [eight] books, a Chronicle of the Times; in two, the Gesta Frederici I., the last of which is inserted in the vith volume of Muratori's historians. [The chronicle is edited by Wilmans in Mon. Germ. Hist. xx. p. 116 *sqq*., and separately in the Script. rer. Germ. 1867 (German translation by Kohl, 1881). The Gesta is also edited by Wilmans in the same volume of the Monumenta; and by Waitz (1884) in the series of the Script. rer. Germ. (German translation by Kohl, 1883). The name of the Chronicle was originally De duabus civitatibus. It is a History of the World, and its object is to prove that, while the secular civitas or kingdom is ephemeral and transitory, the Church, or the kingdom of God, is eternal. Cp. the brief characteristic of Otto in Giesebrecht's Geschichte der deutschen Kaiserzeit, p. 394 *sqq*.]

destruction. The pope and the *Sicilian* are united in an impious league to oppose *our* liberty and *your* coronation. With the blessing of God, our zeal and courage has hitherto defeated their attempts. Of their powerful and factious adherents, more especially the Frangipani, we have taken by assault the houses and turrets; some of these are occupied by our troops, and some are levelled with the ground. The Milvian bridge, which they had broken, is restored and fortified for your safe passage; and your army may enter the city without being annoyed from the castle of St. Angelo. All that we have done, and all that we design, is for your honour and service, in the loyal hope that you will speedily appear in person to vindicate those rights which have been invaded by the clergy, to revive the dignity of the empire, and to surpass the fame and glory of your predecessors. May you fix your residence in Rome, the capital of the world; give laws to Italy and the Teutonic kingdom; and imitate the example of Constantine and Justinian,[66] who, by the vigour of the senate and people, obtained the sceptre of the earth." [67] But these splendid and fallacious wishes were not cherished by Conrad the Franconian, whose eyes were fixed on the Holy Land, and who died without visiting Rome soon after his return from the Holy Land.[67a]

His nephew and successor, Frederic Barbarossa, was more ambitious of the Imperial crown; nor had any of the successors of Otho acquired such absolute sway over the kingdom of Italy. Surrounded by his ecclesiastical and secular princes, he gave audience in his camp at Sutri [68] to the ambassadors of Rome, who thus addressed him in a free and florid oration: "Incline your ear to the queen of cities; approach with a peaceful and friendly mind the precincts of Rome, which has cast away the yoke of the clergy, and is impatient to crown her legitimate emperor. Under your auspicious influence, may the primitive times be restored. Assert the prerogatives of the eternal city, Frederick I. A.D. 1155

[At Sutri, June 7, &c.]

---

[66] We desire (said the ignorant Romans) to restore the empire in eum statum, quo fuit tempore Constantini et Justiniani, qui totum orbem vigore senatus et populi Romani suis tenuere manibus.

[67] Otho Frising. de Gestis Frederici I. l. i. c. 28, p. 662-664.

[67a] [Mr. E. Harrison has pointed out that the repetition of "the Holy Land" in this sentence is un-Gibbonian in style and rhythm. He suggests that the author meant to write "Palestine" in the first clause.]

[68] [For the meeting with Pope Hadrian at Sutri, and the following events, see Giesebrecht's Geschichte der deutschen Kaiserzeit, v. p. 60 *sqq.*]

and reduce under her monarchy the insolence of the world.
You are not ignorant that, in former ages, by the wisdom of the
senate, by the valour and discipline of the equestrian order, she
extended her victorious arms to the East and West, beyond the
Alps, and over the islands of the ocean. By our sins, in the
absence of our princes, the noble institution of the senate has
sunk in oblivion; and, with our prudence, our strength has likewise decreased. We have revived the senate and the equestrian
order; the counsels of the one, the arms of the other, will be
devoted to your person and the service of the empire. Do you
not hear the language of the Roman matron? You were a guest,
I have adopted you as a citizen; a Transalpine stranger, I have
elected you for my sovereign; [69] and given you myself, and all
that is mine. Your first and most sacred duty is, to swear and
subscribe that you will shed your blood for the republic; that
you will maintain in peace and justice the laws of the city and
the charters of your predecessors; and that you will reward with
five thousand pounds of silver the faithful senators who shall
proclaim your titles in the Capitol. With the name, assume the
character, of Augustus." The flowers of Latin rhetoric were not
yet exhausted; but Frederic, impatient of their vanity, interrupted the orators in the high tone of royalty and conquest.
"Famous, indeed, have been the fortitude and wisdom of the
ancient Romans; but your speech is not seasoned with wisdom,
and I could wish that fortitude were conspicuous in your actions.
Like all sublunary things, Rome has felt the vicissitudes of time
and fortune. Your noblest families were translated to the East,
to the royal city of Constantine; and the remains of your strength
and freedom have long since been exhausted by the Greeks and
Franks. Are you desirous of beholding the ancient glory of
Rome, the gravity of the senate, the spirit of the knights, the
discipline of the camp, the valour of the legions? you will find
them in the German republic. It is not empire, naked and
alone, the ornaments and virtues of empire have likewise migrated beyond the Alps to a more deserving people; [70] they will

[69] Hospes eras, civem feci. Advena fuisti ex Transalpinis partibus; principem
constitui.
[70] Non cessit nobis nudum imperium, virtute suâ amictum venit, ornamenta sua
secum traxit. Penes nos sunt consules tui, &c. Cicero or Livy would not have
rejected these images, the eloquence of a barbarian born and educated in the Her-
cynian forest.

be employed in your defence, but they claim your obedience. You pretend that myself or my predecessors have been invited by the Romans : you mistake the word ; they were not invited, they were implored. From its foreign and domestic tyrants, the city was rescued by Charlemagne and Otho, whose ashes repose in our country ; and their dominion was the price of your deliverance. Under that dominion your ancestors lived and died. I claim by the right of inheritance and possession, and who shall dare to extort you from my hands ? Is the hand of the Franks [71] and Germans enfeebled by age ? Am I vanquished ? Am I a captive ? Am I not encompassed with the banners of a potent and invincible army ? You impose conditions on your master ; you require oaths: if the conditions are just, an oath is superfluous ; if unjust, it is criminal. Can you doubt my equity? It is extended to the meanest of my subjects. Will not my sword be unsheathed in the defence of the Capitol ? By that sword the northern kingdom of Denmark has been restored to the Roman empire. You prescribe the measure and the objects of my bounty, which flows in a copious but a voluntary stream. All will be given to patient merit ; all will be denied to rude importunity." [72] Neither the emperor nor the senate could maintain these lofty pretensions of dominion and liberty. United with the pope, and suspicious of the Romans, Frederic continued his march to the Vatican: his coronation was disturbed by a [June 18] sally [73] from the Capitol ; and, if the numbers and valour of the Germans prevailed in the bloody conflict, he could not safely encamp in the presence of a city of which he styled himself the sovereign. About twelve years afterwards he besieged Rome, [A.D. 1167, July] to seat an antipope in the chair of St. Peter ; and twelve Pisan galleys were introduced into the Tiber ; but the senate and people were saved by the arts of negotiation and the progress of disease ; nor did Frederic or his successors reiterate the hostile attempt. Their laborious reigns were exercised by the popes, the crusades, and the independence of Lombardy and Germany ; they courted the alliance of the Romans ; and Frederic the

[71] Otho of Frisingen, who surely understood the language of the court and diet of Germany, speaks of the Franks in the xiith century as the reigning nation (Proceres Franci, equites Franci, manus Francorum) ; he adds, however, the epithet of *Teutonici*.

[72] Otho Frising. de Gestis Frederici I. l. ii. c. 22, p. 720-723. These original and authentic acts I have translated with freedom, yet with fidelity.

[73] [The coronation ceremony was over when the sally was made.]

Second offered in the Capitol the great standard, the *Caroccio* of Milan.[74] After the extinction of the house of Swabia, they were banished beyond the Alps ; and their last coronations betrayed the impotence and poverty of the Teutonic Cæsars.[75]

Wars of the Romans against the neighbouring cities Under the reign of Hadrian, when the empire extended from the Euphrates to the ocean, from Mount Atlas to the Grampian Hills, a fanciful historian [76] amused the Romans with the picture of their infant wars. "There was a time," says Florus, "when Tibur and Præneste, our summer-retreats, were the objects of hostile vows in the Capitol, when we dreaded the shades of the Arician groves, when we could triumph without a blush over the nameless villages of the Sabines and Latins, and even Corioli could afford a title not unworthy of a victorious general." The pride of his contemporaries was gratified by the contrast of the past and the present : they would have been humbled by the prospect of futurity ; by the prediction that after a thousand years Rome, despoiled of empire and contracted to her primæval limits, would renew the same hostilities on the same ground which was then decorated with her villas and gardens. The adjacent territory on either side of the Tiber was always claimed, and sometimes possessed, as the patrimony of St. Peter; but the barons assumed a lawless independence, and the cities too faithfully copied the revolt and discord of the metropolis. In the twelfth and thirteenth centuries the Romans incessantly laboured

[74] From the Chronicles of Ricobaldo and Francis Pipin, Muratori (dissert. xxvi. tom. ii. p. 492) has transcribed this curious fact, with the doggrel verses that accompanied the gift.

> Ave decus orbis ave ! victus tibi destinor, ave !
> Currus ab Augusto Frederico Cæsare justo.
> Væ Mediolanum ! jam sentis spernere vanum
> Imperii vires, proprias tibi tollere vires.
> Ergo triumphorum urbs potes memor esse priorum
> Quos tibi mittebant reges qui bella gerebant.

Ne si dee tacere (I now use the Italian Dissertations, tom. i. p. 444) che nell' anno 1727, una copia desso Caroccio in marmo dianzi ignoto si scopri, nel Campidoglio presso alle carcere di quel luogo, dove Sisto V. l'avea falto [*leg.* fatto] rinchiudere. Stava esso posto sopra quatro colonne di marmo fina colla sequente inscrizione, &c., to the same purpose as the old inscription.

[75] The decline of the Imperial arms and authority in Italy is related with impartial learning in the Annals of Muratori (tom. x. xii.) ; and the reader may compare his narrative with the Histoire des Allemands (tom. iii. iv.) by Schmidt, who has deserved the esteem of his countrymen.

[76] Tibur nunc suburbanum et æstivæ Præneste deliciæ nuncupatis in Capitolio votis petebantur. The whole passage of Florus (l. i. c. 11) may be read with pleasure, and has deserved the praise of a man of genius (Oeuvres de Montesquieu, tom. iii. p. 634, 635, quarto edition).

to reduce or destroy the contumacious vassals of the church and senate; and, if their headstrong and selfish ambition was moderated by the pope, he often encouraged their zeal by the alliance of his spiritual arms. Their warfare was that of the first consuls and dictators, who were taken from the plough. They assembled in arms at the foot of the Capitol; sallied from the gates, plundered or burnt the harvests of their neighbours, engaged in tumultuary conflict, and returned home after an expedition of fifteen or twenty days. Their sieges were tedious and unskilful: in the use of victory, they indulged the meaner passions of jealousy and revenge; and, instead of adopting the valour, they trampled on the misfortunes, of their adversaries. The captives, in their shirts, with a rope round their necks, solicited their pardon. The fortifications and even the buildings of the rival cities were demolished, and the inhabitants were scattered in the adjacent villages. It was thus that the seats of the cardinal bishops, Porto, Ostia, Albanum, Tusculum, Præneste, and Tibur, or Tivoli, were successively overthrown by the ferocious hostility of the Romans.[77] Of these,[78] Porto and Ostia, the two keys of the Tiber, are still vacant and desolate: the marshy and unwholesome banks are peopled with herds of buffaloes, and the river is lost to every purpose of navigation and trade. The hills, which afford a shady retirement from the autumnal heats, have again smiled with the blessings of peace; Frascati has arisen near the ruins of Tusculum; Tibur, or Tivoli, has resumed the honours of a city;[79] and the meaner towns of Albano and Palestrina are decorated with the villas of the cardinals and princes of Rome. In the work of destruction, the ambition of the Romans was often checked and repulsed by the neighbouring cities and their allies; in the first siege of Tibur, they were driven from their

[77] Ne a feritate Romanorum, sicut fuerant Hostienses, Portuenses, Tusculanenses, Albanenses, Labicenses, et nuper Tiburtini destruerentur (Matthew Paris, p. 757). These events are marked in the Annals and Index (the xviiith volume) of Muratori.

[78] For the state or ruin of these suburban cities, the banks of the Tiber, &c., see the lively picture of the P. Labat (Voyage en Espagne et en Italie), who had long resided in the neighbourhood of Rome; and the more accurate description of which P. Eschinard (Roma, 1750, in octavo) has added to the topographical map of Cingolani.

[79] Labat (tom. iii. p. 233) mentions a recent decree of the Roman government, which has severely mortified the pride and poverty of Tivoli: in civitate Tiburtinâ non vivitur civiliter.

Battle of
Tusculum,
A.D. 1167

Battle of
Viterbo,
A.D. 1234

camp; and the battles of Tusculum [80] and Viterbo [81] might be compared, in their relative state, to the memorable fields of Thrasymene and Cannæ. In the first of these petty wars, thirty thousand Romans were overthrown by a thousand German horse, whom Frederic Barbarossa had detached to the relief of Tusculum; and, if we number the slain at three, the prisoners at two, thousand, we shall embrace the most authentic and moderate account. Sixty-eight years afterward, they marched against Viterbo, in the ecclesiastical state, with the whole force of the city; by a rare coalition, the Teutonic eagle was blended, in the adverse banners, with the keys of St. Peter; and the pope's auxiliaries were commanded by a count of Toulouse and a bishop of Winchester.[82] The Romans were discomfited with shame and slaughter; but the English prelate must have indulged the vanity of a pilgrim, if he multiplied their numbers to one hundred, and their loss in the field to thirty, thousand men. Had the policy of the senate and the discipline of the legions been restored with the Capitol, the divided condition of Italy would have offered the fairest opportunity of a second conquest. But in arms the modern Romans were not *above,* and in arts they were far *below,* the common level of the neighbouring republics. Nor was their warlike spirit of any long continuance; after some irregular sallies, they subsided in the national apathy, in the neglect of military institutions, and in the disgraceful and dangerous use of foreign mercenaries.

The election of the popes

Ambition is a weed of quick and early vegetation in the vineyard of Christ. Under the first Christian princes, the chair of St. Peter was disputed by the votes, the venality, the violence, of a popular election; the sanctuaries of Rome were polluted with blood; and, from the third to the twelfth century, the church was distracted by the mischief of frequent schisms. As

[80] I depart from my usual method of quoting only by the date the Annals of Muratori, in consideration of the critical balance in which he has weighed nine contemporary writers who mention the battle of Tusculum (tom. x. p. 42-44).

[81] Matthew Paris, p. 345. This bishop of Winchester was Peter de Rupibus, who occupied the see thirty-two years (A.D. 1206-1238), and is described, by the English historian, as a soldier and a statesman (p. 178, 399).

[82] [Lucas Savelli, who became Senator in 1234, passed an edict claiming Tuscany and the Campagna as the property of the Roman people. Pope Gregory IX. fled from Rome, and Viterbo was his chief support. "What," asks Gregorovius, "would have been the fate of the Papacy, had the city succeeded in becoming a civic power such as Milan or Pisa?" (v. p. 172). Frederic II. saw himself unwillingly forced to assist the Pope.]

long as the final appeal was determined by the civil magistrate, these mischiefs were transient and local; the merits were tried by equity or favour; nor could the unsuccessful competitor long disturb the triumph of his rival. But, after the emperors had been divested of their prerogatives, after a maxim had been established that the vicar of Christ is amenable to no earthly tribunal, each vacancy of the holy see might involve Christendom in controversy and war. The claims of the cardinals and inferior clergy, of the nobles and people, were vague and litigious; the freedom of choice was over-ruled by the tumults of a city that no longer owned or obeyed a superior. On the decease of a pope, two factions proceeded, in different churches, to a double election: the number and weight of votes, the priority of time, the merit of the candidates, might balance each other; the most respectable of the clergy were divided; and the distant princes who bowed before the spiritual throne could not distinguish the spurious from the legitimate idol. The emperors were often the authors of the schism, from the political motive of opposing a friendly to an hostile pontiff; and each of the competitors was reduced to suffer the insults of his enemies, who were not awed by conscience, and to purchase the support of his adherents, who were instigated by avarice or ambition. A peaceful and perpetual succession was ascertained by Alexander the Third,[83] who finally abolished the tumultuary votes of the clergy and people, and defined the right of election in the sole college of cardinals.[84] The three orders of bishops, priests, and deacons were assimilated to each other by this important privilege; the parochial clergy of Rome obtained the first rank in the hierarchy: they were indifferently chosen among the nations of Christendom; and the possession of the richest benefices, of the most important bishoprics, was not incompatible with their title and office. The senators of the Catholic church, the coadjutors and legates of the supreme pontiff, were robed in purple, the symbol of martyrdom or royalty; they claimed a proud equality

Right of the cardinals established by Alexander III.

A.D. 1179 [Lateran Council]

---

[83] See Mosheim, Institut. Histor. Ecclesiast. p. 401, 403. Alexander himself had nearly been the victim of a contested election; and the doubtful merits of Innocent had only preponderated by the weight of genius and learning which St. Bernard cast into the scale (see his life and writings).

[84] The origin, titles, importance, dress, precedency, &c. of the Roman cardinals, are very ably discussed by Thomassin (Discipline de l'Eglise, tom. i. p. 1262-1287); but their purple is now much faded. The sacred college was raised to the definite number of seventy-two, to represent, under his vicar, the disciples of Christ.

with kings; and their dignity was enhanced by the smallness of their number, which, till the reign of Leo the Tenth, seldom exceeded twenty or twenty-five persons.   By this wise regulation all doubt and scandal were removed, and the root of schism was so effectually destroyed that in a period of six hundred years a double choice has only once divided the unity of the sacred college.   But, as the concurrence of two-thirds of the votes had been made necessary, the election was often delayed by the private interest and passions of the cardinals; and, while they prolonged their independent reign, the Christian world was left destitute of an head.   A vacancy of almost three years had preceded the elevation of Gregory the Tenth, who resolved to prevent the future abuse; and his bull, after some opposition, has been consecrated in the code of the canon law.[85]   Nine days are allowed for the obsequies of the deceased pope and the arrival of the absent cardinals.   On the tenth, they are imprisoned, each with one domestic, in a common apartment, or *conclave*, without any separation of walls or curtains; a small window is reserved for the introduction of necessaries; but the door is locked on both sides, and guarded by the magistrates of the city, to seclude them from all correspondence with the world. If the election be not consummated in three days, the luxury of their tables is contracted to a single dish at dinner and supper; and after the eighth day they are reduced to a scanty allowance of bread, water, and wine.   During the vacancy of the holy see, the cardinals are prohibited from touching the revenues, or assuming, unless in some rare emergency, the government of the church; all agreements and promises among the electors are formally annulled; and their integrity is fortified by their solemn oaths and the prayers of the Catholics.   Some articles of inconvenient or superfluous rigour have been gradually relaxed, but the principle of confinement is vigorous and entire: they are still urged by the personal motives of health and freedom to accelerate the moment of their deliverance; and the improvement of ballot, or secret votes, has wrapt the struggles of the conclave [86]

Institution of the conclave by Gregory X. A.D. 1274

---

[85] See the bull of Gregory X. [issued at Lyons, at the Great Council] approbante sacro concilio, in the *Sexte* of the Canon Law (l. i. tit. 6, c. 3), a supplement to the Decretals, which Boniface VIII. promulgated at Rome in 1298, and addressed to all the universities of Europe.

[86] The genius of Cardinal de Retz had a right to paint a conclave (of 1665), in which he was a spectator and an actor (Mémoires, tom. iv. p. 15-57); but I am at

in the silky veil of charity and politeness.[87]   By these institutions the Romans were excluded from the election of their prince and bishop; and in the fever of wild and precarious liberty they seemed insensible of the loss of this inestimable privilege.   The [A.D. 1328] emperor Lewis of Bavaria revived the example of the great Otho. After some negotiation with the magistrates, the Roman people was assembled [88] in the square before St. Peter's; the pope of Avignon, John the Twenty-second, was deposed; the choice of [April 18] his successor was ratified by their consent and applause.   They freely voted for a new law, that their bishop should never be [April 23] absent more than three months in the year and two days' journey from the city; and that, if he neglected to return on the third summons, the public servant should be degraded and dismissed.[89] But Lewis forgot his own debility and the prejudices of the times : beyond the precincts of a German camp, his useless phantom was rejected; the Romans despised their own workmanship; the anti-pope implored the mercy of his lawful sovereign;[90] and [Peter of Corbara]

a loss to appreciate the knowledge or authority of an anonymous Italian, whose history (Conclavi de' Pontifici Romani, in 4to, 1667) has been continued since the reign of Alexander VII.   The accidental form of the work furnishes a lesson, though not an antidote, to ambition.   From a labyrinth of intrigues, we emerge to the adoration of the successful candidate ; but the next page opens with his funeral.

[87] The expressions of Cardinal de Retz are positive and picturesque : On y vécut toujours ensemble avec le même respect et la même civilité que l'on observe dans le cabinet des rois, avec la même politesse qu'on avoit dans la cour de Henri III., avec la même familiarité que l'on voit dans les collèges ; avec la même modestie qui se remarque dans les noviciats ; et avec la même charité, du moins en apparence, qui pourroit être entre des frères parfaitement unis.

[88] Richiesti per bando (says John Villani) sanatori di Roma, e 52 del popolo, et capitani de' 25, e consoli (consoli ?), et 13 buoni huomini, uno per rione.   Our knowledge is too imperfect to pronounce how much of this constitution was temporary, and how much ordinary and permanent.   Yet it is faintly illustrated by the ancient statutes of Rome.   [The meaning of the author's interrogation to consoli is not obvious.]

[89] Villani (l. x. c. 68-71, in Muratori, Script. tom. xiii. p. 641-645) relates this law, and the whole transaction, with much less abhorrence than the prudent Muratori.   Any one conversant with the darker ages must have observed how much the sense (I mean the nonsense) of superstition is fluctuating and inconsistent.   [Gregorovius observes (vi. 160) : "This important revolution was the consequence of the sojourn of the Popes at Avignon, the effect of the quarrel which John XXII. so foolishly invoked with the empire, and of the reforming principles of the monarchy, with which was associated the Franciscan schism.   The high-handed doings of John and Lewis, their tedious actions at law, the extensive researches into the imperial and papal authority, formed the close of this mediæval struggle, which now passed into more intellectual regions.   The age of the reformation began ; the ecclesiastical severance of Germany and Italy was perceptible in the distance and became inevitable as soon as the political severance was accomplished."]

[90] In the first volume of the Popes of Avignon, see the second original Life of John XXII. p. 142-145, the confession of the anti-pope, p. 145-152 ; and the laborious notes of Baluze, p. 714, 715.

the exclusive right of the cardinals was more firmly established by this unseasonable attack.

Had the election been always held in the Vatican, the rights of the senate and people would not have been violated with impunity. But the Romans forgot, and were forgotten, in the absence of the successors of Gregory the Seventh, who did not keep, as a divine precept, their ordinary residence in the city and diocese. The care of that diocese was less important than the government of the universal church; nor could the popes delight in a city in which their authority was always opposed and their person was often endangered. From the persecution of the emperors and the wars of Italy, they escaped beyond the Alps into the hospitable bosom of France ; from the tumults of Rome they prudently withdrew to live and die in the more tranquil stations of Anagni, Perugia, Viterbo, and the adjacent cities. When the flock was offended or impoverished by the absence of the shepherd, they were recalled by a stern admonition that St. Peter had fixed his chair, not in an obscure village, but in the capital of the world ; by a ferocious menace that the Romans would march in arms to destroy the place and people that should dare to afford them a retreat. They returned with timorous obedience ; and were saluted with the account of an heavy debt, of all the losses which their desertion had occasioned, the hire of lodgings, the sale of provisions, and the various expenses of servants and strangers who attended the court.[91] After a short interval of peace, and perhaps of authority, they were again banished by new tumults, and again summoned by the imperious or respectful invitation of the senate. In these occasional retreats, the exiles and fugitives of the Vatican were seldom long or far distant from the metropolis ; but in the beginning of the fourteenth century, the apostolic throne was transported, as it might seem, for ever, from the Tiber to the Rhône ; and the cause of the transmigration may be deduced from the furious contest between Boniface the Eighth and the

---

[91] Romani autem non valentes nec volentes ultra suam celare cupiditatem gravissimam contra papam movere cœperunt questionem, exigentes ab eo urgentissime omnia quæ subierant per ejus absentiam damna et jacturas, videlicet in hospitiis locandis, in mercimoniis, in usuris, in redditibus, in provisionibus, et in aliis modis innumerabilibus. Quod cum audisset papa, præcordialiter ingemuit et se comperiens *muscipulatum*, &c., Matt. Paris, p. 757. For the ordinary history of the popes, their life and death, their residence and absence, it is enough to refer to the ecclesiastical annalists, Spondanus and Fleury.

king of France.[92]   The spiritual arms of excommunication and Boniface VIII. [Benedict Gaetani] A.D. 1294-1303
interdict were repulsed by the union of the three estates and the
privileges of the Gallican church; but the pope was not prepared
against the carnal weapons which Philip the Fair had courage to
employ.   As the pope resided at Anagni, without the suspicion of
danger, his palace and person were assaulted by three hundred
horse, who had been secretly levied by William of Nogaret, [1303]
a French minister, and Sciarra Colonna, of a noble but hostile
family of Rome.   The cardinals fled; the inhabitants of Anagni
were seduced from their allegiance and gratitude; but the dauntless Boniface, unarmed and alone, seated himself in his chair,
and awaited, like the conscript fathers of old, the swords of the
Gauls.   Nogaret, a foreign adversary, was content to execute
the orders of his master: by the domestic enmity of Colonna,
he was insulted with words and blows; and during a confinement
of three days his life was threatened by the hardships which they
inflicted on the obstinacy which they provoked.   Their strange
delay gave time and courage to the adherents of the church, who
rescued him from sacrilegious violence; but his imperious soul
was wounded in a vital part; and Boniface expired at Rome in
a frenzy of rage and revenge.   His memory is stained with the
glaring vices of avarice and pride; nor has the courage of a
martyr promoted this ecclesiastical champion to the honours of
a saint: a magnanimous sinner (say the chronicles of the times),
who entered like a fox, reigned like a lion, and died like a dog.
He was succeeded by Benedict the Eleventh, the mildest of man-
kind.   Yet he excommunicated the impious emissaries of Philip, [The Bull Flagitio-sum, A.D. 1304]
and devoted the city and people of Anagni by a tremendous curse,
whose effects are still visible to the eyes of superstition.[93]

After his decease, the tedious and equal suspense of the con- Transla-tion of the holy see to Avignon, A.D. 1309
clave was fixed by the dexterity of the French faction.   A specious
offer was made and accepted, that, in the term of forty days, they

---

[92] Besides the general historians of the church of Italy and of France, we possess
a valuable treatise, composed by a learned friend of Thuanus, which his last and
best editors have published in the appendix (Histoire particulière du grand Différend entre Boniface VIII. et Philippe le Bel, par Pierre du Puis, tom vii. p. xi. p.
61-82.   [Tosti, Storia di Bonifacio VIII.   The bulls of Boniface have been edited
from the Vatican archives by Degon, Faucon and Thomas, 1884-90.]

[93] It is difficult to know whether Labat (tom. iv. p. 53-57) be in jest or in earnest
when he supposes that Anagni still feels the weight of this curse, and that the corn-
fields, or vineyards, or olive trees, are annually blasted by Nature, the obsequious
handmaid of the popes.

would elect one of the three candidates who should be named by their opponents. The archbishop of Bordeaux, a furious enemy of his king and country, was the first on the list; but his ambition was known; and his conscience obeyed the calls of fortune and the commands of a benefactor, who had been informed by a swift messenger that the choice of a pope was now in his hands. The terms were regulated in a private interview; and with such speed and secrecy was the business transacted that the unanimous conclave applauded the elevation of Clement the Fifth.[94]   The cardinals of both parties were soon astonished by a summons to attend him beyond the Alps; from whence, as they soon discovered, they must never hope to return. He was engaged, by promise and affection, to prefer the residence of France; and, after dragging his court through Poitou and Gascony, and devouring, by his expense, the cities and convents on the road, [A.D. 1308] he finally reposed at Avignon,[95] which flourished above seventy years[96] the seat of the Roman pontiff and the metropolis of Christendom. By land, by sea, by the Rhône, the position of Avignon was on all sides accessible; the southern provinces of France do not yield to Italy itself; new palaces arose for the accommodation of the pope and cardinals; and the arts of luxury were soon attracted by the treasures of the church. They were already possessed of the adjacent territory, the Venaissin county,[97] a populous and fertile spot; and the sovereignty of Avignon was

[94] See in the Chronicle of Giovanni Villani (l. viii. c. 63, 64, 80, in Muratori, tom. xiii.) the imprisonment of Boniface VIII. and the election of Clement V., the last of which, like most anecdotes, is embarrassed with some difficulties.

[95] The original lives of the eight popes of Avignon, Clement V. John XXII. Benedict XII. Clement VI. Innocent VI. Urban V. Gregory XI. and Clement VII., are published by Stephen Baluze (Vitæ Paparum Avenionensium; Paris, 1693, 2 vols. in 4to), with copious and elaborate notes, and a second volume of acts and documents. With the true zeal of an editor and a patriot, he devoutly justifies or excuses the characters of his countrymen.

[96] The exile of Avignon is compared by the Italians with Babylon and the Babylonish captivity. Such furious metaphors, more suitable to the ardour of Petrarch than to the judgment of Muratori, are gravely refuted in Baluze's preface. The Abbé de Sade is distracted between the love of Petrarch and of his country. Yet he modestly pleads that many of the local inconveniences of Avignon are now removed; and many of the vices against which the poet declaims had been imported with the Roman court by the strangers of Italy (tom. i. p. 23-28).

[97] The comtat Venaissin was ceded to the popes, in 1273, by Philip III., king of France, after he had inherited the dominions of the count of Toulouse. Forty years before the heresy of Count Raymond had given them a pretence of seizure, and they derived some obscure claim from the xith century to some lands citra Rhodanum (Valesii Notitia Galliarum, p. 459, 610; Longuerue, Description de la France, tom. i. p. 376-381).

AVIGNON : THE PALACE OF THE POPES

afterwards purchased from the youth and distress of Jane, the first queen of Naples, and countess of Provence, for the inade- [A.D. 1348, June 12] quate price of fourscore thousand florins.[98] Under the shadow of the French monarchy, amidst an obedient people, the popes enjoyed an honourable and tranquil state, to which they long had been strangers; but Italy deplored their absence; and Rome, in solitude and poverty, might repent of the ungovernable freedom which had driven from the Vatican the successor of St. Peter. Her repentance was tardy and fruitless; after the death of the old members, the sacred college was filled with French cardinals,[99] who beheld Rome and Italy with abhorrence and contempt, and perpetuated a series of national and even provincial popes, attached by the most indissoluble ties to their native country.

The progress of industry had produced and enriched the Italian republics: the æra of their liberty is the most flourishing period of population and agriculture, of manufactures and commerce; and their mechanic labours were gradually refined into the arts of elegance and genius. But the position of Rome was less favourable, the territory less fruitful; the character of the inhabitants was debased by indolence, and elated by pride; and they fondly conceived that the tribute of subjects must for ever nourish the metropolis of the church and empire. This prejudice was encouraged in some degree by the resort of pilgrims to the shrines of the apostles; and the last legacy of the popes, the institution of the HOLY YEAR,[100] was not less beneficial to the people than to the clergy. Since the loss of Palestine,

Institution of the Jubilee, or holy year, A.D. 1300

---

[98] If a possession of four centuries were not itself a title, such objections might annul the bargain; but the purchase-money must be refunded, for indeed it was paid. Civitatem Avenionem emit . . . per ejusmodi venditionem pecuniâ redundantes, &c. (2da Vita Clement. VI. in Baluz. tom. i. p. 272; Muratori, Script. tom. iii. p. ii. p. 565). [Recherches historiques concernant les droits du Pape sur la ville et l'état d'Avignon, 1768.] The only temptation for Jane and her second husband was ready money, and without it they could not have returned to the throne of Naples.

[99] Clement V. immediately promoted ten cardinals, nine French and one English (Vita 4ta, p. 63, et Baluz. p. 625, &c.). In 1331, the pope refused two candidates recommended by the king of France, quod xx. Cardinales, de quibus xvii. de regno Franciæ originem traxisse noscuntur, in memorato collegio existant (Thomassin, Discipline de l'Eglise, tom. i. p. 1281). [In the year A.D. 1378 the college consisted of 23 cardinals, 16 of them were at Rome and included 7 Limousins, 4 French, 1 Spaniard, and 4 Italians. See Gregorovius, vi. 491.]

[100] Our primitive account is from Cardinal James Caietan [= Jacopo Stefaneschi, cardinalis S. Georgii ad Velum aureum] (Maxima Bibliot. Patrum, tom. xxv.); and I am at a loss to determine whether the nephew of Boniface VIII. be a fool or a knave; the uncle is a much clearer character.

the gift of plenary indulgences, which had been applied to the crusades, remained without an object; and the most valuable treasure of the church was sequestered above eight years from public circulation. A new channel was opened by the diligence of Boniface the Eighth, who reconciled the vices of ambition and avarice; and the pope had sufficient learning to recollect and revive the secular games, which were celebrated in Rome at the conclusion of every century. To sound, without danger, the depth of popular credulity, a sermon was seasonably pronounced, a report was artfully scattered, some aged witnesses were produced; and on the first of January of the year thirteen hundred the church of St. Peter was crowded with the faithful, who demanded the *customary* indulgence of the holy time. The pontiff, who watched and irritated their devout impatience, was soon persuaded, by ancient testimony, of the justice of their

[Bull of Boniface VIII. A.D. 1300, Feb. 22]

claim; and he proclaimed a plenary absolution to all Catholics who, in the course of that year, and at every similar period, should respectfully visit the apostolic churches of St. Peter and St. Paul. The welcome sound was propagated through Christendom; and at first from the nearest provinces of Italy, and at length from the remote kingdoms of Hungary and Britain, the highways were thronged with a swarm of pilgrims who sought to expiate their sins in a journey, however costly or laborious, which was exempt from the perils of military service. All exceptions of rank or sex, of age or infirmity, were forgotten in the common transport; and in the streets and churches many persons were trampled to death by the eagerness of devotion.[101] The calculation of their numbers could not be easy nor accurate; and they have probably been magnified by a dexterous clergy,

---

[101] [" The way that led from the city across the Bridge of St. Angelo to St. Peter's was too narrow; a new street was therefore opened in the walls along the river, not far from the ancient tomb known as the Meta Romuli. [Gregorovius reads *pontem* for *portum* in the passage in Stefaneschi which describes this.] The bridge was covered with booths which divided it in two, and in order to prevent accidents it was enacted that those going to St. Peter's should keep to one side of the bridge, those returning to the other." This arrangement is referred to by Dante, Inferno, xviii., v. 28 *sqq.* :—

Come i Roman, per l'esercito molto,
L'anno del Giubbileo, su per lo ponte
Hanno a passar la gente modo tolto:
Che dall' un lato tutti hanno la fronte
Verso 'l castello, e vanno a Santo Pietro;
Dall' altra sponda vanno verso 'l Monte.

See Gregorovius, v. p. 560-1.]

well apprised of the contagion of example; yet we are assured by a judicious historian, who assisted at the ceremony, that Rome was never replenished with less than two hundred thousand strangers; and another spectator has fixed at two millions the total concourse of the year. A trifling oblation from each individual would accumulate a royal treasure; and two priests stood night and day, with rakes in their hands, to collect, without counting, the heaps of gold and silver that were poured on the altar of St. Paul.[102] It was fortunately a season of peace and plenty; and, if forage was scarce, if inns and lodgings were extravagantly dear, an inexhaustible supply of bread and wine, of meat and fish, was provided by the policy of Boniface and the venal hospitality of the Romans. From a city without trade or industry, all casual riches will speedily evaporate; but the avarice and envy of the next generation solicited Clement the Sixth[103] to anticipate the distant period of the century. The gracious pontiff complied with their wishes; afforded Rome this poor consolation for his loss; and justified the change by the name and practice of the Mosaic Jubilee.[104] His summons was The second obeyed; and the number, zeal, and liberality of the pilgrims jubilee, A.D. 1350 did not yield to the primitive festival. But they encountered the triple scourge of war, pestilence, and famine;[105] many wives and virgins were violated in the castles of Italy; and many strangers were pillaged or murdered by the savage Romans, no longer moderated by the presence of their bishop.[106] To the impatience of the popes we may ascribe the successive reduction to fifty, thirty-three, and twenty-five years; although the second of these terms is commensurate with the life of Christ. The profusion of indulgences, the revolt of the Protes-

---

[102] See John Villani (l. viii. c. 36) in the xiith, and the Chronicon Astense in the xith volume (p. 191, 192) of Muratori's Collection. Papa innumerabilem pecuniam ab eisdem accepit, nam duo clerici, cum rastris, &c.

[103] The two bulls of Boniface VIII. and Clement VI. are inserted in the Corpus Juris Canonici (Extravagant. Commun. l. v. tit. ix. c. 1, 2).

[104] The sabbatic years and jubilees of the Mosaic law (Car. Sigon. de Republicâ Hebræorum, Opp. tom. iv. l. iii. c. 14, 15, p. 151, 152), the suspension of all care and labour, the periodical release of lands, debts, servitude, &c. may seem a noble idea, but the execution would be impracticable in a *profane* republic; and I should be glad to learn that this ruinous festival was observed by the Jewish people.

[105] [It was shortly after the abdication of Rienzi (1347) and the devastations of the Black Death.]

[106] See the Chronicle of Matteo Villani (l. i. c. 56), in the xivth volume of Muratori, and the Mémoires sur la Vie de Pétrarque, tom. iii. p. 75-89.

tants, and the decline of superstition have much diminished the value of the jubilee; yet even the nineteenth and last festival was a year of pleasure and profit to the Romans; and a philosophic smile will not disturb the triumph of the priest or the happiness of the people.[107]

The nobles
or barons
of Rome   In the beginning of the eleventh century, Italy was exposed to the feudal tyranny, alike oppressive to the sovereign and the people. The rights of human nature were vindicated by her numerous republics, who soon extended their liberty and dominion from the city to the adjacent country. The sword of the nobles was broken; their slaves were enfranchised; their castles were demolished; they assumed the habits of society and obedience; their ambition was confined to municipal honours, and in the proudest aristocracy of Venice or Genoa each patrician was subject to the laws.[108]   But the feeble and disorderly government of Rome was unequal to the task of curbing her rebellious sons, who scorned the authority of the magistrate within and without the walls. It was no longer a civil contention between the nobles and the plebeians for the government of the state; the barons asserted in arms their personal independence; their palaces and castles were fortified against a siege; and their private quarrels were maintained by the numbers of their vassals and retainers. In origin and affection, they were aliens to their country;[109] and a genuine Roman, could such have been produced, might have renounced these haughty strangers, who disdained the appellation of citizens and proudly styled themselves the princes of Rome.[110]   After a dark series of revolutions, all records of pedigree were lost; the distinction of surnames was abolished; the blood of the nations was mingled in a thousand channels; and the Goths and Lombards,

---

[107] The subject is exhausted by M. Chais, a French Minister at the Hague, in his Lettres Historiques et Dogmatiques sur les Jubilés et les Indulgences; la Haye, 1751, 3 vols. in 12mo : an elaborate and pleasing work, had not the author preferred the character of a polemic to that of a philosopher.

[108] Muratori (Dissert. xlvii.) alleges the Annals of Florence, Padua, Genoa, &c., the analogy of the rest, the evidence of Otho of Frisingen (de Gest. Fred. I. l. ii. c. 13), and the submission of the marquis of Este.

[109] As early as the year 824, the emperor Lothaire I. found it expedient to interrogate the Roman people, to learn from each individual by what national law he chose to be governed (Muratori, Dissert. xxii.).

[110] Petrarch attacks these foreigners, the tyrants of Rome, in a declamation or epistle, full of bold truths and absurd pedantry, in which he applies the maxims, and even prejudices, of the old republic, to the state of the xivth century (Mémoires, tom. iii. p. 157-169).

the Greeks and Franks, the Germans and Normans, had obtained the fairest possessions by royal bounty or the prerogative of valour. These examples might be readily presumed; but the elevation of an Hebrew race to the rank of senators and consuls is an event without a parallel in the long captivity of these miserable exiles.[111] In the time of Leo the Ninth, a wealthy and learned Jew was converted to Christianity, and honoured at his baptism with the name of his godfather, the reigning pope. The zeal and courage of Peter, the son of Leo, were signalised in the cause of Gregory the Seventh, who entrusted his faithful adherent with the government of Hadrian's mole, the tower of Crescentius, or, as it is now called, the castle of St. Angelo. Both the father and the son were the parents of a numerous progeny ; their riches, the fruits of usury, were shared with the noblest families of the city ; and so extensive was their alliance that the grandson of the proselyte was exalted, by the weight of his kindred, to the throne of St. Peter. A majority of the clergy and people supported his cause; he reigned several years in the Vatican ; and it is only the eloquence of St. Bernard, and the final triumph of Innocent the Second, that has branded Anacletus with the epithet of antipope. After his defeat and death, the posterity of Leo is no longer conspicuous ; and none will be found of the modern nobles ambitious of descending from a Jewish stock. It is not my design to enumerate the Roman families which have failed at different periods, or those which are continued in different degrees of splendour to the present time.[112] The old consular line of the *Frangipani* discover their name in the generous act of *breaking* or dividing bread in a time of famine ; and such benevolence is more truly glorious than to have inclosed, with their allies the *Corsi*, a spacious quarter of the city in the chains of their fortifications ; the *Savelli*, as it should seem a Sabine race, have

(marginal note:) Family of Leo the Jew. [The Pierleoni]

---

[111] The origin and adventures of this Jewish family are noticed by Pagi (Critica, tom. iv. p. 435, A.D. 1124, No. 3, 4), who draws his information from the Chronographus Maurigniacensis [in Migne, Patr. Lat. 180, p. 131 *sqq.*], and Arnulphus Sagiensis de Schismate (in Muratori, Script. Ital. tom. iii. p. i. p. 423-432). The fact must in some degree be true ; yet I could wish that it had been coolly related, before it was turned into a reproach against the antipope.

[112] Muratori has given two dissertations (xli. and xlii.) to the names, surnames, and families of Italy. Some nobles, who glory in their domestic fables, may be offended with his firm and temperate criticism ; yet surely some ounces of pure gold are of more value than many pounds of base metal.

maintained their original dignity ; [113] the obsolete surname of the *Capizucchi* is inscribed on the coins of the first senators ; the *Conti* preserve the honour, without the estate, of the counts of Signia ; [114] and the *Annibaldi* must have been very ignorant, or very modest, if they had not descended from the Carthaginian hero.[115]

The ColonnaBut among, perhaps above, the peers and princes of the city, I distinguish the rival houses of COLONNA and URSINI, whose private story is an essential part of the annals of modern Rome. I. The name and arms of Colonna [116] have been the theme of much doubtful etymology ; nor have the orators and antiquarians overlooked either Trajan's pillar, or the columns of Hercules, or the pillar of Christ's flagellation, or the luminous column that guided the Israelites in the desert. Their first historical appearance in the year eleven hundred and four attests the power and antiquity, while it explains the simple meaning, of the name. By the usurpation of Cavæ, the Colonna provoked the arms of Paschal the Second ; but they lawfully held in the Campagna of Rome the hereditary fiefs of Zagarola and *Colonna ;* and the latter of these towns was probably adorned with some lofty pillar, the relic of a villa or temple.[117] They likewise possessed one moiety

---

[113] [" The foundation of the house of the Savelli, which was probably German, was due to the nepotism of their member Pope Honorius [III.], and they only rose to power after his time." Gregorovius, v. p. 118.]

[114] [See the references in Gregorovius, v. p. 6.]

[115] The cardinal of St. George, in his poetical, or rather metrical, history of the election and coronation of Boniface VIII. (Muratori, Script. Ital. tom. iii. p. i. p. 641, &c.), describes the state and families of Rome at the coronation of Boniface VIII. (A.D. 1295) :—

Interea titulis redimiti sanguine et armis
Illustresque viri Romanâ a stirpe trahentes
Nomen in emeritos tantæ virtutis honores
Intulerant sese medios festumque colebant
Auratâ fulgentes [*leg.* fulgente] togâ, sociante catervâ.
Ex ipsis devota domus præstantis ab *Ursâ*
Ecclesiæ, vultumque gerens demissius altum
Festa *Columna* jocis, necnon *Sabellia* mitis ;
Stephanides senior, *Comites, Annibalica* [*leg.* Anibalica] proles,
Præfectusque urbis magnum sine viribus nomen.
                                   (l. ii. c. 5, 100, p. 647, 648).

The ancient statutes of Rome (l. iii. c. 59, p. 174, 175) distinguish eleven families of barons, who are obliged to swear in concilio communi, before the senator, that they would not harbour or protect any malefactors, outlaws, &c.—a feeble security ! [The Anibaldi family rose to prominence c. A.D. 1230. See Gregorovius, v. 158.]

[116] It is pity that the Colonna themselves have not favoured the world with a complete and critical history of their illustrious house. I adhere to Muratori (Dissert. xlii. tom. iii. p. 647, 648).

[117] Pandulph. Pisan. in Vit. Paschal. II. in Muratori, Script. Ital. tom. iii. p. i. p. 335. The family has still great possessions in the Campagna of Rome ; but they

of the neighbouring city of Tusculum, a strong presumption of their descent from the counts of Tusculum, who in the tenth century were the tyrants of the apostolic see. According to their own and the public opinion, the primitive and remote source was derived from the banks of the Rhine; [118] and the sovereigns of Germany were not ashamed of a real or fabulous affinity with a noble race, which in the revolutions of seven hundred years has been often illustrated by merit and always by fortune.[119] About the end of the thirteenth century, the most powerful branch was composed of an uncle and six brothers, all conspicuous in arms or in the honours of the church.   Of these, Peter was elected senator of Rome, introduced to the Capitol in a triumphant car, and hailed in some vain acclamations with the title of Cæsar, while John and Stephen were [Nicholas IV. A.D. 1288-92] declared Marquis of Ancona and Count of Romagna, by Nicholas the Fourth, a patron so partial to their family that he has been delineated in satirical portraits imprisoned as it were in a hollow pillar.[120] After his decease, their haughty behaviour provoked the displeasure of the most implacable of mankind. The two cardinals, the uncle and the nephew, denied the election of Boniface the Eighth ; and the Colonna were oppressed for a moment by his temporal and spiritual arms.[121] He proclaimed a crusade against his personal enemies: their estates were confiscated; their fortresses on either side of the Tiber were besieged by the troops of St. Peter and those of the rival nobles ;

have alienated to the Rospigliosi this original fief of *Colonna* (Eschinard, p. 258, 259).

[118]   Te longinqua dedit tellus et pascua Rheni,

says Petrarch ; and, in 1417, a duke of Guelders and Juliers acknowledges (Lenfant, Hist. du Concile de Constance, tom. ii. p. 539) his descent from the ancestors of Martin V. (Otho Colonna) : but the royal author of the Memoirs of Brandenburg observes that the sceptre in his arms has been confounded with the column. To maintain the Roman origin of the Colonna, it was ingeniously supposed (Diario di Monaldeschi, in the Script. Ital. tom. xii. p. 533) that a cousin of the emperor Nero escaped from the city and founded Mentz in Germany.

[119] I cannot overlook the Roman triumph or ovation of Marco Antonio Colonna, who had commanded the pope's galleys at the naval victory of Lepanto (Thuan. Hist. l. vii. tom. iii. p. 55, 56 ; Muret. Oratio x. Opp. tom. i. p. 180-190).

[120] Muratori, Annali d'Italia, tom. x. p. 216, 220.

[121] Petrarch's attachment to the Colonna has authorised the Abbé de Sade to expatiate on the state of the family in the fourteenth century, the persecution of Boniface VIII., the character of Stephen and his sons, their quarrels with the Ursini, &c. (Mémoires sur Pétrarque, tom. i. p. 98-110, 146-148, 174-176, 222-230, 275-280). His criticism often rectifies the hearsay stories of Villani, and the errors of the less diligent moderns. I understand the branch of Stephen to be now extinct.

and after the ruin of Palestrina or Præneste, their principal seat, the ground was marked with a ploughshare, the emblem of perpetual desolation. Degraded, banished, proscribed, the six brothers, in disguise and danger, wandered over Europe without renouncing the hope of deliverance and revenge. In this double hope, the French court was their surest asylum: they prompted and directed the enterprise of Philip; and I should praise their magnanimity, had they respected the fortune and courage of the captive tyrant. His civil acts were annulled by the Roman people, who restored the honours and possessions of the Colonna; and some estimate may be formed of their wealth by their losses, of their losses by the damages of one hundred thousand gold florins, which were granted them against the accomplices and heirs of the deceased pope. All the spiritual censures and disqualifications were abolished [122] by his prudent successors; and the fortune of the house was more firmly established by this transient hurricane. The boldness of Sciarra Colonna was signalised in the captivity of Boniface, and long afterwards in the coronation of Lewis of Bavaria; and by the gratitude of the emperor the pillar in their arms was encircled with a royal crown. But the first of the family in fame and merit was the elder Stephen, whom Petrarch loved and esteemed as an hero superior to his own times and not unworthy of ancient Rome. Persecution and exile displayed to the nations his abilities in peace and war; in his distress, he was an object not of pity, but of reverence; the aspect of danger provoked him to avow his name and country; and when he was asked, "Where is now your fortress?" he laid his hand on his heart, and answered, "Here". He supported with the same virtue the return of prosperity; and, till the ruin of his declining age, the ancestors, the character, and the children of Stephen Colonna, exalted his dignity in the Roman republic, and at the and Ursini court of Avignon. II. The Ursini migrated from Spoleto: [123]

---

[122] Alexander III. had declared the Colonna who adhered to the emperor Frederic I. incapable of holding any ecclesiastical benefice (Villani, l. v. c. 1); and the last stains of annual excommunication were purified by Sixtus V. (Vita di Sisto V. tom. iii. p. 416). Treason, sacrilege, and proscription are often the best titles of ancient nobility.

[123]
————Vallis te proxima misit
Appenninigenæ quâ prata virentia sylvæ
Spoletana metunt armenta gregesque protervi.

Monaldeschi (tom. xii. Script. Ital. p. 533) gives the Ursini a French origin, which may be remotely true. [Cp. Gregorovius, v. p. 39 *sqq.*]

the sons of Ursus, as they are styled in the twelfth century, from some eminent person who is only known as the father of their race. But they were soon distinguished among the nobles of Rome, by the number and bravery of their kinsmen, the strength of their towers, the honours of the senate and sacred college, and the elevation of two popes, Celestin the Third and Nicholas the Third, of their name and lineage.[124] Their riches may be accused as an early abuse of nepotism; the estates of St. Peter were alienated in their favour by the liberal Celestin;[125] and Nicholas was ambitious for their sake to solicit the alliance of monarchs; to found new kingdoms in Lombardy and Tuscany; and to invest them with the perpetual office of senators of Rome. All that has been observed of the greatness of the Colonna will likewise redound to the glory of the Ursini, their constant and equal antagonists in the long hereditary feud which distracted above two hundred and fifty years the ecclesiastical state. The jealousy of pre-eminence and power was the true ground of their quarrel; but, as a specious badge of distinction, the Colonna embraced the name of Ghibelines and the party of the empire; the Ursini espoused the title of Guelphs and the cause of the church. The eagle and the keys were displayed in their adverse banners; and the two factions of Italy most furiously raged when the origin and nature of the dispute were long since forgotten.[126] After the retreat of the popes to Avignon, they disputed in arms the vacant republic; and the mischiefs of discord were perpetuated by the wretched

[Celestine III. A.D. 1191-8. Nicholas III. 1277-80]

Their hereditary feuds

---

[124] In the metrical life of Celestine V. by the Cardinal of St. George (Muratori, tom. iii. p. i. p. 613, &c.), we find a luminous and not inelegant passage (l. i. c. iii. p. 203, &c.) :—

> —— genuit quem nobilis Ursæ (*Ursi ?*)
> Progenies, Romana domus, veterataque magnis
> Fascibus in clero, pompasque experta senatus,
> Bellorumque manu grandi stipata parentum
> Cardineos apices necnon fastigia dudum
> Papatus *iterata* tenens.

Muratori (Dissert. xlii. tom. iii.) observes that the first Ursini pontificate of Celestin III. was unknown; he is inclined to read *Ursi* progenies.

[125] Filii Ursi, quondam Cœlestini papæ nepotes, de bonis ecclesiæ Romanæ ditati (Vit. Innocent. III. in Muratori, Script. tom. iii. p. i.). The partial prodigality of Nicholas III. is more conspicuous in Villani and Muratori. Yet the Ursini would disdain the nephews of a *modern* Pope. [Fra Salimbene of Parma said of Nicholas III. that he built Sion in his kinsfolk (ædificavit Sion in sanguinibus). The expression is quoted by Gregorovius, v. 490. Compare Dante, Inferno, xix. v. 70-2, where he is alluded to as "figliuol dell' orsa".]

[126] In his fifty-first Dissertation on the Italian Antiquities, Muratori explains the factions of the Guelphs and Ghibelines.

compromise of electing each year two rival senators. By their
private hostilities, the city and country were desolated, and the
fluctuating balance inclined with their alternate success. But
none of either family had fallen by the sword, till the most
renowned champion of the Ursini was surprised and slain by
the younger Stephen Colonna.[127] His triumph is stained with
the reproach of violating the truce; their defeat was basely
avenged by the assassination, before the church-door, of an
innocent boy and his two servants. Yet the victorious Colonna,
with an annual colleague, was declared senator of Rome during
the term of five years. And the muse of Petrarch inspired a
wish, a hope, a prediction, that the generous youth, the son of
his venerable hero, would restore Rome and Italy to their
pristine glory; that his justice would extirpate the wolves and
lions, the serpents and *bears*, who laboured to subvert the
eternal basis of the marble COLUMN.[128]

[127] Petrarch (tom. i. p. 222-230) has celebrated this victory according to the
Colonna; but two contemporaries, a Florentine (Giovanni Villani, l. x. c. 220)
and a Roman (Ludovico Monaldeschi [S. R. I. xii.] p. 533, 534), are less favourable to their arms.

[128] The Abbé de Sade (tom. i. notes, p. 61-66) has applied the vith Canzone of
Petrarch, *Spirto Gentil*, &c., to Stephen Colonna the Younger.

> *Orsi*, lupi, leoni, aquile e serpi
> Ad una gran marmorea *colonna*
> Fanno noja sovente e à se damno.

CHAPTER LXX

Character and Coronation of Petrarch—Restoration of the Freedom and Government of Rome by the Tribune Rienzi —His Virtues and Vices, his Expulsion and Death— Return of the Popes from Avignon—Great Schism of the West—Re-union of the Latin Church—Last Struggles of Roman Liberty—Statutes of Rome—Final Settlement of the Ecclesiastical State

IN the apprehension of modern times, Petrarch [1] is the Italian songster of Laura and love. In the harmony of his Tuscan rhymes, Italy applauds, or rather adores, the father of her lyric poetry; and his verse, or at least his name, is repeated by the enthusiasm or affectation of amorous sensibility. Whatever may be the private taste of a stranger, his slight and superficial knowledge should humbly acquiesce in the judgment [1a] of a learned nation; yet I may hope or presume that the Italians do not compare the tedious uniformity of sonnets and elegies with the sublime compositions of their epic muse, the original wild-ness of Dante, the regular beauties of Tasso, and the boundless variety of the incomparable Ariosto. The merits of the lover I am still less qualified to appreciate; nor am I deeply interested in a metaphysical passion for a nymph so shadowy that her existence has been questioned; [2] for a matron so prolific [3] that

Petrarch,
A.D. 1304,
June 19
[July 20]-
A.D. 1374,
July 19

---

[1] The Mémoires sur la Vie de François Pétrarque (Amsterdam, 1764, 1767, 3 vols. in 4to) form a copious, original and entertaining work, a labour of love, composed from the accurate study of Petrarch and his contemporaries; but the hero is too often lost in the general history of the age, and the author too often languishes in the affectation of politeness and gallantry. In the preface to his first volume, he enumerates and weighs twenty Italian biographers, who have professedly treated of the same subject. [Körting, Petrarca's Leben und Werke, 1878; Geiger, Petrarca, 1874. Cp. above, p. 124, note 92.]

[1a] [The author originally wrote *taste*, and afterwards amended it.]

[2] The allegorical interpretation prevailed in the xvth century; but the wise commentators were not agreed whether they should understand by Laura, religion, or virtue, or the blessed Virgin, or ———. See the prefaces to the first and second volumes.

[3] Laura de Noves, born about the year 1307, was married in January 1325 to Hugues de Sade, a noble citizen of Avignon, whose jealousy was not the effect of

she was delivered of eleven legitimate children[4] while her amorous swain sighed and sung at the fountain of Vaucluse.[5] But in the eyes of Petrarch, and those of his graver contemporaries, his love was a sin, and Italian verse a frivolous amusement. His Latin works of philosophy, poetry, and eloquence established his serious reputation, which was soon diffused from Avignon over France and Italy; his friends and disciples were multiplied in every city; and, if the ponderous volume of his writings[6] be now abandoned to a long repose, our gratitude must applaud the man who by precept and example revived the spirit and study of the Augustan age. From his earliest youth, Petrarch aspired to the poetic crown. The academical honours of the three faculties had introduced a royal degree of master or doctor in the art of poetry;[7] and the title of poet-laureat, which custom, rather than vanity, perpetuates in the English court,[8] was first invented by the Cæsars of Germany. In the musical games of antiquity, a prize was be-

love, since he married a second wife within seven months of her death, which happened the 6th of April 1348, precisely one and twenty years after Petrarch had seen and loved her.

[4] Corpus crebris partubus exhaustum; from one of these is issued, in the tenth degree, the Abbé de Sade, the fond and grateful biographer of Petrarch; and this domestic motive most probably suggested the idea of his work, and urged him to inquire into every circumstance that could affect the history and character of his grandmother (see particularly tom. i. p. 122-133, notes, p. 7-58; tom. ii. p. 455-495, notes, p. 76-82).

[5] Vaucluse, so familiar to our English travellers, is described from the writings of Petrarch, and the local knowledge of his biographer (Mémoires, tom. i. p. 340-359). It was, in truth, the retreat of an hermit; and the moderns are much mistaken if they place Laura and an happy lover in the grotto.

[6] Of 1250 pages, in a close print, at Basil, in the xvith century, but without the date of the year. The Abbé de Sade calls aloud for a new edition of Petrarch's Latin works; but I much doubt whether it would redound to the profit of the bookseller, or the amusement of the public. [Petrarch's Epistolæ de rebus familiaribus et variæ have been edited in 3 vols., 1859-63, by G. Fracassetti and translated (with commentary) into Italian by the same scholar (in 5 vols., 1863-7), who has also translated and annotated the Epistolæ seniles (Lettere senili, 2 vols., 1869). The De viris illustribus vitæ has been edited by A. Razzolini, 1874, who has added in a 2nd vol. the Italian translation thereof by Donato degli Albanzani.]

[7] Consult Selden's Titles of Honour, in his works (vol. iii. p. 457-466). An hundred years before Petrarch, St. Francis received the visit of a poet, qui ab imperatore fuerat coronatus et exinde rex versuum dictus.

[8] From Augustus to Louis, the muse has too often been false and venal; but I much doubt whether any age or court can produce a similar establishment of a stipendiary poet, who in every reign, and at all events, is bound to furnish twice a year a measure of praise and verse, such as may be sung in the chapel, and, I believe, in the presence of the sovereign. I speak the more freely, as the best time for abolishing this ridiculous custom is while the prince is a man of virtue and the poet a man of genius.

stowed on the victor;[9] the belief that Virgil and Horace had been crowned in the Capitol inflamed the emulation of a Latin bard;[10] and the laurel [11] was endeared to the lover by a verbal resemblance with the name of his mistress. The value of either object was enhanced by the difficulties of the pursuit ; and, if the virtue or prudence of Laura was inexorable,[12] he enjoyed, and might boast of enjoying, the nymph of poetry. His vanity was not of the most delicate kind, since he applauds the success of his own *labours ;* his name was popular; his friends were active; the open or secret opposition of envy and prejudice was surmounted by the dexterity of patient merit. In the thirty-sixth year of his age, he was solicited to accept the object of his wishes ; and on the same day, in the solitude of Vaucluse, he received a similar and solemn invitation from the senate of Rome [Aug. 30, and the university of Paris. The learning of a theological school, A.D. 1340] and the ignorance of a lawless city, were alike unqualified to bestow the ideal, though immortal, wreath which genius may obtain from the free applause of the public and of posterity ; but the candidate dismissed this troublesome reflection, and, after some moments of complacency and suspense, preferred the summons of the metropolis of the world.

The ceremony of his coronation [13] was performed in the

---

[9] Isocrates (in Panegyrico, tom. i. p. 116, 117, edit. Battie, Cantab. 1729) claims for his native Athens the glory of first instituting and recommending the ἀγῶνας καὶ τὰ ἆθλα μέγιστα μὴ μόνον τάχους καὶ ῥώμης, ἀλλὰ καὶ λόγων καὶ γνώμης. The example of the Panathenæa was imitated at Delphi ; but the Olympic games were ignorant of a musical crown, till it was extorted by the vain tyranny of Nero (Sueton. in Nerone, c. 23 ; Philostrat. apud Casaubon ad locum ; Dion Cassius or Xiphilin, l. lxiii. p. 1032 [c. 9], 1041 [c. 20]. Potter's Greek Antiquities, vol. i. p. 445, 450).

[10] The Capitoline games (certamen quinquennale, *musicum*, equestre, gymnicum) were instituted by Domitian (Sueton. c. 4) in the year of Christ 86 (Censorin. de Die Natali, c. xviii. p. 100, edit. Havercamp), and were not abolished in the ivth century (Ausonius de Professoribus Burdegal. V.). If the crown were given to superior merit, the exclusion of Statius (Capitolia nostræ inficiata lyræ, Sylv. l. iii. v. 31) may do honour to the games of the Capitol ; but the Latin poets who lived before Domitian were crowned only in the public opinion.

[11] Petrarch and the senators of Rome were ignorant that the laurel was not the Capitoline, but the Delphic crown (Plin. Hist. Natur. xv. 39 ; Hist. Critique de la République des Lettres, tom i. p. 150-220). The victors in the Capitol were crowned with a garland of oak-leaves (Martial, l. iv. epigram 54).

[12] The pious grandson of Laura has laboured, and not without success, to vindicate her immaculate chastity against the censures of the grave and the sneers of the profane (tom. ii. notes, p. 76-82).

[13] The whole process of Petrarch's coronation is accurately described by the Abbé de Sade (tom. i. p. 425-435 ; tom. ii. p. 1-6, notes, p. 1-13), from his own writings [see Ep. Poet. ii. 1], and the Roman Diary of Ludovico Monaldeschi, without mixing in this authentic narrative the more recent fables of Sannuccio Delbene.

His poetic
coronation
at Rome,
A.D. 1341,
April 8
Capitol, by his friend and patron the supreme magistrate of the
republic.   Twelve patrician youths were arrayed in scarlet ; six
representatives of the most illustrious families, in green robes,
with garlands of flowers, accompanied the procession ; in the
midst of the princes and nobles, the senator, count of Anguillara,
a kinsman of the Colonna, assumed his throne ; and, at the voice
of an herald, Petrarch arose.   After discoursing on a text of
Virgil,[14] and thrice repeating his vows for the prosperity of
Rome, he knelt before the throne, and received from the senator
a laurel crown, with a more precious declaration, " This is the
reward of merit".   The people shouted, "Long life to the
Capitol and the poet ! "   A sonnet in praise of Rome was accepted as the effusion of genius and gratitude; and, after the
whole procession had visited the Vatican, the profane wreath
was suspended before the shrine of St. Peter.   In the act or
diploma[15] which was presented to Petrarch, the title and prerogatives of poet-laureat are revived in the Capitol, after the
lapse of thirteen hundred years ; and he receives the perpetual
privilege of wearing, at his choice, a crown of laurel, ivy, or
myrtle, of assuming the poetic habit, and of teaching, disputing,
interpreting, and composing in all places whatsoever and on all
subjects of literature.   The grant was ratified by the authority
of the senate and people ; and the character of citizen was the
recompense of his affection for the Roman name.   They did
him honour, but they did him justice.   In the familiar society
of Cicero and Livy, he had imbibed the ideas of an ancient
patriot; and his ardent fancy kindled every idea to a sentiment
and every sentiment to a passion.   The aspect of the seven
hills and their majestic ruins confirmed these lively impressions ;
and he loved a country by whose liberal spirit he had been
crowned and adopted.   The poverty and debasement of Rome
excited the indignation and pity of her grateful son : he dissembled the faults of his fellow-citizens; applauded with partial
fondness the last of their heroes and matrons; and in the remembrance of the past, in the hope of the future, was pleased

14   [Sed me Parnassi deserta per ardua dulcis
          Raptat amor.
                                          Georgics 3, 291.
This address has been published by Attilio Hortis in Scritti inediti di Fr. Petrarca,
1874, p. 311 *sqq.*]
        15 The original act is printed among the Pièces Justificatives in the Mémoires
sur Pétrarque, tom. iii. p. 50-53.

to forget the miseries of the present time. Rome was still the lawful mistress of the world; the pope and the emperor, her bishop and general, had abdicated their station by an inglorious retreat to the Rhône and the Danube; but, if she could resume her virtue, the republic might again vindicate her liberty and dominion. Amidst the indulgence of enthusiasm and eloquence,[16] Petrarch, Italy, and Europe were astonished by a revolution which realised, for a moment, his most splendid visions. The rise and fall of the tribune, Rienzi, will occupy the following pages.[17] The subject is interesting, the materials are rich, and the glance of a patriot-bard [18] will sometimes vivify the copious but simple narrative of the Florentine,[19] and more especially of the Roman,[20] historian.

In a quarter of the city which was inhabited only by mechanics and Jews, the marriage of an innkeeper and a washerwoman produced the future deliverer of Rome.[21] From such parents Nicholas

Birth, character, and patriotic de- otic de- signs of Rienzi [Born, A.D. 1314]

[16] To find the proofs of his enthusiasm for Rome, I need only request that the reader would open, by chance, either Petrarch or his French biographer. The latter has described the poet's first visit to Rome [A.D. 1337] (tom. i. p. 323-335). But, in the place of much idle rhetoric and morality, Petrarch might have amused the present and future age with an original account of the city and his coronation.

[17] It has been treated by the pen of a Jesuit, the P. du Cerceau, whose posthumous work (Conjuration de Nicholas Gabrini, dit de Rienzi, Tyran de Rome, en 1347) was published at Paris, 1748, 12mo. I am indebted to him for some facts and documents in John Hocsemius, canon of Liège, a contemporary historian (Fabricius, Bibliot. Lat. med. Ævi, tom. iii. p. 273; tom. iv. p. 85).

[18] The Abbé de Sade, who so freely expatiates on the history of the xivth century, might treat, as his proper subject, a revolution in which the heart of Petrarch was so deeply engaged (Mémoires, tom. ii. p. 50, 51, 320-417, notes, p. 70-76; tom. iii. p. 221-243, 366-375). Not an idea or a fact in the writings of Petrarch has probably escaped him.

[19] Giovanni Villani, l. xii. c. 89, 104, in Muratori, Rerum Italicarum Scriptores, tom. xiii. p. 969, 970, 981-983.

[20] In his third volume of Italian Antiquities (p. 249-548), Muratori has inserted the Fragmenta Historiæ Romanæ ab Anno 1327 usque ad Annum 1354, in the original dialect of Rome or Naples in the xivth century, and a Latin version for the benefit of strangers. It contains the most particular and authentic life of Cola (Nicholas) di Rienzi, which had been printed at Bracciano, 1627, in 4to, under the name of Tomaso Fortifiocca, who is only mentioned in this work as having been punished by the tribune for forgery. [This Life has been edited by Zeferino Re, 2nd ed. 1854.] Human nature is scarcely capable of such sublime or stupid impartiality; but whosoever is the author of these Fragments, he wrote on the spot and at the time, and paints, without design or art, the manners of Rome and the character of the tribune. [Rienzi's letters have been published by A. Gabrielli, Epistolario di Cola di Rienzo, 1890. Monographs: Papencordt, Cola di Rienzi und seine Zeit, 1841 (and French transl. by Boré, 1845); Rodocanachi, Cola di Rienzo: histoire de Rome de 1342 à 1354, 1888.]

[21] The first and splendid period of Rienzi, his tribunitian government, is contained in the xviiith chapter of the Fragments (p. 399-479) which, in the new division, forms the iid book of the history in xxxviii. smaller chapters or sections. [The more correct form of his name is Rienzo, from Lorenzo. In Latin documents he is called Nicolaus Laurentii.]

Rienzi Gabrini could inherit neither dignity nor fortune; and the gift of a liberal education, which they painfully bestowed, was the cause of his glory and untimely end. The study of history and eloquence, the writings of Cicero, Seneca, Livy, Cæsar, and Valerius Maximus, elevated above his equals and contemporaries the genius of the young plebeian; he perused with indefatigable diligence the manuscripts and marbles of antiquity; loved to dispense his knowledge in familiar language; and was often provoked to exclaim, "Where are now these Romans? their virtue, their justice, their power? why was I not born in those happy times?"[22] When the republic addressed to the throne of Avignon an embassy of the three

[A.D. 1343, Jan.]

orders, the spirit and eloquence of Rienzi recommended him to a place among the thirteen deputies of the commons. The orator had the honour of haranguing Pope Clement the Sixth, and the satisfaction of conversing with Petrarch, a congenial mind; but his aspiring hopes were chilled by disgrace and poverty; and the patriot was reduced to a single garment and

[Becomes notary of the civic camera, A.D. 1344]

the charity of the hospital. From this misery he was relieved by the sense of merit or the smile of favour; and the employment of apostolic notary afforded him a daily [23] stipend of five gold florins, a more honourable and extensive connection, and the right of contrasting, both in words and actions, his own integrity with the vices of the state. The eloquence of Rienzi was prompt and persuasive; the multitude is always prone to envy and censure: he was stimulated by the loss of a brother and the impunity of the assassins; nor was it possible to excuse or exaggerate the public calamities. The blessings of peace and justice, for which civil society has been instituted, were banished from Rome: the jealous citizens, who might have endured every personal or pecuniary injury, were most deeply

[22] The reader may be pleased with a specimen of the original idiom : Fò da soa juventutine nutricato di latte de eloquentia, bono gramatico, megliore rettuorico, autorista bravo. Deh como et quanto era veloce leitore! moito usava Tito Livio, Seneca, et Tullio, et Balerio Massimo, moito li dilettava le magnificentie di Julio Cesare raccontare. Tutta la die se speculava negl' intagli di marmo lequali iaccio intorno Roma. Non era altri che esso, che sapesse lejere li antichi pataffii. Tutte scritture antiche vulgarizzava; quesse fiure di marmo justamente interpretava. Oh come spesso diceva, " Dove suono quelli buoni Romani? dove ene loro somma justitia? poteramme trovare in tempo che quessi fiuriano!"

[23] [Monthly, not daily. See Cola's petition for the office, which was granted to him by the Pope. See Gregorovius, vi. p. 231, note.]

wounded in the dishonour of their wives and daughters;[24] they were equally oppressed by the arrogance of the nobles and the corruption of the magistrates; and the abuse of arms or of laws was the only circumstance that distinguished the lions from the dogs and serpents of the Capitol. These allegorical emblems were variously repeated in the pictures which Rienzi exhibited in the streets and churches; and, while the spectators gazed with curious wonder, the bold and ready orator unfolded the meaning, applied the satire, inflamed their passions, and announced a distant hope of comfort and deliverance. The privileges of Rome, her eternal sovereignty over her princes and provinces, was the theme of his public and private discourse; and a monument of servitude became in his hands a title and incentive of liberty. The decree of the senate, which granted the most ample prerogatives to the emperor Vespasian, had been inscribed on a copper-plate still extant in the choir of the church of St. John Lateran.[25] A numerous assembly of nobles and plebeians was invited to this political lecture, and a convenient theatre was erected for their reception. The notary appeared in a magnificent and mysterious habit, explained the inscription by a version and commentary,[26] and descanted with eloquence and zeal on the ancient glories of the senate and people, from whom all legal authority was derived. The supine ignorance of the nobles was incapable of discerning the serious tendency of such representations: they might sometimes chastise with words and blows the plebeian reformer; but he was often suffered in

---

[24] Petrarch compares the jealousy of the Romans with the easy temper of the husbands of Avignon (Mémoires, tom. i. p. 330).

[25] The fragments of the *Lex Regia* may be found in the inscriptions of Gruter, tom. i. p. 242, and at the end of the Tacitus of Ernesti, with some learned notes of the editor, tom. ii. [See C. I. L. vi. 930. Cp. above, vol. i. p. 72, n. 19. "Cola had discovered this bronze tablet in the Lateran, where it had been employed in the construction of an altar in the time of Boniface VIII. The inscription had then been turned inwards, but it was restored to light either by the fall of the church in consequence of the fire or in process of rebuilding. The use to which Cola turned this monument of imperial despotism was singular and ingenious. He caused the tablet to be built into the wall behind the choir of the Lateran, and round it had the Senate painted in the act of conferring the imperial authority on Vespasian."]

[26] I cannot overlook a stupendous and laughable blunder of Rienzi. The Lex Regia empowers Vespasian to enlarge the Pomœrium, a word familiar to every antiquary. It was not so to the tribune; he confounds it with pom*a*rium, an orchard, translates lo Jardino de Roma cioene Italia, and is copied by the less excusable ignorance of the Latin translator (p. 406) and the French historian (p. 33). Even the learning of Muratori has slumbered 'over the passage. [Gregorovius compares Dante's (Purgatorio, vi. 105) chè il giardin dell' Imperio sia deserto.]

the Colonna palace to amuse the company with his threats and predictions; and the modern Brutus [27] was concealed under the mask of folly and the character of a buffoon. While they indulged their contempt, the restoration of the *good estate*, his favourite expression, was entertained among the people as a desirable, a possible, and at length as an approaching, event; and, while all had the disposition to applaud, some had the courage to assist, their promised deliverer.

He assumes the government of Rome, A.D. 1347, May 20; A prophecy, or rather a summons, affixed on the church-door of St. George, was the first public evidence of his designs; a nocturnal assembly of an hundred citizens on Mount Aventine, the first step to their execution. After an oath of secrecy and aid, he represented to the conspirators the importance and facility of their enterprise; that the nobles, without union or resources, were strong only in the fear of their imaginary strength; that all power, as well as right, was in the hands of the people; that the revenues of the apostolical chamber might relieve the public distress; and that the pope himself would approve their victory over the common enemies of government and freedom. After securing a faithful band to protect his first declaration, he proclaimed through the city, by sound of trumpet, that on the evening of the following day all persons should assemble without arms before the church of St. Angelo, to provide for the re-establishment of the good estate. The whole night was employed in the celebration of thirty masses of the Holy Ghost; and in the morning, Rienzi, bare-headed, but in complete armour, issued from the church, encompassed by the hundred conspirators. The pope's vicar, the simple bishop of Orvieto, who had been persuaded to sustain a part in this singular ceremony, marched on his right hand; and three great standards were borne aloft as the emblems of their design. In the first, the banner of *liberty*, Rome was seated on two lions, with a palm in one hand and a globe in the other; St. Paul, with a drawn sword, was delineated in the banner of *justice;* and in the third, St. Peter held the keys of *concord* and *peace.* Rienzi was encouraged by the presence and applause of an innumerable crowd, who understood little and hoped much; and the procession

---

[27] Priori (*Bruto*) tamen similior, juvenis uterque, longe ingenio quam cujus simulationem induerat, ut sub hoc obtentu liberator ille P. R. aperiretur tempore suo . . . ille regibus, hic tyrannis contemptus (Opp. p. 536).

slowly rolled forwards from the castle of St. Angelo to the Capitol. His triumph was disturbed by some secret emotion, which he laboured to suppress : he ascended without opposition, and with seeming confidence, the citadel of the republic ; harangued the people from the balcony ; and received the most flattering confirmation of his acts and laws. The nobles, as if destitute of arms and counsels, beheld in silent consternation this strange revolution ; and the moment had been prudently chosen, when the most formidable, Stephen Colonna, was absent from the city. On the first rumour he returned to his palace, affected to despise this plebeian tumult, and declared to the messenger of Rienzi that at his leisure he would cast the mad-man from the windows of the Capitol. The great bell instantly rang an alarm, and so rapid was the tide, so urgent was the danger, that Colonna escaped with precipitation to the suburb of St. Laurence ; from thence, after a moment's refreshment, he continued the same speedy career, till he reached in safety his castle of Palestrina, lamenting his own imprudence, which had not trampled the spark of this mighty conflagration. A general and peremptory order was issued from the Capitol to all the nobles, that they should peaceably retire to their estates : they obeyed ; and their departure secured the tranquillity of the free and obedient citizens of Rome.

But such voluntary obedience evaporates with the first trans- *with the title and office of tribune* ports of zeal ; and Rienzi felt the importance of justifying his usurpation by a regular form and a legal title. At his own choice, the Roman people would have displayed their attachment and authority, by lavishing on his head the names of senator or con-sul, of king or emperor : he preferred the ancient and modest appellation of tribune ; [28] the protection of the commons was the essence of that sacred office ; and they were ignorant that it had never been invested with any share in the legislative or executive powers of the republic. In this character, and with the consent *Laws of the good estate* of the Romans, the tribune enacted the most salutary laws for the restoration and maintenance of the good estate. By the first he fulfils the wish of honesty and inexperience, that no civil suit should be protracted beyond the term of fifteen days. The danger of frequent perjury might justify the pronouncing against a false

---

[28] [This was his style : Nicholaus, Severus et Clemens, Libertatis Pacis Justi-tiæque Tribunus, et sacre Romane Reipublice Liberator. (Gregorovius, vi. 249).]

accuser the same penalty which his evidence would have inflicted; the disorders of the times might compel the legislator to punish every homicide with death and every injury with equal retaliation. But the execution of justice was hopeless till he had previously abolished the tyranny of the nobles. It was formally provided that none, except the supreme magistrate, should possess or command the gates, bridges, or towers, of the state; that no private garrisons should be introduced into the towns or castles of the Roman territory; that none should bear arms or presume to fortify their houses in the city or country; that the barons should be responsible for the safety of the highways and the free passage of provisions; and that the protection of malefactors and robbers should be expiated by a fine of a thousand marks of silver. But these regulations would have been impotent and nugatory, had not the licentious nobles been awed by the sword of the civil power. A sudden alarm from the bell of the Capitol could still summon to the standard above twenty thousand volunteers; the support of the tribune and the laws required a more regular and permanent force. In each harbour of the coast, a vessel was stationed for the assurance of commerce; a standing militia of three hundred and sixty horse and thirteen hundred foot was levied, clothed, and paid in the thirteen quarters of the city; and the spirit of a commonwealth may be traced in the grateful allowance of one hundred florins, or pounds, to the heirs of every soldier who lost his life in the service of his country. For the maintenance of the public defence, for the establishment of granaries, for the relief of widows, orphans and indigent convents, Rienzi applied without fear of sacrilege, the revenues of the apostolic chamber; the three branches of hearth-money, the salt-duty, and the customs, were each of the annual produce of one hundred thousand florins;[29] and scandalous were the abuses if in four or five months the amount of the salt-duty could be trebled by his judicious economy. After thus restoring the forces and finances of the republic, the tribune recalled the nobles from their solitary independence; required their personal

[29] In one Ms. I read (l. ii. c. 4, p. 409) perfumante quatro *solli*, in another quatro *florini*: an important variety, since the florin was worth ten Roman *solidi* (Muratori, dissert. xxviii.). The former reading would give us a population of 25,000, the latter of 250,000 families; and I much fear that the former is more consistent with the decay of Rome and her territory. [The population was probably not more than 50,000 in all, at this period. Cp. Gregorovius, vi. 152 note. The hearth tax (*focaticum*) is said to have been 26 denari (*ib.* 256).]

appearance in the Capitol; and imposed an oath of allegiance to the new government and of submission to the laws of the good estate. Apprehensive for their safety, but still more apprehensive of the danger of a refusal, the princes and barons returned to their houses at Rome, in the garb of simple and peaceful citizens; the Colonna and Ursini, the Savelli and Frangipani, were confounded before the tribunal of a plebeian, of the vile buffoon whom they had so often derided, and their disgrace was aggravated by the indignation which they vainly struggled to disguise. The same oath was successively pronounced by the several orders of society, the clergy and gentlemen, the judges and notaries, the merchants and artisans, and the gradual descent was marked by the increase of sincerity and zeal. They swore to live and die with the republic and the church, whose interest was artfully united by the nominal association of the bishop of Orvieto, the pope's vicar, to the office of tribune. It was the boast of Rienzi that he had delivered the throne and patrimony of St. Peter from a rebellious aristocracy; and Clement the Sixth, who rejoiced in its fall, affected to believe the professions, to applaud the merits, and to confirm the title, of his trusty servant. The speech, perhaps the mind, of the tribune was inspired with a lively regard for the purity of the faith: he insinuated his claim to a supernatural mission from the Holy Ghost; enforced by an heavy forfeiture the annual duty of confession and communion; and strictly guarded the spiritual as well as temporal welfare of his faithful people.[30]

Never, perhaps, has the energy and effect of a single mind been more remarkably felt than in the sudden, though transient, reformation of Rome by the tribune Rienzi. A den of robbers was converted to the discipline of a camp or convent: patient to hear, swift to redress, inexorable to punish, his tribunal was always accessible to the poor and stranger; nor could birth or dignity or the immunities of the church protect the offender or his accomplices. The privileged houses, the private sanctuaries in Rome, on which no officer of justice would presume to trespass, were abolished; and he applied the timber and iron of their barricades in the fortifications of the Capitol. The vener-

Freedom and prosperity of the Roman republic

---

[30] Hocsemius, p. 398, apud du Cerceau, Hist. de Rienzi, p. 194. The fifteen tribunician laws may be found in the Roman historian (whom for brevity I shall name) Fortifiocca, l. ii. c. 4.

able father of the Colonna was exposed in his own palace to the
double shame of being desirous, and of being unable, to protect
a criminal.   A mule, with a jar of oil, had been stolen near
Capranica; and the lord of the Ursini family was condemned
to restore the damage, and to discharge a fine of four hundred
florins for his negligence in guarding the highways.   Nor were
the persons of the barons more inviolate than their lands or
houses; and, either from accident or design, the same impartial
rigour was exercised against the heads of the adverse factions.
Peter Agapet Colonna, who had himself been senator of Rome,
was arrested in the street for injury or debt; and justice was
appeased by the tardy execution of Martin Ursini, who, among
his various acts of violence and rapine, had pillaged a shipwrecked vessel at the mouth of the Tiber.[31]   His name, the
purple of two cardinals, his uncles, a recent marriage, and a
mortal disease, were disregarded by the inflexible tribune, who
had chosen his victim.   The public officers dragged him from
his palace and nuptial bed : his trial was short and satisfactory ;
the bell of the Capitol convened the people ; stript of his
mantle, on his knees, with his hands bound behind his back,
he heard the sentence of death ; and, after a brief confession,
Ursini was led away to the gallows.   After such an example,
none who were conscious of guilt could hope for impunity, and
the flight of the wicked, the licentious, and the idle soon
purified the city and territory of Rome.   In this time (says the
historian) the woods began to rejoice that they were no longer
infested with robbers; the oxen began to plough; the pilgrims
visited the sanctuaries; the roads and inns were replenished
with travellers; trade, plenty, and good faith were restored in
the markets; and a purse of gold might be exposed without
danger in the midst of the highway.   As soon as the life and
property of the subject are secure, the labours and rewards of

[Martin
Stefanes-
chi]

---

[31] Fortifiocca, l. ii. c. 11.   From the account of this shipwreck we learn some
circumstances of the trade and navigation of the age. 1. The ship was built and
freighted at Naples for the ports of Marseilles and Avignon. 2. The sailors were
of Naples and the Isle of Oenaria, less skilful than those of Sicily and Genoa.
3. The navigation from Marseilles was a coasting voyage to the mouth of the
Tiber, where they took shelter in a storm, but, instead of finding the current,
unfortunately ran on a shoal; the vessel was stranded, the mariners escaped.
4. The cargo, which was pillaged, consisted of the revenue of Provence for the
royal treasury, many bags of pepper and cinnamon, and bales of French cloth,
to the value of 20,000 florins : a rich prize.

industry spontaneously revive : Rome was still the metropolis of the Christian world ; and the fame and fortunes of the tribune were diffused in every country by the strangers who had enjoyed the blessings of his government.

The deliverance of his country inspired Rienzi with a vast, and perhaps visionary, idea of uniting Italy in a great federative republic, of which Rome should be the ancient and lawful head, and the free cities and princes the members and associates. His pen was not less eloquent than his tongue ; and his numerous epistles were delivered to swift and trusty messengers. On foot, with a white wand in their hand, they traversed the forests and mountains ; enjoyed, in the most hostile states, the sacred security of ambassadors ; and reported, in the style of flattery or truth, that the highways along their passage were lined with kneeling multitudes, who implored Heaven for the success of their undertaking.   Could passion have listened to reason, could private interest have yielded to the public welfare, the supreme tribunal and confederate union of the Italian republic might have healed their intestine discord and closed the Alps against the barbarians of the North.[32]   But the propitious season had elapsed ; and, if Venice, Florence, Sienna, Perugia, and many inferior cities offered their lives and fortunes to the good estate, the tyrants of Lombardy and Tuscany must despise, or hate, the plebeian author of a free constitution. From them, however, and from every part of Italy, the tribune received the most friendly and respectful answers ; they were followed by the ambassadors of the princes and republics ; and in this foreign conflux, on all the occasions of pleasure or business, the low-born notary could assume the familiar or majestic courtesy of a sovereign.[33]   The most glorious circum-

The tribune is respected in Italy, &c. [Idea of a confederation of Italy]

[32] [It is strange that Gibbon should have made no mention of Dante's work De Monarchia, which, though it expressed the Ghibelline ideal and looked for salvation to Germany, was nevertheless animated with the same idea which inspired Rienzi, in so far as it recognised that the rule of the world belonged to Rome. The De Monarchia is an important indication of the mediæval ideals which moved Italians in the fourteenth century, and the reaction against the Popes.   Bryce gives an account of his argument in his Holy Roman Empire, p. 276 *sqq.* (new ed. 1904).   As the work appeared after the Italian expedition of Henry VII.—the last episode in the history of the Empire in Italy—Bryce describes the book as "an epitaph instead of a prophecy".   See also the observations of Gregorovius, vi. p. 19-24.   It is pathetic to see how men like Petrarch looked for the regeneration of Italy to the degenerate rabble of Rome.]

[33] It was thus that Oliver Cromwell's old acquaintance, who remembered his vulgar and ungracious entrance into the House of Commons, were astonished at

stance of his reign was an appeal to his justice from Lewis
king of Hungary, who complained that his brother, and her
husband, had been perfidiously strangled by Jane queen of
Naples: [34] her guilt or innocence was pleaded in a solemn trial
at Rome; but, after hearing the advocates,[35] the tribune adjourned this weighty and invidious cause, which was soon
determined by the sword of the Hungarian. Beyond the
Alps, more especially at Avignon, the revolution was the theme
of curiosity, wonder, and applause. Petrarch had been the
private friend, perhaps the secret counsellor, of Rienzi: his
*and cele-
brated by
Petrarch* writings breathe the most ardent spirit of patriotism and joy;
and all respect for the pope, all gratitude for the Colonna, was
lost in the superior duties of a Roman citizen. The poet-
laureat of the Capitol maintains the act, applauds the hero, and
mingles with some apprehension and advice the most lofty hopes
of the permanent and rising greatness of the republic.[36]

*His vices
and follies* While Petrarch indulged these prophetic visions, the Roman
hero was fast declining from the meridian of fame and power;
and the people, who had gazed with astonishment on the
ascending meteor, began to mark the irregularity of its course
and the vicissitudes of light and obscurity. More eloquent
than judicious, more enterprising than resolute, the faculties
of Rienzi were not balanced by cool and commanding reason;
he magnified in a tenfold proportion the objects of hope and
fear; and prudence, which could not have erected, did not
presume to fortify, his throne. In the blaze of prosperity,
his virtues were insensibly tinctured with the adjacent vices:
justice with cruelty, liberality with profusion, and the desire
of fame with puerile and ostentatious vanity. He might have

the ease and majesty of the Protector on his throne (see Harris's Life of Cromwell,
p. 27-34, from Clarendon, Warwick, Whitelocke, Waller, &c.). The consciousness
of merit and power will sometimes elevate the manners to the station.

[34] See the causes, circumstances, and effects of the death of Andrew, in Giannone
(tom. iii. l. xxiii. p. 220-229), and the Life of Petrarch (Mémoires, tom. ii. p. 143-148,
245-250, 375-379, notes, p. 21-37). The Abbé de Sade *wishes* to extenuate her
guilt.

[35] The advocate who pleaded against Jane could add nothing to the logical force
and brevity of his master's epistle. Johanna! inordinata vita præcedens, retentio
potestatis in regno, neglecta vindicta, vir alter susceptus, et excusatio subsequens,
necis viri tui te probant fuisse participem et consortem. Jane of Naples and Mary
of Scotland have a singular conformity.

[36] See the Epistola Hortatoria de Capessendâ Republicâ, from Petrarch to
Nicholas Rienzi (Opp. p. 535-540), and the fifth eclogue or pastoral, a perpetual
and obscure allegory.

learned that the ancient tribunes, so strong and sacred in the public opinion, were not distinguished in style, habit, or appearance, from an ordinary plebeian;[37] and that, as often as they visited the city on foot, a single *viator*, or beadle, attended the exercise of their office.   The Gracchi would have frowned or smiled, could they have read the sonorous titles and epithets of their successor, "NICHOLAS, SEVERE AND MERCIFUL; DELIVERER OF ROME; DEFENDER OF ITALY;[38] FRIEND OF MANKIND, AND OF LIBERTY, PEACE, AND JUSTICE; TRIBUNE AUGUST": his theatrical pageants had prepared the revolution; but Rienzi abused, in luxury and pride, the political maxim of speaking to the eyes as well as the understanding of the multitude.   From nature he had received the gift of an handsome person,[39] till it was swelled and disfigured by intemperance; and his propensity to laughter was corrected in the magistrate by the affectation of gravity and sternness.   He was clothed, at least on public occasions, in a parti-coloured robe of velvet or satin, lined with fur and embroidered with gold; the rod of justice which he carried in his hand was a sceptre of polished steel, crowned with a globe and cross of gold, and enclosing a small fragment of the true and holy wood.   In his civil and religious processions through the city, he rode on a white steed, the symbol of royalty; the great banner of the republic, a sun with a circle of stars, a dove with an olive-branch, was displayed over his head; a shower of gold and silver was scattered among the populace; fifty guards with halberds encompassed his person; a troop of horse preceded his march; and their tymbals and trumpets were of massy silver.

[37] In his Roman questions Plutarch (Opuscul. tom. i. p. 505, 506, edit. Græc. Hen. Steph.) states, on the most constitutional principles,· the simple greatness of the tribunes, who were not properly magistrates, but a check on magistracy.   It was their duty and interest ὁμοιοῦσθαι σχήματι καὶ στολῇ καὶ διαίτῃ τοῖς ἐπιτυγχάνουσι τῶν πολιτῶν . . . καταπατεῖσθαι δεῖ (a saying of C. Curio) καὶ μὴ σεμνὸν εἶναι τῇ δημάρχου ὄψει . . . ὅσῳ δὲ μᾶλλον ἐκταπεινοῦται τῷ σώματι, τοσούτῳ μᾶλλον αὔξεται τῇ δυνάμει, &c.   Rienzi, and Petrarch himself, were incapable perhaps of reading a Greek philosopher; but they might have imbibed the same modest doctrines from their favourite Latins, Livy and Valerius Maximus.

[38] I could not express in English the forcible though barbarous title of *Zelator* Italiæ, which Rienzi assumed.

[39] Era bell' homo (l. ii. c. 1, p. 399).   It is remarkable that the riso sarcastico of the Bracciano edition is wanting in the Roman Ms. from which Muratori has given the text.   In his second reign, when he is painted almost as a monster, Rienzi travea una ventresca tonna trionfale, a modo de uno Abbate Asiano, or Asinino (l. iii. c. 18, p. 523).

The pomp
of his
knight-
hood, A.D.
1347,
August 1
The ambition of the honours of chivalry [40] betrayed the mean-
ness of his birth and degraded the importance of his office ; and
the equestrian tribune was not less odious to the nobles whom
he adopted than to the plebeians whom he deserted.   All that
yet remained of treasure or luxury or art was exhausted on that
solemn day.   Rienzi led the procession from the Capitol to the
Lateran ; the tediousness of the way was relieved with decora-
tions and games ; the ecclesiastical, civil, and military orders
marched under their various banners; the Roman ladies attended
his wife ; and the ambassadors of Italy might loudly applaud, or
secretly deride, the novelty of the pomp.   In the evening, when
they had reached the church and palace of Constantine, he
thanked and dismissed the numerous assembly, with an invitation to the festival of the ensuing day.   From the hands of a
venerable knight he received the order of the Holy Ghost ; the
purification of the bath was a previous ceremony ; but in no step
of his life did Rienzi excite such scandal and censure as by the
[Vase of
green
basalt]
profane use of the porphyry vase in which Constantine (a foolish
legend) had been healed of his leprosy by Pope Sylvester.[41]
With equal presumption the tribune watched or reposed within
the consecrated precincts of the baptistery ; and the failure of
his state-bed was interpreted as an omen of his approaching
downfall.   At the hour of worship he shewed himself to the
returning crowds in a majestic attitude, with a robe of purple,
his sword, and gilt spurs ; but the holy rites were soon interrupted by his levity and insolence.   Rising from his throne, and
advancing towards the congregation, he proclaimed in a loud
voice, " We summon to our tribunal Pope Clement, and command him to reside in his diocese of Rome ; we also summon

[40] Strange as it may seem, this festival was not without a precedent.   In the
year 1327, two barons, a Colonna and an Ursini, the usual balance, were created
knights by the Roman people : their bath was of rose-water, their beds were decked
with royal magnificence, and they were served at St. Maria of Araceli in the Capitol
by the twenty-eight *buoni huomini*.   They afterwards received from Robert, king of
Naples, the sword of chivalry (Hist. Rom. l. i. c. 2, p. 259).   [On 26th July of this
year, 1347, Rienzi issued an edict, declaring the majesty and supremacy of the
Roman people, and abolishing all the privileges assumed by the Popes.   This edict
was submitted to a council of jurists, and was issued in the name of the Italian
nation.   See Gregorovius, vi. p. 267.]

[41] All parties believed in the leprosy and bath of Constantine (Petrarch. Epist.
Famil. vi. 2), and Rienzi justified his own conduct by observing to the court of
Avignon that a vase which had been used by a pagan could not be profaned by a
pious Christian.   Yet this crime is specified in the bull of excommunication (Hocsemius, apud du Cerceau, p. 189, 190).

the sacred college of Cardinals.[42]   We again summon the two
pretenders, Charles of Bohemia and Lewis of Bavaria, who style
themselves emperors ; we likewise summon all the electors of
Germany, to inform us on what pretence they have usurped the
inalienable right of the Roman people, the ancient and lawful
sovereigns of the empire." [43]   Unsheathing his maiden sword, he
thrice brandished it to the three parts of the world, and thrice
repeated the extravagant declaration, "And this too is mine ! "
The pope's vicar, the bishop of Orvieto, attempted to check this
career of folly ; but his feeble protest was silenced by martial
music ; and, instead of withdrawing from the assembly, he consented to dine with his brother tribune, at a table which had
hitherto been reserved for the supreme pontiff.   A banquet, such
as the Cæsars had given, was prepared for the Romans.   The
apartments, porticoes, and courts of the Lateran were spread
with innumerable tables for either sex and every condition ; a
stream of wine flowed from the nostrils of Constantine's brazen
horse ; no complaint, except of the scarcity of water, could be
heard ; and the licentiousness of the multitude was curbed by
discipline and fear.[44]   A subsoquent day was appointed for the and coro-
coronation of Rienzi ; [45]   seven crowns of different leaves or [Aug. 15]
metals were successively placed on his head by the most eminent of the Roman clergy ; [46]   they represented the seven gifts

[42] This *verbal* summons of Pope Clement VI., which rests on the authority of
the Roman historian and a Vatican Ms., is disputed by the biographer of Petrarch
(tom. ii. not. p. 70-76), with arguments rather of decency than of weight.   The court
of Avignon might not choose to agitate this delicate question.

[43] The summons of the two rival emperors, a monument of freedom and folly, is
extant in Hocsemius (Cerceau, p. 163-166). [Gregorovius (vi. p. 276) well observes :
" The Romans, accustomed to all the spectacles of history, blunted to the distinc-
tions between the sublime and the ridiculous . . . neither laughed at this edict nor
at the figure of the crazy tribune. . . . They loudly shouted their approval.   The
absurd proclamation appeared as the ultimate consequence of the claims of the city
to the Imperial majesty, with which she had formally confronted Conrad the first
of the Hohenstaufens. . . . The errors and theories of Dante and Petrarch in their
theological age explain or excuse the insane dreams of the Tribune."]

[44] [On the next day, 2nd August, a festival of the Unity of Italy was held.   Cola
assigned the banner of Italy to the Florentines, the banner of Constantine to Perugia,
the banner of freedom to Siena.]

[45] It is singular that the Roman historian should have overlooked this sevenfold
coronation, which is sufficiently proved by internal evidence, and the testimony of
Hocsemius, and even of Rienzi (Cerceau, p. 167-170, 229).

[46] [Not exactly seven crowns, but six crowns (of oak, ivy, myrtle, laurel, olive,
silver) and a globe, emblem of the world.   Rienzi believed that the ancient tribunes
were crowned with these six crowns, and thus he characteristically combined classical
antiquity with Christianity.   He was at once (Gregorovius, vi. p. 284) " Tribunus
Augustus and Candidate of the Holy Ghost ".]

of the Holy Ghost; and he still professed to imitate the example of the ancient tribunes. These extraordinary spectacles might deceive or flatter the people; and their own vanity was gratified in the vanity of their leader. But in his private life he soon deviated from the strict rule of frugality and abstinence; and the plebeians, who were awed by the splendour of the nobles, were provoked by the luxury of their equal. His wife, his son, his uncle (a barber in name and profession), exposed the contrast of vulgar manners and princely expense; and, without acquiring the majesty, Rienzi degenerated into the vices, of a king.

Fear and
hatred of
the nobles
of Rome

A simple citizen describes with pity, or perhaps with pleasure, the humiliation of the barons of Rome. "Bare-headed, their hands crossed on their breast, they stood with downcast looks in the presence of the tribune; and they trembled, good God, how they trembled!"[47] As long as the yoke of Rienzi was that of justice and their country, their conscience forced them to esteem the man whom pride and interest provoked them to hate: his extravagant conduct soon fortified their hatred by contempt; and they conceived the hope of subverting a power which was no longer so deeply rooted in the public confidence. The old animosity of the Colonna and Ursini was suspended for a moment by their common disgrace: they associated their wishes, and perhaps their designs; an assassin was seized and tortured; he accused the nobles; and, as soon as Rienzi deserved the fate, he adopted the suspicions and maxims, of a tyrant. On the same day, under various pretences, he invited to the Capitol his principal enemies, among whom were five members of the Ursini,

[Sept. 14,
A.D. 1347]

and three of the Colonna, name. But, instead of a council or a banquet, they found themselves prisoners under the sword of despotism or justice; and the consciousness of innocence or guilt might inspire them with equal apprehensions of danger. At the sound of the great bell the people assembled: they were arraigned for a conspiracy against the tribune's life; and, though some might sympathize in their distress, not a hand nor a voice was raised to rescue the first of the nobility from their impending doom. Their apparent boldness was prompted by despair;

[47] Puoi se faceva stare denante a se, mentre sedeva, li baroni tutti in piedi ritti co le vraccia piecate, e co li capucci tratti. Deh como stavano paurosi! (Hist. Rom. l. ii. c. 20, p. 439.) He saw them, and we see them.

MEDIÆVAL ROME: THE TOR DE' CONTI: 13th CENTURY

they passed in separate chambers a sleepless and painful night ;
and the venerable hero, Stephen Colonna, striking against the
door of his prison, repeatedly urged his guards to deliver him by
a speedy death from such ignominious servitude. In the morning they understood their sentence from the visit of a confessor
and the tolling of the bell. The great hall of the Capitol had
been decorated for the bloody scene with red and white hangings ;
the countenance of the tribune was dark and severe ; the swords
of the executioners were unsheathed ; and the barons were interrupted in their dying speeches by the sound of trumpets.
But in this decisive moment Rienzi was not less anxious or apprehensive than his captives : he dreaded the splendour of their
names, their surviving kinsmen, the inconstancy of the people,
the reproaches of the world ; and, after rashly offering a mortal
injury, he vainly presumed that, if he could forgive, he might
himself be forgiven. His elaborate oration was that of a Christian and a suppliant ; and, as the humble minister of the commons, he entreated his masters to pardon these noble criminals,
for whose repentance and future service he pledged his faith
and authority. " If you are spared," said the tribune, " by the
mercy of the Romans, will you not promise to support the good
estate with your lives and fortunes ? " Astonished by this marvellous clemency, the barons bowed their heads ; and, while they
devoutly repeated the oath of allegiance, might whisper a secret,
and more sincere, assurance of revenge. A priest, in the name
of the people, pronounced their absolution. They received the
communion with the tribune, assisted at the banquet, followed
the procession ; and, after every spiritual and temporal sign of
reconciliation, were dismissed in safety to their respective homes,
with the new honours and titles of generals, consuls, and patricians.[48]

During some weeks they were checked by the memory of their
danger rather than of their deliverance, till the more powerful
of the Ursini, escaping with the Colonna from the city, erected
at Marino the standard of rebellion. The fortifications of the
castle were instantly restored ; the vassals attended their lord ;
the outlaws armed against the magistrate ; the flocks and herds,

They op-
pose
Rienzi in
arms

---

[48] The original letter, in which Rienzi justifies his treatment of the Colonna
(Hocsemius, apud Du Cerceau, p. 222-229), displays, in genuine colours, the
mixture of the knave and the madman.

the harvests and vineyards, from Marino to the gates of Rome, were swept away or destroyed; and the people arraigned Rienzi as the author of the calamities which his government had taught them to forget.   In the camp Rienzi appeared to less advantage than in the rostrum; and he neglected the progress of the rebel barons till their numbers were strong and their castles impregnable.   From the pages of Livy he had not imbibed the art, or even the courage, of a general.   An army of twenty thousand Romans returned, without honour or effect, from the attack of Marino; and his vengeance was amused by painting his enemies, their heads downwards, and drowning two dogs (at least they should have been bears) as the representatives of the Ursini. The belief of his incapacity encouraged their operations: they were invited by their secret adherents; and the barons attempted, with four thousand foot and sixteen hundred horse, to enter Rome by force or surprise.   The city was prepared for their reception; the alarm bell rung all night; the gates were strictly guarded, or insolently open; and after some hesitation

Defeat and death of the Colonna, Nov. 20 they sounded a retreat.   The two first divisions had passed along the walls, but the prospect of a free entrance tempted the headstrong valour of the nobles in the rear; and, after a successful skirmish, they were overthrown and massacred without quarter by the crowds of the Roman people.   Stephen Colonna the younger, the noble spirit to whom Petrarch ascribed the restoration of Italy, was preceded or accompanied in death by his son John, a gallant youth, by his brother Peter, who might regret the ease and honours of the church, by a nephew of legitimate birth, and by two bastards of the Colonna race; and the number of seven, the seven crowns, as Rienzi styled them, of the Holy Ghost, was completed by the agony of the deplorable parent, of the veteran chief, who had survived the hope and fortune of his house.   The vision and prophecies of St. Martin and Pope Boniface had been used by the tribune to animate his troops;[49] he displayed, at least in the pursuit, the spirit of an hero; but he forgot the maxims of the ancient Romans, who abhorred the

---

[49] Rienzi, in the above-mentioned letter, ascribes to St. Martin the tribune, Boniface VIII. the enemy of Colonna, himself, and the Roman people, the glory of the day, which Villani likewise (l. xii. c. 104) describes as a regular battle.   The disorderly skirmish, the flight of the Romans. and the cowardice of Rienzi are painted in the simple and minute narrative of Fortifiocca, or the anonymous citizen (l. ii. c. 34-37).

triumphs of civil war. The conqueror ascended the Capitol; deposited his crown and sceptre on the altar; and boasted with some truth that he had cut off an ear which neither pope nor emperor had been able to amputate.[50] His base and implacable revenge denied the honours of burial; and the bodies of the Colonna, which he threatened to expose with those of the vilest malefactors, were secretly interred by the holy virgins of their name and family.[51] The people sympathized in their grief, repented of their own fury, and detested the indecent joy of Rienzi, who visited the spot where these illustrious victims had fallen. It was on that fatal spot that he conferred on his son the honour of knighthood; and the ceremony was accomplished by a slight blow from each of the horsemen of the guard, and by a ridiculous and inhuman ablution from a pool of water, which was yet polluted with patrician blood.[52]

A short delay would have saved the Colonna, the delay of a single month, which elapsed between the triumph and the exile of Rienzi. In the pride of victory, he forfeited what yet remained of his civil virtues, without acquiring the fame of military prowess. A free and vigorous opposition was formed in the city; and, when the tribune proposed in the public council[53] to impose a new tax and to regulate the government of Perugia, thirty-nine members voted against his measures; repelled the injurious charge of treachery and corruption; and urged him to prove, by their forcible exclusion, that, if the populace adhered to his cause, it was already disclaimed by the most respectable citi-

Fall and flight of the tribune Rienzi, A.D. 1347, Dec. 15

[Tax on salt]

---

[50] In describing the fall of the Colonna, I speak only of the family of Stephen the Elder, who is often confounded by the P. du Cerceau with his son. That family was extinguished, but the house has been perpetuated in the collateral branches, of which I have not a very accurate knowledge. Circumspice (says Petrarch) familiæ tuæ statum, Columniensium *domos :* solito pauciores habeat columnas. Quid ad rem ? modo fundamentale stabile solidumque permaneat.

[51] The convent of St. Silvester was founded, endowed, and protected by the Colonna cardinals, for the daughters of the family who embraced a monastic life, and who, in the year 1318, were twelve in number. The others were allowed to marry with their kinsmen in the fourth degree, and the dispensation was justified by the small number and close alliances of the noble families of Rome (Mémoires sur Petrarque, tom. i. p. 110, tom. ii. p. 401).

[52] Petrarch wrote a stiff and pedantic letter of consolation (Fam. l. vii. epist. 13, p. 682, 683). The friend was lost in the patriot. Nulla toto orbe principum familia carior ; carior tamen respublica, carior Roma, carior Italia.

Je rends grâces aux Dieux de n'être pas Romain.

[53] This council and opposition is obscurely mentioned by Pollistore, a contemporary writer, who has preserved some curious and original facts (Rer. Italicorum, tom. xxv. c. 31, p. 798-804).

zens. The pope and the sacred college had never been dazzled by his specious professions ; they were justly offended by the insolence of his conduct ; a cardinal legate was sent to Italy, and, after some fruitless treaty and two personal interviews, he [Dec. 3] fulminated a bull of excommunication, in which the tribune is degraded from his office and branded with the guilt of rebellion, sacrilege, and heresy.[54] The surviving barons of Rome were now humbled to a sense of allegiance ; their interest and revenge engaged them in the service of the church ; but, as the fate of the Colonna was before their eyes, they abandoned to a private adventurer the peril and glory of the revolution. John Pepin, count of Minorbino,[55] in the kingdom of Naples, had been condemned for his crimes, or his riches, to perpetual imprisonment ; and Petrarch, by soliciting his release, indirectly contributed to the ruin of his friend. At the head of one hundred and fifty soldiers, the count of Minorbino introduced himself into Rome ; barricaded the quarter of the Colonna ; and found the enterprise as easy as it had seemed impossible. From the first alarm, the bell of the Capitol incessantly tolled ; but, instead of repairing to the well-known sound, the people was silent and inactive ; and the pusillanimous Rienzi, deploring their ingratitude with sighs and tears, abdicated the government and palace of the republic.

Revolutions of Rome, A.D. 1347-1354 [Senators : Luca Savelli and Bertoldo Orsini] Without drawing his sword, Count Pepin restored the aristocracy and the church ; three senators were chosen, and the legate, assuming the first rank, accepted his two colleagues from the rival families of Colonna and Ursini. The acts of the tribune were abolished, his head was proscribed ; yet such was the terror of his name that the barons hesitated three days before they would trust themselves in the city, and Rienzi was [Rienzi leaves Rome for Naples, March, A.D. 1348] left above a month in the castle of St. Angelo, from whence he peaceably withdrew, after labouring, without effect, to revive the affection and courage of the Romans. The vision of freedom and empire had vanished ; their fallen spirit would have ac-

[54] The briefs and bulls of Clement VI. against Rienzi are translated by the P. du Cerceau (p. 196, 232), from the Ecclesiastical Annals of Rodericus Raynaldus (A.D. 1347, No. 15, 17, 21, &c.), who found them in the archives of the Vatican.

[55] Matteo Villani describes the origin, character, and death of this count of Minorbino, a man da natura inconstante e senza sede, whose grandfather, a crafty notary, was enriched and ennobled by the spoils of the Saracens of Nocera (l. vii. c. 102, 103). See his imprisonment, and the efforts of Petrarch, tom. ii. p. 149-151.

quiesced in servitude, had it been smoothed by tranquillity and order ; and it was scarcely observed that the new senators derived their authority from the Apostolic See ; that four cardinals were appointed to reform, with dictatorial power, the state of the republic.[56]   Rome was again agitated by the bloody feuds of the barons, who detested each other and despised the com- [A.D. 1350-3] mons ; their hostile fortresses, both in town and country, again rose and were again demolished ; and the peaceful citizens, a flock of sheep, were devoured, says the Florentine historian, by these rapacious wolves.   But, when their pride and avarice had exhausted the patience of the Romans, a confraternity of the Virgin Mary protected or avenged the republic ; the bell of the Capitol was again tolled, the nobles in arms trembled in the presence of an unarmed multitude ; and of the two senators, Colonna escaped from the window of the palace, and Ursini was [Orsini stoned at the foot of the altar.   The dangerous office of tribune Feb. 15, was successively occupied by two plebeians, Cerroni and Baron- A.D. 1353] celli.   The mildness of Cerroni was unequal to the times ; and, [Cerroni, after a faint struggle, he retired with a fair reputation and A.D. 1351-2] a decent fortune to the comforts of rural life.   Devoid of eloquence or genius, Baroncelli was distinguished by a resolute [Baron- spirit : he spoke the language of a patriot, and trod in the " second footsteps of tyrants ; his suspicion was a sentence of death, and A.D. 1453] his own death was the reward of his cruelties.   Amidst the public misfortunes, the faults of Rienzi were forgotten ; and the Romans sighed for the peace and prosperity of the good estate.[57]

After an exile of seven years, the first deliverer was again Adven- restored to his country.   In the disguise of a monk or a pilgrim, Rienzi he escaped from the castle of St. Angelo, implored the friendship of the king of Hungary at Naples, tempted the ambition of every bold adventurer, mingled at Rome with the pilgrims of the jubilee, lay concealed among the hermits of the Apennine,[58]

[56] [One of these cardinals asked Petrarch his opinion on the question. Petrarch's advice was : " Snatch all this pestilential tyranny from the hands of the nobles ; not only give the *Plebs Romana* a share of the public dignities, but deprive the unworthy Senators of the office which they have so badly administered " (Gregorovius, vi. p. 330).]

[57] The troubles of Rome, from the departure to the return of Rienzi, are related by Matteo Villani (l. ii. c. 47 ; l. iii. c. 33, 57, 78) and Thomas Fortifiocca (l. iii. c. 1-4).   I have slightly passed over these secondary characters, who imitated the original tribune.

[58] [The Fraticelli of Monte Majella in the Abruzzi. Rienzi stayed there above two years, doing penance for his sins.]

and wandered through the cities of Italy, Germany, and Bohemia. His person was invisible, his name was yet formidable; and the anxiety of the court of Avignon supposes, and even magnifies, his personal merit. The emperor Charles the Fourth gave

[At Prague, July, A.D. 1350]

audience to a stranger, who frankly revealed himself as the tribune of the republic and astonished an assembly of ambassadors and princes by the eloquence of a patriot and the visions of a prophet, the downfall of tyranny and the kingdom of the

[Prisoner at Rand- nitz, A.D. 1351-2]

Holy Ghost.[59] Whatever had been his hopes, Rienzi found himself a captive; but he supported a character of independence and dignity, and obeyed, as his own choice, the irresistible summons of the supreme pontiff. The zeal of Petrarch, which had been cooled by the unworthy conduct, was rekindled by the sufferings and the presence, of his friend; and he boldly complains of the times in which the saviour of Rome was delivered

[A prisoner at Avig- non, A.D. 1351 [1352]]

by her emperor into the hands of her bishop. Rienzi was transported slowly, but in safe custody, from Prague to Avignon; his entrance into the city was that of a malefactor; in his prison he was chained by the leg; and four cardinals were named to inquire into the crimes of heresy and rebellion. But his trial and condemnation would have involved some questions which it was more prudent to leave under the veil of mystery: the temporal supremacy of the popes; the duty of residence; the civil and ecclesiastical privileges of the clergy and people of

[Death of Clement VI. Dec. 6, A.D. 1352]

Rome. The reigning pontiff well deserved the appellation of Clement; the strange vicissitudes and magnanimous spirit of the captive excited his pity and esteem; and Petrarch believes that he respected in the hero the name and sacred character of a poet.[60] Rienzi was indulged with an easy confinement and the

---

[59] These visions, of which the friends and enemies of Rienzi seem alike ignorant, are surely magnified by the zeal of Pollistore, a Dominican inquisitor (Rer. Ital. tom. xxv. c. 36, p. 819). Had the tribune taught that Christ was succeeded by the Holy Ghost, that the tyranny of the pope would be abolished, he might have been convicted of heresy and treason without offending the Roman people. [The letters of Rienzi at this time (given in Papencordt's work, cited above, p. 269, note 20) are very important. They portray the state of Rome; indict the Pope; and are thoroughly Ghibelline in spirit, expressing the need of keeping the secular and ecclesiastical powers apart. Gregorovius says (vi. 346): "The tribune in chains at Prague was more dangerous to the Papacy than he had been when at the height of his power in the Capitol. He now expressed, like the Monarchists, the necessity for mankind of a reformation; and this constitutes the serious importance of this extraordinary Roman, and secures him a place in history."]

[60] The astonishment, the envy almost, of Petrarch is a proof, if not of the truth of this incredible fact, at least of his own veracity. The Abbé de Sade (Mémoires,

use of books ; and in the assiduous study of Livy and the Bible
he sought the cause and the consolation of his misfortunes.

The succeeding pontificate of Innocent the Sixth opened a
new prospect of his deliverance and restoration ; and the court
of Avignon was persuaded that the successful rebel could alone
appease and reform the anarchy of the metropolis.   After a
solemn profession of fidelity, the Roman tribune was sent into
Italy with the title of senator ; but the death of Baroncelli appeared to supersede the use of his mission ; and the legate, Cardinal Albornoz,[61] a consummate statesman, allowed him, with
reluctance, and without aid, to undertake the perilous experiment.
His first reception was equal to his wishes : the day of his entrance was a public festival, and his eloquence and authority
revived the laws of the good estate.   But this momentary sun-
shine was soon clouded by his own vices and those of the people :
in the Capitol, he might often regret the prison of Avignon ; and,
after a second administration of four months, Rienzi was massacred in a tumult which had been fomented by the Roman
barons.   In the society of the Germans and Bohemians, he is
said to have contracted the habits of intemperance and cruelty ;
adversity had chilled his enthusiasm, without fortifying his reason
or virtue ; and that youthful hope, that lively assurance, which is
the pledge of success, was now succeeded by the cold impotence
of distrust and despair.   The tribune had reigned with absolute
dominion, by the choice and in the hearts of the Romans ; the
senator was the servile minister of a foreign court ; and, while
he was suspected by the people, he was abandoned by the prince.
The legate Albornoz, who seemed desirous of his ruin, inflexibly
refused all supplies of men and money ; a faithful subject could
no longer presume to touch the revenues of the apostolic chamber ; and the first idea of a tax was the signal of clamour and
sedition.   Even his justice was tainted with the guilt or reproach
of selfish cruelty ; the most virtuous citizen of Rome was sacrificed to his jealousy ; and in the execution of a public robber,

*Rienzi,
senator of
Rome, A.D.
1354*

[August 1]

---

tom. iii. p. 242) quotes the vith epistle of the xiiith book of Petrarch, but it is of the
royal Ms., which he consulted, and not of the ordinary Basil edition (p. 920).

[61] Ægidius or Giles Albornoz, a noble Spaniard, archbishop of Toledo, and
cardinal legate in Italy (A.D. 1353-1367), restored, by his arms and counsels, the
temporal dominion of the popes. His life has been separately written by Sepulveda ;
but Dryden could not reasonably suppose that his name, or that of Wolsey, had
reached the ears of the Mufti in Don Sebastian.

[Execution of Monreale, August 29] from whose purse he had been assisted, the magistrate too much forgot, or too much remembered, the obligations of the debtor.[62] A civil war exhausted his treasures, and the patience of the city; the Colonna maintained their hostile station at Palestrina; and his mercenaries soon despised a leader whose ignorance and fear were envious of all subordinate merit. In the death as in the life of Rienzi, the hero and the coward were strangely mingled. When the Capitol was invested by a furious multitude, when he was basely deserted by his civil and military servants, the intrepid senator, waving the banner of liberty, presented himself on the balcony, addressed his eloquence to the various passions of the Romans, and laboured to persuade them that in the same cause himself and the republic must either stand or fall. His oration was interrupted by a volley of imprecations and stones; and, after an arrow had transpierced his hand, he sunk into abject despair, and fled weeping to the inner chambers, from whence he was let down by a sheet before the windows of the prison. Destitute of aid or hope, he was besieged till the evening: the doors of the Capitol were destroyed with axes and fire; and, while the senator attempted to escape in a plebeian habit, he was discovered and dragged to the platform of the palace, the fatal scene of his judgments and executions. A whole hour, without voice or motion, he stood amidst the multitude, half naked and half dead; their rage was hushed into curiosity and wonder; the last feelings of reverence and compassion yet struggled in his favour; and they might have prevailed, if a bold assassin had not plunged a dagger in his breast. He fell senseless with the first stroke; the impotent revenge of his enemies inflicted a thousand wounds; and the senator's body was [His death, A.D. 1354, Sept. [Oct.] 8] abandoned to the dogs, to the Jews, and to the flames. Posterity will compare the virtues and the failings of this extraordinary man; but in a long period of anarchy and servitude the name of Rienzi has often been celebrated as the deliverer of his country and the last of the Roman patriots.[63]

---

[62] From Matteo Villani and Fortifiocca, the P. du Cerceau (p. 344-394) has extracted the life and death of the Chevalier Montreal, the life of a robber, and the death of an hero. At the head of a free company, the first that desolated Italy, he became rich and formidable; he had money in all the banks, 60,000 ducats in Padua alone.

[63] The exile, second government, and death of Rienzi are minutely related by the anonymous Roman who appears neither his friend nor his enemy (l. iii. c. 11-25). Petrarch, who loved the *tribune*, was indifferent to the fate of the *senator*.

The first and most generous wish of Petrarch was the restora- Petrarch invites and upbraids the emperor Charles IV. A.D. 1355, January-May
tion of a free republic ; but, after the exile and death of his
plebeian hero, he turned his eyes from the tribune to the king
of the Romans. The Capitol was yet stained with the blood of
Rienzi, when Charles the Fourth descended from the Alps to
obtain the Italian and Imperial crowns. In his passage through
Milan he received the visit, and repaid the flattery, of the poet-
laureat ; accepted a medal of Augustus ; and promised, without [Coronation, April 5, Easter Day]
a smile, to imitate the founder of the Roman monarchy. A false
application of the names and maxims of antiquity was the source
of the hopes and disappointments of Petrarch ; yet he could not
overlook the difference of times and characters : the immeasurable
distance between the first Cæsars and a Bohemian prince, who by
the favour of the clergy had been elected the titular head of the
German aristocracy. Instead of restoring to Rome her glory and
her provinces, he had bound himself, by a secret treaty with the
pope, to evacuate the city on the day of his coronation ; and his
shameful retreat was pursued by the reproaches of the patriot
bard.[64]

After the loss of liberty and empire, his third and more humble He solicits the popes of Avignon to fix their residence at Rome
wish was to reconcile the shepherd with his flock ; to recall the
Roman bishop to his ancient and peculiar diocese. In the fervour of youth, with the authority of age, Petrarch addressed his
exhortations to five successive popes, and his eloquence was
always inspired by the enthusiasm of sentiment and the freedom
of language.[65] The son of a citizen of Florence invariably preferred the country of his birth to that of his education ; and
Italy, in his eyes, was the queen and garden of the world.
Amidst her domestic factions, she was doubtless superior to
France both in art and science, in wealth and politeness ; but
the difference could scarcely support the epithet of barbarous,
which he promiscuously bestows on the countries beyond the
Alps. Avignon, the mystic Babylon, the sink of vice and corruption, was the object of his hatred and contempt; but he

[64] The hopes and the disappointment of Petrarch are agreeably described in his own words by the French biographer (Mémoires, tom. iii. p. 575-413) ; but the deep though secret wound was the coronation or Zanubi, the poet-laureat, by Charles IV.

[65] See, in his accurate and amusing biographer, the application of Petrarch and Rome to Benedict XII. in the year 1334 (Mémoires, tom. i. p. 261-265), to Clement VI. in 1342 (tom. ii. p. 45-47), and to Urban V. in 1366 (tom. iii. p. 677-691) ; his praise (p. 711-715) and excuse (p. 771) of the last of these pontiffs. His angry contro-versy on the respective merits of France and Italy may be found (Opp. p. 1068-1085).

forgets that her scandalous vices were not the growth of the
soil, and that in every residence they would adhere to the power
and luxury of the papal court.   He confesses that the successor
of St. Peter is the bishop of the universal church ; yet it was not
on the banks of the Rhône, but of the Tiber, that the apostle
had fixed his everlasting throne ; and, while every city in the
Christian world was blessed with a bishop, the metropolis alone
was desolate and forlorn.   Since the removal of the Holy See,
the sacred buildings of the Lateran and the Vatican, their altars
and their saints, were left in a state of poverty and decay ; and
Rome was often painted under the image of a disconsolate
matron, as if the wandering husband could be reclaimed by the
homely portrait of the age and infirmities of his weeping spouse.[66]
But the cloud which hung over the seven hills would be dispelled
by the presence of their lawful sovereign : eternal fame, the
prosperity of Rome, and the peace of Italy would be the recompense of the pope who should dare to embrace this generous
resolution.   Of the five whom Petrarch exhorted, the three first,
John the Twenty-second, Benedict the Twelfth, and Clement
the Sixth, were importuned or amused by the boldness of the
orator ; but the memorable change which had been attempted
by Urban the Fifth was finally accomplished by Gregory the
Eleventh.   The execution of their design was opposed by weighty
and almost insuperable obstacles.   A king of France, who has
deserved the epithet of Wise, was unwilling to release them
from a local dependence : the cardinals, for the most part his
subjects, were attached to the language, manners, and climate
of Avignon ; to their stately palaces ; above all, to the wines of
Burgundy.[67]   In their eyes, Italy was foreign or hostile ; and
they reluctantly embarked at Marseilles, as if they had been
sold or banished into the land of the Saracens.   Urban the
Fifth resided three years in the Vatican with safety and honour ;
his sanctity was protected by a guard of two thousand horse ;
and the king of Cyprus, the queen of Naples, and the emperors

Return of
Urban V.
A.D. 1367,
October 16-
A.D. 1370,
April 17

[66]   Squalida sed quoniam facies, neglectaque cultu
            Cæsaries ; multisque malis lassata senectus
            Eripuit solitam effigiem : vetus accipe nomen ;
            Roma vocor.   (Carm. l. ii. p. 77).
He spins this allegory beyond all measure or patience.   The epistles to Urban V.
in prose are more simple and persuasive (Senilium, l. vii. p. 811-827 ; l. ix. epist. i.
p. 844-854).
        [67] [*Vinum Bennense*, " Beaune ".]

of the East and West devoutly saluted their common father in the chair of St. Peter. But the joy of Petrarch and the Italians was soon turned into grief and indignation. Some reasons of public or private moment, his own impatience or the prayers of the cardinals, recalled Urban to France; and the approaching election was saved from the tyrannic patriotism of the Romans. The powers of Heaven were interested in their cause: Bridget of Sweden, a saint and pilgrim, disapproved the return, and foretold the death, of Urban the Fifth; the migration of Gregory the Eleventh was encouraged by St. Catherine of Sienna, the spouse of Christ and ambassadress of the Florentines; and the popes themselves, the great masters of human credulity, appear to have listened to these visionary females.[68] Yet those celestial admonitions were supported by some arguments of temporal policy. The residence of Avignon had been invaded by a hostile violence: at the head of thirty thousand robbers, an hero had extorted ransom and absolution from the vicar of Christ and the sacred college; and the maxim of the French warriors, to spare the people and plunder the church, was a new heresy of the most dangerous import.[69] While the pope was driven from Avignon, he was strenuously invited to Rome. The senate and people acknowledged him as their lawful sovereign, and laid at

Final return of Greg. XI. A.D. 1377, Jan. 17

---

[68] I have not leisure to expatiate on the legends of St. Bridget or St. Catherine, the last of which might furnish some amusing stories. Their effect on the mind of Gregory XI. is attested by the last solemn words of the dying pope, who admonished the assistants, ut caverent ab hominibus, sive viris, sive mulieribus, sub specie religionis loquentibus visiones sui capitis, quia per tales ipse seductus, &c. (Baluz. Not. ad Vit. Pap. Avenionensium, tom. i. p. 1223). [St. Bridget was the wife of a great Swedish noble, Ulf Gudmarson. Her life by Bartholdus de Roma is published in the Acta Sanctorum, 8th October, iv. p. 495 *sqq.* Her revelations have been frequently edited, most recently (Revel. Selectæ) by A. Heuser, 1851. There is also an English translation: "Certayne revelacyons of St. Brigitte," by Th. Godfrey (London, no date). The most important monograph is by a Swede, F. Hammerich, and has been done into German by A. Michelsen: St. Brigitta die nördische Prophetin und Ordensstifterin, 1872. There is also a Danish monograph by A. Brinkmann (1893); and a French by the Comtesse de Flavigny: Sainte Brigitte de Suede, 1892.—There is an immense literature on Catherine of Siena. Chavin de Malan's Histoire de Sainte Catherine de Sienne, 2 vols., 1846, and Augusta T. Drane's History of St. Catherine of Siena with her companions (with a translation of her treatise on Consummate Perfection), 2 vols., 1887 (3rd ed., 1899), may be mentioned. The letters of the saint have been edited by N. Tommaseo in 4 vols., 1860.]

[69] This predatory expedition is related by Froissart (Chronique, tom. i. p. 230), and in the life of du Guesclin (Collection Générale des Mémoires Historiques, tom. iv. c. 16, p. 107-113). As early as the year 1361, the court of Avignon had been molested by similar freebooters, who afterwards passed the Alps (Mémoires sur Pétrarque, tom. iii. p. 563-569).

his feet the keys of the gates, the bridges, and the fortresses; of the quarter at least beyond the Tiber.[70] But this loyal offer was accompanied by a declaration that they could no longer suffer the scandal and calamity of his absence; and that his obstinacy would finally provoke them to revive and assert the primitive right of election.   The abbot of Mount Cassin had been consulted whether he would accept the triple crown[71] from the clergy and people: "I am a citizen of Rome,"[72] replied that venerable ecclesiastic, "and my first law is the voice of my country." [73]

His death,
A.D. 1378

If superstition will interpret an untimely death,[74] if the merit of counsels be judged from the event, the heavens may seem to frown on a measure of such apparent reason and propriety. Gregory the Eleventh did not survive above fourteen months

[70] Fleury alleges, from the annals of Odericus Raynaldus, the original treaty which was signed the 21st of December, 1376, between Gregory XI. and the Romans (Hist. Ecclés. tom. xx. p. 275).

[71] The first crown or regnum (Ducange, Gloss. Latin. tom. v. p. 702) on the Episcopal mitre of the popes is ascribed to the gift of Constantine [to Pope Sylvester] or Clovis.   The second was added by Boniface VIII. as the emblem, not only of a spiritual, but of a temporal, kingdom.   The three states of the church are represented by the triple crown which was introduced by John XXII. or Benedict XII. (Mémoires sur Pétrarque, tom. i. p. 258, 259).   [The regnum or pointed tiara "originally consisted of white peacock's feathers, and was later ornamented with precious stones, encircled by a gold rim, and afterwards by three diadems; the whole was surmounted by a carbuncle".   Gregorovius, v. p. 8 (where there is a description of the papal coronation).   The three diadems are said to have been added by Nicholas I., Boniface VIII., and Urban V.   Monograph: Zöpffel, Die Papstwahlen und die mit ihnen im nächsten Zusammenhang stehenden Ceremonien vom 11 bis 14 Jahrhundert, 1871.]

[72] Baluze (Not. ad Pap. Avenion. tom. i. p. 1194, 1195) produces the original evidence, which attests the threats of the Roman ambassadors, and the resignation of the abbot of mount Cassin, qui ultro se offerens respondit se civem Romanum esse, et illud velle quod ipsi vellent.

[73] The return of the popes from Avignon to Rome, and their reception by the people, are related in the original Lives of Urban V. and Gregory XI. in Baluze (Vit. Paparum Avenionensium, tom. i. p. 363-486) and Muratori (Script. Rer. Italicarum, tom. iii. p. i. p. 610-712).   In the disputes of the schism, every circumstance was severely though partially scrutinised, more especially in the great inquest which decided the obedience of Castile, and to which Baluze, in his notes, so often and so largely appeals, from a Ms. volume in the Harley library (p. 1281, &c.).   [See the works of Theodoricus de Niem: De scismate (ed. Erler, 1890); Vitæ Pontificum Romanorum a Nicolao IV. usque ad Urbanum V. with an anonymous continuation to A.D. 1418 (in Eccard, Corpus hist. medii ævi, i. p. 1461 sqq.); Nemus Unionis (collection of documents for Gregory XII. and Benedict XIII.), ed. Schard (with the De scismate), 1566.   Monograph: G. Erler, Dietrich von Nieheim; sein Leben und seine Schriften, 1887.]

[74] Can the death of a good man be esteemed a punishment by those who believe in the immortality of the soul?   They betray the instability of their faith.   Yet, as a mere philosopher, I cannot agree with the Greeks, ὃν οἱ θεοὶ φιλοῦσιν ἀποθνῄσκει νέος (Brunck, Poetæ Gnomici, p. 231).   See in Herodotus (l. i. c. 31) the moral and pleasing tale of the Argive youths.

his return to the Vatican; and his decease was followed by the great schism of the West, which distracted the Latin church above forty years. The sacred college was then composed of twenty-two cardinals: six of these had remained at Avignon; eleven Frenchmen, one Spaniard, and four Italians entered the conclave in the usual form. Their choice was not yet limited to the purple; and their unanimous votes acquiesced in the arch-bishop of Bari, a subject of Naples, conspicuous for his zeal and learning, who ascended the throne of St. Peter under the name of Urban the Sixth. The epistle of the sacred college affirms his free and regular election, which had been inspired, as usual, by the Holy Ghost; he was adored, invested, and crowned, with the customary rights; his temporal authority was obeyed at Rome and Avignon, and his ecclesiastical supremacy was acknowledged in the Latin world. During several weeks, the cardinals attended their new master with the fairest professions of attachment and loyalty, till the summer-heats permitted a decent escape from the city. But, as soon as they were united at Anagni and Fundi, in a place of security, they cast aside the mask, accused their own falsehood and hypocrisy, excommunicated the apostate and antichrist of Rome, and proceeded to a new election of Robert of Geneva, Clement the Seventh, whom they announced to the nations as the true and rightful vicar of Christ. Their first choice, an involuntary and illegal act, was annulled by the fear of death and the menaces of the Romans; and their complaint is justified by the strong evidence of probability and fact. The twelve French cardinals, above two-thirds of the votes, were masters of the election; and, whatever might be their provincial jealousies, it cannot fairly be presumed that they would have sacrificed their right and interest to a foreign candidate, who would never restore them to their native country. In the various and often inconsistent narratives,[75] the shades of popular violence are more darkly or faintly coloured; but the licentiousness of the seditious Romans was inflamed by a sense of their privileges, and the danger of a second emigration. The conclave was intimidated by the shouts, and encompassed by the

(margin note: Election of Urban VI. April 9)

(margin note: Election of Clement VII. Sept. 21)

---

[75] In the first book of the Histoire du Concile de Pise, M. Lenfant has abridged and compared the original narratives of the adherents of Urban and Clement, of the Italians and Germans, the French and Spaniards. The latter appear to be the most active and loquacious, and every fact and word in the original Lives of Gregory XI. and Clement VII. are supported in the notes of their editor Baluze.

arms, of thirty thousand rebels ; the bells of the Capitol and St.
Peter's rang in alarm : "Death, or an Italian pope !" was the
universal cry ; the same threat was repeated by the twelve bannerets or chiefs of the quarters, in the form of charitable advice ;
some preparations were made for burning the obstinate cardinals ;
and, had they chosen a Transalpine subject, it is probable that
they would never have departed alive from the Vatican. The
same constraint imposed the necessity of dissembling in the eyes
of Rome and of the world ; the pride and cruelty of Urban presented a more inevitable danger ; and they soon discovered the
features of the tyrant, who could walk in his garden and recite
his breviary, while he heard from an adjacent chamber six cardinals groaning on the rack. His inflexible zeal, which loudly
censured their luxury and vice, would have attached them to
the stations and duties of their parishes at Rome ; and, had he
not fatally delayed a new promotion, the French cardinals would
have been reduced to an helpless minority in the sacred college.
For these reasons, and in the hope of repassing the Alps, they
rashly violated the peace and unity of the church ; and the merits
of their double choice are yet agitated in the Catholic schools.[76]
The vanity, rather than the interest, of the nation determined
the court and clergy of France.[77] The states of Savoy, Sicily,
Cyprus, Arragon, Castille, Navarre, and Scotland were inclined
by their example and authority to the obedience of Clement the
Seventh, and, after his decease, of Benedict the Thirteenth.
Rome and the principal states of Italy, Germany, Portugal, England,[78] the Low Countries, and the kingdoms of the North, adhered to the prior election of Urban the Sixth, who was succeeded by Boniface the Ninth, Innocent the Seventh, and
Gregory the Twelfth.

From the banks of the Tiber and the Rhône, the hostile

[76] The ordinal numbers of the popes seem to decide the question against
Clement VII. and Benedict XIII. who are boldly stigmatized as anti-popes by the
Italians, while the French are content with authorities and reasons to plead the
cause of doubt and toleration (Baluz. in Præfat.). It is singular, or rather it is not
singular, that saints, visions, and miracles should be common to both parties.

[77] Baluze strenuously labours (Not. p. 1271-1280) to justify the pure and pious
motives of Charles V., king of France : he refused to hear the arguments of Urban ;
but were not the Urbanists equally deaf to the reasons of Clement, &c. ?

[78] An epistle, or declamation, in the name of Edward III. (Baluz. Vit. Pap.
Avenion. tom. i. p. 553) displays the zeal of the English nation against the Clementines. Nor was their zeal confined to words ; the bishop of Norwich led a crusade
of 60,000 bigots beyond sea (Hume's History, vol. iii. p. 57, 58).

pontiffs encountered each other with the pen and the sword; Great schism of the West, A.D. 1378-1418
the civil and ecclesiastical order of society was disturbed; and
the Romans had their full share of the mischiefs, of which they
may be arraigned as the primary authors.[79] They had vainly
flattered themselves with the hope of restoring the seat of the
ecclesiastical monarchy, and of relieving their poverty with the
tributes and offerings of the nations; but the separation of
France and Spain diverted the stream of lucrative devotion; Calamities of Rome
nor could the loss be compensated by the two jubilees which
were crowded into the space of ten years. By the avocations
of the schism, by foreign arms and popular tumults, Urban the
Sixth and his three successors were often compelled to interrupt
their residence in the Vatican. The Colonna and Ursini still
exercised their deadly feuds; the bannerets of Rome asserted
and abused the privileges of a republic; the vicars of Christ,
who had levied a military force, chastised their rebellion with
the gibbet, the sword, and the dagger; and, in a friendly conference, eleven deputies of the people were perfidiously murdered
and cast into the street. Since the invasion of Robert the Norman, the Romans had pursued their domestic quarrels without
the dangerous interposition of a stranger. But, in the disorders
of the schism, an aspiring neighbour, Ladislaus king of Naples,
alternately supported and betrayed the pope and the people;
by the former he was declared *gonfalonier*, or general of the
church, while the latter submitted to his choice the nomination
of their magistrates. Besieging Rome by land and water, he
thrice entered the gates as a barbarian conqueror; profaned the
altars, violated the virgins, pillaged the merchants, performed
his devotions at St. Peter's, and left a garrison in the castle of
St. Angelo. His arms were sometimes unfortunate, and to a
delay of three days he was indebted for his life and crown; but
Ladislaus triumphed in his turn, and it was only his premature
death that could save the metropolis and the ecclesiastical state
from the ambitious conqueror, who had assumed the title, or at
least the powers, of king of Rome.[80]

[79] Besides the general historians, the Diaries of Delphinus Gentilis, Peter
Antonius, and Stephen Infessura, in the great Collection of Muratori, represent the
state and misfortunes of Rome.

[80] It is supposed by Giannone (tom. iii. p. 292) that he styled himself Rex
Romæ, a title unknown to the world since the expulsion of Tarquin. But a nearer
inspection has justified the reading of Rex Ramæ, of Rama, an obscure kingdom
annexed to the crown of Hungary.

I have not undertaken the ecclesiastical history of the schism; but Rome, the object of these last chapters, is deeply interested in the disputed succession of her sovereigns. The first counsels for the peace and union of Christendom arose from the university of Paris, from the faculty of the Sorbonne, whose doctors were esteemed, at least in the Gallican church, as the most consummate masters of theological science.[81] Prudently waiving all invidious inquiry into the origin and merits of the dispute, they proposed, as an healing measure, that the two pretenders of Rome and Avignon should abdicate at the same time, after qualifying the cardinals of the adverse factions to join in a legitimate election; and that the nations should *subtract* [82] their obedience, if either of the competitors preferred his own interest to that of the public. At each vacancy, these physicians of the church deprecated the mischiefs of an hasty choice; but the policy of the conclave and the ambition of its members were deaf to reason and entreaties; and whatsoever promises were made, the pope could never be bound by the oaths of the cardinal. During fifteen years, the pacific designs of the university were eluded by the arts of the rival pontiffs, the scruples or passions of their adherents, and the vicissitudes of French factions that ruled the insanity of Charles the Sixth. At length a vigorous resolution was embraced; and a solemn embassy, of the titular patriarch of Alexandria, two archbishops, five bishops, five abbots, three knights, and twenty doctors, was sent to the courts of Avignon and Rome, to require, in the name of the church and king, the abdication of the two pretenders, of Peter de Luna, who styled himself Benedict the Thirteenth, and of Angelo Corrario, who assumed the name of Gregory the Twelfth. For the ancient honour of Rome and the success of their com-

---

[81] The leading and decisive part which France assumed in the schism is stated by Peter du Puis, in a separate history, extracted from authentic records, and inserted in the seventh volume of the last and best edition of his friend Thuanus (p. xi. p. 110-184).

[82] Of this measure, John Gerson, a stout doctor, was the author or the champion. The proceedings of the university of Paris [of which he was chancellor] and the Gallican church were often prompted by his advice, and are copiously displayed in his theological writings, of which Le Clerc (Bibliothèque Choisie, tom. x. p. 1-78) has given a valuable extract. John Gerson acted an important part in the councils of Pisa and Constance. [The collective works of Gerson were issued several times in the 15th century. The best edition is that of Ellies Du Pin, 1706. Monographs : J. B. Schwab, Johannes Gerson, 1858 ; A. L. Masson, Jean Gerson, sa vie, son temps, ses œuvres, 1894.]

mission, the ambassadors solicited a conference with the magistrates of the city, whom they gratified by a positive declaration that the most Christian king did not entertain a wish of transporting the holy see from the Vatican, which he considered as the genuine and proper seat of the successor of St. Peter.   In the name of the senate and people, an eloquent Roman asserted their desire to co-operate in the union of the church, deplored the temporal and spiritual calamities of the long schism, and requested the protection of France against the arms of the king of Naples.   The answers of Benedict and Gregory were alike edifying and alike deceitful; and, in evading the demand of their abdication, the two rivals were animated by a common spirit.   They agreed on the necessity of a previous interview, but the time, the place, and the manner could never be ascertained by mutual consent.   " If the one advances," says a servant of Gregory, " the other retreats; the one appears an animal fearful of the land, the other a creature apprehensive of the water.   And thus, for a short remnant of life and power, will these aged priests endanger the peace and salvation of the Christian world." [83]

The Christian world was at length provoked by their obstinacy and fraud: they were deserted by their cardinals, who embraced each other as friends and colleagues; and their revolt was supported by a numerous assembly of prelates and ambassadors.   With equal justice the council of Pisa deposed the popes of Rome and Avignon; the conclave was unanimous in the choice of Alexander the Fifth,[84] and his vacant seat was soon filled by a similar election of John the Twenty-third, the most profligate of mankind.[85]   But, instead of extinguishing the schism, the rashness of the French and Italians had given a third pretender to the chair of St. Peter.   Such new claims of the synod and conclave were disputed; three kings, of Germany,

Council of Pisa, A.D. 1409

[June 5]

[Greek Pope]

[Baldassarre Cossa]

[A.D. 1410]

[83] Leonardus Brunus Aretinus, one of the revivers of classic learning in Italy, who, after serving many years as secretary in the Roman court, retired to the honourable office of chancellor of the republic of Florence (Fabric. Bibliot. medii Ævi, tom. i. p. 290).   Lenfant has given the version of this curious epistle (Concile de Pise, tom. i. p. 192-195).   [The Letters of Leonardus were edited in eight books by L. Mehns, 1741.]

[84] [Pietro Filargo was a native of Candia.   The last Greek Pope was John VII. (elected A.D. 705).]

[85] [Theodoric of Niem, Historia de vita Johannis XXIII., in Meibomius, Scr. rer. Germ. i. p. 5 sqq.   C. Hunger, Zur Geschichte Papst Johanns xxiii., 1876.]

Hungary, and Naples, adhered to the cause of Gregory the Twelfth; and Benedict the Thirteenth, himself a Spaniard, was acknowledged by the devotion and patriotism of that powerful nation. The rash proceedings of Pisa were corrected by the council of Constance; the emperor Sigismond acted a conspicuous part as the advocate or protector of the Catholic church; and the number and weight of civil and ecclesiastical members might seem to constitute the states-general of Europe. Of the three popes, John the Twenty-third was the first victim: he fled, and was brought back a prisoner; the most scandalous charges were suppressed; the vicar of Christ was only accused of piracy, murder, rape, sodomy, and incest; and, after subscribing his own condemnation, he expiated in prison the imprudence of trusting his person to a free city beyond the Alps. Gregory the Twelfth, whose obedience was reduced to the narrow precincts of Rimini, descended with more honour from the throne, and his ambassador convened the session in which he renounced the title and authority of lawful pope. To vanquish the obstinacy of Benedict the Thirteenth, or his adherents, the emperor in person undertook a journey from Constance to Perpignan. The kings of Castille, Arragon, Navarre, and Scotland obtained an equal and honourable treaty; with the concurrence of the Spaniards, Benedict was deposed by the council; but the harmless old man was left in a solitary castle to excommunicate twice each day the rebel kingdoms which had deserted his cause. After thus eradicating the remains of the schism, the synod of Constance proceeded, with slow and cautious steps, to elect the sovereign of Rome and the head of the church. On this momentous occasion, the college of twenty-three cardinals was fortified with thirty deputies; six of whom were chosen in each of the five great nations of Christendom, the Italian, the German, the French, the Spanish, and the *English*: [86] the interference of strangers

Council of Constance, A.D. 1414-1418

[July 4, A.D. 1415]

[Benedict at Peniscola; dies A.D. 1423]

---

[86] I cannot overlook this great national cause, which was vigorously maintained by the English ambassadors against those of France. The latter contended that Christendom was essentially distributed into the four great nations and votes of Italy, Germany, France, and Spain; and that the lesser kingdoms (such as England, Denmark, Portugal, &c.) were comprehended under one or other of these great divisions. The English asserted that the British islands, of which they were the head, should be considered as a fifth and co-ordinate nation with an equal vote; and every argument of truth or fable was introduced to exalt the dignity of their country. Including England, Scotland, Wales, the four kingdoms of Ireland,

was softened by their generous preference of an Italian and a
Roman; and the hereditary as well as personal merit of Otho Election of
Colonna recommended him to the conclave. Rome accepted Martin V.
with joy and obedience the noblest of her sons, the ecclesiastical
state was defended by his powerful family, and the elevation of
Martin the Fifth is the æra of the restoration and establishment of the popes in the Vatican.[87]

The royal prerogative of coining money, which had been Martin V.
exercised near three hundred years by the senate, was *first* re- A.D. 1417,
sumed by Martin the Fifth,[88] and his image and superscription Eugenius
introduce the series of the papal medals. Of his two immedi- 1431,
ate successors, Eugenius the Fourth was the *last* pope expelled Nicholas
by the tumults of the Roman people,[89] and Nicholas the Fifth, Last revolt
the *last* who was importuned by the presence of a Roman of Rome,
emperor.[90] I. The conflict of Eugenius with the fathers of A.D. 1434,
Basil, and the weight or apprehension of a new excise, em- May 29-Oct.
26

---

and the Orkneys, the British islands are decorated with eight royal crowns, and
discriminated by four or five languages, English, Welsh, Cornish, Scotch, Irish, &c.
The greater island, from north to south, measures 800 miles, or 40 days' journey;
and England alone contains 32 counties, and 52,000 parish churches (a bold
account!), besides cathedrals, colleges, priories and hospitals. They celebrate
the mission of St. Joseph of Arimathea, the birth of Constantine, and the legatine
powers of the two primates, without forgetting the testimony of Bartholemy de
Glanville (A.D. 1360), who reckons only four Christian kingdoms, 1. of Rome,
2. of Constantinople, 3. of Ireland, which had been transferred to the English
monarchs, and 4. of Spain. Our countrymen prevailed in the council, but the
victories of Henry V. added much weight to their arguments. The adverse plead-
ings were found at Constance by Sir Robert Wingfield, ambassador from Henry VIII.
to the emperor Maximilian I. and by him printed in 1517, at Louvain. From a
Leipsic Ms. they are more correctly published in the Collection of von der Hardt,
tom. v.; but I have only seen Lenfant's abstract of these acts (Concile de Constance,
tom. ii. p. 447, 453, &c.).

[87] The histories of the three successive councils, Pisa, Constance, and Basil,
have been written with a tolerable degree of candour, industry, and elegance, by a
Protestant minister, M. Lenfant, who retired from France to Berlin. They form
six volumes in quarto; and, as Basil is the worst, so Constance is the best, part of
the Collection. [See above, p. 105, note 40.]

[88] See the xxviith Dissertation of the Antiquities of Muratori, and the ist Instruction of the Science des Médailles of the Père Joubert and the Baron de la Bastie.
The Metallic History of Martin V. and his successors has been composed by two
monks, Moulinet a Frenchman, and Bonanni an Italian; but I understand that the
first part of the series is restored from more recent coins.

[89] Besides the lives of Eugenius IV. (Rerum Italic. tom. iii. p. i. p. 869, and
[the Life by Vespasianus Florentinus] tom. xxv. p. 256), the Diaries of Paul
Petroni and Stephen Infessura are the best original evidence for the revolt of the
Romans against Eugenius IV. The former, who lived at the time and on the spot,
speaks the language of a citizen equally afraid of priestly and popular tyranny.

[90] The coronation of Frederic III. is described by Lenfant (Concile de Basle,
tom. ii. p. 276-288) from Æneas Sylvius, a spectator and actor in that splendid
scene.

boldened and provoked the Romans to usurp the temporal government of the city. They rose in arms, selected seven governors of the republic and a constable of the Capitol; imprisoned the pope's nephew; besieged his person in the palace; and shot volleys of arrows into his bark as he escaped down the Tiber in the habit of a monk. But he still possessed in the castle of St. Angelo a faithful garrison and a train of artillery: their batteries incessantly thundered on the city, and a bullet more dexterously pointed broke down the barricade of the bridge and scattered, with a single shot, the heroes of the republic. Their constancy was exhausted by a rebellion of five months. Under the tyranny of the Ghibeline nobles, the wisest patriots regretted the dominion of the church; and their repentance was unanimous and effectual. The troops of St. Peter again occupied the Capitol; the magistrates departed to their homes; the most guilty were executed or exiled; and the legate, at the head of two thousand foot and four thousand horse, was saluted as the father of the city. The synods of Ferrara and Florence, the fear or resentment of Eugenius, prolonged his absence: he was received by a submissive people; but the pontiff understood from the acclamations of his triumphal entry that, to secure their loyalty and his own repose, he must grant, without delay, the abolition of the odious excise.

II. Rome was restored, adorned, and enlightened by the peace-

Last coronation of a German emperor, Frederick III. A.D. 1452, March 18

ful reign of Nicholas the Fifth. In the midst of these laudable occupations, the pope was alarmed by the approach of Frederic the Third of Austria; though his fears could not be justified by the character or the power of the Imperial candidate. After drawing his military force to the metropolis and imposing the best security of oaths [91] and treaties, Nicholas received, with a smiling countenance, the faithful advocate and vassal of the church. So tame were the times, so feeble was the Austrian, that the pomp of his coronation was accomplished with order and harmony; but the superfluous honour was so disgraceful to an independent nation that his successors have excused themselves from the toilsome pilgrimage to the Vatican, and rest their Imperial title on the choice of the electors of Germany.

[91] The oath of fidelity imposed on the emperor by the pope is recorded and sanctified in the Clementines (l. ii. tit. ix.); and Æneas Sylvius, who objects to this new demand, could not foresee that in a few years he should ascend the throne and imbibe the maxims of Boniface VIII.

A citizen has remarked, with pride and pleasure, that the king of the Romans, after passing with a slight salute the cardinals and prelates who met him at the gate, distinguished the dress and person of the senator of Rome ; and, in this last farewell, the pageants of the empire and the republic were clasped in a friendly embrace.[92]   According to the laws of Rome,[93] her first magistrate was required to be a doctor of laws, an alien, of a place at least forty miles from the city ; with whose inhabitants he must not be connected in the third canonical degree of blood or alliance.   The election was annual ; a severe scrutiny was instituted into the conduct of the departing senator ; nor could he be recalled to the same office till after the expiration of two years.   A liberal salary of three thousand florins was assigned for his expense and reward ; and his public appearance represented the majesty of the republic.   His robes were of gold brocade or crimson velvet, or in the summer season of a lighter silk ; he bore in his hand an ivory sceptre ; the sound of trumpets announced his approach ; and his solemn steps were preceded at least by four lictors or attendants, whose red wands were enveloped with bands or streamers of the golden colour or livery of the city.   His oath in the Capitol proclaims his right and duty to observe and assert the laws, to control the proud, to protect the poor, and to exercise justice and mercy within the extent of his jurisdiction.   In these useful functions he was assisted by three learned strangers, the two *collaterals* and the judge of criminal appeals ; their frequent trials of robberies, rapes, and murders are attested by the laws ; and the weakness of these laws connives at the licentiousness of private feuds and armed associations for mutual defence.   But the senator was confined to the administration of justice ; the Capitol, the treasury, and the government of the city and its territory were entrusted to the three *conservators*,[94] who were changed four

Marginal notes:
The statutes and government of Rome
[Senator Forensis, foreign Senator]
[Collateralis = assessor]

---

[92] Lo senatore di Roma, vestito di brocarto con quella beretta, e con quelle maniche, et ornamenti di pelle, co' quali va alle feste di Testaccio e Nagone, might escape the eye of Æneas Sylvius, but he is viewed with admiration and complacency by the Roman citizen (Diario di Stephano Infessura, p. 1133). [See Gregorovius, v. p. 289 *sqq.*]

[93] See, in the statutes of Rome, *the senator and three judges* (l. i. c. 3-14), the *conservators* (l. i. c. 15-17 ; l. iii. c. 4), the *caporioni* (l. i. c. 18 ; l. iii. c. 8), the *secret council* (l. iii. c. 2), the *common council* (l. iii. c. 3).   The title of *feuds, defiances, acts of violence,* &c. is spread through many a chapter (c. 14-40) of the second book.

[94] [Urban V. introduced the three Conservators of the Civic Camera—"a civic council with judicial and administrative power whose office endures to the present

times in each year ; the militia of the thirteen regions assembled
under the banners of their respective chiefs, or *caporioni ;* and
the first of these was distinguished by the name and dignity of
[Consilium the*prior*.   The popular legislature consisted of the secret and
Speciale,
Consilium the common councils of the Romans.   The former was composed
Generale]
of the magistrates and their immediate predecessors, with some
fiscal and legal officer, and three classes of thirteen, twenty-six,
and forty counsellors, amounting in the whole to about one
hundred and twenty persons.   In the common council, all male
citizens had a right to vote; and the value of their privilege
was enhanced by the care with which any foreigners were prevented from usurping the title and character of Romans.   The
tumult of a democracy was checked by wise and jealous precautions: except the magistrates, none could propose a question;
none were permitted to speak, except from an open pulpit or
tribunal; all disorderly acclamations were suppressed; the sense
of the majority was decided by a secret ballot; and their decrees
were promulgated in the venerable name of the Roman senate
and people.   It would not be easy to assign a period in which
this theory of government has been reduced to accurate and
constant practice, since the establishment of order has been
gradually connected with the decay of liberty.   But in the year
one thousand five hundred and eighty the ancient statutes were
collected, methodized in three books, and adapted to present
use, under the pontificate, and with the approbation, of Gregory
the Thirteenth: [95] this civil and criminal code is the modern
law of the city; and, if the popular assemblies have been abolished, a foreign senator, with the three conservators, still resides
in the palace of the Capitol. [96]   The policy of the Cæsars has
been repeated by the popes; and the bishop of Rome affected

day," Gregorovius, v. p. 439.   At the same time, Urban abolished the Council of
Seven Reformatores, who had been elected in 1358 to advise the Senators, and
suppressed the " Banderesi," the heads of military companies which had been
organized in 1356.   These Banderesi executed justice (like the Gonfalonieri in
Florence), and their power had become very tyrannical.   See Gregorovius, *ib.* p. 403.]
    [95] *Statuta almae Urbis Romae Auctoritate S. D. N. Gregorii XIII. Pont.
Max. a Senatu Populoque Rom. reformata et edita.   Romae,* 1580, *in folio.*   The
obsolete repugnant statutes of antiquity were confounded in five books, and Lucas
Pætus, a lawyer and antiquarian, was appointed to act as the modern Tribonian.
Yet I regret the old code, with the rugged crust of freedom and barbarism.
    [96] In my time (1765), and in M. Grosley's (Observations sur l'Italie, tom. ii. p.
361), the senator of Rome was M. Bielke, a noble Swede, and a proselyte to the
Catholic faith.   The pope's right to appoint the senator and the conservator is
implied rather than affirmed in the statutes.

to maintain the form of a republic, while he reigned with the absolute powers of a temporal as well as spiritual monarch.

It is an obvious truth that the times must be suited to extra- Conspiracy of Porcaro. A.D. 1453, Jan. 9 ordinary characters, and that the genius of Cromwell or Retz might now expire in obscurity. The political enthusiasm of Rienzi had exalted him to a throne; the same enthusiasm, in the next century, conducted his imitator to the gallows. The birth of Stephen Porcaro was noble, his reputation spotless; his tongue was armed with eloquence, his mind was enlightened with learning; and he aspired, beyond the aim of vulgar ambition, to free his country and immortalise his name. The dominion of priests is most odious to a liberal spirit: every scruple was removed by the recent knowledge of the fable and forgery of Constantine's donation; Petrarch was now the oracle of the Italians; and, as often as Porcaro revolved the ode which describes the patriot and hero of Rome, he applied to himself the visions of the prophetic bard. His first trial of the popular feeling was at the funeral of Eugenius the Fourth: in an elaborate speech, he called the Romans to liberty and arms; and they listened with apparent pleasure, till Porcaro was interrupted and answered by a grave advocate, who pleaded for the church and state. By every law the seditious orator was guilty of treason; but the benevolence of the new pontiff, who viewed his character with pity and esteem, attempted, by an honourable office, to convert the patriot into a friend. The inflexible Roman returned from Anagni with an increase of reputation and zeal; and on the first opportunity, the games of the place Navona, he tried to inflame the casual dispute of some boys and mechanics into a general rising of the people. Yet the humane Nicholas was still averse to accept the forfeit of his life; and the traitor was removed from the scene of temptation to Bologna, with a liberal allowance for his support, and the easy obligation of presenting himself each day before the governor of the city. But Porcaro had learned from the younger Brutus that with tyrants no faith or gratitude should be observed: the exile declaimed against the arbitrary sentence; a party and a conspiracy were gradually formed; his nephew, a daring youth, assembled a band of volunteers; and on the appointed evening a feast was prepared at his house for the friends of the republic. Their leader, who had escaped from Bologna, appeared among them in a robe of

purple and gold : his voice, his countenance, his gestures, be-
spoke the man who had devoted his life or death to the glorious
cause.   In a studied oration, he expatiated on the motives and
the means of their enterprise; the name and liberties of Rome;
the sloth and pride of their ecclesiastical tyrants; the active or
passive consent of their fellow-citizens; three hundred soldiers
and four hundred exiles, long exercised in arms or in wrongs;
the licence of revenge to edge their swords, and a million of
ducats to reward their victory.   It would be easy (he said) on
the next day, the festival of the Epiphany, to seize the pope and
his cardinals before the doors, or at the altar, of St. Peter's; to
lead them in chains under the walls of St. Angelo; to extort by
the threat of their instant death a surrender of the castle; to
ascend the vacant Capitol; to ring the alarm-bell; and to restore
in a popular assembly the ancient republic of Rome.   While he
triumphed, he was already betrayed.   The senator, with a strong
guard, invested the house; the nephew of Porcaro cut his way
through the crowd; but the unfortunate Stephen was drawn from
a chest, lamenting that his enemies had anticipated by three
hours the execution of his design.   After such manifest and
repeated guilt, even the mercy of Nicholas was silent.   Porcaro,
and nine of his accomplices, were hanged without the benefit of
the sacraments ; and, amidst the fears and invectives of the
papal court, the Romans pitied, and almost applauded, these
martyrs of their country.[97]   But their applause was mute, their
pity ineffectual, their liberty for ever extinct ; and, if they have
since risen in a vacancy of the throne or a scarcity of bread,
such accidental tumults may be found in the bosom of the most
abject servitude.

Last dis-
orders of
the nobles
of Rome

But the independence of the nobles, which was fomented by
discord, survived the freedom of the commons, which must be

[97] Besides the curious though concise narrative of Machiavel (Istoria Fiorentina,
l. vi. Opere, tom. i. p. 210, 211, edit. Londra, 1747, in 4to), the Porcarian conspiracy is related in the Diary of Stephen Infessura (Rer. Ital. tom. iii. p. ii. p.
1134, 1135), and in a separate tract by Leo Baptista Alberti (Rer. Ital. tom. xxv.
p. 609-614).   It is amusing to compare the style and sentiments of the courtier and
citizen.   Facinus profecto quo . . . neque periculo horribilius, neque audaciâ de-
testabilius, neque crudelitate tetrius, a quoquam perditissimo uspiam excogitatum
sit. . . . Perdette la vita quell' huomo da bene, e amatore dello bene e libertà di
Roma.   [Another source: Petrus de Godis, Dyalogon de conjuratione Porcaria, was
first published by M. Perlbach in 1879.   See also Tommasini, Documenti relativi a
Stefano Porcari, in the Arch. della Soc. rom. di storia patria, iii. p. 63 sqq., 1879 ;
Sanesi, Stefano Procari e la sua congiura, 1887.]

founded in union.   A privilege of rapine and oppression was
long maintained by the barons of Rome ; their houses were a
fortress and a sanctuary ; and the ferocious train of banditti and
criminals whom they protected from the law repaid the hospitality with the service of their swords and daggers.   The private
interest of the pontiffs, or their nephews, sometimes involved
them in these domestic feuds.   Under the reign of Sixtus the
Fourth, Rome was distracted by the battles and sieges of the
rival houses ; after the conflagration of his palace, the protonotary Colonna was tortured and beheaded ; and Savelli, his
captive friend, was murdered on the spot, for refusing to join in
the acclamations of the victorious Ursini.[98]   But the popes no
longer trembled in the Vatican : they had strength to command,
if they had resolution to claim, the obedience of their subjects ;
and the strangers, who observed these partial disorders, admired
the easy taxes and wise administration of the ecclesiastical state.[99]

The spiritual thunders of the Vatican depend on the force of
opinion ; and, if that opinion be supplanted by reason or passion,
the sound may idly waste itself in the air ; and the helpless priest
is exposed to the brutal violence of a noble or a plebeian adversary.
But after their return from Avignon the keys of St. Peter were
guarded by the sword of St. Paul.   Rome was commanded by
an impregnable citadel ; the use of cannon is a powerful engine
against popular seditions ; a regular force of cavalry and infantry
was enlisted under the banners of the popes ; his ample revenues
supplied the resources of war ; and, from the extent of his domain,
he could bring down on a rebellious city an army of hostile
neighbours and loyal subjects.[100]   Since the union of the duchies

*The popes
acquire the
absolute
dominion
of Rome,
A.D. 1500,
&c.*

[98] The disorders of Rome, which were much inflamed by the partiality of Sixtus
IV., are exposed in the diaries of two spectators, Stephen Infessura and an anony-
mous citizen.   See the troubles of the year 1484, and the death of the protonotary
Colonna, in tom. iii. p. ii. p. 1083, 1158.

[99] Est toute la terre de l'église troublée pour cette partialité (des Colonnes et des
Ursins), come nous dirions Luce et Grammont, ou en Hollande Houc et Caballan ;
et quand ce ne seroit ce différend la terre de l'église seroit la plus heureuse habitation
pour les sujets, qui soit dans tout le monde (car ils ne payent ni tailles ni guères
autres choses), et seroient toujours bien conduits (car toujours les papes sont sages
et bien conseillés) ; mais très souvent en advient de grands et cruels meurtres et
pilleries.

[100] By the economy of Sixtus V. the revenue of the ecclesiastical state was raised
to two millions and a half of Roman crowns (Vita, tom. iii. p. 291-296) ; and so
regular was the military establishment that in one month Clement VIII. could invade the duchy of Ferrara with three thousand horse and twenty thousand foot
(tom. iii. p. 64).   Since that time (A.D. 1597) the papal arms are happily rusted ;
but the revenue must have gained some nominal increase.

of Ferrara and Urbino, the ecclesiastical state extends from the
Mediterranean to the Adriatic, and from the confines of Naples
to the banks of the Po ; and, as early as the sixteenth century,
the greater part of that spacious and fruitful country acknowledged the lawful claims and temporal sovereignty of the Roman
pontiffs.   Their claims were readily deduced from the genuine
or fabulous donations of the darker ages ; the successive steps of
their final settlement would engage us too far in the transactions
of Italy, and even of Europe : the crimes of Alexander the Sixth,
the martial operations of Julius the Second and the liberal policy
of Leo the Tenth, a theme which has been adorned by the pens
of the noblest historians of the times.[101]   In the first period of
their conquests, till the expedition of Charles the Eighth, the
popes might successfully wrestle with the adjacent princes and
states, whose military force was equal, or inferior, to their own.
But, as soon as the monarchs of France, Germany, and Spain,
contended with gigantic arms for the dominion of Italy, they
supplied with art the deficiency of strength, and concealed, in
a labyrinth of wars and treaties, their aspiring views and the
immortal hope of chasing the barbarians beyond the Alps.   The
nice balance of the Vatican was often subverted by the soldiers
of the North and West, who were united under the standard of
Charles the Fifth ; the feeble and fluctuating policy of Clement
the Seventh exposed his person and dominions to the conqueror ;
and Rome was abandoned seven months to a lawless army, more
cruel and rapacious than the Goths and Vandals.[102]   After this
severe lesson, the popes contracted their ambition, which was
almost satisfied, resumed the character of a common parent, and
abstained from all offensive hostilities, except in an hasty quarrel,
when the vicar of Christ and the Turkish sultan were armed at
the same time against the kingdom of Naples.[103]   The French

[101] More especially by Guicciardini and Machiavel : in the general history of the
former, in the Florentine history, the Prince, and the political discourses of the
latter.   These, with their worthy successors, Fra Paolo and Davila, were justly
esteemed the first historians of modern languages, till, in the present age, Scotland
arose to dispute the prize with Italy herself.

[102] In the history of the Gothic siege, I have compared the barbarians with the
subjects of Charles V. (vol. iii. p. 347-348) : an anticipation which, like that of the
Tartar conquests, I indulged with the less scruple, as I could scarcely hope to reach
the conclusion of my work.

[103] The ambitious and feeble hostilities of the Caraffa pope, Paul IV., may be
seen in Thuanus (l. xvi.-xviii.) and Giannone (tom. iv. p. 149-163).   Those Catholic
bigots, Philip II. and the duke of Alva, presumed to separate the Roman prince

and Germans at length withdrew from the field of battle: Milan, Naples, Sicily, Sardinia, and the sea-coast of Tuscany were firmly possessed by the Spaniards; and it became their interest to maintain the peace and dependence of Italy, which continued almost without disturbance from the middle of the sixteenth to the opening of the eighteenth century.   The Vatican was swayed and protected by the religious policy of the Catholic king; his prejudice and interest disposed him in every dispute to support the prince against the people; and, instead of the encouragement, the aid, and the asylum, which they obtained from the adjacent states, the friends of liberty or the enemies of law were inclosed on all sides within the iron circle of despotism.   The long habits of obedience and education subdued the turbulent spirit of the nobles and commons of Rome.   The barons forgot the arms and factions of their ancestors, and insensibly became the servants of luxury and government.   Instead of maintaining a crowd of tenants and followers, the produce of their estates was consumed in the private expenses, which multiply the pleasures, and diminish the power, of the lord.[104]   The Colonna and Ursini vied with each other in the decoration of their palaces and chapels; and their antique splendour was rivalled or surpassed by the sudden opulence of the papal families.   In Rome the voice of freedom and discord is no longer heard; and, instead of the foaming torrent, a smooth and stagnant lake reflects the image of idleness and servitude.

A Christian, a philosopher,[105] and a patriot will be equally scandalized by the temporal kingdom of the clergy; and the local majesty of Rome, the remembrance of her consuls and triumphs, may seem to embitter the sense, and aggravate the shame, of her slavery.   If we calmly weigh the merits and de-

The ecclesiastical government

from the vicar of Christ; yet the holy character, which would have sanctified his victory, was decently applied to protect his defeat. [For the Popes of the 16th century, see Ranke, History of the Popes, their Church and State (Eng. translations by Kelly, 1843; E. Foster, 3 vols., 1847-8; J. H. Merle d'Aubigne, 2 vols., 1851).]

[104] This gradual change of manners and expense is admirably explained by Dr. Adam Smith (Wealth of Nations, vol. i. p. 495-504), who proves, perhaps too severely, that the most salutary effects have flowed from the meanest and most selfish causes.

[105] Mr. Hume (Hist. of England, vol. i. p. 389) too hastily concludes that, if the civil and ecclesiastical powers be united in the same person, it is of little moment whether he be styled prince or prelate, since the temporal character will always predominate.

fects of the ecclesiastical government, it may be praised in its present state as a mild, decent, and tranquil system, exempt from the dangers of a minority, the sallies of youth, the expenses of luxury, and the calamities of war.   But these advantages are overbalanced by a frequent, perhaps a septennial, election of a sovereign, who is seldom a native of the country; the reign of a *young* statesman of threescore, in the decline of his life and abilities, without hope to accomplish, and without children to inherit, the labours of his transitory reign.   The successful candidate is drawn from the church, and even the convent; from the mode of education and life the most adverse to reason, humanity, and freedom.   In the trammels of servile faith, he has learnt to believe because it is absurd, to revere all that is contemptible, and to despise whatever might deserve the esteem of a rational being; to punish error as a crime, to reward mortification and celibacy as the first of virtues; to place the saints of the calendar [106] above the heroes of Rome and the sages of Athens; and to consider the missal or the crucifix as more useful instruments than the plough or the loom.   In the office of nuncio, or the rank of cardinal, he may acquire some knowledge of the world, but the primitive stain will adhere to his mind and manners: from study and experience he may suspect the mystery of his profession; but the sacerdotal artist will imbibe some portion of the bigotry which he inculcates.   The genius of Sixtus the Fifth [107] burst from the gloom of a Franciscan cloister. In a reign of five years, he exterminated the outlaws and banditti, abolished the *profane* sanctuaries of Rome,[108] formed a

Sixtus V.
A.D. 1585-
1590

---

[106] A Protestant may disdain the unworthy preference of St. Francis or St. Dominic, but he will not rashly condemn the zeal or judgment of Sixtus V. who placed the statues of the apostles St. Peter and St. Paul on the vacant columns of Trajan and Antonine.

[107] A wandering Italian, Gregorio Leti, has given the Vita di Sisto-Quinto (Amstel. 1721, 3 vols. in 12mo), a copious and amusing work, but which does not command our absolute confidence.   Yet the character of the man, and the principal facts, are supported by the annals of Spondanus and Muratori (A.D. 1585-1590), and the contemporary history of the great Thuanus (l. lxxxii. c. 1, 2; l. lxxxiv. c. 10; l. c. c. 8).   [The source of Leti was a collection of anecdotes, of apocryphal character, entitled Detti e fatti di papa Sisto V., of which the Ms. is in the Corsini library at Rome.   This discovery was made by Ranke.   See his Sämmtliche Werke, vol. 39, pp. 59-65 (in Appendix to his Lives of the Popes).]

[108] These privileged places, the *quartieri* or *franchises*, were adopted from the Roman nobles by the foreign ministers.   Julius II. had once abolished the abominandum et detestandum franchitiarum hujusmodi nomen; and after Sixtus V. they again revived.   I cannot discern either the justice or magnanimity of Louis XIV. who, in 1687, sent his ambassador, the marquis de Lavardin, to Rome, with an

naval and military force, restored and emulated the monuments of antiquity, and, after a liberal use and large increase of the revenue, left five millions of crowns in the castle of St. Angelo. But his justice was sullied with cruelty, his activity was prompted by the ambition of conquest : after his decease, the abuses revived ; the treasure was dissipated ; he entailed on posterity thirty-five new taxes, and the venality of offices ; and, after his death, his statue was demolished by an ungrateful or an injured people.[109] The wild and original character of Sixtus the Fifth stands alone in the series of the pontiffs : the maxims and effects of their temporal government may be collected from the positive and comparative view of the arts and philosophy, the agriculture and trade, the wealth and population, of the ecclesiastical state. For myself, it is my wish to depart in charity with all mankind ; nor am I willing, in these last moments, to offend even the pope and clergy of Rome.[110]

armed force of a thousand officers, guards, and domestics, to maintain this iniquitous claim, and insult Pope Innocent XI. in the heart of his capital (Vita di Sisto V. tom. iii. p. 260-278 ; Muratori, Annali d'Italia, tom. xv. p. 494-496 ; and Voltaire, Siècle de Louis XIV. tom. ii. c. 14, p. 58, 59).

[109] This outrage produced a decree, which was inscribed on marble and placed in the Capitol. It is expressed in a style of manly simplicity and freedom : Si quis, sive privatus, sive magistratum gerens de collocandâ *vivo* pontifici statuâ mentionem facere ausit, legitimo S. P. Q. R. decreto in perpetuum infamis et publicorum munerum expers esto. MDXC. mense Augusto (Vita di Sisto V. tom. iii. p. 469). I believe that this decree is still observed, and I know that every monarch who deserves a statue should himself impose the prohibition.

[110] The histories of the church, Italy, and Christendom have contributed to the chapter which I now conclude. In the original Lives of the Popes, we often discover the city and republic of Rome ; and the events of the xivth and xvth centuries are preserved in the rude and domestic chronicles which I have carefully inspected, and shall recapitulate in the order of time.

1. Monaldeschi (Ludovici Boncomitis) Fragmenta Annalium Roman. A.D. 1328, in the Scriptores Rerum Italicarum of Muratori, tom. xii. p. 525. *N.B.* The credit of this fragment is somewhat hurt by a singular interpolation, in which the author relates *his own death* at the age of 115 years. [The work seems to be a forgery ; and Labruzzi (Arch. della Società Romana di storia patria, ii. p. 281 *sqq.*, 1879) ascribes it to Alfonso Ceccarelli (who was executed in 1583).]

2. Fragmenta Historiæ Romanæ (vulgo Thomas Fortifioccæ), in Romana Dialecto vulgari (A.D. 1327-1354), in Muratori, Antiquitat. medii Ævi Italiæ, tom. iii. p. 247-548 ; the authentic ground-work of the history of Rienzi. [See above, p. 269, note 20.]

3. Delphini (Gentilis) Diarium Romanum (A.D. 1370-1410), in the Rerum Italicarum, tom. iii. p. ii. p. 846.

4. Antonii (Petri) *Diarium* Rom. (A.D. 1404-1417), tom. xxiv. p. 969. [See Savignoni, Giornale d'Antonio di Pietro dello Schiavo, in the Arch. della Società Rom. di stor. patr. xiii. p. 295 *sqq.*]

5. Petroni (Pauli) Miscellanea Historica Romana (A.D. 1433-1446), tom. xxiv. p. 1101.

6. Volaterrani (Jacob.) Diarium Rom. (A.D. 1472-1484), tom. xxiii. p. 81.

7. Anonymi Diarium Urbis Romæ (A.D. 1481-1492), tom. iii. p. ii. p. 1069.

8. Infessuræ (Stephani) Diarium Romanum (A.D. 1294, or 1378-1494), tom. iii. p. ii. p. 1109. [New edition by O. Tommasini, 1890.]

9. Historia Arcana Alexandri VI. sive Excerpta ex Diario Joh. Burcardi (A.D. 1492-1503), edita a Godefr. Guilelm. Leibnizio, Hanover, 1697, in ¦4to. The large and valuable Journal of Burcard might be completed from the Ms. in different libraries of Italy and France (M. de Foncemagne, in the Mémoires de l'Acad. des Inscrip. tom. xvii. p. 597-606). [Best, and only complete edition by L. Thuasne, 3 vols., 1883-5.]

Except the last, all these fragments and diaries are inserted in the Collections of Muratori, my guide and master in the history of Italy. His country and the public are indebted to him for the following works on that subject : 1. *Rerum Italicarum Scriptores* (A.D. 500-1500), *quorum potissima pars nunc primum in lucem prodit*, &c. xxviii. vols. in folio, Milan, 1723-1738, 1751. A volume of chronological and alphabetical tables is still wanting as a key to this great work, which is yet in a disorderly and defective state. [After the lapse of nearly a century and a half this great Collection has been supplied with Chronological Indices by J. Calligaris and others : Indices Chronologici ad Script. Rer. Ital., 1885. A new ed. of the collection, by Carducci and Fiorini, is in course of publication, 1900- .] 2. *Antiquitates Italiæ medii Ævi*, vi. vols. in folio, Milan, 1738-1743, in lxxv. curious dissertations on the manners, government, religion, &c. of the Italians of the darker ages, with a large supplement of charters, chronicles, &c. [Also published in 17 quarto volumes at Arezzo, 1777-80. Chronological Indexes have been prepared to this work too by Battaglino and Calligaris, 1889, &c.] 3. *Dissertazioni sopra le Antiquità Italiane*, ii. vols. in 4to, Milano, 1751, a free version by the author, which may be quoted with the same confidence as the Latin text of the Antiquities. 4. *Annali d' Italia*, xviii. vols. in octavo, Milan, 1753-1756, a dry, though accurate and useful, abridgment of the history of Italy, from the birth of Christ to the middle of the xviiith century. 5. *Dell' Antichità Estense ed Italiane*, ii. vols. in folio, Modena, 1717, 1740. In the history of this illustrious race, the parent of our Brunswick kings, the critic is not seduced by the loyalty or gratitude of the subject. In all his works, Muratori proves himself a diligent and laborious writer, who aspires above the prejudices of a Catholic priest. He was born in the year 1672, and died in the year 1750, after passing near sixty years in the libraries of Milan and Modena (Vita del Proposto Ludovico Antonio Muratori, by his nephew and successor, Gian. Francesco Soli Muratori, Venezia, 1756, in 4to). [Several biographies of Muratori have appeared since ; *e.g.* by Reina in 1819 ; by Brigidi in 1871. In 1872, the centenary of his birth, were published : Belviglieri, La vita, le opere, i tempi di L. A. Muratori ; and Roncaglia, Vita di L. A. Mur.]

CHAPTER LXXI

Prospect of the Ruins of Rome in the Fifteenth Century—Four Causes of Decay and Destruction—Example of the Coliseum—Renovation of the City—Conclusion of the whole Work

IN the last days of Pope Eugenius the Fourth, two of his servants, the learned Poggius[1] and a friend, ascended the Capitoline Hill; reposed themselves among the ruins of columns and temples; and viewed from that commanding spot, the wide and various prospect of desolation.[2] The place and the object gave ample scope for moralising on the vicissitudes of fortune, which spares neither man nor the proudest of his works, which buries empires and cities in a common grave; and it was agreed that in proportion to her former greatness the fall of Rome was the more awful and deplorable. "Her primæval state, such as she might appear in a remote age, when Evander entertained the stranger of Troy,[3] has been delineated by the fancy of Virgil. This Tarpeian rock was then a savage and solitary thicket: in the time of the poet, it was crowned with the golden roofs of a temple: the temple is overthrown, the gold has been pillaged, the wheel of fortune has accomplished

[margin note] View and discourse of Poggius from the Capitoline Hill, A.D. 1430

---

[1] I have already (not. 58, 59, on chap. lxv.) mentioned the age, character, and writings of Poggius; and particularly noticed the date of this elegant moral lecture on the varieties of fortune. [On the subject of this chapter the following works may be consulted: Gregorovius, Rome in the Middle Ages (notices of the fortunes of the ancient monuments are scattered throughout the work; consult Index); Jordan's Topographie der Stadt Rom im Alterthum, 1871-1885; J. H. Middleton, The Remains of Ancient Rome, 2 vols., 1892; above all, the works of R. Lanciani: Pagan and Christian Rome, 1892; The Ruins and Excavations of Ancient Rome, 1897; Destruction of Ancient Rome, 1899; O. Richter, Topographie der Stadt Rom, 1901.]

[2] Consedimus in ipsis Tarpeiæ arcis ruinis, pone ingens portæ cujusdam, ut puto, templi, marmoreum limen, plurimasque passim confractas columnas, unde magnâ ex parte prospectus urbis patet (p. 5).

[3] Æneid, viii. 97-369. This ancient picture, so artfully introduced and so exquisitely finished, must have been highly interesting to an inhabitant of Rome; and our early studies allow us to sympathize in the feelings of a Roman.

her revolution, and the sacred ground is again disfigured with thorns and brambles. The hill of the Capitol, on which we sit, was formerly the head of the Roman empire, the citadel of the earth, the terror of kings; illustrated by the footsteps of so many triumphs, enriched with the spoils and tributes of so many nations. This spectacle of the world, how is it fallen! how changed! how defaced! The path of victory is obliterated by vines, and the benches of the senators are concealed by a dunghill. Cast your eyes on the Palatine hill, and seek, among the shapeless and enormous fragments, the marble theatre, the obelisks, the colossal statues, the porticoes of Nero's palace: survey the other hills of the city, the vacant space is interrupted only by ruins and gardens. The forum of the Roman people, where they assembled to enact their laws and elect their magistrates, is now inclosed for the cultivation of pot-herbs or thrown open for the reception of swine and buffaloes. The public and private edifices, that were founded for eternity, lie prostrate, naked, and broken, like the limbs of a mighty giant; and the ruin is the more visible, from the stupendous relics that have survived the injuries of time and fortune." [4]

His description of the ruins

These relics are minutely described by Poggius, one of the first who raised his eyes from the monuments of legendary, to those of classic, superstition.[5] 1. Besides a bridge, an arch, a sepulchre, and the pyramid of Cestius, he could discern, of the age of the republic, a double row of vaults in the salt-office of the Capitol, which were inscribed with the name and munificence of Catulus. 2. Eleven temples were visible in some degree, from the perfect form of the Pantheon, to the three arches and a marble column [6] of the temple of Peace, which Vespasian erected after the civil wars and the Jewish triumph. 3. Of the number, which he rashly defines, of seven *thermæ*, or public baths, none were sufficiently entire to represent the use and distribution of the several parts; but those of Diocletian and Antoninus Caracalla still retained the titles of the founders, and astonished the curious spectator, who, in observing their solidity

---

[4] Capitolium adeo . . . immutatum ut vineæ in senatorum subsellia successerint, stercorum ac purgamentorum receptaculum factum. Respice ad Palatinum montem . . . vasta rudera . . . cæteros colles perlustra omnia vacua ædificiis, ruinis vineisque oppleta conspicies (Poggius de Varietat. Fortunæ, p. 21).

[5] See Poggius, p. 8-22.

[6] [The column was moved by Paul V. to the church of S. Maria Maggiore.]

SIENA, PALAZZO PUBBLICO. PLAN OF MEDIÆVAL ROME; FRESCO
BY TADDEO BARTOLI

and extent, the variety of marbles, the size and multitude of the columns, compared the labour and expense with the use and importance. Of the baths of Constantine, of Alexander,[7] of Domitian, or rather of Titus,[8] some vestige might yet be found. 4. The triumphal arches of Titus, Severus,[9] and Constantine were entire, both the structure and the inscriptions; a falling fragment was honoured with the name of Trajan; and two arches, then extant in the Flaminian Way, have been ascribed to the baser memory of Faustina and Gallienus.[10] 5. After the wonder of the Coliseum, Poggius might have overlooked a small amphitheatre of brick, most probably for the use of the prætorian camp. The theatres of Marcellus [11] and Pompey were occupied, in a great measure, by public and private buildings; and in the Circus, Agonalis, and Maximus, little more than the situation and the form could be investigated. 6. The columns of Trajan and Antonine [12] were still erect; but the Egyptian obelisks were broken or buried.[13] A people of gods and heroes, the workmanship of art, was reduced to one equestrian figure of gilt brass,

[7] [Thermæ Neronianæ et Alexandrinæ, baths built by Nero and enlarged by Alexander Severus, were close to the Stadium (discovered in 1869), south of the Piazza Navona—south-west of the Pantheon.]

[8] [It has been proved only quite recently (by excavations in 1895) that the Baths of Titus and Trajan were distinct; it was not a case of baths built by Titus and restored or improved by Trajan. The Propylæa of the Thermæ of Titus have been found on the north side of the Coliseum; the Baths of Trajan were to the north-east, almost adjoining. See Lanciani, Ruins and Excavations, p. 365-6. On the Aventine there were other large Baths, the Thermæ Decianæ. See Lanciani, *ib.* p. 544-6.]

[9] [An interesting sketch of the history of this arch will be found in Lanciani, *op. cit.* p. 284-6.]

[10] [He also mentions the Arch of Claudius (in the Piazza Sciarra) and the Arch of Lentulus (on the Aventine). Lanciani has shown that an old Church of St. Stephen, which was excavated in the Piazza di Pietra, was built of spoils taken from the triumphal Arch of Claudius and from the Temple of Neptune (in the Piazza di Pietra). Cp. his Pagan and Christian Rome, p. 99. Fragments of the Arch of Tiberius at the foot of the Capitoline have been discovered. Foundations of the Arch of Augustus were found in 1888. Lanciani had shown in 1882 that "this arch had been found and destroyed by the workmen of the fabbrica di S. Pietro between 1540 and 1546 exactly in that place, and that the inscription *Corpus*, vol. vii. no. 872, belonged to it". Ruins and Excavations, p. 271.]

[11] [See below, p. 328, note 54.]

[12] [It is interesting to observe that in the Middle Ages it was usual to ascend the Column of Marcus Aurelius for the sake of the view, by the spiral staircase within, and a fee of admission was charged. See Gregorovius, iii. p. 549.]

[13] [Poggio saw on the Capitol a small obelisk which is now in the Villa Mattei. And there was the obelisk in the Vatican Circus, which Sixtus V. removed to the Piazza di S. Pietro where it now stands. Since then several obelisks have been set up again; *e.g.*, the great red granite obelisk in the Piazza of St. John in the Lateran; the obelisks in the Piazza del Popolo and the Piazza di Monte Citorio. See Parker's Twelve Egyptian Obelisks. And cp. above, vol. ii. p. 278, note 48.]

and to five marble statues, of which the most conspicuous were the two horses of Phidias and Praxiteles.   7. The two mausoleums or sepulchres of Augustus [14] and Hadrian could not totally be lost; but the former was only visible as a mound of earth; and the latter, the castle of St. Angelo, had acquired the name and appearance of a modern fortress.   With the addition of some separate and nameless columns, such were the remains of the ancient city; for the marks of a more recent structure might be detected in the walls, which formed a circumference of ten miles, included three hundred and seventy-nine turrets, and opened into the country by thirteen gates.

Gradual
decay of
Rome

This melancholy picture was drawn above nine hundred years after the fall of the Western empire, and even of the Gothic kingdom of Italy.   A long period of distress and anarchy, in which empire, and arts, and riches had migrated from the banks of the Tiber, was incapable of restoring or adorning the city; and, as all that is human must retrograde if it do not advance, every successive age must have hastened the ruin of the works of antiquity.   To measure the progress of decay, and to ascertain, at each æra, the state of each edifice, would be an endless and a useless labour; and I shall content myself with two observations, which will introduce a short inquiry into the general causes and effects.   1. Two hundred years before the eloquent complaint of Poggius, an anonymous writer composed a description of Rome.[15]   His ignorance may repeat the same objects

---

[14] [The Mausoleum of Augustus was taken as a stronghold by the Colonnas and destroyed in 1167 when they were banished.   It was refortified in 1241, and it was used as a pyre for the body of Rienzi.   See Lanciani, Pagan and Christian Rome, p. 177-80.   The Soderini family converted it into a hanging garden in 1550.   The ancient *ustrinum* or cremation enclosure, and a number of monuments, were found in excavations in 1777.]

[15] Liber de Mirabilibus Romæ, ex Registro Nicolai Cardinalis de Arragoniâ, in Bibliothecâ St. Isidori Armario IV. No. 69.   This treatise, with some short but pertinent notes, has been published by Montfaucon (Diarium Italicum, p. 283-301), who thus delivers his own critical opinion : Scriptor xiiimi circiter sæculi, ut ibidem notatur; antiquariæ rei imperitus, et, ut ab illo ævo, nugis et anilibus fabellis refertus : sed quia monumenta quæ iis temporibus Romæ supererant pro modulo recenset, non parum inde lucis mutuabitur qui Romanis antiquitatibus indagandis operam navabit (p. 283).   [Mirabilia Romæ, ed Parthey, 1867 ; The Marvels of Rome or Picture of the Golden City, Eng. tr. by F. M. Nicholls, 1889.   The Mirabilia is a 12th century recension of an older guide-book, probably of the 10th century, of which the Graphia aureæ urbis Romæ (Publ. in Ozanam's Documents inédits, p. 155 *sqq.*) is another recension.   The Ordo Romanus, or itinerary, of Benedict (12th cent.) is based on the Mirabilia.   We have a still older description, of about A.D. 900, in the Collection of inscriptions by the Anonymous of Einsiedeln (based on a map of Rome, of 4th or 5th century).   It is published in Jordan's Topo-

under strange and fabulous names. Yet this barbarous topo-
grapher had eyes and ears : he could observe the visible remains ;
he could listen to the tradition of the people; and he distinctly
enumerates seven theatres, eleven baths, twelve arches, and
eighteen palaces, of which many had disappeared before the
time of Poggius. It is apparent that many stately monuments
of antiquity survived till a late period,[16] and that the principles
of destruction acted with vigorous and increasing energy in the
thirteenth and fourteenth centuries. 2. The same reflection
must be applied to the three last ages ; and we should vainly
seek the Septizonium of Severus,[17] which is celebrated by Petrarch and the antiquarians of the sixteenth century. While the
Roman edifices were still entire, the first blows, however weighty
and impetuous, were resisted by the solidity of the mass and
the harmony of the parts ; but the slightest touch would precipitate the fragments of arches and columns that already nodded
to their fall.

After a diligent inquiry, I can discern four principal causes Four
causes of
of the ruin of Rome, which continued to operate in a period of destruction;
more than a thousand years. I. The injuries of time and
nature. II. The hostile attacks of the barbarians and Christians. III. The use and abuse of the materials. And, IV. The
domestic quarrels of the Romans.

I. The art of man is able to construct monuments far more I. The injuries of
permanent than the narrow span of his own existence ; yet these nature;
monuments, like himself, are perishable and frail ; and, in the
boundless annals of time, his life and his labours must equally
be measured as a fleeting moment. Of a simple and solid
edifice, it is not easy, however, to circumscribe the duration.
As the wonders of ancient days, the pyramids [18] attracted the

graphie der Stadt Rom im Alterthum, vol. ii. Cp. the accounts of this topographical
literature in Jordan, *op. cit.*, Gregorovius, iii. p. 516 *sqq.*, and Lanciani, Destruction
of Ancient Rome.]
    [16] The Père Mabillon (Analecta, tom. iv. p. 502) has published an anonymous
pilgrim of the ixth century, who, in his visit round the churches and holy places of
Rome, touches on several buildings, especially porticoes, which had disappeared
before the xiiith century. [The Anonymous of Einsiedeln, see last note.]
    [17] On the Septizonium, see the Mémoires sur Pétrarque (tom. i. p. 325), Donatus
(p. 338), and Nardini (p. 117, 414). [The existing remains of the Palace of Severus
on the Palatine are about sixty yards high. In the eighth century, two-fifths of the
building in the centre collapsed. The siege of Henry IV. in 1084 (see below, p. 327)
destroyed many pillars, and in 1257 Brancaleone destroyed the larger extremity.
For its use by Sixtus V. see below, p. 325.]
    [18] The age of the pyramids is remote and unknown, since Diodorus Siculus (tom.

curiosity of the ancients: an hundred generations, the leaves of autumn,[19] have dropped into the grave; and, after the fall of the Pharaohs and Ptolemies, the Cæsars and Caliphs, the same pyramids stand erect and unshaken above the floods of the Nile.   A complex figure of various and minute parts is more accessible to injury and decay; and the silent lapse of time is often accelerated by hurricanes and earthquakes, by fires and inundations.   The air and earth have doubtless been shaken; and the lofty turrets of Rome have tottered from their foundations; but the seven hills do not appear to be placed on the great cavities of the globe; nor has the city, in any age, been exposed to the convulsions of nature which, in the climate of Antioch, Lisbon, or Lima, have crumbled in a few moments the works of ages into dust.   Fire is the most powerful agent of life and death: the rapid mischief may be kindled and propagated by the industry or negligence of mankind; and every period of the Roman annals is marked by the repetition of similar calamities.   A memorable conflagration, the guilt or misfortune of Nero's reign, continued, though with unequal fury, either six or nine days.[20]   Innumerable buildings, crowded in close and crooked streets, supplied perpetual fuel for the flames; and, when they ceased, four only of the fourteen regions were left entire; three were totally destroyed, and seven were deformed by the relics of smoking and lacerated edifices.[21]   In the full

[marginal notes: hurricanes and earthquakes; fires;]

i. l. i. c. 44, p. 72) is unable to decide whether they were constructed 1000 or 3400 years before the clxxxth Olympiad.   Sir John Marshman's contracted scale of the Egyptian dynasties would fix them about 2000 years before Christ (Canon. Chronicus, p. 47).   [Most of the pyramids belong to the 4th millennium B.C.   The Great Pyramid of Gizeh was the tomb of Khufu (Cheops), the second king of the 4th dynasty said to have flourished in B.C. 3969-3908.   See Petrie, History of Egypt, i. p. 38 *sqq.*   For the earlier pyramid of Sneferu, *ib.* p. 32-3; and for the pyramids of the successors of Khufu, and the following dynasties, the same volume *passim.*]

[19] See the speech of Glaucus in the Iliad (z, 146).   This natural but melancholy image is familiar to Homer.

[20] The learning and criticism of M. des Vignoles (Histoire Critique de la République des Lettres, tom. viii. p. 74-118; ix. p. 172-187) dates the fire of Rome from A.D. 64, 19th July, and the subsequent persecution of the Christians from 15th November of the same year.

[21] Quippe in regiones quatuordecim Roma dividitur, quarum quatuor integræ manebant, tres solo tenus dejectæ; septem reliquis pauca tectorum vestigia supererant, lacera et semiusta.   Among the old relics that were irreparably lost, Tacitus enumerates the temple of the Moon of Servius Tullius; the fane and altar consecrated by Evander præsenti Herculi; the temple of Jupiter Stator, a vow of Romulus; the palace of Numa; the temple of Vesta, cum Penatibus populi Romani.   He then deplores the opes tot victoriis quæsitæ et Græcarum artium decora . . . multa quæ seniores meminerant, quæ reparari nequibant (Annal. xv. 40, 41).

meridian of empire, the metropolis arose with fresh beauty from her ashes; yet the memory of the old deplored their irreparable losses, the arts of Greece, the trophies of victory, the monuments of primitive or fabulous antiquity.   In the days of distress and anarchy, every wound is mortal, every fall irretrievable; nor can the damage be restored either by the public care of government or the activity of private interest.   Yet two causes may be alleged, which render the calamity of fire more destructive to a flourishing than a decayed city.   1. The more combustible materials of brick, timber, and metals are first melted or consumed ; but the flames may play without injury or effect on the naked walls and massy arches that have been despoiled of their ornaments.   2. It is among the common and plebeian habitations that a mischievous spark is most easily blown to a conflagration ; but, as soon as they are devoured, the greater edifices which have resisted or escaped are left as so many islands in a state of solitude and safety.   From her situation, Rome is exposed to the danger of frequent inundations.   Without excepting the Tiber, the rivers that descend from either side of the Apennine have a short and irregular course ; a shallow stream in the summer heats ; an impetuous torrent, when it is swelled in the spring or winter by the fall of rain and the melting of the snows.   When the current is repelled from the sea by adverse winds, when the ordinary bed is inadequate to the weight of waters, they rise above the banks, and overspread, without limits or control, the plains and cities of the adjacent country. Soon after the triumph of the first Punic war, the Tiber was increased by unusual rains ; and the inundation, surpassing all former measure of time and place, destroyed all the buildings that were situate below the hills of Rome.   According to the variety of ground, the same mischief was produced by different means ; and the edifices were either swept away by the sudden impulse, or dissolved and undermined by the long continuance, of the flood.[22]   Under the reign of Augustus, the same calamity

inunda-tions (margin note)

---

[22] A. U. C. 507, repentina subversio ipsius Romæ prævenit triumphum Romanorum . . . diversæ ignium aquarumque clades pene absumsere urbem.   Nam Tiberis insolitis auctus imbribus et ultra opinionem, vel diurnitate vel magnitudine redundans, *omnia* Romæ ædificia in plano posita delevit.   Diversæ qualitates locorum ad unam convenere perniciem : quoniam et quæ segnior inundatio tenuit madefacta dissolvit, et quæ cursus torrentis invenit impulsa dejecit (Orosius, Hist. l. iv. c. 11, p. 244, edit. Havercamp).   Yet we may observe that it is the plan and study of the Christian apologist to magnify the calamities of the pagan world.

was renewed : the lawless river overturned the palaces and temples on its banks ;[23] and, after the labours of the emperor in cleansing and widening the bed that was encumbered with ruins,[24] the vigilance of his successors was exercised by similar dangers and designs. The project of diverting into new channels the Tiber itself, or some of the dependent streams, was long opposed by superstition and local interests ;[25] nor did the use compensate the toil and cost of the tardy and imperfect execution. The servitude of rivers is the noblest and most important victory which man has obtained over the licentiousness of nature ;[26] and, if such were the ravages of the Tiber under a firm and active government, what could oppose, or who can enumerate, the injuries of the city after the fall of the Western empire ? A remedy was at length produced by the evil itself : the accumulation of rubbish and the earth that had been washed down from the hills is supposed to have elevated the plain of Rome fourteen or fifteen feet, perhaps, above the ancient level ;[27] and the modern city is less accessible to the attacks of the river.[28]

II. The hostile attacks of the barbarians and Christians

II. The crowd of writers of every nation, who impute the destruction of the Roman monuments to the Goths and the Christians, have neglected to inquire how far they were animated by an hostile principle and how far they possessed the means and the leisure to satiate their enmity. In the preceding volumes

[23]
> Vidimus flavum Tiberim retortis
> Littore Etrusco violenter undis
> Ire dejectum monumenta Regis
> Templaque Vestæ.   (Horat. Carm. i. 2).

If the palace of Numa and temple of Vesta were thrown down in Horace's time, what was consumed of those buildings by Nero's fire could hardly deserve the epithets of vetustissima or incorrupta.

[24] Ad coercendas inundationes alveum Tiberis laxavit ac repurgavit, completum olim ruderibus, et ædificiorum prolapsionibus coarctatum (Suetonius in Augusto, c. 30).

[25] Tacitus (Annal. i. 79) reports the petitions of the different towns of Italy to the senate against the measure; and we may applaud the progress of reason. On a similar occasion local interests would undoubtedly be consulted; but an English House of Commons would reject with contempt the arguments of superstition, " that nature had assigned to the rivers their proper course," &c.

[26] See the Epoques de la Nature of the eloquent and philosophic Buffon. His picture of Guyana in South America is that of a new and savage land, in which the waters are abandoned to themselves, without being regulated by human industry (p. 212, 561, quarto edition).

[27] In his Travels in Italy, Mr. Addison (his works, vol. ii. p. 98, Baskerville's edition) has observed this curious and unquestionable fact.

[28] Yet, in modern times, the Tiber has sometimes damaged the city; and in the years 1530, 1557, 1598, the Annals of Muratori record three mischievous and memorable inundations, tom. xiv. p. 268, 429 ; tom. xv. p. 99, &c.

of this History, I have described the triumph of barbarism and religion; and I can only resume, in a few words, their real or imaginary connexion with the ruin of ancient Rome. Our fancy may create, or adopt, a pleasing romance, that the Goths and Vandals sallied from Scandinavia, ardent to avenge the flight of Odin,[29] to break the chains, and to chastise the oppressors, of mankind; that they wished to burn the records of classic literature and to found their national architecture on the broken members of the Tuscan and Corinthian orders. But, in simple truth, the northern conquerors were neither sufficiently savage nor sufficiently refined to entertain such aspiring ideas of destruction and revenge. The shepherds of Scythia and Germany had been educated in the armies of the empire, whose discipline they acquired, and whose weakness they invaded; with the familiar use of the Latin tongue, they had learned to reverence the name and titles of Rome; and, though incapable of emulating, they were more inclined to admire than to abolish, the arts and studies of a brighter period. In the transient possession of a rich and unresisting capital, the soldiers of Alaric and Genseric were stimulated by the passions of a victorious army; amidst the wanton indulgence of lust or cruelty, portable wealth was the object of their search; nor could they derive either pride or pleasure from the unprofitable reflection that they had battered to the ground the works of the consuls and Cæsars. Their moments were indeed precious: the Goths evacuated Rome on the sixth,[30] the Vandals on the fifteenth, day;[31] and, though it be far more difficult to build than to destroy, their hasty assault would have made a slight impression on the solid piles of antiquity. We may remember that both Alaric and Genseric affected to spare the buildings of the city; that they subsisted in strength and beauty under the auspicious government of Theodoric;[32] and that the momentary resentment of Totila[33] was disarmed by his own temper and the advice of his friends and enemies. From these innocent barbarians the reproach may be transferred to the Catholics of Rome. The statues,

---

[29] I take this opportunity of declaring that in the course of twelve years I have forgotten, or renounced, the flight of Odin from Azoph to Sweden, which I never very seriously believed (vol. i. p. 260). The Goths are apparently Germans; but all beyond Cæsar and Tacitus is darkness or fable in the antiquities of Germany.

[30] History of the Decline, &c., vol. iii. p. 348.

[31] *Ibid.* vol. iv. p. 6.   [32] *Ibid.* vol. iv. p. 203-204.   [33] *Ibid.* vol. iv. p. 432.

altars, and houses of the dæmons were an abomination in their eyes; and in the absolute command of the city they might labour with zeal and perseverance to erase the idolatry of their ancestors. The demolition of the temples of the East [34] affords to *them* an example of conduct, and to *us* an argument of belief; and it is probable that a portion of guilt or merit may be imputed with justice to the Roman proselytes. Yet their abhorrence was confined to the monuments of heathen superstition; and the civil structures that were dedicated to the business or pleasure of society might be preserved without injury or scandal. The change of religion was accomplished, not by a popular tumult, but by the decrees of the emperor, of the senate, and of time. Of the Christian hierarchy, the bishops of Rome were commonly the most prudent and least fanatic; nor can any positive charge be opposed to the meritorious act of saving and converting the majestic structure of the Pantheon.[35]

III. The use and abuse of the materials

III. The value of any object that supplies the wants or pleasures of mankind is compounded of its substance and its form, of the materials and the manufacture. Its price must depend on the number of persons by whom it may be acquired and used; on the extent of the market; and consequently on the ease or difficulty of remote exportation, according to the nature of the commodity, its local situation, and the temporary circumstances of the world. The barbarian conquerors of Rome usurped in a moment the toil and treasure of successive ages; but, except the luxuries of immediate consumption, they must view without desire all that could not be removed from the city in the Gothic waggons or the fleet of the Vandals.[36] Gold and silver were the

---

[34] History of the Decline, &c., vol. iii. c. xxviii. p. 205-209.

[35] Eodem tempore petiit a Phocate principe templum, quod appellatur *Pantheon*, in quo fecit ecclesiam Sanctæ Mariæ semper Virginis et omnium martyrum; in quâ ecclesiæ [misprint for ecclesiâ] princeps multa bona obtulit (Anastasius vel potius Liber Pontificalis in Bonifacio IV. in Muratori, Script. Rerum Italicarum, tom. iii. p. i. p. 135). According to the anonymous writer in Montfaucon, the Pantheon had been vowed by Agrippa to Cybele and Neptune, and was dedicated by Boniface IV. on the kalends of November to the Virgin, quæ est mater omnium sanctorum (p. 297, 298). [It is now established that the existing Pantheon was not the work of Agrippa but of Hadrian (A.D. 120-5). The original building of Agrippa was rectangular. See Lanciani, Ancient Rome, p. 476-88. Urban VIII. removed the bronze roof from the portico of the Pantheon. Raphael's coffin and bones were discovered here in 1833.]

[36] Flaminius Vacca (apud Montfaucon, p. 155, 156; his Memoir is likewise printed, p. 21, at the end of the Roma Antica of Nardini), and several Romans, doctrinâ graves, were persuaded that the Goths buried their treasures at Rome, and bequeathed the secret marks filiis nepotibusque. He relates some anecdotes to

first objects of their avarice; as in every country, and in the
smallest compass, they represent the most ample command of
the industry and possessions of mankind. A vase or a statue of
those precious metals might tempt the vanity of some barbarian
chief; but the grosser multitude, regardless of the form, was
tenacious only of the substance; and the melted ingots might
be readily divided and stamped into the current coin of the
empire. The less active or less fortunate robbers were reduced
to the baser plunder of brass, lead, iron, and copper; whatever
had escaped the Goths and Vandals was pillaged by the Greek
tyrants; and the emperor Constans, in his rapacious visit,
stripped the bronze tiles from the roof of the Pantheon.[37] The
edifices of Rome might be considered as a vast and various mine:
the first labour of extracting the materials was already performed;
the metals were purified and cast; the marbles were hewn and
polished; and, after foreign and domestic rapine had been
satiated, the remains of the city, could a purchaser have been
found, were still venal. The monuments of antiquity had been
left naked of their precious ornaments, but the Romans would
demolish with their own hands the arches and walls, if the hope
of profit could surpass the cost of the labour and exportation.
If Charlemagne had fixed in Italy the seat of the Western empire,
his genius would have aspired to restore, rather than to violate,
the works of the Cæsars; but policy confined the French monarch
to the forests of Germany; his taste could be gratified only by
destruction; and the new palace of Aix la Chapelle was decorated
with the marbles of Ravenna [38] and Rome.[39] Five hundred years

prove that, in his own time, these places were visited and rifled by the Transalpine
pilgrims, the heirs of the Gothic conquerors.

[37] Omnia quæ erant in ære ad ornatum civitatis deposuit : sed et ecclesiam B.
Mariæ ad martyres quæ de tegulis æreis [erat] cooperta discooperuit (Anast. in
Vitalian. p. 141). The base and sacrilegious Greek had not even the poor pretence
of plundering an heathen temple ; the Pantheon was already a Catholic church.

[38] For the spoils of Ravenna (musiva atque marmora) see the original grant of
Pope Hadrian I. to Charlemagne (Codex Carolin. epist. lxvii. in Muratori, Script.
Ital. tom. iii. p. ii. p. 223).

[39] I shall quote the authentic testimony of the Saxon poet (A.D. 887-899), de
Rebus gestis Caroli Magni, l. v. 437-440, in the Historians of France, tom. v. p.
180 :—

> Ad quæ marmoreas præstabat Roma columnas,
> Quasdam præcipuas pulchra Ravenna dedit.
> De tam longinquâ poterit regione vetustas
> Illius ornatum Francia ferre tibi.

And I shall add, from the Chronicle of Sigebert (Historians of France, tom. v. p.
378), extruxit etiam Aquisgrani basilicam plurimæ pulchritudinis, ad cujus struc-

after Charlemagne, a king of Sicily, Robert, the wisest and most
liberal sovereign of the age, was supplied with the same materials
by the easy navigation of the Tiber and the sea ; and Petrarch
sighs an indignant complaint that the ancient capital of the
world should adorn, from her own bowels, the slothful luxury
of Naples.[40]   But these examples of plunder or purchase were
rare in the darker ages ; and the Romans, alone and unenvied,
might have applied to their private or public use the remaining
structures of antiquity, if in their present form and situation
they had not been useless in a great measure to the city and
its inhabitants.   The walls still described the old circumference, but the city had descended from the seven hills into the
Campus Martius ; and some of the noblest monuments which
had braved the injuries of time were left in a desert, far remote
from the habitations of mankind.   The palaces of the senators
were no longer adapted to the manners or fortunes of their indigent successors ; the use of baths [41] and porticoes was forgotten ;
in the sixth century, the games of the theatre, amphitheatre,
and circus had been interrupted ; some temples were devoted to
the prevailing worship ; but the Christian churches preferred the
holy figure of the cross ; and fashion or reason had distributed,
after a peculiar model, the cells and offices of the cloister.   Under
the ecclesiastical reign, the number of these pious foundations
was enormously multiplied ; and the city was crowded with forty

turam a Roma et Ravennâ columnas et marmora devehi fecit. [See above, vol. v.
p. 292.]
    [40] I cannot refuse to transcribe a long passage of Petrarch (Opp. p. 536, 537, in
Epistolâ hortatoriâ ad Nicolaum Laurentium [Var. epist. 48, ed. Fracassetti, vol.
iii. p. 427]), it is so strong and full to the point: Nec pudor aut pietas continuit
quominus impii spoliata Dei templa, occupatas arces, opes publicas, regiones urbis,
atque honores magistratuum inter se divisos; (*habeant ?*) quam [misprint for quâ]
unâ in re, turbulenti ac seditiosi homines et totius reliquæ vitæ consiliis et rationi-
bus discordes, inhumani fœderis stupendâ societate convenirent, in pontes et mœnia
atque immeritos lapides desævirent.   Denique post vi vel senio collapsa palatia,
quæ quondam ingentes tenuerunt viri, post diruptos arcus triumphales (unde majores
horum forsitan corruerunt), de ipsius vetustatis ac propriæ impietatis fragminibus
vilem quæstum turpi mercimonio captare non puduit.   Itaque nunc, heu dolor ! heu
scelus indignum ! de vestris marmoreis columnis, de liminibus templorum (ad quæ
nuper ex orbe toto concursus devotissimus fiebat), de imaginibus sepulchrorum sub
quibus patrum vestrorum venerabilis civis (*cinis ?*) erat, ut reliquas sileam, desidiosa
Neapolis adornatur.   Sic paullatim ruinæ ipsæ deficiunt.   Yet king Robert was the
friend of Petrarch.
    [41] Yet Charlemagne washed and swam at Aix la Chapelle with an hundred of
his courtiers (Eginhart, c. 22, p. 108, 109); and Muratori describes, as late as the
year 814, the public baths which were built at Spoleto in Italy (Annali, tom. vi. p.
416).

monasteries of men, twenty of women, and sixty chapters and colleges of canons and priests,[42] who aggravated, instead of relieving, the depopulation of the tenth century. But, if the forms of ancient architecture were disregarded by a people insensible of their use and beauty, the plentiful materials were applied to every call of necessity or superstition, till the fairest columns of the Ionic and Corinthian orders, the richest marbles of Paros and Numidia, were degraded, perhaps, to the support of a convent or a stable. The daily havoc which is perpetrated by the Turks in the cities of Greece and Asia may afford a melancholy example ; and, in the gradual destruction of the monuments of Rome, Sixtus the Fifth may alone be excused for employing the stones of the Septizonium in the glorious edifice of St. Peter's.[43] A fragment, a ruin, howsoever mangled or profaned, may be viewed with pleasure and regret; but the greater part of the marble was deprived of substance, as well as of place and proportion ; it was burnt to lime for the purpose of cement. Since the arrival of Poggius, the temple of Concord[44] and many capital structures had vanished from his eyes ; and an epigram of the same age expresses a just and pious fear that the continuance of this practice would finally annihilate all the monuments of antiquity.[45] The smallness of their numbers was the sole check on the demands and depredations of the Romans. The imagination of Petrarch might create the presence of a mighty people ;[46] and I hesitate to believe that even in the fourteenth century they

---

[42] See the Annals of Italy, A.D. 988. For this and the preceding fact, Muratori himself is indebted to the Benedictine history of Père Mabillon.

[43] Vita di Sisto Quinto, da Gregorio Leti, tom. iii. p. 50.

[44] Porticus ædis Concordiæ, quam cum primum ad urbem accessi vidi fere integram opere marmoreo admodum specioso: Romani postmodum ad calcem ædem totam et porticus partem disjectis columnis sunt demoliti (p. 12). The temple of Concord was therefore *not* destroyed by a sedition in the xiiith century, as I have read in a Ms. treatise del' Governo civile de Rome [Roma], lent me formerly at Rome, and ascribed (I believe falsely) to the celebrated Gravina. Poggius likewise affirms that the sepulchre of Cæcilia Metella was burnt for lime (p. 19, 20).

[45] Composed by Æneas Sylvius, afterwards Pope Pius II. and published by Mabillon from a Ms. of the Queen of Sweden (Musæum Italicum, tom. i. p. 97) :—

Oblectat me, Roma, tuas spectare ruinas :
Ex cujus lapsu gloria prisca patet.
Sed tuus hic populus muris defossa vetustis
Calcis in obsequium marmora dura coquit.
Impia tercentum si sic gens egerit annos,
Nullum hinc indicium nobilitatis erit.

[46] Vagabamur pariter in illâ urbe tam magnâ ; quæ, cum propter spatium vacua videretur, populum habet immensum (Opp. p. 605 ; Epist. Familiares, ii. 14).

could be reduced to a contemptible list of thirty-three thousand inhabitants. From that period to the reign of Leo the Tenth, if they multiplied to the amount of eighty-five thousand,[47] the increase of citizens was in some degree pernicious to the ancient city.

IV. The domestic quarrels of the Romans

IV. I have reserved for the last and most potent and forcible cause of destruction, the domestic hostilities of the Romans themselves.[47a] Under the dominion of the Greek and French emperors, the peace of the city was disturbed by accidental though frequent seditions : it is from the decline of the latter, from the beginning of the tenth century, that we may date the licentiousness of private war, which violated with impunity the laws of the Code and the Gospel, without respecting the majesty of the absent sovereign or the presence and person of the vicar of Christ. In a dark period of five hundred years, Rome was perpetually afflicted by the sanguinary quarrels of the nobles and the people, the Guelphs and Ghibelines, the Colonna and Ursini ; and, if much has escaped the knowledge, and much is unworthy of the notice, of history, I have exposed in the two preceding chapters the causes and effects of the public disorders. At such a time, when every quarrel was decided by the sword and none could trust their lives or properties to the impotence of law, the powerful citizens were armed for safety or offence against the domestic enemies whom they feared or hated. Except Venice alone, the same dangers and designs were common to all the free republics of Italy ; and the nobles usurped the prerogative of fortifying their houses, and erecting strong towers [48] that were capable of resisting a sudden attack. The cities were filled with these

[47] These states of the population of Rome, at different periods, are derived from an ingenious treatise of the physician Lancisi, de Romani Cœli Qualitatibus (p. 122). [Cp. above p. 274, note 29. The population at beginning of the 16th century was 85,000 ; in 1663, it was 105,433. Gregorovius, *op. cit.* vi. p. 731.]

[47a] [It would be truer to say that the author's third cause, the use and abuse of materials by the Romans, including the construction of fortresses by rival nobles, was the most potent. This has been clearly shown in Lanciani's investigation of the subject in his Destruction of Ancient Rome. As he says, the part of the barbarians in the work of demolition is "hardly worth considering when compared with the guilt of others". In his remarks, however, on hostile attacks, Gibbon should have noted the effects of the Norman pillage of the city in 1084 (see Lanciani, *op. cit.* p. 159 *sqq.*).]

[48] All the facts that relate to the towers at Rome, and in other free cities of Italy, may be found in the laborious and entertaining compilation of Muratori, Antiquitates Italiæ medii Ævi, dissertat. xxvi. (tom. ii. p. 493-496, of the Latin, tom. i. p. 446, of the Italian, work).

hostile edifices; and the example of Lucca, which contained three hundred towers, her law, which confined their height to the measure of fourscore feet, may be extended, with suitable latitude, to the more opulent and populous states.   The first step of the senator Brancaleone in the establishment of peace and justice was to demolish (as we have already seen) one hundred and forty of the towers of Rome; and in the last days of anarchy and discord, as late as the reign of Martin the Fifth, forty-four still stood in one of the thirteen or fourteen regions of the city.[49] To this mischievous purpose, the remains of antiquity were most readily adapted: the temples and arches afforded a broad and solid basis for the new structures of brick and stone; and we can name the modern turrets that were raised on the triumphal monuments of Julius Cæsar, Titus, and the Antonines.[50]   With some slight alterations, a theatre, an amphitheatre, a mausoleum, was transformed into a strong and spacious citadel.   I need not repeat that the mole of Hadrian has assumed the title and form of the castle of St. Angelo;[51] the Septizonium of Severus was capable of standing against a royal army;[52] the sepulchre of Metella has sunk under its outworks;[53] the theatres of Pompey and Marcellus were occupied by the Savelli[54] and Ursini families; and the rough

[49] [Thirteen regions in the 14th century.   Their names and armorial bearings in Gregorovius, vi. p. 727-8.]

[50] As for instance, Templum Jani nunc dicitur, turris Centii Frangapanis; et sane Jano impositæ turris lateritiæ conspicua hodieque vestigia supersunt (Montfaucon, Diarium Italicum, p. 186).   The anonymous writer (p. 285) enumerates, arcus Titi, turris Cartularia; arcus Julii Cæsaris et Senatorum, turres de Bratis; arcus Antonini, turris de Cosectis, &c.   [There is an account of these towers and fortresses in Gregorovius, v. p. 657 sqq.]

[51] Hadriani molem . . . magnâ ex parte Romanorum injuria . . . disturbavit: quod certe funditus evertissent, si eorum manibus pervia, absumptis grandibus saxis, reliqua moles exstitisset (Poggius de Varietate Fortunæ, p. 12).   [In A.D. 1379, the mausoleum of Hadrian, which held out for Pope Clement, was destroyed by the Romans.   It was "pulled down to the central part which encloses the vault" (Gregorovius, vi. 516).   The ruins lay for about twenty years till it was restored by Boniface IX. A.D. 1398, with a tower.   In the 14th century there was a covered passage connecting St. Angelo with the Vatican.]

[52] Against the emperor Henry IV. (Muratori, Annali d'Italia, tom. ix. p. 147).   [See above, p. 317, note 17.]

[53] I must copy an important passage of Montfaucon: Turris ingens rotunda . . . Cæciliæ Metellæ . . . sepulchrum erat, cujus muri tam solidi, ut spatium perquam minimum intus vacuum supersit: et Torre di Bove [or Capo di Bove] dicitur, a boum capitibus muro inscriptis.   Huic sequiori ævo, tempore intestinorum bellorum, ceu urbecula adjuncta fuit, cujus mœnia et turres etiamnum visuntur; ita ut sepulchrum Metellæ quasi arx oppiduli fuerit.   Ferventibus in urbe partibus, cum Ursini atque Columnenses mutuis cladibus perniciem inferrent civitati, in utriusve partis ditionem cederet magni momenti erat (p. 142).   [The sepulchre of Caecilia Metella still stands, a conspicuous object on the Appian Way.]

[54] See the testimonies of Donatus, Nardini, and Montfaucon.   In the Savelli

fortress has been gradually softened to the splendour and elegance of an Italian palace. Even the churches were encompassed with arms and bulwarks, and the military engines on the roof of St. Peter's were the terror of the Vatican and the scandal of the Christian world. Whatever is fortified will be attacked; and whatever is attacked may be destroyed. Could the Romans have wrested from the popes the castle of St. Angelo, they had resolved, by a public decree, to annihilate that monument of servitude. Every building of defence was exposed to a siege; and in every siege the arts and engines of destruction were laboriously employed. After the death of Nicholas the Fourth, Rome, without a sovereign or a senate, was abandoned six months to the fury of civil war. "The houses," says a cardinal and poet of the times,[55] "were crushed by the weight and velocity of enormous stones;[56] the walls were perforated by the strokes of the battering-ram; the towers were involved in fire and smoke; and the assailants were stimulated by rapine and revenge." The work was consummated by the tyranny of the laws; and the factions of Italy alternately exercised a blind and thoughtless vengeance on their adversaries, whose houses and castles they rased to the ground.[57] In comparing the *days* of foreign, with the *ages* of

palace, the remains of the theatre of Marcellus are still great and conspicuous. [The theatre of Marcellus, towards end of 11th century, was converted into a fortress by the Pierleoni. In the 14th century it was purchased by the Savelli. In 1712 it passed into the hands of the Orsini. "The section of the outside shell visible at present, a magnificent ruin in outline and colour, is buried 15 feet in modern soil and supports the Orsini palace erected upon its stage and ranges of seats. What stands above ground of the lower or Doric arcades is rented by the Prince for the most squalid and ignoble class of shops." Lanciani, Ruins and Excavations, p. 494. The Theatre of Balbus became the fortress of the Cenci.]

[55] James, cardinal of St. George ad velum aureum, in his metrical life of Pope Celestin V. (Muratori, Script. Ital. tom. i. p. iii. p. 621; l. i. c. 1. ver. 132, &c.).

> Hoc dixisse sat est, Romam caruisse Senatu
> Mensibus exactis heu sex; belloque vocatum (*vocatus*)
> In scelus, in socios fraternaque vulnera patres;
> Tormentis jecisse viros immania saxa;
> Perfodisse domus trabibus, fecisse ruinas
> Ignibus; incensas turres, obscuraque fumo
> Lumina vicino, quo sit spoliata supellex.

[56] Muratori (Dissertazione sopra le Antiquità Italiane, tom. i. p. 427-431) finds that stone bullets, of two or three hundred pounds weight, were not uncommon; and they are sometimes computed at xii or xviii *cantari* of Genoa, each *cantaro* weighing 150 pounds.

[57] The vith law of the Visconti prohibits this common and mischievous practice; and strictly enjoins that the houses of banished citizens should be preserved pro communi utilitate (Gualvaneus de la Flamma, in Muratori, Script. Rerum Italicarum, tom. xii. p. 1041).

domestic, hostility, we must pronounce that the latter have been far more ruinous to the city; and our opinion is confirmed by the evidence of Petrarch. "Behold," says the laureat, "the relics of Rome, the image of her pristine greatness! neither time nor the barbarian can boast the merit of this stupendous destruction: it was perpetrated by her own citizens, by the most illustrious of her sons; and your ancestors (he writes to a noble Annibaldi) have done with the battering-ram, what the Punic hero could not accomplish with the sword." [58] The influence of the two last principles of decay must, in some degree, be multiplied by each other; since the houses and towers, which were subverted by civil war, required a new and perpetual supply from the monuments of antiquity.

These general observations may be separately applied to the amphitheatre of Titus, which has obtained the name of the COLISEUM,[59] either from its magnitude or from Nero's colossal statue: an edifice, had it been left to time and nature, which might, perhaps, have claimed an eternal duration. The curious antiquaries, who have computed the numbers and seats, are disposed to believe that, above the upper row of stone steps, the amphitheatre was encircled and elevated with several stages of wooden galleries, which were repeatedly consumed by fire and restored by the emperors. Whatever was precious, or portable, or profane, the statues of gods and heroes, and the costly ornaments of sculpture, which were cast in brass, or overspread with leaves of silver and gold, became the first prey of conquest or fanaticism, of the avarice of the barbarians or the Christians. In the massy stones of the Coliseum many holes are discerned;

---

[58] Petrarch thus addresses his friend, who, with shame and tears, had shewn him the mœnia, laceræ specimen miserabile Romæ, and declared his own intention of restoring them (Carmina Latina, l. ii. epist. Paulo Annibalensi, xii. p. 97, 98):

> Nec te parva manet servatis fama ruinis
> Quanta quod integræ fuit olim gloria Romæ
> Reliquiæ testantur adhuc; quas longior ætas
> Frangere non valuit; non vis aut iræ cruenti
> Hostis, ab egregiis franguntur civibus, heu! heu!
> . . . Quod *ille* nequivit (*Hannibal*)
> Perficit hic aries. . . .

[59] The fourth part of the Verona Illustrata of the Marquis Maffei, professedly treats of amphitheatres, particularly those of Rome and Verona, of their dimensions, wooden galleries, &c. It is from magnitude that he derives the name of *Colosseum*, or *Coliseum* : since the same appellation was applied to the amphitheatre of Capua, without the aid of a colossal statue; since that of Nero was erected in the court (*in atrio*) of his palace, and not in the Coliseum (p. iv. p. 15-19; l. i. c. 4).

and the two most probable conjectures represent the various accidents of its decay.   These stones were connected by solid links of brass or iron, nor had the eye of rapine overlooked the value of the baser metals : [60] the vacant space was converted into a fair or market ; the artisans of the Coliseum are mentioned in an ancient survey ; and the chasms were perforated or enlarged, to receive the poles that supported the shops or tents of the mechanic trades.[61]   Reduced to its naked majesty, the Flavian amphitheatre was contemplated with awe and admiration by the pilgrims of the North ; and their rude enthusiasm broke forth in a sublime proverbial expression, which is recorded in the eighth century, in the fragments of the venerable Bede : " As long as the Coliseum stands, Rome shall stand ; when the Coliseum falls, Rome will fall ; when Rome falls, the world will fall ".[62]   In the modern system of war, a situation commanded by three hills would not be chosen for a fortress ; but the strength of the walls and arches could resist the engines of assault ; a numerous garrison might be lodged in the enclosure ; and, while one faction occupied the Vatican and the Capitol, the other was intrenched in the Lateran and the Coliseum.[63]

Games of Rome

The abolition at Rome of the ancient games must be understood with some latitude ; and the carnival sports of the Testacean Mount and the Circus Agonalis [64] were regulated by the law [65]

---

[60] Joseph Maria Suarés, a learned bishop, and the author of an history of Præneste, has composed a separate dissertation on the seven or eight probable causes of these holes, which has been since reprinted in the Roman Thesaurus of Sallengre. Montfaucon (Diarium, p. 233) pronounces the rapine of the barbarians to be the unam germanamque causam foraminum. [The travertine blocks were connected by iron clamps, run with lead ; and the holes, as the author says, are due to the removal of these clamps in the Middle Ages.   Cp. Middleton, Remains of Ancient Rome, ii. 87 *note*.]

[61] Donatus, Roma Vetus et Nova, p. 285.

[62] Quamdiu stabit Colyseus, stabit et Roma ; quando cadet Colyseus, cadet Roma ; quando cadet Roma, cadet et mundus (Beda in Excerptis seu Collectaneis apud Ducange Glossar. med. et infimæ Latinitatis, tom. ii. p. 407, edit. Basil). This saying must be ascribed to the Anglo-Saxon pilgrims who visited Rome before the year 735, the æra of Bede's death ; for I do not believe that our venerable monk ever passed the sea.

[63] I cannot recover, in Muratori's original Lives of the Popes (Script. Rerum Italicarum, tom. iii. p. i.), the passage that attests this hostile partition, which must be applied to the end of the xith or the beginning of the xiith century.

[64] Although the structure of the Circus Agonalis be destroyed, it still retains its form and name (Agona, [in Agona], Nagona, Navona) : and the interior space affords a sufficient level for the purpose of racing.   But the Monte Testaceo, that strange pile of broken pottery, seems only adapted for the annual practice of hurling from top to bottom some waggon-loads of live hogs for the diversion of the populace (Statuta Urbis Romæ, p. 186).

[65] See the Statuta Urbis Romæ, l. iii. c. 87, 88, 89, p. 185, 186.   I have already given an idea of this municipal code.   The races of Nagona and Monte Testaceo

or custom of the city.   The senator presided with dignity and pomp to adjudge and distribute the prizes, the gold ring, or the *pallium*,[66] as it was styled, of cloth or silk.   A tribute on the Jews supplied the annual expense ; [67] and the races, on foot, on horseback, or in chariots, were ennobled by a tilt and tournament of seventy-two of the Roman youth.   In the year one thousand three hundred and thirty-two, a bull-feast, after the fashion of the Moors and Spaniards, was celebrated in the Coliseum itself ; and the living manners are painted in a diary of the times.[68]   A convenient order of benches was restored ; and a general proclamation, as far as Rimini and Ravenna, invited the nobles to exercise their skill and courage in this perilous adventure.   The Roman ladies were marshalled in three squadrons, and seated in three balconies, which on this day, the third of September, were lined with scarlet cloth.   The fair Jacova di Rovere led the matrons from beyond the Tiber, a pure and native race, who still represent the features and character of antiquity.   The remainder of the city was divided, as usual, between the Colonna and Ursini ; the two factions were proud of the number and beauty of their female bands : the charms of Savella Ursini are mentioned with praise ; and the Colonna regretted the absence of the youngest of their house, who had sprained her ankle in the garden of Nero's tower.   The lots of the champions were drawn by an old and respectable citizen ; and they descended into the *arena* or pit, to encounter the wild bulls on foot, as it should seem, with a single spear.   Amidst the crowd, our annalist has selected the names, colours, and devices, of twenty of the most conspicuous knights.   Several of the names are the most illustrious of Rome and the ecclesiastical state ; Malatesta, Polenta, della Valle, Cafarello, Savelli, Capoccio, Conti, Anni-

A bull-feast in the Coliseum, A.D. 1332, Sept. 3

---

are likewise mentioned in the Diary of Peter Antonius, from 1404 to 1417 (Muratori, Script. Rerum Italicarum, tom. xxiv. p. 1124).

[66] The *Pallium*, which Menage so foolishly derives from *Palmarium*, is an extension of the idea and the words from the robe or cloak to the materials, and from thence to their application as a prize (Muratori, dissert. xxxiii.).

[67] For these expenses, the Jews of Rome paid each year 1130 florins, of which the odd thirty represented the pieces of silver for which Judas had betrayed his master to their ancestors.   There was a foot-race of Jewish as well as of Christian youths (Statuta Urbis, ibidem).

[68] This extraordinary bull-feast in the Coliseum is described, from tradition rather than memory, by Ludovico Buonconte Monaldesco, in the most ancient fragments of Roman annals (Muratori, Script. Rerum Italicarum, tom. xii. p. 525, 536) ; and, however fanciful they may seem, they are deeply marked with the colours of truth and nature.

baldi, Altieri, Corsi; the colours were adapted to their taste and situation; the devices are expressive of hope or despair, and breathe the spirit of gallantry and arms. " I am alone like the youngest of the Horatii," the confidence of an intrepid stranger; "I live disconsolate," a weeping widower; "I burn under the ashes," a discreet lover; "I adore Lavinia, or Lucretia," the ambiguous declaration of a modern passion; " My faith is as pure," the motto of a white livery; "Who is stronger than myself?" of a lion's hide; "If .I am drowned in blood, what a pleasant death!" the wish of ferocious courage. The pride or prudence of the Ursini restrained them from the field, which was occupied by three of their hereditary rivals, whose inscriptions denoted the lofty greatness of the Colonna name: "Though sad, I am strong;" "Strong as I am great;" "If I fall," addressing himself to the spectators, "you fall with me;"—intimating (says the contemporary writer) that, while the other families were the subjects of the Vatican, they alone were the supporters of the Capitol. The combats of the amphitheatre were dangerous and bloody. Every champion successively encountered a wild bull; and the victory may be ascribed to the quadrupeds, since no more than eleven were left on the field, with the loss of nine wounded, and eighteen killed, on the side of their adversaries. Some of the noblest families might mourn, but the pomp of the funerals, in the churches of St. John Lateran and Sta. Maria Maggiore, afforded a second holiday to the people. Doubtless it was not in such conflicts that the blood of the Romans should have been shed; yet, in blaming their rashness, we are compelled to applaud their gallantry; and the noble volunteers, who display their magnificence and risk their lives under the balconies of the fair, excite a more generous sympathy than the thousands of captives and malefactors who were reluctantly dragged to the scene of slaughter.[69]

Injuries,   This use of the amphitheatre was a rare, perhaps a singular, festival: the demand for the materials was a daily and continual want, which the citizens could gratify without restraint or remorse. In the fourteenth century, a scandalous act of concord secured to both factions the privilege of extracting stones from the free and common quarry of the Coliseum;[70] and Poggius

[69] Muratori has given a separate dissertation (the xxixth) to the games of the Italians in the middle ages.

[70] In a concise but instructive memoir, the Abbé Barthélemy (Mémoires de

laments that the greater part of these stones had been burnt to lime by the folly of the Romans.[71] To check this abuse, and to prevent the nocturnal crimes that might be perpetrated in the vast and gloomy recess, Eugenius the Fourth surrounded it with a wall; and, by a charter long extant, granted both the ground and edifice to the monks of an adjacent convent.[72] After his death, the wall was overthrown in a tumult of the people; and, had they themselves respected the noblest monument of their fathers, they might have justified the resolve that it should never be degraded to private property. The inside was damaged; but, in the middle of the sixteenth century, an æra of taste and learning, the exterior circumference of one thousand six hundred and twelve feet was still entire and inviolate; a triple elevation of fourscore arches, which rose to the height of one hundred and eight feet. Of the present ruin the nephews of Paul the Third are the guilty agents; and every traveller who views the Farnese palace may curse the sacrilege and luxury of these upstart princes.[73] A similar reproach is applied to the Barberini; and the repetition of injury might be dreaded from every reign, till the Coliseum was placed under the safeguard of religion by the most liberal of the pontiffs, Benedict the Fourteenth, who consecrated a spot which persecution and fable had stained with the blood of so many Christian martyrs.[74]

and consecration of the Coliseum

l'Académie des Inscriptions, tom. xxviii. p. 585) has mentioned this agreement of the factions of the xivth century de Tiburtino faciendo in the Coliseum, from an original act in the archives of Rome.

[71] Coliseum . . . ob stultitiam Romanorum *majori ex parte* ad calcem deletum, says the indignant Poggius (p. 17): but his expression, too strong for the present age, must be very tenderly applied to the xvth century. [It may be inferred with tolerable certainty that the chief injury which the shell of the Coliseum sustained, the falling of the whole western half towards the Cælian Hill, happened in the great earthquake of A.D. 1348. These ruins were then freely used as a quarry. Cp. Lanciani, Ruins and Excavations, p. 375-6. In A.D. 1386 the senate and people gave one-third of the Coliseum to the Compagnia del Salvatore ad Sancta Sanctorum.]

[72] Of the Olivetan monks. Montfaucon (p. 142) affirms this fact from the memorials of Flaminius Vacca (No. 72). They still hoped, on some future occasion, to revive and vindicate their grant.

[73] After measuring the priscus amphitheatri gyrus, Montfaucon (p. 142) only adds that it was entire under Paul III.; tacendo clamat. Muratori (Annali d'Italia, tom. xiv. p. 371) more freely reports the guilt of the Farnese Pope and the indignation of the Roman people. Against the nephews of Urban VIII. I have no other evidence than the vulgar saying, " Quod non fecerunt Barbari, fecere Barbarini," which was perhaps suggested by the resemblance of the words. [The spelling Barbarini here is intentional and should not be changed.]

[74] As an antiquarian and a priest, Montfaucon thus deprecates the ruin of the Coliseum; Quod si non suopte merito atque pulchritudine dignum fuisset quod

Ignorance
and bar-
barism of
the Ro-
mans

When Petrarch first gratified his eyes with a view of those monuments whose scattered fragments so far surpass the most eloquent descriptions, he was astonished at the supine indifference [75] of the Romans themselves; [76] he was humbled rather than elated by the discovery that, except his friend Rienzi and one of the Colonna, a stranger of the Rhône was more conversant with these antiquities than the nobles and natives of the metropolis.[77] The ignorance and credulity of the Romans are elaborately displayed in the old survey of the city, which was composed about the beginning of the thirteenth century; and, without dwelling on the manifold errors of name and place, the legend of the Capitol [78] may provoke a smile of contempt and indignation. "The Capitol," says the anonymous writer, "is so named as being the head of the world; where the consuls and senators formerly resided for the government of the city and the globe. The strong and lofty walls were covered with glass and gold, and crowned with a roof of the richest and most curious carving. Below the citadel stood a palace, of gold for the greatest part, decorated with precious stones, and whose value might be estimated at one third of the world itself. The statues of all the provinces were arranged in order, each with a small bell suspended from its neck; and such was the contrivance of art magic [79]

improbas arceret manus, indigna res utique in locum tot martyrum cruore sacrum tantopere saevitum esse.

[75] Yet the Statutes of Rome (l. iii. c. 81, p. 182) impose a fine of 500 *aurei* on whosoever shall demolish any ancient edifice, ne ruinis civitas deformetur, et ut antiqua aedificia decorem urbis perpetuo repraesentent.

[76] In his first visit to Rome (A.D. 1337; see Mémoires sur Pétrarque, tom. i. p. 322, &c.), Petrarch is struck mute miraculo rerum tantarum, et stuporis mole obrutus. . . . Praesentia vero, mirum dictu, nihil imminuit: vere major fuit Roma majoresque sunt reliquiae quam rebar. Jam non orbem ab hâc urbe domitum, sed tam sero domitum, miror (Opp. p. 605; Familiares, ii. 14; Joanni Columnae).

[77] He excepts and praises the *rare* knowledge of John Colonna. Qui enim hodie magis ignari rerum Romanarum, quam Romani cives? Invitus dico, nusquam minus Roma cognoscitur quam Romae.

[78] After the description of the Capitol, he adds, statuae erant quot sunt mundi provinciae; et habebat quaelibet tintinnabulum ad collum. Et erant ita per magicam artem dispositae, ut quando aliqua regio Romano Imperio rebellis erat, statim imago illius provinciae vertebat se contra illam; unde tintinnabulum resonabat quod pendebat ad collum; tuncque vates Capitolii qui erant custodes senatui, &c. He mentions an example of the Saxons and Suevi, who, after they had been subdued by Agrippa, again rebelled; tintinnabulum sonuit; sacerdos qui erat in speculo in hebdomadâ senatoribus nuntiavit; Agrippa marched back and reduced the —— Persians (Anonym. in Montfaucon, p. 297, 298).

[79] The same writer affirms that Virgil captus a Romanis invisibiliter exiit ivitque Neapolim. A Roman magician, in the xith century, is introduced by William of Malmesbury (de Gestis Regum Anglorum, l. ii. p. 86); and in the time of Flaminus Vacca (No. 81, 103) it was the vulgar belief that the strangers (the *Goths*) invoked the daemons for the discovery of hidden treasures.

that, if the province rebelled against Rome, the statue turned round to that quarter of the heavens, the bell rang, the prophet of the Capitol reported the prodigy, and the senate was admonished of the impending danger." A second example of less importance, though of equal absurdity, may be drawn from the two marble horses, led by two naked youths, which have since been transported from the baths of Constantine to the Quirinal Hill. The groundless application of the names of Phidias and Praxiteles may perhaps be excused ; but these Grecian sculptors should not have been removed above four hundred years from the age of Pericles to that of Tiberius ; they should not have been transformed into two philosophers or magicians, whose nakedness was the symbol of truth and knowledge, who revealed to the emperor his most secret actions, and, after refusing all pecuniary recompense, solicited the honour of leaving this eternal monument of themselves.[80] Thus awake to the power of magic, the Romans were insensible to the beauties of art : no more than five statues were visible to the eyes of Poggius ; and, of the multitudes which chance or design had buried under the ruins, the resurrection was fortunately delayed till a safer and more enlightened age.[81] The Nile, which now adorns the Vatican, had been explored by some labourers in digging a vineyard near the temple, or convent, of the Minerva ; but the impatient proprietor, who was tormented by some visits of curiosity, restored the unprofitable marble to its former grave.[82] The discovery of a statue of Pompey, ten feet in length, was the occasion of a law-suit. It had been found under a partition-wall : the equitable judge had pronounced that the head should be separated from the body, to satisfy the claims of the con-

---

[80] Anonym. p. 289. Montfaucon (p. 191) justly observes that, if Alexander be represented, these statues cannot be the work of Phidias (Olympiad lxxxiii.), or Praxiteles (Olympiad civ.), who lived before that conqueror (Plin. Hist. Natur. xxxiv. 19).

[81] William of Malmesbury (l. ii. p. 86, 87) relates a marvellous discovery (A.D. 1046) of Pallas, the son of Evander, who had been slain by Turnus : the perpetual light in his sepulchre, a Latin epitaph, the corpse, yet entire, of a young giant, the enormous wound in his breast (pectus perforat ingens), &c. If this fable rests on the slightest foundation, we may pity the bodies, as well as the statues, that were exposed to the air in a barbarous age.

[82] Prope porticum Minervæ, statua est recubantis, cujus caput integrâ effigie tantæ magnitudinis, ut signa omnia excedat. Quidam ad plantandas arbores scrobes faciens detexit. Ad hoc visendum cum plures in dies magis concurrerent, strepitum adeuntium fastidiumque pertæsus, horti patronus congestâ humo texit (Poggius de Varietate Fortunæ, p. 12).

tiguous owners; and the sentence would have been executed, if the intercession of a cardinal and the liberality of a pope had not rescued the Roman hero from the hands of his barbarous countrymen.[83]

Restoration and ornaments of the city, A.D. 1420, &c.

But the clouds of barbarism were gradually dispelled; and the peaceful authority of Martin the Fifth and his successors restored the ornaments of the city as well as the order of the ecclesiastical state. The improvements of Rome, since the fifteenth century, have not been the spontaneous produce of freedom and industry. The first and most natural root of a great city is the labour and populousness of the adjacent country, which supplies the materials of subsistence, of manufactures, and of foreign trade. But the greater part of the Campagna of Rome is reduced to a dreary and desolate wilderness; the overgrown estates of the princes and the clergy are cultivated by the lazy hands of indigent and hopeless vassals; and the scanty harvests are confined or exported for the benefit of a monopoly. A second and more artificial cause of the growth of a metropolis is the residence of a monarch, the expense of a luxurious court, and the tributes of dependent provinces. Those provinces and tributes had been lost in the fall of the empire; and, if some streams of the silver of Peru and the gold of Brazil have been attracted by the Vatican, the revenues of the cardinals, the fees of office, the oblations of pilgrims and clients, and the remnant of ecclesiastical taxes afford a poor and precarious supply, which maintains, however, the idleness of the court and city. The population of Rome, far below the measure of the great capitals of Europe, does not exceed one hundred and seventy thousand inhabitants; [84] and, within the spacious inclosure of the walls, the largest portion of the seven hills is overspread with vineyards and ruins. The beauty and splendour of the modern city may be ascribed to the abuses of the government, to the influence of superstition. Each reign (the exceptions are rare) has been marked by the rapid elevation of a new family, enriched by the

[83] See the Memorials of Flaminius Vacca, No. 57, p. 11, 12, at the end of the Roma Antica of Nardini (1704, in 4to).

[84] In the year 1709, the inhabitants of Rome (without including eight or ten thousand Jews) amounted to 138,568 souls (Labat, Voyages en Espagne et en Italie, tom. iii. p. 217, 218). In 1740 they had increased to 146,080; and in 1765, I left them, without the Jews, 161,899. I am ignorant whether they have since continued in a progressive state.

childless pontiff at the expense of the church and country.   The palaces of these fortunate nephews are the most costly monuments of elegance and servitude; the perfect arts of architecture, painting, and sculpture have been prostituted in their service; and their galleries and gardens are decorated with the most precious works of antiquity, which taste or vanity has prompted them to collect.   The ecclesiastical revenues were more decently employed by the popes themselves in the pomp of the Catholic worship; but it is superfluous to enumerate their pious foundation of altars, chapels, and churches, since these lesser stars are eclipsed by the sun of the Vatican, by the dome of St. Peter, the most glorious structure that ever has been applied to the use of religion.   The fame of Julius the Second, Leo the Tenth, and Sixtus the Fifth is accompanied by the superior merit of Bramante and Fontana, of Raphael and Michael-Angelo; and the same munificence which had been displayed in palaces and temples was directed with equal zeal to revive and emulate the labours of antiquity.   Prostrate obelisks were raised from the ground and erected in the most conspicuous places; of the eleven aqueducts of the Cæsars and Consuls, three were restored; the artificial rivers were conducted over a long series of old or of new arches, to discharge into marble basins a flood of salubrious and refreshing waters; and the spectator, impatient to ascend the steps of St. Peter's, is detained by a column of Egyptian granite, which rises between two lofty and perpetual fountains to the height of one hundred and twenty feet.   The map, the description, the monuments of ancient Rome have been elucidated by the diligence of the antiquarian and the student;[85] and the footsteps of heroes, the relics, not of super-

[85] The Père Montfaucon distributes his own observations into twenty days, he should have styled them weeks, or months, of his visits to the different parts of the city (Diarium Italicum, c. 8-20, p. 104-301).   That learned Benedictine reviews the topographers of ancient Rome; the first efforts of Blondus, Fulvius, Martianus, and Faunus, the superior labours of Pyrrhus Ligorius, had his learning been equal to his labours; the writings of Onuphrius Panvinius, qui omnes obscuravit, and the recent but imperfect books of Donatus and Nardini.   Yet Montfaucon still sighs for a more complete plan and description of the old city, which must be attained by the three following methods : 1. The measurement of the space and intervals of the ruins.   2. The study of inscriptions and the places where they were found.   3. The investigation of all the acts, charters, diaries of the middle ages, which name any spot or building of Rome.   The laborious work, such as Montfaucon desired, must be promoted by princely or public munificence; but the great modern plan of Nolli (A.D. 1748) would furnish a solid and accurate basis for the ancient topography of Rome. [We have now Lanciani's great plan in forty-six sheets : Forma

stition, but of empire, are devoutly visited by a new race of pilgrims from the remote, and once savage, countries of the North.

Final con-
clusion

Of these pilgrims, and of every reader, the attention will be excited by an History of the Decline and Fall of the Roman Empire: the greatest, perhaps, and most awful scene in the history of mankind.   The various causes and progressive effects are connected with many of the events most interesting in human annals: the artful policy of the Cæsars, who long maintained the name and image of a free republic; the disorder of military despotism; the rise, establishment, and sects of Christianity; the foundation of Constantinople; the division of the monarchy; the invasion and settlements of the Barbarians of Germany and Scythia; the institutions of the civil law; the character and religion of Mahomet; the temporal sovereignty of the popes; the restoration and decay of the Western empire of Charlemagne; the crusades of the Latins in the East; the conquests of the Saracens and Turks; the ruin of the Greek empire; the state and revolutions of Rome in the middle age.   The historian may applaud the importance and variety of his subject; but, while he is conscious of his own imperfections, he must often accuse the deficiency of his materials.   It was among the ruins of the Capitol that I first conceived the idea of a work which has amused and exercised near twenty years of my life, and which, however inadequate to my own wishes, I finally deliver to the curiosity and candour of the public.

LAUSANNE,
June 27, 1787.

Urbis Romæ, 1893 *sqq.* (published by the Academy of the Lincei).   See also Formæ Urbis Romæ antiquæ, by Kiepert and Hülsen, 1896.   For excavations in recent times see especially the series of the Bullettino della Commissione archeologica comunale di Roma, 1872 *et sqq.*; Notizie degli Scavi di Antichità, 1876 *et sqq.*; Mittheilungen of the German archæol. Institute, Römische Abtheilung, 1886 *et sqq.*]

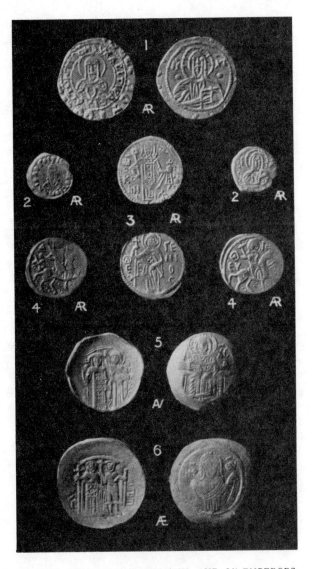

COINS OF JOHN VIII PALAEOLOGUS, AND OF EMPERORS
OF TREBIZOND NICAEA AND THESSALONICA
See List of Illustrations

APPENDIX

ADDITIONAL NOTES BY THE EDITOR

1. AUTHORITIES

LAONICUS CHALCONDYLES[1] belonged to a good Athenian family. He went twice as an ambassador to the Sultan Murad, and was on both occasions imprisoned. His History in 10 books covers the period 1298-1463, and thus includes the fall of the Empire of Trebizond. He was a man of great ability, and, though we may wish that he had not set it before himself to imitate Herodotus and Thucydides, we must recognise the talent which he displayed in handling a most intractable period of history. It is very interesting to pass from his predecessors in the series of the Byzantine historians to this writer. We no longer watch events from the single and simple standpoint of Constantinople. The true theme of Chalcondyles is not the decline of the diminished empire, but the growth and development of the Ottoman State.[2] The centre of events shifts with the movements of the sultan. The weakest point of Chalcondyles is his chronology. (Ed. Baumbach (Geneva), 1615; ed. Bekker (Bonn), 1843.)

DUCAS was a grandson of Michael Ducas (a scion of the imperial family of that name), who is mentioned as having taken part in the struggle between Cantacuzenus and John Palæologus in the 14th century. He was secretary of the Genoese podestà at Phocæa, before the siege of Constantinople, and afterwards he was employed by the Gattilusi of Lesbos as an ambassador to the sultan. His connexion with the Genoese helped, probably, to determine his ecclesiastical views; he was a hearty supporter of union with the Latin Church, as the great safeguard against the Turks. His History covers the period 1341-1462; he is more accurate than Chalcondyles. In language he is not a purist; his work is full of foreign words. (Ed. Bullialdus (Paris), 1649; ed. Bekker (Bonn), 1834, with a 15th cent. Italian translation, which fills up some gaps in the Greek.)

George PHRANTZES (cp. above p. 102 note), born 1401, was secretary of the Emperor Manuel, whose son Constantine he rescued at Palias in 1429. In 1432 Protovestiarios, he was made Prefect of Sparta in 1448, and then elevated to the post of Great Logothete. See further, above p. 102 and p. 162 sqq. Taken prisoner on the capture of Constantinople (cp. above p. 204), he fled to the Peloponnesus, visited Italy, and ended his life as Brother Gregory in a monastery of Corfu, where he composed his Chronicle. This work, when Gibbon wrote, was accessible only in the Latin translation of Pontanus (1604). The Greek original was first published by F. K. Alter (Vienna, 1796), from an inferior Ms. An improved text was issued by Bekker in the Bonn series, 1838.[3] The history covers a longer period than that of Chalcondyles; beginning A.D. 1258, it comes

---

[1] Chalcondyles, for Chalc⟨oc⟩ondyes, is explained by Krumbacher as meaning the man with the bronze handle (Gesch. der byz. Litt., p. 305).

[2] This has been excellently brought out by Krumbacher, op. cit., p. 302.

[3] There is also extant an abbreviated version of the Chronicle in colloquial Greek, and it seems to have been prepared by Phrantzes himself. Cp. Krumbacher, op. cit., p. 308. It has been edited in Mai's Class. Auct. ix. p. 594 sqq., 1837, and reprinted in Migne, P.G., 156.

down to A.D. 1476, the year before the work was completed. Bk. 1 comes down to the death of Manuel; Bk. 2 to the death of John; Bk. 3 treats of the reign of Constantine and the capture of the city; Bk. 4 the events of the following twenty-three years. The high position which he held in the State and his opportunities of knowledge render Bks. 2 and 3 especially valuable. He is naturally a good hater of the Turks, from whom he had suffered so much. His style is not pedantic like that of Chalcondyles. (Biographical Monograph by G. Destunis in the Zhurnal Ministerstva narodn. prosv., vol. 287, p. 427 *sqq.*, 1893.)

CRITOBULUS of Imbros wrote a history of the deeds of Mohammad II. from A.D. 1451 to 1467. Although he is not out of sympathy with his countrymen, he has thrown in his lot with the conquerors, and he writes from the Turkish point of view. This is the interesting feature of his work, which is thus sharply contrasted with the histories of Chalcondyles and Ducas. He inscribes the book, in a dedicatory epistle, to Mohammad himself, whom he compares to Alexander the Great. Like Ducas and Chalcondyles, he describes the siege of Constantinople at second hand; but like theirs his very full description is a most valuable source for comparison with the accounts of the eye-witnesses. He can indeed be convicted of many small inaccuracies. For example, he states that Giustiniani was wounded in the chest, and that Constantine was slain near the Cercoporta; and in other parts of his work his chronology is at fault. He was an imitator of Thucydides, and puts Thucydidean speeches into the mouth of Mohammad. But he does not scruple to use a "modern" foreign word like τούφακες, "guns" (from the Turkish; cp. modern Greek τουφέκι, a gun). The history of Critobulus is extant in an Ms. at Constantinople, and it was first published by C. Müller, in the 2nd part of vol. v. of Fragmenta Historicorum Græcorum, p. 40 *sqq.*, 1870, with very useful notes.

The description of Murad's siege of Constantinople by JOHN CANANUS is mentioned above p. 80, note 93; and that of the siege of Thessalonica in 1430, by JOHN ANAGNOSTES, on p. 145, note 14.

The chronicle of the last years of the empire is briefly told in the anonymous EKTHESIS CHRONIKE, a work of the 16th century, published by C. Sathas in Bibl. Græc. Med. Ævi. vii. p. 556 *sqq.* (1894). A new edition of this little work by Prof. Lampros was published in 1902 (London).

It remains to mention the Anonymous Dirge concerning Tamurlane, Θρῆνος περὶ Ταμυρλάγγου, written during the campaign of Timur into Asia Minor. It is published by Papadimitriu in the Lietopis ist.-phil. obschestva of Odessa (Vizant. Otdiel.), ii. p. 173 *sqq.* (Older, bad ed., in Wagner's Medieval Greek Texts, p. 105 *sqq.*) Timur's name also appears in this poem as Ταμυρλάνης (l. 47) and Τεμύρης (l. 41).

RASHĪD AD-DĪN, born 1247 at Hamadān, was originally a physician, but became Vizir of Persia, 1298. He was executed by Abū Said in 1318. In the preface to his Jāmi at-Tawārīkh he acknowledges his obligations to a minister of Mongol birth and name, who was versed in Turkish and Mongolian history. He refers to the *Altan depter*, a book of Mongol annals which was in the Khan's treasury, text and Russian translation by J. N. Berezin, 1858 *sqq.*

Alā ad-Dīn Ata-mulk JUVAINĪ composed a work entitled Jahān Kushāi (a history of the Conqueror of the World) on the last ten years of Chingiz, and coming down as far as A.D. 1257. Born in Khorāsān in A.D. 1227-8, he visited the court of Mangū Khān c. A.D. 1249. His work (of which there is a Ms. in the British Museum) has never been printed, though he is one of the best authorities on the history of his time. But it has been largely used by D'Ohsson and others. For his biography see Fundgruben des Orients, i. 220-34.

Minhāj-i-Sirāj JŪZJĀNĪ, son of a cadi of the army of Mohammad Ghōrī, lived c. A.D. 1200-70, and wrote his history, the Tabākāt-i-Nāsirī, about the middle of the century, at the court of Nāsir ad-Dīn Mahmūd, King of Delhi. Beginning with the Patriarchs, he brought his history down to his own day, and Bk. 23 is occupied with the incursions of the Turks and Mongols,—the Karā-Khitāy Chingiz and his successors, to A.D. 1259. The author writes in a clear straightforward style, and supports his narrative by references to sources. The work was translated by Major Raverty in the Bibliotheca Indica (1848, etc.), and there are large extracts in Elliot and Dowson, History of India as told by its own historians, ii. 266 *sqq*.

The second and third Books of the Memoirs of Tīmūr are the Institutions and Designs which were translated by Major Davy (1783) and used by Gibbon. Book iv. coming down to 1375 A.D. has since been translated by Major Charles Stewart, 1830 (the Mulfuzāt Timūry, or autobiographical Memoirs of the Moghul Emperor Timūr). The original memoirs were written in Turkish (in the "Jagtay Tūrky language") and were rendered into Persian by Abū Tālib Husainī. The English translations are made from the Persian version.

Mirza HAIDAR lived in the 16th century and was a cousin of the famous Bābar. His Tarīkh-i-Rashīdī (transl. by Elias and Ross, see above p. 5, note 12, with learned apparatus of introduction and notes) is "the history of that branch of the Moghul Khans who separated themselves, about the year 1321, from the main stem of the Chaghatai, which was then the ruling dynasty in Transoxiana; and it is the only history known to exist of this branch of the Moghuls" (Elias, *ib.* p. 7). There are two parts of the work; the second contains memoirs of the author's life, etc., which do not concern any events touched upon by Gibbon. In the first part, written in 1544-6 in Cashmir, the author follows the history of two dynasties: the Khans of Moghulistān, beginning with Tughluk Tīmūr; and their vassals the Dughlāt amīrs of Eastern Turkestan, from one of whom Haidar was descended. This part of the work is based largely on oral traditions, but the author also made use of the work of Sharaf ad-Dīn. Elias criticizes "the weakness of the chronology and the looseness with which numbers and measurements are made".

Of Chinese authorities for the history of the Mongols, the most important is the annals entitled YUAN SHI, of which Bretschneider (Mediæval Researches for Eastern Asiatic Sources, 1888) gives the following account (vol. i. p. 180 *sqq*.). In 1369 "the detailed records of the reigns of the thirteen Yüan emperors were procured, and the emperor (Hungwu) gave orders to compile the history of the Yüan [Mongols], under the direction of *Sung Lien* and *Wang Wei*. The work, which occupied sixteen scholars, was begun in the second month of 1369 and finished in the eighth month of the same year. But as at that time the record of the reign of Shun ti (the last Mongol emperor in China) was not yet received, the scholar *Ou yang Yu* and others were sent to *Pei p'ing* to obtain the required information. In the sixth month of 1370 the Yüan Shi was complete." There were various subsequent editions. "The Yüan Shi has been compiled from official documents. Perhaps we must except the biographies, for which the information was probably often derived from private sources. It seems that the greater part of the documents on which the Chinese history of the Mongols is based had been drawn up in the Chinese language; but in some cases they appear to have been translated from the Mongol. I conclude this from the fact that in the Yüan Shi places are often mentioned, not, as usually, by their Chinese names, but by their Mongol names represented in Chinese characters" (p. 183). The Yüan Shi (p. 185 *sqq*.) is divided into four sections: (1) consists of the lives of the 13 Mongol Khans in Mongolia and China, and the annals of their reigns from Chingiz to Shun ti (1368); (2) memoirs (geographical, astronomical, politico-economical notices; regulations on dress, rites, public appointments, etc.; military ordinances, etc.); (3) genealogical tables and lists; (4) about a thousand biographies of eminent men of the period [Bretschneider observes that these biographies "bear evidence to the liberal views of the Mongol emperors as to the acknowledgment of merit. They seem never to have been influenced by national considerations"]; and notices of foreign lands and nations south and east of China (*e.g.*, Korea, Japan, Burma, Sumatra).

An abstract of the annals of the Yüan shi is contained in the first ten chapters of the YUAN SHI LEI PIEN (an abbreviated History of the Mongols) which were translated by Gaubil in his Histoire de Gentchiscan (see above p. 5, note 11). From this abstract, and the Yüan shi and another work entitled the Shi Wei (Woof of History), R. K. Douglas compiled his Life of Jinghiz Khān, 1877.

The YÜAN CH'AO PI SHI, Secret History of the Mongol dynasty, is a Chinese translation of a Mongol work, which was completed before 1240. It contains the early history of the Mongols, the reign of Chingiz, and part of the reign of Ogotai ; and it was translated into Chinese in the early period of the Ming dynasty. An abridgment of this work was translated into Russian by Palladius, and published in 1866 in the Records of the Russian Ecclesiastical Mission at Peking, vol. 4. It was only six years later that Palladius found that the work was extant in a fuller form. Bretschneider says : This document " corroborates generally Rashid-eddin's records, and occasionally we find passages in it which sound like a literal translation of the statements of the Persian historiographer. This proves that Rashid had made use of the same source of information as the unknown author of the Yüan ch'ao pi shi. As to the dates in the latter work, they are generally in accordance with the dates given by the Mohammadan authors : but in a few cases the Yüan ch'ao pi shi commits great chronological blunders and misplacements of events, as, for instance, with respect to the war in the west."

In his work cited above Bretschneider has rendered accessible other Chinese documents bearing on Mongol history, especially some relations of Chinese travellers and envoys ; for example, an extract (i. p. 9 sqq.) from the Si Yu Lu (Description of Journey to the West) of Ye-lü Ch'u ts'ai, a minister of Chingiz who attended him to Persia, 1219-24. (There is a biography of this Ye-lü in the Yüan Shi.) Bretschneider makes valuable contributions to the difficult subject of geographical identifications, and discusses among other documents the account of the Armenian prince Haithon's visit to Mongolia, written by Guiragos Gandsaketsi. This Haithon I. must not be confounded with Haithon, the monk of Prémontré, mentioned by Gibbon (above, p. 6, note 13). The account of Guiragos was translated into French by Klaproth (Nouv. Journ. Asiat., p. 273 sqq., 1833) from a Russian version by Argutinski ; but the history of Guiragos has since been translated by Brosset.

See also above, p. 5, n. 11.

SSANANG SSETSEN, a prince of the tribe of Ordus and a descendant of Chingiz, born A.D. 1604, wrote in Turkish a history of the eastern Mongols which he finished in 1662. It was thus written after the Manchus had conquered China and overthrown the Mongols. The earlier part of the book is practically a history of Tibet. The account of the origin of the Mongols is translated from Chinese sources. The author is a zealous Buddhist and dwells at great length on all that concerned the interests of his religion ; other matters are often dismissed far too briefly. The relation of the career of Chingiz is marked by many anachronisms and inaccuracies. The work was made accessible by the German translation of I. J. Schmidt, under the title, Geschichte der Ostmongolen und ihres Fürstenhauses, 1829.

MODERN WORKS. Finlay, History of Greece, vol. iii. J. von Hammer, Geschichte des osmanischen Reiches, vol. i., 1834. J. W. Zinkeisen, Geschichte des osmanischen Reiches in Europa, vol. i., 1840. E. Pears, The Destruction of the Greek Empire and the Story of the Capture of Constantinople by the Turks, 1903. N. Jorga, Geschichte des osmanichen Reiches, vols. i. and ii., 1908-9. Sir H. H. Howorth, History of the Mongols (see above, p. 5, note 12). Gregorovius, History of the City of Rome in the Middle Ages (see above, p. 219, note 2).

For sketches of the history of the Ottoman Turks : S. Lane-Poole, Turkey (Story of the Nations), 1888 ; La Jonquière, Histoire de l'empire Ottoman, 1897.

For the laws, constitution, etc., of the Ottoman empire, the chief work is Mouradja d'Ohsson's Tableau général de l'empire Ottoman, 7 vols., 1788-1824.

For Mongols, see above, p. 5, note 12. For Servia : C. Jireček, Geschichte der Serben, I. (bis 1371), 1911. For the schism of the Greek and Latin Churches, see above, p. 87, note 1. For the capture of Constantinople, see below, Appendix 3.

2. THE MONGOL INVASION OF EUROPE, A.D. 1241—(P. 15-17)

It is only recently that European history has begun to understand that the successes of the Mongol army which overran Poland and occupied Hungary in the spring of A.D. 1241 were won by consummate strategy and were not due to a mere overwhelming superiority of numbers. But this fact has not yet become a matter of common knowledge ; the vulgar opinion which represents the Tartars as a wild horde carrying all before them solely by their multitude, and galloping through Eastern Europe without a strategic plan, rushing at all obstacles and overcoming them by mere weight, still prevails. It will therefore not be amiss to explain very briefly the plan and execution of the Mongol campaign. The nominal commander-in-chief was Batu, but there is no doubt that the management of the expedition was in the hands of Subutai.

The objective of Subutai was Hungary,—the occupation of Hungary and the capture of Gran (Strigonium), which was then not only the ecclesiastical capital but the most important town in the country. In advancing on Hungary, his right flank was exposed to an attack from the princes of Poland, behind whom were the forces of Bohemia and North Germany. To meet this danger, Subutai divided his host into two parts, which we may call the northern and the southern army. The duty of the northern army was to sweep over Poland, advance to Bohemia, and effectually prevent the princes of the north from interfering with the operations of the southern army in Hungary. Thus strategically the invasion of Poland was subsidiary to the invasion of Hungary, and the northern army, when its work was done, was to meet the southern or main army on the Danube.

The northern army advanced in three divisions. The main force under Baidar marched through the dominions of Boleslaw the Chaste, and took Cracow ; then bearing north-westward it reached Oppeln on the Oder, where it defeated prince Mieczyslaw ; and descended the Oder to Breslau. At the same time Kaidu advanced by a more northerly route through the land of Conrad, prince of Mosovia and Cujavia ; while on the extreme right a force under Ordu terrified the Lithuanians and Prussians and crossed the Lower Vistula. The three divisions reunited punctually at Breslau, the capital of Henry II. of Lower Silesia ; and all took part in the battle of Liegnitz (April 9), for which King Wenzel of Bohemia arrived too late. Just one day too late : the Mongol generals had skilfully managed to force Prince Henry to fight before his arrival. Wenzel discreetly withdrew beyond the mountains into Bohemia ; all he could hope to do was to defend his own kingdom. Saxony now lived in dread that its turn had come. But it was no part of the plan of Subutai to launch his troops into Northern Germany. They had annihilated the forces of Poland ; it was now time for them to approach the main army in Hungary. The Mongols therefore turned their back upon the north, and marched through Upper Silesia and Moravia, capturing town after town as they went. Upon Wenzel who watched them with a large army, expecting them to invade Bohemia, they played a trick. He was posted near the defile of Glatz and the Mongols were at Ottmachau. They were too wary to attack him in such a position ; it was necessary to remove him. Accordingly they marched back as if they purposed to invade Bohemia by the pass of the Königstein in the north. Wenzel marched to the threatened point ; and when the Mongols saw him safely there, they rapidly retraced their steps and reached Moravia (end of April, beginning of May).

Meanwhile the main army advanced into Hungary in three columns converging on the Upper Theiss. The right wing was led by Shaiban, a younger brother of Batu, and seems to have advanced on the Porta Hungariae—the north-western entrance to Hungary, in the Little Carpathians. The central column under Subutai himself, with Batu, marched on the Porta Rusciae, the defile which leads from Galicia into the valley of the Theiss. The left column, under Kadan and Buri, moved through Transylvania towards the Körös.

The Porta Rusciae was carried, its defenders annihilated, on March 15 ; and a flying column of Tartars shot across Hungary, in advance of the main army. On March 15 they were half a day's journey from Pest, having ridden about 180 miles in less than three days. On the 17th they fought and defeated an Hunga-rian force, and on the same day Shaiban's right column captured Waitzen, a fort near the angle where the Danube bends southward. The object of Subutai in sending the advance squadron Pestward was doubtless to multiply difficulties for the Hungarians in organizing their preparations. These preparations were already hampered by the conflicts and jealousies between the king and his nobles ; and then towards the end of March befell the murder of Kutan, the chief of the Cumans, and the consequent revolt of the Cumans,—mentioned by Gibbon,—which demolished the defence of Eastern Hungary. Meanwhile Kadan's left column had advanced through Transylvania and passed the Körös and Theiss ; in the first days of April it advanced to the Danube, in the neighbourhood of Pest. Subutai had in the meantime arrived himself with the main central column, and the three columns of the central army were now together in position on the left bank of the Danube from Waitzen to Pest. But the Hungarian army with its German allies and Slavonic contingents had united at Pest, about 100,000 strong ; and it was impossible for the Mongols to cross in the face of such a host. Accordingly Subutai began a retreat, drawing the enemy after him. He retired behind the Sajó, not far from the confluence of that river with the Theiss, —a central position on the route from Pest to Galicia, where he was in touch with his own base of operations near Unghvar and the Porta Rusciae. The Hungarians took up their position on the opposite bank in the plain of Mohi. By skilful tactics the Mongols surrounded their camp and cut them to pieces on April 11, two days after the northern army had gained the battle of Liegnitz.

It was wonderful how punctually and effectually the arrangements of the commander were carried out in operations extending from the Lower Vistula to Transylvania. Such a campaign was quite beyond the power of any European army of the time ; and it was beyond the vision of any European commander. There was no general in Europe, from Frederick II. downward, who was not a tiro in strategy compared to Subutai. It should also be noticed that the Mongols embarked upon the enterprise, with full knowledge of the political situation of Hungary and the condition of Poland ; they had taken care to inform themselves by a well-organized system of spies : on the other hand, the Hungarians and Christian powers, like childish barbarians, knew hardly anything about their enemies.

The foregoing summary is founded on the excellent study of G. Strakosch-Grassmann, Der Einfall der Mongolen, in Mitteleuropa in den Jahren 1241 und 1242, 1893, and the vivid account of L. Cahun, in his Introduction à l'Histoire de l'Asie, p. 352 sqq. The chief defect in Strakosch-Grassmann's book is that he does not give to Subutai his proper place. The important Chinese biography of Subutai is translated in the first vol. of Bretschneider's Mediæval Researches from Eastern Asiatic Sources, 1888. All the western authorities have been carefully studied and analysed by Strakosch-Grassmann. (The account of the Mongol campaigns in Köhler's Die Entwicklung des Kriegswesens und der Kriegführung in der Ritterzeit, vol. 3, pt. 3, 1889, may also be compared.) For a short and good sketch of the Mongol invasions, see F. H. Skrine and E. D. Ross, The Heart of Asia, 1899.

3. SOURCES FOR THE SIEGE OF CONSTANTINOPLE, A.D. 1453— (CHAP. LXVIII.)

For the siege of Constantinople, Gibbon had only three accounts by eye-witnesses, that of Phrantzes, that of Leonardus of Chios, and that of Cardinal Isidore (see above p. 170, note 12). The most important new source is the history of Critobulus (see above p. 340), though he was not an eye-witness. Several other relations by persons who were in the city during the siege have been published during the present century.

Chief among these is the Journal of a Venetian, Nicolò Barbaro : Giornale dell' assedio di Constantinopoli 1453, edited by E. Cornet, 1856.[1] It is invaluable for determining the diary of the siege ; but it is marked by hostility and spite towards the Genoese, especially Giustiniani, and by contempt for the Greeks.

An " Informacion " sent by Francesco de Tresves to the Cardinal d'Avignon, and also by Jehan Blanchin and Jacques Tedardi (or Tedaldi) of Florence, on the

[1] There is a good analysis of the contents in Ellissen's Analekten, vol. iii., Appendix, p. 84 sqq.

capture of Constantinople. Edited in Martene and Durand, Thesaurus, i. p. 1819 *sqq.* (1717), and in Chartier's Chroniques de Charles VII., iii. p. 20 *sqq.*, 1858. Tedardi was an eye-witness. He escaped by throwing himself into the water, and was rescued by a Venetian boat.

Ubertino Pusculo of Brescia, who was also fortunate enough to escape, has left an account of the last episode of the history of the Empire in four Books of Latin hexameters. It contributes little enough to our knowledge of facts. The description of the siege does not begin till the middle of the Third book. In the First book there is an account of the battle of Varna, and much about the ecclesiastical antagonism of the Greeks and Latins. The Second begins with the death of John Palæologus and the accession of Constantine, and contains a virulent description of the moral degeneration of the people of Constantinople (v. 117 *sqq.*) :—

> obscæna sanctæ pietatis in urbe
> nec species nec forma fuit, nec gratia recti,
> nec virtutis amor (v. 141).

The work is published in Ellissen's Analekten, vol. iii., as an Appendix, 1857.

An anonymous Greek poem, in political verses, under the title of Capture of Constantinople (ʽΑλωσις Κωνσταντινουπόλεος) is misnamed, for it touches only incidentally on the facts of the siege and is in this respect of little historical importance. It is really an appeal to the powers of the West—

> αὐθένταις εὐγενέστατοι, τῆς Δύσης μεγιστᾶνες—

French and English, Spanish and Germans

> Φραζζέζους καὶ ʼΑγκέζιδες, Σπανιόλους, ʼΑλαμάνους—

to combine and recover Constantinople from the unbelievers. The Venetians are especially encouraged and urged to set the example—

> ʼΩ Βενετζιάνοι φρόνιμοι, πρακταῖοι κ' ἐπιδέξιοι.

The Hungarians, Servians, and Walachians are incited to avenge the defeat of Varna :—

> ʼΩ Βλαχία πολύθλιβη, Σερβία πονεμένη,
> θυμεῖσθε ταῖς αἰχμαλωσιαῖς, Οὐγκρία λυπημένη.

The author, though orthodox, was not extreme in his ecclesiastical views. He probably lived within reach of Mohammad's arm, for he will not disclose his name :—

> Τώρα σκεπάζω τόνομα καὶ κρύβω τόνομά μου,
> νὰ μὴ τὸ 'ξεύρουν οἱ πολλοὶ τίς ὁ τοιαῦτα γράψας,

but gives his friends the means of knowing his identity by mentioning two bodily marks—a black mole on the little finger of his right hand, and another of the same size on his left hand (vv. 10, 20 *sqq.*). The work was first edited by Ellissen in vol. iii. of his Analekten (1857), with introduction, translation, and analysis, under the title Dirge of Constantinople (Θρῆνος Κωνσταντινοπόλεως)—a misnomer, for it is not a dirge but a tearful appeal. Legrand published an improved text in 1880 in vol. i. of his Bibl. grecque vulgaire, p. 169 *sqq.*

There are five other laments (θρῆνοι) known. See Papadopulos-Kerameus, in Byzantinische Zeitschrift, xii. 267 *sqq.* (1) ἀνακάλημα τῆς Κπόλεως, Legrand, Collection de monuments pour servir à l'étude de la langue néo-hellénique, N.S., No. 5, 1875. (2) A dialogue between the four Eastern Patriarchs, published by Krumbacher, Ein dialogischer Threnos auf den Fall von Konstantinopel, 1901. (3) Θρῆνος, published by S. Lampros in ʽΕστία, 1886, 821 *sqq.* from a Ms. of Mt. Athos. (4) Μοιρολόγιν θλιβερόν, not printed, found by Papadopulos-K. in a Ms. of the Patriarchal Library at Cairo. (5) Θρῆνος, in a Ms. of the Patriarchal Library at Jerusalem, published by Papadopulos-K., *loc. cit.*

A Slavonic account, written probably by a Slav of some of the Balkan countries, is also preserved, and has been published by Sreznevski under the title, Skazaniia o vziatii Tsargrada bezbozhnym turetskym sultanom, in the Zapiski of the 2nd Division of the St. Petersburg Academy of Science, vol. i. p. 99 *sqq.*, 1854.

We have another Slavonic account, written in a mixture of Polish and Servian, by a Janissary of Mohammad, named Michael, who took part in the siege. He was a Servian of Ostrovica, and in his later years he went to Poland and wrote his Memoirs, which were edited, as "Pamietniki Janiczara," by Galezowsky in 1828, in vol. v. of his collection of Polish writers (Zbior Pisarzow Polskieh). This relation is especially valuable as written from outside, by one who knew what was going on in the camp of the besiegers. It has been utilised by Mijatovich in his account of the siege (see below).

A report by the Father Superior of the Franciscans who was at Galata during the siege was printed by Muratori in vol. 18 (p. 701) of the Scr. Rer. It. : Rapporto del Superiore dei Franciscani presente all' assedio et alla presa di Constantinopoli. It seems to have escaped the notice of Gibbon.

An account by Christoforo Riccherio (La presa di Constantinopoli) is inserted in Sansovino's Dell' Historia Universale dell' origine et imperio de Turchi (1564), p. 343 *sqq.*

Abraham, an Armenian monk, who was present at the siege, wrote a " Mélodie élégiaque," which was translated into French by Brosset and printed in St. Martin's ed. of Lebeau's Histoire du Bas-Empire (xxi. p. 307 *sqq.*) which Brosset completed.

Adam de Montaldo, of Genoa : De Constantinopolitano excidio ad nobilissimum juvenem Melleducam Cicalam, amicum optimum; edited by C. Desimoni, in the Atti della Società Ligure di storia patria, x. p. 325 *sqq.*, 1874.

Besides these relations of eye-witnesses we have some additional contemporary accounts which were not accessible to Gibbon. The most important of these sources, Critobulus, has been spoken of in Appendix 1.

Zorzi Dolphin wrote an account of the "siege and capture of Constantinople in 1453," which was published by G. M. Thomas in the Sitzungsberichte of the Bavarian Academy, 1868. His sources were the reports of Leonardo of Chios, Philip da Rimano, and anonymous eye-witnesses. He adds little to the story.

A letter of the Genoese " Podestà of Pera," written on June 23, 1853, giving a brief account of the capture, was published by Sylvestre de Sacy in Notices et extraits des manuscrits de la bibliothèque du Roi, xi. 1, p. 74, 1827.

Documents throwing light on the policy of the Genoese in the fatal year will be found in Vigna's Codice diplomatico delle Colonie Tauro-Liguri, durante la Signoria dell' ufficio de S. Georgio (1453-1475), 1868.

Of little importance for the siege is the Amyris of Filelfo—on the life and deeds of Mohammad in 4 Books—published in Hopf's Chroniques gréco-romanes.

A Monody of Andronicus Callistus, in Migne's Patr. Gr., 161, p. 1124, teaches us, as Paspates has pointed out, that there was water in the ditch outside the western wall.

The final scene of the siege is briefly described in Spandugino Cantacusino's Della origine de principi Turchi (which is included in Bk ii. of Sansovino's Dell' Historia Universale, p. 187 *sqq.*), p. 195-6.

There are a number of other documents extant which have not yet been printed. C. Hopf and A. Dethier had designed and prepared the publication of these in the Monumenta Hungar. Hist., along with many sources which had been already published. Two volumes lie in Ms.; two have been printed, but were never in the market, and are almost impossible to procure. A description of their contents is given by Krumbacher in his Gesch. der byzantinischen Litteratur, p. 311-12. Cp. Pears, Destruction of the Greek Empire, xiii. *sq.*

Brosset gathered some material from Armenian and Georgian sources; see the last vol. of St. Martin's edit. of Lebeau's Histoire du Bas-Empire.

The Turkish authorities are of very little value for the siege; they were utilised by Hammer. The earliest Ottoman historians belong to the end of the 15th century, *viz.*, the History of the great-grandson of Ashīk-Pasha (who lived under Murad I.); the anonymous chronicle, Tarīkhi Ali Osmān; the World-view of Neshri. See Hammer's Introduction to his History. These earlier works were used by the most famous of Ottoman historians, Sad ad-Dīn, in his Crown of Histories (written under Murad III., end of 16th cent.). His account of the siege has been translated by E. J. W. Gibb, 1879. For Ahmad Muktar Pasha's work see Pears, *op. cit.* xiv.

The following is a list of the chief modern accounts of the siege that have appeared since Gibbon wrote:—

Hammer, Geschichte des osmanischen Reiches, i. p. 398 *sqq.*, 1834.

Zinkeisen, Geschichte des osmanischen Reiches, i. p. 811 *sqq.*, 1840.

Stassulevich (J.), Osada i Vziatie Vizantii Turkami, 1854.

Sreznevski, Poviest o Tsargradie, 1855.

Mordtmann (A. D.), Belagerung und Eroberung Constantinopels durch die Türken im Jahre 1453; 1858. (This had two advantages over previous accounts. Mordtmann knew the ground; and he made use of the diary of Barbaro.)

Finlay, History of Greece, vol. iii. p. 503 *sqq.*

Krause (J. H.), Die Eroberungen von Constantinopel im dreizehnten und fünfzehnten Jahrhundert, 1870.

Broadribb and Besant, Constantinople, a sketch of its history from its foundation to its conquest by the Turks, 1879.

Vlasto (E. H.), Les derniers jours de Constantinople, 1883.

Paspatês (A. G.) Πολιορκία καὶ ἅλωσις τῆς Κωνσταντινουπόλεως ὑπὸ τῶν Ὀθωμανῶν ἐν ἔτει, 1453; 1890.

Mijatovich (Ch.) Constantine, Last Emperor of the Greeks, 1892.

Pears (E.), The Destruction of the great Empire and the Story of the Capture of Constantinople by the Turks, 1903.

The sources have been dealt with in an article by P. Pogodin in the Zhurnal min. narod. prosv., vol. 283, August, 1889.

A. van Millingen's Byzantine Constantinople (1899) contains much material for the study of the siege, and many difficulties in the episode are discussed. Pears (*op. cit.* vi.) refers to "two valuable papers" entitled Die letzten Tage von Byzanz, by A. Mordtmann, in the Mitteilungen des deutschen Exkursions-Klubs in Konstantinopel, 1895.

BIBLIOGRAPHY

(By H. M. Beatty, M.A., LL.D., F.R.Hist.S.)

BIBLIOGRAPHY OF GIBBON'S HISTORY, MINOR AND MISCELLANEOUS WORKS, AND LETTERS; AND OF THE CONTROVERSIAL REPLIES TO HISTORY

ABBREVIATED REFERENCES

Bury = the present edition.
Misc. Works = the 1814 edition (unless otherwise stated) of Gibbon's Miscellaneous Works.
Murray = The Autobiographies of E. G., edited by John Murray (1896).
Prothero = Private Letters of E. G., edited by R. E. Prothero (1896).
Read = Historic Studies in Vaud . . . by General Meredith Read (1897).
Sévery = La Vie de Société dans le Pays de Vaud (1911-12).
Hill = The Memoirs of E. G., edited by G. B. Hill (1900).
Graesse = Trésor de livres rares (1859-69).
Oettinger = Historisches Archiv (1841).
Quérard = (unless otherwise stated) La France littéraire (1827-64).
Brunet = Manuel du Libraire (1860-65).
Lowndes and Allibone = the well-known bibliographies.
B.M. = British Museum.
D.N.B. = Dict. Natl. Biography.

CONTENTS

The place of publication is London, when not otherwise stated.

THE DECLINE AND FALL: EDITIONS IN ENGLISH

" The moment of conception ; the fifteenth of October, 1764 " (Murray, p. 270).
" As early as 1771 . . . a rough draught " (Bury, iii. p. 283).

Volume The First (chapters 1-16) :

1776, February 16th, The | History | Of The | Decline And Fall | Of The | Roman Empire. | By Edward Gibbon Esq. ; | Volume The First. |
    Jam provideo animo . . . videbatur [Livy, xxxi.-l., motto omitted in later editions].

London: | Printed For W. Strahan; And T. Cadell, In The Strand. | MDCCLXXVI. |

Preface (pp. v-viii), "Bentinck St., Feb. 1, 1776"; Contents (3 pp.); History (pp. 1-586); "Advertisement" [to Notes, one page]; Notes (pp. i-lxxxviii); Errata (one page). 1000 copies. "The volume (a handsome quarto) costs one guinea unbound" (Read, ii. p. 387). "On February 16, I gave myself to the universe" (Read, *ibid.*). In Murray, p. 311, Gibbon says "February 17," and this was the date appointed (Prothero, i. p. 279); but the 17th was a Saturday, and perhaps therefore abandoned. The dates in the Memoirs are often contradictory. "It sold like a threepenny pamphlet"; "in a fortnight not a single copy remained" (Read, *ibid.*).

1776, June 3rd, Second Edition, 1500 copies, 4to (Strahan & Cadell). The notes are still at the end of the book. "My new birth happened last Monday, 700 of the 1500 were gone yesterday" ("June the 6th, 1776, from Almack's, where I was chose last week," Prothero, i. p. 284).

Dublin, 1776, two volumes, 8vo (printed for Wm. Hallhead, 63 Dame St.). "The bookseller's property was twice invaded by the pyrates of Dublin" (Murray, p. 311). "The natives have printed it very well, and the notes at the bottom take up much less space than I could have imagined" (Prothero, i. p. 288).

1777, April (Strahan & Cadell). "We are now printing a third edition in quarto of 1000 copies (in all 3500) with the notes at the bottom" (March 29, 1777; Prothero, i. p. 304). Evidently revised :—" I shall usually refer to the third edition, unless there are any various readings" (*Vindication*, 1779, in Misc. Works, iv. p. 526). Gibbon's two-thirds profits on this edition were £326 13s. 4d. (Misc. Works, ii. p. 167; where the price given, 16s., was no doubt for the trade; the sale price, as shown by an advertisement at the end of *A Vindication*, was £1 1s. in boards).

1781 (Strahan & Cadell). The Fourth Edition, with engraving ("Publish'd as the Act directs Febry. 1st 1780") by Jno. Hall of portrait [1779] by Reynolds of "Edward Gibbon Esqr. born the 8th May 1737". Preface and P.S. ("Bentinck-Street, March 1, 1781"), "Advertisement," detailed Table of Contents (12 pp.), History, pp. 1 to 704. Notes at the bottom of page.

This edition and the Dublin of 1776 are recorded in G.'s own catalogue of his library (on the backs of playing cards) in the B.M.; which, in spite of his personal preference, records no edition with the notes at the end.

SECOND AND THIRD VOLUMES (CHAPS. 17-26 AND 27-38) :

"The commencement of my Second Volume, 1777, December" (Murray, p. 315).

1781, March 1st, vols. ii. and iii., 4to (printed for W. Strahan and T. Cadell, in the Strand, £2 2s.).

Second Volume : portrait by Reynolds and map of the Eastern part of the Roman Empire; pp. 1-640, with notes at the bottom of the pages; Errata.

Third Volume : map of the Western part of the Roman Empire; pp. 1-640; Table of Contents of vols. i., ii., iii.; Errata.

1781, vols. ii. and iii., 4to, Second Edition (Strahan & Cadell), no portrait, maps as before, but Table of Contents and Errata at the *beginning* of each vol.

Dublin, 1781, chaps. 17-38, in four volumes, 8vo (printed for Wm. Hallhead).

FIRST, SECOND, AND THIRD VOLUMES (CHAPS. 1-38) :

1782 (Preface dated March 1), Vols. 1, 2, 3, 4to (Strahan & Cadell). For the variants introduced by Gibbon into the text, see vol. i., pp. 506-9 of the present edition.

1783, six volumes, first octavo edition of chaps. 1-38, portrait and map; not further revised, see "Advertisement," dated Bentinck St., April 20, 1783 (Strahan & Cadell).

1788, six volumes, 8vo (Strahan & Cadell).

1789, three volumes, 4to. "New edition" (Strahan & Cadell).

FOURTH, FIFTH, AND SIXTH VOLUMES (CHAPS. 39-47; 48-57; 58-71):

Vol. iv. " begun March 1, 1782—ended June, 1784 ".

Vol. v. " begun July, 1784—ended May 1, 1786 ".

Vol. vi. " begun May 18, 1786—ended June 27, 1787 ".

" These three volumes were sent to press August 15, 1787, and the whole impression was concluded April following."

" The day of publication was delayed that it might coincide with the fifty-first anniversary of my own birthday " (Misc. Works, i. pp. 256 and 260).

1788, May 8th, vols. iv., v., vi., 4to ; printed for A. Strahan and T. Cadell, in the Strand ; 3000 copies ; £3 3s. in boards.

Fourth Volume : Preface, pp. i-vi ; P.S., pp. vii-viii ; Table of Contents ; pp. 1-620.

Fifth Volume : Table of Contents ; pp. 1-684.

Sixth Volume : Table of Contents ; pp. 1-646 ; General Index to the entire work. Errata to vols. 4, 5, 6.

1790, 6 vols., 8vo (Strahan & Cadell, £1 10s.).

" I do not propose making any improvements or corrections in the octavo edition which you meditate " (Letter of 11th February, 1789, to Cadell, Misc. Works, edn. 1796, i. p. 684).

EDITIONS OF THE COMPLETE WORK IN ENGLISH

Basil, 1787-9, 13 vols., 8vo (J. J. Tourneisen). The notes of vols. i.-vi. are at the end of each vol. ; those of vols. vii.-xii. form the contents of vol. xiii. No map or portrait.

Quérard places this edition as : " Basil (Strasbourg)į".

Basil, 1789, 14 vols., 8vo (J. J. Tourneisen).

" The type is neat, the paper tolerable, and the text *wonderfully* correct " (Letter 11th February, 1789, *ut supra*).

" I cannot be displeased with the two numerous and correct impressions of the English original, which have been published for the use of the Continent at Basil in Switzerland. Of their fourteen octavo Volumes, the two last include the whole body of the notes. The public importunity had forced *me* to remove them from the end of the Volume to the bottom of the page, but I have often repented of my complyance " (Murray, p. 339).

Dublin, 1788-9, 6 vols., 8vo, portrait and two maps (printed for Luke White, No. 86, Dame Street). Vol. v. is dated 1788. This has apparently misled Lowndes and Graesse.

1791, 12 vols., 8vo, portrait and maps (Strahan & Cadell, £3 12s.).

1796, 6 vols., 4to, adorned with the Head of the Author and Maps adapted to the Work (printed for T. Cadell, Jun., and W. Davies, successors to Mr. Cadell, £7 10s.).

1797, 12 vols., 8vo, portrait and maps (printed for A. Strahan ; and T. Cadell, Jun., and W. Davies in the Strand).

1802, 12 vols., 8vo, portrait and folding maps, £3 12s. ; large paper in royal 8vo, £6 6s. (printed by A. Strahan, Printers St., for T. Cadell, Jun., and W. Davies).

1806, 12 vols., 8vo, portrait and maps (Vernor, Hood & Sharpe in the Poultry and others).

1807, 12 vols., royal 18mo, with some account of the life of the author, portrait and maps (printed for Cadell & Davies and others).

1809, 9 vols., 8vo, new edition with numerous embellishments, portrait, and map (with a second title engraved, bearing date 1808 ; Oddy & Co. and Maxwell).

Edinburgh, 1811, 12 vols., 8vo, with a life of the author, portrait, and maps (printed for Bell & Bradfute, Peter Hill, Silvester Doig and A. Stirling and John Ogle).

1813, 12 vols., 8vo, portrait after Reynolds and maps (T. Cadell and W. Davies and others).

1815, 12 vols., 8vo, with portrait, memoir, and maps (printed for Lackington, Allen & Co., W. Otridge, R. Scholey, and G. Cowie & Co., London ; and for P. Hill, Doig & Stirling, and Oliver & Boyd, Edinburgh).

1816, 12 vols., 8vo, portrait and map (W. Allason and others).

1818, 12 vols., 8vo, portrait and maps (W. Allason and others).

1819, 12 vols., 8vo, portrait (W. Allason and others).

1820, 12 vols., 8vo, maps of Eastern and Western parts of Empire (W. Allason and others).

1820, 12 vols., 8vo, with Life, portrait, and map (printed at Edinburgh for Lackington, Harding, etc.).

1820, 12 vols., 8vo, portrait and maps (Cadell & Davies and others).

1821, 8 vols., 8vo, with maps and portrait (printed for R. Priestley and others by J. F. Dove, St. John's Square).

Leipzig, 1821-22, 12 vols., 8vo (E. Fleischer).

1822, 8 vols., 8vo, portrait and maps (Priestley & Weale and others).

1823, 8 vols., 8vo, portrait and maps, with "Advertisement" by J. Sleath, D.D. (St. Paul's School), stating that "great care has been taken with the present *complete* edition" and that "the Greek and Latin quotations have been attentively examined" (printed by J. F. Dove, St. John's Square, for W. Baynes & Son and others).

1825, 8 vols., 8vo, portrait, memoir, and maps (G. Cowie & Co. and others, Poultry ; printed by J. F. Dove, St. John's Square).

1825, 12 vols., 12mo.

1827, 12 vols., 8vo, Life, portrait, and maps (Thomas McLean and others).

1827, 11 vols., 12mo ; the title page of each volume is engraved and contains a vignette (printed by Thomas Davison for Thomas Tegg, No. 73, Cheapside).

Oxford, 1827, 8 vols., 8vo, with steel portrait, £3 3s. ; 50 copies in large paper, royal 8vo, £8 8s. (" Oxford Classics Edition," Pickering, printed by Talboys & Wheeler). An issue of 1828 is frequently recorded in bibliographies,—questionable. "Professes to have been carefully revised" (Lowndes). No maps.

Edinburgh, 1828 *et seq.*, 12 vols., 8vo, illustrated with maps designed for the work (printed by Ballantyne & Co. for John Thomson, etc.).

1828, 4 vols., 8vo, engraved frontispiece dated 1825 (Jones & Co.).

1828, 8 vols., 8vo, with Life, portrait, and maps (Cadell and others).

Leipzig, 1828-9, 12 vols., 8vo.

1830, 8vo, printed from the edition in twelve volumes, with an introductory memoir of the author by William Youngman (Joseph Ogle Robinson, 42 Poultry ; Liverpool, A. C. Baynes, Waterloo Place. Stereotyped and printed by J. R. & C. Childs). Portrait.

Edinburgh, 1831, 12 vols., 8vo, with portrait by Lizars and maps.

Edinburgh, 1832, 12 vols., royal 8vo, illustrated with three large maps designed for the work (Crusades, Provinces from Adriatic to Propontis, Empire of Charlemagne), and with memoir (Thomas Nelson and Peter Brown).

1837, 8vo, with memoir by Chalmers and portrait.

1838, 8 vols., 8vo, with Life, portrait, and maps (Cadell and others).

1838-9, 12 vols., 8vo, with notes by Guizot, edited by Milman, and original historical maps (John Murray, 9s. each).

Paris, 1840, 8 vols., 8vo, with portrait and three maps and notes by Guizot and Milman (Baudry's European Library, 3 Quai Malaquais, near the Pont des Arts).

1840, thick royal 8vo, with portrait after Reynolds, engraved by W. C. Edwards, and introductory memoir by William Youngman (Ball, Arnold & Co., 34 Paternoster Row. Bungay : printed by John Childs & Son).

Derby, 1842, 4 vols., 8vo, with Life, portrait and maps (printed for Thomas Richardson).

1844, royal 8vo, with memoir by W. Youngman, stereotyped in one vol. (Bohn).

Halifax, 1844-5, 4 vols., 8vo, Life, portrait and four maps (printed and published by William Milner, Cheapside).
    Subsequent issues in 1847 and 1848.

1846, 6 vols., 8vo, with notes by Guizot, edited by Milman, Second edition (John Murray, £3 3s.).

1847, 8vo, with memoir by W. Youngman, new edition (Bohn, 18s.) ; also in 1865 and 1866.

1847, 8vo, with Life by A. Chalmers (Longman) ; also in 1862.

1848, 8 vols., 8vo, Life, portrait, and maps (Longman, Brown, Green & Longmans and others, £3).

London and New York, 1850, 2 vols., imp. 8vo, with 57 engravings and maps ; notes and memoir by F. A. Guizot (Virtue, £1 16s.).

Reissued 1863 ; 4th issue in 1870.

1853-5, 7 vols., cr. 8vo, with copious index, two maps, portrait of Gibbon, and variorum notes : including those of Guizot, Wenck, Schreiter, and Hugo, edited with further illustrations from the most recent sources by an English Churchman [*i.e.* H. G. Bohn], (Bohn, £1 4s. 6d.).

[The first volume having been criticised for careless printing, a corrected impression was issued in 1854. The book passed to Messrs. Bell & Sons in 1864, and has since that date been reprinted about thirteen times ; in later issues the words " an English Churchman " have been omitted. Reissued also in New York, Boston, Philadelphia.]

1854 (vols. 1-5), 1855 (vols. 6-8), 8 vols., 8vo, with portrait by E. Scriven after Reynolds and fourteen maps, notes by Milman and Guizot, edited with additional notes by William Smith, LL.D. (John Murray, 7s. 6d. each vol.).

[This, the third of the Milman editions, includes also the Autobiography, and has been repeatedly reprinted since. The Milman editions have been also reprinted about a dozen times in New York, Boston or Philadelphia.]

1860, imp. 8vo (Tegg).

1869, 3 vols., cr. 8vo (Alexander Murray).

London and New York, 1873, 4 vols., cr. 8vo (Chandos Classics, Frederick Warne & Co.).

Reissued 1887.

1875, thick royal 8vo, with portrait.

New York, 1880, 5 vols., 16mo (American Book Exchange).

1890, 4 vols., large 8vo.

1892, 2 vols., 8vo (Lubbock's Hundred Books).

1895, 4 vols., 8vo (Gibbings, Standard British Classics).

1896-1900, 7 vols., cr. 8vo, with maps, edited with introduction, notes, appendices, and index by J. B. Bury ; also 7 vols., demy 8vo (Methuen & Co.) ; also New York (Macmillan Co.).

1903-6, 7 vols., 6 ins. by 4 (The World's Classics).

1905-6, 7 vols., cr. 8vo, edited by J. B. Bury (Methuen's Standard Library).

1910, 6 vols., cr. 8vo, edited by Oliphant Smeaton (Everyman's Library) ; also New York (Dutton).

1909 *et seq.*, 7 vols., demy 8vo, edited with introduction, notes, and appendices by J. B. Bury, with maps ; and with illustrations selected by O. M. Dalton (Methuen & Co.). The present edition.

UNDATED EDITIONS

3 vols., large cr. 8vo (Warne & Co.).

2 vols., large 8vo, with Milman's notes and full-page illustrations (Ward, Lock & Co.).

New York, 5 vols., cr. 8vo, with notes by Milman and index (International Book Company, 310-318 Sixth Avenue).

New York, Pittsburg, and Cincinnati, 6 vols, in twelve, 8vo, Milman's and Smith's notes, illustrated " Edition de luxe " (Euclid Press).

" The conquests of our language and litterature (*sic*) are not confined to Europe alone ; and the writer who succeeds in London is speedily read on the banks of the Delaware and Ganges " (Murray, p. 339).

MUTILATIONS, ABRIDGMENTS, AND SELECTIONS OF THE HISTORY

1826, 5 vols., 8vo, reprinted for the use of families and young persons, with the careful omission of all passages of an irreligious or immoral tendency, by Thomas Bowdler, F.R.S.S.A. (Longman, £1 11s. 6d.), with motto :—

O Hamlet, thou has cleft my heart in twain.
O throw away the worser part of it
And live the purer with the other half.

1789, 2 vols., 8vo, Gibbon's History. . . . Abridged (printed for G. Kearsley, Johnson's Head, Fleet St.); by J. Adams (B.M. Catalogue), or Rev. Charles Here-
ford (Lowndes, D.N.B., Allibone and Graesse). Possibly, "J. Adams" was
the *nom de guerre* by which the anonymous and Reverend abridger was known
to his publisher in his unorthodox undertaking, or, to use his own words, "the
delicacy of his situation". "Much religious disquisition has been carefully
rejected."
Dublin, 1790, 2 vols., 8vo (printed, vol. i., by William Porter; vol. ii., by Robert
Rhames; for H. Chamberlaine, P. Wogan and seven others). Matter apparently as in English abridgment.
1807, 2 vols., 8vo, Second edition (of London Abridgment).
1856, 8vo, abridged by William Smith, LL.D. (The Student's Gibbon), illustrated
by one hundred engravings on wood (John Murray); and subsequent impressions.
1899-1901, 2 vols., 8vo, abridged by Sir W. Smith, revised edition by A. H. J.
Greenidge and J. G. C. Anderson (John Murray).

1840, 12mo, The Beauties of Gibbon, selected from his works by A. Howard,
portrait.
1869, post 8vo, History of the Crusades (chaps. 58-61 of the History), (Alexander
Murray).
1869, post 8vo, Rise and Fall of the Saracen Empire (chaps. 50, 51, 52), (Alexander
Murray).
1870, post 8vo, The Saracen Empire (chaps. 50, 51, 52), with Ockley's History
(Alexander Murray).
1870, post 8vo, The Crusades (chaps. 58-61), with Siege of Rhodes and Scott's Essay
on Chivalry (Alexander Murray).
1880, cr. 8vo, History of the Crusades (1095-1261), with Gibbon's Life and Letters
(Chandos Library, Warne).
Münster, 1881-2, 16mo, History of the first and fourth Crusades;
History of the heroes of Old Germany, Alaric, Odoacer, Theodoric the
Great, Clovis and Alboin (Werke der Englischen Literatur. Ausgewählt und
ausgestattet von Ant. Goebel).
New York, 1883, 12mo, History of Christianity: all that relates to the progress of
the Christian religion in the History . . .; with Life, preface and notes,
illustrated (Peter Eckler).
New York, 1896, Birth, character and doctrine of Mahomet (Peter Eckler).
1899, 8vo, History of the Crusades, with Life and Letters, verbatim reprint, with
copious index by W. J. Day (C. Arthur Pearson).
1905, 8vo, Selections from Gibbon (The Arnold Prose Books).
1906, 8vo, The Age of the Antonines (chaps. i., ii., iii. of the History), edited by
W. H. D. Rouse (Blackie's English Texts).
1907, 8vo, The Age of the Antonines, edited by J. H. Fowler (English Literature
for Secondary Schools, Macmillan & Co.).
1910, Narratives from the History of the Decline and . . ., selected and edited by
J. H. Fowler (English Literature for Secondary Schools, Macmillan & Co.).

TRANSLATIONS OF THE HISTORY

FRENCH

Paris, 1777-95, 18 vols., 8vo, Histoire de la décadence et de la chute de l'Empire
Romain, traduite de l'Anglois (*sic*) par M. Le Clerc de Sept-Chênes; continuée
par MM. Démeunier et Boulard, finie par MM. Cantwel et Marinié, et revue
quant aux derniers volumes par M. Boulard (Moutard et Maradan).
"The first volume had been feebly though faithfully translated by M.

Le Clerc de Septchênes" (Murray, p. 339 note); or, according to Brunet, Quérard (*Les Supercheries Littéraires*), and Sainte-Beuve (*Causeries*, viii. p. 454), by Louis XVI., at least in part. But see the letters to and from Septchênes (Prothero, i. p. 296, and Misc. Works, ii. p. 190).

Paris, 1790-2, 12 vols., 12mo, Histoire . . . par M. de Sept-Chênes, nouvelle edition.

    Graesse says that "la première version p. Mokarky" (*sic*), *i.e.* the two editions just mentioned, "est moins complète" than the Guizot edn. of 1812.

Paris, 1812, 13 vols., 8vo, Histoire . . . trad. par Le Clerc de Sept-Chênes, nouvelle edition, revue et corrigée [par Mme Guizot], précédée d'une lettre sur la vie et le caractère de Gibbon par Suard, et accompagnée de notes par M. Guizot (Maradan).

Paris, 1819, 13 vols., 8vo (Lefèvre).

Paris, 1828-9, 13 vols., 8vo, accompagnée de notes par F. Guizot, relatives pour la plupart à l'histoire de la propagation du Christianisme (Ledentu).

Paris, 1835-6, 2 vols., royal 8vo, avec une notice par J. A. C. Buchon (A. Desrez, rue Saint-Georges).

Paris, 1843, 2 vols., 8vo, avec une introduction par J. A. C. Buchon (Société du Panthéon Littéraire, Hennuyer et Turpin, 20 fr.).

Abridgments and Extracts in French

Paris, 1804, 3 vols., 8vo, Histoire de la décadence . . . abrégée et réduite à ce qu'elle contient d'essentiel et d'utile par Adam[s], et traduite de l'Anglais par P. C. Briand.

Paris, 1810, 10 vols., 18mo, Histoire de l'empire Romain jusqu'à la prise de Constantinople par les Turcs, précédée d'une Introduction par Meiners; trad. de l'angl. par J. B. J. Breton (Bibliothèque historique, à l'usage des jeunes gens, 12 fr.).

Paris, 1821, 8vo, Aperçus historiques sur le droit romain par Gibbon, avec les Aperçus sur l'origine du droit français par Fleury; recueil à l'usage des élèves du cours de l'histoire du droit romain et du droit français (Gillet et Mlle. Leloir, 4 fr.).

Liége, 1821, 8vo, Précis de l'histoire du droit romain, traduction adoptée par M. Guizot, rev. et rectifiée par Warkonning [*sic* Quérard; Warnkoenig?] (P. J. Collardin, 3 fr.).

GERMAN

Leipzig, 1779 *et seq.*, 19 parts, 8vo, Geschichte des Verfalls und Untergangs des Römischen Reichs, aus d. Engl. übersetzt mit Anmerkungen von Fr. Aug. W. Wenck [first incl. only], Schreiter, Beck, und Müller.

    "I wish it were in my power to read the German, which is praised by the best Judges" (Murray, p. 339).

Magdeburg and Vienna, 1788-92, 16 vols., large 8vo, Geschichte der Abnahme und des Falls des Römischen Reichs aus d. Engl. übersetzt (von Chr. Wlh. v. Riemberg), sammt d. einleit. u. Register. Mit 3 Karten.

Frankfort and Leipzig, 1800-3, 13 vols., large 8vo, Geschichte des Verfalls . . . von Fr. A. Wenck.

Frankfort, 1800, 12 vols., small 8vo, Geschichte des Verfalls . . ., aus d. Engl., mit Anmerkungen und Abhandlungen von Fr. A. Wenck.

Leipzig, 1805-7, 19 vols., 8vo, Geschichte des Verfalls (Wenck, etc.), new issue of 1779 edition (Hinrichs).

Leipzig, 1835-7, 1 vol. (12 parts), 4to, with portrait, Geschichte des ehemaligen Sinkens und endlichen Untergangs des römischen Weltreichs, nebst biograph. Skizze über den Verfasser von Joh. Sporschil.

Leipzig, 1837-41, 12 vols., 16mo, the same, neue Taschenausgabe.

Leipzig, 1842-4, 12 vols., 8vo, the same, second octavo edition. With portrait.

Leipzig, 1854, 12 vols., same, third edition.

Leipzig, 1861-3, 12 vols., same, fourth edition.

Abridgments and Selections in German

Lüneburg, 1787, 8vo, Leben Attilas, Königs der Hunnen, aus dem Englischen übersetzt.

Hamburg, 1788, 8vo, Ausbreitung d. Christenthums aus natürl. Ursachen, aus d. Engl. (Matthiessen).

Göttingen, 1790, 8vo, Histor. Uebersicht d. Röm. Rechts, aus d. Engl. mit Anmerkungen von G. Hugo. Reissued 1839.

Berlin, 1790, 3 vols., 8vo, Geschichte d. Verfalls u. Unterg. d. Röm. Reichs, im Auszüge, von G. K. F. Seidel (Voss).

Dessau, 1797, 8vo, Bekehrung d. Kaiser Constantin d. Grossen, aus d. Engl.

ITALIAN

Lausanne [= Florence ?], 1779, 3 vols., 8vo, Istoria . . . tradotta dal Francese del Signore Le Clerc de Sept-chênes.

Apparently discontinued after the sixteenth chapter ; Oettinger says "15 Bände," but Graesse says "non terminée". Spedalieri (Confutazione, 1798) mentions two Italian translations, but does not say if complete.

Pisa, 1779-86, vols. 1-9, 8vo, Istoria della decadenza e rovina dell' Impero Romano tradotta dall' Inglese di Edoardo Gibbon. (Vols. 1-3, Per Carlo Ginesi, Con Licenza de' Superiori ; Vols. 4-8, Presso Jacopo Grazioli, Con Licenza de' Superiori ; vol. 9, Presso Luigi Raffaelli, Con Approvazione.)

This translation was planned by Monsignor Angelo Fabroni, at his own expense ; ten vols. (chaps. 1-43) were translated, the first by Gonnella, the others by Professor Foggi. Fabroni's co-operation was disapproved at Rome ; the tenth volume (chaps. 39-43), though printed, was not published and was afterwards destroyed ; and after Fabroni's death the other nine were, except 200 copies, sold for waste paper. See Bertocci, *Repertorio Bibliografico* (1880) and the preface to Bertolotti's translation, *infra ;* also the leaflet inserted in the British Museum copy. "The superior merit of the Interpreter, or his language, inclines me to prefer the Italian version " (Murray, p. 339). " The critical Essay at the end of the iiid Volume was furnished by the Abbate Nicola Spedalieri. The vth and viith Volumes are armed with five letters from an anonymous Divine " (*ibid.* p. 322). Gibbon's own copy is in the British Museum, with his book-plate in the first volume. This translation appears, as professed, to be made from the English original (first edition, except in one sentence at beginning of chap. i.).

Milan, 1820-4, 13 vols., 8vo, with copious index, brief Life of Gibbon, and a compendium of Spedalieri's confutation, Storia della decadenza e rovina dell' Impero Romano di Edoardo Gibbon. Traduzione dall' Inglese [by Davide Bertolotti].

It is translated from the 8vo London edition of 1791, and dedicated by the publisher, Nicolò Bettoni, to Lady Fanny Harvey. The first half is founded on the Pisa translation, which is severely criticised, revised " parola per parola " (Biblioteca Storica di tutte le nazioni, 20 lire).

Lugano, 1841, 3 vols., 4to, Storia della decadenza. . . .

Abridgments in Italian

Bastia, 1835, with map, Storia . . . compendiata da Fran. Inghirami.

Florence, 1875, 16mo, with map, Storia . . . [to the middle of the Twelfth Century] compendiata ad uso delle scuole da Gugl. Smith (Barbèra, 4 lire). Fifth edition in 1884.

SPANISH

Barcelona, 1847-8, 8 vols., 8vo, Histria [*sic*, Graesse] de la decadencia del Imperio Rom. trad. del ingles con notas p. J. Mor. de Fuentes (130 rs. de la cortina).

RUSSIAN

Moscow, 1883-6, Исторія упалка и разрушенія Римской Имперіи . . . Перевелъ
. . . В. Н. Невѣломскій, 7 parts, 8vo.

HUNGARIAN (chapters 1-38)

Pest, 1868-9, A Római Birodalon hanyatlásának és bukásának története . . .
Azangol eredetiböl átdolgozta Hegyessy K., 2 vols., 8vo.

POLISH (chapter 44)

Cracow, 1830, E. Gibbona rys historyczny Prawa Rzymskiego. Przetozyl z
Angielskiego i uwagami G. Hugona powiększyl J. H. S. Rzesińki. 8vo.
Reissued 1844.

GREEK (chapter 44)

Athens, 1840, 'E. Γιββωνος 'Ιστοριας της Παρακμης και πτωσεως του ρωμαϊκου κρατουι
κεφαλαιον μδ., περιεχον την ιστοριαν του ρωμαικου δικαιου. 'Οι προσετεθησαν as
σημειωσεις του Ούγωνος, Βαρνκοινιγου και τινες των μεταφραστων 'Α. 'Ερτσογ και
Π. Παππαρρηγοπουλου, 8vo.

CZECH (chapter 44)

Prague, 1880, E. Gibbon: o Právu Římském. Z anglického jazyka přeložil J.
Váňa, 8vo (Anglo-Slavonic Library, Part 3: Anglicko-slovanská Knihovna
zábavy i poučení).

GIBBON'S MINOR WORKS

ESSAI SUR L'ETUDE DE LA LITTÉRATURE

London, 1761, [" I received the first copy (June the 23rd) at Alresford " (Murray,
p. 170)], Essai | sur | l'Etude | de la | Littérature | , chez T. Becket et P. A.
de Hondt, " in a small Volume in duodecimo," " the primitive value of half
a crown ".
　　Errata, p. ii ; " To Edward Gibbon, Esq.," by " E. Gibbon, Junior " (in
English, dated May 28th, 1761), pp. iii-vii ; " Avis au Lecteur, Le 26 Avril
[16 Avril in Misc. Works], 1761," pp. ix-xiii ; " A. L'Auteur " signed " M.
Maty," xv-xxxii ; Essai, pp. 1-159.
　　Begun, March 8, 1758 ; resumed July 11 ; continued February 11, 1759 ;
revised April 23, 1761. [A copy with inscription : " To Mrs. Jolliffe from the
Author," was sold in March, 1912, for £3 12s. 6d.] The Essai is reprinted in
Misc. Works, iv. pp. 1-93, " with corrections and additions from an interleaved
copy " (Misc. Works, i. p. xix)—apparently all in the notes : e.g. pp. 30, 34, 54.
London and Paris, 1762, Essai . . . 12mo (Duchesne). [Recorded by Quérard,
La France Littéraire.]
[Genève ?] 1762, small 8vo, paper cover, Essai . . . suivant la Copie, à Londres :
chez T. Becket and P. A. de Hondt, s.l. [Priced in a recent catalogue at
£5 5s., May, 1911.] Errata corrected and two indexes added.
　　" The next year (1762) a new Edition (I believe at Geneva) extended the
fame, or at least the circulation, of the work " (Murray, p. 171).
　　It is possible that these two 1762 editions are the same, and that Gibbon
was mistaken.
London, 1764, 8vo, An essay on the study of literature, written originally in
French . . . now first translated into English (T. Becket and P. A. de Hondt,
2s.) ; also a large paper edition, 4s.
　　" The author might have wept over the blunders and the baldness of the
English translation " (Murray, p. 171).

[Apparently translated by Becket : " his translation," Misc. Works, i. p. 157 note ; Murray, p. 256.]

There is another translation, " an entirely new one," in " The Miscellaneous Works " of 1837.

Dublin, 1777, 12mo, An essay . . . " The publication of my History revived the memory. I refused the permission of reprinting it : the public curiosity was imperfectly satisfied by a pyrated copy of the booksellers of Dublin " (Murray, p. 171).

Translations (German) of the Essai

Hamburg, 1792, 8vo, Versuch über d. Studium d. Literatur ; aus d. Französ. von Eschenburg.

Leipzig, 1794, mit neuem Titel.

MÉMOIRES LITTÉRAIRES

London, 1768, 12mo, Mémoires Littéraires de la Grande Bretagne pour l'an 1767 (Londres : Chez T. Becket et P. A. de Hondt, dans le Strand).

Deyverdun was apparently the responsible editor (Read, ii. pp. 380-3). For plan and contents, see Misc. Works, ii. pp. 68-71.

London, 1769, 12mo, Mémoires Littéraires pour l'an 1768 (Chez C. Heydinger dans Grafton St., Soho ; Et se vend chez P. Elmsley, vis-à-vis Southampton Street dans le Strand).

[Both of these are now in the British Museum. The two vols., in one, have been recently catalogued at nine guineas and again at twelve.]

One article, " Doutes Historiques par M. Horace Walpole," by Gibbon, with supplementary " réflexions " by Hume, is reprinted in Misc. Works, iii. pp. 331-49.

CRITICAL OBSERVATIONS

1770, 8vo, Critical Observations on the Sixth Book of the Aeneid : " were sent, without my name, to the press " ; " my first English publication " (Murray, p. 282).

1794, 8vo, Critical Observations. . . .

Reprinted in Misc. Works, iv. pp. 467-514.

A VINDICATION, ETC.

1779, January 14th [Walpole's Letters, edn. Toynbee, x. p. 363]. A | Vindication | Of | Some Passages | In The | Fifteenth And Sixteenth Chapters | Of The | History of the Decline and Fall of | the Roman Empire. | By the Author.

" in octavo—for I would not print it in quarto, lest it should be bound and preserved with the History itself " (Murray, p. 316).

Pp. 1-158 ; Errata (Printed for W. Strahan ; and T. Cadell In The Strand).

1779 (" we have a second edition in the press," February 6th, Prothero, i. p. 357), 8vo. A Vindication . . . " Bentinck St., February 3, 1779 ".

The same number of pages as first edition, but on larger and better paper ; fully revised : some passages (e.g. at the end about A Gentleman) which formed a " Postscript " in 1st edn., are now incorporated and a few passages added. In Misc. Works, iv. pp. 515-648, Sheffield follows 2nd edn. as a rule, but reinserts a compliment to Bishop Lowth, omitted in 2nd edn. of Vindication.

Dublin, 1779, 8vo. A Vindication. . . .

MÉMOIRE JUSTIFICATIF

1779, May, small 4to of 32 pages [without name of author or place], | Mémoire Justificatif | pour servir de | Réponse | à | L'Exposé &c. | de la | Cour de France | MDCCLXXIX.

The " Exposé " referred to was a pamphlet entitled : " Exposé des motifs de la conduite du Roi de France relativement à l'Angleterre ". G.'s Mémoire was "delivered as a state paper to the Courts of Europe" (Murray, 320), and was "translated even into the Turkish language" (Misc. Works, i. p. xx). Reprinted in Misc. Works (1796), ii. pp. 531-550, and in Misc. Works (1814), v. pp. 1-34; with, however, initial title in both editions thus: Mémoire Justificatif pour servir de Réponse à l'Exposé des Motifs de la Conduite du Roi de France relativement à l'Angleterre. A copy of the original is in the B.M.

1779, The Annual Register, pp. 397-412, English translation of the Mémoire. (Preceded by translations of the Spanish and French manifestoes.)

AN HISTORICAL VIEW OF CHRISTIANITY

1806, 4to, An Historical View of Christianity, containing select passages from Scripture, with a commentary by the late Edward Gibbon, Esq., and notes by the late Lord Viscount Bolingbroke, Monsieur de Voltaire, and others (Cadell & Davies).
Not included in Misc. Works.

MISCELLANEOUS WORKS

1796, 2 vols., 4to, Miscellaneous Works of Edward Gibbon, Esquire. With Memoirs of his Life and Writings, composed by Himself: illustrated from his letters, with occasional notes and narrative, by John Lord Sheffield [printed for A. Strahan, and T. Cadell, Jun., and W. Davies (successors to Mr. Cadell) in the Strand. £2 10s.].
Vol. i., p. 17, has the silhouette of Gibbon "cut with scissars (sic) by Mrs. Brown" (i. p. 435).
"The most important part consists of Memoirs . . . of which he left Six different sketches. From all these the following Memoirs have been carefully selected and put together," vol. i. p. iv.

Dublin, 1796, 3 vols., 8vo, Miscellaneous Works . . . (printed for P. Wogan and twelve others). Silhouette of G. Errata of London edition corrected.
Contains (vol. i., pp. 277-8) matter not found in any other edition, although an English translation appears in the 1837 edition. Sévery (vol. ii., pp. 322-3) says: "Lord Sheffield faisait paraître à Dublin l'édition dite irlandaise des Miscellanées de Gibbon, et il pria M. le ministre Levade de lui remettre une notice sur Mme de Sévery [died Jan. 17, 1796] qu'il désirait placer après la lettre [Misc. Works, i., pp. 392-7] dans laquelle Gibbon raconte à son ami Sheffield la mort de M. de Sévery". "Faisait paraître" can hardly be fact; even thus to countenance a cheap rival reprint is strange. Presumably the copyright was still in Sheffield's hands, for which in 1812 John Murray paid him, as executor, £1000 (Hill, p. 315 and also p. 195).

Basil, 1796 (1-4), 1797 (5-7), 7 vols., 8vo, Miscellaneous Works . . . (J. J. Tourneisen, 28 fr.).
A curiously arranged book. Vols. i. and ii. contain the text of vol. i., 4to; vols. iii.-v. of vol. ii., 4to; vols. vi. and vii. contain translations into English of the Essai and other pieces in French, but not of the Mémoire Justificatif; while all the notes, even the most minute, are massed at the end of vol. vii. The Errata of the 4to edn. are corrected. Quérard places this edition as "Basil (Strasbourg)".

1814, 8vo, "A new edition with considerable additions in Five Volumes," The Miscellaneous Works of Edward Gibbon, Esq. With Memoirs of . . . by the Right Honourable John, Lord Sheffield (printed for John Murray, 50 Albemarle Street, By C. Roworth, Bell-yard, Temple-Bar, £3 5s.; also in royal 8vo, £4 10s.).
I., Memoirs and Letters; II., Letters; III., Historical and Critical; IV., Classical and Critical; V., Miscellaneous.
Contains plates of Gibbon (Warton, 1774, "by far the best likeness," p. xi), The Pavilion and Terrace at Lausanne, Sheffield Place, Fletching Church, The Mausoleum.

The additional matter in this edition is detailed in Sheffield's " Advertisement," pp. iv. *seq.* There are various minor alterations in the Memoirs, especially in the first few pages ; *e.g.* the compliment to " Our immortal Fielding" now first appears. Many additional letters ; though omits an important letter of Feb. 11, 1789, to Cadell, probably withheld from rival publisher.

1814, 4to, Antiquities of the House of Brunswick [extracted and printed privately for presents].

  (Mr. Toovey, of Piccadilly, catalogued a copy in morocco at £1 16s.)
1815, 4to, Miscellaneous Works . . . vol. iii. [uniform with vols. i. and ii. of 1796, to complete the set] with portrait by Warton (John Murray, £2 8s.).
1837, 8vo, Silhouette, The Miscellaneous Works. . . . " Complete in one volume " (B. Blake, 13 Bell Yard, Temple Bar, 10s. 6d.). Also New York, same year.

  This is really only the two first volumes of the 1796 edition ; and all in English, including " Essai," " Mémoire Justificatif " and the Sévery notice, *ut supra.*

TRANSLATIONS OF MISCELLANEOUS WORKS

French

Paris, 1797, 2 vols., 8vo, Mémoires de Gibbon, suivis de quelques ouvrages posthumes et de quelques lettres du même auteur, recueillis et publiés par Lord Sheffield ; trad. de l'angl. (par J. E. F. Marignié), Paris, An V., 10 fr.
  Apparently reissued in An VI. (1798), see Quérard.

German

Leipzig, 1801-2, 2 vols., 8vo, Vermischte Werke, mit Anmerkungen, herausgegeben von J. Lord Sheffield ; aus d. Engl. mit Zusätzen.
  Graesse says : " n'est pas complète " ; " on y ajoute ; J. Wilkes, *Supplement to Misc. Works of Gibbon* " ; which, according to Brunet, was an anonymous, privately printed piece, which had already appeared in the Observer in 1780. This piece is not in B.M. Library under Wilkes.

THE MEMOIRS SEPARATELY

1827, 2 vols., small 8vo, Memoirs of the Life and Writings of Edward Gibbon, composed by himself and illustrated. . . .
  (" A collection of the most instructive and amusing lives.")
1831, 8vo, Autobiography and correspondence (Ward & Locke).
  Reissued in 1869.
1839, 8vo, The Life of Edward Gibbon, with selections from his correspondence and illustrations by H. H. Milman (John Murray, 9s.).
  Uniform with the first issue of Milman's *Decline and Fall.*
Paris, 1840, 8vo, with Essay on the Study of Literature. Portrait.
1854, Memoirs of my Life and Writings (prefixed to Smith's edition of *Decline and Fall,* 8vo).
1869, post 8vo, The Autobiography and Correspondence, reprint of the original 4to edition, cr. 8vo (Alexander Murray, 3s. 6d.).
Boston, 1877-8, 12mo, with a critical and biographical essay by W. D. Howells (" Famous Autobiographies "). Reissued 1905 by Houghton, Mifflin & Co.
1880, cr. 8vo, The Life and Letters, with index, by W. J. Day (with History of the Crusades, Chandos Classics).
1891, 8vo, Memoirs and a selection from his letters, edited by Henry Morley, with introduction. Printed from the 1796 edn. (Routledge, Carisbrooke Library).
1896, 8vo, with portrait from an enamel by H. Bone, R.A., after Reynolds. The Autobiographies of Edward Gibbon, printed verbatim from hitherto unpublished MSS., with an introduction by the Earl of Sheffield, edited by John Murray (John Murray) ; also New York, 1897 (Scribner).

Memoirs F (and Appendix), B, C, E, A, D ; Memoranda and Fragments ; Will of 1788 (not of 1791) ; Index.

Passages hitherto unpublished are so marked, not always correctly, *e.g.* on p. 417, the passage " We seem—society " appeared in the second edition, and the first clause in both editions.

1897, The same, Second edition.

Boston, 1898, 12mo, Memoirs, with introduction and notes by Oliver Farrar Emerson (Athenæum Press Series, Ginn).

1899, 8vo, Life and Letters (with History of the Crusades), verbatim reprint, with copious index by W. J. Day (C. Arthur Pearson).

1900, cr. and demy 8vo, The Memoirs of The Life of Edward Gibbon, with various observations and excursions by Himself, edited by George Birkbeck Hill (Methuen & Co.). Preface ; elaborate notes and 68 Appendixes.

" My text, with the exception of a few words, is Lord Sheffield's. It does not, however, exactly correspond with either his first or his second edition " (p. xvii). An indispensable edition. Also New York (Putnam).

1907, pott 8vo, Autobiography of Edward Gibbon, as originally edited by Lord Sheffield, with an introduction by J. B. Bury (The World's Classics, Henry Frowde). Follows the readings of the 1814 edition.

1911, foolscap 8vo, The Autobiography of Edward Gibbon, edited by Oliphant Smeaton (Everyman's Library, Dent) ; also New York (Dutton).

TRANSLATIONS OF THE MEMOIRS

German

Brunswick, 1796-7, 2 parts, 8vo, Leben, von ihm selbst beschrieben ; übersetzt von Ziegenbein.

Leipzig, 1797, 8vo, Leben . . . mit Anmerkungen herausgegeben von J. Lord Sheffield, aus dem Englischen übersetzt und mit erläuternden Anmerkungen begleitet [by F. G. S.]. Portrait.

Leipzig, 1801, 8vo, portrait.

Italian

Milan, 1825, 8vo, Memorie scritte da lui medesimo.

GIBBON'S LETTERS, ETC.

1896, 2 vols., 8vo, Private Letters of Edward Gibbon (1753-1794), edited by Rowland E. Prothero (John Murray).

The frontispieces are the Silhouette of Gibbon and The Pavilion and Terrace, Lausanne.

Letters garbled or truncated in Misc. Works are here printed entire. This, however, is not a complete collection of Gibbon's Letters, and must be supplemented by the other works below and also by the Misc. Works, both editions.

1897, Same, Second edition.

1896, 8vo, The Girlhood of Maria Josepha Holroyd. Recorded in letters . . . edited by J. H. Adeane (Longmans, Green & Co.).

Contains two letters, one portion hitherto unpublished (p. 201).

1897, 2 vols., 8vo, Historic Studies in Vaud, Berne, and Savoy, by General Meredith Read (Chatto & Windus). Thirty-one illustrations, including portraits of Gibbon and Deyverdun from the originals at La Grotte.

Contains unpublished letters, etc., of Gibbon, but (except one letter) translated into English.

Paris, 1882, 2 vols., small 8vo, Le Salon de Madame Necker d'après des documents tirés des archives de Coppet par Le Comte D'Haussonville (Calmann Lévy).

Contains unpublished letters and verse from Gibbon to Suzanne Curchod.

1882, 2 vols., small 8vo, The Salon of Madame Necker, translated by H. M. Trollope.

Lausanne and Paris, 1911-12, 2 vols., 8vo, La Vie de Société dans le Pays de Vaud
à la fin du dix-huitième siècle. Par M. et Mme. William de Sévery (Lausanne,
Georges Bridel & Cie ; Paris, Librairie Fischbacher).

Many illustrations, connected with Gibbon.

In vol. ii. are two chapters (i. and ii.) devoted to Gibbon, containing
letters, etc., in the French original, many of which Meredith Read had translated in his book.

Not in the B.M. I have not seen vol. i., which is out of print.

1895, cr. 4to, Proceedings of the Gibbon Commemoration (1794-1894), by R. H. T.
Ball (Longmans, Green & Co.).

Contains catalogue of the Gibbon exhibition, with quotations, etc.

There appears to be no complete uniform edition of Gibbon's Works.
The "Edition Lausanne" (Fred. de Fau & Co., New York, 1907) includes
History, 7 vols., 12mo, Autobiographies and Private Letters.

CONTROVERSIAL REPLIES TO THE HISTORY

1776, October (Misc. Works, iv. p. 602), Anonymous [James Chelsum, D.D.]. Remarks on the two last chapters of Mr. Gibbon's History of . . . . In a Letter
to a Friend, 8vo.

Second edition, enlarged, with additional remarks by Dr. Randolph, Lady
Margaret Professor, was published under Chelsum's name in 1778, Oxford,
12mo. Translated into Italian, though probably unpublished (Spedalieri,
Confutazione, 1827, Preface, p. 10).

Cambridge, 1776, Richard Watson, D.D., F.R.S., and Regius Professor of Divinity.
An Apology for Christianity in a series of letters to Edward Gibbon, Esq.,
12mo. Six Letters, with an "Appendix" by R. Wynne, Rector of St. Alphage,
London.

Also Cambridge, 1777, 12mo; Dublin, 1777, 8vo; 1791, 12mo; 1797,
12mo. Also included in "Two Apologies," 1806, 8vo ; 1816, 8vo; 1820, 8vo ;
Edinburgh, 1821, 12mo ; 1839, Bohn. Translated into Italian, though probably
unpublished (Spedalieri, *ut supra*).

1776, William Salisbury, B.D. Strictures on Mr. Gibbon's Account of Christianity
and its First Teachers.

Inserted in his translation of J. B. Bullet's Histoire de l'établissement du
Christianisme, 8vo.

York, 1778, William Burgh, LL.D. An inquiry into the belief of the Christians of
the first three centuries respecting the one Godhead of the Father, Son, and
the Holy Ghost, 8vo.

Dublin, 1778, Smyth Loftus, M.A., Vicar of Coolock. A Reply to the Reasonings
of Mr. Gibbon in History of . . . ; which seem to affect the Truth of Christianity ; but have not been noticed in the Answer which Dr. Watson hath given
to that Book, 8vo.

1778, East Apthorp, M.A., Vicar of Croydon. Letters on the Prevalence of Christianity before its Civil Establishment. With Observations on a late History
of . . ., 8vo.

1778, Henry Edwards Davis, B.A., of Balliol College, Oxford. An Examination of
the fifteenth and sixteenth chapters of Mr. Gibbon's History of the . . . . In
which his view of the Progress of the Christian Religion is shewn to be founded
on the Misrepresentation of the Authors he cites : and Numerous Instances of
his Inaccuracy and Plagiarism are produced, 8vo (J. Dodsley in Pall-Mall). In
my copy, which bears the book-plate of I. Baker Holroyd, there is on title page,
in old writing resembling Sheffield's : "supposed by some to be written by
Douglas Bishop of Salisbury ". He was at this time only Canon of Windsor
(D.N.B.).

1778, A Gentleman [Francis Eyre]. A few remarks on the History of . . . , relative
chiefly to the two last chapters, 8vo.

An anonymous Roman Catholic.

[Gibbon's *Vindication* appeared on January 14th, 1779.]

1779, [Francis Eyre]. A short Appeal to the Public. By the Gentleman who is particularly addressed in the Postscript of the Vindication . . ., 8vo.

1779, Henry Edwards Davis, B.A. A Reply to Mr. Gibbon's Vindication, wherein the charges brought against him in the "Examination" are confirmed, and further instances given of his Misrepresentation, Inaccuracy, and Plagiarism, 8vo (J. Dodsley).

1780, George Laughton, D.D. The Progress and Establishment of Christianity, in reply to the 15th Chapter of the Decline . . . 4to. Also 1786, 4to.

[1780 ?], not published. Lord Hailes. "That which is placed in the foremost rank, etc," 8vo. (Being observations on the account of the early Christians given by Gibbon.)

[1780 ?], not published. Lord Hailes. "To the virtues of the Primitive Christians, etc.," 8vo. (Further observations on the same.)

York, 1781, Joseph Milner, A.M. Gibbon's Account of Christianity considered; together with some strictures on Hume's Dialogues concerning Natural Religion, 8vo.

1781, Henry Taylor, Rector of Crawley and Vicar of Portsmouth. Thoughts on the Nature of the Grand Apostacy, with Reflections and Observations on the Fifteenth Chapter of Mr. Gibbon's History, 8vo.

Birmingham, 1782. Joseph Priestley, LL.D. An History of the Corruptions of Christianity, 2 vols., 8vo.

Also Birmingham, 1793, 2 vols., 8vo. See also Correspondence between Gibbon and Priestley in Misc. Works, ii. pp. 265-72.

1783, J. Ogilvie, D.D. An inquiry into the Causes of the Infidelity . . . of the Times: with observations on the writings of . . . Gibbon, 8vo.

Norwich, [1784], Thomas Howes. A Discourse on the Abuse of the Talent of Disputation in Religion, particularly as practiced (*sic*) by Dr. Priestly (*sic*), Mr. Gibbon and others of the modern sect of philosophic Christians. Preached at the Cathedral Church, Norwich, June 23, 1784.

Reprinted in Critical Observations on Books antient and modern [by Thomas Howes], 4 vols., 8vo, London, 1776-1800.

Chester, 1784, George Travis, A.M. Letters to Edward Gibbon, Esq., in defence of the Authenticity of the 7th Verse of the 5th Chapter of the First Epistle of St. John, 4to.

Three of these Letters had been published in 1782 in the Gentleman's Magazine. There were enlarged editions of the book in 1785, 8vo, London; and 1794, 8vo, London. See Preface to Porson's *Letters*, p. ix, where the second edition is given as 1786, apparently wrongly.

Oxford, 1784, Joseph White, D.D. Sermons preached before the University of Oxford in 1784 [Bampton Lectures: A Comparison of Mahometism (*sic*) and Christianity, in their History, their Evidence, and their Effects], 8vo.

Second edition, London, 8vo, 1785; fourth edition, 1792; new edition, 1811, 8vo (with title: A Comparison . . . .). As to the authorship of these lectures, see Hill, p. 320.

Winchester, 1785, James Chelsum, D.D. A Reply to Mr. Gibbon's Vindication of . . . Containing a review of the Errors still retained in these chapters, 8vo.

Edinburgh, 1786, David Dalrymple, Lord Hailes. An Inquiry into the Secondary Causes which Mr. Gibbon has assigned for the rapid Growth of Christianity, 4to.

Second edition, Edinburgh, 1808, 12mo.

Birmingham, 1787, Joseph Priestley, LL.D., F.R.S. Letters to a Philosophical Unbeliever, Part ii., containing a State of the Evidence of revealed Religion, with Animadversions on the two last Chapters of the first Volume of *Mr. Gibbon's History of the Decline and Fall of the Roman Empire*, 8vo (printed by Pearson & Rollason for J. Johnson, No. 72 St. Paul's Churchyard, London). Part i., referring to Hume, had been published at Bath in 1780. The second edition of Part i. and the first edition of Part ii. (referring to Gibbon) were both published at Birmingham in 1787.

1788, [Anonymous], Observations on the three last Volumes of the Roman History by Edward Gibbon, Esq., 12mo.

1790, Letters to Mr. Archdeacon Travis, in answer to his Defence of the Three Heavenly Witnesses, 1 John v. 7, 8vo (printed for T. & J. Egerton, Whitehall).

Of the xii Letters, five had appeared in seven issues of the Gentleman's Magazine (Oct. and Dec., '88; Feb., April, May, June, Aug., '89). The famous criticism of Gibbon is in Preface, pp. xxvii-xxxii.

1790, W. Disney, D.D. Sermon preached before the University of Cambridge, 28th June, 1789; with some strictures on the licentious notions avowed or enumerated in Mr. Gibbon's Roman History, 4to.

1791, Simplex. Letters addressed to Soame Jenyns, Esq. . . ., containing Strictures on the writings of Edward Gibbon, Esq., 12mo. Second edition. Date of first edition?

1791, Rev. John Whitaker. Gibbon's History of . . ., vols. iv., v., and vi., 4to, reviewed, 8vo.

Previously "published in the English Review, Oct., 1788, etc."; "malignant and illiberal"; "he has allotted the first month's review to an attack on the first three volumes, or rather on the first" (Misc. Works, i. p. 243, Sheffield's note). "Whitaker was as dirty a cur as I remember" (Macaulay's Journal, 9th Oct., '50).

Oxford, 1791, Henry Kett, M.A. Sermons preached before the University of Oxford in the year 1790 [Bampton Lectures]. A representation of the conduct and opinions of Primitive Christians, with remarks on certain assertions of Mr. Gibbon and Dr. Priestley, 8vo.

Second edition, with corrections . . . additions, London, 1792, 8vo.

1792, John Milner, D.D., F.S.A., Bishop of Castabala. An historical and critical Inquiry into the Existence and Character of Saint George, Patron of England, of the Order of the Garter, and of the Antiquarian Society; in which the assertions of Edward Gibbon, Esq., History of Decline and Fall, cap. 23 . . . are discussed, 8vo.

Canterbury, [1792], N. Nisbett, M.A. The Scripture Doctrine concerning the Coming of Christ . . . in answer to the objections of Mr. Gibbon, etc., 8vo.

Shrewsbury, 1796 [Anonymous]. A letter to the Right Honourable John Lord Sheffield on the publication of the Memoirs and Letters of the late Edward Gibbon, Esq., 8vo.

A general attack on "our Heathenish Historian" (p. 40).

1797, John Evans, LL.D., of Islington. An attempt to account for the Infidelity of the late Edward Gibbon, Esq., founded on his own Memoirs . . ., 8vo.

Canterbury, 1800, N. Nisbett. The Coming of the Messiah the true Key to the right understanding of the most difficult passages of the New Testament . . . in answer to . . . objections of the Historian of the Decline . . ., 8vo.

Deal, 1802, N. Nisbett, M.A. The Triumphs of Christianity over Infidelity displayed; being a full answer to the objections of Mr. Gibbon, that our Lord and his Apostles predicted the near approach of the end of the world in their own time, 8vo.

Chatham, [1805], N. Nisbett, M.A. A concise and interesting View of the objection of Mr. Gibbon, that our Lord foretold his second coming in the clouds of Heaven, in the generation in which he lived, which the revolution of seventeen centuries has proved not to be agreeable to experience, 8vo.

1808, The Author of Christian Knowledge in theological extracts and abridgments. An Antidote to Infidelity insinuated in the Works of E. Gibbon, containing expositions on the prophecies of our Blessed Saviour, in Matthew 24, Mark 13, and Luke 21, with other interesting disquisitions to similar effect, 8vo.

New edition. Date of first edition?

1809, Wm. Cockburn, M.A., Fellow of St. John's College, Cambridge. The Credibility of the Jewish Exodus defended against some remarks of Edward Gibbon, Esq., and the Edinburgh Reviewers, 8vo (J. Hatchard).

Faversham, 1812, N. Nisbett, M.A. Letters illustrative of the Gospel History and of the Epistles. . . . In reply to Mr. Gibbon, Mr. Faber and others, 12mo.

Coventry [printed], 1860, Miss Sara Sophia Hennell. The early Christian anticipa-

tion of an approaching end of the World. . . . Including an . . . examination
. . . of the fifteenth chapter of Gibbon (Fifth Baillie Prize Essay), 8vo.
[New York ?, 1868], James Madison MacDonald. Irony in History; or the true
position of Gibbon in respect to Christianity . . . (reprinted from Bibliotheca
Sacra, July, 1868), 8vo.

FRENCH

Paris, 1842, Marie Nicolas Silvestre Guillon, Bishop of Morocco. Examen critique
des doctrines de Gibbon . . . sur Jésus-Christ . . . 2 tom., 8vo.

ITALIAN

Rome, 1779, Abate Nicola Spedalieri. Confutazione dell' esame del cristianesimo
fatto dal sig. Eduardo Gibbon nella sua Storia della . . . (Salvioni).
Pisa, 1782, Nicola Spedalieri. Saggio di Confutazione de' due capi xv. e xvi.
di Gibbon spettanti all' esame del Cristianesimo (inserted in vol. iii., dated
1780, of the Pisa translation of the History; also epitomised in Bertolotti's
Milan translation, 1820-4, after chap. 16).
Pisa, 1783 [Anonymous]. Riflessioni sopra il tomo v. e vi. della Storia della . . .
divise in III. lettere dirette al Sigg. Foothead e Kirk, Inglesi Cattolici (inserted in vol. v. pp. 363-435 of the Pisa translation).
Pisa, 1783 [Anonymous]. Riflessioni sopra il tomo vii. della . . . divise in II.
lettere . . . (inserted in vol. vii. of the Pisa translation).
    " The piety or prudence of my Italian translator has provided an antidote
against the poison of his original " (Murray, p. 322). " Risoluti però di non
mai presentare agl' incauti il veleno senza l'antidoto " (vol. iii. p. 4). Letters
to Foothead and Kirk are also inserted in Bertolotti's Milan translation
after chap. 25.
Rome, 1784, Nicola Spedalieri. Confutazione dell' esame del Cristianesimo fatto
. . . 2 vols., 4to.
    The author trusts that he is " gratifying the faithful in depositing at the
foot of the altar the spolia opima of three foes [Watson, Chelsum, and Gibbon],
although they had hoped to see him return victorious over one only " (Preface).
Piacenza, 1798, Nicola Spedalieri. Confutazione dell' esame . . ., 2 vols., 4to.
Rome, 1827, Nicola Spedalieri. Confutazione dell' esame . . ., 2 vols. (4 parts),
12mo. Stampata a spese della società dell' Amicizia Cattolica. This edition
was published to combat the popularity of the " Italian Republics " of Sis-
mondi, into whom the Anti-Catholic spirit of the " Scotch " Gibbon had now
entered (Publisher's note).
    The history of Spedalieri's book is enigmatical. The 1779 edn., *supra*, is
recorded on the specific authority of Rivista d'Italia, November, 1903, p. 793,
but is inconsistent with statement in Cimbali, Vita di Spedalieri, and also in
Pisa translation (iii. pp. 4-5 of Saggio) ; where it is explained that Spedalieri
had now completed, but not published, his work, of which, however, he allowed
an epitome to be inserted in the Pisa translation, " for the errors in which epitome
the author was not responsible ". On the other hand, in the Pisa translation,
ix. p. 400, and in the Preface to the Confutazione, the epitome is described as
by Spedalieri himself. Probably the Saggio was a *ballon d'essai;* and the
statement therein " a voluntary error ".

    " At the distance of twelve years, I calmly affirm my judgement of Davies,
Chelsum, etc. A victory over such antagonists was a sufficient humiliation "
(Murray, pp. 316-7).

INDEX

of the Greek Church by the Otto-
mans, 211 and *note*.
Canterbury, Emperor Manuel at, vii., 97.
Capelianus, i., 194.
Capernaum, Latin pilgrims besieged in,
vi., 266.
Caphargamala, village near Jerusalem,
iii., 222.
Capiculi, Turkish troops, vii., 180 and
note.
Capistran (John Capistrano), vii., 156
note.
Capitation tax in Gaul, i., 444; levied
on the Jews, ii., 96; under Constan-
tine, 207 and *note*; levied by Leo
III., v., 278 and *note*.
Capito, Ateius, iv., 486, 489 and *note*.
Capitol of Rome, ii., 95 and *notes*; *see*
Rome.
Capitoline games, *see* Games.
Capitoline Mount, i., 322 *note*.
Capitolinus, i., 106 *note*, 110 *note*.
Capizucchi family, vii., 260.
Capoccia family, vii., 331.
Caporioni, chiefs of militia, vii., 304.
Cappadocia, invaded by Alaric, i., 348;
domains of, ii., 198 *sq*. and *note*;
proconsul of, iv., 272; Paulicians
of, vi., 120.
Capranica, vii., 276.
Caprara, iv., 444.
Capraria (Island), monks in, iii., 248.
Capreolus, Bishop of Carthage, on de-
solation of Africa, iii., 480 *note*.
Capsia, taken by Roger of Sicily, vi., 220.
Captain, title of, in Rome, v., 323 *note*.
Capua, i., 23; amphitheatre at, 48, 53;
vii., 329 *note*; destroyed by Alaric,
iii., 348 and *note*; Belisarius at, iv.,
333; Lombard princes of, vi., 177;
besieged by the Saracens, 179; taken
by Roger, 218.
Caput Vada, Belisarius at, iv., 299 and
note.
Capuzzi, Roman family of, vii., 238 *note*.
Caracalla, i., 133 *note*; names of, 139
note; reign, 143 *sqq.*; titles of, 143
note; edict concerning freemen, 171
and *note*; taxation of Roman citizens by, 179; baths of, iii., 321 *sq.*;
laws of, iv., 482 *note*; edict of, concerning the name of Romans, vi.,
105.
Caracorum or Holin, residence of Zingis
Khan, vii., 19 and *note sq*.
Caractacus, i., 4.
Caracullus for Caracalla, i., 140 *note*; in
the poems of Ossian, 141 *note*.
Caramania, Emir of, military force of
the, vii., 27; state of, rivals the

Ottomans in Asia, *ib. note*; Sultan
of, defeated by Murad, *ib.*; con-
quered by Bajazet, 35; war with
the Ottoman Turks, 148, 150.
Carausius, i., 385 *sqq*.
Carashar Nevian, ancestor of Timour,
vii., 45.
Caravans, Sogdian, iv., 246.
Carbeas, the Paulician, vi., 123 *sq*.
Carbonarian forest, iii., 479 and *note*.
Carcassonne, iv., 126 *note*; Church of St.
Mary at, v., 510; taken by Anbasa,
vi., 14 *note*.
Carche, ii., 547 and *note*.
Cardinals, titles of, v., 316 and *note*;
their right to elect a Pope, vii., 249;
sacred college of, *ib. note*; conclave
of, 250 and *note*; predominance of
French, 255 and *note*.
Cardonne, De, his History of Africa, v.,
488 *note*; on Aglabites and Edrisites,
vi., 55.
Carduchians, subdued by Trajan, i., 7,
404.
Carduene (Corduene), i., 404 and
note.
Caribert, King of Paris, iv., 170 *note*.
Carinus (M. Aurelius), i., 364; Cæsar,
365, 366 *note*; emperor, 368; character, 368 and *note*; celebrates the
Roman games, 369; death, 375 and
note.
Carizme [Khwārizm], city of, taken by
the Saracens, v., 441 and *note*; reduced by Malek Shah, vi., 254; province of, invaded by Mongols, vii.,
8; city of, taken by Mongols, 9;
by Timour, 73.
Carizmians, invade Syria, vi., 373.
Carloman, brother of Charlemagne, v.,
303.
Carlovingian dynasty, v., 286 *sqq*.
Carmath, an Arabian preacher, vi., 51
and *note*.
Carmathians, Arabian sect, rise and progress of, vi., 52 *sqq.*, 53 *note*.
Carmel, Mount, battles near, vi., 363.
Carmelites, iv., 63 *note*.
Carnuntum, on the Danube, Severus declared emperor at, i., 122 *note*; Con-
gress of, 439 *note*.
Carocium, standard of the Lombards, v.,
323 *note*; placed in Capitol by
Frederic II., vii., 246.
Carpi, i., 263, 391 and *note*, 470 *note*.
Carpilio, son of Aetius, educated in the
camp of Attila, iii., 474 and *note*,
503 *note*.
Carpini, John de Plano, friar, visits court
of the great Khan, vii., 6 *note*.

deposed at Council of Basil, 117;
receives Oriental embassies, 119;
forms league against the Turks, 147
sq.; spurious epistle of, to King of
Ethiopia, 161 *note*; expelled, 301;
funeral of, 305; builds wall round
the Coliseum, 333.

Eugenius, the rhetorician, made emperor
by Arbogastes, iii., 190; paganism
of, *ib. note*; death, 194.

Eugippius, Life of St. Severinus by, iv.,
54 *note*, 60 *note*.

Eugraphia, widow at Constantinople,
persecutes Chrysostom, iii., 397 *note*.

Eugubine Tables, iv., 473 and *note*.

Eulalia, St., of Merida, iv., 13.

Eulalius, count of the domestics, testament of, iv., 255.

Eulalius, philosopher, iv., 284.

Eulogia, sister of Michael Palæologus,
vi., 485; conspires against her
brother, 494.

Eulogies and *benedictions* at Constantinople, v., 126.

Eulogius, Patriarch of Alexandria, account of, v., 171 and *note*.

Eulogius, St., of Cordova, v., 523 *note*.

Eumenius, the orator, i., 57 *note*, 386
note; Professor of Rhetoric at
Autun, 423 *note*; panegyric of, ii.,
309 *note*.

Eunapius, history of the Sophists, ii.,
461 *note*, 513 *note*; on the Gothic
war, iii., 63 *note*; on the ravages of
the Goths, 123 *note*; fanaticism of,
218.

Eunomians, disabilities of the, under
Theodosius, iii., 160.

Eunomius, ii., 372 and *note*; shelters
Procopius, iii., 13 *note*, 149.

Eunuchs, i., 412; power of, ii., 260
sq.; character of, 261; power of,
under Arcadius, iii., 380 and *note*.

Euphemia, daughter of John of Cappadocia, iv., 257.

Euphemia, daughter of Marcian, marries
Anthemius, iv., 33.

Euphemia, St., church of, council held
in, v., 132.

Euphemius, expedition of, to Sicily, vi.,
40 and *note*; death, 41.

Euphrates, victories of M. Antoninus on
the, i., 10; navigation of, ii., 536,
537 *note*; source of, iv., 273 and
note.

Euphrosyne, daughter of Constantine
VI., marries Michael the Second,
v., 203, 209.

Euphrosyne, wife of Alexius Angelus, vi.,
392.

Euric, King of the Visigoths, assassinates his brother Theodoric, iv., 41;
persecutes the Orthodox party, 88;
dominions of, 107 *sq.*; first Gothic
prince who wrote laws, 132.

Euripides, i., 281.

Europe, population of, i., 46 and *note*;
change in climate of, 231; present
state of, iv., 176 *sq.*; political system
of, in fifteenth century, vii., 300 *note*.

Europus, i., 223 *note*; iv., 184 *note*; Belisarius at, 395.

Eusebia, wife of Constantius II., friendship of, to Julian, ii., 270, 271;
friendly reception of Julian, 272;
her supposed jealousy of Julian,
274 and *note*; death, 430 and *note*.

Eusebius, Bishop of Vercellæ, ii., 395.

Eusebius, chamberlain of Honorius, his
death, iii., 333.

Eusebius, Count of Ticinum, orders
execution of Boethius, iv., 216 *note*.

Eusebius, neo-Platonist, ii., 464.

Eusebius of Cæsarea, as a historian, i.,
470 and *note*; ii., 125 and *note*; on
Palestine martyrs, 146 *note*; remark on his style, *ib.*; silence on
death of Crispus, 223 *note*; account
of Constantine's conversion, 323 and
note; friendship with Constantine,
326; description of the Church at
Jerusalem, 340 *note*; supports Arius,
365; accepts the Homoousion, 377;
character of, *ib. note*; at the Council of Tyre, 387.

Eusebius of Nicomedia, supports Arius,
ii., 365; exile, 377; recall, 378;
educates Julian, 457 and *note*;
Bishop of Constantinople, iii., 150
note.

Eusebius Scholasticus, poem on the
Gothic war, iii., 394 *note*.

Eusebius, the eunuch, chamberlain of
Constantius, ii., 261; questions
Gallus, 268; fall of, 440; death, 447.

Eustace, the elder brother of Godfrey of
Bouillon, vi., 289.

Eustathius, Archbishop of Thessalonica,
vi., 110, 227 *note*.

Eustathius, Bishop of Antioch, ii., 378;
death, 404.

Eustathius of Cappadocia, ii., 283 *note*.

Eustathius of Epiphania, iv., 271 *note*.

Eustochium, daughter of Paula, iv., 69.

Euthalites or Nephthalites (White Huns),
iii., 91 and *note*, 92; conquests of,
iv., 274; defeat Perozes, King of
Persia, 275; conquered by the Turks,
376; by Nushirvan, 411; in Transoxiana, v., 441 *note*.

INDEX

Valturio, Robert, his de Re Militari, vii., 167 *note*.
Valvassors, order of, at Rome, v., 323 and *note*; or *bannerets*, in diocese of Coustances, vi., 192.
Van (city of, Salban), v., *sq. note*.
Van Dale, de Consecratione Principum, i., 75 *note*.
Vandale, physician, ii., 492 *note*.
Vandals, in Germany, i., 253 *note*, 261 and *note*, 317 *note*; settle in Britain, 358; ally themselves with the Sarmatians, ii., 229; invade Italy, iii., 277; defeated by the Franks, 284; in Gaul and Spain, 365; defeated by Wallia, 368; take Seville and Carthagena, 424; in Africa, 425 *sqq.*; maritime power, iv., 1; treaty with Empire, 2 *note*; plunder Rome, 5 *sqq.* and *notes*; on the coasts of the Mediterranean, 29; their conversion, 83; persecute the African Christians, 88 *sqq.*; number of, under Gelimer, 301; fate of, 309 *sqq.*; become extinct in Africa, 314; revolt of, in Africa, 416; complete disappearance of, 421; effect of their capture on the buildings of Rome, vii., 321.
Vannes, diocese of, subdued by the Britons of Armorica, iv., 161.
Vapincum, ii., 258 *note*.
Varanes, general of Honorius, iii., 301.
Varanes, or Bahram, usurper, exploits of, v., 48; rebellion of, 50 *sqq.*; interviews with Chosroes, 52 *note*; death of, 55.
Varanes, or Bahram, King of Persia (Varahran II.), i., 365 and *note*.
Varanes, son of Yezdegerd, King of Persia, persecutes the Christians, iii., 412; ruin of the Armenian kingdom under, 415 *note*.
Varangians, in the Byzantine service, vi., 86, 155; name of, *ib. note*; acclamations of, 89 *note*; serve under Alexius Comnenus, 206; composed of Danes and English, 412 and *note*; serve under the Emperors of Nicæa, 483, 484.
Varchonites, *see* Ogors.
Varna, battle of, vii., 151 *sq.*
Varni, or Varini, iv., 169.
Varro, on fall of Rome, iii., 506 and *note*; on comets, iv., 462 and *note*.
Varronian, Count, father of Jovian, ii., 546.
Varronian, infant son of Jovian, iii., 6.
Varus, Alfenus, Roman lawyer, iii., 371 *note*.

Varus, i., 3 *note*, 22 *note*.
Vasinobroncæ, iii., 61 *note*.
Vataces, John Ducas, Emperor of Nice, vi., 450; besieges Constantinople, 452; conquests, 457; death, 458; administration, 476 *sqq.*; treasures of, 482 and *note*; interview with the Sultan of Iconium, vii., 23; his account of the Mongol invasion, 87.
Vatari, village of, iv., 417 *note*.
Vatican, library of the, vii., 134. *See* Rome.
Vaucluse, retreat of Petrarch, vii., 266 and *note*.
Vayvods, or Hungarian chiefs, vi., 144; vii., 155. *See* Voivode.
Veccus, Johannes, Patriarch of Constantinople, vi., 493 and *note*.
Vedastus, St., Life of, iv., 113 *note*.
Vegetius, his description of Roman legions, i., 17 *note*; iii., 197 and *note*.
Veii, siege of, i., 172; position of, *ib. note*, 407 *note*.
Velleda, German prophetess, i., 246.
Venantius, consul, v., 136.
Venaissin, county, ceded to the Popes, vii., 254 and *note*.
Velleius, Paterculus, i., 121 *note*.
Venedi, i., 263 *sq.* and *note*; subdued by Hermanric, iii., 61.
Venerianus, i., 285 *note*.
Venetians, recover Ravenna, v., 283; alliance with Alexius Comnenus, vi., 215; war with Emperor Manuel, 225; commerce, 397; government, 398; treaty with the crusaders, 399 *sqq.*; treachery of, to crusaders, 400 *note*; territory after conquest of Constantinople, 434; settlements in Constantinople, *ib.*; war with the Genoese, 535; treaty with Cantacuzene, *ib.*; their defeat, 536; use of gunpowder by, vii., 86; transport of ships from Adige to Lake Garda, 193 *note*. *See* Venice.
Veneti, i., 23 and *note*.
Venice, or Venetia, foundation of the republic of, iii., 495 *sqq.*; history of, by Maffei, 496 *note*; infant dominion of, v., 25; ally of Lombardy, 324; trade of, with Egypt and Palestine, vi., 263 *note*; History of, 396 *sqq.*; bronze horses of Constantinople taken to, 429 *note*; her monopoly of trade with the East, vii., 16 *note*; John Palæologus at, 110; knowledge of Turkish political affairs at, 217 *note*; holds aloof from factions of Italy, 326.

INDEX

INDEX

ERRATA, ETC. IN VOLS. I.-VII.

(*A great number of the corrigenda and emendations in the following list are due to Mr. E. Harrison, of Trinity College, Cambridge.*)

VOL. I.

P. 7, l. 8. read " ravaged ".
P. 79, l. 17. read " policy " with 1st 4to ed.
P. 89, n. 64, l. 2. read " Crispus ".
P. 147, l. 14. the 1st 4to ed. has " office," which is probably correct.
P. 148, n. 36, l. 3. after " 75 " insert " [*leg.* ' 74 '] ".
P. 169, l. 2. for " states " read " state ".
P. 237, l. 1. read " villages " with 1st 4to ed.
P. 373, n. 108, l. 3. for " *colonis* " read " *coronis* ".
P. 403, n. 79, l. 1. " Victor " should have small initial.
P. 405, n. 87, l. 1. read " Sarmatam ".
P. 434, l. 14 from foot. read " benefactor ".
P. 471, l. 6 from foot. for " war-like " read " warlike ".

VOL. II.

P. 21, l. 9. insert comma after " powers ".
P. 51, n. 135 ad fin. for " Prudent," read " Prudent.".
P. 52, n. 137. read " Cyprian."
P. 52, n. 138. read " Tertullian."
P. 100, l. 5 from foot. read " or the theatre " with 1st 4to ed.
P. 128, l. 2. possibly read " the " for " their " with 1st 4to ed.
P. 133, n. 156, l. 3. for " Anthemius " read " Anthimius [*leg.* Anthimus] ".
P. 264, n. 18, l. 1. for " quidem " read " quaedam ".
P. 264, n. 18, l. 6. after " concideret " insert " [*leg.* ' arbitrium r.v. succideret '] ".
P. 283, l. 8. omit " the " after " from ".
P. 320, l. 16. for " former " read " formal ".
P. 344, n. 116, l. 4. for " poor " read " pure ".
P. 353, n. 7, l. 1. for " agitur " read " igitur ".
P. 356, l. 16. for " of " read " as ".
P. 360, l. 9. read " dialectics ".
P. 369, l. 10. read " counsels ".
P. 370, l. 7 from foot. for " fears " read " fear ".
P. 375, l. 3. insert comma after " memory ".
P. 381, n. 92, l. 3. after " excitaret " insert " [*leg.* ' excitavit '] ".
P. 401, n. 141, l. 1. read " supererat " in one word.
P. 441, n. 49, l. 3. after " ours " insert " [but see Plato, Laws, IV. 713] ".
P. 445, n. 58, ll. 4 and 5. insert comma after " avium " and after " nives ".
P. 452, n. 79, l. 1. read ἰσχὺς ψυχή.
P. 506, l. 2. insert comma after " Augustus ".
P. 518, n. 43, l. 1. read " flumen ".
P. 547, l. 7. insert semicolon after " Jovian ".
P. 558, l. 10. read " appeared ".

VOL. III.

P. 36, l. 9. insert comma after "cruelty".
P. 47, n. 120, l. 2. for "procorum" read "porcorum".
P. 77, l. 13. for "enured" read "inured".
P. 120, l. 16. for "sacred" read "secret".
P. 133, n. 127, l. 4. read "scaturiente".
P. 144, n. 11, l. 4. read "orbis".
P. 149, n. 22, l. 2. insert comma after "sanctionem".
P. 152, n. 32, l. 4. read "Βυζαντιναὶ".
P. 160, n. 50, l. 3. delete "to" before "the Roman".
P. 169, n. 69, l. 4. for "increase" read "decrease".
P. 226, n. 96, l. 2. for "had" read "has".
P. 246, n. 40, l. 2. insert comma after "court".
P. 261, n. 24. for "civibus" read "civilibus".
P. 280, n. 79, l. 1. read "Augustin."
P. 280, n. 79, l. 2. read "Grot.)".
P. 299, last l. read "versification".
P. 304, l. 2. delete "so".
P. 309, n. 26, l. 3. read "Numatian."
P. 310, n. 30, l. 4. read "Quadringenties".
P. 358, n. 152, l. 3. read "repeated|".
P. 370, l. 4 from foot. for "appeared" read "appear".
P. 373, n. 182, l. 1. read "οὐκέτι".
P. 379, n. 2, l. 2. for "night;" read "night."
P. 382, l. 3. Notice that by "the last year of the fourth century" is meant "A.D. 399".
P. 385, n. 16. insert comma after "report".
P. 387, l. 7 from foot. read "cities".
P. 395, n. 41, l. 2 from end. read "Opera Chrysostom."
P. 412, l. 18. read "fire-temples".
P. 414, n. 82, l. 5. read "Aedificiis".
P. 423, n. 12, l. 2. read "revolt".
P. 427, n. 21, l. 3. for "514" read "414".
P. 444, n. 8, l. 3. read "praesulem".
P. 471, l. 2 from foot. for "Lord" read "lord".
P. 490, n. 45, l. 3. after "simili" insert "[leg. ' simile ']".
P. 490, n. 45, l. 4. after "referuntur" insert "[referantur, Mommsen with better MSS.]".
P. 507, n. 80, l. 4. after "tamen" insert "[leg. ' tantum ']".

VOL. IV.

P. 32, n. 79. insert comma after "Barbarians".
P. 35, n. 86, l. 5. for "heretics" read "heresies".
P. 40, l. 11 from foot. "antagonists" seems to be an error for "antagonist".
P. 49, n. 118, l. 2. for comma read point before "Sigonius".
P. 65, l. 13. for "angelic" read "angelic".
P. 68, n. 25, l. 6. for "this" read "his".
P. 92, l. 10 from foot. for "field" read "fields".
P. 100, l. 6. for "rights" read "rites".
P. 106, n. 2, l. 2. for exclamation read colon.
P. 110, l. 3 from foot. for "Soissons," read "Soissons;" and for "Belgic." read "Belgic,".
P. 120, n. 46, l. 3. read "Burgundian".
P. 121, marg. note, l. 6. for "332" read "532".
P. 123, l. 20. for "should" read "would".
P. 123, l. 21. for "would" read "should".
P. 140, l. 1. read "loyal".
P. 144, n. 108, l. 3. read "Lemanum".

P. 157, l. 18. for "justify" read "satisfy".
P. 162, n. 145, l. 2. for exclamation read semicolon.
P. 205, l. 6 from foot. read "Campania".
P. 208, ll. 16, 17. transpose "at his summons" to follow "appeared".
P. 244, n. 64, l. 2. after "21" insert "[22 (26)]".
P. 251, n. 84. after "parenti" insert "[parente]", and after "persolvit" insert "[*leg.* 'persolvit genitoris ']".
P. 274, n. 132, l. 1. read "the tone".
P. 274, n. 132, ll. 2, 3. for "lie" read "lye".
P. 275, n. 135, l. 3. read "Texeira".
P. 283, n. 151, l. 3. read "βασιλέως".
P. 294, l. 5 from foot. for "patrons" read "patron".
P. 297, n. 18, l. 5. for "at" read "of".
P. 316, n. 46, l. 3. insert comma after "soldiers".
P. 317, l. 2. read "respectful".
P. 331, n. 80, l. 4. read "successively".
P. 345, l. 23. for "smile," read "smile ;" and for "possess ;¦" read "possess,".
P. 354, l. 1. read "treasure".
P. 372, l. 17. Potidaea was a Corinthian not an Athenian colony.
P. 379, l. 16. "their" seems to be an error for "his".
P. 387, l. 4. read "questions".
P. 399, n. 82, l. 2. after "et a" insert "[omit a]".
P. 403, l. 7. read "immemorial".
P. 423, l. 6. "freedmen" is evidently an error for "freemen".
P. 447, l. 3. insert comma after "hill".
P. 459, n. 109, l. 3. read "Lycophront."
P. 487, n. 56, l. 3. after "nimis" insert "[*leg.* 'nimias ']".
P. 498, n. 86, l. 2. read "Mucius".
P. 504, n. 108, l. 2. read "actionibus, patrum jura".
P. 513, n. 134. after "invisit" insert "[*leg.* 'dimisit. Cp. below, vol. vi. p. 90, n. 66 ']".

VOL. V.

P. 22, l. 14 from foot. "invention" seems to be an error for "intervention".
P. 92, n. 115, l. 4. for "cera" read "sera".
P. 117, n. 26, l. 6. after "scraped" add ": ὄστρακον means a sherd."
P. 136, l. 5 from foot. "freedmen" should be "freemen" (liberos).
P. 144, n. 89, l. 2. "has" seems to be an error for "had".
P. 177, l. 6. "immoveable" seems to be an error for "moveable".
P. 216, n. 58, l. 3 from end. for "Roman" read "Russian".
P. 277, n. 35. read "βασιλεῖαι".
P. 278, l. 6. "the powers" may be an error for "his powers".
P. 281, n. 44, l. 1. after "Longobardi" insert "[*leg.* 'Langobardi ']".
P. 294, n. 71, l. 1. read "Italiae".
P. 294, n. 75, l. 2. read "[by] Constantine".
P. 296, n. 80, l. 4. read "μιᾷ".
P. 313, n. 125, l. 1. read "Francofurt."
P. 334, l. 3 from foot. read "sequestered".
P. 356, l. 5. for "had" read "has".
P. 359, n. 74, l. 2. read "Fénelon".
P. 398, l. 7 from foot. for "bid" read "bade.".
P. 402, l. 1. for "cruelty" read "credulity".
P. 408, n. 82, l. 3. "recapitulated" may be an error for "recapitulates".
P. 432, n. 23, l. 4. for "on" read "under".
P. 432, n. 23, l. 5. for "darts" read "dust".
P. 448, l. 9 from foot. We should expect "imprudent" instead of "prudent".
P. 471, l. 4 from foot. for "of the" read "or the".
P. 493, n. 168, l. 2. read "κτείνουσι".
P. 498, n. 186, l. 2. read "fuggirono".

P. 498, n. 187, l. 5. read " forget ".
P. 501, ll. 4, 3 from foot. no paragraph.
P. 504, n. 203, l. 6. for " state " read " date ".
P. 508, n. 211, l. 2. " tables " seems to be an error for " table ".
P. 512, n. 219, l. 3. insert comma after " chief ".

VOL. VI.

P. 4, n. 6, l. 1. for " deserved " read " deserves ".
P. 12, n. 24, l. 4. for " the text " read " that text ".
P. 44, l. 2. delete " and ".
P. 45, l. 5. for " fishermen " read " fisherman ".
P. 60, n. 136, l. 3. for " cast " read " casts ".
P. 65, n. 2, l. 4. for " slavish " read " lavish ".
P. 69, n. 10, l. 10. for " Brunk," read " Brunk."
P. 77, l. 11. for " manufactures of " read " manufacturers to ".
P. 80, n. 35, l. 3. read " Bas-Empire ".
P. 81, n. 36, l. 1. for " potentissime " read " potentissimus [leg. ' potentissime ']".
P. 90, l. 18. read " Such had ever been ".
P. 90, l. 1. from foot. read " Berenice ".
P. 131, l. 17. for " Jew " read " Jews ".
P. 134, l. 5. insert comma after " limits ".
P. 159, n. 69, l. 4. read " d'Ukranie ".
P. 160, n. 72. after " τοῖς " insert " [leg. ' ταῖς ']".
P. 161, l. 18. for " prince " read " princes ".
P. 168, n. 96, l. 1. insert point after " Montacut ".
P. 189, l. 3. from foot. for " natural " read " martial ".
P. 191, n. 44. read " are produced ".
P. 191, n. 48, l. 3. read " περιφανής ".
P. 197, l. 13. for " were " read " was ".
P. 200, l. 12. for " successors " read " successor ".
P. 222, l. 11. for " unfortunate " read " fortunate ".
P. 230, l. 11. from foot. read " measure of policy or reason ".
P. 235, n. 6, l. 4. read colon for comma before " 300 ".
P. 261, n. 60, l. 2. read " le sac ".
P. 272, n. 6, l. 9. read " commisisse ".
P. 291, n. 51, l. 2. after " vix " insert " [leg. ' ut vix ']".
P. 297, n. 62, l. 1. after " Scodras " insert " [leg. ' Scodra ']".
P. 297, n. 62, l. 5. delete comma after " Beglerbeg ".
P. 298, n. 68, l. 3. read " stone bridge ".
P. 302, l. 7. for " trode " read " trod ".
P. 309, n. 89, l. 3. for " trode " read " trod ".
P. 320, l. 13 from foot. for " future " read " fortune ".
P. 322, l. 6. read " Cedron ".
P. 326, l. 7 from foot. for " pilgrims " read " pilgrim ".
P. 326, n. 124, l. 5. for " potens " read " potius ".
P. 340, l. 11. for " their " read " her ".
P. 343, l. 5. for " actions " read " action ".
P. 347, n. 38, l. 1. read " iste [leg. ' isti ']".
P. 348, l. 12. for " in Jerusalem " read " of Jerusalem ".
P. 353, n. 52, l. 3. for " Abhed " read "Adhed ".
P. 355, n. 58. delete " He did not—Aleppo ".
P. 367, l. 6 from foot. for " neutral " read " neuter ".
P. 393, l. 5 from foot. for " usurpers " read " usurers ".
P. 396, l. 8 from foot. for " claim " read " claims ".
P. 408, n. 72, l. 1. read " piscatorum ".
P. 411, l. 5 from foot. read " stone bridge ".
P. 411, ll. 16-18. So author's text, but the sense requires that " former " and " latter " should be interchanged.
P. 428, l. 2. for " his " read " this ".

P. 429, l. 13. for " form " read " forms ".
P. 437, l. 17. for " a merit " read " the merit ".
P. 440, l. 8 from foot. for " their " read " the ".
P. 453, l. 16. read " adoptive ".
P. 465, l. 5. for " success " read " increase ".
P. 526, n. 36, l. 1. read " some true pearls ".

VOL. VII.

P. 7, n. 22. for " Chang-Tsong " read " Chang Tsung "; and for " Niu-Chi "
read " Nü-chih ". Niu-chi is the French translation. The term Nü-chih was
substituted in 1031 for Nü-chên, the chên being part of the personal name of the
Kitan Emperor of that time, to whom the Nü-chên Tartars were subject. When
the Kitans were overthrown the original name was revived. The name Manchu
dates from 1616. I am indebted to Professor H. W. Giles for this note.

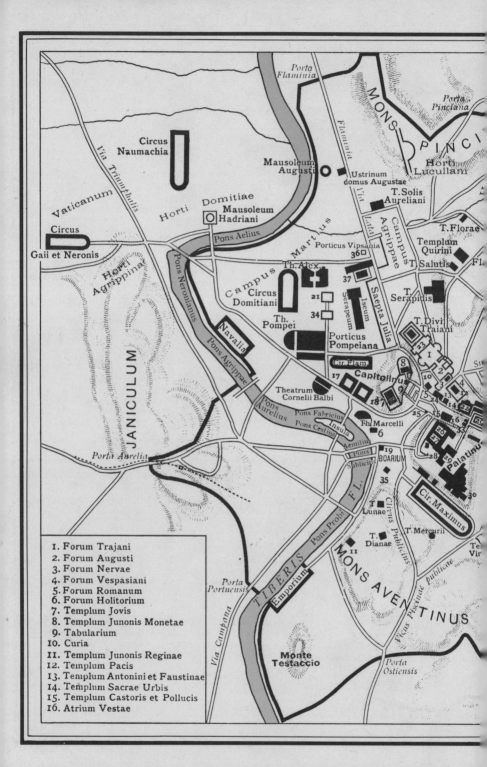

Porta
Flaminia

Porta
Pinciana

MONS

Circus
Naumachia

Mausoleum
Augusti

PINCI

Horti
Lucullani

Vaticanum

Horti   Domitiae

Ustrinum
domus Augustae

T. Solis
Aureliani

Mausoleum
Hadriani

T. Florae

Circus

Pons Aelius

Porticus Vipsania

Templum
Quirini

Gaii et Neronis

36

T. Salutis

Fl.

Th. Alex.

Horti
Agrippinae

Campus

Martius

Campus
Agrippae

37

T.
Serapidis

Circus
Domitiani

21

Saepta Julia

Iseum
Serapeum

Navalia

Th.
Pompei

34

T. Divi
Traiani

Porticus
Pompeiana

Cir. Flam.

23

I

8

2

JANICULUM

17

Capitolinus

10

Pons Agrippae

Theatrum
Cornelii Balbi

18   7

5

13

14   22

Pons Aurelius

Insula

Fh. Marcelli

25

15

16

Pons Fabricius
Pons Cestius

6

27

26

Aemilius

19

Porta Aurelia

Pons
Sublicius

BOARIUM

28   29

Palatium

35

Cir. Maximus

Lunae

T.
Dianae

T. Mercurii

MONS

Cir. Maximus

Pons Probi

30

11

AVEN

Te.
Vir

1. Forum Trajani
2. Forum Augusti
3. Forum Nervae
4. Forum Vespasiani
5. Forum Romanum
6. Forum Holitorium
7. Templum Jovis
8. Templum Junonis Monetae
9. Tabularium
10. Curia
11. Templum Junonis Reginae
12. Templum Pacis
13. Templum Antonini et Faustinae
14. Templum Sacrae Urbis
15. Templum Castoris et Pollucis
16. Atrium Vestae

Porta
Portuensis

TIBERIS

Emporium

TINUS

Via Campana

Monte
Testaccio

Porta
Ostiensis